Paradox

Thomas M. Cook
American Airlines, Inc.

Robert A. Russell
The University of Tulsa

Introduction to Management Science

PRENTICE HALL, Englewood Cliffs, New Jersey 07632

Library of Congress Cataloging-in-Publication Data

Cook, Thomas M.
   Introduction to management science / Thomas M. Cook, Robert A.
Russell,—4th ed.
     p. cm.
   Includes bibliographies and index.
   ISBN 0-13-486317-8
   1. Management—Mathematical models. 2. Operations research.
I. Russell, Robert A.   II. Title.
HD30.25.C67 1989
658.4′034—dc19

                    88-25259
                     CIP

The corporate logos reproduced on the cover and with the chapter opening scenarios are done so with permission, courtesy of the following: Homart Development Co.; U.S. Air Force; North American Van Lines, Inc.; American Airlines, Inc.; The Southland Corporation; General Motors Corporation; E. I. du Pont de Nemours and Company; The LTV Corporation; Mobil Oil Corporation; Phillips Petroleum Company; National Railroad Passenger Corp. (Amtrak); Ohio Edison Co.; Manitoba Telephone System; The Xerox Corporation (Xerox is a registered trademark of the Xerox Corporation); United Airlines; Bethlehem Steel Corporation; and Digital Equipment Corporation.

Editorial/production supervision: Eleanor Perz
Interior design: Christine Gehring-Wolf
Cover design: Levavi & Levavi
Manufacturing buyer: Margaret Rizzi

 © 1989, 1985, 1981, 1977 by Prentice-Hall, Inc.
A Division of Simon & Schuster
Englewood Cliffs, New Jersey 07632

Printed in the United States of America
10 9 8 7 6 5 4 3 2 1

ISBN 0-13-486317-8

Prentice-Hall International (UK) Limited, *London*
Prentice-Hall of Australia Pty. Limited, *Sydney*
Prentice-Hall Canada Inc., *Toronto*
Prentice-Hall Hispanoamericana, S.A., *Mexico*
Prentice-Hall of India Private Limited, *New Delhi*
Prentice-Hall of Japan, Inc., *Tokyo*
Simon & Schuster Asia Pte. Ltd., *Singapore*
Editora Prentice-Hall do Brasil, Ltda., *Rio de Janeiro*

Contents

5 Sensitivity Analysis   158

6 Distribution and Assignment Problems   197

7 Network Models   260

8 Project Scheduling   290

9 Integer and Goal Programming   339

10 Dynamic Programming   380

11 Probability Concepts and Distributions   407

15 Discrete Digital Simulation **586**

United Airlines, 586

16 Inventory Systems **630**

Standard Brands, Inc., 630

17 Decision Support Systems   692

18 Heuristics, AI, and Expert Systems   708

Appendix A
Cases

Appendix B
Solving Simultaneous Linear Equations, with Gaussian Elimination,   758

Preface

This text is designed to introduce the reader to the field of operations research/management science (OR/MS). Although the book can be used by practitioners or students of any discipline, it is aimed at the business student who will most likely pursue a career in an organization requiring some managerial ability and decision-making skill. The book is written to support the introductory course, whose purpose is to introduce future consumers of OR/MS to the discipline. It is written at a level that is appropriate for both the undergraduate and graduate student.

We have written the book with a balanced emphasis on not only the quantitative techniques, but also their application and strengths and weaknesses. To stress applications, we have begun each chapter with a real world scenario featuring a well-known organization and how it used OR/MS to its benefit. These applications were obtained from success stories in the OR/MS literature and the authors' personal experiences. Additional applications are cited through examples in the individual chapters, as well as in the problems section at the end of each chapter. A section called computer implications is also included in those chapters that present computer-based methods. In this particular section we discuss practical information, such as the availability of software packages or inherent shortcomings or advantages of the relevant computer-based methodology. The computer implications section could also be called "what the manager needs to know."

One of the current trends in the OR/MS discipline is the integration of microcomputer software in the teaching of OR/MS. It is clear that computer-based OR/MS techniques are now available to a much wider range of people. This allows us to focus more on application and interpretation, and less on algorithmic calculations. In this fourth edition we have expanded our presentations of computer output for the various OR/MS techniques and integrated the QSB OR/MS software package as well as the LINDO software package.

The fourth edition continues the effort at being a very student-oriented text. It is designed so that readers without a rigorous mathematical background can learn about and gain appreciation of quantitative methods for decision making. A course in college algebra or finite mathematics is sufficient mathematical preparation. An introductory course in statistics is recommended, but certainly not a necessity. As a further aid to students, important terms are italicized in the text and highlighted as key words in the margin at the point of definition. Review questions and problems are presented at the end of each chapter, as well as answers to selected problems that are given in Appendix J. These problem numbers are printed in black within the chapter text.

Although the fourth edition retains the same basic philosophy and features of the third edition, it contains the following enhancements.

□ New chapter on Artificial Intelligence—This chapter presents an overview of the emerging field of artificial intelligence and discusses the key issues surrounding the Management Science/Artificial Intelligence interface.

□ New cases and more challenging problems—Eight new cases and many more challenging end-of-chapter problems have been included to provide the pedagogical tools to assist the instructor in following the TIMS Education Committee's recommendations on the first core course in OR/MS.

□ Expanded software usage and illustrations—The popular QSB software package has been further integrated in the text. This package was top rated in *OR/MS Today*. It is available from Prentice Hall for individual student purchase or as a site license. The site license is free to adopters of fifty or more *Introduction to Management Science* texts from Prentice Hall.

The widely used LINDO package has been incorporated in the linear and integer programming chapters. Additionally, illustrations of spreadsheets have been introduced in the linear programming and simulation chapters. They are particularly effective for illustrating deterministic simulation often used in business applications.

☐ Chapter updates—All chapters have been thoroughly updated. Topics such as Karmarkar's interior point method, decision support systems, expert systems, and new directions in PC technology are presented. In addition, many new applications of OR/MS have been added throughout the book.

Popular pedagogical aids such as solved problems at the end of each chapter have been preserved. The optional Study Guide has been revised and updated for this fourth edition. The separate paperback guide will include a summary of the key points of each chapter as well as a review of key terms, solved problems, and sample exams with solutions.

We would like to thank the staff at Prentice Hall for their assistance, particularly Editor Dennis Hogan and Production Editor Eleanor Perz. Our thanks also to Kim Rose and Dianne Mooty who typed the manuscript as well as the Instructor's Manual, and to Bill Stripling, graduate assistant.

T.M.C.
R.A.R.

1

Introduction

HOMART DEVELOPMENT CO.[1]

Homart Development Co. is one of the largest commercial land developers in the United States. The firm currently owns or is developing over 50 regional shopping centers and 19 major office buildings and is involved in land development of properties that total over 1000 acres. Homart is a consolidated, wholly owned subsidiary of Sears, Roebuck and Co. Were the firm independent, its assets would qualify it to rank in "The Fortune 500."

Homart's business involves the full cycle of real estate operations: identifying opportunities for development, analyzing their feasibility, obtaining the necessary governmental approvals, overseeing design and construction, leasing, and then managing the properties as long-term investments.

One of the most important strategic issues for Homart is the divestiture of shopping malls and office buildings. In the 1986 strategic plan, 170 assets were analyzed for possible divestiture over 10 years. The problem is complicated by requirements imposed by the parent corporation that Homart meet a minimum aggregate return on equity each year. In the past, divestiture planning was done only every third year. Real estate has typically been an entrepreneurial business that has had little use for man-

[1] J. C. Bean, C. E. Noon, and G. J. Salton, "Asset Divestiture at Homart Development Co.," *Interfaces,* 17 (January–February 1987), 48–64.

agement science techniques at any level. However, Homart decided to develop a mathematical modeling approach to complement their asset evaluation and corporate financial planning modules for strategic planning.

The management science model has had a major impact on the strategic planning process at Homart. A stringent policy not to sell assets at a loss has been analyzed and revoked. This is resulting in substantial changes in the schedule of assets to be divested in the next few years. While few of the monetary effects of these policy changes are quantifiable, what has been measured is estimated to have a monetary impact of $40 million.

The divestiture planning process has been changed to a biannual process. Improved speed and accuracy allow sensitivity analysis on economic factors. Encouraged by the success of the divestiture analysis, Homart has a stated strategy of exploiting its quantitative capabilities as a means of achieving a competitive advantage. Other management science projects are currently underway.

INTRODUCTION

Prior to the twentieth century, business and other organizations functioned in a less complex environment than that of today. Managers of contemporary organizations (such as Homart) must cope with a dynamic world of increased population, inflation, recession, social consciousness, and shortages of resources such as energy and capital. Consequently, the decision-making task of modern management is more demanding and more important than ever.

Fortunately, we human beings can use our ingenuity to find new ways to handle the problems that confront us. Even though contemporary institutions face an increasingly complex and uncertain environment, they also have available innovative approaches to dealing with decision problems. This book is concerned with some of the new tools and technology that have been developed specifically to help management in the decision-making process.

management science
operations research

Management science is the discipline devoted to studying and developing procedures to help in the process of making decisions. It is also commonly called *operations research*. The two terms have come to be used interchangeably, and we shall use both throughout the text. The principal characteristic of operations research/management science (OR/MS) is its use of the scientific method for decision making. Management can approach complex decision problems in several ways. Managers may resort to intuitive or observational approaches that depend on subjective analyses. Or, putting faith in "proven" procedures, they may simply repeat other managers' solutions. Such attempts at handling problems are sometimes called *seat-of-the-pants* approaches. They may not attack the problems in a systematic manner, and they do little to improve or advance the managerial decision process. On the other hand, a management science approach provides a rational, systematic way to handle decision problems. Using a systematic approach, the decision maker has a better chance to make a proper decision.

Our greatest technical accomplishments have been achieved by utilizing the scientific method. Only recently, however, have we begun to apply this methodology outside the laboratory environment of physics and chemistry. Even though these new environments are less controlled, the operations of organizations and their decision-making processes still lend themselves to analysis through scientific methodology.

How did scientific methodology come to be applied to decision problems? The answer to that question will further your comprehension of the field of management science.

HISTORICAL OVERVIEW

Operations research/management science (OR/MS) is an interdisciplinary field comprising elements of mathematics, economics, computer science, and engineering. Its specific content expanded enormously after the twentieth-century invention of electronic computers. Its fundamental philosophical principle, however—the use of scientific methodology to solve problems—was a recorded management technique much earlier. Venetian shipbuilders of the fifteenth century, for example, are known to have used an assembly line of sorts in outfitting ships.

Progress was not consistent until the Industrial Revolution, however. Based on his analysis of the manufacture of straight pins, Adam Smith proclaimed the merits of division of labor in 1776. Charles Babbage, an English mathematician and mechanical genius, wrote a seminal treatise titled *On Economy of Machines and Manufactures* (1832). In it, Babbage discussed such issues relevant to management science as skill differential in wages and concepts of industrial engineering.

In the late nineteenth century, an American engineer, Frederick Taylor, formally advocated a scientific approach to the problems of manufacturing. Taylor, sometimes called the father of scientific management, was largely responsible for developing industrial engineering as a profession. It was his philosophy that there was one ''best way'' or most efficient way to accomplish a given task. He used time studies to evaluate worker performance and to analyze work methods.

Henry L. Gantt, a contemporary of Taylor, refined the content of early scientific management by bringing into consideration the human aspect of management's attitude toward labor. He espoused the importance of the personnel department to the scientific approach to management. Perhaps his greatest contribution, however, was his scheduling system for loading jobs on machines. Basically a recording procedure, Gantt's system was devised to minimize job completion delays; it permitted machine loadings to be planned months in advance.

The early scientific management era was an important stage of development for OR/MS. However, its progress was mostly limited to establishing or improving efficient performance of specific tasks in the lower levels of organizations. It may not be possible to pinpoint the first true application of management science, but several pioneers should be noted. As early as 1914, an Englishman named Frederick W. Lanchester attempted to predict the outcome of military battles based on the numerical strength of personnel and weaponry. Lanchester's predicting equation may represent the first attempt to model an organizational decision problem mathematically. In 1915, Ford W. Harris published a simple lot-size formula that constituted the basis for inventory control for several decades and still finds wide use today. Just as Harris helped establish inventory control theory, a Danish mathematician, A. K. Erlang, founded modern waiting-line, or queuing, theory. He developed mathematical formulas to predict waiting times for callers using automatic telephone exchanges.

One of the first to apply sophisticated mathematical models to business problems in the United States was Horace C. Levinson, an astronomer by training. In the 1930s, Levinson studied such market-oriented applications as the relationship between advertising and sales and the effect of income and residential location upon customer purchases.

Despite such advances in the scientific approach to quantitative management problems before 1940, OR/MS did not emerge as a recognized discipline until World War II. In the late 1930s, the British assembled a team of specialists to investigate the effective use of radar. Subsequently, the British military establishment increasingly called upon the British scientific establishment to study other problems, such as antisubmarine warfare, civilian defense, and the optimal deployment of convoy vessels to accompany supply ships.

This approach to military problem solving called upon experts from various areas of specialization. Perhaps the most famous British group was headed by the distinguished physicist P. M. S. Blackett. Blackett's Circus, so-called, consisted of three physiologists, two mathematical physicists, an Army officer, a surveyor, two mathematicians, an astrophysicist, and a general physicist. This multidiscipline team approach has become a characteristic of OR/MS. The highly successful British operational research was credited with helping to win the Battle of Britain and the Battle of the North Atlantic.

Such successes influenced the United States military establishment to include "operations analysis" groups on its staff. During World War II, the United States gathered mathematicians, statisticians, probability theorists, and computer experts to work on operations analysis. During the period, John von Neumann made immense contributions in the area of game theory and utility theory, and George Dantzig worked on the simplex method of linear programming.

linear programming After the war, the military establishment increased its research programs and retained some operations research personnel, but industry largely ignored the methodology of the discipline. Many operations research ideas naturally had a military orientation, and nonmilitary managers tended to regard the techniques either as irrelevant to their problems or impossible to implement. Two events helped to bring operations research to industry. In 1947, George Dantzig developed *linear programming,* a technique that uses linear algebra to determine the optimal allocation of scarce resources. Obviously, such a method could be applied profitably to many business problems. Operations research began to be regarded as sometimes relevant to industry.

The second, and more important, occurrence to enhance the acceptability of nonmilitary operations research was the development and production of high-speed electronic computers. Some operations research techniques entailed long, complex calculations to solve real-world problems. Computers, capable of performing such calculations millions of times faster than people, were invaluable tools for the operations research profession. With the advent of electronic instruments to perform functions that were previously impossible or unprofitable, OR/MS could be perceived as valid to, and valuable for, business and industry. The dependence of OR/MS methodology on computers cannot be overemphasized. Even today, certain large-scale problems cannot be solved with current techniques and existing computer hardware. Research will undoubtedly improve the methodology, but it is ultimately the future generations of computers that will allow operations researchers and management scientists to extend the successful applications of their discipline.

Given the favorable climate engendered by industry's acceptance of OR/MS in the 1950s, the discipline developed rapidly. One measure of its formalization was the establishment of professional associations. Chief among these are Operational Research Society (British, 1950), Operations Research Society of America (1952), The Institute of Management Science (United States, 1953), and Decision Sciences Institute (1969).

By the end of the 1950s, many of the standard tools of OR/MS, such as linear programming, dynamic programming, inventory control theory, and queuing theory, were relatively well developed. However, in the 1950s most of the OR/MS applications focused on specialized and very well-defined problems. Since the early 1960s, formal OR/MS endeavors have dealt increasingly with planning problems that are less well structured and more realistic. Decision analysis emerged as a process for dealing with decisions associated with much uncertainty. Goal programming and multiobjective linear programming were developed to deal with decision problems that have multiple and sometimes conflicting goals.

During the 1970s and into the 1980s, OR/MS has become increasingly concerned with the interface with management information systems (MIS). Computerized data bases play a vital role in supporting OR/MS models as well as in everyday decision making. The marriage of OR/MS and MIS has resulted in a special kind of information system called a decision support system (DSS). This type of system holds great promise for the enhancement of the decision-making process at all levels of management. Among the latest developments in the 1980s is the emergence of expert systems and artificial intelligence (AI). Expert systems have evolved to handle decision problems that require human knowledge or expertise. In the more general field of artificial intelligence, OR/MS models and techniques are sometimes useful in developing heuristic search procedures. It will be interesting to observe future developments between OR/MS and AI.

Since 1950, the field of OR/MS has progressed steadily. Currently more than 20,000 people are involved in applying, teaching, or researching the field. Most *Fortune 500* companies practice OR/MS. Smaller companies may not require full-time OR/MS programs and personnel, but they often hire management consultants for OR/MS projects. Given such exposure, business is finding increasingly desirable the employee who has OR/MS training. As a result, many universities offer undergraduate and graduate degrees in the field, and most business schools have requirements in the subjects of operations research, management science, decision science, or quantitative methods.

THE NATURE OF MANAGEMENT SCIENCE

You have probably gained some insight into the nature of management science from the preceding brief historical overview. In this section we define the actual content of this discipline more specifically. Harvey Wagner, past president of The Institute of Management Sciences, has described OR/MS simply and yet precisely. Wagner states that operations research is a scientific approach to problem solving for executive management. The Operations Research Society of America amplifies this basic definition by calling operations research an experimental and applied science devoted to observing, understanding, and predicting the behavior of purposeful human/machine systems. It is logically applied, therefore, to the practical problems of government, business, and society.

As the foregoing definitions suggest, the fundamental characteristic of OR/MS is its scientific or systematic approach to decision making. But how can we apply the scientific method to the often uncontrollable and imprecise environment of the real world? In laboratory experiments, data are rejected unless they are demonstrably accurate, and all conditions are strictly controlled. In modern organizations, data are often imperfect, and the outside world exerts a significant influence on many of the variables under study. Factors relevant to a management science experiment are often impossible to manipulate. Furthermore, the functioning and profitability of the firm usually take precedence over artificial changes induced for the sake of experimentation. For example, a company would not temporarily close its warehouses in order to determine the exact shortage costs for its inventory.

Even though the management scientist usually cannot perform a "pure" scientific experiment, this does not preclude using a scientific approach. The management scientist works in a situation analogous to an astronomer's: Each has little control over a constantly changing universe and yet each performs scientific experiments and builds mathematical models to account for the observed phenomena.

THE SCIENTIFIC METHOD

To see how the management scientists may use a scientific approach, you must recall the basic steps of the scientific method. These are

1. Observation
2. Definition of the problem
3. Formulation of a hypothesis
4. Experimentation
5. Verification

As you would suppose, the first three steps of the scientific method can be carried out by the management scientist much as they would be by a chemist or a biologist. However, experimentation and verification can pose special problems in real-world applications.

Let us consider a hypothetical problem for the manager of a manufacturing firm to see how the scientific method can be applied to the analysis of a business problem. The first step of the scientific method requires the recognition of a particular phenomenon. Suppose that the manager of the manufacturing firm has observed a significant rise in inventory costs over the past year. This observation suggests the existence of a problem that can perhaps be treated, yielding benefits to the firm.

Thus, it is necessary to pinpoint the exact nature of the problem. The manager has observed rising costs. These may simply be due to inflation. Some observations may be directly related to the symptoms of the problem rather than to the problem itself. It is important that the decision maker formulate the problem precisely and address the truly relevant issues. Much time, effort, and money can be wasted looking at the wrong problem.

In our example, suppose that the manager has determined that inventory costs have risen even faster than the national rate of inflation. The manager suspects that a significant part of the increased cost is caused by the firm's current inventory policy and thus is potentially amenable to change. The manager's problem can now be clearly defined: It is necessary to determine a new inventory policy that will reduce inventory costs.

The inventory costs of the company are comprised primarily of inventory holding costs (costs of carrying and storing) and inventory replenishing costs (costs of ordering and restocking). A closer examination by the manager yields the fact that replenishing costs have increased more rapidly than holding costs. This is true primarily because transportation costs and the clerical costs of placing orders have risen sharply. The manager now has a hypothesis: Ordering larger quantities fewer times per year will decrease overall inventory costs. This new policy will increase holding costs somewhat, but it will lower replenishing costs at the same time.

Now the manager needs to determine how much larger the orders should be. A trial-and-error approach can be implemented by changing the order quantity and observing the effects on total inventory costs. Observations will then confirm or disprove the initial hypothesis. Another approach is to use a mathematical inventory model (Chapter 16) that "fits" the particular problem. This approach, if applicable, eliminates the need for trial and error, for the model determines the order quantity. A third approach is computer simulation (Chapter 15). In any of these situations, the manager ultimately determines whether the hypothesis is valid by comparing the cost of the new solution with the cost before experimentation. Higher costs may indicate that the original hypothesis is incorrect. In that case, further experiments are called for to try to develop a better hypothesis.

Verification of the conclusions of the experiment can be made in several ways. The most accurate, of course, is actually to implement the new solution within the company and then observe its effects. This procedure can be very dangerous in practice, and it may have far-reaching consequences throughout the organization. Usually, it is best to try to forecast the success of the new solution by applying it to hypothetical data or data that represent past transactions of the firm. However, since costs, prices, and demand are constantly changing, success on past data does not necessarily guarantee success in future inventory transactions for the company. Thus, complete verification in the real world is not always possible.

A SYSTEMS APPROACH

systems approach   The scientific method is extremely useful for trying to solve certain very specific problems the management scientist encounters. It is usually applied, however, within a much broader context known as the *systems approach.* The word *system* is much used in our society. We hear of computer systems, solar systems, nervous systems, political systems, and systems we usually cannot beat. In this book, we shall refer to a system as a whole comprising interrelated parts intended to accomplish a specific objective. Thus, a computer system is made up of hardware components (such as the central processing unit, terminals, and disk and tape drives) and software components (such as the operating system software and various compilers). These components interact to accomplish the objective of processing computer jobs.

Organizations, too, conform to our definition of a system. One kind of organization that can use management science to its advantage—the kind with which we will be concerned primarily—is a human/machine system comprising components such as machinery, departments, divisions, and individual people. The main purpose of the management scientist is to aid in the achievement of the goals of the organization as a whole. Viewing the organization as a system permits us to consider the individual components in relation to the entire organization.

This perspective is essential, for the good of the whole may not necessarily derive from the greatest good for each of the parts. In other words, concentrating only on a particular component of the organizational system may result in *optimization,* or best achievement of goals, for that component but a less than optimal solution, or *suboptimization,* for the organization as a whole. Optimizing the organization's goals is sometimes accomplished by optimizing its subsystems. In other cases, however, suboptimization of various components is necessary for the sake of the organization's greatest good. A systems approach best equips the decision maker to determine which alternative actually will maximize the realization of the goals of the organization.

Just as a systems approach helps us to have a balanced perspective concerning an organization's components, it also helps us to view the organization as a component, or subsystem, of the environment in which it exists. Today's human/machine organizations operate under conditions of rapid change and ever-increasing complexity. Good decision making, therefore, requires that management take a broad view. Just as an inventory problem, for example, within a single component may affect an organization's production, finance, accounting, and personnel functions, so too the organization's inventory decisions can affect external supply, demand, and prices in the general market.

Usually, no single decision maker is sufficiently multitalented to understand the ramifications of proposed solutions on all aspects of the organization, including its internal and external environments. Often, a team of specialists is formed to attack quantitative management problems. The concept of the team approach to decision making is a key characteristic of the OR/MS approach. You may recall that one of the first operations research teams, Blackett's Circus, consisted of 11 different specialists. Depending on the type of application, an OR/MS team might include experts in mathematical programming, accounting, finance, marketing research, engineering, mathematics, behavioral science, statistics, computer programming, and other fields. This interdisciplinary approach tends to treat the individual phases of a problem most effectively; consequently, the success of the entire project is enhanced.

To summarize, management science applications include any approach to problem solving that incorporates all, or most, of the following characteristics:

1. Viewing the problem within a systems perspective
2. Applying the scientific method to develop the solution methodology
3. Using a team, or interdisciplinary, approach
4. Using a mathematical model
5. Using a high-speed electronic computer

We have not yet said much about the fourth essential characteristic of management science, model building. Your introduction to mathematical models is in the following section. Most of the topics you will encounter in this text involve some use of a mathematical model.

MODELS IN MANAGEMENT SCIENCE

In general terms, a model is a representation or an abstraction of an object or a particular real-world phenomenon. A good model accurately displays the key properties of the entity it represents. Many different disciplines employ the use of models. For example, aeronautical engineers use scale-model airplanes in wind tunnels, and civil engineers may use scale models of bridges, buildings, or river systems. More abstract models are used by economists to predict future economic activity and by ecologists to estimate potential effects on the environment. In each of these applications, the model represents an abstraction of reality, and the purpose of the model is to gain specific information about, and general insight into, the phenomenon it represents. By using models, we can investigate certain cause-and-effect relationships and the interaction between key variables.

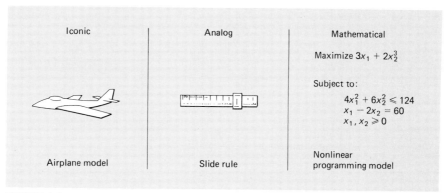

Iconic	Analog	Mathematical

Maximize $3x_1 + 2x_2^3$

Subject to:
$$4x_1^2 + 6x_2^2 \leqslant 124$$
$$x_1 - 2x_2 = 60$$
$$x_1, x_2 \geqslant 0$$

Airplane model	Slide rule	Nonlinear programming model

FIGURE 1.1 **Three examples of models**

Many different models exist, but each may be classified as belonging to one of three types. (Figure 1.1) An *iconic model* is a physical representation that actually looks like the object it represents. Examples of iconic models include model airplanes and cars, or photographs.

An *analog model* substitutes one property for another; it can represent dynamic situations statically. For example, a slide rule is an analog model because it substitutes physical distances for numerical quantities. A frequency polygon is an analog model in statistics because it represents numerical data pictorially. Why is a flow chart an analog model in computer programming? The third class of models consists of *symbolic, or mathematical, models*. This type of model is important to the management scientist. Mathematical models attempt to represent nonmathematical reality by means of equations and other mathematical statements. These models translate the essential features of a given situation into mathematical symbols. Then, the symbols can be manipulated in ways that the actual personnel, production, inventory, and so on, cannot. A mathematical model is thus a formal structure that creates a framework within which a problem can be analyzed. *Simulation models* are an alternative to mathematical models in analyzing complex systems. Simulation models statistically describe system behavior by replicating system performance for a specified number of trials.

Building useful models for management science applications requires a delicate balance between accuracy and simplicity. The model must be detailed enough to represent the essential realities of the problem and yet manageable in terms of computation and implementation. No mathematical model can capture all characteristics, properties, and uncertainties of a real situation. Attempting to build such a total model results in outright failure or in a model that is too cumbersome to use.

Some management science models involve relationships that cannot be expressed as a system of equations. An example is a model based on proper-

iconic model

analog model

symbolic, or mathematical, model

simulation model

TABLE 1.1 *Knapsack problem data*

Item	Weight (lbs)	Value
1 Water	3.00	60
2 Tent	5.00	60
3 Food	4.00	40
4 Matches	.01	10
5 Fishing tackle	4.00	20
6 Sleeping bag	3.00	10
7 Snake bite kit	.50	3

ties of mathematical group structures. (A group is a collection of elements having certain properties; matrices and real numbers are examples of groups.) However, most models created for management science applications do consist of a system of equations. A single equation, called the *objective function*, is used to measure the effectiveness of proposed solutions. The remaining equations, called the *constraints*, ensure that the solution satisfies certain requirements dictated by the nature of the problem. To illustrate the nature of a mathematical model, let us consider a small mathematical model that has an objective function and only one constraint.

objective function

constraints

Our problem is well known in OR/MS literature. It is called the knapsack problem, or sometimes the cargo-loading problem, and it has many applications. Let us consider seven items that we would like to take on a camping trip. Table 1.1 lists the weight and the subjective value we have assigned to each item. We further assume that our knapsack has a 10-pound capacity, which means that we cannot take all seven items on the camping trip. The problem is to choose the items that maximize the sum of their values to us and yet do not exceed the 10-pound limit.

Before we create a mathematical model of this problem, we need to define some decision variables. Decision variables have two characteristics: They are the variables whose solution values actually indicate the solution to the problem, and those variables over which the decision maker has control. Our problem is to decide which items to take on the trip. Therefore, let

$$x_i = \begin{cases} 1 & \text{if we take item } i, \text{ for } i = 1, 2, \ldots, 7 \\ 0 & \text{otherwise} \end{cases}$$

Thus $x_4 = 1$ means that we take item 4, and $x_4 = 0$ means that we do not take item 4. Our measure of effectiveness is total value; therefore, our objective function is to maximize $60x_1 + 60x_2 + 40x_3 + 10x_4 + 20x_5 + 10x_6 + 3x_7$. Our only restraint is the weight capacity, which can be represented by $3x_1 +$

$5x_2 + 4x_3 + .01x_4 + 4x_5 + 3x_6 + .50x_7 \leq 10$. Our final mathematical model is thus

Maximize $\quad 60x_1 + 60x_2 + 40x_3 + 10x_4 + 20x_5 + 10x_6 + 3x_7 \qquad$ (value)

subject to $\quad 3x_1 + 5x_2 + 4x_3 + .01x_4 + 4x_5 + 3x_6 + .50x_7 \leq 10$ (weight)

where $\quad x_i = 0$ or 1 for $i = 1, 2, \ldots, 7$.

Solving the foregoing mathematical model is not as easy as deriving it, but this time the answer is given to you. The best solution is to take items 1, 2, 4, and 7, and the associated value is 133. This means that we would take water, a tent, matches, and a snake bite kit on the camping trip. Once the model and a solution procedure are established, we can investigate various properties of the problem if we want. For example, we can study the effect of capacity on maximum value by changing the capacity from 10 to other values (such as 9 or 11) and re-solving the model. In this way, a model can be manipulated to reveal various relationships among key variables in the problem.

Many models of interest consist of nonlinear relationships. In the sciences, well-known descriptive models include Kepler's law of planetary orbit and Galileo's quantification of Newton's observation on gravity. Galileo's model states that a falling body falls a distance of

$$D = \frac{gt^2}{2}$$

feet in t seconds, where g is called the constant of acceleration. The model specifically describes the relationship between distance traveled and time. Like most models, it is only an approximation of reality. For instance, the model ignores the effects of air friction, wind, and other possible factors. Nevertheless, the model is extremely useful to scientists and engineers in design considerations.

A useful nonlinear model in business applications is the economic order quantity, or EOQ, model. Given a rate of demand r, a variable carrying cost C_1, and a fixed ordering cost C_3, the EOQ model states that

$$q = \sqrt{2C_3 r / C_1}$$

where q is the order quantity that will minimize the combined costs of ordering and carrying inventory. The EOQ is based on many assumptions and is only an approximation of reality. These assumptions are specified in Chapter 16, on inventory control systems.

The objective function that the EOQ model minimizes is

$$\text{cost} = \frac{C_1 q}{2} + \frac{C_3 r}{q}$$

This is a function of one variable, namely, q. The function is unconstrained in that there are no restrictions on the value of q other than it be greater than zero. The EOQ formula can be derived from the objective function using differential calculus. This derivation is shown in the appendix to Chapter 16.

Given some constraints on the value of q, the unconstrained problem becomes one of constrained optimization. Suppose that warehouse space limits the number of inventory items to 200. Suppose further that a sales contract requires the purchase of at least 130 items. A constrained nonlinear model can be expressed as

$$\text{Minimize} \quad \frac{C_1 q}{2} + \frac{C_3 r}{q}$$

$$\text{subject to} \quad q \leq 200$$
$$q \geq 130$$

Given specific values for the parameters C_1, C_3, and r, the solution of the model will yield the order quantity q that minimizes costs and satisfies all constraints.

Another approach to modeling complex systems is called simulation. Simulation differs from mathematical models in that specific relationships between variables and input and output are not always explicitly stated. Simulation models establish logical relationships between different modules in the system. IF/THEN and other well-defined logical relationships move entities through the system to be simulated. Statistics on relevant variables are captured, and descriptions of system phenomena can be studied.

Simulation models are generally used when the system of interest is too complex for mathematical modeling or too large for analytical solution on a computer. Simulation models offer more flexibility than do mathematical models; they view the system from a basic elemental level. Simulation, however, tends to describe system behavior rather than prescribe specific *descriptive* solutions or courses of action. Thus, simulation models are typically labeled as *descriptive* models, and mathematical programming models are *normative* *normative* or prescriptive.

Mathematical modeling and simulation are complementary approaches to solving real-world decision problems. Part of the learning experience in this course involves learning when each of the basic techniques are appropriate for application. Figure 1.2 depicts two of the most common approaches to modeling in OR/MS.

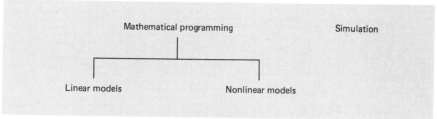

FIGURE 1.2 **Two widely used modeling approaches in OR/MS**

Although model building is an integral part of OR/MS procedures, it is still more an art than a science. Successful model building comes with experience and practice at relating situations to mathematical equations. A few standard models have been created that can be used in certain commonly occurring problem situations. However, most quantitative problems are unique simply because every organization has its own restrictions, limitations, and goals. Most of the time, therefore, models have to be built from scratch.

No model is perfect, and no model can truly represent the situation it symbolizes. Thus, successful management science projects do not depend solely upon models and scientific techniques. As the discipline becomes more sophisticated, greater emphasis is being placed on human factors. There is awareness of the need to balance purely quantitative approaches with the experience, judgment, and insight provided by management. This is a progressive step.

BASIC STEPS IN THE OR/MS APPROACH

Not all OR/MS projects follow the exact steps shown in Figure 1.3, but most do approximate the general process. The first step is problem formulation. We have already mentioned this important step in conjunction with the scientific method. Even though problem formulation sounds easy, it is a critical and nontrivial step. Defining the real problem and not just the symptoms of the problem requires insight, some imagination, and time.

It is general practice (although not required) to use a model in the quantitative analysis process. Once the problem has been well defined, we might find a model that has previously been developed to solve that kind of problem. If one is not available, it will be necessary to develop a model that will accurately reflect the essence of the decision-making problem.

The next step is to solve or manipulate the model to obtain a solution and hopefully a prescription for the problem. The model solution requires the necessary input data. The preparation of data to make it usable to the model often requires a major effort. Often the data are not readily available,

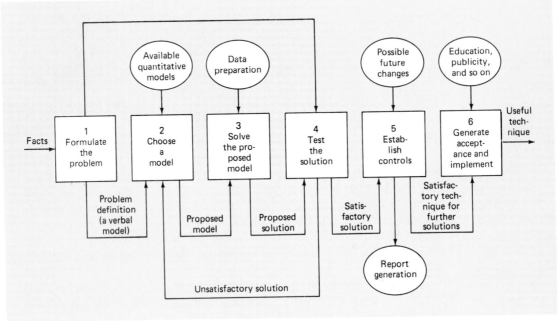

FIGURE 1.3 **Flow diagram of a typical six-stage OR/MS study (after Ackoff)**

and must be obtained from the accounting, production, or engineering departments. Even when available, the data often have to be transformed to a different form to be usable by the model.

The actual solution of the model is usually accomplished by a solution procedure called an *algorithm*. The calculations are usually performed on a high-speed computer, although small problems can sometimes be solved by hand. Once the solution is obtained, it must be tested for accuracy. Generally, tests of reasonableness are applied, and the solution is checked to see if it really "solves" the decision problem. An inaccurate or unreasonable solution usually implies that the model used does not accurately reflect the true nature of the problem. In this case the model must be modified or replaced by a more appropriate choice.

Given a satisfactory solution, the next step is to establish controls for the use of the model. Guidelines as to the assumptions and limitations of the model need to be established, as well as procedures to guarantee input data integrity and solution quality. Another important consideration is the design of flexibility within the model and the entire OR/MS process. The model and general procedure should not only be useful in solving today's problem but also future problems with some variations in problem characteristics. This "flexibility planning" will ensure the usefulness of the model for a much longer period of time.

The last step of the OR/MS process is often the most difficult. Implementing and generating acceptance for a new procedure often meets with resistance to change. There are many stories concerning potentially useful models that were never implemented because of politics, lack of communication between analyst and user, or fear of change. This is why education, publicity, and documentation of the new procedure are important in implementation. A close working relationship and involvement on the part of the model user as well as an understanding of human and organizational behavior are invaluable prerequisites to the emergence of a useful technique.

MANAGEMENT SCIENCE AND THE FUNCTIONAL AREAS OF BUSINESS

Most of you reading this book are majoring in business and have interests in one of its primary functional areas. In this section, we relate management science to each of these areas. As you will see, these are basically two-way relationships: Management science needs information, policy, and other guidance from the functional areas, and each area has specific problems for which management science can help to generate solutions.

Accounting and Finance

Management science models and techniques are virtually useless without accurate data. An organization's accounting department can be vital in providing the necessary data. Woolsey and Swanson have advised the practicing management scientist to make friends with a cost accountant, who "can be the greatest ally for which the up-and-coming OR man can hope."[2]

Management science, in return, can make significant contributions to the field of accounting. The study of management information systems has been applied to automate and improve various accounting procedures. An MIS is a formal system (usually computerized) for collecting, analyzing, and reporting information to managers. Statistical sampling theory has been used to improve the reliability and systematization of auditing procedures. Linear programming has been used to assign audit staff personnel to audit engagements, and goal programming has been used for broad planning purposes in CPA firms. Management science procedures have also been used to resolve transfer pricing and by-product costing and to develop standard costs. Other applications include inventory control and forecasting future transactions.

The management scientist needs the financial analyst to provide input concerning cash-flow restrictions and policies. The OR/MS practitioner also

---

[2] R. E. D. Woolsey and H. S. Swanson, *Operations Research for Immediate Application: A Quick and Dirty Manual* (New York: Harper & Row Publishers, Inc., 1975), p. 168.

needs data about the cost of capital and facts concerning long-range capital requirements. Successful management science applications in the financial realm include capital budgeting, a procedure that assesses various projects requiring cash outlays in order to maximize net benefits in limited-budget situations. Computer simulation models have been used to build corporate financial-planning models. These simulation models are manipulated to answer various "what if" questions concerning the future of the firm. Management science has also been used to design investment portfolios. Portfolio selection procedures are used primarily to choose investment vehicles and mixes that will interact to minimize risk or maximize gain. Other financial applications include equipment-replacement analysis and determination of dividend policies.

Marketing

Marketing research applications are numerous. They include determination of product mix, product selection, and forecasting future demand. Advertising applications include the selection of media in order to maximize a product's effective exposure to a particular market segment at lowest cost. Management science techniques have also been used to assign salespeople to territories, to determine the appropriate number of accounts for them to serve, and to establish their travel routes in order to minimize the distances they must cover. Physical distribution problems are especially suited to resolution by management science techniques. Models have been developed to determine least-cost shipping patterns from plant to market. Location theory has been used to determine optimal locations and sizes for warehouses so that the cost of the distribution of goods is minimal. Other marketing applications include assessing competitive marketing strategies and analyzing packaging effectiveness.

Production/Operations

The production/operations area is probably the richest functional area for OR/MS applications. Applications abound at all three levels of managerial decision making and in both the public and private sectors. At the strategic level, OR/MS models have been used to aid in plant location decisions and distribution system design. Simulation and queuing models have been used in manufacturing and service system design and planning for long-term capacity. At the tactical level, we find analysis of inventory policies and procedures as well as aggregate production planning. At the operational level there are numerous applications in forecasting and scheduling. Some of the more common scheduling applications include heuristics for job shop scheduling, models for personnel assignment and scheduling, and models for vehicle and rail car scheduling and routing. Statistical analysis is used routinely to study quality-control problems.

Information Systems

Although some might argue whether information systems are a functional area of business, it is undeniable that they are playing an increasing role in strategic and competitive business practices. Coupled with OR/MS models, information systems can provide much needed decision support for all the functional areas. The models provide much needed analytical support, while information systems and data bases provide OR/MS models with timely data and the capability to be more responsive to decision maker needs. Systems that aid in sophisticated financial planning and projection are probably the most common. The ability to do "what if" analysis on multimillion-dollar decisions is extremely valuable to financial planners. Decision support systems have also been utilized in marketing strategy and market response models. Personnel-related applications include systems for human resource management.

Relationship to Behavioral Sciences

With a discipline title such as management science, you might wonder about the relationship between management science and traditional management or behavioral science disciplines. In some circles, management science and behavioral management are contrasted as quantitative and qualitative management, respectively. By behavioral management, we mean the body of knowledge devoted to understanding human and organizational behavior. Each mode, however, is less effective without the other. Behavioral scientists utilize quantitative techniques to draw conclusions concerning observed human or organizational behavior. Management science relies upon the fundamentals of behavioral management to solve real-world problems successfully. The solutions proposed by management scientists almost always require some changes within the organization. These changes often have behavioral ramifications. In fact, it is entirely accurate to describe the management scientist as an agent of change.

Management science exists ultimately for people. As a collection of techniques and models isolated from a human context, the discipline is meaningless. If management science is to be implemented successfully, human factors and behavioral aspects must receive careful consideration. After all, what good is an optimally balanced assembly line if the workers are poorly motivated or on strike?

MANAGEMENT SCIENCE IN ACTION

There are obviously multitudes of management science applications, ranging from traditional military and production concerns to more contemporary ones in the fields of environmental engineering, the social sciences, and even sports. In this section, we discuss three specific applications of management science in which concrete results were achieved.

Fleet Control System

Hertz Rent-A-Car is number one in the car rental business and trying hard to stay that way. Hertz operates a substantial fleet of vehicles in more than 100 cities in the United States and Canada. Most of the major Hertz field operations are organized as pools consisting of from 2 to 10 cities with fleets of 2,000 to 6,000 cars.[3] The major benefit of the pool arrangement is the potential for improving fleet utilization through the shifting of cars from cities with surplus to cities with shortages.

Imagine, though, the complexity of Hertz's short-term planning problem. How would you allocate cars to each city on a daily basis? Keep in mind the dual and conflicting goals of the Hertz management—assuring adequate vehicle availability for the customer and, at the same time, maintaining a high degree of utilization for each car in the fleet.

The distribution problem has both a "city dimension" and a "time dimension." City demand for cars can vary significantly, and the planning horizon must extend well beyond the current day. Arrangements for transfers of cars must be made days in advance. A further complication is that the capacity or available number of cars is highly complex and uncertain. New cars are always being installed and other cars retired; some are moving to and from the maintenance shop. Finally, the Hertz Rent-It-Here, Leave-It-There policy means that future rentals can occur anywhere and return anywhere.

The complexity and importance of the short-range planning problem has long been recognized by the Hertz management. However, until recently their decisions were based on "gut feelings," with heavy reliance on sometimes distorted hand-computed averages and statistics. Spurred by competition and the desire to be more profitable, Hertz decided to turn to a sound analytical approach to the short-range planning problem.

The Hertz Operations Research group responded by developing the Pool Control System (PCS). PCS is an interactive model-oriented management tool. It is a descriptive rather than a prescriptive analytical tool, whose purpose is to clarify and evaluate alternatives. Ultimate decision making is left to the manager. (PCS provides the information and reports to aid in the decision.) The PCS system uses a model (a system of equations) to calculate estimates for key variables, such as capacity and demand. It is a time-sharing–based system that answers the following kinds of questions for each city: How many cars will be needed? How many cars will be available or can be moved in from other pool cities? How many reservations can be ac-

[3] Martin Edelstein and Myron Melnyk, "The Pool Control System," *Interfaces*, 8 (November 1977), 21–36.

cepted? How will the actions taken for any city on any day affect future days and other cities?

PCS is an example of a successful decision support system that combines an analytical model with a computerized information system. All levels of management at Hertz have attributed dramatic improvements in both customer service and fleet utilization to PCS. Approximately 50 cities representing over 60 percent of Hertz's car fleet use PCS daily. Those cities using the system have realized an increase of at least 10 percent in the average number of rentals per car. This directly affects bottom-line performance. This is all accomplished by a system whose total operating cost for each pool city never exceeds $10 a day.

PCS has been used most successfully in handling the Florida winter season, the Olympics, the Super Bowl, the summer peak on the West Coast, the presidential inauguration, and major conventions as well as normal business periods. The next time you find yourself walking (not running) through an airport, you might have the Pool Control System to thank.

Production Distribution and Inventory

The Agrico Chemical Company is a subsidiary of The Williams Companies, one of the nation's 350 largest industrial companies.[4] Agrico is one of the largest manufacturers of chemical fertilizers in the United States. Led by progressive management, Agrico had grown from a relatively small firm to a company with sales exceeding $500 million in less than a decade.

By the mid-1970s, however, sharply escalating distribution costs, together with the highly seasonal demand pattern of chemical fertilizers, were creating a complex problem that standard techniques involving charts and cost figures could not handle. The complexity of the situation affected the three major segments of the company's operation—production, distribution, and inventory. In response to its problems, management decided to develop an integrated computer-based planning system.

To aid in its problem solution, Agrico enlisted an outside team of management science consultants. The consultants brought on board the knowledge of advanced network methodology to deal with the multiple-time-period distribution problem. The Agrico distribution problem was indeed large in scale, as it consisted of 4 production plants, 78 distribution centers, and approximately 2,000 customers.

An integral part of the production, distribution, and inventory (PDI) system is a transshipment network model.

A state-of-the-art transshipment algorithm enabled the production, distribution, and inventory problem, with approximately 2,400,000 decision

---

[4] Fred Glover, Gene Jones, David Karney, Darwin Klingman, and John Mote, "An Integrated Production, Distribution, and Inventory Planning System," *Interfaces*, 9, no. 5 (November 1979), 21–35.

variables, to be solved in less than 1 minute of CPU time. The efficiency of the algorithm enabled the PDI system to be used extensively to evaluate the benefit/cost impact of alternative capital investments.

Some of the areas of cost savings generated by use of the model include

1. The early completion of a distribution center would save $175,000.
2. The location of a distribution center on the upper Ohio River would save $100,000 per month in transportation costs.
3. Changing the capacity of some distribution centers while doubling the capacity of a nitrogen chemical plant would save $12,000 annually.

However, the most significant impact of the PDI system is in the increased planning capability and the rescheduling of all production and distribution activities. Within a two-year period, the PDI system resulted in a savings of $4 million. When all decision alternatives suggested by the system have been implemented, it is expected that Agrico's $70 million annual distribution and inventory costs will be reduced by more than $8 million.

Designing and Streamlining Restaurant Operations

The Burger King Corporation has the second largest restaurant system in the world.[5] There are now 3,000 Burger King restaurants across the United States and in many other nations; new units open at the rate of 300 annually and total sales exceed $2 billion.

The management of the fast-food restaurant business is much more complex than in the earlier days of day-to-day operations. The addition of drive-thru windows, larger menus, and the changes in building and equipment all contribute to making management's experience base, obtained in the original restaurant system, unsuitable for decision making in today's environment. The alternative has been to rely increasingly on the analyses provided by the Operations Research Department.

Early efforts by the operations research group included a computer model to purchase meat that saved .75 cents per pound on 3 million pounds of meat per week. Next, the drive-thru operations were analyzed to improve the speed of service. The resulting efficiency package has increased the annual sales capacity of a Burger King restaurant by $35,000. Based on cost escalations and the success of previous OR/MS studies, Burger King committed to a productivity improvement program.

---

[5] William Swart and Luca Donno, "Simulation Modeling Improves Operations, Planning, and Productivity of Fast Food Restaurants," *Interfaces*, 11, no. 6 (December 1981), 35–47.

At the heart of the productivity improvement program is a general-purpose restaurant simulation model. The productivity program allows the restaurant operator to predict his return on investment and a five-year sales estimate. Specific applications of the simulation model determined the optimal stack size or distance between order station and pick-up window. The longer stack accommodates an additional 13 customers per hour for an annual benefit of $10,000 per restaurant. Another study showed that a second drive-thru window could increase sales by 15 percent during peak lunch hours; net benefits are $13,000 per year per restaurant. The model has also been useful in examining the operational impact of the introduction of new products. The model showed that the introduction of small specialty sandwiches would generate a delay of 8 seconds per customer. This would result in an annual loss of $13,000 in sales capacity for an average restaurant. On this basis the sandwiches were not introduced, and Burger King avoided a $39 million loss in capacity to the entire system. Operations research has become an integral part of the planning process at Burger King Corporation.

SUMMARY

You have been introduced to operations research/management science in this chapter. As an interdisciplinary field, OR/MS has existed only a little more than 45 years, but its body of knowledge draws upon related fields as old as human communication. The earliest formal OR/MS activities were military applications by the British during World War II. The field has grown greatly since the early 1940s, and OR/MS is now widely practiced in business and government.

In principle, OR/MS is the application of scientific or systematic methods to improve the decision-making process. The OR/MS approach assumes a systems viewpoint from which scientific procedures can be applied to various aspects of an entire problem. The advantage of the systems approach is that it allows the optimization of an organization's overall goals, not just those of isolated departments or components of the human/machine system.

The characteristic most distinguishing the OR/MS approach is its use of models. Mathematical models attempt to translate the essential qualities of real-world situations into systems of equations. Manipulating or solving the mathematical models can engender effective strategies or courses of action for the decision maker. Simulation models are used to gain descriptions of system behavior under a variety of conditions.

The real-world applications of OR/MS are numerous. In this chapter, we presented three applications in which specific improvements over previous operations were achieved. OR/MS procedures are distinguished from other theoretical scientific endeavors in that they must ultimately be useful or implementable in the real world.

LOOKING AHEAD

In the chapters to follow we shall examine certain basic OR/MS methods. These methods include some of the most widely used OR/MS techniques today. That is the main reason for your exposure to them in an introductory text.

For example, a recent survey of 500 large corporations yielded some interesting facts about the usage of OR/MS in large companies.[6] Table 1.2 indicates the frequency of use of the listed techniques by the 125 responding firms. As you can see, the main topics of this text are widely used among large U.S. corporations.

The techniques listed in the table and all other OR/MS procedures fall into one of three categories. These three categories are defined according to the nature of the environment in which a decision must be made. The environment or the data for a problem can be one of the following:

1. Deterministic
2. Stochastic
3. Uncertain

deterministic problems *Deterministic problems* are those in which data are known with certainty. For example, the knapsack problem we examined earlier is a deterministic problem since all values, weights, and capacities were known exactly. *Stochastic problems* *chastic problems* are those in which the data are not known with certainty, but a probability distribution is known. For example, consider an inventory problem in which the customer demand for a product each month is not known exactly. However, past records for the company indicate a reliable frequency distribution for this stable product. Thus, we can specify the probability that future demand will exceed a specified amount. The majority of mathematical models employed in practice are deterministic. Simulation models, on the other hand, are typically applied to stochastic decision problems.

uncertain problems Problems that must be dealt with when data are *uncertain* are the most difficult of all. An example of this type of problem is the determination of a bid in a competitive-bidding situation. In bidding for a contract, the uncer-

---

[6] Guisseppi A. Forgionne, "Corporate Management Science Activities: An Update," *Interfaces*, 13 (June 1983), 20–23.

TABLE 1.2 *Usage of ORIMS techniques among 125 large corporations*

Methodology	Frequency of use (% of respondents)		
	Never	Moderate	Frequent
Statistical Analysis	1.6	38.7	59.7
Computer Simulation	12.9	53.2	33.9
PERT/CPM	25.8	53.2	21.0
Linear Programming	25.8	59.7	14.5
Queuing Theory	40.3	50.0	9.7
Nonlinear Programming	53.2	38.7	8.1
Dynamic Programming	61.3	33.9	4.8
Game Theory	69.4	27.4	3.2

tainty hinges around the bids to be submitted by the competition. Future demand or future sales are often uncertain quantities, too.

In subsequent chapters we first look at deterministic decision models. Beginning with linear programming, we then examine transportation and assignment models along with other network-type models. Next, we study project scheduling, and finally some more advanced mathematical programming topics, such as goal, dynamic, and integer programming.

The remainder of the book deals with stochastic decision models. We begin this part of the text with a review of probability concepts and then move to decision analysis or decision making under uncertainty. Forecasting comes next, followed by queuing theory or the analysis of waiting lines. We next study the very valuable tool of computer simulation, and then inventory control. Following this, we deal with the management information system interface and the emerging areas of decision support systems and expert systems. Finally, we look at current trends and the potential for synergism between OR/MS and the emerging area of artificial intelligence.

Each chapter will begin with a scenario featuring a well-known organization and its experience in applying OR/MS to its real-world problems. We hope these scenarios will stimulate your interest in and appreciation of OR/MS. Each of the following chapters will end with a solved problem section. In this section, additional problems are solved to illustrate further the techniques presented in the chapter and to help you with the homework problems. At the end of the text you will find cases dealing with many of the topics covered in the text. The cases are more involved and more challenging than the typical homework problems. They do, however, provide you the opportunity to develop your realistic problem-solving skills and to apply the newly learned techniques from the text.

REVIEW QUESTIONS

1. Management science attempts to apply scientific methodology in solving decision problems. How does this methodology differ from the scientific method used in the physical science laboratory?

2. What characteristics distinguish the OR/MS approach to problem solving?

3. In what ways does management science contribute to the functional areas of business? In what ways does it borrow from these areas?

4. What are the advantages of adopting a systems perspective in making decisions for an organization?

5. Several applications of management science are mentioned in this chapter. List as many others as you can.

6. Recall the story of the three blind men who each examined a different part of an elephant. Draw an analogy between their conclusions and the systems approach.

7. List some applications of OR/MS to your major field of interest.

8. What does it mean to "solve" a model?

9. Explain how data can be a serious problem in the application of OR/MS methodology.

10. In the context of decision making, explain the differences in the terms *deterministic, stochastic,* and *uncertain.*

11. To employ management science applications successfully in the real world, more than just a good mathematical model is necessary. What else is needed?

12. What are some of the factors responsible for the rapid growth of OR/MS after 1950?

13. Does management science benefit all levels of management? Explain.

14. Pick some organization with which you are familiar and describe the organization as a whole, and its related components.

15. What are some advantages of using mathematical models? What are some potential pitfalls?

PROBLEMS

1.1 *Simple sales forecasting model.* An appliance manufacturer has developed a small mathematical model that forecasts potential sales given price and advertising expenditures. Let y represent sales and x_1 and x_2 represent advertising expenditures and price, respectively. The model predicts that $y = 8.14 + .66x_1 - .17x_2$. Determine the sales forecast if the price is $250 and advertising expenditures are $40,000. Comment on the possible accuracy or inaccuracy of the model. What variables or relationships may have been omitted?

1.2 Three OR/MS applications are listed as follows. In each case, state the variables relevant to the problem, the data that are required, and what form the output, or answer to the problem, should take.

a. Scheduling commercial airlines between major U.S. cities

b. Determining the location and size of regional warehouses for a retail manufacturer

c. Selecting an investment portfolio for an insurance company

1.3 Recall the knapsack example from Table 1.1. Suppose that it will not be necessary to take water on the trip. Formulate the new model and determine a solution.

1.4 Is your model in Problem 1.3 deterministic or stochastic? Explain.

1.5 *Newsboy problem.* Consider an example of the classical newsboy problem. Suppose that you manage a newstand which buys papers for 12 cents and sells them for 20 cents. The demand for newspapers is variable each day, but past sales records reveal the relative frequencies of demand shown in the table.

Demand	Probability
50	.10
75	.40
100	.35
125	.15

How many papers should you stock considering that leftover papers are worthless the next day? What kind of systematic decision procedure can you think of to solve the problem?

1.6 Is the newsboy problem (Problem 1.5) deterministic or stochastic? Explain.

1.7 *Econometric model.* Consider the following econometric model for forecasting national income:

$$C_t = cY_{t-1} + b \qquad (1)$$
$$I_t = k(Y_{t-1} - Y_{t-2}) + A \qquad (2)$$
$$Y_t = C_t + I_t \qquad (3)$$

where the subscripts refer to time periods. Equation (1) says that consumption equals the marginal propensity to consume c times the income in the preceding period Y_{t-1}, plus a constant b. Equation (2) says that current investment I_t equals the product of the accelerator k

and the change in income that occurred in the preceding period, $(Y_{t-1} - Y_{t-2})$ plus autonomous investment, A. Equation (3) simply defines current income as the sum of consumption and investment.

Using the model requires collecting data on the past values of C, I, and Y. Furthermore, it is necessary to estimate the constants or parameters of the model, c, b, and k. Comment on the accuracy of the model in estimating national income.

1.8 Which is preferable, a simple model that is a relatively good approximation of the problem or a very complex and large model that captures nearly all the relevant aspects of the decision problem?

1.9 *Demand model.* The marketing analyst for a company has determined that the price-demand relationship for their product is linear for a price between \$12 and \$20. That is,

$$\text{demand } D = 1,500 - 30p$$

where $p = $ price.

a. How many units can it expect to sell with a price of \$15?

b. Given a variable cost of \$10 for each unit, what price will maximize profit?

1.10 *Location model.* Three workstations are located along an assembly line as indicated below. All three stations use the same type of parts from an in-process inventory bin that is to be located somewhere along the line. Develop a model to determine the optimum location to minimize the sum of the squares of the distances from the bin to each workstation. Solve your model.

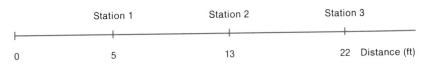

1.11 *Purchase decision.* An airline company is considering the purchase of a sophisticated inspection machine to help identify structural defects in their airplanes. The device will cost \$1,000,000 a year to own and operate but will make the airplanes approximately 10 percent safer. If the average value of a jet airliner is \$6 million and the limits of liability per passenger are \$75,000, should the airlines purchase the device considering that airliners very rarely crash?

1.12 *Car rental model.* Recall the Hertz Rent-A-Car problem from the "Management Science in Action" section of the chapter. One of the equations in their PCS model relates to estimation of completed rentals in city n on day d. This variable CR_{nd} is estimated by

$$CR_{nd} = \overline{CR}_{nd} + \min(CAP_{nd}, DMND_{nd}) \cdot LFE_{nd}$$

where

$$\overline{CR}_{nd} = \sum_{i=1}^{28} RNT_{n,d-i} \cdot LFE_{in,d-i}$$

$$RNT_{in,d-i} = \text{number of rentals in city } n \text{ on day } d - i$$
$$LFE_{in,d-i} = \text{percentage of rentals due back on day } d - i$$
$$CAP_{nd} = \text{rental capacity of city } n \text{ on day } d$$
$$DMND_{nd} = \text{estimated demand at city } n \text{ on day } d$$

Some of the assumptions of the model are that no car will be rented more than twice on a given day and that LFE data supplied by the customer are a good estimate of rental life.

a. Do you think that these assumptions significantly reduce the usefulness of the model?

b. Can you think of any other implicit assumptions or limitations of the portion of the model shown?

BIBLIOGRAPHY

Ackoff, Russell L., and Patrick Rivett, *Manager's Guide to Operations Research*. New York: John Wiley & Sons, Inc., 1963.

————, and Maurice W. Sasieni, *Fundamentals of Operations Research*. New York: John Wiley & Sons, Inc., 1968.

Anderson, D. R., D. J. Sweeney, and T. A. Williams, *An Introduction to Management Science: Quantitative Approaches to Decision Making*, 5th ed. St. Paul, Minn.: West Publishing Company, 1988.

Churchman, C. West, Russell L. Ackoff, and E. L. Arnoff, *Introduction to Operations Research*. New York: John Wiley & Sons, Inc., 1957.

Hillier, F. S., and Gerald J. Lieberman, *Introduction to Operations Research*, 4th ed. San Francisco: Holden-Day, Inc., 1986.

Levin, Richard I., David S. Rubin, and Joel P. Stinson, *Quantitative Approaches to Management*, 6th ed. New York: McGraw-Hill Book Company, 1986.

Littauer, S. B., "What's OR/MS?" *Management Science*, Application Series, 17 (October 1970).

McCloskey, Joseph F., ''The Beginnings of Operations Research: 1934–1941,'' *Operations Research*, 35 (January–February 1987).

Miller, David W., and Martin K. Starr, *Executive Decisions and Operations Research*, 2nd ed. Englewood Cliffs, N.J.: Prentice Hall, 1969.

Simon, Leonard S., ''What Is a Management Scientist?'' *Interfaces*, 1 (February 1971).

Taha, Hamdy A., *Operations Research: An Introduction*, 4th ed. New York: Macmillian Publishing Company, 1987.

Wagner, Harvey M., ''The ABC's of OR,'' *Operations Research*, 19 (December 1969).

2

Linear Programming: Formulation and Applications

UNITED STATES AIR FORCE[1]

Each year the Air Force must make recommendations to Congress regarding how much of the Air Force procurement budget should be spent on the many different aircraft and types of munitions. These procurement decisions concern such aircraft as the F-16, A-10, F-111, and F-15E. The munitions include the maverick, LLGB, MK-82, and MK-84. At stake is the cost and effectiveness against various targets, such as tanks, bridges, and logistics facilities.

The decision process is complicated by the type of conflict, aircraft attrition, effectiveness of the enemy, and even the weather. Decisions with this degree of uncertainty have not traditionally been approached with a mathematical programming or optimization approach. Current planning procedures at the Air Force have been in place for 10 years and have withstood the test of time. However, a linear programming model has been developed to help support the procurement process. The main benefit of the model over past approaches is that it accounts for budget constraints and existing resource quantities in the planning process.

[1] Robert J. Might, "Decision Support for Aircraft and Munitions Procurement," *Interfaces*, 17 (September–October 1987), 55–63.

The results of a series of runs of the linear program are of two types:

1. Detailed listing of aircraft and munitions using both existing and procured to destroy the target set. The list can be explained to show the effects of weather conditions.
2. Graphical displays showing trade-offs, such as the ratio of funds expended on aircraft versus munitions and target value destroyed versus funds expended as a function of the conflict duration.

The linear programming computer runs were made on an IBM 3081-GX computer using IBM's MPSX package or Ketron's MPS3 package. Problem sizes ranged from 1,293 constraints and 6,019 decision variables to 3,179 constraints and 299,885 decision variables. Run times ranged from 3.5 to 261 minutes.

The new methodology (under direction from Air Force senior leadership) is currently being run in parallel with the old system. It is currently being used by the Fighter Division of the Air Force Center for Studies and Analysis. It is anticipated that the new methodology will form the core of a new munitions procurement planning process.

WHAT IS LINEAR PROGRAMMING?

Of all the available techniques and decision tools in management science, linear programming (LP) is one of the most widely used. It is primarily concerned with the determination of the best allocation of scarce resources. Usually, a firm's scarce resources include capital, labor, raw materials, finished goods, or time. For instance, a marketing department may suggest several new products that its firm can sell successfully. However, each new product contributes a different amount to profit and requires a different amount of each of the scarce resources. Furthermore, there are not enough resources to produce all the new products suggested. Which new products and how much of each one should the firm produce? Linear programming can be used to aid in this decision process. In this case, it would probably be used to show what product mix will maximize profits but not exceed the available resources.

mathematical programming   Linear programming (LP) is a component of the more general field of *mathematical programming*. Mathematical programming is concerned with the development of modeling and solution procedures for the purpose of maximizing the extent to which the goals and objectives of the decision maker are realized. Very special conditions must hold before a general mathematical programming problem is actually an LP problem. These special linearity conditions will be described later in the chapter.

Despite the implication of its name, LP has little to do with computer programming. In LP, the word *programming* is related to planning. Specifically, it refers to modeling a problem and subsequently solving it by mathematical techniques. As we shall see, LP is very similar to setting up and solving a system of linear equations.

Even though LP is quite different from computer programming, computer development has played an integral part in the successful application of LP. Real-world LP problems often involve hundreds of variables and equations. These problems would be impossible to solve without a high-speed computer.

Historically, significant contributions to LP were Leontief's input-output analysis in 1936 and the publication, in 1947, of George Dantzig's technique for, and mathematical proof of, the simplex solution procedure. Today, LP is the most widely used mathematical programming and optimization technique. In surveying *Fortune 500* companies, the authors found that of those responding, 95 percent claimed to use LP at least to some extent. More specifically, 37.5 percent claimed to use it very frequently, 32.5 percent used it frequently, 25 percent used it rarely, and only 5 percent never used it. Undoubtedly, smaller companies use LP less. In some cases, it is simply not needed; in other cases, managers may not understand LP or realize its potential. In appropriate situations, LP can be a very powerful tool.

GENERAL AREAS OF APPLICATION

As you can imagine, LP has many business applications. But LP is also often used as a tool for developing economic theory and for the systematic analysis of problems both in the physical and social sciences. When a problem can be looked at as a matter of effectively allocating scarce resources, LP can often be used in its solution.

Industrial, agricultural, and military applications of LP are the most extensive. Some of these include scheduling military and industrial oil tanker fleets, dietary planning, agricultural land use and farm management, urban traffic control, oil refinery operation, scheduling blast furnace operations, and minimizing trim losses in paper mills.

Each of the functional areas of business has its own relationship to LP. In accounting, this relationship is multifaceted. In an LP analysis, the accountant supplies required data. Some public accounting firms employ teams of management consultants as advisors to clients. These consultants sometimes use LP to help solve clients' problems. Moreover, certain LP applications are directed to the accounting function itself. These are usually in the areas of budgeting and financial planning. Applications in finance include portfolio selection models and financial mix strategies in which LP is used to select the best means for financing company projects.

Marketing applications of LP are numerous and include effective media selection for advertising strategies, development of least-cost distribution patterns, warehouse location, and optimal allocation of sales forces. Management applications of LP include production scheduling, human-resource planning, and other kinds of resource allocations.

The list of applications is continually growing as more decision makers are becoming aware of the utility of LP, and the availability of computers increases. The development of more powerful computers will also pave the way for applications that are currently beyond the capability of existing hardware.

PROBLEMS LP CAN BE USED ON

In this section, we discuss some of the general problem situations to which LP can be applied. The following five areas represent the kinds of problems for which LP is now widely used. Can you think of other examples, perhaps innovative ones?

Blending   In blending problems, several raw ingredients are mixed into a final product that must fulfill certain specifications. Each of the raw ingredients contributes certain properties to the final product and entails a given cost. Examples of blending problems are blending petroleum products, mixing cattle feed, mixing meats to make sausage, and mixing paint. Many different combinations of these ingredients will result in satisfactory end products; the objective is to determine the blend of ingredients that does not exceed available supply, meets all technical specifications, and minimizes costs.

Determining product mix   In these problems, it is necessary to determine the kinds and quantities of products to be manufactured to maximize profits. A firm can almost always manufacture several different products; each of these requires the use of limited production resources and contributes a certain amount toward profit. The final product mix must take into consideration the limited resources, expected demand for each product, and various management policies.

Physical distribution and assignment   In physical distribution problems it is necessary to ship goods from supply points or production facilities to warehouses or centers of customer demand. Each supply point has a specified capacity, and each point of demand has a specified level of demand. Furthermore, shipping and/or production costs vary for the different plant-to-market alternatives. The problem is to determine the shipping pattern that minimizes shipping costs, meets all demand, and does not exceed available supply. In assignment problems, the objective is to assign facilities or people to specified jobs to maximize performance or minimize costs or time.

Production scheduling and inventory planning   Many firms produce products that are subject to fluctuations in demand. Widely varying production rates have proven to be very costly. The objective is basically to determine a production schedule that meets anticipated demand and yet maintains reasonable inventory levels and minimizes the overall costs of production and carrying inventory.

Purchasing   Linear programming can be used to help confront the kind of purchasing decisions in which products are available at different quantities, qualities, and prices. The objective is profit maximization, and the purchase decision must take into consideration the output requirements and specifications as well as budget limitations. Linear programming can also be used in "make-or-buy" situations. In these cases the question is whether to produce a product or purchase it from an outside source.

THE LP MODEL

linear pro-gramming model

Linear programming is a mathematical technique that will maximize or minimize a linear function subject to a system of linear constraints. This linear function, together with the system of linear constraints, forms what is called the *linear programming model*. The canonical form of an LP model is as follows:

$$\text{Maximize} \quad c_1 x_1 + c_2 x_2 + \cdots + c_n x_n \qquad (2.1)$$

$$\text{subject to restrictions} \quad a_{11} x_1 + a_{12} x_2 + \cdots + a_{1n} x_n \leq b_1 \qquad (2.2)$$

$$a_{21} x_1 + a_{22} x_2 + \cdots + a_{2n} x_n \leq b_2$$

$$\vdots$$

$$a_{m1} x_1 + a_{m2} x_2 + \cdots + a_{mn} x_n \leq b_m$$

$$\text{and} \quad x_1 \geq 0, x_2 \geq 0, \ldots, x_n \geq 0 \qquad (2.3)$$

Any problem whose mathematical formulation fits this general model is an LP problem.

objective function

An LP model consists of two basic parts—an objective function and a set of constraints. The function (2.1) being maximized, $c_1 x_1 + c_2 x_2 + \cdots + c_n x_n$, is called the *objective function*. It is simply a mathematical expression that measures the effectiveness of a particular solution for the LP problem.

constraints   The restrictions (2.2) in the foregoing model are called *constraints*. These mathematical statements specify such elements of the problem as the limita-
nonnegativity   tions of available resources or the demand that must be met. Conditions (2.3)
conditions   are called the *nonnegativity conditions*.

decision   The x_j variables are *decision variables;* that is, they are the variables
variables   whose value is determined when the LP model is solved. Their values provide the answers that are being sought in the LP analysis. To determine the values of the decision variables, the LP model needs data. The input data
parameters   constants are often referred to as *parameters*. The a_{ij}, c_j, and b_i in the general model are all parameters of the model.

Not all valid LP models fit the exact form of the canonical model. Variations include an objective function that is to be minimized and constraints that are equations rather than inequalities.

FORMULATING LP MODELS

There are many different types of models. You may be familiar with econometric models, civil engineering prototype models, iconic and analog models, even models of the world. In this section, we shall deal with mathematical models. Before any problem can be solved by LP analysis, it must be formulated as a mathematical model that fits the general form set forth in the preceding section. In any mathematical model, the decision maker is attempting to represent the essence of some problem in terms of relationships among symbols. In LP formulations, the real-world problem is translated into mathematical equations.

Model building is more an art than a science; thus, formulating successful models depends greatly upon the model builder's own ingenuity and experience. Formulation can often be the most difficult part of an LP analysis. It is also the most important, for once the problem has been formulated correctly, it can be solved on a computer by an LP computer code. We shall state several business problems and show how to formulate them as LP models. In this way, you will begin to gain a feeling for how to approach the formulation of an LP model.

PRODUCT MIX EXAMPLE   The Faze Linear Company is a small manufacturer of high-fidelity components for the discriminating audiophile. It currently manufactures power amplifiers and preamplifiers; it has the facilities to produce only power amps, only preamps, or a combination of both. Production resources are limited, and it is critical that the firm produce the appropriate number of power amps and/or preamps to maximize profit. Currently, the power amp is selling for $799.95 and is contributing $200 toward profit. The preamp sells for $1,000 and contributes $500 to profit. Figure 2.1 illustrates the product mix problem.

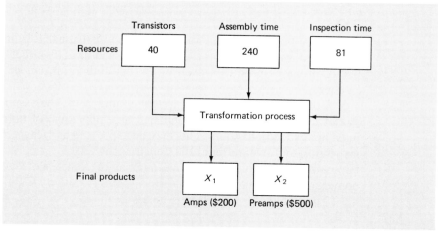

FIGURE 2.1 **Faze Linear product mix problem**

We shall assume that the firm can sell all the components that it can produce and that plant equipment and labor skills are interchangeable between the power amps and preamps.

Constructing the objective function   Given its limited production capacities, Faze Linear would like to produce the exact number of power amps and/or preamps each day that maximize its profits. The objective function of the LP model must evaluate the profit potential of any proposed product mix. The first step in the construction of the objective function is the determination of the appropriate decision variables. What is the manufacturer trying to decide? Specifically, the answer to the question, How many power amps and how many preamps should be produced each day? Thus, let the decision variable x_1 equal the number of power amps to be produced each day, and let x_2 equal the number of preamps to be produced each day. Since x_1 and x_2 contribute \$200 and \$500, respectively, to profit, we may state the objective function as "Maximize $200x_1 + 500x_2$." Preamps contribute more to profit, so it may seem that only preamps should be produced. However, this may not be true since preamps also require more production resources.

Constructing the constraints   In this simplified example, we shall assume that there are only three production resources. The production process is limited by scarcity of high-quality transistors for the preamps, assembly worker hours, and inspection and testing worker hours. Because of a shortage of high-quality transistors, at most 40 preamps can be manufactured on a daily basis; all other electronic components are in adequate supply. There are only 240 hours of assembly worker time available each day. Furthermore, each power amp requires 1.2 hours for assembly and each preamp requires 4 hours. Finally, there are 81 worker hours available for inspection and testing each day, and the two components require .5 and 1 hour, respectively.

Since power amps do not require the transistor that is in short supply, the limited availability of these transistors will directly affect only the number of preamps produced each day. This constraint can be expressed as $x_2 \leq 40$.

Both components require assembly time; thus, the assembly time constraint must ensure that the combined assembly time of both components must not exceed 240 hours. This may be expressed as $1.2x_1 + 4x_2 \leq 240$. For inspection and testing time, the constraint is $.50x_1 + 1x_2 \leq 81$. Since it is impossible to produce a negative number of components, we impose the nonnegativity conditions $x_1, x_2 \geq 0$.

The final LP formulation is thus

$$\text{Maximize}\quad 200x_1 + 500x_2$$

$$\begin{aligned}
\text{subject to}\qquad\quad x_2 &\leq\ 40 \\
1.2x_1 +\ \ 4x_2 &\leq 240 \\
.50x_1 +\ \ 1x_2 &\leq\ 81 \\
x_1, x_2 &\geq 0
\end{aligned}$$

This problem is simple, and LP is not necessary to solve it. However, product mix problems involving hundreds of products and constraints are impossible to solve intuitively, and the use of LP is necessary. As an exercise, try to solve the Faze Linear problem intuitively. How high is your profit? Later, we shall determine the optimum product mix by LP.

GUIDELINES FOR CONSTRUCTING LP MODELS

To formulate an LP model successfully, the decision maker must

1. Understand the problem.
2. Identify the decision variables.
3. Choose a numerical measure of effectiveness for the objective function.
4. Represent this measure of effectiveness as a linear expression involving the decision variables.
5. Identify and represent all constraints as linear expressions involving the decision variables.
6. Collect data or make appropriate estimations for all parameters of the model.

It is not possible to give a magic formula for success in LP model formulation, but the following suggestions can help.

Understand the problem   Make sure that you understand the problem fully. Is the objective clear? Is the problem a maximization or a minimization?

Determine variables   Decide what the decision variables should be. What, precisely, is being sought in the problem? Is it a production schedule, a resource allocation, a shipping pattern, or something else? Remember that the optimum values of the decision variables must provide the answers to the problem. The most common error beginning students make is defining decision variables incorrectly and thus developing invalid models.

Identify and represent all constraints   A constraint must be constructed for each limited resource. Be certain that each decision variable that affects the given resource is included in the constraint. Formulate constraints for all technical specifications or requirements, such as usage or production in fixed proportions. Finally, check for other types of constraints, such as management policies, demand, or other pertinent conditions.

Collect relevant data   All parameters of the model must be defined as numerical constants. Are all relevant data available? In LP analysis, the collection and estimation of relevant data is often the most time-consuming part of the project.

DIET PROBLEM EXAMPLE   In this example, we present a simplification of the classical diet problem. This is a minimization rather than a maximization problem. The objective is to determine the type and amount of foods to include in a daily diet to meet certain nutritional requirements at minimum cost. The foods we include are tuna fish, milk, spinach, and whole-wheat bread; the only nutrients we consider are vitamins A, C, and D, and iron. We are given the nutritional and cost data shown in Table 2.1. Figure 2.2 illustrates the diet minimization problem. The decision to be made is simply to

TABLE 2.1   *Nutrition and cost data for diet problem*

Nutrient	Gallon of milk	Pound of tuna fish	Loaf of bread	Pound of spinach	Recommended daily allowance (RDA)
Vitamin A	6,400	237	0	34,000	5,000 IU
Vitamin C	40	0	0	71	75 mg
Vitamin D	540	0	0	0	400 IU
Iron	28	7	13	8	12 mg
Cost	$1.95	$1.80	$.75	$.80	

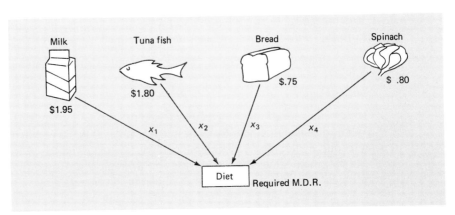

FIGURE 2.2 **The diet problem**

determine the amount of each type of food to include in the daily diet. Thus, let x_1 = number of gallons of milk, x_2 = number of pounds of tuna fish, x_3 = number of loaves of bread, and x_4 = number of pounds of spinach. The objective function, therefore, is to minimize $1.95x_1 + 1.80x_2 + .75x_3 + .80x_4$.

The constraints must ensure that the RDA for each vitamin is met. For vitamin A, each gallon of milk contains 6,400 IU, each pound of tuna fish contains 237 IU, bread contains none, and each pound of spinach contains 34,000 IU. Hence, the RDA constraint for vitamin A is written $6,400x_1 + 237x_2 + 0x_3 + 34,000x_4 \geq 5,000$.

The other three constraints and nonnegativity conditions are written

$$40x_1 + 0x_2 + 0x_3 + 71x_4 \geq 75$$

$$540x_1 + 0x_2 + 0x_3 + 0x_4 \geq 400$$

$$28x_1 + 7x_2 + 13x_3 + 8x_4 \geq 12$$

$$x_1, x_2, x_3, x_4 \geq 0$$

PRODUCTION/DISTRIBUTION EXAMPLE   In this example, two production plants located in different parts of the country must produce and distribute a product to three regional warehouses. The three warehouses have demands of 500, 2,000, and 900, respectively. The cost of shipping, based primarily on distance, is given in Table 2.2. The labor and power costs are less at plant 1; each unit is produced at a cost of $1.50. Each unit at plant 2 is produced at a cost of $2.

The objective in this problem is to meet all demand and minimize the combined cost of production and distribution. The decision to be made concerns how much should be shipped from each plant to each warehouse. Figure 2.3 depicts the combined production and distribution problem.

TABLE 2.2 *Cost ($) of shipping one unit*

From plant	To warehouse		
	1	2	3
1	.30	.90	.80
2	.70	.20	.40

It is more convenient (although not essential) to represent these decision variables as variables with two subscripts. Let

$$x_{ij} = \text{amount shipped from plant } i \text{ to warehouse } j$$

where

$$i = 1, 2$$
$$j = 1, 2, 3$$

Since each unit that is shipped must first be produced, we develop an objective function to minimize $(1.50 + .30)x_{11} + (1.50 + .90)x_{12} + (1.50 + .80)x_{13} + (2.00 + .70)x_{21} + (2.00 + .20)x_{22} + (2.00 + .40)x_{23}$.

The only restriction in this model is that demand must be met. To meet the demand at warehouse 1, all the shipments sent to warehouse 1 must sum to 500. Thus, the first constraint is $x_{11} + x_{21} = 500$. The other two demand constraints are $x_{12} + x_{22} = 2,000$ and $x_{13} + x_{23} = 900$. The nonnegativity

FIGURE 2.3 The production and distribution problem

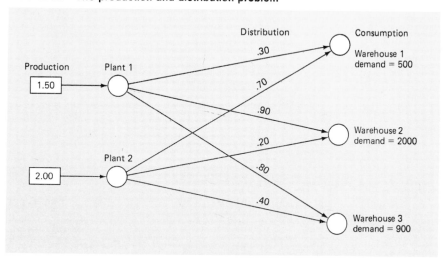

TABLE 2.3   *Cost and composition of fertilizer components*

Mixing component	Cost	Nitrogen (%)	Phosphorous (%)
1	$.20	60	10
2	.30	10	40

condition is $x_{ij} \geq 0$ for all i and j. The complete formulation of the model is thus

Minimize $1.80x_{11} + 2.40x_{12} + 2.30x_{13} + 2.70x_{21} + 2.20x_{22} + 2.40x_{23}$

subject to $x_{11} + x_{21} = 500$

$x_{12} + x_{22} = 2{,}000$

$x_{13} + x_{23} = 900$

$x_{ij} \geq 0$ for all i and j

BLENDING EXAMPLE   The Green Turf Lawn and Garden Store is trying to sell its own brand of lawn fertilizer this year. It plans to sell two types of fertilizer, one high in nitrogen content and the other an all-purpose fertilizer. The fertilizers are mixed from two different components that contribute nitrogen and phosphorus in different amounts. The composition of each component and cost per pound is given in Table 2.3. Figure 2.4 shows the blending problem.

This season's demand is estimated to be 5,000 25-pound bags of high-nitrogen fertilizer and 7,000 25-pound bags of all-purpose fertilizer. The fertilizer high in nitrogen is to contain between 40 and 50 percent nitrogen,

FIGURE 2.4   **The fertilizer blending problem**

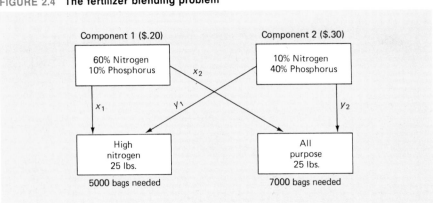

and the all-purpose fertilizer is to contain, at most, 20 percent phosphorus. How many pounds of each mixing component should Green Turf purchase to satisfy estimated demand at minimum cost?

Let x_1 and x_2 be the number of pounds of mixing component 1 that are purchased for the high-nitrogen and all-purpose fertilizers, respectively. Similarly, let y_1 and y_2 be the number of pounds of mixing component 2 that are obtained for the high-nitrogen and all-purpose fertilizers. The objective function is then formulated to be

$$\text{Minimize } .20x_1 + .30y_1 + .20x_2 + .30y_2$$

Assuming that Green Turf wants at least to meet its estimated demand, we can specify the demand on high-nitrogen fertilizer by $x_1 + y_1 \geq 25$ (5,000). Similarly, the demand for all-purpose fertilizer is specified by $x_2 + y_2 \geq 25$ (7,000).

Since the different mixing components contribute different amounts of nitrogen and phosphorus, we must calculate a weighted average to represent the content of a particular blend. The high-nitrogen fertilizer must contain at least 40 percent nitrogen. Thus, $(.60x_1 + .10y_1)/(x_1 + y_1) \geq .40$. This constraint is not a linear expression, but it can be turned into one by eliminating the fraction; thus,

$$.60x_1 + .10y_1 \geq .40(x_1 + y_1)$$
$$.20x_1 - .30y_1 \geq 0$$

The upper limit of 50 percent nitrogen can be written $(.60x_1 + .10y_1)/(x_1 + y_1) \leq .50$, or $.10x_1 - .40y_1 \leq 0$.

Finally, the 20 percent phosphorus restriction on the all-purpose fertilizer is represented $(.10x_2 + .40y_2)/(x_2 + y_2) \leq .20$, or $-.10x_2 + .20y_2 \leq 0$.

The final LP model, then, is stated

$$\text{Minimize} \quad .20x_1 + .30y_1 + .20x_2 + .30y_2$$
$$\text{subject to} \quad x_1 + y_1 \geq 125{,}000$$
$$x_2 + y_2 \geq 175{,}000$$
$$.20x_1 - .30y_1 \geq 0$$
$$.10x_1 - .40y_1 \leq 0$$
$$-.10x_2 + .20y_2 \leq 0$$
$$x_1, x_2, y_1, y_2 \geq 0$$

CONSTRAINED BREAK-EVEN ANALYSIS   The Braden Co. has decided to add one new product line and is considering the addition of two other products. Part of their decision process is to perform a standard break-even analysis to determine what volume of sales is needed for revenue to equal total fixed and variable costs.

One of the firm's accountants has determined the break-even point for product x to be 1,000 units. The graph in Figure 2.5 illustrates the calculation of the break-even point given the following data on product x:

Product	Selling price per unit	Variable cost per unit	Fixed cost
x	$20	$10	$10,000
y	25	12	10,000
z	15	8	10,000

In considering the addition of products y and z, management would like to know what sales volumes of x, y, and z would be necessary to break even and furthermore minimize total capital outlay. Braden currently has contracted to provide 750 units of product x. The same customer has also requested 400 units of z if the product is produced. Braden management is reluctant to produce over 300 units of product y initially, as the market for this product is unproven.

It is not possible to graph the break-even chart for this problem in two dimensions, and the constraints on the sales volume of products x, y, and z preclude using standard break-even analysis. However, linear programming can be used to solve the problem.

FIGURE 2.5 **Break-even graph for product x**

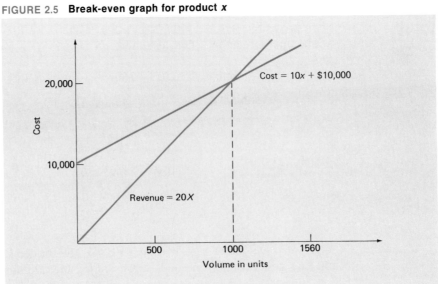

Since management is interested in determining the break-even quantities of x, y, and z (given the stated restrictions), let

$$x_1 = \text{number of units of product } x \text{ to produce}$$
$$x_2 = \text{number of units of product } y \text{ to produce}$$
$$x_3 = \text{number of units of product } z \text{ to produce}$$

The objective function must represent total variable and fixed costs and can be written as

$$\text{Minimize } 10x_1 + 12x_2 + 8x_3 + 30{,}000$$

Since the 30,000 fixed cost is independent of the decision variables, it can be omitted from the objective function, yielding

$$\text{Minimize } 10x_1 + 12x_2 + 8x_3$$

The first constraint forces the total revenue to equal total costs and can be stated as

$$20x_1 + 25x_2 + 15x_3 = 10x_1 + 12x_2 + 8x_3 + 30{,}000$$

or

$$10x_1 + 13x_2 + 7x_3 = 30{,}000$$

The other constraints reflecting sales contracts and demand limitations are expressed as

$$x_1 \geq 750$$
$$x_2 \leq 300$$
$$x_3 \geq 400$$

The complete model with nonnegativity conditions is thus

$$
\begin{aligned}
\text{Minimize} \quad & 10x_1 + 12x_2 + 8x_3 \\
\text{subject to} \quad & 10x_1 + 13x_2 + 7x_3 = 30{,}000 \\
& x_1 \qquad\qquad\qquad \geq \quad 750 \\
& \qquad\ x_2 \qquad\qquad \leq \quad 300 \\
& \qquad\qquad\ x_3 \geq \quad 400 \\
& x_1,\, x_2,\, x_3 \geq 0
\end{aligned}
$$

The solution to the problem is left as an exercise in Chapter 3.

TABLE 2.4 *Machine loading cost and production time data*

Machine	Product	Cost of producing one unit of product j on machine i ($)			Time required to produce one unit of product j on machine i (hr)		
		1	2	3	1	2	3
1		13	9	10	.4	1.1	.9
2		11	12	8	.5	1.2	1.3

MACHINE LOADING EXAMPLE   Nickelson Machine Shop wants to develop a math model to help decide which jobs should be processed on which machines so as to minimize total cost. Initially, the manager wants to try LP on a small example to see if the results are satisfactory. The first consideration, then, is loading three jobs; two machines are available for processing. The jobs correspond to producing 3, 7, and 4 units, respectively, for products 1, 2, and 3. Machine 1 has 8 hours available during each day, but machine 2 has only 6. Table 2.4 gives relevant cost and production time data, and Figure 2.6 illustrates the jobs queuing up for processing on the two machines.

If we let x_{ij} = the number of units of product j to be allocated for production to machine i, then we can formulate the objective function to minimize $13x_{11} + 9x_{12} + 10x_{13} + 11x_{21} + 12x_{22} + 8x_{23}$. The time constraints on machine availability are

$$\text{Machine 1:} \quad .4x_{11} + 1.1x_{12} + .9x_{13} \leq 8$$
$$\text{Machine 2:} \quad .5x_{21} + 1.2x_{22} + 1.3x_{23} \leq 6$$

FIGURE 2.6 **Three jobs to be processed on two machines**

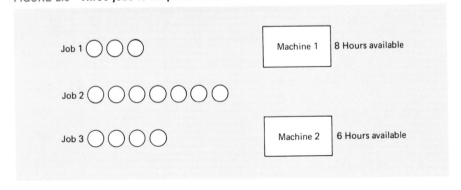

The production requirements specify that the appropriate number of units be produced for each product. These constraints are

$$Product\ 1:\quad x_{11} + x_{21} = 3$$
$$Product\ 2:\quad x_{12} + x_{22} = 7$$
$$Product\ 3:\quad x_{13} + x_{23} = 4$$

The final LP model is

$$Minimize\quad 13x_{11} + 9x_{12} + 10x_{13} + 11x_{21} + 12x_{22} + 8x_{23}$$
$$subject\ to\quad .4x_{11} + 1.1x_{12} + .9x_{13} \le 8$$
$$.5x_{21} + 1.2x_{22} + 1.3x_{23} \le 6$$
$$x_{11} + x_{21} = 3$$
$$x_{12} + x_{22} = 7$$
$$x_{13} + x_{23} = 4$$
$$x_{ij} \ge 0;\ i = 1,\ 2;\ j = 1,\ 2,\ 3$$

PLYWOOD MANUFACTURING   In this example we present a more complex model that represents the LP formulation of an actual plywood manufacturing process. Plywood Ponderosa de Mexico, S.A., is the primary plywood manufacturer in Mexico.[2] The company manufactures a large number of different panel grades and thicknesses and has the capacity to produce 85 million square feet of $\frac{1}{4}$ inch plywood per year.

In the production process, logs are cut or peeled into thin sheets called green veneer. Green veneers are classified into five types depending on their quality and thickness. In the second stage of production, the green veneer is dried and cut into different standard sizes. The next stage involves gluing together pieces of veneer of different thicknesses and grades and pressing them in a hot press. The semifinal products are of three different grades. Finally, the rough plywood is sawed into an exact size and polished. Figure 2.7 illustrates the production process.

Since the company manufactures a large number of different panel grades and thicknesses, the choice of product mix is a very complex issue which has a significant effect on profits. The process needs to balance the available wood mix and the projected sales requirements within given production constraints. Additionally, the planning horizon usually covers two

---

[2] A. Roy, E. De Falomir, and L. Lasdon, "An Optimization-Based Decision Support System for a Product Mix Problem," *Interfaces*, 12 (April 1982), 26–33.

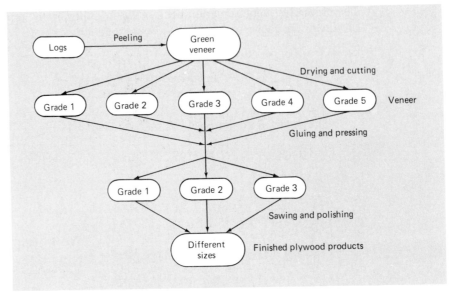

FIGURE 2.7   **The plywood manufacturing process**

periods (months) in which the ending inventory for the first month is the beginning inventory for the next. The LP formulation of the two-time-period model has 90 variables and 45 constraints.

Listed below is the multiple-time-period formulation of the plywood manufacturing problem.

X_{it} = Amount of product i in period t $(i = 1, \ldots, n), (t = 1, \ldots, T)$
C_{it} = Contribution margin of product i in period t
Y_{jt} = Amount of veneer sheet type j produced in period t $(j = 1, \ldots, n_1)$
Z_{kt} = Amount of green veneer type k produced in period t $(k = 1, \ldots, n_2)$
C_{pt} = Consumption of log type p in period t $(p = 1, \ldots, n_3)$
F_{pt} = Final inventory of log type p in period t
S_{pt} = Supply of log type p in period t
P_i = Pressing hours required per unit of product i
G_i = Polishing hours required per unit of product i
A_t = Total polishing hours available in period t
B_t = Total pressing hours available in period t
D_{ij} = Amount of type j veneer sheet required per unit of product i
E_{pT} = Final inventory requirement coefficients for log type p in period T
Q_{kp} = Green veneer type k yield per unit of log type p

H_{kj} = Green veneer type k required per unit of veneer sheet of type j
U_{it} = Upper limit on market demand for product i in period t
L_{it} = Lower limit on market demand for product i in period t
T = Number of periods in planning horizon
n_1 = Number of different types of veneers
n_2 = Number of different types of green veneer
n_3 = Number of different types of logs

The objective is

$$\text{Maximize} \sum_i \sum_t C_{it} X_{it}.$$

The constraints are

Polishing capacity limit:

$$\sum_i G_i X_{it} \leq A_t, \, t = 1, \ldots, T$$

Pressing capacity limit:

$$\sum_i P_i X_{it} \leq B_t, \, t = 1, \ldots, T$$

Veneer sheets required:

$$\sum_i D_{ij} X_{it} = Y_{jt}, \, j = 1, \ldots, n_1, t = 1, \ldots, T$$

Material balance on logs:

$$C_{pt} + F_{pt} - F_{pt-1} = S_{pt}, \, p = 1, \ldots, n_3, t = 1, \ldots, T$$

Final inventory composition requirement:

$$\sum_p E_{pT} F_{pT} = 0$$

Green veneer yield from logs:

$$\sum_p Q_{kp} C_{pt} = Z_{kt}, \, k = 1, \ldots, n_2, t = 1, \ldots, T$$

Green veneers required:

$$\sum_j H_{kj} Y_{jt} = Z_{kt}, \; k = 1, \ldots, n_2, \; t = 1, \ldots, T$$

Market constraints:

$$L_{it} \leq X_{it} \leq U_{it}$$

The constraints in the model reflect the limited production capacity of the pressing and polishing processes. There are also constraints on the market demand for the final plywood products and the availability of the raw material (logs). Another set of constraints specifies the amount of each type of veneer that is required per each final product. Another set of constraints specifies the yield of green veneer types from the different types of logs. Finally, there is a set of constraints specifying the amount of green veneer required and another constraint forcing the final log inventory to be zero.

Plywood Ponderosa uses the IFPOS software package to solve the model. IFPOS is an optimization program that is used with IFPS, the interactive financial planning system. The use of the optimization package within the financial planning language facilitates the integration of financial models with production models.

MATHEMATICAL ASSUMPTIONS AND LIMITATIONS OF LP

Now that you are more familiar with LP, we can discuss the requirements for an LP model. It is tacitly assumed that there is a single goal we can represent by a linear objective function and that all restrictions are linear in nature. Given these prior conditions, any LP model has two basic properties: certainty and linearity.

certainty   *Certainty* requires that all parameters of the model be known. In the realm of decision-making problems, LP falls into the class of decision making under certainty. In other words, the objective function coefficients, c_j, the coefficients of the constraints, a_{ij}, and the right-hand side values, b_i, must all be known constants. When a decision maker cannot determine exact values for some of these parameters, specific numerical values must be estimated and assigned, nonetheless, to use LP. This requirement bears repeating: Specific numerical values are necessary to solve an LP model. By using sensitivity analysis (a technique discussed in Chapter 5), the decision maker can explore the effects of changing some parameters over a range of values. This capability is particularly important when some parameters have been estimated or are known to change over time.

linearity   *Linearity* is a property of mathematical functions. The term denotes the stable relationship between dependent and independent variables that are graphically expressed by straight lines. Suppose that y is a variable whose value depends on the value of an independent variable x. If y is linearly related to x, the graph of y versus x results in a straight line.

In LP, we generally use more than two variables. Suppose that we have n variables $x_1, x_2, \ldots, x_n$. Then a linear expression in terms of these variables is of the form $a_1x_1 + a_2x_2 + \ldots + a_nx_n$. Note that in a linear expression the coefficients are constants, all variables have an exponent of 1, and no variables are multiplied together.

The linearity assumption of LP means that it is necessary for the objective function and the left-hand side of every constraint to be a linear expression. For example, $8x_1 + 17x_2$ is a linear expression, but $8x_1^2 + 17x_2x_3$ is nonlinear since x_1 has an exponent of 2 and x_2 and x_3 form a product of variables.

Three properties of linearity help to clarify the implications of linearity. These properties are proportionality, additivity, and divisibility.

proportionality   *Proportionality* requires that the amount of each resource used must be proportional to the value of the decision variable. This must be true over the entire range of values for the decision variable. Thus, there can be no special costs that raise a decision variable's value above zero, such as a fixed, or start-up, charge associated with beginning an activity. In the objective function, the contribution to profit must also be proportional to the value of the decision variable. For example, in an objective function to maximize profit, $3x_1 + 7x_2$, each unit of x_1 contributes \$3 (a proportional amount) to the value of the objective function.

additivity   *Additivity* postulates that the value of the objective function and the amount of resource used is equal to the sum of the contributions of all decision variables. Using the same objective function, maximize $3x_1 + 7x_2$, suppose that $x_1 = 1$ and $x_2 = 1$. Additivity asserts that the contributions of 3 and 7, respectively, must add together to form a sum of 10.

divisibility   *Divisibility* simply means that the decision variables are allowed to assume a continuous range of values. Thus, the decision variable values may be fractional or any decimal value. The point here is that LP generally will not provide integer, or whole number, solutions. Of course, we know that it is impossible to manufacture a fractional number of automobiles. In problems where integer solutions are required, LP may be used to provide approximate answers by rounding off the solution to integers. However, doing so may cause significant departure from optimality. If optimal integer solutions are required, you must resort to another, more difficult, branch of *integer programming* mathematical programming known as *integer programming*.

Obviously, then, conditions compatible with linear expression must exist before LP can be used. Many mathematical programming models are nonlinear, and other techniques must be used to solve these types of prob-

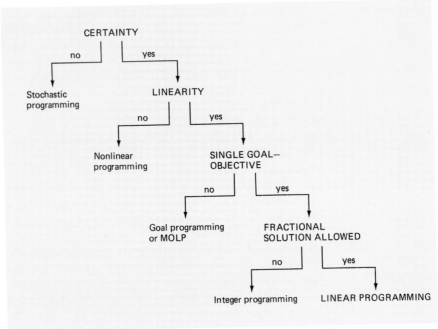

FIGURE 2.8 **LP as related to other math programming approaches**

lems. In some cases, however, LP is used to get approximate solutions to nonlinear problems. This is done since LP is generally much faster and can solve much larger problems than the nonlinear techniques. Figure 2.8 summarizes the assumptions of linear programming and shows what other types of mathematical programming approaches are applicable when certain assumptions are not satisfied. Whenever multiple objectives exist, there is an extension of ordinary linear programming which can be used in addition to goal programming. This extension is multiple objective linear programming or MOLP and is discussed in Chapter 9.

SUMMARY

Linear programming is a method for dealing with decision problems that can be expressed as constrained linear models. The primary assumptions of all linear programming models are certainty of the parameters and linearity of the objective function and all constraints.

In this chapter, we have focused on how to formulate LP models and on the many applications of linear programming. Even though model building is more of an art than a science, you can gain competence through practice and the following of the six steps listed in the chapter. The formulation of models is still one step that requires human insight and is not solvable by a computer.

We have seen how the U.S. Air Force has used linear programming to their advantage in managing their aircraft and munitions procurement. Several other prototype examples have been presented in the chapter; these examples have application to the functional areas of business, including production, marketing, finance, and accounting. Specifically, these examples have dealt with product mix, diet, blending, production/distribution, break-even analysis, and machine loading. In the solved problem section that follows we examine a portfolio selection problem. Additionally, the problems at the end of the chapter deal with several other types of applications.

SOLVED PROBLEM

PROBLEM STATEMENT

Portfolio selection is a financial decision problem in which specific investment alternatives must be selected given a certain budget. The alternatives generally consist of common stocks, bonds, and other securities. The objective is usually to maximize return or minimize risk or the variation in return. Several mathematical programming approaches have been used in designing portfolios. Some of these approaches are beyond the scope of this book; however, linear programming can be applied when the relationships involved are linear.

The United Credit Union has $500,000, which has accrued from previous investments. The management at United would like to reinvest the $500,000 in a portfolio that would maximize yield while maintaining an acceptable level of risk. The investment opportunities, rates of return, and risk measurements are shown in the table.

Investment alternative	Expected rate of return	Estimated variation (σ) in rate of return
Municipal bonds	7.5	0.2
Government bonds	6.5	0.0
Midland Oil stock	11.9	6.0
Western Coal stock	8.8	4.5
Northern Automotive stock	10.0	5.0

The management has decided that the weighted average risk factor (σ) for the entire portfolio should not exceed 3.0. They also want to invest at least 20 percent in bonds, but at least 30 percent of the bond investment must be in government bonds. Their final policy is to invest no more than $250,000 in Western Coal stock.

SOLUTION

The formulation of the portfolio selection problem as a linear programming model requires the expression of the objective and all policies and restrictions as linear relationships. The first step is to determine the decision variables; these should reflect the basic question that needs to be answered: How much should United invest in each of the five alternatives?

Therefore, let

x_1 = amount invested in municipal bonds
x_2 = amount invested in government bonds
x_3 = amount invested in Midland Oil stock
x_4 = amount invested in Western Coal stock
x_5 = amount invested in Northern Automotive stock

The linear programming model can be written as

Maximize $7.5x_1 + 6.5x_2 + 11.9x_3 + 8.8x_4 + 10.0x_5$

subject to $.2x_1 + 0x_2 + 6x_3 + 4.5x_4 + 5x_5 \leq 3.0(500,000)$
(average risk constraint)

$x_1 + x_2 \geq .2(500,000)$
(total bond requirement)

$-.3x_1 + .7x_2 \geq 0$
(government bond percentage)

$x_4 \leq 250,000$
(coal restriction)

$x_1 + x_2 + x_3 + x_4 + x_5 = 500,000$ (total budget)

$x_1, x_2, \ldots, x_5 \geq 0$

The first and third constraints perhaps require some explanation. The coefficients of the first constraint are obtained by dividing each associated standard deviation of return σ by 500,000 (the total weight) to ensure that the weighted average is ≤ 3.0. The third constraint is formed by $x_2 \geq .3(x_1 + x_2)$, or $-.3x_1 + .7x_2 \geq 0$.

REVIEW QUESTIONS

1. How does LP differ from just solving a system of equations?
2. Interpret the difference between an equality constraint and an inequality constraint.

3. The nonnegativity conditions are not always imposed in every LP model. Give some situations in which they might not be enforced.
4. What does "linearity" mean?
5. Can you think of any LP applications other than those discussed in the chapter?
6. What are three properties of linearity?
7. Explain what is meant by the phrase, "Model building is more an art than a science."
8. What assumptions must be satisfied for a problem to be solved by LP?

PROBLEMS

√2.1 *Product mix.* The Ace Manufacturing Company produces two lines of its product, the super and the regular. Resource requirements for production are given in the table. There are 1,600 hours of assembly worker hours available per week, 700 hour of paint time, and 300 hours of inspection time. Regular customers will demand at least 150 units of the regular line and 90 of the super. Formulate an LP model that will determine the optimal product mix on a weekly basis.

Product line	Profit contribution	Assembly time (hr)	Paint time (hr)	Inspection time (hr)
Regular	$50	1.2	.8	.2
Super	75	1.6	.9	.2

2.2 *Product mix.* The Crazy Nut Company wishes to market two special nut mixes during the holiday season. Mix 1 contains $\frac{1}{2}$ pound of peanuts and $\frac{1}{2}$ pound of cashews; mix 2 contains $\frac{3}{5}$ pound of peanuts, $\frac{1}{4}$ pound of cashews, and $\frac{3}{20}$ pound of almonds. Mix 1 sells for $1.49 per pound; mix 2 sells for $1.69 per pound. The data pertinent to the raw ingredients appear in the table. Assuming that Crazy can sell all cans of either mix that it produces, formulate an LP model to determine how much of mixes 1 and 2 to produce.

Ingredient	Amount available (lb)	Cost per lb
Peanuts	30,000	$.35
Cashews	12,000	.50
Almonds	9,000	.60

√2.3 *Break-even analysis.* A firm is considering the production of two new products. Data pertaining to sales price and costs are shown in the table. The firm has already contracted to provide 500 units of product *A* and would like to calculate the break-even quantities for products *A* and *B*. Formulate an LP model to determine the break-even points for products *A* and *B* at minimal total capital outlay.

Product	Selling price per unit	Variable cost per unit	Fixed cost
A	$30	$16	$10,000
B	35	18	12,000

2.4 *Portfolio selection.* Western Trust Co. invests in various types of securities. They have $5 million for immediate investment and wish to maximize the interest earned over the next year. Risk is not a factor. There are four investment possibilities, as outlined in the table. To structure the portfolio further, the Board of Directors of Western has specified that at least 40 percent of the investment must be placed in corporate bonds and common stock. Furthermore, no more than 20 percent of the investment can be in real estate. Formulate an LP model to meet their objectives.

Investment	Expected interest earned (%)	Maximum allowable investment (000,000's)
Corporate bonds	8.5	$3
Common stock	9.0	3
Gold certificates	10.0	2
Real estate	13.0	1

2.5 *Investment and budget allocation.* The Viscus Oil Company must decide how to allocate its budget from windfall profits. The government grants certain tax breaks if the company invests funds in research concerned with energy conservation. However, the government stipulates that at least 60 percent of the funds must be funneled into research for automobile efficiency. Viscus has a $1 million budget for energy research and development this year; the research proposal data are shown in the table. Assuming Viscus wants to maximize return on its investments and receive the government tax break, how should the budget be allocated? Formulate as an LP model.

Project	Management policy on upper limit of expenditures	Forecast return on investment (%)
Methanol fuel research	$300,000	4.0
Electrically operated cars	100,000	0.1
Emission reduction	300,000	3.0
Solar cells	200,000	2.0
Windmills	100,000	1.0

2.6 *Production and distribution.* The Leiz Manufacturing Company produces small chips for use in pocket calculators. Leiz has two plants that produce the chips and then distribute them to five different wholesalers. The costs of production at plants 1 and 2 are $2.19 and $2.38, respectively. Forecast demand indicates that shipments will have to be 2,000 to wholesaler 1, 3,000 to wholesaler 2, 1,000 to wholesaler 3, 5,000 to wholesaler 4, and 4,000 to wholesaler 5. The distribution costs of shipping a chip from plant to wholesaler are shown in the table. Production capacity at each plant is 8,000 units. Formulate an LP model to determine how many chips each plant supplies each wholesaler.

	To wholesaler				
From plant	*1*	*2*	*3*	*4*	*5*
1	.03	.02	.05	.04	.02
2	.06	.04	.02	.03	.05

2.7 *Loan planning.* Mydlend Mortgage Company makes four types of loans, as listed in the table. The company is trying to decide how to allocate $5 million in funds. The company president has decided that the average risk must not exceed 3.7 percent. Formulate an LP model to maximize yield in allocating the $5 million.

Type of loan	Yield (%)	Risk (%)
First mortgage	7	3.5
Remodeling	1	2.0
Auto	8	3.8
Signature	14	4.0

2.8 *Diet planning.* An agriculture student wants to determine what quantities of various grains to feed cattle to meet minimum nutritional requirements at lowest cost. The student is considering the use of corn, barley, oats, and wheat. The table relates the relevant dietary information per pound of grain. Formulate an LP model to determine the dietary mix that minimizes cost.

Nutrient	Corn	Barley	Oats	Wheat	Recommended daily allowance
Protein	10	9	11	8	20 mg
Calcium	50	45	58	50	70 mg
Iron	9	8	7	10	12 mg
Calories	1,000	800	850	9,000	4,000
Cost per lb	$.55	$.47	$.45	$.52	

2.9 *Marketing media selection.* A manufacturer of tennis rackets would like to introduce its new line of poly-play rackets. The firm may advertise in leading tennis magazines or on television during the World Championship Tennis pro tour and major international tournaments. The feeling is that those players whose annual income exceeds $15,000 will be 1.8 times more likely to buy this new racket. The objective in the advertising scheme is to maximize potential sales. One unit of TV advertising costs $35,000 and reaches approximately 2 million people, half of whom make more than $15,000 annually. One unit of advertising in tennis magazine 1 costs $25,000 and reaches 1 million people, three-fourths of whom are in the higher income bracket. One unit of advertising in tennis magazine 2 costs $15,000 and reaches 600,000 people, two-thirds of whom have incomes exceeding $15,000. The total advertising budget is $250,000. Formulate the problem as an LP model.

2.10 *Purchasing.* McKisson Co. purchases two components for the assembly of its block-and-tackle sets. A total of four suppliers can supply the components.,However, each supplier has a different per unit purchase price, distribution cost, and available supply. Purchase prices and freight costs are given in the table. Additionally, suppliers 1, 2, 3, and 4 have the capacity to supply 2,000, 3,000, 4,000, and 4,000 components, respectively. (Their production capacity is equally taxed by either component.) McKisson has a demand of 5,000 units for component 1 and 6,000 units for component 2. How many units of each component should McKisson order from each supplier to minimize costs?

| | Purchase price | | | |
	Supplier 1	Supplier 2	Supplier 3	Supplier 4
Component 1	$5	$7	$6	$4
Component 2	8	8	9	7
	Freight cost			
	Supplier 1	Supplier 2	Supplier 3	Supplier 4
Component 1	$1.65	$1.25	$ .95	$1.10
Component 2	1.75	1.35	1.10	1.15

2.11 *Financing decision.* Consider the problem faced by a major city, of financing various capital improvement projects. Of highest priority are the renovation of existing sewage treatment plants and the development of a water pipeline from another region to ensure a good-quality water supply. The projects will cost $200 million and will be funded by the sale of a proposed bond issue, and loans from an insurance company and a bank. Underwriters in Chicago have stated that no more than $110 million in bonds can be sold at the proposed rate of 10 percent. The bank will loan no more than $100 million at a rate of 13 percent and insists that its loan be no larger than one-half the bond debt. Finally, the insurance company will loan up to $80 million but at a rate of 15 percent. Formulate a linear programming model to determine the best financing strategy for the city.

2.12 *Transportation.* The Normal Distribution Company supplies five major metropolitan areas from three of its regionally located warehouses. It would like to minimize the transportation costs of shipping from warehouse to market. Transportation costs are shown in the table. Formulate an LP model to meet all demand at minimum transportation cost.

	To city					
From warehouse	1	2	3	4	5	Supply
1	$ 7	$ 5	$12	$11	$ 9	500
2	13	12	6	3	8	300
3	7	6	5	4	14	350
Demand	150	200	100	300	400	

2.13 *Production/product mix.* A manufacturer of office equipment would like to optimize the company's product mix. Currently, the firm produces desks, chairs, tables, and filing cabinets. Each product's resource requirements are given in the table. The desks, chairs, tables, and cabinets contribute $150, $45, $100, and $40 to profit, respectively. The minimum monthly demand requirements are 75 desks, 120 chairs, 100 tables, and 50 filing cabinets. Additionally, management does not want the number of filing cabinets to exceed 10 percent of the total number of items produced. Formulate as an LP model.

Product	Wood (board ft)	Plastic (sq ft)	Steel alloy (lb)	Administrative worker hours
Desks	0	6	9	2.5
Chairs	3	1	1	1.2
Tables	5	2	2	2.2
Cabinets	0	0	15	1.9
Availability	1,000	1,200	1,000	1,500

2.14 *Blending.* The Smelly Oil Company produces all three major types of gasoline: regular, premium, and unleaded. Its gasoline is produced by blending two petroleum components and a high-octane lead additive. Minimum octane ratings must be met as provided in the following table of data:

Gasoline	Minimum octane	Selling price per gal.
Regular	89	$1.50
Premium	94	1.57
Unleaded	87	1.55

Cost and availability for the ingredients in the blends are shown in the next table:

Blending ingredients	Octane	Cost per gal	Per month (gal)
Component 1	130	$1.24	76,000
Component 2	75	1.18	95,000
Lead additive	1,100	2.50	60,000

Formulate an LP problem to determine the blends that maximize profit and meet all technical specifications. Assume that octane values mix linearly.

2.15 *Capital rationing.* The Zink Fuel Company is confronted with five projects competing for the firm's fixed budget of $300,000. The net investment and estimated present values of future cash inflows for each project are listed in the table. Each of the projects is of the type that can be funded partially. That is, it is not necessary to fund all or none of the project (as is often the case). Formulate an LP model to maximize the total present value of the projects selected.

Project	Net investment	Present value of inflows at 10 percent
1	$ 80,000	$115,000
2	100,000	150,000
3	70,000	85,000
4	90,000	110,000
5	120,000	133,000

2.16 *Shopping center design.* Lincoln Properties has invested in the development of an indoor shopping center mall in the Kansas City suburbs. It must now plan for the size and quantity of stores to lease to in the mall. Smaller stores having 2,500 square feet are more profitable, but large "anchor" stores (approximately 250,000 square feet) are necessary to attract sufficient volumes of traffic. Medium-sized stores average around 100,000 square feet. The mall will contain 1 million square feet, and Lincoln Properties wants at least one large anchor store in the mall. Furthermore, it wants a 3 : 1 ratio of medium to large stores and the total square footage of small stores to be 1.5 times that of medium and large stores combined. Leasing rates are anticipated to be $265,000, $170,000, and $20,000 per year for large, medium-sized, and small stores, respectively. Formulate an LP model to determine the most profitable store configuration in the new mall.

2.17 *Production and inventory planning.* The Coldman Company has a production planning problem. Management wants to plan production for the ensuing year so as to minimize the combined cost of production and inventory storage costs. In each quarter of the year, demand is anticipated to be 65, 80, 135, and 75, respectively. The product can be manufactured during regular time at a cost of $16 per unit produced, or during overtime at a cost of $20 per unit. The table gives data pertinent to production capacities. The cost of carrying one unit in inventory per quarter is $2. The inventory level at the beginning of the first quarter is zero. Formulate an LP model to minimize the production plus storage costs for the year.

Capacities (units)			
Quarter	Regular time	Overtime	Quarterly demand
1	80	10	65
2	90	10	80
3	95	20	135
4	70	10	75

2.18 *Machine loading.* Jiffy Job Shop would like to try a quantitative approach to its machine loading problem. There are three machines in the shop, and they are used to produce five different products. Each machine has an 8-hour time availability each working day. Today, the demand is 6, 3, 2, 1, and 5 for products 1 through 5, respectively. The table gives relevant cost and production time data. Formulate an LP model to determine the units of product j to be allocated for production on machine i.

Machine	Product	Cost of producing one unit of product j on machine i					Time required to produce one unit of product j on machine i (hr)				
		1	2	3	4	5	1	2	3	4	5
1		$12	$10	$13	$ 9	$8	1	.8	1.5	.5	.6
2		7	6	12	11	9	1.5	.9	.7	.4	.9
3		14	8	5	3	2	1.2	1.1	.9	.8	.5

√ 2.19 *Refinery operation.* An American oil company uses crude oil from around the world to produce its final petroleum products. The different input mixes of the crude oils are shown in the table. The fractions indicate the optimal usage of each crude as a component of each final product. Thus, the input of Gulf crude is best utilized when 15 percent is used for regular gas, 40 percent for unleaded, and so on. The prices per barrel of the crudes are $34, $35, $33, $34, and $37, respectively, for the Gulf, North Atlantic, Alaskan, Mexican, and OPEC oil. The objective is to meet market demand at minimum cost. Formulate the refinery optimization problem as a linear optimization model.

	Optimal fraction of allocation				
Crude oil	*Regular*	*Unleaded*	*Premium*	*Diesel*	*Fuel oil*
Gulf	.15	.40	.30	.10	.05
North Atlantic	.20	.30	.20	.15	.15
Alaskan	.40	.10	.10	.20	.20
Mexican	.25	.30	.30	.10	.05
OPEC	.10	.40	.40	.10	—
Demand *(barrels/day)*	30,000	50,000	20,000	25,000	35,000

2.20 *Personnel scheduling.* Ma-Bell Corporation has a scheduling problem. Operators are needed according to the schedule shown in the table. Operators work 8-hour shifts and can begin work at either midnight, 4 A.M., 8 A.M., noon, 4 P.M. or 8 P.M. Let x_j equal the number of operators beginning work in time period j, $j = 1, 2, \ldots, 6$. Formulate an LP model to hire the minimum number of operators the company needs.

Time period	*Operators needed*
Midnight to 4 A.M.	4
4 A.M. to 8 A.M.	6
8 A.M. to noon	90
Noon to 4 P.M.	85
4 P.M. to 8 P.M.	55
8 P.M. to midnight	20

2.21 *Cutting stock (trim loss).* Potluck Forests, Inc., produces paper products. In one of its processes, reels of 100 inch wide paper are cut into smaller-width reels of the same length. Each week, orders for different width reels are received. Currently, the cutting patterns are manually estimated by an experienced operator. Potluck wishes to apply linear programming to this classical OR problem. This week the company has orders for 30, 50, 25, and 90 reels, respectively, of the 60, 48, 36, and 24-inch widths. The objective is to cut the original 100-inch reels to meet demand and minimize waste. Waste is defined as both trim loss and surplus. Trim loss is the leftover portion of a 100-inch reel. For example, if a 100-inch reel is cut into two 36-inch reels and a 24-inch reel, there are 4 inches of leftover trim loss, as shown.

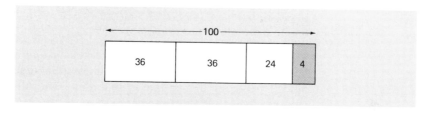

Surplus waste is generated when more reels of a certain type are cut than are demanded. For example, if there are 5 extra 24-inch reels cut, there is a waste of $5 \times 24 = 120$. Determine all possible ways to cut the 100-inch reels to yield reels of sizes 60, 48, 36, and 24. Let x_j represent the number of 100 inch reels to be cut in pattern j. Calculate the trim loss for each pattern and formulate an LP model to minimize total trim and surplus waste.

2.22 *Production scheduling.* The Akron Tire Company currently produces four lines of tires: the economy, glass-belted, snow tire, and steel radial. Recent recessionary trends have caused a decline in demand, and the company is laying off workers and discontinuing its third shift.

   The problem it faces is that of rescheduling production during the first and second shifts for the remaining quarter of the year. The production process primarily involves the use of vulcanization, fabrication, and plastometer machines. However, the limiting resource in production is the availability of machine hours on the vulcanization machines. The economy, glass-belted, snow tire, and steel radial require 4, 5, 5, and 7 hours, respectively, of vulcanizing time.

   The sales manager has forecast the expected sales for each of the four tires in the last quarter of the year. These estimates are shown in the following table:

Month	Forecast sales			
	Economy	Glass-belted	Snow tire	Steel radial
October	8,000	19,000	4,000	7,000
November	7,000	19,000	15,000	7,000
December	6,000	18,000	17,000	7,000

The production capacity in terms of vulcanizing hours available is expressed by month and shift in the next table:

	Vulcanizing hours available	
Month	Shift 1	Shift 2
October	110,000	100,000
November	130,000	120,000
December	115,000	116,000

The labor cost of operating the vulcanizing machines is $10 per hour during the first shift. The shift differential requires that the wages be $12 per hour during the second shift. The other relevant cost is storage: It costs $4 per month to store a tire, regardless of its type. Note that it will be necessary to store some tires in the problem, as there is not enough labor available during December to meet December demand.

Assuming that the company wishes to produce exactly as many tires as the sales manager has forecast, formulate an LP model to determine a production schedule that will meet demand at minimum total cost.

2.23 *Air cleaner design.* A tractor manufacturer in Bombay, India, needs to design an air cleaner for its 60-hp tractor. The limiting specifications are that the diameters of the main body (x_2) and the exit duct (x_1) should not exceed $6\frac{1}{4}$ and $2\frac{1}{2}$ inches, respectively. To maintain pressure drop, these same diameters should not go below $3\frac{3}{4}$ and $1\frac{1}{2}$ inches, respectively. The tractor manufacturer has contracted to supply a minimum of 50 air cleaners per month. There is a national shortage of sheet metal, as the Indian government will only sanction 15,000 square inches of material per month. Other technical air cleaner requirements dictate that the total amount of metal per air cleaner should be no less than 250 square inches. Other parts and scrap require that all areas must be multiplied by 1.6 to obtain total metal requirements. The area of metal required by each air cleaner (including scrap) is given by $1.6(2.75\pi x_1 + 10\pi x_2)$, where $\pi = 3.1416$. Formulate an LP model to minimize the metal used in each air cleaner and to determine diameters x_1 and x_2.

2.24 *Agricultural land allocation.* Agricultural applications of LP are numerous. The optimal use of agricultural land resources is becoming increasingly important to feed the world's people. This case is based on an actual model used to allocate land optimally given a set of agronomic and institutional constraints specific to the foreign country. We consider a group of 11 possible crops and 8 agricultural regions in which the crops may be cultivated. Each region is currently supporting a certain acreage of one or more of the 11 crops. However, a reallocation of the land may result in more efficient utilization, and also a higher net revenue per acre of crop, in each region.

The 11 crops are categorized as follows:

Winter crops	Summer crops
1 Wheat	5 Cotton variety 1
2 Barley	6 Cotton variety 2
3 Broad beans	7 Rice
4 Lentils	8 Corn
	9 Millet
	10 Sesame
	11 Sugar cane

The following variables are relevant to the model:

i = region number (8)
j = crop number (11)
r_{ij} = net revenue factor per acre of crop j in region i
x_{ij} = acreage to be assigned to crop j in region i
y_{ij} = actual current acreage of crop j in province i
w_i = total area in winter crops in region i
s_i = total area in summer crops in region i
y_i = total cultivated area in region i
(note that $w_i \leq y_i$ and $s_i \leq y_i$)
y_{i11} = actual acreage of sugar cane in region i

The objective function of the model defines net revenue in terms of crop yield, a_{ij}, crop price, p_j, and cultivation costs, c_{ij}. Thus $r_{ij} = a_{ij}p_j - c_{ij}$. Assuming that all parameters, a_{ij}, p_j, and c_{ij} are known, we can then calculate the r_{ij} for the objective function.

The constraints relate to the following restrictions:

☐ The total acreage of winter crops in region i must equal w_i.
☐ The total acreage of summer crops in region i must equal s_i.
☐ The total acreage of cotton crops in each region i must not exceed one-third of the total cultivated area in region i.
☐ Even though the objective is to maximize net revenue, there exists a constraint that the new acreage of the staple crops, wheat, broad beans, and corn, must be at least .3, .3, and .85, respectively, as large as the current acreage of these three crops.
☐ Each region must cultivate the same amount of sugar cane as is currently being cropped.

Formulate an LP model to maximize the net revenue, subject to the foregoing constraints.

2.25 *Multiperiod production planning.* The Zilco Co. has forecasted demand for its leading product line for the next six months as indicated:

Month	1	2	3	4	5	6
Demand	800	1,200	1,600	2,400	1,200	800

Zilco's policy is to meet all demand if at all possible. It currently has 100 units in inventory; all other demand must be met by production. If on-hand inventory plus production exceeds demand in any given month, the excess is subject to an inventory carrying cost of $50 per unit per month.

At the beginning of the first month, there are 30 workers currently employed. Regular labor cost averages $1,500 per month per worker. Each worker can produce 1 unit per day. Assume each month has 22 workdays. Laying off a worker at the beginning of any month costs $500. Hiring and training a new worker at the beginning of any month costs $750. Daily overtime is limited to 2 hours in excess of the normal 8 hour workday. Overtime is compensated at 1.5 times regular labor costs. Zilco has a total monthly budget of $150,000 to cover all expenses relating to this production-planning problem.

Formulate an LP model to determine optimal production and inventory levels plus hiring and firing policies for the next six months.

2.26 *Multiperiod investment planning.* As investment analyst for a partnership, you have been asked to make recommendations concerning real estate investments over the next three years. The partnership currently has $2 million to invest and is considering investing in three alternatives. These alternatives include condominiums, a shopping center, and a commercial office complex. The general partners have estimated the following cash flows over the three-year period.

Project	Month						
	0	6	12	18	24	30	36
Condos	-$2,000,000	-$1,000,000	-$ 500,000	$ 0	$ 600,000	$2,000,000	$4,500,000
Shopping center	-3,000,000	-800,000	1,000,000	1,500,000	1,500,000	4,000,000	-1,000,000
Office building	-1,500,000	-1,000,000	-1,000,000	500,000	1,800,000	2,000,000	3,000,000

The partnership is expecting the following cash inflows at 6-month intervals from previous investments: $600,000 (in 6 months), $400,000, $450,000, $300,000, $360,000, and $320,000 at the end of 36 months. Additional money is available from borrowing at 6-month intervals at 5 percent interest per half year. The partnership does not want the total amount borrowed to ever exceed $2.5 million. Excess funds available in any period can be invested at 4 percent per half year.

Formulate an LP model to optimize decisions regarding investing and borrowing over the next three years. The partnership's goal is to maximize net worth at the end of three years.

BIBLIOGRAPHY

Anderson, David, Dennis Sweeney, and Thomas Williams, *Linear Programming for Decision Making: An Applications Approach.* New York: West Publishing Company, 1974.

Charnes, A., and W. W. Cooper, *Management Models and Industrial Applications of Linear Programming.* New York: John Wiley & Sons, Inc., 1968.

Eppen, G. D., F. J. Gould, and C. P. Schmidt, *Introductory Management Science,* 2nd ed. Englewood Cliffs, N.J.: Prentice Hall, 1987.

Levin, Richard I., David S. Rubin, and Joel P. Stinson, *Quantitative Approaches to Management,* 6th ed. New York: McGraw-Hill Book Company, 1986.

Schrage, Linus, *Linear, Integer, and Quadratic Programming with LINDO,* 3rd ed. Palo Alto, Calif.: The Scientific Press, 1986.

Taha, H. A., *Operations Research: An Introduction,* 4th ed. New York: Macmillan Publishing Company, 1987.

3

Solving LP Problems: Graphical Method

NORTH AMERICAN VAN LINES

North American Van Lines, Inc., is one of the nation's largest truck transportation companies, with over 3,700 vehicles in its independent owner-operator fleet.[1] The Fleet Service Division has the primary responsibility for planning and controlling the company's fleet of tractors. Fleet Service's primary objective is to minimize the company's cost of maintaining and carrying equipment. The process is extremely complex due to the hundreds of variables and constraints which must be considered.

Prior to the implementation of a decision support system, Fleet Service used a manual financial planning and forecasting system which was highly labor intensive (120 person-hours) and took one to two weeks to generate each month. Thus, the manual method was very costly and unable to consider a wide variety of scenarios or sales-mix alternatives.

A decision support system was developed which included a large-scale linear programming model as the heart of the system. The LP model was used to suggest a mix of tractors to sell to contract truckers and to trade in to manufacturers during each four-week period of the fiscal year. The model thus generated a new/used sales mix which would result in the

[1] D. Avramovich, T. Cook, G. Langston, and F. Sutherland, "A Decision Support System for Fleet Management: A Linear Programming Approach," *Interfaces*, 12 (June 1982), 1–9.

lowest level of net expense. The model contained 400–500 decision variables and enabled fleet management to review plans in half a day instead of one to two weeks.

Based upon forecast parameters and the suggested new/used sales mix, the decision support system outputs a series of descriptive reports which illustrate the financial impact of adopting the sales mix. Sensitivity reports enable management to assess the impact of certain parameter changes without rerunning the model.

In addition to work force savings and improved timeliness of the planning process, management feels that the new system has significantly improved profit contribution due to better decisions about the buying, selling, and trading in of tractor units. For example, they were able to reduce the tractor inventory by 100 units. This represents a reduction in the average value of inventory of $3,000,000 and an approximate savings of $600,000 a year in inventory carrying cost.

INTRODUCTION

In Chapter 2, we examined some of the mathematical assumptions of LP, described how to formulate LP problems, and indicated typical areas of application. In this chapter, we investigate how these formulated LP models can be solved by the graphical method. The graphical method is limited to problems with no more than three variables, since we cannot draw graphs in more than three dimensions. In fact, it is very awkward to graph problems with more than two variables.

graphical method   The *graphical method* is valuable mainly from an instructional point of view. It provides a "picture" of how LP solutions are determined, and yields insight into the nature of an LP problem. By studying the graphical method we will have a more intuitive understanding of linear programming analysis involving the simplex method, and also of sensitivity analysis. The simplex method is a practical method for solving larger, more realistic LP problems, and is the subject of Chapter 4.

THE GRAPHICAL SOLUTION METHOD

The graphical method of LP solution simply involves plotting each of a problem's constraints to form a region of possible solutions. We then examine this region to select the best alternative. To illustrate the graphical method, let us return to the Faze Linear product mix example of Chapter 2.

Recall that the objective is to produce the appropriate number of power amplifiers and preamplifiers to maximize the profit. The two components contribute $200 and $500, respectively, to profit. The model we derived is

Maximize $200x_1 + 500x_2$ (profit)

subject to $x_2 \leq 40$ (transistor availability)

$1.2x_1 + 4x_2 \leq 240$ (assembly time)

$.5x_1 + 1x_2 \leq 81$ (inspection/testing time)

$x_1, x_2 \geq 0$

where

x_1 = number of amplifiers to be produced
x_2 = number of preamplifiers to be produced

To use the graphical solution method we must establish a coordinate grid system on which to display the possible values of x_1 and x_2. Whenever the nonnegativity conditions ($x_1 \geq 0$ and $x_2 \geq 0$) apply to both decision variables, our graph will be confined to the positive quadrant. Figure 3.1 illustrates the coordinate system for the Faze Linear problem. Any point (x_1, x_2) in the first quadrant is a potential solution to the Faze Linear problem, where x_1 = number of amps to be produced and x_2 = number of preamps to

FIGURE 3.1 Coordinate system for Faze Linear problem

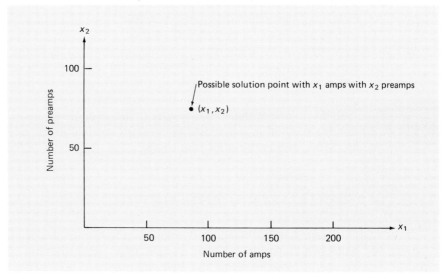

be produced. We must determine which points in the first quadrant are feasible (i.e., satisfy all the constraints) and then determine which feasible point provides the maximum profit contribution.

The set of all feasible points can be determined by graphing the region defined by the three constraints. The first constraint $x_2 \leq 40$ pertains to transistor availability and can be graphed by initially graphing the equation form of the constraint

$$x_2 = 40$$

A simple procedure for graphing the equation of a line is to locate the x_1 and x_2 intercepts (since any two points determine a line). The x_1 intercept is determined by setting $x_2 = 0$ and solving for x_1. Likewise, the x_2 intercept is determined by setting $x_1 = 0$ and solving for x_2. Returning to our equation $x_2 = 40$ and solving for the x_2 intercept, we have

$$0 + x_2 = 40$$
$$x_2 = 40$$

Thus, the x_2 intercept is 40. Since the equation does not contain an x_1 variable, there will not be an x_1 intercept and the graph of the line will be parallel to the x_1 axis, and will intersect the x_2 axis at the point (0,40). Figure 3.2 illustrates the graph of $x_2 = 40$.

Although the graph of $x_2 = 40$ is a line, the graph of $x_2 \leq 40$ is a half space or region defined by the points on one side of the line $x_2 = 40$. To determine which half space is defined by $x_2 \leq 40$ it is only necessary to check a point on either side of the line $x_2 = 40$. The easiest check involves substi-

FIGURE 3.2   **Graph of $x_2 = 40$**

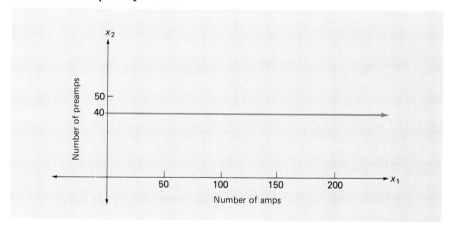

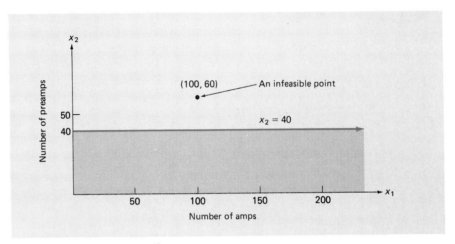

FIGURE 3.3 **Graph of $x_2 \leq 40$**

tuting the origin ($x_1 = 0$, $x_2 = 0$) into the constraint, Thus,

$$0 + 0 \leq 40$$
$$0 \leq 40$$

and the origin satisfies the inequality. The region below the line $x_2 = 40$ and containing the origin is the graph of $x_2 \leq 40$. Note that we could have chosen a point such as ($x_1 = 100$, $x_2 = 60$) to illustrate that points lying above the line $x_2 = 40$ are infeasible. In other words

$$0(100) + 1(60) \not\leq 40$$

Figure 3.3 shows the graph of $x_2 \leq 40$.

In the second constraint, involving assembly time, we determine the x_1 intercept by setting $x_2 = 0$ and solving

$$1.2x_1 + 4(0) = 240$$
$$x_1 = 200$$

Setting $x_1 = 0$ we determine the x_2 intercept

$$1.2(0) + 4x_2 = 240$$
$$x_2 = 60$$

The two points that determine the graph of $1.2x_1 + 4x_2 = 240$ are (200, 0) and (0, 60).

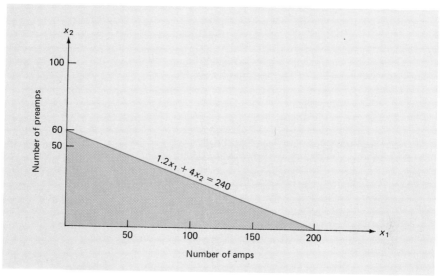

FIGURE 3.4   **Graph of 1.2x₁ + 4x₂ ≤ 240 (assembly time)**

Plotting the line that passes through (200, 0) and (0, 60) yields the line shown in Figure 3.4. Checking to see whether the origin satisfies the constraint yields the following:

$$1.2(0) + 4(0) \leq 240$$
$$0 \leq 240$$

Therefore we shade the area between the line $1.2x_1 + 4x_2 = 240$ and the origin. Figure 3.4 shows the region that satisfies the second constraint.

At this point we are interested in only those points that satisfy both the first and the second constraint. Figure 3.5 illustrates the region that satisfies both $x_2 \leq 40$ and $1.2x_1 + 4x_2 \leq 240$.

To determine the set of all points that satisfy all three constraints, we must supplement the graph in Figure 3.5 with the region confined to constraint three, or $.5x_1 + 1x_2 \leq 81$. Solving for the x_1 and x_2 intercepts we have

$$.5x_1 + 1(0) = 81$$
$$x_1 = 162$$
$$.5(0) + 1x_2 = 81$$
$$x_2 = 81$$

Plotting the line which passes through (162, 0) and (0, 81) and observing that the origin satisfies the constraint, we have the region shown in Figure 3.6.

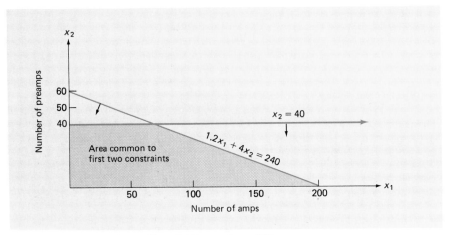

FIGURE 3.5 **Graph of $x_2 \leq 40$ and $1.2\,x_1 + 4x_2 \leq 240$**

feasible region   Superimposing the graph of the third constraint on the region defined by the first two constraints yields the *feasible region* or the set of points that satisfy all constraints. Figure 3.7 shows the feasible region for the Faze Linear problem. Notice that point X lies completely outside the feasible region. Point W does not satisfy any of the three constraints. Point X satisfies the first constraint but violates the second and third. Both X and W are infeasible points. Point Y satisfies all three constraints, is part of the feasible region, and therefore is a feasible point.

FIGURE 3.6 **Graph of $.5x_1 + 1x_2 \leq 81$**

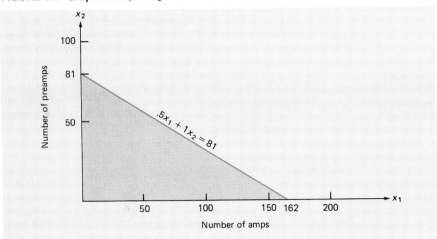

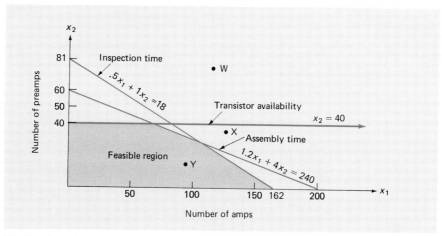

FIGURE 3.7 **Graph of all three Faze Linear constraints**

FINDING THE OPTIMAL SOLUTION

optimal solution   In Figure 3.7 we have graphed the set of all feasible points to the Faze Linear problem. We have enough resources in terms of transistors, assembly time, and inspection time to produce any combination of amps and preamps that falls in the feasible region. However, we are interested in an optimal solution rather than one that is only feasible. An *optimal solution* is a solution that is not only feasible, but also achieves the best possible value for the objective function. If we are trying to increase profit, an optimal solution is a feasible solution that maximizes profit. Similarly, if we are minimizing, an optimal solution is a feasible solution that minimizes cost or whatever criterion of effectiveness the objective function measures. The goal of LP is to determine an optimal solution. Therefore, let us proceed to find the optimal solution to the Faze Linear problem.

At first, the determination of an optimal solution might seem to be a difficult task. You can see that the feasible region in Figure 3.7 encompasses an infinite number of feasible solutions. How, then, can we find the one or ones that are optimal? Fortunately, LP theory provides a result that allows us to exclude all but a finite number of feasible points.

extreme points   In Figure 3.8, notice that the feasible region contains five vertices; *A*, *B*, *C*, *D*, and *O*. These vertices, or corner points, are called *extreme points* of the feasible region. These extreme points play an integral part in LP optimization. The following fundamental theorem of LP states the role of extreme points in LP optimization.

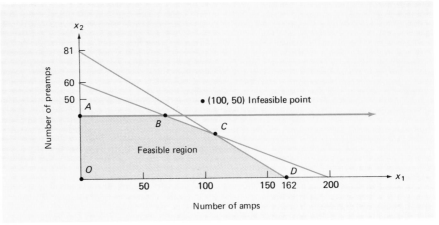

FIGURE 3.8 **Graph of feasible region and extreme points**

extreme point theorem *Extreme Point Theorem* If an optimal solution to a linear programming problem exists, then at least one such optimal solution must be an extreme point solution.

The importance of the extreme point theorem is that it restricts our search for an optimal solution from an infinite number of possibilities to a finite number of extreme points, no matter how large the problem. Thus, in our search for the best solution, we can limit our analysis to only extreme points. Of course, really large LP problems have an astronomical (although finite) number of extreme points.

In our small example with the Faze Linear Company, we have only five extreme points; A, B, C, D, and O; the point O is the origin $(0, 0)$. One approach to determining the optimal solution is to find the coordinates of the other four extreme points and then simply find the profit associated with each of these. The point with the highest profit is the optimal solution to the Faze Linear problem.

Finding the coordinates of all five extreme points, however, is laborious and unnecessary. We can make use of the objective function to single out the extreme point that is the optimum. The objective function is the measuring device we use to determine the relative worth of any proposed solution. Let Z = the value of the objective function; then we wish to

$$\text{Maximize} \quad Z = 200x_1 + 500x_2$$

The objective function is now in the form of a linear equation. If we pick any particular level of profit, say, $Z = \$20,000$, we can plot the graph of

$$\$20,000 = 200x_1 + 500x_2$$

on the feasible region of Figure 3.8. Doing this, we get the result shown in Figure 3.9. All points lying on the dashed line segment in Figure 3.9 yield a profit of \$20,000. To plot the objective function for a specific value of Z, we can simply calculate the x_1 and x_2 intercepts as we did for the constraint equations. You can perform the calculations to verify that the x_1 intercept is (100, 0) and the x_2 intercept is (0, 40).

We can also plot the objective function by converting it to slope-intercept form. This involves solving for x_2 in terms of x_1. Starting with the objective function

$$Z = 200x_1 + 500x_2$$

and solving for x_2 we obtain

$$500x_2 = -200x_1 + Z$$
$$x_2 = -200/500x_1 + Z/500$$

or

$$x_2 = -.4x_1 + .002Z$$

FIGURE 3.9   **Graph of objective function for Z = \$20,000**

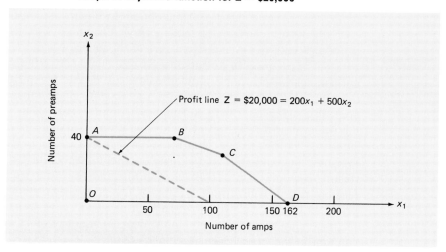

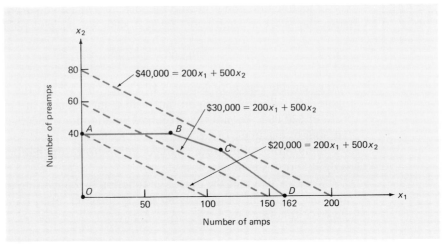

FIGURE 3.10 **Alternative profit lines for various values of Z**

The coefficient of x_1, $-.4$, is the slope of the objective function and the term $.002Z$ is the x_2 intercept.

We can plot profit lines for various profit values by using either the axis intercepts or the slope-intercept form of the line. Letting $Z = \$30,000$ we can plot the profit line

$$\$30,000 = 200x_1 + 500x_2$$

as shown in Figure 3.10. Any point on the line $\$30,000 = 200x_1 + 500x_2$ and within the feasible region will yield a profit of $\$30,000$. Points outside the region violate at least one constraint and are infeasible. Trying for more profit, we can set $Z = \$40,000$ and obtain the dashed line in Figure 3.10 that is totally outside the feasible region. Thus, it is not possible to obtain a profit of $\$40,000$ with the given parameters of the problem.

From Figure 3.10 we can observe that all objective function profit lines are parallel and the more profitable lines are farther from the origin. Given this information, can you determine a method for finding the most profitable point in the feasible region? Suppose we move the profit line away from the origin in the direction of increasing profit. Moving the profit line with slope $= -.4$ toward the "northeast" will increase profit. How far can we move the line and still have at least one point on the line be in the feasible region? It might be intuitively clear at this time that an extreme point of the feasible region will always be one of the points that yield the maximum profit. In Figure 3.11 we show that extreme point C is the point that yields the maximum profit and is still in the feasible region. Point C is the optimum solution to the Faze Linear problem.

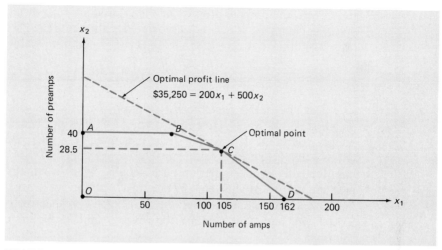

FIGURE 3.11   Optimal solution for the Faze Linear problem

Precisely how does point C yield the optimum solution? By determining the x_1 and x_2 coordinates of point C we obtain the daily production levels for power amps and preamps, respectively. Examining the graph we can estimate approximate x_1 and x_2 values for the point C. However, it is much more precise to calculate an exact solution for the coordinates of point C.

To calculate the coordinates of C, we must first notice that point C occurs at the intersection of the two lines: $1.2x_1 + 4x_2 = 240$ and $.5x_1 + 1x_2 = 81$. The coordinates can now be determined by solving these two equations simultaneously.

$$1.2x_1 + 4x_2 = 240$$
$$.5x_1 + 1x_2 = 81$$

Using the method of elimination we can eliminate the variable x_2 by multiplying the second equation by 4 and subtracting the result from the first equation. We can then solve for x_1.

$$
\begin{array}{rcr}
1.2x_1 + 4x_2 &=& 240 \\
-2.0x_1 - 4x_2 &=& -324 \\
\hline
-.8x_1 &=& -84 \\
x_1 &=& 105
\end{array}
$$

Substituting 105 for x_1 in the first equation, we obtain

$$4x_2 = 240 - 1.2(105)$$
$$x_2 = \tfrac{1}{4}(240 - 126)$$
$$x_2 = 28.5$$

Thus, the optimal product mix is to produce 105 power amps and 28.5 preamps each day. The profit associated with the optimal solution is found by substituting x_1 and x_2 into the objective function to yield

$$Z = 200(105) + 500(28.5) = \$35{,}250$$

Did you notice that the LP solution suggests the production of 28.5 preamps daily? As we have said before, LP does not necessarily generate integer solutions. It is impossible to manufacture 28.5 preamps per day unless a unit is half-completed one day and then finished the next day, and so on. If whole-number solutions are sought, what is wrong with trying to produce 105 power amps and 29 preamps? Alternatively, we could round off the LP optimal solution and produce 105 and 28, respectively, for a profit of \$35,000 per day. This solution, however, might not be the optimal integer solution.

SUMMARY OF THE GRAPHICAL SOLUTION METHOD

At this point let us summarize the graphical solution procedure. The steps for a maximization problem are:

1. Plot each of the constraints as an equation.
2. For those constraints which are inequalities, determine the feasible area confined to each constraint, and then determine the feasible region that is common to all constraints.
3. Plot the objective function for a specific level of profit.
4. Move the objective function profit line in the direction of increasing profit. This direction is usually (but not always) away from the origin. (You may need to construct two profit lines to determine which direction maximizes.)
5. The extreme point that lies on the maximum feasible profit line is the optimal solution point.
6. Determine which constraint equations intersect at the extreme point in step 5. Solve these constraint equations simultaneously to find the optimal solution values.

It is possible to implement a more brute force approach in determining the optimal solution. In this case you can skip steps 3 through 6 and simply solve simultaneous equations at each extreme point to find the solution values at each point. Substituting these values into the objective function will determine which extreme point yields the maximum objective function value. This alternative approach has obvious disadvantages when there are many extreme points to evaluate.

GRAPHICAL SOLUTION
OF MINIMIZATION PROBLEMS

Minimization LP problems are solved in much the same way as maximization problems. Only steps 4 and 5 of the maximization methodology have to be modified. Minimization problems occur naturally as cost minimization problems. Typically, minimization problems involve some greater than or equal to constraints to ensure that demand or technological specifications are met. Let's demonstrate the graphical approach to minimization problems through a simple example.

Consider the production and distribution problem faced by the Reed Pump Co. The company manufactures pumping apparatus for the petroleum industry. It is trying to determine an optimal production and distribution plan for its new submersible pump. They have one main plant and two regional warehouses. Warehouse 1 has demand for at least 80 pumps this month, and warehouse 2 has demand for at least 100 units. The following are the combined costs of producing and shipping to the two warehouses:

	Cost of producing and shipping	
From plant	Warehouse 1	Warehouse 2
	$240	$280

To achieve economies of scale, the company wants to produce at least 300 pumps this month. The only resource limitation involves manufacturing-resource hours. Pumps sent to regional warehouse 1 need an extra-fine filter and require 5 hours of manufacturing time. Those pumps sent to warehouse 2 require only 4 hours of manufacturing time. The company has 2,000 hours of manufacturing-resource time available per month. What is the optimal production and distribution plan for the Reed Pump Co.?

To solve the Reed Company problem, we must first formulate the problem as an LP model. Let

x_1 = number of pumps to be produced and shipped to warehouse 1

x_2 = number of pumps to be produced and shipped to warehouse 2

We can represent the objective function as

$$\text{Minimize} \quad 240x_1 + 280x_2$$

since the total costs of producing and shipping to warehouses 1 and 2 are $240 and $280, respectively. The demand requirements at each warehouse can be expressed as

$$x_1 \geq 80$$
$$x_2 \geq 100$$

The minimum production run quantity of 300 requires that

$$x_1 + x_2 \geq 300$$

Finally, the limitation on manufacturing-resource hours can be expressed as

$$5x_1 + 4x_2 \leq 2{,}000$$

Incorporating the nonnegativity conditions we have the following complete formulation of the Reed Pump Co. problem:

$$\text{Minimize} \quad Z = 240x_1 + 280x_2$$
$$\text{subject to} \quad x_1 \qquad\qquad \geq \quad 80$$
$$x_2 \geq \quad 100$$
$$x_1 + \quad x_2 \geq \quad 300$$
$$5x_1 + \quad 4x_2 \leq 2000$$
$$x_1, x_2 \geq 0$$

Since we have only two decision variables we can solve the problem graphically. The first step is to graph all four constraints as equations. The graphs of the four constraint equations are shown in Figure 3.12.

The arrows indicate in which direction to shade each respective constraint to indicate feasibility. Notice that in this problem the $\geq$ constraints are to be shaded away from the origin. Figure 3.13 shows the feasible region which is common to all four constraints.

Given the feasible region and the four extreme points which are shown in Figure 3.13, the next step is to plot objective function cost lines to determine the optimal point. If we pick an arbitrary cost figure such as $100,000 we can plot the objective function cost line as shown in Figure 3.13. To find

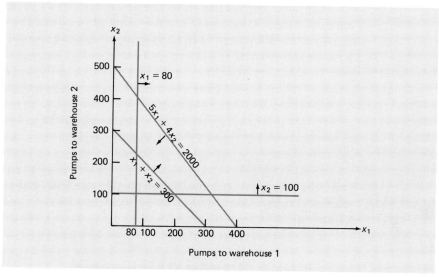

FIGURE 3.12 **Constraint lines for Reed Pump Co.**

the optimal extreme point we need to move the cost line in the direction of decreasing cost. In this problem the direction of decreasing cost is toward the origin. Moving the cost line toward the origin, we find that the last point it touches in the feasible region is point D. Thus, point D is the optimal extreme point for the problem.

FIGURE 3.13 **Feasible region and optimal point**

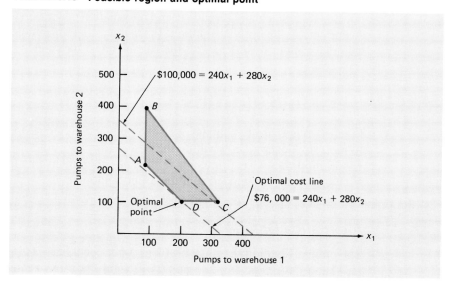

The final step in the graphical solution approach is to solve for the values of x_1 and x_2 at point D. Since point D occurs at the intersection of constraint equations $x_2 = 100$ and $x_1 + x_2 = 300$, we solve these two equations simultaneously:

$$0x_1 + 1x_2 = 100$$
$$\underline{1x_1 + 1x_2 = 300}$$
$$x_2 = 100$$
$$x_1 = 300 - 1(100)$$
$$x_1 = 200$$

Thus, the point D is specified by the coordinates (200, 100) and the optimal solution is to produce and ship 200 pumps to warehouse 1 and 100 pumps to warehouse 2.

The minimum cost associated with the optimal solution is calculated as

$$Z = 240(200) + 280(100)$$
$$Z = 48,000 + 28,000$$
$$Z = \$76,000$$

binding
constraint   Substituting the optimal solution values into the original constraints we find that only the second and third constraints are *binding;* that is, the constraint left-hand side value precisely equals the right-hand side value. In constraint 1 the demand lower limit of 80 is exceeded, and in constraint 4 there are $2,000 - [5(200) + 4(100)] = 600$, that is, 600 hours of manufacturing capacity left unused. These excess quantities in nonbinding constraints are referred to as slack and provide useful information concerning resources and constraints in the optimal solution. In Chapter 4 on the simplex method, we will take a more formal look at the role of slack variables.

SPECIAL CASES IN SOLVING LP PROBLEMS

In our two graphical examples we have obtained a unique optimal solution. In most applications this will be the case. However, other terminations for LP solutions do exist. For example, it is possible to have an infinite number of solutions, an unbounded solution, or no solution at all. Next we show you how to approach these special cases using the graphical method.

Alternative Optima

The optimal solution to an LP problem is not necessarily unique. It is possible that an adjacent extreme point will yield the same value. Graphically,

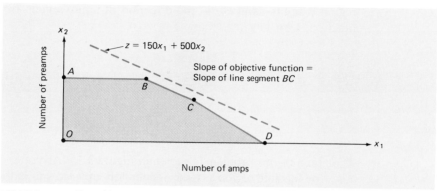

FIGURE 3.14 Faze Linear problem with alternative optima

this happens whenever the slope of the objective function equals the slope of a constraint equation that passes through an optimal extreme point. Suppose we modify the Faze Linear maximization problem to illustrate the concept. Let us change the profit contribution of amplifiers from $200 to $150. The objective function becomes

$$\text{Maximize} \quad Z = 150x_1 + 500x_2$$

solving for the slope we get

$$x_2 = -.3x_1 + .002Z$$

The slope is now $-.3$ and is equal to the slope of the second constraint. In Figure 3.14 we show the optimal objective function line in relation to the feasible region.

Notice that the objective function is parallel to the line segment BC. In this modified problem both points C (105, 28.5) and B (66.66, 40) are optimal and yield a maximum profit of $30,000. When we have alternative optima, we actually have an infinite number of optimal solutions. Not only are points C and B optimal, but also every point lying on the line segment BC.

Having alternative optima in the LP solution is good in that it offers the decision maker a choice of optimal alternatives. It is possible that one optimal solution is preferred to another based on some criterion that is not explicitly stated in the objective function.

Unbounded Solution

It is possible for an LP problem to have a nonempty set of feasible solutions and yet have no finite optimal solution. This can occur whenever the feasible region extends infinitely in the direction of improvement for the objective function. Consider the example

$$\text{Maximize} \quad x_1 + x_2$$
$$\text{subject to} \quad 5x_1 - x_2 \geq 10$$
$$3x_1 - 2x_2 \leq 9$$
$$x_1, x_2 \geq 0$$

The graph of this problem is shown in Figure 3.15. As you can see in Figure 3.15, the feasible region extends indefinitely upward within the cone-shaped shaded area. We can pick arbitrarily large values of x_1 and x_2 to make the objective function value $x_1 + x_2$ as large as desired. If the objective function represents profit, then we could achieve unlimited profit! Thus, there exists no finite optimum. Clearly there is something wrong in this situation. Linear programming inherently deals with the allocation of scarce resources, but in this case we can produce an unlimited number of x_1 and x_2.

An unbounded problem implies that the model has been formulated incorrectly. Usually a constraint has been omitted or the signs on some of the coefficients have been reversed. In any case it's back to the drawing board to try to correct the model before a new solution is attempted.

Note that an unbounded feasible region alone does not imply an unbounded solution. In this example, if we were minimizing the same objective function $x_1 + x_2$, the finite optimum would occur at $x_1 = 2$ and $x_2 = 0$.

FIGURE 3.15 **Unbounded LP problem**

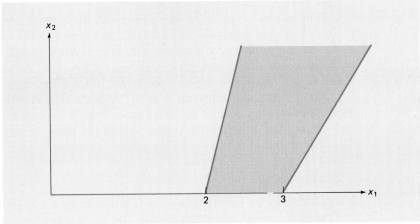

No Feasible Solution

It is also possible to have an LP problem in which *no feasible solution* exists. This situation corresponds to a problem that is formulated incorrectly or has conflicting restrictions within the constraint set. Consider the example

$$\text{Minimize} \quad x_1 + x_2$$
$$\text{subject to} \quad x_1 - x_2 \geq 1$$
$$-x_1 + x_2 \geq 1$$
$$x_1,\ x_2 \geq 0$$

It is obvious from inspecting the model that it is impossible to satisfy both constraints simultaneously. In this case the constraints are said to be inconsistent. The graph in Figure 3.16 shows the nature of the inconsistency. No point satisfies both constraints. In this case the feasible region is empty. Notice that no area has been shaded.

It is possible to have an LP model with no careless mistakes that has no solution. In this case the decision maker is trying to satisfy conditions in the constraints which are incompatible. For example, we might be trying to reduce operating costs while at the same time trying to double production output. In some cases infeasibility can be resolved by determining which constraints are in conflict and in some way loosening the constraint restrictions enough to allow a feasible solution to exist. In situations where this constraint-relaxation process is not successful, the original intended use of the model must be abandoned.

FIGURE 3.16　**Example of no feasible solution**

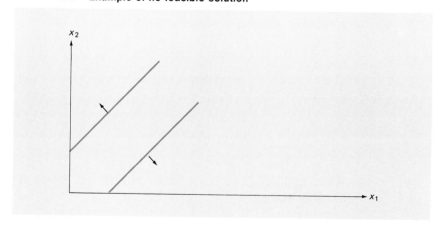

SUMMARY

In this chapter we have looked at the graphical method of solving LP problems. Since accurate graphical analysis is limited to two dimensions, we can only apply the graphical method to problems having two variables. The methodology is useful for instructional purposes.

We learned an important theoretical result in the extreme point theorem. That is, an optimal solution (if it exists) occurs at an extreme point of the feasible region. The optimal extreme point can be determined by moving the objective function line in the direction of increasing (maximization) or decreasing (minimization) value. Solving simultaneous equations yields the exact coordinates of the optimal point. The solution of a systematic series of simultaneous equations will also be the basis for the simplex method to be covered in the next chapter.

Not all LP models have a unique optimal solution. Some problems have alternative optima while others are unbounded or have no solution at all.

Finally, in the Solved Problem section, we illustrate the concepts of a binding constraint and slack in a constraint. These concepts will be important in the next two chapters on LP analysis.

SOLVED PROBLEM

PROBLEM STATEMENT

a. Solve the following minimization problem graphically:

$$\text{Minimize} \quad 2x_1 + 3x_2$$
$$\text{subject to} \quad x_2 \geq 2$$
$$4x_1 + 3x_2 \geq 12$$
$$x_1 + 2x_2 \leq 8$$
$$x_1, x_2 \geq 0$$

b. Which of the constraints are binding; i.e. active? Which of the constraints are nonbinding?

c. Suppose we add an additional constraint of the form $3x_1 + 9x_2 \leq 45$. What is the new optimal solution?

SOLUTION

a. Plotting each of the constraints, we obtain the region shown. The feasible region is the shaded triangular area defined by the constraints. It contains

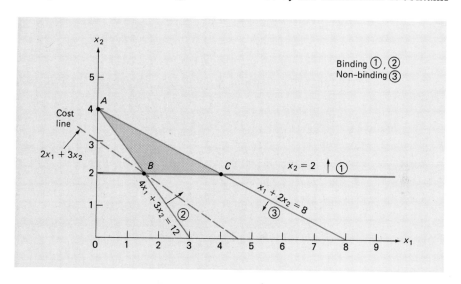

only three extreme points A, B, and C. The slope of the objective function is $-\frac{2}{3}$, and sliding the cost line down from the northeast toward the origin, we find that extreme point B is the optimum. The coordinates for B are found by solving simultaneously the two equations that represent the two lines defining point B.

$$\begin{aligned} x_2 &= 2 \\ \underline{4x_1 + 3x_2} &= \underline{12} \\ x_2 &= 2 \\ x_1 &= \tfrac{3}{2} \end{aligned}$$

Thus, the optimal solution is $x_1 = \frac{3}{2}$, $x_2 = 2$ with a minimum objective function value of 9.

b. The constraints which are active or binding are those whose left-hand side equals their right-hand side when the optimal solution is substituted into the constraint. Checking the three constraints we have

Constraint 1: $2 = 2$ binding (slack $= 0$)
Constraint 2: $4(\frac{3}{2}) + 2(3) = 12$ binding (slack $= 0$)
Constraint 3: $\frac{3}{2} + 2(3) < 8$ nonbinding (slack $= \frac{1}{2}$)

Binding constraints can be easily detected in graphical analysis. They are the constraints that pass through the optimal solution point. Examining the graph, we see that constraints 1 and 2 pass through the optimal point *B*, whereas nonbinding constraint 3 does not. Thus, constraint 3 will have nonzero slack. However, to determine the amount of slack present in the third constraint, we must calculate this quantity algebraically. For the third constraint, we have

$$\text{slack} = 8 - (\tfrac{3}{2} + 2(3)) = 8 - 7\tfrac{1}{2} = \tfrac{1}{2} \text{ unit}$$

c. Adding the constraint $3x_1 + 9x_2 \leq 45$, we get the following graph:

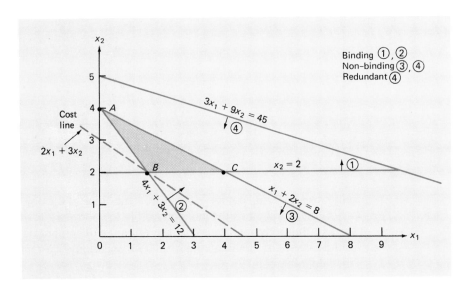

Notice that the newly added fourth constraint does not alter the previously determined feasible region. In this problem the added constraint is redundant; that is, it has no effect on the feasible region. Redundant constraints can be deleted from the graphical analysis without affecting the solution. Thus, the optimal solution remains $x_1 = \tfrac{3}{2}$ and $x_2 = 2$.

REVIEW QUESTIONS

1. Under what conditions can you use the graphical method to solve an LP problem?
2. What are the geometric characteristics of an optimal solution to an LP problem?

3. What is the difference between a feasible solution and an optimal solution in an LP problem?
4. In the graphical method, how can you determine that the solution is unbounded?
5. What does an unbounded solution indicate?
6. How can you graphically determine if the LP problem has alternative optima?
7. How can you determine that a problem has no feasible solution when solving via the graphical method?

PROBLEMS

3.1 Plot the set of points that satisfy the following conditions.
  a. $3x_1 + 5x_2 = 15$
  b. $3x_1 + 5x_2 \leq 15$
  c. $3x_1 + 5x_2 \geq 15$
  d. $3x_1 - 5x_2 = 15$

3.2 A manufacturing firm produces two products. Each product must go through an assembly and a paint process. The first product requires 4 hours to assemble and 1 hour to paint. The second product requires 2 hours to assemble and 3 hours to paint. There are 40 hours per week of assembly and paint time.
  a. Plot the constraints for assembly time and paint time
  b. Graph the feasible region and identify all extreme points

3.3 Suppose in Problem 3.2 that the profit contributions of products 1 and 2 are 30 and 20, respectively.
  a. What is the optimal solution?
  b. If the profit contribution of product 2 increases to 30, does the optimal solution change?

3.4 Solve the following problem graphically.

$$\text{Maximize} \quad 6x_1 + 8x_2$$
$$\text{subject to} \quad x_1 \qquad\qquad \leq 12$$
$$x_2 \leq 10$$
$$2x_1 + 3x_2 \leq 36$$
$$x_1, x_2 \geq 0$$

3.5   Solve the following minimization problem by the graphical method.

$$\text{Minimize} \quad x_1 + x_2$$
$$\text{subject to} \quad x_2 \geq 2$$
$$2x_1 - x_2 \geq 0$$
$$3x_1 + 2x_2 \leq 12$$
$$x_1, x_2 \geq 0$$

3.6   Solve Problem 2.1 (product mix) by the graphical method.

3.7   An Iowa farmer has a 1,000 acre farm on which corn and soybeans are planted. He has 1,900 tons of fertilizer and insecticide to cover at most 800 acres of corn and 600 acres of soybeans. Letting x_1 and x_2 represent acres of corn and soybeans, respectively, the following LP model was developed to determine how the farmer should plant to maximize profit.

$$\text{Maximize} \quad 250x_1 + 190x_2 \qquad \text{(profit)}$$
$$\text{subject to} \quad x_1 + x_2 \leq 1000 \qquad \text{(acres)}$$
$$2x_1 + 1.5x_2 \leq 1900 \qquad \text{(fertilizer)}$$
$$x_1 \qquad\quad \leq 800 \qquad \text{(insecticide)}$$
$$x_2 \leq 600 \qquad \text{(insecticide)}$$
$$x_1, x_2 \geq 0$$

   a. Solve this model graphically.
   b. Are any constraints redundant?
   c. Which constraints are binding?
   d. What are the slack values in the nonbinding constraints?

3.8   Solve Problem 2.3 (break-even analysis) graphically.

3.9   Consider the following LP problem:

$$\text{Maximize} \quad 6x_1 + 8x_2$$
$$\text{subject to} \quad 4x_1 + 8x_2 \leq 48$$
$$-2x_1 + 3x_2 \leq 18$$
$$3x_1 + 1.5x_2 \leq 24$$
$$x_1, x_2 \geq 0$$

Use the graphical method to find the optimal solution and the objective function value.

3.10 *Product mix.* Home Products, Inc., specializes in home cooking devices. They are trying to plan production for their electric skillets and crock pots. The company works a 40-hour week and has its production limited only by productive capacity. The table indicates production capacity in terms of units of final product. The profit contribution is $5 for a skillet and $7 for a crock pot. Formulate and solve the product mix problem. You may want to convert the capacity values to hours of production capacity required per unit.

	Weekly capacity (units)	
Department	Skillets	Crock pots
Casting	400	—
Wiring	250	250
Assembly	500	400

3.11 Solve Problem 2.2 (product mix) by the graphical method.

3.12 Consider the following LP model:

$$\text{Minimize} \quad 6x_1 + 10x_2$$
$$\text{subject to} \quad 4x_1 + 3x_2 \geq 12$$
$$3x_1 + 6x_2 \geq 12$$
$$10x_1 + 4x_2 \geq 20$$
$$x_1, x_2 \geq 0$$

Solve the model graphically.

3.13 Given the following linear programming problem:

$$\text{Maximize} \quad 3x_1 + 2x_2$$
$$\text{subject to} \quad x_1 \qquad \leq 5$$
$$x_2 \leq 5$$
$$x_1 + x_2 \leq 5$$
$$x_1, x_2 \geq 0$$

a. Graphically show the feasible region for the problem.

b. Find all extreme points of the problem.

c. Determine the optimal solution.

d. If the objective function were changed to $3x_1 + 3x_2$, what would the optimal solution be?

3.14 Given the following constraint set,

$$x_2 \leq 2$$

$$2x_1 + x_2 \leq 8$$

$$2x_1 - x_2 \geq 2$$

$$x_1, x_2 \geq 0$$

the associated graph is

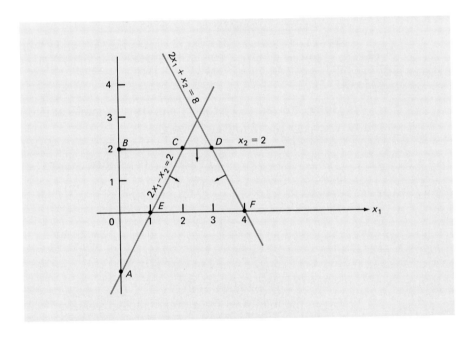

a. Fill in the following table.

Point	x_1	x_2
A		
B		
C		
D		
E		
F		

    b. Which of the points are feasible?

    c. If the objective function is Maximize $3x_1 + 4x_2$, what are the objective function values at points C, D, and F?

    d. What is the optimal solution point?

3.15 The Weed Beater Company produces two weed-trimming models, electric and gasoline. In its master production schedule, it plans to assemble at least 100 units for each day's delivery.\The electric weed beater requires 1 hour of assembly and costs \$20, whereas the gas model requires 2 hours and costs \$45. The company's objective is to minimize total assembly costs and produce at least 35 electric models per day.

    a. Formulate the Weed Beater problem as an LP model.

    b. Solve the problem graphically

3.16 Solve the following problem graphically.

$$\text{Minimize} \quad 6x_1 + 12x_2$$
$$\text{subject to} \quad 7x_1 + 1x_2 \geq 7$$
$$2x_1 - 3x_2 \leq 6$$
$$3x_1 + 2x_2 \geq 6$$
$$2x_1 + 5x_2 \geq 10$$
$$x_1, x_2 \geq 0$$

3.17 The McMichael Concrete Co. produces bags of concrete from river sand and inland sand from quarry mining. Each pound of river sand costs 8 cents and contains 5 units of fine sand, 4 units of coarse sand, and 6 units of gravel. Each pound of quarry sand costs 10 cents and contains 2 units of fine sand, 5 units of coarse and 10 units of gravel. Each bag of concrete must contain at least 12 units of fine sand, 14 units of coarse sand, and 9 units of gravel. Formulate an LP model which will find the best combination of river sand and quarry sand which will meet the requirements of fine sand, coarse sand, and gravel at least cost. Solve the model graphically. What is the minimum cost per bag of concrete mix?

3.18 Solve the following LP problem graphically.

$$\text{Maximize} \quad 7x_1 + 9x_2$$
$$\text{subject to} \quad x_1 + x_2 \leq 1$$
$$2x_1 + 3x_2 \geq 12$$
$$x_1, x_2 \geq 0$$

√ 3.19 Solve the following linear programming problem graphically:

$$\text{Maximize} \quad 4x_1 + 6x_2$$

$$\text{subject to} \quad x_1 + x_2 \leq 4$$

$$3x_1 + x_2 \geq 4$$

$$x_1 + 5x_2 \geq 4$$

$$x_1 \qquad \leq 3$$

$$x_1, x_2 \geq 0$$

3.20 Solve the following problem graphically:

$$\text{Maximize} \quad -2x_1 + 4x_2$$

$$\text{subject to} \quad -x_1 + x_2 \leq 1$$

$$x_1 - 2x_2 \geq -4$$

$$x_1, x_2 \geq 0$$

3.21 Graph each of the following objective functions, and determine the direction in which the graph of the objective function should be moved to maximize the objective

a. $Z = 4x_1 + 5x_2$.

b. $Z = 6x_1 - 3x_2$.

c. $Z = -3x_1 + 2x_2$.

3.22 Given the following graph of a feasible region, determine the constraints which have been graphed. Are any constraints redundant?

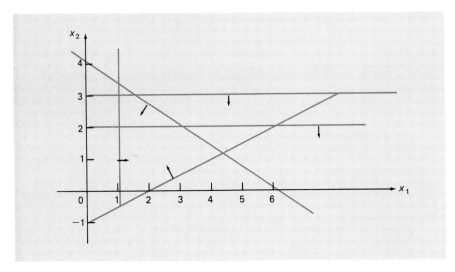

3.23 Consider the Faze Linear problem that we solved earlier in this chapter. Determine the optimal solution and profit for each of the following changes in the problem. Assume that each change is relative to the original problem, that is, the changes are not cumulative.

    a. A decrease in the cost of heavy duty power supplies has increased the profit contribution of amplifiers from $200 to $350.

    b. The availability of transistors is increased from 40 to 50 per day.

    c. The availability of assembly time is reduced from 240 to 220 hours.

3.24 The Friskie Dog Food Co. makes dry dog food from several ingredients. Two of the ingredients, fish and oats, provide protein and vitamin D. The company needs to know how many pounds of fish and oats to mix in each bag of dog food in order to meet minimum nutritional requirements at minimum cost. The following LP model has been formulated to solve this problem:

$$\text{Minimize} \quad .89x_1 + .20x_2$$
$$\text{subject to} \quad 8x_1 + 2x_2 \geq 80 \quad \text{(units protein)}$$
$$2x_1 + 4x_2 \geq 48 \quad \text{(units vitamin D)}$$
$$x_1, x_2 \geq 0$$

Solve this problem graphically.

3.25 Solve the following LP model graphically:

$$\text{Minimize} \quad 8x_1 + 12x_2$$
$$\text{subject to} \quad x_1 + x_2 \geq 10$$
$$5x_1 + 3x_2 \geq 45$$
$$x_2 \leq 18$$
$$x_1, x_2 \geq 0$$

3.26 Consider the following LP model:

$$\text{Minimize} \quad x_1 + x_2$$
$$\text{subject to} \quad 6x_1 + 3x_2 \geq 18$$
$$4x_1 + 5x_2 \geq 20$$
$$x_1 + 4x_2 \geq 8$$
$$5x_1 + 6x_2 \leq 60$$
$$x_1, x_2 \geq 0$$

a. Solve the problem graphically.

b. Determine the number of extreme points in the feasible region.

c. Which constraints are binding? nonbinding?

d. What are the slack values associated with each constraint?

e. Does the solution change if the objective function is modified to minimize $x_1 + 3x_2$?

3.27 In Problem 3.26, suppose that the objective function is maximize $2x_1 + 3x_2$. What is the new optimal solution? Do any of the answers to parts b, c, and d change relative to Problem 3.26?

3.28 MICRO-TEK sells IBM-compatible microcomputers. It sells a desktop and a portable unit. The firm makes $900 on each desktop it sells and $700 on each portable. Because of limited production, the manufacturer cannot ship more than 50 desktop units or more than 80 portable units next month. Dealer assembly and customer checkout time requires 3 hours for a desktop and 2 hours for a portable unit. Assuming that MICRO-TEK has 200 work hours available next month, how many desktop and how many portable units should it order so that profit is maximized? Assume that it can sell all that are ordered.

3.29 From your solution to Problem 3.28, determine

a. Which constraints are binding.

b. What the slack values are for each constraint.

c. A competitive market has forced MICRO-TEK to lower its prices so that profit contributions are reduced to $650 for the desktop and $500 for the portable. Does this change affect the optimal solution?

3.30 Suppose in Problem 3.28 that the availability of portable units is reduced to 60 for next month. Does this affect the optimal solution? Instead, suppose the availability of desktops is reduced to 40. Does this affect the optimal solution?

3.31 Consider the following LP model:

$$\text{Maximize} \quad 100x_1 + 75x_2 \qquad \text{(profit)}$$
$$\text{subject to} \quad 3x_1 + x_2 \leq 18 \qquad \text{(resource 1)}$$
$$4x_1 + 3x_2 \leq 36 \qquad \text{(resource 2)}$$
$$x_1, x_2 \geq 0$$

Solve the problem graphically and compute the objective function value.

3.32 The following LP model is related to the maximization Problem 3.31. This minimization problem is called the dual of the maximization Problem 3.31.

$$\text{Minimize} \quad 18y_1 + 36y_2$$

$$\text{subject to} \quad 3y_1 + 4y_2 \geq 100$$

$$y_1 + 3y_2 \geq 75$$

$$y_1, y_2 \geq 0$$

Solve this dual problem graphically.

a. What is the optimal solution?

b. How does the minimum objective function value correspond to the maximum objective function value found in Problem 3.31?

c. The optimal values of y_1 and y_2 tell us something about the marginal values of the right-hand side coefficients in the associated maximization problem. Given this information, which resource is "worth more" in Problem 3.31?

BIBLIOGRAPHY

Anderson, David R., Dennis J. Sweeney, and Thomas A. Williams, *An Introduction to Management Science,* 5th ed. St. Paul, Minn.: West Publishing Company, 1988.

Eppen, G. D., F. J. Gould, and C. P. Schmidt, *Introductory Management Science,* 2nd ed. Englewood Cliffs, N.J.: Prentice Hall, 1987.

Levin, Richard I., David S. Rubin, and Joel P. Stinson, *Quantitative Approaches to Management,* 6th ed. New York: McGraw-Hill Book Company, 1986.

Taylor, Bernard W. III, *Introduction to Management Science,* 2nd ed. Dubuque, Iowa: Wm. C. Brown, Publishers, 1986.

4

Solving LP Problems: Simplex Method

AMERICAN AIRLINES INC.

During 1988 American purchased over 1.5 billion gallons of flight fuel and spent in excess of $1 billion on fuel (more than 15 percent of total expenses). With the airline growing at more than 15 percent per year and fuel prices continuing to climb, it is absolutely critical to manage fuel purchases carefully. The impact on the "bottom line" is very significant. For example, if average fuel costs were decreased by 1 cent per gallon, American would have spent approximately $15 million less for fuel during 1988.

In addition to negotiating good contracts with vendors selling flight fuel, most large airlines ferry fuel into airports where fuel is either in short supply or expensive. American utilizes a large-scale linear programming model to optimize the fuel ferry decision process. The model minimizes a total cost function that includes incremental fuel burn associated with carrying additional weight. The decision variables are how much fuel to put on an airplane over and above what is needed for a single flight segment. Constraints on the decision-making process include aircraft capacity constraints and fuel availability constraints.

The model is used in the following modes:

□ **Planning mode** The output from this mode assists fuel planners in deciding how much fuel should be contracted for each station airport. It also provides a tool for negotiating price with the various flight fuel vendors at a specific airport.

☐ **Operational mode** The output from the fuel ferry model is used by Flight Dispatch on a daily basis to determine the fuel "topping factors" for each flight. Those topping factors determine the amount of fuel to be ferried. The operational model has been estimated to save American in excess of $3,000,000 per year.

INTRODUCTION

In Chapter 3 we studied the graphical method for solving linear programming problems with two decision variables. The graphical method is useful for explaining the extreme point theorem and illustrating important linear programming concepts. However, to solve actual business problems involving many variables (usually hundreds or thousands), an easily computerized systematic procedure is needed.

The most widely used method for solving LP problems is the simplex method. This method was developed by George Dantzig in 1947 and has since been refined and specialized for various applications. The simplex method is a solution algorithm. An algorithm is an iterative procedure with specific computational rules that solves a problem in a finite number of steps. The simplex algorithm is a systematic algebraic procedure for examining the extreme points of the LP feasible region. The extreme points are examined in a sequence such that each successive point yields a solution that is at least as effective as the previous point. The simplex method is very similar to solving a system of linear equations. In fact the computational steps are closely related to the Gaussian elimination procedure for solving systems of linear equations. Gaussian elimination is explained in Appendix B at the end of this text. If you are not familiar with this method for solving linear equations, you should review Appendix B before studying this chapter on the simplex method.

In this chapter we first present an algebraic review of the simplex method. We refer again to the familiar Faze Linear problem to show how to convert the LP model into standard form and apply the simplex steps. Basic feasible solutions are defined and related to the extreme points described in the graphical method. We first show the calculations for a maximization problem and then extend the method to the minimization case. The handling of special cases is discussed, and finally we look at computer-generated solutions for the simplex method.

ALGEBRAIC OVERVIEW OF THE SIMPLEX METHOD

The simplex method requires that all constraints be expressed as equations. Mathematically, it is easier to solve systems of equations than systems of inequalities. Therefore, we shall have to convert less-than-or-equal-to and greater-than-or-equal-to constraints into equations. The process of converting the constraints to equations is called transforming the problem to standard form.

First we shall learn how to convert $\leq$ constraints to equations. The transformation process involves adding "dummy variables" to the inequalities. Suppose that we have the constraint $x_1 + x_2 \leq 5$. We can convert this inequality to an equation by adding an additional variable s_1, called a *slack variable*. Thus we have

slack variable

$$x_1 + x_2 + s_1 = 5$$

where $s_1 \geq 0$. A slack variable, as the name implies, represents unused resources. In the foregoing equation, if $x_1 = 2$ and $x_2 = 1$, then s_1 must equal 2. Thus, $x_1 + x_2 < 5$ and s_1 represents two units of the right-hand side resource that are left over.

Notationally, we distinguish between slack and decision variables. The x_i represent decision variables and refer to actual activities; the s_i denote slack variables that represent unused capacity.

To illustrate the transformation of an entire model to standard form, we return to the Faze Linear product mix problem. The annotated model is

$$\text{Maximize} \quad 200x_1 + 500x_2 \qquad \text{(profit)}$$

$$\begin{aligned} \text{subject to} \quad && x_2 &\leq 40 && \text{(transistor constraint)} \\ 1.2x_1 + && 4x_2 &\leq 240 && \text{(assembly constraint)} \\ .5x_1 + && x_2 &\leq 81 && \text{(inspection constraint)} \end{aligned}$$

$$x_1, x_2 \geq 0$$

standard form

We convert the LP formation of the Faze Linear problem to *standard form* by adding a slack variable for each $\leq$ constraint:

$$\text{Maximize} \quad 200x_1 + 500x_2 + 0s_1 + 0s_2 + 0s_3$$

$$\begin{aligned} \text{subject to} \quad && x_2 + s_1 && &= 40 && (4.1) \\ 1.2x_1 + && 4x_2 && + s_2 && = 240 && (4.2) \\ .5x_1 + && x_2 && + s_3 &= 81 && (4.3) \end{aligned}$$

$$x_1, x_2, s_1, s_2, s_3 \geq 0$$

We have thus transformed a system of inequalities into a system of equations ready to be solved by the simplex method. Notice that the slack variables are given an objective function coefficient of zero. Thus, the slack variables affect the profit only indirectly through their values in the constraints; there is no profit obtained from having resources left over.

In the process of converting the Faze Linear problem to standard form, we have added three more variables, for a total of five. Since we add a slack variable for each constraint, we can conclude that linear programming problems in standard form will always have more variables than equations. Linear systems with more variables than equations will have an infinite number of solutions, provided that a solution exists. That is, the system will either have no solution or an infinite number of solutions. The simplex method does not consider all possible solutions. It looks only at a special type of solution called a basic solution. There are only a finite number of basic solutions, although for large problems the number of basic solutions can be quite large. We now examine the nature of basic solutions that are feasible.

BASIC FEASIBLE SOLUTIONS

To illustrate how we might obtain an infinite number of solutions to an LP problem, let's reconsider the Faze Linear problem with x_1, x_2, and s_1 solved in terms of s_2 and s_3.

$$105 + 11.5 \neq 40$$

$$
\begin{aligned}
x_2 + s_1 &= 40 & (4.4) \\
1.2x_1 + 4x_2 &= 240 - s_2 & (4.5) \\
.5x_1 + x_2 &= 81 - s_3 & (4.6)
\end{aligned}
$$

We can solve Equations (4.4)–(4.6) by arbitrarily setting s_2 and s_3 to any value and solving for the resulting values of x_1, x_2, and s_1. The simplex method simplifies this problem by setting s_2 and s_3 equal to zero. Solving the resulting system of equations with Gaussian elimination we obtain $x_1 = 105$, $x_2 = 28.5$, and $s_1 = 11.5$. This particular solution is called a basic solution. To see some other solutions, you can set s_2 and s_3 to values other than zero and solve the resulting 3×3 system.

To learn more about the nature of basic solutions, let's consider the general LP problem statement with $m \leq$ type constraints and n decision variables. In the process of converting to standard form, we add a slack variable for each $\leq$ constraint. Adding m slack variables, we obtain $m + n$ total variables in m equations. Thus, any LP model in standard form will always have more variables than constraints. Having n more variables than constraints gives us n degrees of freedom in solving the $m \times (m + n)$ system of equations.

In our Faze Linear problem in standard form we have $n = 2$ decision variables, $m = 3$ equations, and $m = 3$ slack variables. We are solving three equations in five unknowns. We have $n = 2$ degrees of freedom and can set any two variables equal to zero and solve for the remaining three variables. In the general $m \times (m + n)$ LP problem in standard form, we can set n of the variables equal to zero and solve the m equations in terms of the remaining m

basic variables. A solution derived by setting n of the variables equal to zero is
solution called a *basic solution*.

Setting n of the variables equal to zero essentially removes them from the system of m equations in $m + n$ unknowns, which reduces to m equations in m unknowns. If the n unknowns to be set to zero are selected properly, the resulting $m \times m$ system of equations will have a unique solution.[1] A unique solution implies that precisely one set of values for the remaining m variables will solve the $m \times m$ system of equations.

How many ways can we select m variables out of $m + n$ variables? The answer lies in the number of combinations which can be formed by taking m selections out of a possible $m + n$. The formula for the number of possible combinations is

$$\binom{m + n}{m} = \frac{(m + n)!}{m!(m + n - m)!} = \frac{(m + n)!}{m!n!}$$

Thus, there is a maximum of $\binom{m + n}{m}$ possible basic solutions to an LP problem. In the Faze Linear problem with $m = 3$ and $n = 2$, we have

$$\binom{3 + 2}{3} = \frac{5!}{3!2!} = \frac{5 \cdot 4 \cdot 3 \cdot 2 \cdot 1}{(3 \cdot 2 \cdot 1)(2 \cdot 1)} = \frac{120}{12} = 10$$

different possible basic solutions. Even though the maximum number of basic solutions is finite, the number can be astronomically large for large m and n.

Fortunately the simplex method only considers those basic solutions that are also feasible. To illustrate a basic solution that is not feasible, consider selecting the three variables x_1, x_2, and s_2 to solve the Faze Linear equations (4.1)–(4.3). Setting s_1 and s_3 equal to zero we obtain

$$\begin{aligned} x_2 &= 40 \\ 1.2x_1 + 4x_2 + s_2 &= 240 \\ .5x_1 + x_2 &= 81 \end{aligned}$$

[1] In the general case of solving an $m \times n$ system of equations, three conditions can exist: (1) a unique solution, (2) an infinite number of solutions, or (3) no solution.

Solving this system we obtain $x_2 = 40$, $x_1 = 82$, and $s_2 = -18.4$. The negative value of -18.4 renders this solution infeasible. Thus, even though the solution is basic (there are $m = 3$ variables used to solve the problem), it is not feasible (because all variables must be nonnegative).

basic feasible solutions   Basic solutions that are also feasible are called *basic feasible solutions*. These solutions not only involve m variables, but also satisfy all constraints, including the nonnegativity conditions. In the simplex method we have a systematic procedure that examines only basic feasible solutions. Basic feasible solutions are calculated algebraically, but have a very interesting geometric interpretation. Consider the following fundamental property in linear programming.

> There is a one-to-one correspondence between basic feasible solutions and extreme points of the feasible region

Basic feasible solutions and extreme points are one in the same and provide the optimal solution to an LP problem.

To illustrate the relationship between basic feasible solutions and extreme points, consider the graph in Figure 4.1.

The graph shows the five extreme points, *A, B, C, D,* and *O* associated with the Faze Linear problem. Consider also the basic feasible solutions listed in Table 4.1.

Notice how each extreme point corresponds to a basic feasible solution

basic and nonbasic variables in which exactly two of the five variables have a value of zero and three have a nonzero solution. Those n variables whose values are set to zero are called *nonbasic variables*. The remaining m variables are called *basic variables* and

FIGURE 4.1   Faze Linear feasible region and associated extreme points

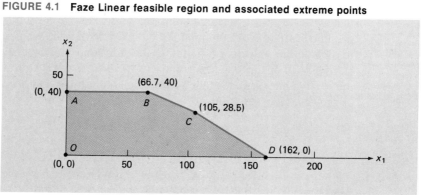

TABLE 4.1 *Basic feasible solutions for the Faze Linear problem*

Extreme point (in Fig. 4.1)	Power amps x_1	Preamps x_2	Transistor slack s_1	Assembly slack (hr) s_2	Inspection slack (hr) s_3	Profit
A	.0	40.0	.0	80.0	41.0	$20,000
B	66.7	40.0	.0	.0	7.7	33,333
C	105.0	28.5	11.5	.0	.0	35,250
D	162.0	.0	40.0	45.6	.0	32,400
O	.0	.0	40.0	240.0	81.0	0

are used to solve the system of equations. Observe which of the variables are basic and nonbasic in each of the five solutions shown in Table 4.1.

The calculations of the simplex method involve the successive generation of basic feasible solutions until the optimal one is found. The simplex method is an adjacent-extreme-point solution procedure in that it moves around the feasible region from one adjacent extreme point to another. For example, when we solve the Faze Linear problem our calculations will start at the origin O in Figure 4.1 and move sequentially to point A, then to point B, and finally to the optimal point C. In moving to an adjacent extreme point, the simplex method only examines points whose objective function value is at least as good as the value at the previous point. In determining the optimal solution, the simplex method will usually examine a mere fraction of all possible basic feasible solutions.

At this point let us review what we have learned and what we need to learn to execute the simplex method. With Gaussian elimination (in Appendix B) we have a method using elementary row operations to solve systems of linear equations. These solutions, however, are not necessarily basic feasible solutions and can yield negative solution values. We have learned that we need basic feasible solutions and that these solutions correspond geometrically to extreme points of the feasible region. We need to learn how to include the objective function in the solution procedure. We also need to learn how to ensure that the solutions are basic feasible solutions and how to move from one basic feasible solution to another one that improves the value of the objective function.

INCORPORATING THE OBJECTIVE FUNCTION

The simplex method is basically a method for solving systems of linear equations that also optimizes an associated objective function. Letting $Z =$

objective function value, we restate the Faze Linear in standard form as

$$\text{Maximize} \quad Z = 200x_1 + 500x_2 + 0s_1 + 0s_2 + 0s_3 \qquad (4.7)$$

$$\text{subject to} \qquad\qquad x_2 + s_1 \qquad\qquad\qquad = 40 \qquad (4.8)$$

$$1.2x_1 + 4x_2 \qquad + s_2 \qquad\quad = 240 \qquad (4.9)$$

$$.5x_1 + x_2 \qquad\qquad\qquad + s_3 = 81 \qquad (4.10)$$

$$x_1, x_2, s_1, s_2, s_3 \geq 0$$

If we let the three slack variables be basic and the two decision variables x_1 and x_2 be nonbasic, we can obtain an initial basic feasible solution. Setting x_1 and x_2 to zero, equations (4.8)–(4.10) reduce to

$$1s_1 + 0s_2 + 0s_3 = 40$$

$$0s_1 + 1s_2 + 0s_3 = 240$$

$$0s_1 + 0s_2 + 1s_3 = 81$$

The solution can be read immediately as $s_1 = 40$, $s_2 = 240$, and $s_3 = 81$. The objective function profit is $Z = 0(40) + 0(240) + 0(81) = 0$.

Notice how the solution can be read immediately from the right-hand side coefficients. You may observe that the basic variables have a coefficient of 1 in one equation and a 0 coefficient in every other row. Notice also that the column vectors associated with each basic variable are unit vectors; that is, the vectors are

$$\begin{pmatrix} 1 \\ 0 \\ 0 \end{pmatrix} \begin{pmatrix} 0 \\ 1 \\ 0 \end{pmatrix} \quad \text{and} \quad \begin{pmatrix} 0 \\ 0 \\ 1 \end{pmatrix}$$

for s_1, s_2, and s_3, respectively. Unit vectors have a component of 1 in one position and a component of 0 in every other position. The foregoing observations can be generalized to characterize basic feasible solutions in the simplex method. The following properties can be stated to help guide our simplex calculations.

i. Each basic variable appears in exactly one equation, in which it has a coefficient of 1.

ii. In the constraint equations, the column vectors associated with basic variables are unit vectors.

iii. The right-hand sides of the constraint equations are nonnegative constants that are the solution values for the basic variables.

Incorporating information from the objective function, we can now use elementary row operations to illustrate an intuitive approach for the simplex calculations. The elementary row operations on the equations will be executed to preserve properties i–iii.

elementary row operations
We studied elementary row operations in Appendix B on Gaussian elimination. To refresh your memory we restate the two most useful *elementary row operations:*

> 1. Multiplication of any equation (row) by a nonzero number.
> 2. Replacing any equation (row) by adding to it any other equation (row) in the system multiplied by a nonzero number.

Systems of linear equations that are manipulated by elementary row operations will change form through changes in their coefficients; however, all mathematical properties including the solutions to the system remain unchanged.

Let's now return to the initial basic feasible solution to the Faze Linear problem. This first solution corresponds to the origin extreme point O in Figure 4.1. The variable values are $x_1 = 0$, $x_2 = 0$, $s_1 = 40$, $s_2 = 240$, and $s_3 = 81$; the objective function profit is zero.

How can we improve the solution to yield a profit greater than zero? Looking at the objective function we have

$$\text{Maximize} \quad Z = 200x_1 + 500x_2$$

For every unit of x_2 (preamps) introduced into the solution the profit will increase by \$500. Let's explore how many units of x_2 we can produce and still maintain a basic feasible solution. It is useful to state another property of basic feasible solutions.

> An LP problem with m constraint equations will have exactly m basic variables

Given the foregoing property, it is apparent that if we introduce x_2 into the solution, one of the slack variables must become nonbasic and assume a zero value, since we may have only $m = 3$ basic variables. To see which slack variable must leave the solution, let's see what happens as the value of x_2 is increased. Expressing the slack variables in equations (4.8)–(4.10) in terms of x_2 we obtain

$$s_1 = 40 - x_2$$
$$s_2 = 240 - 4x_2$$
$$s_3 = 81 - x_2$$

how large can x_2 get before a basic variable goes to zero?

$$0 = 40 - x_2 \Rightarrow x_2 = 40$$
$$0 = 240 - 4x_2 \Rightarrow x_2 = 60$$
$$0 = 81 - x_2 \Rightarrow x_2 = 81$$

The calculations show that as the value of x_2 is increased in the constraint equations, slack variable s_1 is the first basic variable to be driven to zero. Slack s_1 is forced to 0 when x_2 assumes a value of 40. Thus, to prevent any basic variable from becoming negative, we can introduce only 40 units of x_2 into the solution at this time, since setting x_2 to any value greater than 40 will cause a variable to become negative.

If we do introduce 40 units of x_2 the new profit will be

$$Z = \$500(40) = \$20,000$$

When we introduce x_2 as a basic variable and make s_1 a nonbasic variable, we must update the constraint equation coefficients and the objective function. This is accomplished using elementary row operations.

USING ELEMENTARY ROW OPERATIONS TO TRANSFORM THE EQUATIONS

Rewriting the Faze linear equations in standard form expressing the objective function Z as an equation with profit equal to zero, we have

$$
\begin{array}{llllll}
Z - 200x_1 - 500x_2 & & & = & 0 & (4.11) \\
& 1x_2 + 1s_1 & & = & 40 & (4.12) \\
1.2x_1 + & 4x_2 + & 1s_2 & = & 240 & (4.13) \\
.5x_1 + & 1x_2 & + 1s_3 = & 81 & & (4.14)
\end{array}
$$

Notice the highlighted column vector $\begin{pmatrix} 1 \\ 4 \\ 1 \end{pmatrix}$ associated with variable x_2. Since x_2 is to become a basic variable and replace s_1, we must use elementary row operations to eliminate x_2 from every equation except the equation in which s_1 exists. Thus, we must use elementary row operations to transform the column vector associated with x_2 from $\begin{pmatrix} 1 \\ 4 \\ 1 \end{pmatrix}$ to the unit vector $\begin{pmatrix} 1 \\ 0 \\ 0 \end{pmatrix}$.

Variable x_2 has a coefficient of 1 in equation (4.12) so equation (4.12) remains unchanged. We must, however, eliminate the coefficient of 4 (for x_2)

in equation (4.13) and the coefficient of 1 in equation (4.14) in such a way that the original system is maintained. That is, each row must be updated by using elementary row operations. Here are the steps of the calculations:

Step 1: Obtain a coefficient of 1 for x_2 in equation (4.12). (This is already done in this problem):

$$\text{New eq. (4.12)}\quad 1x_2 + 1s_1 = 40$$

Step 2: Eliminate the coefficient of 4 in equation (4.13):

$$
\begin{array}{lrl}
\text{Old eq. (4.13)} & 1.2x_1 + 4x_2 \phantom{{}+{}} + s_2 = & 240 \\
-4 \times \text{New eq. (4.12)} & \underline{0x_1 - 4x_2 - 4s_1 \phantom{{}+s_2} = } & \underline{-160} \\
\text{New eq. (4.13)} & 1.2x_1 + 0x_2 - 4s_1 + s_2 = & 80
\end{array}
$$

Step 3: Eliminate the coefficient of 1 in equation (4.14):

$$
\begin{array}{lrl}
\text{Old eq. (4.14)} & .5x_1 + 1x_2 \phantom{{}+{}} + s_3 = & 81 \\
-1 \times \text{New eq. (4.12)} & \underline{0x_1 - 1x_2 - s_1 \phantom{{}+s_3} = } & \underline{40} \\
\text{New eq. (4.14)} & .5x_1 + 0x_2 - s_1 + s_3 = & 41
\end{array}
$$

To update the objective function equation we must also eliminate the coefficient of -500 in equation (4.11).

Step 4: Eliminate the coefficient of -500 in equation (4.11):

$$
\begin{array}{lrl}
\text{Old eq. (4.11)} & Z - 200x_1 - 500x_2 \phantom{{}+500s_1} = & 0 \\
500 \times \text{New eq. (4.12)} & \underline{ 0x_1 + 500x_2 + 500s_1 = } & \underline{20{,}000} \\
\text{New eq. (4.11)} & Z - 200x_1 \phantom{{}+500x_2} + 500s_1 = & 20{,}000
\end{array}
$$

The completely updated set of equations can be written as

$$
\begin{array}{rl}
Z - 200x_1 + + 500s_1 = & 20{,}000 \\
0x_1 + 1x_2 + 1s_1 + 0s_2 + 0s_3 = & 40 \\
1.2x_1 + 0x_2 - 4s_1 + 1s_2 + 0s_3 = & 80 \\
.5x_1 + 0x_2 - 1s_1 + 0s_2 + 1s_3 = & 41
\end{array}
$$

This second set of equations is equivalent to equations (4.11)–(4.14). The solution to this second set, however, is $x_2 = 40$, $s_2 = 80$, $s_3 = 41$, $x_1 = 0$, and $s_1 = 0$. The profit has improved from $Z = 0$ to $Z = \$20{,}000$. Notice also that this new basic feasible solution corresponds to extreme point A in Figure 4.1. Studying the updated set of equations, we can see that the column vectors of the basic variables x_2, s_2, and s_3 are indeed unit vectors.

How can we improve the solution further? Examining the new objective function equation we can see that

$$Z = 200x_1 - 500s_1 + 20{,}000$$

Since x_1 and s_1 are nonbasic, their current values are 0, and Z simply equals $20,000 by virtue of basic variable $x_2 = 40$. Notice that increasing the value of x_1 will increase profit by $200 per unit; likewise increasing the value of s_1 will decrease profit by $500 per unit.

In maximizing the profit for the Faze Linear Co. we would now want to introduce variable x_1 into the solution. We would have to determine which basic variable to remove from the solution and then update the equations using elementary row operations. Executing this plan would move our solution to extreme point B in Figure 4.1. However, at this point we shall stop and introduce a slightly more formal approach to the simplex calculations. Our goal in the first part of this chapter has been to relate the algebraic calculations of the simplex method to the geometric observations of the graphical method and to the equation manipulations of the Gaussian elimination method. This algebraic development should facilitate your understanding of the mechanics of the simplex method.

BASIC STEPS

Now that you have some familiarity with the basic algebraic calculations in the simplex method, we shall try to formalize these procedures to specify a complete algorithm. Specifically, we shall present an overview of the basic steps and introduce the simplex tableau for facilitating calculations. Exact rules for preserving feasibility and basic feasible solutions will be covered, as well as rules for determining entering and leaving variables at each iteration.

We shall first consider an LP model with all $\leq$ constraints. Later we will show how to transform $\geq$ and $=$ constraints to standard form. Assuming that we have converted the model to standard form, the simplex method encompasses the following basic steps:

1. Determine an initial basic feasible solution. The initial basic variables will be slack or dummy variables.

entering variable 2. Determine an *entering variable* that can improve the value of the objective function. If no such variable can be found then stop; the current solution is optimal.

leaving variable 3. Determine the basic variable to leave the solution. The *leaving variable* is the basic variable whose value first reaches zero as the value of the entering variable is increased.

4. Update the coefficients of the system of equations to reflect the fact

that the entering variable has replaced the leaving variable. The updating is accomplished using elementary row operations and is called

pivoting   *pivoting*.

iteration   Notice the loop from step 4 to step 2. Each repetition of steps 2 through 4 is called an *iteration* in the simplex method. Large-scale LP problems require hundreds or thousands of iterations. The completion of each iteration corresponds to the determination of a new improved extreme point (basic feasible solution).

THE SIMPLEX TABLEAU

Computers execute the simplex method by storing the appropriate information and operating on it whenever it is needed. When we execute the simplex method by hand, calculations are more conveniently dealt with in tabular

simplex   form. The table consisting of the system equations and other relevant infor-
tableau   mation is called a *simplex tableau*. The general form of an initial tableau is shown in Tableau 4.1.

The terms in the initial tableau are defined as follows:

c_j = objective function coefficient of variable j
b_i = right-hand side coefficient of constraint i
a_{ij} = constraint coefficient of variable j in equation i
c_B = objective function coefficients of the basic variables

TABLEAU 4.1   *Form for initial simplex tableau*

		decision variables				slack variables				Solution values
	c_j	c_1	c_2	$\cdots$	c_n	0	0	$\cdots$	0	
c_B	Basic variables	x_1	x_2	$\cdots$	x_n	s_1	s_2	$\cdots$	s_m	Solution values
0	s_1	a_{11}	a_{12}	$\cdots$	a_{1n}	1	0	$\cdots$	0	b_1
0	s_2	a_{21}	a_{22}	$\cdots$	a_{2n}	0	1			b_2
$\vdots$	$\vdots$	$\vdots$				$\vdots$	$\vdots$		$\vdots$	$\vdots$
0	s_m	a_{m1}	a_{m2}	$\cdots$	a_{mn}	0	0		1	b_m
	z_j									
	$c_j - z_j$									

solutions of basic variables

The initial simplex tableau represents the original LP equations in standard form supplemented by some additional rows and columns. Looking first at the rows, we have the c_j row at the top of the tableau; the c_j are simply the objective function coefficients of the variables listed in the row below. After the header row which describes the column headings are m rows which represent the m constraint coefficients. The leftmost column in the tableau represents the objective function coefficients of the basic variables. With all $\leq$ constraints the initial tableau will contain m slack variables with c_B values equal to 0. The next column headed by ''Basic Variables'' is a list of those m variables that are in the solution, or basic. The rightmost column displays the solution values of the basic variables.

THE BASIC STEPS APPLIED

Determine an Initial Basic Feasible Solution

For convenience let's restate the Faze Linear problem in standard form and illustrate the associated initial tableau.

$$\text{Maximize} \quad 200x_1 + 500x_2 + 0s_1 + 0s_2 + 0s_3$$

$$\text{subject to} \quad 0x_1 + \quad 1x_2 + 1s_1 + 0s_2 + 0s_3 = \quad 40$$

$$1.2x_1 + \quad 4x_2 + 0s_1 + 1s_2 + 0s_3 = 240$$

$$.5x_1 + \quad 1x_2 + 0s_1 + 0s_3 + 1s_3 = \quad 81$$

Transferring the equations to the initial tableau we have Tableau 4.2:

TABLEAU 4.2 *Initial simplex tableau for Faze Linear*

objective function coefficients

	c_j	200	500	0	0	0	
c_B	Basic variables	x_1	x_2	s_1	s_2	s_3	Solution
0	s_1	0	1	1	0	0	40
0	s_2	1.2	4	0	1	0	240
0	s_3	.5	1	0	0	1	81

objective function coefficients of basic variables →

← value of s_1
← value of s_2
← value of s_3

The initial tableau requires no calculations, but merely the construction of the appropriate table headings and columns.

The initial basic feasible solution for an LP model with all $\leq$ constraints always consists of the m slack variables. Notice the slack variables s_1, s_2, and s_3 listed in the "Basic variables" column. We can also observe that the column vectors under s_1, s_2, and s_3 in the initial tableau are unit vectors. The starting variables for any LP model will be dummy variables. Later in the chapter we shall describe how to establish an initial basic feasible solution for models having $\geq$ and $=$ type constraints. In this case we will have to employ another type of dummy variable called an artificial variable.

Improving the Current Solution

The simplex method achieves an improved solution by bringing one nonbasic variable into the solution to replace a current basic variable. The basic variable that leaves the solution becomes nonbasic and assumes a value of zero. Each time a new variable is brought into the solution, a new basic feasible solution is achieved; this corresponds to moving to a new extreme point.

How can we determine which nonbasic variables have the potential to improve the solution? To answer this question let's rewrite the current equations of the Faze Linear problem of Tableau 4.2. Rewriting the equations, we can express the slack variables (which are basic) in terms of the nonbasic variables, x_1 and x_2.

$$s_1 = 40 - 0x_1 - 1x_2 \qquad (4.15)$$
$$s_2 = 240 - 1.2x_1 - 4x_2 \qquad (4.16)$$
$$s_3 = 81 - .5x_1 - 1x_2 \qquad (4.17)$$

We can observe in equation (4.16), for example, that increasing the value of x_1 decreases the value of s_2 at 1.2 per unit of x_1 increase. Likewise, increasing the value of x_2 causes a four-per-unit decrease in the value of s_2. Observing the highlighted columns in equations (4.15)–(4.17), we can see that these are simply the columns under x_1 and x_2 from Tableau 4.2. Those *substitution* coefficients in the tableau that are directly under a variable x_j are sometimes *coefficients* called *substitution coefficients*. These substitution coefficients indicate the per unit change in the associated basic variable for each unit of increase in variable x_j.

By using the substitution coefficients, we can now calculate the economic impact of increasing any nonbasic variable. The c_B column indicates the objective function value of each unit of the associated basic variable. Multiplying the c_B column times the column of substitution coefficients for a nonbasic variable x_j yields the net decrease in profit attributed to bringing x_j into solution. This net decrease in profit for variable x_j is called a z_j value. The z_j value is defined as the amount of profit that is given up for each unit of variable x_j that enters the solution. The z_j values for x_1 and x_2 are calculated as follows:

c_B		x_1		
0	×	0	=	0
0	×	1.2	=	0
0	×	.5	=	0
		z_1	=	0

sum these to get z_1

c_B		x_2		
0	×	1	=	0
0	×	4	=	0
0	×	1	=	0
		z_2	=	0

sum these to get z_2

Since the slack variables have zero objective function coefficients, both z_1 and z_2 are zero. In other words, we give up no profit if x_1 or x_2 enter the solution. (When the basic variables have nonzero objective function coefficients, the z_j values are usually >0.)

The z_j values indicate the per unit loss from bringing a nonbasic variable x_j into solution. The loss reflects the fact that the value of some of the current basic variables must be reduced to accommodate the increase in nonbasic variable x_j, since some resources must go to the new variable. The per unit gain for bringing x_j into the solution is represented by the associated objective function coefficient c_j. The net opportunity cost of bringing x_j into the solution is calculated as $c_j - z_j$ (gain − loss). The $c_j - z_j$ values are called *reduced costs* opportunity costs or *reduced costs*. Making the $c_j - z_j$ calculations for all five variables in the simplex tableau we have

$$
\begin{aligned}
c_1 - z_1 &= 200 - [0(0) + 0(1.2) + 0(.5)] = 200 \\
c_2 - z_2 &= 500 - [0(1) + 0(4) + 0(1)\,] = 500 \\
c_3 - z_3 &= 0 - [0(1) + 0(0) + 0(0)\,] = 0 \\
c_4 - z_4 &= 0 - [0(0) + 0(1) + 0(0)\,] = 0 \\
c_5 - z_5 &= 0 - [0(0) + 0(0) + 0(1)\,] = 0
\end{aligned}
$$

For completeness we have calculated the $c_j - z_j$ values for the three basic variables as well as the two nonbasic variables. However, the $c_j - z_j$ value for a basic variable will always be zero.

TABLEAU 4.3 *Complete initial tableau with $c_j - z_j$ rows*

		c_j	200	500	0	0	0	
c_B		Basic variables	x_1	x_2	s_1	s_2	s_3	Solution
0		s_1	0	1	1	0	0	40
0		s_2	1.2	4	0	1	0	240
0		s_3	.5	1	0	0	1	81
		z_j	0	0	0	0	0	0
		$c_j - z_j$	200	500	0	0	0	

← profit of solution

opportunity costs

Expanding our initial simplex tableau to include the z_j and $c_j - z_j$ rows, we have the completed initial tableau in Tableau 4.3. The $c_j - z_j$ value of 500 for x_2 indicates that the objective function will increase by 500 for each unit of x_2 brought into solution. To improve our current basic feasible solution and move to a more profitable extreme point, we can bring into solution any nonbasic variable whose $c_j - z_j > 0$.

In maximization problems we generally choose the nonbasic variable whose $c_j - z_j$ value is largest, to improve the solution. This choice of entering variable gives the fastest *rate* of improvement, though not necessarily the greatest *amount* of improvement. We can state the rule for the entering variable as follows:

In a maximization problem we increase the value of the objective function by selecting (as the entering variable) the nonbasic variable that has the largest positive $c_j - z_j$ value. If there is no positive $c_j - z_j$, no improvement is possible.

In the Faze Linear problem we shall select variable x_2 to enter the solution. Since only three variables can be basic in this problem, we must now determine a variable to leave the solution.

Determine the Leaving Variable

The variable to leave the solution and become nonbasic is that basic variable whose value first reaches zero as the value of the entering variable (here x_2)

TABLEAU 4.4   *Illustration of columns involved in ratio test*

							column of entering variable	
	c_j	200	500	0	0	0	solution column	
	Basic variables	x_1	x_2	s_1	s_2	s_3	Solution	Ratio
	c_B							
leaving variable $s_1 \rightarrow$ 0	s_1	0	1	1	0	0	40	$\frac{40}{1}$ ← minimum
0	s_2	1.2	4	0	1	0	240	$\frac{240}{4}$ ratio
0	s_3	.5	1	0	0	1	81	$\frac{81}{1}$
	z_j	0	0	0	0	0	0	
	$c_j - z_j$	200	500	0	0	0		

↑

is increased. In the algebraic overview section of this chapter we showed why s_1 is the leaving variable for this first iteration. Let's review our reasoning and show a shortcut method to determine the leaving variable (Tableau 4.4).

First, assuming that $x_1 = 0$, we can express the basic variables s_1, s_2, and s_3 as a function of x_2:

$$
\begin{aligned}
s_1 &= 40 - x_2 \\
s_2 &= 240 - 4x_2 \\
s_3 &= 81 - x_2
\end{aligned}
$$

Setting each of these basic slack variables to zero and solving for x_2 determines the maximum value x_2 can attain without forcing a basic variable to a negative value.

$$
\begin{aligned}
0 &= 40 - x_2 \Rightarrow x_2 = \tfrac{40}{1} = 40 \leftarrow \text{maximum feasible value for } x_2 \\
0 &= 240 - 4x_2 \Rightarrow x_2 = \tfrac{240}{4} = 60 \\
0 &= 81 - x_2 \Rightarrow x_2 = \tfrac{81}{1} = 81
\end{aligned}
$$

We can see that s_1 will be zero when x_2 reaches a value of 40. If x_2 assumes a value larger than 40, s_1 will assume a negative value. Thus 40 is the value of x_2 when it enters the solution, and s_1 is the variable that must leave the solution at a zero value.

We can determine the leaving variable easily by forming ratios between two columns in the simplex tableau. Consider the column headed by the entering variable x_2 and the right-hand side solution column. Dividing the coefficients in the x_2 column into the values in the solution column we get the same ratios that we found in our previous analysis. The minimum ratio determines the value of the entering variable. The row in which the minimum ratio occurs determines the leaving variable. Since the minimum ratio occurred in row 1, the basic variable that is associated with row 1, or s_1, is the leaving variable. Tableau 4.4 shows the results of the minimum ratio test in the context of a full simplex tableau.

x_2	Solution	Ratio	
1	40	$\frac{40}{1} = 40$	← minimum ratio
4	240	$\frac{240}{4} = 60$	
1	81	$\frac{81}{1} = 81$	

We can formalize the choice of the leaving variable with the following decision rule:

leaving
variable

> Calculate the ratios of the coefficients in the "Solution" column divided by the coefficients in the simplex column of the entering variable. Consider only those ratios whose denominator is greater than zero. The resulting minimum ratio is the new value of the entering variable. The basic variable in the row with the minimum positive ratio is the *leaving variable*.

Updating the Simplex Tableau

Having decided which variable is to enter the solution and which variable is to leave the solution, we must update the simplex tableau. The updating process not only involves the transformation of the constraint equations, but also the updating of the additional information in the c_B column and the z_j and $c_j - z_j$ rows. The procedure used to perform the updating utilizes elementary row operations and is traditionally called pivoting.

In Tableau 4.4 we have used two arrows along the perimeter of the tableau to point out the column of the entering variable and the row of the leaving variable. At the intersection of the x_2 column and the s_1 row is a
pivot element circled number called the *pivot element*. The pivot element will play a key role in the updating process. The row in which the pivot element occurs is
pivot row called the *pivot row*. The entering variable will always assume its position in the "Basic variables" list where the leaving variable was located. (This position will always correspond to the pivot row.)

The pivoting or updating process consists of two basic steps. In one step we update the pivot row so that the pivot element becomes a one. In the other step we update the other rows (using the pivot row) so that all other constraint coefficients in the pivot column are zero.

The pivot row is simple to update; we simply multiply all coefficients in the pivot row by the reciprocal of the pivot element. This elementary row operation will yield an updated pivot element of one. In our example in Tableau 4.4 the pivot element is already a 1. However, for completeness we show the calculation.

$$\text{New pivot row} = \tfrac{1}{1} \times \text{old pivot row}$$
$$= 1 \times (0 \quad 1 \quad 1 \quad 0 \quad 0 \quad 40)$$
$$= \quad (0 \quad 1 \quad 1 \quad 0 \quad 0 \quad 40)$$

In Tableau 4.5 we show the updated pivot row in the partially completed simplex tableau. Notice that the c_B column has been updated to in-

TABLEAU 4.5 *First iteration with pivot row updated*

c_B	Basic variables	c_j						
		200	500	0	0	0		
		x_1	x_2	s_1	s_2	s_3	Solution	
500	x_2	0	1	1	0	0	40	← updated pivot row
0	s_2							
0	s_3							
	z_j							
	$c_j - z_j$							

clude the $500 profit contribution of x_2. We now use the updated pivot row to update the other rows in the tableau. Recall from the algebraic overview section that the constraint coefficients of a basic variable should be a unit vector. Thus we want the column vector of x_2 to appear as the highlighted unit vector:

Basic variables	x_2
x_2	1
s_2	0
s_3	0

We can use elementary row operations to eliminate the second and third coefficients in the x_2 column. We define the pivot intersection number of a row to be the number in the row that is in the pivot column. In Tableau 4.4, the pivot intersection numbers for rows 2 and 3, respectively, are 4 and 1. Using the updated pivot row we can update the other rows using the formula

new row = old row − pivot intersection number × new pivot row

To illustrate the pivoting process, let us update rows 2 and 3 in the tableau:

$$
\begin{array}{rrrrrrr}
\text{old row 2} = (1.2 & 4 & 0 & 1 & 0 & 240) \\
-4 \times \text{updated pivot row} = (0 & -4 & -4 & 0 & 0 & -160) \\
\hline
\text{new row 2} = 1.2 & 0 & -4 & 1 & 0 & 80
\end{array}
$$

We have now eliminated the 4 in the x_2 column of row 2. Updating the third row we have

$$
\begin{array}{rrrrrrr}
\text{old row 3} = & (.5 & 1 & 0 & 0 & 1 & 81) \\
-1 \times \text{updated pivot row} = & (\,0 & -1 & -1 & 0 & 0 & -40) \\
\hline
\text{new row 3} = & .5 & 0 & -1 & 0 & 1 & 41
\end{array}
$$

Once these rows have been updated, we can calculate the z_j values as

$$
\begin{array}{rlll}
z_1 = & 500(0) & + 0(1.2) + 0(.5) = & 0 \\
z_2 = & 500(1) & + 0(0) \quad + 0(0) = & 500 \\
z_3 = & 500(1) & + 0(-4) + 0(-1) = & 500 \\
z_4 = & 500(0) & + 0(1) \quad + 0(0) = & 0 \\
z_5 = & 500(0) & + 0(0) \quad + 0(1) = & 0 \\
\text{profit} = & 500(40) & + 0(80) \quad + 0(41) = & 20{,}000
\end{array}
$$

The $c_j - z_j$ reduced costs are calculated by subtracting the z_j values from the objective function coefficients.

$$
\begin{array}{llll}
c_1 - z_1 = & 200 - & 0 = & 200 \\
c_2 - z_2 = & 500 - & 500 = & 0 \\
c_3 - z_3 = & 0 - & 500 = & -500 \\
c_4 - z_4 = & 0 - & 0 = & 0 \\
c_5 - z_5 = & 0 - & 0 = & 0
\end{array}
$$

In Tableau 4.6, the completed tableau for the second solution is presented. The solution corresponds to extreme point A in Figure 4.1. The current solution value in the lower right-hand side of the tableau is calculated by

TABLEAU 4.6   *Updated tableau after first iteration*

c_B	c_j Basic variables	200 x_1	500 x_2	0 s_1	0 s_2	0 s_3	Solution	Minimum ratio
500	x_2	0	1	1	0	0	40	—
0	s_2	1.2	0	−4	1	0	80	$\frac{80}{1.2} = 66.67$
0	s_3	.5	0	−1	0	1	41	$\frac{41}{.5} = 82$
	z_j	0	500	500	0	0	20,000	
	$c_j - z_j$	200	0	−500	0	0		

taking the c_B column times the "Solution" column to yield profit = 500(40) + 0(80) + 0(41) = 20,000.

The pivoting process merely involves multiplying one equation by a constant and adding it to another equation. However, certain rules involving elementary row operations are observed so that the solution to the updated system of equations is the same as for the original LP model. Thus, the rows in Tableau 4.6 still represent equations equivalent to the original system.

Returning to our calculations, we can see that the second solution in Tableau 4.6 is not optimal since $c_1 - z_1 = 200$. Thus, x_1 will be the entering variable, and the leaving variable is calculated by forming the ratios $\frac{80}{1.2}$ and $\frac{41}{.5}$. No ratio is formed for row 1 since it has a zero in the x_1 column. Row 2 yields the minimum ratio, and s_2 becomes the leaving variable. Thus, 1.2 becomes the pivot element.

We must now update the entire simplex tableau to represent accurately the new basic feasible solution. The first step is always to update the pivot row. In this case, row 2 is the pivot row. Multiplying by the reciprocal of the pivot element 1.2, we have

$$\text{new pivot row} = \frac{1}{1.2} \times \text{old pivot row}$$

$$= \frac{1}{1.2} \times (1.2 \quad 0 \quad -4 \quad 1 \quad 0 \quad 80\ )$$

$$= \quad (1 \quad 0 \quad -\tfrac{10}{3} \quad \tfrac{5}{6} \quad 0 \quad 66\tfrac{2}{3})$$

In updating rows 1 and 3 we must remember that the new substitution coefficients under x_1 must become the unit vector

$$x_1$$

$$0$$
$$1$$
$$0$$

Since row 1 already has a zero coefficient in the x_1 column, row 1 does not need to be changed. Thus

$$\text{new row } 1 = (0 \quad 1 \quad 1 \quad 0 \quad 0 \quad 40)$$

Eliminating the .5 in the x_1 column of row 3 (in terms of the new pivot row), we have

$$
\begin{array}{rrrrrrr}
\text{old row 3} = (& .5 & 0 & -1 & 0 & 1 & 41\ ) \\
-.5 \times \text{updated pivot row} = (& -.5 & 0 & +\tfrac{5}{3} & -\tfrac{5}{12} & 0 & -33\tfrac{1}{3}) \\
\hline
\text{new row 3} = & 0 & 0 & \tfrac{2}{3} & -\tfrac{5}{12} & 1 & 7\tfrac{2}{3}
\end{array}
$$

TABLEAU 4.7   *Updated tableau after second iteration*

c_B	Basic variables	c_j x_1	200 x_2	500 s_1	0 s_2	0 s_3	0 Solution	Minimum ratio
500	x_2	0	1	1	0	0	40	$\frac{40}{1} = 40$
200	x_1	1	0	$-\frac{10}{3}$	$\frac{5}{6}$	0	$66\frac{2}{3}$	—
0	s_3	0	0	$\frac{2}{3}$	$-\frac{5}{12}$	1	$7\frac{2}{3}$	$7\frac{2}{3}/\frac{3}{3} = 11.5$
	z_j	200	500	$-166\frac{2}{3}$	$166\frac{2}{3}$	0	$33,333\frac{1}{3}$	
	$c_j - z_j$	0	0	$166\frac{2}{3}$	$-166\frac{2}{3}$	0		

↑

We can also treat the $c_j - z_j$ row like any other row in the updating process. In this case we must eliminate the coefficient of 200 in the $c_j - z_j$ row

$$
\begin{array}{rrrrrr}
\text{old } c_j - z_j = (& 200 & 0 & -500 & 0 & 0) \\
-200 \times \text{updated pivot row} = (-200 & 0 & +666\frac{2}{3} & -166\frac{2}{3} & 0) \\
\hline
\text{new } c_j - z_j = & 0 & 0 & 166\frac{2}{3} & -166\frac{2}{3} & 0
\end{array}
$$

Given the new $c_j - z_j$ row it is not necessary to compute the z_j values; however, for completeness the z_j's are

$$
\begin{aligned}
z_1 &= 500(0) & + \; 200(1) & + \; 0(0) & = & \quad 200 \\
z_2 &= 500(1) & + \; 200(0) & + \; 0(0) & = & \quad 500 \\
z_3 &= 500(1) & + \; 200(-\tfrac{10}{3}) & + \; 0(\tfrac{2}{3}) & = & -166\tfrac{2}{3} \\
z_4 &= 500(0) & + \; 200(\tfrac{5}{6}) & + \; 0(-\tfrac{5}{12}) & = & \quad 166\tfrac{2}{3} \\
z_5 &= 500(0) & + \; 200(0) & + \; 0(1) & = & \quad 0 \\
\text{profit} &= 500(40) & + \; 200(66\tfrac{2}{3}) & + \; 0(7\tfrac{2}{3}) & = & 33,333\tfrac{1}{3}
\end{aligned}
$$

The value of the new solution is $33,333\frac{1}{3}$. The basic feasible solution corresponds to extreme point B in Figure 4.1. The updated tableau is shown in Tableau 4.7.

One more iteration is required before optimality is reached. The next and final solution is presented in Tableau 4.8. This solution corresponds to the optimal extreme point C in Figure 4.1. The tableau indicates optimality since all solution values are nonnegative and all $c_j - z_j$ are less than or equal to zero, which indicates that no higher profit can be achieved. That is, if all $c_j - z_j$ are ≤ 0, then there is no nonbasic variable that can enter the solution

TABLEAU 4.8 *Optimal tableau for Faze Linear problem*

c_B	Basic variables	c_j	200	500	0	0	0	
			x_1	x_2	s_1	s_2	s_3	Solution
500	x_2		0	1	0	$\frac{5}{8}$	$-\frac{3}{2}$	$28\frac{1}{2}$
200	x_1		1	0	0	$-\frac{5}{4}$	5	105
0	s_1		0	0	1	$-\frac{5}{8}$	$\frac{3}{2}$	$11\frac{1}{2}$
	z_j		200	500	0	$62\frac{1}{2}$	250	35,250
	$c_j - z_j$		0	0	0	$-62\frac{1}{2}$	-250	

optimality criterion and improve the value of the objective function. We use this fact to state our stopping rule or *optimality criterion.*

> The optimal solution to an LP maximization problem has been achieved when all reduced costs ($c_j - z_j$ values) are $\leq$ zero

The optimality criterion assumes of course that the candidate for the optimal solution is feasible. The feasibility of the solution can be checked by substituting the solution into the original constraints of the model.

From Tableau 4.8, we can see that variables x_2, x_1, and s_1 are in the final solution at values 28.5, 105, and 11.5, respectively. This corresponds to real conditions of producing 28.5 preamps and 105 amps and having 11.5 surplus transistors. The optimal profit is found in the lower right-hand corner at the value of $35,250. This solution is precisely the same solution as determined by the graphical method.

Which of the three resources are being fully utilized? From the optimal tableau, we can see that slack variables s_2 and s_3 are nonbasic and therefore have value zero. Consequently, there is no surplus assembly or inspection time, and these two resources are being fully utilized.

MINIMIZATION PROBLEMS

The solution of a minimization problem is identical to the solution of a maximization problem with one exception. The rule for selecting the entering variable must be changed to effect a decrease in the value of the objective function at each iteration. There are two ways to determine the entering variable for a minimization problem.

1. First, we can simply formulate the minimization problem, then change the signs of all coefficients in the objective function and solve the problem as a maximization problem. The resulting values of the decision variables will be correct, and multiplying the final objective function value by -1 yields the correct minimum value. Some computer codes only maximize (or minimize), and the decision maker must sometimes use this reversing trick to solve an LP problem on the computer.

2. The second approach to minimization involves changing the simplex solution procedure. Again, the alteration is simple; it involves only a change in the selection criterion for the entering variable. Instead of picking the variable with the most positive $c_j - z_j$ to enter the solution, we simply pick the variable with the most negative $c_j - z_j$. Such a selection decreases rather than increases the value of the objective function.

The optimality criterion for a minimization problem is achieved when all $c_j - z_j \geq 0$. The minimum ratio, determination of the leaving variable, and the pivoting process remain the same as the maximization case.

In the following section we will solve an example of a minimization problem. First, let us learn how to handle = and $\geq$ type constraints in the simplex method.

HANDLING OTHER TYPES OF CONSTRAINTS

It is quite common for LP models to contain equality constraints as well as greater-than-or-equal-to constraints. Thus far, we have dealt only with less-than-or-equal-to constraints. Conversion to standard form has involved the addition of one slack variable to each constraint. Let us see how to convert equality and greater-than-or-equal-to constraints to standard form.

Equality Constraints

Consider the constraint

$$7x_1 + 5x_2 = 10$$

This constraint is already an equation, and it appears to be ready for the simplex method. However, it is not clear what the starting value of x_1 and x_2

should be in the initial solution. To answer this would require solving the
artificial system of constraints. We can avoid having to solve the system if we add a
variable dummy variable, called an *artificial variable*. Thus, we convert the initial
equality to

$$7x_1 + 5x_2 + A_1 = 10$$

The solution of $A_1 = 10$ in the initial solution is obvious because A_1 will not
appear in any other equations. Like the slack variables, the column of constraint coefficients of an artificial variable forms a unit vector. Unlike slack
variables, artificial variables are not allowed to assume a nonzero value in
the optimal solution. For example, if A_1 were to equal 2 in the preceding
equation, then $7x_1 + 5x_2$ would equal 8 rather than 10.

Artificial variables are used only to obtain a starting (*pseudofeasible*)
solution for the simplex method and must eventually be forced out of the
solution. We shall do this by assigning artificial variables extremely low
objective function coefficients in maximization problems and extremely high
objective function coefficients in minimization problems.

Greater-than-or-Equal-to Constraints

In a greater-than-or-equal-to constraint, the left-hand side of the inequality is
allowed to exceed the right-hand side value. Consider the constraint

$$7x_1 + 5x_2 \geq 10$$

To allow $7x_1 + 5x_2$ to exceed 10 we introduce a slack variable. The slack
variable must be subtracted from the left hand side to obtain an equation.
Thus we have

$$7x_1 + 5x_2 - s_1 = 10$$

However, the starting solution in terms of the slack variable requires $s_1 = -10$. Basic variables are not allowed to assume a negative value; therefore
we add an artificial variable A_1 to obtain a positive starting solution in terms
of the dummy variables. Thus the constraint in standard form is

$$7x_1 + 5x_2 - s_1 + A_1 = 10$$

In the initial solution A_1 would equal 10. Subsequently the simplex method
negative will have to force the artificial to have a value of zero.
right-hand The simplex method requires that all right-hand side values be non-
side negative. What happens if we have a constraint with a *negative right-hand*

side? We must multiply the entire constraint by -1 to achieve a positive right-hand side. For example, if we have

$$7x_1 - 5x_2 \leq -10$$

then we multiply by -1 to obtain

$$-7x_1 + 5x_2 \geq 10$$

Notice that the sign of each coefficient changed and that the direction of the inequality is reversed.

Let us now consider the solution of a minimization problem with all three types of constraints.

EXAMPLE   Consider an oil company that produces a petroleum product requiring the input of crude oil A and crude oil B. Each barrel of the final product must contain at least 50 gallons. In this final mix, at least 20 gallons must be crude oil A and, at most, 30 gallons can be crude oil B. Crude oil B costs $.75 per gallon, and crude oil A cost $1.00 per gallon. How many gallons of crude A and B should be in each barrel of the petroleum product in order to meet specifications and minimize costs?

If we let x_1 equal the number of gallons of crude B in a barrel of final product and x_2 the number of gallons of crude A, then the problem is formulated thus:

$$
\begin{aligned}
\text{Minimize} \quad & .75x_1 + 1.00x_2 \\
\text{subject to} \quad & x_1 + x_2 \geq 50 \\
& x_1 \leq 30 \\
& x_2 \geq 20 \\
& x_1, x_2 \geq 0
\end{aligned}
$$

Converting the constraints to standard form, we have

$$
\begin{aligned}
x_1 + x_2 - s_1 + A_1 &= 50 \\
x_1 + s_2 &= 30 \\
x_2 - s_3 + A_2 &= 20
\end{aligned}
$$

phase 1/ phase 2 approach   In the simplex method we must force the artificial variables out of the solution to a value of zero. There are two approaches to this problem: the two-phase approach and the penalty approach. The *two-phase approach* is a method where in phase 1 the artificials are forced out of the solution and in phase 2 the original problem is solved. In phase 1 the objective function consists of only the artificial variables. Thus, in our example the phase 1 objective function would be

$$\text{Minimize} \quad A_1 + A_2$$

subject to the problem constraints. If phase 1 achieves an objective function value of zero (that is, the artificials have a value of zero), phase 2 is begun with an objective function of Minimize $.75x_1 + 1.00x_2$. Phase 2 benefits from the advanced starting solution determined during phase 1. If the artificials cannot all be forced to a value of zero in phase 1, the problem has no feasible solution and phase 2 is not attempted.

In our solution to the example minimization problem we shall use a penalty approach instead of the two-phase method. That is, we penalize the artificial variables so that they will not appear in the final solution. Assigning the artificials an arbitrarily high cost accomplishes this for a minimization problem. For a maximization problem we would assign the artificials an arbitrarily low profit. If we let M ($-M$ for a maximization) represent a very large number, we can write the objective function as

$$\text{Minimize} \quad .75x_1 + 1.00x_2 + 0s_1 + 0s_2 + 0s_3 + MA_1 + MA_2$$

The problem is now in standard form and can be solved by the simplex method. The big M is simply treated as a number; thus, the basic simplex procedure does not change.

To help you visualize the nature of the minimization problem, let us consider a brief graphical analysis. In Figure 4.2, the oil company's minimi-

FIGURE 4.2   **Graphical solution of oil company's minimization problem**

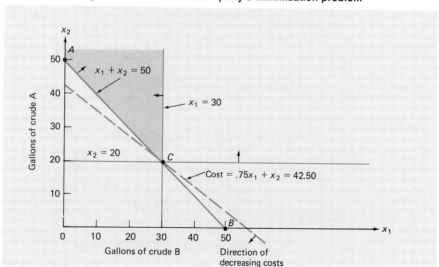

zation problem is graphed. The constraints $x_1 \le 30$, $x_2 \ge 20$, and $x_1 + x_2 \ge 50$ each define a half-space in the plane. The set of points satisfying all three constraints and defining the feasible region is indicated by the shaded area in the graph.

The objective function, cost = $.75x_1 + 1.00x_2$, is represented by the dashed line in Figure 4.2. Points A and C are the only extreme points of the feasible region. The direction of decreasing costs is toward the southwest; thus point $C = (30, 20)$ is the optimal extreme point. The associated solution is to mix 30 gallons of crude B and 20 gallons of crude A per barrel for a minimum cost of $42.50.

Now let us solve the same problem with the simplex method. Since some variables that have coefficients of zero are not shown in each constraint, we rewrite the initial LP model to demonstrate the existence of each variable in each constraint. The problem is thus restated as

Minimize $.75x_1 + 1.00x_2 + 0s_1 + 0s_2 + 0s_3 + MA_1 + MA_2$

subject to $1x_1 + \quad 1x_2 - 1s_1 + 0s_2 + 0s_3 + 1A_1 + 0A_2 = 50$

$1x_1 + \quad 0x_2 + 0s_1 + 1s_2 + 0s_3 + 0A_1 + 0A_2 = 30$

$0x_1 + \quad 1x_2 + 0s_1 + 0s_2 - 1s_3 + 0A_1 + 1A_2 = 20$

$x_1, x_2, s_1, s_2, s_3, A_1, A_2 \ge 0$

In developing the initial tableau, it is important to know which dummy variables will be basic. The variables to enter the initial solution will be those slacks and artificials with a positive 1 coefficient in the constraint equation in which they appear. This will include all artificials and only those slacks in $\le$ type constraints. Slacks in $\ge$ type constraints have a minus sign and will not be in the initial solution. In our example problem, A_1, S_2, and A_2 are the initial basic variables.

Notice that their position in the basic solution column is dictated by the position of the 1 in their column of substitution coefficients. That is, A_1 is

first with $\begin{pmatrix} 1 \\ 0 \\ 0 \end{pmatrix}$, s_2 is second with $\begin{pmatrix} 0 \\ 1 \\ 0 \end{pmatrix}$, and A_2 is third with $\begin{pmatrix} 0 \\ 0 \\ 1 \end{pmatrix}$.

The initial simplex tableau is shown in Tableau 4.9. The M's are treated simply as numbers; thus, a sample z_j calculation yields

$$z_1 = M(1) + 0(1) + M(0) = M$$

The current cost is calculated as

$$\text{cost} = M(50) + 0(30) + M(20) = 70M$$

TABLEAU 4.9   *Initial tableau for minimization problem*

	c_j	.75	1.00	0	0	M	0	M		Mini-mum ratio
c_B	Basic variables	x_1	x_2	s_1	s_3	A_1	s_2	A_2	Solution	
M	A_1	1	1	−1	0	1	0	0	50	$\frac{50}{1}$
0	s_2	1	0	0	0	0	1	0	30	—
M	A_2	0	1	0	−1	0	0	1	20	$\frac{20}{1}$
	z_j	M	2M	−M	−M	M	0	M	70M	
	$c_j - z_j$	.75 − M	1.00 − 2M	M	M	0	0	0		

↑

As far as procedure goes, the only change from our maximization example is that we pick the variable with the most negative $c_j - z_j$ to enter the solution. In this case, $1.00 - 2M$ is more negative than $.75 - M$; thus, x_2 is the entering variable. The ratios of $\frac{50}{1}$ and $\frac{20}{1}$ are calculated for rows 1 and 3, respectively. Since $20 < 50$, we find that A_2 will leave the solution.

From Tableau 4.9 we can see that the pivot element is 1; thus, the updated pivot row remains unchanged.

$$\text{updated pivot row} = \text{old row 3}$$
$$= (0 \quad 1 \quad 0 \quad -1 \quad 0 \quad 0 \quad 1 \quad 20)$$

The other rows are updated thus:

$$
\begin{array}{l}
\text{old row 1} = (1 \quad\;\; 1 \quad -1 \quad\;\; 0 \quad 1 \quad 0 \quad\;\; 0 \quad\;\; 50) \\
-1 \times \text{updated pivot row} = (0 \quad -1 \quad\;\; 0 \quad +1 \quad 0 \quad 0 \quad -1 \quad -20) \\
\hline
\text{new row 1} = \;1 \quad\;\; 0 \quad -1 \quad\;\; 1 \quad 1 \quad 0 \quad -1 \quad\;\; 30
\end{array}
$$

Since row 2 has a zero pivot intersection number, row 2 does not need to be changed. Thus,

$$\text{new row 2} = (1 \quad 0 \quad 0 \quad 0 \quad 0 \quad 1 \quad 0 \quad 30) = \text{old row 2}$$

$$
\begin{array}{l}
\text{old } c_j - z_j \text{ row} = (.75 - M \quad\;\; 1 - 2M \quad M \quad\;\;\;\; M \quad\;\; 0 \;\; 0 \quad\;\;\;\; 0 \quad\;\;) \\
-(1 - 2M) \times \text{updated pivot row} = (\quad\;\; 0 \quad\quad\; -1 + 2M \quad 0 \quad 1 - 2M \quad 0 \;\; 0 \quad -1 + 2M) \\
\hline
\text{new } c_j - z_j \text{ row} = \;.75 - M \quad\quad\;\; 0 \quad\quad\; M \quad 1 - M \quad 0 \;\; 0 \quad -1 + 2M
\end{array}
$$
$$\text{cost} = M(30) + 0(30) + 1.00(20) = 30M + 20$$

The completed tableau is shown in Tableau 4.10. Note that we have succeeded in driving one of the artificials from the solution.

In the next iteration, x_1 has the most negative $c_j - z_j$. Its $c_j - z_j$ value is $.75 - M$, meaning that for every unit of x_1 brought into solution, we can

TABLEAU 4.10 *Tableau after first iteration for minimization problem*

c_B	Basic variables	c_j .75 x_1	1.00 x_2	0 s_1	0 s_3	M A_1	0 s_2	M A_2	Solution	Minimum ratio
M	A_1	1	0	−1	1	1	0	−1	30	$\frac{30}{1}$
0	s_2	1	0	0	0	0	1	0	30	$\frac{30}{1}$
1.00	x_2	0	1	0	−1	0	0	1	20	—
	z_j	M	1.00	−M	M − 1.00	M	0	1.00 − M	30M + 20	
	$c_j - z_j$	.75 − M	0	M	1.00 − M	0	0	−1.00 + 2M		

→ (indicates row 1 leaving); ↑ (indicates x_1 entering column)

increase our cost by $.75 - M$; actually, this is a decrease since $.75 - M < 0$. The minimum ratio test provides an interesting situation. We have ratios of $\frac{30}{1}$ and $\frac{30}{1}$ in rows 1 and 2. (Why isn't a ratio for row 3 calculated?) The fact that the ratios for rows 1 and 2 are the same means that either A_1 or s_2 may be chosen as the leaving variable. This tie also means that one of the basic variables will assume a zero value in the updated tableau. This situation is *degeneracy* referred to as *degeneracy*. We shall discuss it later in the chapter. For the moment, we chose A_1 as the leaving variable. The pivot element is 1, and the updated pivot row is unchanged from row 1.

$$\text{updated pivot row} = \text{old row 1}$$
$$= (1 \quad 0 \quad -1 \quad 1 \quad 1 \quad 0 \quad -1 \quad 30)$$

The other rows are as

$$
\begin{array}{llllllllr}
\text{old row 2} = (& 1 & 0 & 0 & 0 & 0 & 1 & 0 & 30) \\
-1 \times \text{updated pivot row} = (& -1 & 0 & +1 & -1 & -1 & 0 & +1 & -30) \\
\hline
\text{new row 2} = & 0 & 0 & 1 & -1 & -1 & 1 & 1 & 0
\end{array}
$$

Since the pivot intersection number of row 3 is zero, row 3 remains unchanged.

$$\text{new row 3} = (0 \quad 1 \quad 0 \quad -1 \quad 0 \quad 0 \quad 1 \quad 20) = \text{old row 3}$$

$$
\begin{array}{llllllllr}
\text{old } c_j - z_j \text{ row} = (& .75 - M & 0 & M & 1 - M & 0 & 0 & -1 + 2M) \\
-(.75 - M) \times \text{updated pivot row} = (& -.75 + M & 0 & .75 - M & -.75 + M & -.75 + M & 0 & .75 - M) \\
\hline
\text{new } c_j - z_j \text{ row} = & 0 & 0 & .75 & .25 & -.75 + M & 0 & -.25 + M)
\end{array}
$$

$$\text{cost} = .75(30) + 0(0) + 1.00(20) = 42.50$$

TABLEAU 4.11   *Optimal tableau for minimization problem*

c_B	Basic variables	c_j →							
		.75	1.00	0	0	M	0	M	
		x_1	x_2	s_1	s_3	A_1	s_2	A_2	Solution
.75	x_1	1	0	−1	1	1	0	−1	30
0	s_2	0	0	1	−1	−1	1	1	0
1.00	x_2	0	1	0	−1	0	0	1	20
	z_j	.75	1.00	−.75	−.25	.75	0	.25	42.50
	$c_j - z_j$	0	0	.75	.25	−.75 + M	0	−.25 + M	

In Tableau 4.11 we find the updated, and optimal, tableau. All the $c_j - z_j$ values are greater than or equal to zero, all basic variable values are non-negative, and the constraints are satisfied; the solution is optimal. The constraints will be satisfied (the current solution will be feasible) throughout the simplex method because of the rule for selecting the leaving variable. The pivoting iterations are performed in order to find the optimal solution. The solution indicates that we should mix 30 gallons of crude oil B and 20 gallons of crude oil A in each 50-gallon barrel of the petroleum product. The total cost per barrel is $42.50. In this example, all artificials have been driven from the solution. If any artificials remain at nonzero value in a final solution, the original problem does not have a feasible solution.

SUMMARY OF SIMPLEX PROCEDURE

The following steps summarize the procedures we have discussed for solving LP problems by the simplex method:

1. Assuming that the LP model has been correctly formulated, it must first be converted to standard form.
2. Make sure that all right-hand side values are nonnegative by multiplying both sides of the equations by −1 whenever necessary. (This reverses the direction of the inequality.)
3. Convert ≤ constraints to standard form by adding a slack variable, equality constraints by adding an artificial variable, and ≥ constraints by subtracting a slack and adding an artificial variable.
4. Choose the initial basic feasible solution by placing in solution those slack and/or artificial variables that have a positive 1 coefficient in the original constraints in standard form.

5. Fill in the initial tableau by simply entering the constraint equations as they appear in standard form. Calculate the $c_j - z_j$ values for the solution.

6. Check the $c_j - z_j$ values for the solution. If the problem is a maximization and all $c_j - z_j$ values are ≤ 0, *stop,* for the solution is optimal. (If the problem is a minimization and all $c_j - z_j$ values are ≥ 0, *stop,* for the solution is optimal.)

7. Otherwise, determine the entering variable by selecting the variable whose $c_j - z_j$ value is most positive (or most negative in a minimization).

8. Determine the variable to leave the solution by forming the ratios between the entries in the solution column and associated positive entries in the column of the variable entering the solution. The row in which the minimum ratio occurs designates the basic variable that is to leave the solution. (Select uppermost row in case of a tie.)

9. Bring the entering variable into solution and update the tableau by pivoting. First, update the pivot row by multiplying the entire pivot row by the reciprocal of the pivot element. Next, update the other rows by elementary row operations using the new pivot row to make their pivot intersection number a zero. Go to step 6.

SPECIAL CASES IN THE SIMPLEX METHOD

In many applications of LP, a unique optimal solution is obtained. However, variations do exist. In Chapter 3 on the graphical method we looked at the graphical analysis of situations in which the problem was unbounded, or there was no feasible solution, or there were alternative optima. In this section we focus on the recognition of the special conditions in simplex calculations. We also look at the implications of degeneracy.

UNBOUNDED SOLUTION

As we have seen in Chapter 3, it is possible for an LP problem to have a nonempty feasible region and yet have no finite optimal solution. This can occur whenever the feasible region extends infinitely in the direction of improvement for the objective function. You can see from the graph in Figure 4.3 that we can pick arbitrarily large values of x_1 and x_2 to make the value of an objective function such as

$$\text{Maximize} \quad x_1 + x_2$$

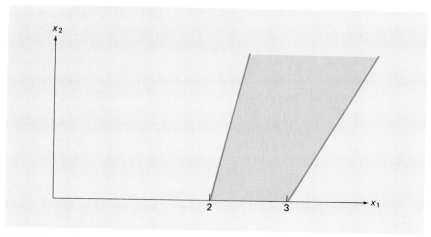

FIGURE 4.3 **Unbounded feasible region**

as large as desired. Thus, there exists no finite optimum. Note however, that an infinite feasible region does not necessarily imply an unbounded solution. In this example, if we were minimizing the same objective function, the finite optimum would occur at $x_1 = 2$ and $x_2 = 0$.

The simplex method can detect the existence of an *unbounded solution* during the process of selecting the entering variable. If a variable with a promising $c_j - z_j$ opportunity cost has been chosen, the next step is to calculate the ratios and select the minimum ratio to determine the leaving variable. However, if no entries in the pivot column are positive, no positive ratio can be formed and the problem is identified as unbounded. Thus, we can identify an unbounded problem in the simplex method when all the substitution coefficients of an entering variable are nonpositive (≤ 0). To visualize this situation, look at the second simplex tableau in standard form as shown in Tableau 4.12. At this iteration, it would pay $\frac{6}{5}$ for every unit of x_2

TABLEAU 4.12 *Unbounded solution*

c_B	Basic variables	c_j	1	1	0	$-M$	0	
			x_1	x_2	s_1	A_1	s_2	Solution
1	x_1		1	$-\frac{1}{5}$	$-\frac{1}{5}$	$\frac{1}{5}$	0	2
0	s_2		0	$-\frac{7}{5}$	$\frac{3}{5}$	$-\frac{3}{5}$	0	3
	z_j		1	$-\frac{1}{5}$	$-\frac{1}{5}$	$\frac{1}{5}$	0	2
	$c_j - z_j$		0	$\frac{6}{5}$	$\frac{1}{5}$	$-M - \frac{1}{5}$	0	

brought into solution, but the solution is unbounded since the entries $-\frac{1}{5}$ and $-\frac{7}{5}$ are both negative in the potential pivot column under x_2.

The detection of unbounded solutions in the simplex tableau can be explained by reinterpreting the meaning of tableau elements in a given column. We have called these elements substitution coefficients, for they represent the per unit decrease of the solution values for every unit of the associated variable brought into solution. For example, the $-\frac{1}{5}$ and $-\frac{7}{5}$ under variable x_2 in Tableau 4.12 represent the reduction in the solution values 2 and 3 for every unit of x_2 brought into solution. Since $-\frac{1}{5}$ and $-\frac{7}{5}$ are negative, this means that the solution values 2 and 3 will actually increase by $\frac{1}{5}$ and $\frac{7}{5}$, respectively, for every unit of x_2 brought into solution. Thus, no matter how much of x_2 is brought into solution, the solution values of the basic variables will never become negative or infeasible and no basic variable will be forced to zero. Therefore, an unlimited amount of x_2 can enter the solution, causing the problem to be unbounded.

Unbounded solutions usually mean that the LP model has been formulated incorrectly. No meaningful real-world LP problems exist in which the decision variables can assume infinite values.

NO FEASIBLE SOLUTION

An LP problem has no feasible solution when the constraints are inconsistent and the feasible region is empty. Figure 4.4 illustrates an inconsistent constraint set that has no feasible region.

In the simplex method it is very easy to recognize when a problem has no feasible solution.

FIGURE 4.4 **No feasible region**

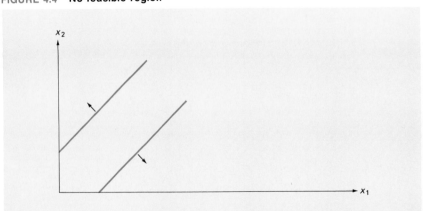

> In the simplex method, the condition of no feasible solution is indicated whenever the final solution contains an artificial variable whose value is greater than zero.

The condition of no feasible solution is determined during phase 1 of the two-phase approach to the simplex method. In this case not all artificials can be driven to zero. In the big M penalty approach, infeasibility is indicated in the final tableau where an artificial variable is basic and has a positive value.

ALTERNATIVE OPTIMA

The optimal solution to an LP problem is not necessarily unique. It is possible that an adjacent extreme point will yield the same profit (or cost). Graphically, this happens whenever the slope of the objective function equals the slope of a constraint equation that passes through an optimal extreme point. In Figure 4.5, we show a modified version of the Faze Linear problem. The problem was modified by changing the profit of x_2 (preamps) to 400 rather than 500. With this modification, both points $C = (105, 28.5)$ and $D = (162, 0)$ yield a profit of $32,400, which is optimal. In Figure 4.5, if the dashed line representing the objective function were moved toward the feasible region, it would eventually intersect the entire line segment between points C and D rather than at a single extreme point.

Alternative optima are also easy to detect in the simplex tableau. Let us consider the modified Faze Linear problem in Tableau 4.13. The solution remains unchanged from Tableau 4.8; only the $c_j - z_j$ values and the cost for x_2 have changed. The $c_j - z_j$ row indicates that the solution is still optimal.

FIGURE 4.5 Faze Linear problem with alternative optima

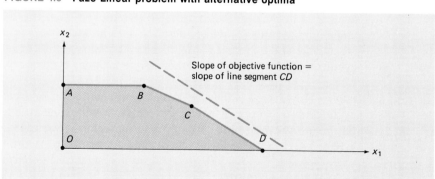

TABLEAU 4.13 *Modified Faze Linear problem at optimality*

c_B	c_j / Basic variables	200 x_1	400 x_2	0 s_1	0 s_2	0 s_3	Solution
400	x_2	0	1	0	$\frac{5}{8}$	$-\frac{3}{2}$	28.5
200	x_1	1	0	0	$-\frac{5}{4}$	5	105.0
0	s_1	0	0	1	$-\frac{5}{8}$	$\frac{3}{2}$	11.5
	z_j	200	400	0	0	400	32,400
	$c_j - z_j$	0	0	0	0	-400	

But since the $c_j - z_j$ for s_2 is zero, we can pivot in s_2 for x_2 and change the profit by zero. The resulting solution also yields a profit of \$32,400 and thus is an alternative optimum.

In general, if a nonbasic variable has a $c_j - z_j$ of zero at optimality, it indicates an alternative optimal solution exists and can be obtained by simply bringing this nonbasic variable into the solution.

Degeneracy

We have already run across the notion of *degeneracy* in the minimization example. In a nondegenerate solution, the nonbasic variables have zero values and the *m* basic variables in solution have positive values. In a degenerate solution, at least one basic variable has a zero value. Thus, at a degenerate extreme point, fewer than *m* basic variables are positive. Degeneracy does not really pose a serious problem. If you check back to Tableau 4.11, you will see that the basic variable s_2 has a zero value, and therefore, the solution is degenerate. All this means is that there is no slack in the second constraint.

Theoretically, degeneracy could pose a potential problem. Early researchers were afraid that *cycling* could occur in a degenerate solution. In cycling, a degenerate basic variable is removed from the solution at zero value only to return at a later iteration with no improvement, thereby creating a cycle and an infinite loop. Techniques were established to assure that cycling would never occur. Practically speaking, cycling rarely occurs because of the inherent numerical round off errors present in digital computers. However, a simple tie-breaking procedure can be used to ensure that cycling never occurs. A degenerate solution will result whenever there is a tie in the minimum ratio to determine the entering variable. (See Tableaus 4.10 and 4.11 to verify this.) The cycling prevention procedure specifies that whenever a tie in the minimum ratio occurs, select the uppermost row in the tableau as the pivot row. This procedure has been proven mathematically to prevent cycling.

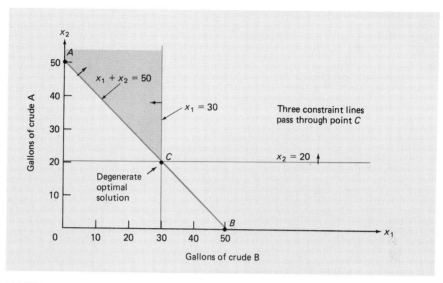

FIGURE 4.6 **Graph of oil company's minimization problem**

Graphically we can see that in two dimensions degeneracy implies that there is a redundant constraint which passes through the solution point. In greater than two dimensions this is not necessarily the case. Let us return to the oil company's minimization problem that has a degenerate solution. Notice in Figure 4.6 that three constraint lines pass through the optimum point C. Only two lines are needed to determine completely the optimum point in two dimensions. Thus, the point is said to be overdetermined and the constraint $x_2 \geq 20$ is actually redundant. The fact that all three constraints are satisfied exactly at point C implies that there is no slack in any constraint. Hence $s_1 = 0$, $s_3 = 0$, and $s_2 = 0$ even though it is "in solution."

An Alternative to the Simplex Method—Karmarkar's Algorithm

Since its initial development in 1947, the simplex method has remained the only practical method for solving linear programming problems. Other methods have been conceived by mathematicians, but all these methods were too inefficient for practical applications.

In 1984 N. Karmarkar, a researcher at AT&T Bell Laboratories, developed a new algorithm which appears to be superior to the simplex method at least for some applications. The algorithm has the very desirable and unique property of polynomial running time. That is, the running time is bounded by a polynomial expression $n^{3.5}L^2$, where n = the dimension of the problem and L = the number of bits in the input.

An interesting feature of Karmarkar's algorithm is that it is an interior point method. The simplex method, by contrast, deals only with extreme

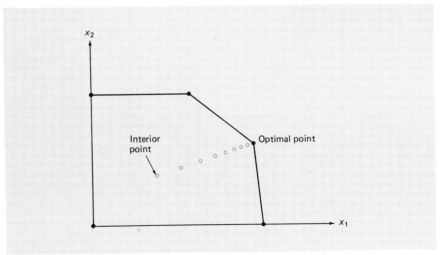

FIGURE 4.7   Illustration of Karmarkar's LP algorithm

points on the outside surface of the feasible region. Figure 4.7 illustrates the fact that Karmarkar's algorithm starts at a strictly interior point and converges to the optimal extreme point. The method parallels the method of steepest descent in classical calculus-based optimization. To speed convergence, Karmarkar's method uses projective transformations to map the current point into another geometric space. The alternative space facilitates the convergence of the steepest descent method. The direction in which to move to find a better solution is preserved through the inverse image of this direction when mapped back to the original feasible region in Euclidean n space. Karmarkar's algorithm consists of repeated application of such projective transformations followed by optimization over an inscribed sphere to create a sequence of points that converges to the optimal solution in polynomial time.

   Some researchers have not been able to make the algorithm perform as well as the simplex method. However, researchers at AT&T Bell Labs claim that the method is 200 times faster than the simplex method on several types of large-scale problems. Their implementation consists of a combination of hardware and software, which takes advantage of parallel processing.

   The practical benefits of an algorithm that is many times faster than the simplex method are far reaching. Many problems that could not be solved optimally because of economic or time considerations can now be solved. Without the speed and efficiency offered by the Karmarkar algorithm, many problems in industry have to be solved heuristically, resulting in suboptimal solutions; the cost of running the problem long enough to get an optimal solution often outweighs the marginal benefit of a slightly better solution. In addition, there are real-world problems in which there is a time window of decision opportunity, and if the problem cannot be solved within that time window, the solution is worthless. For these types of problems, Karmarkar's new algorithm might render some applications amenable to an LP approach that previously could only be solved heuristically. Future research and experimentation will reveal the true contribution of this method to optimization and the field of operations research/management science.

USING SPREADSHEETS IN LP ANALYSIS

Computerized spreadsheet models such as Lotus 1-2-3[2] have become quite popular as tools for analyzing a wide variety of quantitative business problems. Applications seem to be most prevalent in finance and accounting but are also common in the production and operations areas. Spreadsheets are productivity improvement vehicles that facilitate calculations and report generation. Additionally, they allow ''what if'' questions to be answered by merely changing entries in the spreadsheet. Together with word processing, spreadsheets are key software tools that have helped to fuel the microcomputer revolution.

A spreadsheet is a rectangular array of rows and columns. At the intersection of each row and column is a spreadsheet cell. The spreadsheet user can place various types of entries in each cell. The possible entries include labels, numbers, or formulas.

Labels are used to provide headings and name variables or clarify the output shown on the spreadsheet. User-supplied numbers constitute data supplied to the problem and can represent resource availability, costs, rate of return, and so on. Formulas are developed by the user to perform certain calculations on the data contained in various cells of the spreadsheet. Formulas can perform calculations on numbers entered directly into the spreadsheet or on the contents of other cells which themselves might contain formulas. The use of formulas and the automatic calculation feature of spreadsheets allow the user to develop an application program rather efficiently compared to general-purpose programming languages. However, spreadsheets lack some of the flexibility of traditional programming languages and are not appropriate for all types of quantitative analysis.

Spreadsheets are useful in LP analysis because they allow the user to perform ''what if'' analysis on the value of the decision variables while observing the effects on the constraints. This ad hoc analysis does not necessarily yield an optimal solution. However, software packages exist which can operate on spreadsheets to yield an optimal LP solution.

---

[2] Lotus 1-2-3 is a trademark of Lotus Development Corporation.

┌─ Decision values supplied by user

	A	B	C AMPS	D PREAMPS	E	F	G	H
1	Product		AMPS	PREAMPS		************		
2						Total Profit		
3	Quantity					(C5*C3)+(D5*D3)		
4								
5	Profit/Unit		200.00	500.00		************		
6								
7								
8								
9			Resource	Usage		LHS	RHS	Slack
10			AMPS	PREAMPS		Constraint	Value	
11	-------		--------	----------		------------	-------	-----------
12	Transistors		0.0	1.0		(C12*C3)+(D12*D3)	40	+G12-F12
13	Assembly Time		1.2	4.0		(C13*C3)+(D13*D3)	240	+G13-F13
14	Inspection Time		0.5	1.0		(C14*C3)+(D14*D3)	81	+G14-F14
15	-------							-----------
16								
17								

FIGURE 4.8   **Symbolic spreadsheet for Faze Linear problem**

To learn more about using spreadsheets in LP analysis, look at Figure 4.8 in which the Faze Linear problem has been represented in a symbolic spreadsheet. The spreadsheet consists of 15 rows and 8 columns. The rows are numbered 1 to 15, and the columns are represented by the letters A through H. The symbolic spreadsheet shows the content of the cells and not the standard output that would be seen by the user. Many of the 15×8 cells are empty while the remainder contain a label, a number, or a formula. The layout of the spreadsheet is at the user's discretion so that another user would have probably designed the layout and location of labels differently.

The first row contains only labels. In column C, row 1 is a label that associates column C with the decision variable AMPS. The profit contribution of AMPS is entered in cell C5. In cells C12–C14 are the resource requirements of AMPS. These numbers or parameters of the model can be changed at any time during a "what if" analysis. The formulas in the spreadsheet are found in columns F and H. Cell F4 shows the calculation of total profit as a function of the cells containing the decision variables and their associated profit contribution. Cells C3 and D3 represent the value of the decision variables AMPS and PREAMPS, respectively. The user must enter his or her own choice for these values. Given the user choice for AMPS and PREAMPS, the formulas in cells F12–F14 calculate the left-hand side (LHS) of each of the three constraints. These calculations represent how much of the three resources—transistors, assembly time, and inspection time—are used through the production of C3 AMPS and D3 PREAMPS. Cells H12–H14 show the RHS-LHS calculation which equals slack. For the user-developed solution to be feasible, the slack in each constraint must be nonnegative. Even though the spreadsheet provides the user with immediate

	A	B	C	D	E	F	G	H
1	Product		AMPS	PREAMPS				
2						************		
3	Quantity		66.0	40.0		Total Profit		
4						33200 ← Calculated profit		
5	Profit/Unit		200.00	500.00		************		
6								
7			\					
8								
9			Resource	Usage		LHS	RHS	Slack
10			AMPS	PREAMPS		Constraint	Value	
11	----							
12	Transistors		0.0	1.0		40.0	40	0.0
13	Assembly Time		1.2	4.0		239.2	240	0.8
14	Inspection Time		0.5	1.0		73.0	81	8.0
15	----							
16								
17						Constraints evaluated		

FIGURE 4.9   **Actual spreadsheet output for Faze Linear**

calculations pertaining to total profit and slack in the constraints, it does not show the user how to obtain a more effective solution. Thus, a stand-alone spreadsheet model is really a deterministic simulation model that describes certain values or conditions given the user-specified input. Figure 4.9 shows the actual spreadsheet output for user-selected values of 66 and 40 for AMPS and PREAMPS.

OPTIMIZATION VIA SPREADSHEETS

A spreadsheet is useful for decision-maker exploration and ad hoc analysis but does not necessarily achieve optimization. Fortunately, several software packages exist for optimizing LP models embedded in a Lotus 1-2-3 spreadsheet model. Among these packages are Optimal Solutions,[3] What's Best![4] and VINO.[5] Obtaining an optimal solution from these packages requires little effort beyond the construction of the spreadsheet. For example, Optimal Solutions will prompt the user for the values to be maximized or minimized and the relevant constraints. A menu-driven template is exhibited within the spreadsheet to facilitate specification of the LP model. The package is limited to a size of 300 variables and 80 constraints. Problems much larger than this are more suited for solution by specialized LP computer codes.

---

[3] Optimal Solutions is a trademark of Enfin Software Corporation.

[4] What's Best! is a trademark of General Optimization, Inc.

[5] VINO is a trademark of LINDO Systems, Inc.

Spreadsheet models have achieved popularity partly because they allow the user direct control over the decision process, user involvement, and a sense of personal ownership. Summarizing their usefulness in LP analysis, we have the following:

1. Spreadsheets aid in model representation and exploratory analysis of changes in decision variable values and observation of effects on profits, costs, and resources.
2. Optimization of small to medium-sized problems is possible through the use of a spreadsheet optimization package.
3. Spreadsheets are also useful for creating the data that are necessary input to an LP model. Cumbersome calculations can be performed repetitively once the spreadsheet model has been created and debugged.

In spite of the usefulness of spreadsheets, a final caveat is in order. Since the formulas in spreadsheets are not visible to the end user of a spreadsheet model, logic errors can be very difficult to discover. Models created by a single user should be subjected to the same level of scrutiny and validation that is appropriate for other types of models and software projects.

COMPUTER IMPLICATIONS

Applications of LP in the real world inevitably involve the use of electronic digital computers. In these cases, extensive information, data manipulation, and numerical computation require high-speed computers.

Although LP analysis using spreadsheets is appropriate for small end-user problems, large-scale models are typically solved on mainframe computers using highly refined LP computer codes. The advent of powerful minicomputers and 32-bit microcomputers, however, provides the technology to solve some rather large LP models in a nonmainframe environment.

Major computer manufacturers can usually provide computer software packages that perform LP on their machines. For example, IBM, Control Data, Univac, and Honeywell, among others, have standard LP packages. However, it is not necessary to have your own computer in order to use LP. Commercial computer time-sharing companies with available software packages have made it rather easy to use a computer without having to own one. Data input and program output will vary slightly from one software package to another, but are relatively standardized.

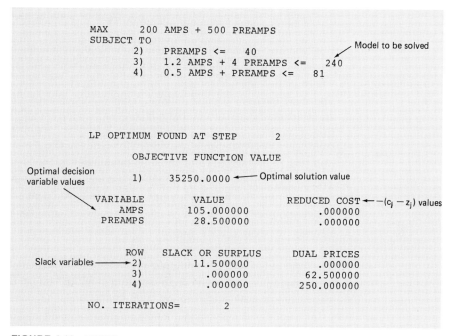

```
        MAX     200 AMPS + 500 PREAMPS
        SUBJECT TO
             2)    PREAMPS <=    40
             3)    1.2 AMPS + 4 PREAMPS <=    240
             4)    0.5 AMPS + PREAMPS <=   81
```

Model to be solved

```
        LP OPTIMUM FOUND AT STEP      2

              OBJECTIVE FUNCTION VALUE

             1)     35250.0000
```

Optimal decision variable values

Optimal solution value

```
        VARIABLE         VALUE          REDUCED COST
        AMPS          105.000000          .000000
        PREAMPS        28.500000          .000000
```

$-(c_j - z_j)$ values

```
          ROW    SLACK OR SURPLUS    DUAL PRICES
          2)        11.500000          .000000
          3)          .000000         62.500000
          4)          .000000        250.000000

        NO. ITERATIONS=       2
```

Slack variables

FIGURE 4.10 **LINDO computer solution to Faze Linear problem**

There are many software packages available that support the solution of LP problems on a microcomputer. Among the many "user-friendly" packages are the LINDO computer package and the QSB computer package.[6] LINDO is a widely used mathematical programming package for solving linear, integer, and quadratic programming problems. It is available in both mainframe and microcomputer versions. The Quantitative Systems for Business (QSB) package is a personal computer package that contains an LP module as well as 13 other modules for supporting many of the quantitative techniques covered in this text.

To illustrate the computer output from an LP computer package, consider the LINDO solution of the familiar Faze Linear product mix problem. Figure 4.10 shows the model to be solved followed by the LINDO solution output. Keep in mind that any model to be solved by an LP computer package must meet two requirements. First, all variables in the constraints must appear on the left with the constants or right-hand side values on the right. Second, the variables must be nonnegative in value. The computer program always assumes this condition, and you do not have to enter the nonnegativity conditions as constraints.

---

[6] LINDO is available from The Scientific Press; QSB is available from Prentice Hall.

In Figure 4.10 we can make the following observations:

1. The first line of output reports the number of iterations required in the simplex method followed by the optimal objective function value, which in this case is 35250.

2. The next two sections of output provide information on the decision variables and constraints, respectively. The optimal values of the decision variables are provided in the "VALUE" column. The "RE-DUCED COST" column provides the values of the $z_j - c_j$ values. Note that this is the negative of the $c_j - z_j$ values discussed in the text.

3. The LINDO output considers the objective function to be row 1 of the model. Thus, the first constraint is labeled row 2 and so on.

4. The values of the slack variables are associated with the row (constraint) in which they appear. The slack values are found in the "SLACK OR SURPLUS" column.

5. The "DUAL PRICES" column provides useful information regarding the marginal value of the RHS quantities. More will be said about dual prices or shadow prices in the next chapter.

Model input for the mainframe or PC version of LINDO can be entered directly through the system's interactive mode. However, large problems are more conveniently created building input files in MPS format. The MPS format is the widely accepted LP input format of the IBM MPSX/370 system for solving large-scale linear programming models. For medium and especially large-scale problems, a matrix generator is generally used to input the model parameters accurately and efficiently. A matrix generator is a program that, given certain parameters, outputs the data in the exact form required as input by a specific LP model.

While matrix generators facilitate LP model input, report generators facilitate the interpretation of LP model output. Report generators take standard output such as that shown in Figure 4.10 and create a report for management that is less technical and more relevant to the specific decision-making environment. Thus, the decision maker or manager does not need to be an expert in linear programming to interpret the output for his or her particular decision.

LP analysis can be very cost effective. Computing costs are steadily dropping, and the use of microcomputers can make computing costs extremely low. Large-scale problems must still be handled on mainframe computers, but computer time is often less than the costs of data collection and personnel. LP analysis requires personnel who know how to model the problem correctly, possibly create a matrix generator, load the model on the computer, and interpret the output. The potential payoff from using LP analysis can be quite high. Several of the application scenarios at the beginning of the chapters in this text illustrate that the returns can be in the thousands or even millions of dollars for really significant applications.

SUMMARY

In Chapter 3 we studied the graphical method for solving LP problems. The graphical method is useful only for illustrative purposes. In this chapter we have examined the simplex method, which is the method typically used for solving LP problems. Using the simplex method and a computer, we can solve problems having thousands of variables and constraints.

To use the simplex method, we learned how to convert $\leq$, $=$, and $\geq$ type constraints to standard form. We learned that basic feasible solutions are fundamental to the simplex method and that they correspond geometrically to extreme points. Early in the chapter we took an intuitive approach to the simplex method in which the LP model was solved algebraically and related to Gaussian elimination. We next attempted to formalize the simplex procedures and solve LP problems via the simplex tableau. We looked at the four basic steps in the simplex method: determining an initial basic feasible solution, determining an entering variable, determining a leaving variable, and updating the simplex tableau through pivoting.

We looked at how to identify and handle special cases such as unboundedness, infeasibility, alternative optima, and degeneracy. Spreadsheet models were examined, and we learned that they can be useful in analyzing small- and medium-scale LP problems. Finally we considered the implications of computer based solutions. Most LP applications are solved on large mainframe computers, but there is an increasing source of LP software and hardware for solving smaller LP models on microcomputers.

Understanding the principles of the simplex method will not only enhance your understanding of constrained optimization, but also your understanding of postoptimality analysis. In Chapter 5, we will look at some of the questions that can be answered once the optimal solution has been obtained.

SOLVED PROBLEM

PROBLEM STATEMENT

Solve the following maximization problem by the simplex method:

$$\begin{aligned}
\text{Maximize} \quad & 3x_1 + 5x_2 + 4x_3 \\
\text{subject to} \quad & x_2 + 2x_3 \leq 6 \\
& 3x_1 + 2x_2 + x_3 \leq 18 \\
& x_1, x_2 \geq 0
\end{aligned}$$

SOLUTION

We first convert the problem to standard form:

$$\text{Maximize} \quad 3x_1 + 5x_2 + 4x_3 + 0s_1 + 0s_2$$

$$\text{subject to} \qquad x_2 + 2x_3 + s_1 \qquad\quad = 6$$

$$3x_1 + 2x_2 + x_3 \qquad + s_2 = 18$$

$$x_1, x_2, x_3, s_1, s_2 \geq 0$$

The problem now has five variables and two equations; there will be two variables in the solution. Placing the two slack variables in the initial tableau, we obtain

		c_j	3	5	4	0	0		Minimum ratio
	c_B	Basic variables	x_1	x_2	x_3	s_1	s_2	Solution	
→	0	s_1	0	1	2	1	0	6	$\frac{6}{1}$
	0	s_2	3	2	1	0	1	18	$\frac{18}{2}$
		z_j	0	0	0	0	0	0	
		$c_j - z_j$	3	5	4	0	0		

In the next tableau, x_2 replaces s_1 in the solution:

		c_j	3	5	4	0	0		Minimum ratio
	c_B	Basic variables	x_1	x_2	x_3	s_1	s_2	Solution	
	5	x_2	0	1	2	1	0	6	—
→	0	s_2	3	0	-3	-2	1	6	$\frac{6}{3}$
		z_j	0	5	10	5	0	30	
		$c_j - z_j$	3	0	-6	-5	0		

In the final tableau, x_1 replaces s_2:

c_B	Basic variables	c_j	3	5	4	0	0	
			x_1	x_2	x_3	s_1	s_2	Solution
5	x_2		0	1	2	1	0	6
3	x_1		1	0	-1	$-\frac{2}{3}$	$\frac{1}{3}$	2
	z_j		3	5	7	3	1	36
	$c_j - z_j$		0	0	-3	-3	-1	

The optimal solution is $x_1 = 2$, $x_2 = 6$, and the maximal objective function value is 36.

REVIEW QUESTIONS

1. What method is effective for solving linear systems of equations?
2. What does an extreme point of the feasible region correspond to algebraically?
3. What characterizes an iterative procedure?
4. Why are slack variables added to $\leq$ constraints? What is the purpose of artificial variables?
5. Given an LP problem with $m + n$ variables and n constraints, how many basic variables (variables in solution) will there always be?
6. What is the meaning of a $c_j - z_j$, and what is the rationale for picking the nonbasic variable with the largest positive $c_j - z_j$ to enter the solution when maximizing?
7. Why are slacks and/or artificial variables used in the starting solution?
8. What is the purpose of the minimum ratio test in the simplex method?
9. How does the simplex method detect when the optimal solution has been achieved?
10. What is the difference between a degenerate and a nondegenerate solution?
11. Can there be more than one optimal solution to an LP problem? How is this recognized?
12. How does the simplex method detect an unbounded solution?
13. Why is it that some nonlinear problems are solved approximately by the use of LP?

PROBLEMS

4.1 Solve the following problem by the simplex method.

$$\text{Maximize} \quad 6x_1 + 8x_2$$
$$\text{subject to} \quad x_1 \quad\quad \leq 12$$
$$x_2 \leq 10$$
$$2x_1 + 3x_2 \leq 36$$
$$x_1,\, x_2 \geq 0$$

4.2 Solve Problem 2.1 (product mix) by the simplex method.

4.3 Consider this problem:

$$\text{Maximize} \quad 2x_1 + 6x_2 + 5x_3$$
$$\text{subject to} \quad x_1 + x_2 + x_3 = 3$$
$$x_1 + 2x_2 + 3x_3 \leq 10$$
$$2x_1 + 6x_2 + 1x_3 \geq 5$$
$$x_1,\, x_2,\, x_3 \geq 0$$

    a. Convert this system to standard form.

    b. What is the maximum number of possible basic solutions?

4.4 Use the simplex method to solve the following problem:

$$\text{Maximize} \quad 3x_1 + 5x_2 + 4x_3$$
$$\text{subject to} \quad\quad x_2 + 2x_3 \leq 6$$
$$3x_1 + 2x_2 + x_3 \leq 24$$
$$x_1 + x_2 + x_3 \leq 12$$
$$x_1,\, x_2,\, x_3 \geq 0$$

4.5 *Sales territory assignment.* The marketing manager of Computate, a manufacturer of minicomputers, is trying to decide how to assign his sales staff to three market regions. Region 1 is an industrial area of a large city and can be expected to yield sales of eight minicomputers per salesperson per week. Regions 2 and 3 yield approximately seven and five sales per salesperson per week. Because of turnover, only seven salespeople are available for assignment. The travel budget is set at

$700 per week, and travel plus selling expenses in the three regions are $90, $70, and $60 per salesperson per week, respectively. The profit contribution per computer is $250.

a. Formulate an LP model to determine the optimal allocation of sales-people to regions.

b. Solve the model by the simplex method.

4.6 Solve by the simplex method.

$$\text{Maximize} \quad 8x_1 + 7x_2$$

$$\text{subject to} \quad 3x_1 + 4x_2 \leq 15$$

$$7x_1 + 5x_2 \leq 20$$

$$x_1, x_2 \geq 0$$

4.7 Solve Problem 2.2 (product mix) by the simplex method.

4.8 Solve the following minimization problem by the simplex method.

$$\text{Minimize} \quad 12x_1 + 18x_2$$

$$\text{subject to} \quad 2x_1 + 3x_2 \geq 6$$

$$5x_1 + x_2 \geq 10$$

$$x_1, x_2 \geq 0$$

4.9 Given the following incomplete simplex tableau for a maximization problem, answer (a)–(d).

	c_j	6	8	10	0	0	
c_B	Basic variables	x_1	x_2	x_3	s_1	s_2	Solution
		.10	.25	0	1	0	120
		.50	.75	1	0	2.50	650
	z_j						
	$c_j - z_j$						

a. Which variables are basic?

b. Complete the partial tableau.

c. Is the solution optimal? If not, which variable should enter?

d. Finish solving the problem.

4.10 Use the simplex method to solve the following minimization problem.

$$\text{Minimize} \quad 40y_1 + 240y_2 + 81y_3$$
$$\text{subject to} \qquad 1.2y_2 + .5y_3 \geq 200$$
$$y_1 + \quad 4y_2 + \quad y_3 \geq 500$$
$$y_1, y_2, y_3 \geq 0$$

4.11 Convert the following problem to standard form.

$$\text{Maximize} \quad 2x_1 + 4x_2$$
$$\text{subject to} \quad 3x_1 + \quad x_2 = 3$$
$$4x_1 + 3x_2 \geq 6$$
$$x_1 + 2x_2 \leq 3$$
$$x_1, x_2 \geq 0$$

4.12 Solve Problem 4.11 by the simplex method.

4.13 Determine the optimal solution to the following problem.

$$\text{Maximize} \quad 3x_1 + 2x_2 + 5x_3$$
$$\text{subject to} \quad 5x_1 + 4x_2 + \quad x_3 \leq 40$$
$$11x_1 - 4x_2 \qquad = \quad 0$$
$$-4x_1 + 5x_2 + 3x_3 \geq 10$$
$$x_1, x_2, x_3 \geq 0$$

4.14 Use the simplex method to determine the optimal solution to the problem in the production distribution example (refer to Table 2.2) in Chapter 2.

4.15 Consider the following problem with only one constraint:

$$\text{Maximize} \quad 5x_1 + 2x_2 + 3x_3 + x_4$$
$$\text{subject to} \quad 4x_1 + 3x_2 + 3x_3 + x_4 \geq 7$$
$$x_i \geq 0, \text{ for all } i$$

a. How many variables will be in any basic solution?

b. Find the optimal solution by inspection.

c. Verify your results with criteria from the simplex method.

4.16 Consider the LP problem

$$\text{Maximize} \quad 2x_1 + 3x_2 + 5x_3 + 1x_4$$

$$\text{subject to} \quad 3x_1 + 1x_2 + 1x_3 + 3x_4 = 5$$

$$2x_1 - 1x_2 + 1x_3 + 1x_4 = 3$$

$$5x_1 + 2x_3 + 3x_4 \leq 8$$

$$x_1, x_2, x_3, x_4 \geq 0$$

After the model has been converted to standard form and solved, the optimal tableau is

c_B	c_j Basic variables	2 x_1	3 x_2	5 x_3	1 x_4	$-M$ A_1	$-M$ A_2	0 S_3	Solution
1	x_4	0	0	0	1	1	1	-1	0
5	x_3	2.5	0	1	0	-1.5	-1.5	2	4
3	x_2	.5	1	0	0	$-.5$	-1.5	1	1
	$c_j - z_j$	-12	0	0	0	$8 - M$	$11 - M$	-12	23

a. What is the optimal solution?

b. Is it degenerate?

c. Are there any alternative optima?

d. Is the solution unbounded?

√ 4.17 *Product mix.* Home Products, Inc., specializes in home cooking devices. They are trying to plan production for their electric skillets and crock pots. The company works a 40-hour week and has its production limited only by productive capacity. The table indicates production capacity in terms of units of final product. The profit contribution is $5 for a skillet and $7 for a crock pot. Formulate and solve the product mix problem by the simplex method. You may want to convert the capacity values to hours of production capacity required per unit.

Department	Weekly capacity (units)	
	Skillets	Crock pots
Casting	400	
Wiring	250	250
Assembly	500	400

4.18 *Petroleum blending.* The Slik Oil Company produces two lines of motor oil and a special engine additive called Motor Honey. All three products are produced by blending two components. These components contribute various properties, including viscosity. The viscosity in the product is proportional to the viscosities of the blending components. The pertinent data appear in the following tables. Assuming no limitation on the demand, determine how many barrels of each oil product Slik should produce each week.

Blending component	Viscosity	Cost per barrel	Availability per week (bbl)
1	20	$36.50	10,000
2	60	41.00	4,000

Product	Viscosity required	Revenue per barrel
30W oil	30	$38
40W oil	40	39
Motor Honey	50	41

4.19 *Inventory/purchasing.* A stereo mail-order warehouse has 8,000 feet available for storage of loudspeakers. The jumbo speakers cost $295 each and require 4 square feet of space, the midsize speakers cost $110 and require 3 square feet of space, and the economy speakers cost $58 and require 1 square foot of space. The demand for the jumbo speakers is, at most, 20 per month. The wholesaler has $10,000 to invest in loudspeakers this month. Assuming that the jumbo speakers contribute $105 to profit, the midsize contribute $50, and the economy contribute $28, how many units of each type should the wholesaler buy and stock?

4.20 *Product mix.* The Green Country Lumber Company produces two wood products, interior wood paneling and plywood. The resource requirements for each product are provided in the table. Assuming that production time is limited to 4,000 hours per week, use the simplex method to maximize Green Country's profit.

Wood product	Production time per sq yd (hr)	Demand	Profit contribution per sq yd
Plywood	.025	At least 6,000 sq yd per week	$.30
Paneling	.040	At most 4,000 sq yd per week	.45

4.21 Consider the following maximization problem and an associated simplex tableau.

Maximize $4x_1 + 5x_2 + 6x_3 + 5x_4$

subject to $2x_1 + 5x_2 + 4x_3 + 3x_4 \leq 224$ resource 1 *Binding*

$\qquad\qquad 5x_1 + 4x_2 - 5x_3 + 10x_4 \leq 280$ resource 2 *Binding*

$\qquad\qquad 2x_1 + 4x_2 + 4x_3 - 2x_4 \leq 184$ resource 3 *Binding*

$\qquad\qquad x_1, x_2, x_3, x_4 \geq 0$

c_j		4	5	6	5	0	0	0	
c_B	Basic variables	x_1	x_2	x_3	x_4	s_1	s_2	s_3	Solution
5	x_4	0	$\frac{1}{5}$	0	1	$\frac{1}{5}$	0	$-\frac{1}{5}$	8
6	x_3	0	$\frac{3}{5}$	1	0	$\frac{1}{5}$	$-\frac{1}{15}$	$-\frac{1}{30}$	20
4	x_1	1	1	0	0	$-\frac{1}{5}$	$\frac{2}{15}$	$\frac{11}{30}$	60
	z_j	4	$\frac{43}{5}$	6	5	$\frac{7}{5}$	$\frac{2}{15}$	$\frac{8}{30}$	400
	$c_j - z_j$	0	$-\frac{18}{5}$	0	0	$-\frac{7}{5}$	$-\frac{2}{15}$	$-\frac{8}{30}$	

a. What is the solution? Is it optimal?

b. Which constraints are binding; that is, which are being met exactly?

c. Which resources are fully utilized?

d. What would happen to the value of the objective function if one unit of x_2 were brought into solution?

e. Which special cases in the simplex method apply here: degeneracy, alternative optima, no solution, unbounded?

4.22 Solve Problem 2.21 (cutting stock) on a computer using an LP computer code.

4.23 Each of the following tableaus represents a possible solution to a maximization problem. Label each tableau with any of the following conditions that apply: (a) feasible, (b) optimal, (c) unbounded, (d) no feasible solution, (e) degeneracy, (f) alternative optima, (g) infeasible.

a.

c_j		9	7	0	0	
c_B	Basic variables	x_1	x_2	s_1	s_2	Solution
9	x_1	1	$\frac{1}{2}$	$\frac{1}{4}$	0	15
0	s_2	0	3	$-\frac{1}{2}$	1	18
	z_j	9	4.5	2.25	0	135
	$c_j - z_j$	0	2.5	-2.25	0	

b.

	c_j	6	12	16	0	0	0	
c_B	Basic variables	x_1	x_2	x_3	s_1	s_2	s_3	Solution
16	x_3	0	0	1	$\frac{1}{2}$	0	$-\frac{1}{3}$	200
0	s_2	0	0	0	$-\frac{3}{2}$	1	$-\frac{1}{3}$	200
12	x_2	$\frac{1}{2}$	1	0	$-\frac{1}{2}$	0	$\frac{2}{3}$	200
	z_j	6	12	16	2	0	2.67	5600
	$c_j - z_j$	0	0	0	-2	0	-2.67	

c.

	c_j	4	12	16	0	0	0	
c_B	Basic variables	x_1	x_2	x_3	s_1	s_2	s_3	Solution
16	x_3	0	0	1	$\frac{1}{2}$	0	$-\frac{1}{3}$	200
0	s_2	0	0	0	$-\frac{3}{2}$	1	$-\frac{1}{3}$	200
12	x_2	$\frac{1}{2}$	1	0	$-\frac{1}{2}$	0	$\frac{2}{3}$	0
	z_j	6	12	16	2	0	2.67	3200
	$c_j - z_j$	-2	0	0	-2	0	-2.67	

d.

	c_j	4	10	0	0	$-M$	$-M$	
c_B	Basic variables	x_1	x_2	s_2	s_1	A_1	A_2	Solution
0	s_1	0	24	24	1	-12	0	24
4	x_1	1	1	1	0	1	0	0
$-M$	A_2	0	-1	-1	0	0	1	1
	z_j	4	$4 + M$	$4 + M$	0	4	$-M$	$-M$
	$c_j - z_j$	0	$6 - M$	$-4 - M$	0	$-4 - M$	0	

e.

	c_j	9	7	0	0	
c_B	Basic variables	x_1	x_2	s_1	s_2	Solution
9	x_1	1	$-\frac{1}{2}$	$\frac{1}{4}$	0	15
0	s_2	0	-3	$-\frac{1}{2}$	1	18
	z_j	9	-4.5	2.25	0	135
	$c_j - z_j$	0	11.5	-2.25	0	

f.

c_B	Basic variables	c_j	9	7	0	0	
			x_1	x_2	s_1	s_2	Solution
9	x_1		1	0	$\frac{1}{3}$	$-\frac{1}{6}$	-15
7	x_2		0	1	$-\frac{1}{6}$	$\frac{1}{3}$	18
	z_j		9	7	$\frac{11}{6}$	$\frac{5}{6}$	-9
	$c_j - z_j$		0	0	$-\frac{11}{6}$	$-\frac{5}{6}$	

4.24 *Concrete mix.* The McMichael Concrete Co. is trying to optimize its concrete mix. Different hardening qualities are needed for various applications. The primary ingredients are limestone and clay, which cost $8 and $11 per ton, respectively. McMichael mixes its concrete in 20-ton batches. For its hardest mix, it needs at least 8 tons of clay and no more than 14 tons of limestone. Formulate the problem, and use the simplex method to determine the optimal blend for the hard mix.

4.25 Solve Problem 2.9 (media selection) by the simplex method.

4.26 The computer solution accompanies the following problem:

$$\text{Maximize} \quad 5x_1 + 2x_2 + 8x_3$$

$$\text{subject to} \quad x_1 - 2x_2 + x_3 \le 440$$

$$2x_1 + 3x_2 - x_3 \le 600$$

$$6x_1 - x_2 + 3x_3 \le 120$$

$$x_1, x_2, x_3 \ge 0$$

```
LP OPTIMUM FOUND AT STEP        2

        OBJECTIVE FUNCTION VALUE

    1)      1440.00000

    VARIABLE          VALUE          REDUCED COST
      X1            .000000           18.000000
      X2         240.000000             .000000
      X3         120.000000             .000000


      ROW     SLACK OR SURPLUS       DUAL PRICES
      2)         800.000000             .000000
      3)            .000000            1.750000
      4)            .000000            3.250000

  NO. ITERATIONS=        2
```

    a. Which variables are basic?

    b. What is the solution and its objective function value?

    c. Which constraints are binding?

    d. What are the $c_j - z_j$ values of slack 2 and slack 3? (Refer to the negatives of the dual prices of slacks 2 and 3.)

4.27 Solve the constrained break-even analysis problem that was formulated in Chapter 2, page 45.

4.28 Assuming that you have formulated the LP model for Problem 2.22 about the Akron Tire Company, solve the model by the use of an LP computer code. What is the optimum production schedule and its associated minimum quarterly cost?

4.29 *Land allocation.* Using an LP computer code, find the optimum land allocation for Problem 2.24 based on the data in the two tables that follow.

Net revenue factor (r_{ij})

	Crop										
Region	Wheat	Barley	Broad beans	Lentils	Cotton type 1	Cotton type 2	Rice	Corn	Millet	Sesame	Sugar cane
1	1.4	2.9	2.8	4.1	.2	.7	1.0	2.3	.7	1.7	.8
2	1.1	2.7	2.9	3.9	.1	.8	1.1	2.1	.6	1.8	.9
3	1.3	2.8	3.0	2.8	.1	.6	.9	2.2	.5	2.0	1.1
4	1.5	2.6	2.9	4.3	.1	.8	1.2	2.3	1.0	2.7	1.2
5	1.1	2.9	3.1	4.4	.2	.8	.8	2.0	1.3	2.2	.8
6	1.2	3.0	2.8	4.4	.1	.9	.7	2.0	1.2	2.5	1.7
7	1.3	2.6	2.7	5.0	.1	.8	.9	2.1	.7	2.6	1.0
8	1.1	2.6	2.6	4.5	.2	.8	.8	1.9	.9	2.1	1.9

Area presently cropped (1,000's of acres)

	Winter crops				Summer crops						
Region	Wheat	Barley	Broad beans	Lentils	Cotton type 1	Cotton type 2	Rice	Corn	Millet	Sesame	Sugar cane
1	201		17		230		216	103			
2	94	10	4				138	76			
3	106		9		143		201	41			
4	8		38			55		42		27	
5	15		76			89		13	133		
6	21	98	8			108		15			
7	30		51	80		58		97			
8	105		13					13	123	6	62

4.30 Solve the air cleaner design, Problem 2.23.

4.31 Using an LP computer package, solve the multiperiod production planning problem (Problem 2.25).

4.32 Using an LP computer package, solve the multiperiod investment planning problem (Problem 2.26).

BIBLIOGRAPHY

Best, Michael J., and Klaus Ritter, *Linear Programming: Active Set Analysis and Computer Programs.* Englewood Cliffs, N.J.: Prentice Hall, 1985.

Charnes, Abraham, and W. W. Cooper, *Management Models and Industrial Applications of Linear Programming.* New York: John Wiley & Sons, Inc., 1961.

Dantzig, George B., *Linear Programming and Extensions.* Princeton, N.J.: Princeton University Press, 1963.

Gass, Saul I., *Linear Programming,* 5th ed. New York: McGraw-Hill Book Company, 1985.

Hadley, George, *Linear Programming.* Reading, Mass.: Addison-Wesley Publishing Company, Inc., 1962.

Hillier, Frederick, and Gerald J. Lieberman, *Introduction to Operations Research,* 4th ed. San Francisco: Holden-Day, Inc., 1986.

Solow, Daniel, *Linear Programming: An Introduction to Finite Improvement Algorithms.* New York: North-Holland, 1984.

Taha, H. A., *Operations Research: An Introduction,* 4th ed. New York: Macmillan Publishing Company, 1986.

Wagner, Harvey M., *Principles of Management Science with Applications to Executive Decisions,* 2nd ed. Englewood Cliffs, N.J.: Prentice Hall, 1975.

5

Sensitivity Analysis

**THE
SOUTHLAND
CORPORATION**

CITGO PETROLEUM CORPORATION[1]

In 1983, Southland Corporation, the 7-Eleven convenience store giant, acquired Citgo Petroleum Corporation. Its goal was to establish management priorities and procedures that would make Citgo as successful in the downstream petroleum business (refining and marketing) as Southland was in the convenience store industry.

With top management support, a task force composed of Southland personnel, Citgo personnel, and external consultants was formed. The strategies that the task force developed resulted in the application of possibly the most comprehensive combination of management science disciplines within a single organization. These management science applications involved

1. A comprehensive combination of mathematical programming, statistics, forecasting, expert systems, artificial intelligence, organizational theory, and cognitive psychology.
2. The support of top management and operational managers.
3. The involvement of diverse business areas, including acquisitions, refining, supply and distribution, market planning, accounts receiv-

[1] Darwin Klingman, Nancy Phillips, David Steiger, and Warren Young, "The Successful Deployment of Management Science Throughout Citgo Petroleum Corporation," *Interfaces*, 17, no. 1 (January–February 1987).

able and payable, inventory control, and individual performance objectives.

4. Timely project development and implementation.

5. Integration of information systems and management science technologies, multiplying the potentials of each.

The results of this comprehensive application of management science disciplines have been impressive. Management was able to reduce working capital requirements by approximately $150 million. The resulting benefits include an annual decrease in interest expense of $18 million and a substantial reduction in Citgo's vulnerability to falling crude oil and product prices. Citgo also estimates that marketing profits improved by $2.5 million and refining profit improved by $50 million in 1985. Thus, total dollar benefits were approximately $70 million in 1985 alone.

Systems implementation required two years with a total cost of $20–30 million. The systems include several major information systems used to gather, store, and analyze data. The incremental costs of adding management science technologies to these computers and systems was very small in light of the enormous benefits they provided.

THE NATURE OF SENSITIVITY ANALYSIS

sensitivity analysis In preceding chapters, we have studied how to model an LP problem and how to calculate an optimal solution by using the simplex method. These two phases, however, generally do not complete an LP analysis; a third phase, called *sensitivity analysis* or *postoptimality analysis,* is usually undertaken. In this chapter we discuss sensitivity analysis and the kinds of questions it allows the decision maker to answer.

In basic terms, sensitivity analysis involves the exploration of changes in model output in response to changes in input parameters. This kind of "what if" analysis is not limited to linear programming, but it is applicable to all types of mathematical programming models, simulation models, and even spreadsheet models. Sensitivity analysis in a simulation or spreadsheet model would involve the systematic varying of input parameters with observation of the effects on key output values in the model. In this way the analyst is exploring how "sensitive" the model is to certain parameters that affect model output.

In the domain of mathematical programming, linear programming is a particularly rich area in which to do sensitivity analysis. Fortunately, in LP there is an underlying mathematical theory which supports postoptimality analysis. Thus, in LP it is possible to infer a great deal about model sensitivity by examining the standard output of LP simplex analysis. Sensitivity analysis for LP is thus more efficient and more convenient than are many other applications of management science.

Fundamental to LP sensitivity analysis is duality theory. We look first at an LP model called the *dual problem* to learn what information it can provide concerning the value of our limited resources. Then, we examine some basic procedures in sensitivity analysis and explore the sensitivity of an optimal LP solution to changes in the data or parameters of the model.

If all the parameters for LP models were perfectly accurate or never changed over time, there would be little need for sensitivity analysis. However, the parameters (the c_j, a_{ij}, and b_i) used in real-world LP models are often only estimates. These parameters are often approximated by means of subjective estimates, limited sampling, or observations subject to human error. Even if the parameters are accurately measured or predicted at a particular time, they may be subject to change. Businesses operate in a dynamic environment, and data pertaining to demand, prices, or resource availability may change significantly in short periods of time. Thus, management and the quantitative decision maker should not consider the original, computer-generated simplex solutions to be final or sacred in any sense. A problem's "optimal" solution is only as accurate as the original data from which it is derived. Thus, it is important to be able to investigate the possible effects on the optimal solution as the various a_{ij}, b_i, and c_j parameters change.

Some LP models may be relatively insensitive to changes in the parameters. In these cases, the original solution may remain optimal even as the parameters are varied over a wide range of values. On the other hand, some models are acutely sensitive to even minor changes in a single parameter. For these models, it is very important to identify the critical parameters so that special care may be taken in estimating their values and investigating their total effect on the optimal solution.

Through the use of sensitivity analysis, new insights can be obtained from the LP model without its having to be re-solved. For example, management may ask, "If the net profit on our deluxe product were to drop 20 percent in the year, would our current production schedule remain optimal, and, if so, by how much would our total profit change?" Or a firm may want to know by how much it can reduce the availability of a particular resource before endangering its ability to meet next month's demand. Or the manager of a product development division might ask, "Given our current limited resources, if we were to introduce a new product, how much must it contribute to profit and overhead in order to make it worthwhile to produce?"

Answers to these questions and many others can be investigated through sensitivity analysis. There are some who claim that there is really no such thing as "the optimal solution." Given limiting assumptions, imperfect data, and the inability to anticipate the future totally, one solution is unlikely to cover all possibilities. What is really needed, they say, is a range of alternatives (with advantages and disadvantages of each alternative), so that management or the decision maker can make a logical choice. Sensitivity analysis can aid in generating alternatives and in planning for responses to unpredictable changes. In this way, sensitivity analysis is a direct tool to aid in flexibility planning. Recall from Chapter 1 that there is a need for management scientists to generate not only models and solutions that are currently effective, but also solutions that are flexible and adaptable to future conditions.

To illustrate the need for sensitivity analysis and flexibility planning, let's consider an LP model used by American Airlines to determine an optimal strategy for fueling aircraft. Given a pricing structure, fuel allotments, and other data, the LP model specifies the best fueling station and vendor for each flight. What happens if a particular vendor cannot meet the planned allotment? Fuel must be purchased from another vendor at a higher cost. Sensitivity analysis can be used to determine what fueling decision should be made to keep the additional cost at a minimum.

Suppose now that a particular vendor can meet his allotment but raises his price per gallon for fuel. How much can the price vary before the previous fueling decisions are no longer optimal? At American Airlines, sensitivity analysis has proven valuable in day-to-day operations by allowing management to evaluate the effect of price changes and respond immediately.

Management should be aware of the types of questions it can pose and reasonably expect to answer through sensitivity analysis. It is more important for you to understand the nature of sensitivity analysis than to be able to work through the calculations of the simplex method in this respect: Once the model is established, the simplex method is completely computerized in real-world applications. Sensitivity analysis, however, is valueless unless you understand what kinds of insight it can yield. With such understanding, you can perceive decision problems in terms of the questions sensitivity analysis can answer.

DUALITY

dual Every LP problem has a counterpart problem called the *dual*. We shall discuss the dual problem and duality primarily as they apply to *shadow prices,* which tell us something about the value of limited resources. But you should be aware that the notion of duality is central to optimization theory, not only for LP but for all mathematical programming. Duality provides the theoretical basis for many sophisticated solution procedures and algorithms for solving special classes of mathematical programming problems. Indeed, duality provides the foundation for sensitivity analysis.

In the next section, you will learn how the dual is formed from the *primal* original, or *primal,* LP problem. You will also discover that solving the original LP model yields the optimal solution to the dual problem, and vice versa. Thus, in solving any LP problem, we can solve either the primal or the dual, whichever is computationally easier. (Generally, the problem with fewer constraints is easier to solve.)

The Dual Problem

Let us explore the dual problem for an LP problem that has all inequality constraints. Consider the primal problem:

Primal

$$\text{Maximize} \quad 5x_1 + 4x_2 + 9x_3$$
$$\text{subject to} \quad 7x_1 + 6x_2 + 3x_3 \leq 20$$
$$1x_1 + 4x_2 + 8x_3 \leq 15$$
$$x_1, x_2, x_3 \geq 0$$

The associated dual is stated

Dual

$$\text{Minimize} \quad 20y_1 + 15y_2$$
$$\text{subject to} \quad 7y_1 + 1y_2 \geq 5$$
$$6y_1 + 4y_2 \geq 4$$
$$3y_1 + 8y_2 \geq 9$$
$$y_1, y_2 \geq 0$$

Can you determine how the dual was formed from the primal problem? All the coefficients in the dual are derived from the primal. Actually, the dual constitutes something of a flip-flopped version of the primal. To take the dual of a primal problem that has all inequalities in the same direction, we follow these steps:

1. Form the dual objective function from the primal right-hand side (RHS) coefficients.
2. Form the ith dual constraint from the ith column of coefficients in the primal constraints.
3. Form the dual RHS coefficients from the primal objective function coefficients.

4. If the primal is a maximization, form the dual as a minimization (and vice versa), and reverse the direction of the inequalities in the constraints.

We associate a dual variable y_i with the ith primal constraint. Thus, the number of variables in the dual problem depends upon the number of primal constraints, not the number of primal variables. The one-to-one correspondence between entries in the dual problem and those in the primal is further illustrated by Table 5.1.

Let us take the dual of the Faze Linear example of previous chapters. Its primal problem is

$$\text{Maximize} \quad 200x_1 + 500x_2$$

$$
\begin{aligned}
\text{subject to} \quad && x_2 &\le 40 && \text{(transistors)} \\
1.2x_1 + && 4x_2 &\le 240 && \text{(assembly hours)} \\
.5x_1 + && x_2 &\le 81 && \text{(inspection hours)} \\
&& x_1, x_2 &\ge 0
\end{aligned}
$$

The dual problem is

$$\text{Minimize} \quad 40y_1 + 240y_2 + 81y_3$$

$$
\begin{aligned}
\text{subject to} \quad && 1.2y_2 + .5y_3 &\ge 200 \\
y_1 + && 4y_2 + y_3 &\ge 500 \\
&& y_1, y_2, y_3 &\ge 0
\end{aligned}
$$

If you understand the economic situations represented by the primal and dual problems, you will better understand the conceptual relationship between the two. Recall that x_1 represents the number of power amps, and x_2 the number of preamps, to produce each day. The y_i variables of the dual represent the marginal value of primal resource i. Thus, y_1 represents the amount by which profit in the primal objective function can be increased per

TABLE 5.1 *Relationship between primal and dual coefficients*

Primal		Dual
*i*th primal constraint	↔	*i*th dual variable y_i
Objective function coefficient c_j	↔	RHS coefficient for *j*th dual constraint

additional unit of transistor made available. Likewise, y_2 measures the potential contribution of an additional assembly hour, and y_3 measures the potential contribution of each additional inspection hour. In the primal problem, the objective function maximizes the total contribution to profit. In the dual problem, the objective function minimizes the total marginal value of all resources.

Similarly, a primal constraint ensures that the availability of a primal resource is not exceeded, and a dual constraint ensures that the marginal value of the required resources for each product must be at least that of the product's profit contribution. For example, in the first dual constraint to the Faze Linear problem, we have $0y_1 + 1.2y_2 + .5y_3 \geq 200$. This constraint specifies that the number of transistors required to produce a power amp (zero) times the marginal value of a transistor (y_1) plus the time required to assemble a power amp (1.2) times the marginal value of assembly hours (y_2) plus the time required to inspect a power amp (.5) times the marginal value of inspection hours (y_3) must be greater than or equal to 200, which is the profit contribution of a power amp. The second dual constraint is interpreted in a similar manner.

Forming the Dual with Mixed Constraints

In the previous section we formed the dual of a maximization problem which consisted of all $\leq$ type constraints. We now consider how to form the dual of an LP model that contains $=$ as well $\geq$ constraints.

One of the requirements for transforming a primal problem into its dual is that the primal be in a standard form. For maximization problems this form requires that all constraints be $\leq$ or $=$ type constraints. For minimization problems we must have $\geq$ or $=$ type constraints. Let us consider two example problems.

First consider the following maximization problem

EXAMPLE 1

$$\text{Maximize}\quad 20x_1 + 35x_2$$
$$\text{subject to}\quad x_1 + x_2 \leq 100$$
$$3x_1 - 5x_2 \geq 50$$
$$x_1, x_2 \geq 0$$

We must convert the second constraint to $\leq$ form by multiplying by -1 to obtain

$$-3x_1 + 5x_2 \leq -50$$

The primal problem can now be stated as

$$\text{Maximize} \quad 20x_1 + 35x_2 \qquad \text{dual variables}$$

$$\text{subject to} \quad x_1 + x_2 \leq 100 \qquad y_1$$

$$-3x_1 + 5x_2 \leq -50 \qquad y_2$$

$$x_1, x_2 \geq 0$$

Notice that a dual variable is associated with each primal constraint. The dual can be stated as

$$\text{Minimize} \quad 100y_1 - 50y_2$$

$$\text{subject to} \quad y_1 - 3y_2 \geq 20$$

$$y_1 + 5y_2 \geq 35$$

$$y_1, y_2 \geq 0$$

EXAMPLE 2

$$\text{Minimize} \quad 40x_1 + 50x_2 \qquad \text{dual variables}$$

$$\text{subject to} \quad 2x_1 + 3x_2 \geq 70 \qquad y_1$$

$$x_1 + x_2 = 1{,}000 \qquad y_2$$

$$5x_1 - 8x_2 \geq 60 \qquad y_3$$

$$x_1, x_2 \geq 0$$

To form the dual of this problem with an equality constraint, we need the following rule regarding the nonnegativity conditions associated with the dual variable.

If the primal constraint is an inequality, the associated dual variable is required to be $\geq$ zero.
If the primal constraint is an equation, the associated dual variable is unrestricted in sign.

The dual is

$$\text{Maximize} \quad 70y_1 + 1{,}000y_2 + 60y_3$$

$$\text{subject to} \quad 2y_1 + y_2 + 5y_3 \leq 40$$

$$3y_1 + y_2 - 8y_3 \leq 50$$

$$y_1, y_3 \geq 0$$

$$y_2 \text{ unrestricted}$$

Notice that since the second primal constraint is an equation, the second dual variable is unrestricted in sign. Similarly, if we take the dual of a primal problem with an unrestricted variable, the associated dual constraint must be an equation.

Since the simplex method requires all variables to be nonnegative, how can we solve a problem with unrestricted variables? The need for unrestricted variables does occur occasionally, especially in financial applications involving positive and negative cash flows.

We handle the unrestricted variable problem in the simplex method by simply splitting the variable into two variables, each of which is required to be nonnegative. In our previous example we would have

$$y_2 = y_2^+ - y_2^-.$$

Everywhere that y_2 appears in the model we replace it with $y_2^+ - y_2^-$, which is a difference of two nonnegative values. The model is rewritten as

$$\text{Maximize} \quad 70y_1 + 1000y_2^+ - 1000y_2^- + 60y_3$$

$$\text{subject to} \quad 2y_1 + y_2^+ - y_2^- + 5y_3 \le 40$$

$$3y_1 + y_2^+ - y_3^- - 8y_3 \le 50$$

$$y_1, y_2^+, y_2^-, y_3 \ge 0$$

The final solution for y_2 must be interpreted by constructing the difference $y_2^+ - y_2^-$. If y_2 should be positive, then y_2^+ will be in solution; if y_2 should be negative, then y_2^- will be in solution.

Shadow Prices

Earlier in the chapter, we stated that it is possible to solve an LP problem in either its primal or dual form. As a matter of fact, an optimal simplex tableau contains the solution to both the primal and its associated dual. To see this, refer to the optimal tableau for the Faze Linear problem that is reconstructed in Tableau 5.1. The optimal primal solution is found in the "Solution" column; the optimal values of x_2, x_1, and s_1 are 28.5, 105, and 11.5, respectively. But where is the optimal dual solution? If you enjoy working puzzles, you may want to explore Tableau 5.1 a bit before reading further.

Recall that there are as many dual variables as there are primal constraints. If there are m primal constraints, we seek m dual variable values. In Tableau 5.1, there are three primal constraints, and we seek the values of the dual variables y_1, y_2, and y_3. You will always find the optimal dual variable values in the $c_j - z_j$ row corresponding to m particular variables. These variables are precisely those m variables that are in solution in the initial tableau. In this example, s_1, s_2, and s_3 were initially in solution. To deter-

TABLEAU 5.1   *Optimal tableau for Faze Linear problem*

c_B	Basic variables	c_j				
		200	500	0	0	0
		x_1	x_2	s_1	s_2	s_3	Solution

c_B	Basic variables	x_1	x_2	s_1	s_2	s_3	Solution
500	x_2	0	1	0	$\frac{5}{8}$	$-\frac{3}{2}$	$28\frac{1}{2}$
200	x_1	1	0	0	$-\frac{5}{4}$	5	105
0	s_1	0	0	1	$-\frac{5}{8}$	$\frac{3}{2}$	$11\frac{1}{2}$
	z_j	200	500	0	$62\frac{1}{2}$	250	35,250
	$c_j - z_j$	0	0	0	$-62\frac{1}{2}$	-250	

negatives of the optimal dual variables y_i

mine the optimal value of y_1, y_2, and y_3, we simply change the signs of the $c_j - z_j$ values associated with s_1, s_2, and s_3. Thus, $y_1 = 0$, $y_2 = 62.5$, and $y_3 = 250$. You can check the feasibility of these values by substituting them into the dual constraints.

Whenever an artificial variable is in the initial solution, an M coefficient may appear in the $c_j - z_j$ row. For example, suppose that an artificial has a $c_j - z_j$ value of $-1.6 - 3M$ in the final tableau. To obtain the optimal dual variable associated with the constraint in which the artificial appears, we simply change the sign and ignore the M coefficient. Thus, the associated dual variable is 1.6. In Chapter 4, Tableau 4.11 contains two artificial variables and depicts the optimal solution to the primal. The associated dual solutions are $y_1 = .75$, $y_2 = 0$, and $y_3 = .25$.

The values of the optimal dual variables are quite important because they provide a measure of the marginal value of the primal resources. A term called a shadow price (or dual price) is derived directly from the optimal dual variable values. For a maximization problem, the shadow price equals the optimal dual variable value. For a minimization problem, the shadow price equals the negative of the optimal dual variable value. Thus, the shadow prices for the Faze Linear problem (a maximization) are 0, 62.5, and 250, respectively. For the minimization problem from Tableau 4.11, the shadow prices are $-.75$, 0, and $-.25$.

A shadow price is associated with each primal constraint. The usefulness of the shadow price can be stated as follows:

shadow price or dual price

> The *shadow price* associated with a primal constraint shows the amount of improvement in the optimal objective function value as the value of the RHS of that constraint is increased one unit, with all other model parameters unchanged.

Be aware that improvement in a maximization problem means objective function increase; in a minimization problem, it means objective function decrease. A shadow price is meaningful only so long as changes in the availability of primal resources do not cause some current basic variable to be pivoted out of solution. To illustrate, let us return to Tableau 5.1. We have already found that $y_1 = 0$, $y_2 = 62.5$, and $y_3 = 250$. Thus, an additional unit (hour) of assembly time is worth $62.50 to the value of the objective function. The manager, however, must be aware that a shadow price measures gross contribution, not necessarily net contribution. The net value of assembly time also has to reflect the cost of procuring that additional hour (if that cost is not already accounted for in the objective function coefficient.) Assuming that you were production manager at Faze Linear and that additional assembly and inspection hours cost roughly the same, which department would you choose to expand? Why?

To answer that question knowledgeably, you would require an analysis to determine how much each department could be expanded before the basis would change and the shadow prices become meaningless. Such an investigation is called sensitivity analysis, and it is the topic to which we now turn.

SENSITIVITY ANALYSIS

Now that you have some idea of the kinds of information conveyed by the primal and dual aspects of an LP problem, let us explore how the optimal solution changes with respect to changes in the various parameters of the model. We have already seen how useful shadow prices can be in giving insight into the economic aspects of the LP model. Using sensitivity analysis, we can determine the range over which shadow prices remain valid as well as answer many other meaningful questions.

Specifically, we address three types of basic sensitivity analysis:

1. RHS ranging
2. Adding a new variable
3. Changes in the objective function coefficients

Other kinds of analysis, which we shall not address in this introductory text, include changes in the constraint coefficients and adding another constraint.

RHS Ranging

The objective of *RHS ranging analysis* is to determine how much the right-hand side of a particular constraint can be increased or decreased without affecting the feasibility of the optimal solution. In some cases a change in the RHS coefficient will not affect the optimal extreme point, and in other cases the change will exclude the previous optimal extreme point from the feasible region. In this latter case, the previous solution and associated shadow prices are no longer valid, and a new optimal solution must be determined.

We can best illustrate the effects of changing the RHS value by graphically analyzing changes in the now familiar Faze Linear problem. Figure 5.1(a) illustrates the feasible region and extreme points for the original Faze Linear problem. Let us explore changing the RHS value of the first constraint:

$$x_2 \leq 40$$

Figure 5.1(b) shows the feasible region if the first constraint is changed to $x_2 \leq 50$. Notice that the feasible region has changed but the optimal point C is unaffected. As we make the RHS value larger, the graph of the constraint moves upward until it becomes redundant. Thus, we can make the RHS value of constraint one as large as desired without affecting the optimal solution.

Now let us explore the effects of decreasing the RHS value to 20. The new feasible region with the constraint $x_2 \leq 20$ is shown in Figure 5.1(c). In this case the feasible region has "shrunk" to the extent that point C is no longer feasible. You can see that the point C is feasible until the RHS value is decreased below 28.5. Thus, the amount or value which the first constraint's RHS value can become without affecting the feasibility of the optimal solution is 28.5 to infinity.

How can we perform RHS ranging analysis in the context of the simplex method? The analysis is relatively straightforward if the effect of slack in a constraint is understood.

Consider the constraint $x_1 + x_2 \leq 10$. If we introduce a slack variable s_1, we obtain $x_1 + x_2 + s_1 = 10$. If $s_1 = 0$, then $x_1 + x_2$ must sum to 10. On the other hand, if $s_1 = 2$, then the sum of $x_1 + x_2$ is 8, and, effectively, their sum has been reduced. The point to be made is that introducing positive slack in a constraint is tantamount to decreasing the right-hand side. Likewise, introducing negative slack is equivalent to increasing the right-hand side. [A negative slack $(-s_i)$ variable is one that is subtracted in a constraint equation, whereas a positive slack is added $(+s_i)$.] For example, if $s_1 = 3$ in the equation $x_1 + x_2 - s_1 = 10$, then $x_1 + x_2$ must sum to 13 in the equation. This is equivalent to allowing the RHS value 10 to increase. To summarize,

---

In a constraint equation,

increasing positive slack $(+s_i)$ = decreasing the right-hand side by the same amount

increasing negative slack $(-s_i)$ = increasing the right-hand side by the same amount

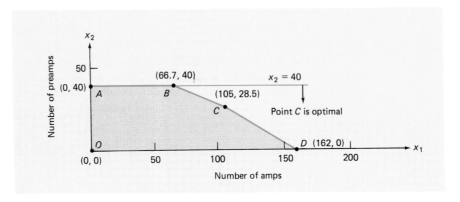

(a)

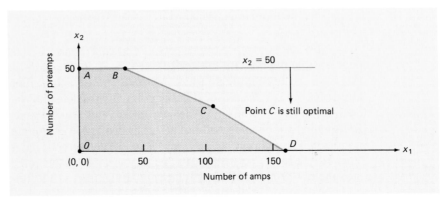

(b)

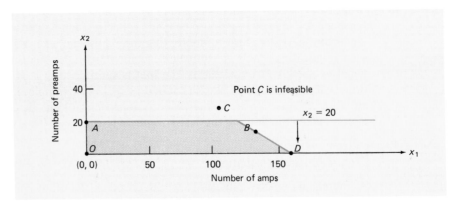

(c)

FIGURE 5.1 **Graphical analysis of RHS ranging**

Given the fact that introducing positive or negative slack is equivalent to decreasing or increasing the right-hand side, then RHS ranging for a particular constraint simply boils down to determining the maximum amount of positive and negative slack that can be introduced. To see how to do this, refer to Tableau 5.1, the optimal simplex tableau associated with the Faze Linear problem.

The right-hand side of the second constraint in the original primal model is 240, indicating that 240 hours of assembly time is available. Let us investigate how much the 240 can be decreased before some variable currently basic is pivoted out of the basis. As we have said, this amounts to determining how much positive slack can be brought into the second constraint.

In Tableau 5.1, the second slack s_2 is associated with the second constraint. How much of positive s_2 can be introduced in the second constraint without changing the basis? The maximum amount is easily determined in exactly the same manner that we determined how much of the entering variable could be brought into solution in the simplex procedures of Chapter 4. To do so, we must simply perform the minimum ratio test!

Consider Tableau 5.2, which is a shortened version of Tableau 5.1. The maximum amount of s_2 we can introduce is found by determining the minimum ratio between the entries in the "Solution" column and their associated positive entries in the s_2 column. Since $\frac{5}{8}$ is the only positive entry, the minimum ratio, by default, is $28\frac{1}{2} \div \frac{5}{8} = 45\frac{3}{5}$. Hence, we may decrease the right-hand side by a maximum of $45\frac{3}{5}$; any larger decrease causes basic variable x_2 to have a negative value. In terms of the Faze Linear problem, this means that the 240 assembly hours can be reduced to $194\frac{2}{5}$ before the basis changes and the shadow prices become invalid.

To determine how much the RHS entry of 240 can be increased, we consider introducing $-s_2$ into the solution (see Tableau 5.3). You should be aware that the variable $-s_2$ is not actually a part of the simplex tableau; it is introduced at this point only as a means of performing RHS ranging. Notice that the signs on the entries in the s_2 column have also been changed. The minimum ratio is clearly $11\frac{1}{2} \div \frac{5}{8} = 18\frac{2}{5}$. Thus, we may increase the right-hand

TABLEAU 5.2 *Short version of Faze Linear optimal tableau*

c_B	Basic variables	Positive slack, s_2	Solution	Minimum ratio	
500	x_2	$\frac{5}{8}$	$28\frac{1}{2}$	$28\frac{1}{2} \div \frac{5}{8} = 45.6$	minimum ratio yields ← max RHS decrease for positive slack
200	x_1	$-\frac{5}{4}$	105	—	
0	s_1	$-\frac{5}{8}$	$11\frac{1}{2}$	—	

TABLEAU 5.3 *Tableau with $-s_2$ introduced for RHS ranging*

c_B	Basic variables	Negative slack, $-s_2$	Solution	Minimum ratio	
500	x_2	$-\frac{5}{8}$	$28\frac{1}{2}$	—	
200	x_1	$\frac{5}{4}$	105	$105 \div \frac{5}{4} = 84$	minimum ratio yields maximum RHS increase for negative
0	s_1	$\frac{5}{8}$	$11\frac{1}{2}$	$11\frac{1}{2} \div \frac{5}{8} = 18.4$ ←	slack

side of 240 by $18\frac{2}{5}$ before the basis changes. In terms of the Faze Linear problem, this means that the assembly hours can be increased to $258\frac{2}{5}$ before s_1 is forced to a negative value.

We have now determined the total range over which the shadow prices are valid. As long as the amount of assembly hours is between $194\frac{2}{5}$ and $258\frac{2}{5}$, the y_2, or marginal value of assembly hours, is \$62.50 per unit.

We can also perform RHS ranging for the other two constraints in the Faze Linear problem. For the first constraint, the analysis is even simpler. The decrease is determined by $11\frac{1}{2} \div 1 = 11\frac{1}{2}$. The amount of increase is unbounded since no minimum ratio can be formed with nonpositive entries from the s_1 column. This makes sense intuitively, for slack s_1 is already in solution; that is, we already have $11\frac{1}{2}$ transistors left over. It should not affect the current solution no matter how many transistors might be made available; they would only be surplus. For the third constraint, the range of inspection time over which the shadow price remains valid is $73\frac{1}{3}$ to 100. Table 5.2 summarizes our RHS ranging analysis.

Adding a New Variable

It is not unusual to want to introduce a new variable into an existing LP model. It is very helpful to know whether such a variable (or product) will be active in the solution or what its objective function coefficient must be

TABLE 5.2 *Analysis of RHS ranging summarized*

Resource	Original RHS value	Shadow price	Range Minimum	Range Maximum
Transistors	40	\$ 0	$28\frac{1}{2}$	No limit
Assembly time	240	62.50	$194\frac{2}{5}$	$258\frac{2}{5}$
Inspection time	81	250.00	$73\frac{1}{3}$	100

for it to be in solution. Given the new variable's resource requirements, it is possible to determine such information without having to re-solve the problem.

Since the shadow prices give us the marginal value of each scarce resource, we may use them to calculate the opportunity cost of bringing a new variable into solution. That is, we can use the shadow prices to calculate the total value in terms of resources that must be given up to bring each unit of the new variable into solution.

Let us return to the Faze Linear example and introduce a new, high-quality digital tuner that is sure to tickle the fancy of many an audiophile. Suppose that, in addition to the power amp (x_1) and the preamp (x_2), the management at Faze Linear is also considering the production of a new tuner (x_3). In terms of the scarce resources, the new tuner would require 1 high-quality transistor, 5 hours of assembly, and 2 hours of inspection. The marketing department forecasts that this tuner should enter the market with a price of approximately $1,500. If markup is 100 percent—that is, profit contribution is $750—should Faze Linear produce this product?

The opportunity cost of producing the tuner can be calculated by multiplying the shadow price of each scarce resource times the amount of the resource required by the production of the tuner. Summing these opportunity costs gives us the amount of profit that must be forfeited to produce the tuner. This is equivalent to the z_j we used in the simplex calculations. The analysis is not completed until the c_j, or the amount of profit gained, is also considered.

For the tuner, we have an opportunity cost of

$$z_3 + 0(1) + 62.5(5) + 250(2) = \$812.50$$

If the profit contribution is only $750, then the $c_j - z_j$ for the tuner is

$$c_3 - z_3 = \$750 - \$812.50 = \$-62.50$$

and it should not be produced and sold at this price.

Table 5.3 summarizes the analysis. It is clear from Table 5.3 that if Faze Linear wants to produce the tuner, its profit contribution must be

TABLE 5.3 *New product analysis*

Resource	Shadow price		Amount of resource required		Opportunity cost
Transistors	$ 0	×	1	=	$ 0
Assembly hours	62.5	×	5	=	312.50
Inspection hours	250.0	×	2	=	500.00
Total opportunity cost (z_3)					$812.50

increased from \$750 to more than \$812.50. This could be accomplished by cutting corners on production costs or increasing the selling price.

Changes in the Objective Function Coefficients

The objective function coefficients (usually profits or costs) may change over time, or they may originally have been rough estimates. In either case, it might be necessary for management to investigate the effects that changes in the objective function coefficients have on the optimal solution. Unlike changes in the right-hand side, changes in the objective function coefficients do not change the values of the basic variables so long as the basis does not change. Thus, changes in the objective function coefficients can only affect the optimality of the current solution and the objective function value itself. Changes in optimality are signaled by the $c_j - z_j$ values.

It is instructive to graphically examine the effects of changing the objective function. In Figure 5.2 we show the feasible region with three different objective functions. The original objective function

$$\text{Maximize} \quad 200x_1 + 500x_2$$

yields extreme point C as the optimal solution. Suppose that the profit contribution c_1 of amplifiers is increased from \$200 to \$400. Then in Figure 5.2 we can see that the slope of the associated profit line is altered to the extent that point D becomes the new optimal solution. Suppose now that we decrease the profit contribution of amplifiers from \$200 to \$150. We can see in Figure 5.2 that the slope of the objective function changes but not quite enough to make point B the optimal extreme point. In this case point C remains optimal.

FIGURE 5.2 **Graphical analysis of objective function changes**

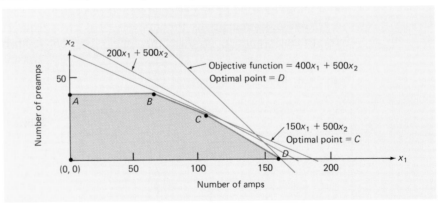

We can conclude that changes in the objective function coefficients change the slope of the objective function and may or may not affect optimality. In either case, the feasible region is unchanged and the feasibility of the optimal solution is unaffected.

To analyze objective function ranging in the context of the simplex method, we will separate the analysis into two parts: first, we deal with nonbasic objective function coefficients; then, we approach basic objective function coefficients.

Nonbasic objective function coefficient   Such a coefficient is one whose associated decision variable is nonbasic and not in solution. Thus, the decision variable associated with a nonbasic objective function coefficient is automatically zero, and its $c_j - z_j \leq 0$ if we are maximizing and $c_j - z_j \geq 0$ if we are minimizing. This must be true, for otherwise we could pivot the decision variable into solution and improve the objective function value.

Changing a nonbasic objective function coefficient, then, affects the value of the $c_j - z_j$ indicator. The basis does not change unless $c_j - z_j$ becomes greater than zero if maximizing and less than zero if minimizing. The amount that c_j can change is governed by the current $c_j - z_j$ value. Thus, we have the following rules:

---

1. If you are maximizing, you may decrease the value of any nonbasic c_j to minus infinity. You may increase c_j up to the value of z_j.
2. If you are minimizing, you may increase the value of any nonbasic c_j to infinity. You may decrease c_j down to the value of z_j.

To illustrate these rules, refer again to Tableau 5.1. The only nonbasic variables are s_2 and s_3. Currently, the objective function coefficients of s_2 and s_3 are both zero. Let us denote the objective function coefficients as c_{s2} and c_{s3}, respectively. Then, the first rule specifies that c_{s2} may decrease to $-\infty$ and may increase to 62.5. If c_{s2} were to increase to, say, 63, then its associated $c_j - z_j$ would become $+.5$, and s_2 would be brought into solution, thus changing the current basis. Similarly, we can decrease c_{s3} to $-\infty$ and increase c_{s3} to 250.

Basic objective function coefficient   If we consider changing an objective function coefficient whose associated decision variable is basic, the same principles apply as in the case of a nonbasic. However, changing a basic objective function coefficient can affect the $c_j - z_j$ of all nonbasic variables. Thus, a more lengthy analysis is required when the objective function coefficient is basic. To begin with, let us consider changing the profit contribution of preamps in the Faze Linear example. Presently, the objective function

TABLEAU 5.4 *Changed preamp profit contribution*

	c_j	200	$500 + \Delta$	0	0	0	
c_B	Basic variables	x_1	x_2	s_1	s_2	s_3	Solution
$500 + \Delta$	x_2	0	1	0	$\frac{5}{8}$	$-\frac{3}{2}$	$28\frac{1}{2}$
200	x_1	1	0	0	$-\frac{5}{4}$	5	105
0	s_1	0	0	1	$-\frac{5}{8}$	$\frac{3}{2}$	$11\frac{1}{2}$
	z_j	200	$500 + \Delta$	0	$62\frac{1}{2} + \frac{5}{8}\Delta$	$250 - \frac{3}{2}\Delta$	$35{,}250 + 28\frac{1}{2}\Delta$
	$c_j - z_j$	0	0	0	$-62\frac{1}{2} - \frac{5}{8}\Delta$	$-250 + \frac{3}{2}\Delta$	

this change in the c_B affects the z_j value of all nonbasic → variables having a nonzero entry in row 1 of the tableau

coefficient $c_2 = 500$. Let us denote the change in c_2 by Δ. Incorporating this change into Tableau 5.1, we establish the values of Tableau 5.4.

In Tableau 5.4, notice the new $c_j - z_j$ values for the nonbasic variables s_2 and s_3. These new values are determined by calculating a new z_j value in precisely the same manner that we did in Chapter 4 in the section headed, "The Basic Steps Applied."

The value of Δ may vary so long as no $c_j - z_j$ for a nonbasic variable becomes greater than zero. Thus, we need to solve for Δ such that

$$-62\frac{1}{2} - \tfrac{5}{8}\Delta \leq 0$$
$$-250 + \tfrac{3}{2}\Delta \leq 0$$

The first inequality yields $\Delta \geq -100$, and the second one requires that $\Delta \leq 166\frac{2}{3}$. Thus, the allowable range on Δ is $-100 \leq \Delta \leq 166\frac{2}{3}$. The c_2 coefficient that was originally 500 may vary from 400 to $666\frac{2}{3}$ before the basis changes.

If there were many nonbasic variables, the foregoing analysis would become tedious. Fortunately, there is an equivalent shortcut procedure. This procedure refers to the optimal tableau and simply forms ratios between the $c_j - z_j$ row and the tableau entries in the row associated with the current basic variable whose objective function coefficient is being analyzed. Suppose that we are considering changes in a basic objective function coefficient c_j. Let i denote the tableau row in which the associated basic variable x_j appears. Let a_{ij} denote the entries in the tableau. Then for i fixed, we find

Minimum $(c_j - z_j)/a_{ij} > 0,$ for the maximum positive change

and

Minimum $|(c_j - z_j)/a_{ij} < 0|,$ for the maximum negative change

Thus, in the previous example where we considered changing c_2, we divide the $c_j - z_j$ row by the tableau row in which x_2 (associated with c_2) is the basic variable. Thus, we get

$$\frac{c_j - z_j \text{ row}}{x_2 \text{ row}} = \frac{0 \ \ 0 \ \ 0 \ \ -62.5 \ \ -250}{0 \ \ 0 \ \ 0 \ \ \frac{5}{8} \ \ -\frac{3}{2}}$$

We ignore any fractions with a zero in the numerator or the denominator. We have only one fraction greater than zero, so that the maximum positive change is

$$\frac{-250}{-\frac{3}{2}} = 166\frac{2}{3}$$

We have only one negative fraction, so that the maximum negative change is

$$\left| \frac{-62.5}{\frac{5}{8}} \right| = |-100| = 100$$

Note that if there were more than one positive or negative fraction, we would have to choose the minimum value among the positive fractions for the maximum positive change and the minimum absolute value among the negative fractions for the maximum negative change.

In Table 5.4 this analysis, together with an analysis on basic objective function coefficient c_1, is summarized. When you are sure you understand the analysis for c_2, work through the analysis for $c_1 = 200$ to see if your results agree with those in Table 5.4.

TABLE 5.4   *Sensitivity analysis for basic objective function coefficients**

	Basic variables	
	Power amps, x_1	*Preamps, x_2*
Tableau row i	2	1
Original c_j	200	500
Minimum $(c_j - z_j)/a_{ij} > 0$	50	$166\frac{2}{3}$
Upper limit for c_j	250	$666\frac{2}{3}$
Minimum $|(c_j - z_j)/a_{ij} < 0|$	50	100
Lower limit for c_j	150	400
Range for c_j	150 to 250	400 to $666\frac{2}{3}$

* This shortcut method is not necessarily valid for the special case of alternative optima. (See explanation in the paragraph below.)

In the special case of alternative optima, the shortcut method needs to be slightly modified. Under conditions of alternative optima, some nonbasic variable, say, variable *r*, has a zero $c_j - z_j$ value. If its associated $a_{ir} > 0$, then the maximum negative (positive) change for the basic objective function coefficient in question is zero when maximizing (minimizing). On the other hand, if $a_{ir} < 0$, then the maximum positive (negative) change is zero when maximizing (minimizing). Remaining upper and lower limits are calculated as in Table 5.4.

INTERPRETATION OF COMPUTER OUTPUT

The types of sensitivity analysis that we have discussed (with the exception of adding a new variable) are often standard LP computer code output, or at least a report option. To illustrate the interpretation of sensitivity analysis output, let us look again at the computer output for the Faze Linear product mix problem.

Figure 5.3 shows the standard LINDO solution output as well as the optional sensitivity analysis output. The shadow prices are part of the standard solution output and are found under the column ''DUAL PRICES.'' Notice that a shadow price is associated with each of the model's constraints.

The optional sensitivity analysis output is shown under the heading ''RANGES IN WHICH THE BASIS IS UNCHANGED.'' Again, the basis refers to the current mix of variables that are ''in solution.'' The sensitivity analysis output shows allowable changes in objective function coefficients and RHS values. Changes outside these ranges will cause the current basis to be suboptimal or infeasible.

The objective function coefficient range analysis is shown for each decision variable. The report shows the current value of the coefficient and the maximum allowable increase and decrease in the coefficient's value. As long as a change in the coefficient is no less than the allowable decrease or no more than the allowable increase (assuming all other parameters remain fixed), the current solution will remain optimal. Of course, a change in a basic objective function coefficient would change the value of the optimal objective function; it is the value of the decision variables that remains unchanged as an objective function coefficient varies over its allowable range.

The RHS ranging analysis is shown immediately below the objective function ranging analysis. The allowable increase and decrease is shown for each RHS value in the original model. Applying the allowable increase and decrease to the current RHS value for constraint 2 (row 3), we find that the allowable range is 194.4 to 258.4. As long as an RHS value stays within its

```
LP OPTIMUM FOUND AT STEP        2

        OBJECTIVE FUNCTION VALUE

    1)    35250.0000

   VARIABLE          VALUE          REDUCED COST
      AMPS         105.000000         .000000
   PREAMPS          28.500000         .000000


      ROW    SLACK OR SURPLUS    DUAL PRICES ◄———— Shadow prices
       2)        11.500000          .000000
       3)          .000000        62.500000
       4)          .000000       250.000000

NO. ITERATIONS=        2

RANGES IN WHICH THE BASIS IS UNCHANGED:    Objective function ranging

                          OBJ COEFFICIENT RANGES ◄
   VARIABLE        CURRENT       ALLOWABLE        ALLOWABLE
                    COEF         INCREASE         DECREASE
      AMPS       200.000000     49.999990        50.000000
   PREAMPS       500.000000    166.666700        99.999990

                          RIGHTHAND SIDE RANGES ◄—— RHS ranging
      ROW         CURRENT       ALLOWABLE        ALLOWABLE
                    RHS          INCREASE         DECREASE
       2          40.000000       INFINITY        11.500000
       3         240.000000      18.400000        45.599990
       4          81.000000      19.000000         7.666668
```

FIGURE 5.3   **Computer sensitivity analysis for Faze Linear problem**

allowable range (assuming all other parameters remain fixed), the optimal basis will not change. However, changes in an RHS value can affect the decision variable values as well as the objective function value. Thus, objective function changes can affect only optimality, but RHS changes can affect feasibility as well as optimality.

Even though the output does not include the analysis of adding a new variable, it does provide the shadow prices, thereby enabling the user to easily analyze the addition of a new variable by hand calculations.

SUMMARY

In this chapter, we have examined the closely related topics of the dual problem and sensitivity analysis. In more advanced topics, duality plays a very important role in the development of optimization techniques. We studied the dual problem primarily as a means for better understanding shadow prices. Shadow prices provide valuable information about the marginal value of scarce resources.

Sensitivity analysis allows us to determine the range over which these shadow prices are valid. A sensitivity analysis can actually be more useful to management than the optimal LP solution itself. It can help management make better decisions regarding such problems as capacity expansion, adding new products, changes in resource availabilities, and price fluctuations. In general, it is a technique that helps management to better relate the economics of the firm to the LP model being analyzed.

In RHS ranging, we determined the range over which a right-hand side can be varied without causing the basis to change. In adding a new variable, we determined whether the variable is worthwhile to introduce to the solution, or what its objective function coefficient must be to make it worthwhile. The final kind of sensitivity analysis involved a ranging analysis on the objective function coefficients. In two separate procedures, we determined the range over which nonbasic and basic objective function coefficients can change before the basis changes.

RHS ranging and objective coefficient analysis are often standard output of LP computer codes. The addition of a new product, however, generally requires a separate analysis.

SOLVED PROBLEMS

PROBLEM STATEMENT

The Faze Linear Company abandoned the idea of producing an expensive state-of-the-art digital tuner, but decided to produce a high-quality and more reasonably priced tuner which sells for $795. The profit contribution of this tuner is $400. The manufacture of this tuner requires no special high-quality transistors, but requires 2 hours of assembly and 1 hour of inspection. To determine an optimal product mix, Faze Linear reformulated their model as follows:

$$\text{Maximize} \quad 200x_1 + 500x_2 + 400x_3$$

$$
\begin{aligned}
\text{subject to} \quad && x_2 && &\leq 40 \\
1.2x_1 + && 4x_2 + && 2x_3 &\leq 240 \\
.5x_1 + && 1x_2 + && 1x_3 &\leq 81 \\
&& x_1, x_2, x_3 &\geq 0
\end{aligned}
$$

where x_1, x_2, and x_3 represent the numbers of amps, preamps, and tuners to be produced, respectively.

Solving the model yields the following optimal tableau:

	c_j	200	500	400	0	0	0	
c_B	Basic variables	x_1	x_2	x_3	s_1	s_2	s_3	Solution
500	x_2	$\frac{1}{10}$	1	0	0	$\frac{1}{2}$	-1	39
400	x_3	$\frac{2}{5}$	0	1	0	$-\frac{1}{2}$	2	42
0	s_1	$-\frac{1}{10}$	0	0	1	$-\frac{1}{2}$	1	1
	z_j	210	500	400	0	50	300	36,300
	$c_j - z_j$	-10	0	0	0	-50	-300	

a. What is the new solution and its profit?

b. Which resources are fully utilized?

c. How much would the profit contribution of amplifiers have to increase before they would be produced?

d. The management at Faze Linear is concerned about the availability of the special high-quality transistors. How much could the availability of transistors change before the current product mix is no longer optimal?

e. Determine the new product mix if the number of inspection hours decreases from 81 to 80.

SOLUTION

a. The new solution is to produce 39 preamps and 42 tuners per day for a profit contribution of $36,300. It is no longer profitable to produce the amplifiers.

b. Resources 2 and 3, or the assembly and inspection time. This is evident by the fact that only slack s_1 (transistors) is in solution at a positive value (therefore having excess or underutilized resources).

c. Currently, the $c_1 - z_1$ value of amplifiers (x_1) is -10. Therefore, the profit contribution of amplifiers would have to increase by more than $10 to be profitable to produce.

d. Transistor availability comprises the first constraint. Slack s_1 is associated with the first constraint; thus consider the s_1 column and the "Solution" column:

s_1	Solution	Minimum ratio	$-s_1$	Solution	Minimum ratio
0	39	—	0	39	—
0	42	—	0	42	—
1	1	1	-1	1	—

Forming the minimum ratio with the positive slack s_1 yields a value of 1. Thus, the 40 available transistors can decrease to 39 without changing the basic variables. Changing the sign of s_1 and its column creates a column of zero and negative numbers. The minimum ratio cannot be calculated as the amount of $-s_1$ that could be brought into solution is unbounded. No amount of extra transistors will affect the solution. The range for transistors is 39 to ∞.

e. The long way to solve this part would be to solve the entire problem from scratch. However, by using the definition of the substitution coefficients, we can easily determine the new solution. Consider the slack s_3 associated with inspection hours. Since s_3 is a positive slack, bringing it into solution is equivalent to decreasing the right-hand side. Consider the s_3 column and the "Solution" column:

s_3	Solution	New solution
-1	39	$39 - (-1)1 = 40$
2	42	$42 - 2(1) = 40$
1	1	$1 - 1(1) = 0$

The substitution coefficients in the s_3 column tell us how much of the solution value for each basic variable we must sacrifice for each unit of s_3 brought into solution. Thus, the new solution is $x_2 = 40$, $x_3 = 40$, and $s_1 = 0$.

PROBLEM STATEMENT

The management of the Faze Linear Company in the previous problem would like to explore systematically other questions and options in their product mix problem. However, they prefer the convenience of a computer output and its various reports. Listed here are the computer solution and sensitivity analysis of the new product mix problem of the previous problem.

a. What are the shadow prices?

b. The management at Faze Linear has earmarked some funds for capital expansion. Which of the three resources in the LP model are recommended for expansion?

c. They are also considering the marketing of a new graphic equalizer. This unit would require no special transistors and 1 hour each of assembly and inspection. It would contribute $320 to profit. Should it be produced?

d. To meet the price cuts of competition, Faze Liner may have to drop the prices on their preamp and tuner. How much could each of these profit contributions decrease (holding all other prices fixed) before the current product mix is no longer optimal?

e. The RHS ranging analysis suggests that the allowable range on inspection time is 80 to 120 hours per day. What does this mean? That is, what if labor shortages reduced the total number of inspection hours per day to less than 80?

SOLUTION

a. The shadow prices are shown in the "DUAL PRICES" column. There is slack in the transistor constraint so that the associated shadow price = 0. The assembly and inspection constraints have shadow prices of 50 and 300, respectively.

```
MAX      200 AMPS + 500 PREAMPS + 400 TUNERS
SUBJECT TO
      2)   PREAMPS <=    40
      3)   1.2 AMPS + 4 PREAMPS + 2 TUNERS <=    240
      4)   0.5 AMPS + PREAMPS + TUNERS <=    81



LP OPTIMUM FOUND AT STEP      2

         OBJECTIVE FUNCTION VALUE

     1)     36300.0000

     VARIABLE          VALUE        REDUCED COST
        AMPS          .000000        10.000000
     PREAMPS        39.000000          .000000
      TUNERS        42.000000          .000000


      ROW    SLACK OR SURPLUS     DUAL PRICES
       2)         1.000000          .000000
       3)          .000000        50.000000
       4)          .000000       300.000000

NO. ITERATIONS=        2

RANGES IN WHICH THE BASIS IS UNCHANGED:

                        OBJ COEFFICIENT RANGES
     VARIABLE        CURRENT        ALLOWABLE        ALLOWABLE
                      COEF          INCREASE         DECREASE
        AMPS       200.000000       10.000000         INFINITY
     PREAMPS       500.000000      300.000000        99.999980
      TUNERS       400.000000      100.000000        25.000000

                        RIGHTHAND SIDE RANGES
      ROW          CURRENT        ALLOWABLE        ALLOWABLE
                     RHS          INCREASE         DECREASE
       2          40.000000       INFINITY         1.000000
       3         240.000000        2.000000        78.000000
       4          81.000000       39.000000         1.000000
```

b. As seen by the shadow prices in part (a), the marginal value of inspection time is highest (300), followed by assembly time (50). Since there are surplus transistors, their marginal value is 0. Therefore, the inspection hours should first be considered for expansion, followed by assembly hours.

c. The equalizer should be produced only if its profit contribution exceeds the value of the current production it would replace. In calculating its $c_j - z_j$ value, we first determine its z_j value by multiplying its resource requirements times their marginal values at optimality.

$$
\begin{array}{lrr}
\text{transistors} & 0 \times & 0 \\
\text{assembly} & 1 \times & 50 \\
\text{inspection} & 1 \times & \underline{300} \\
& z_4 = & \$350
\end{array}
$$

Thus, $c_4 - z_4 = \$320 - \$350 = -\$30$ and the equalizer should not be produced at a profit contribution of only $320.

d. Looking at the sensitivity of the objective function coefficients, we see that the profit contribution of preamps can decrease by 100 to $400 and the profit contribution of tuners can decrease to $375 before the current basic variables would no longer be optimal and some nonbasic variable would enter the solution, replacing a basic variable and changing the product mix.

e. If the number of inspection hours drops below 80, the current three basic variables can no longer be used to comprise a feasible solution to the product mix problem. The three variables could be used to solve the constraint equations, but at least one of the basic variables would assume a negative value (infeasible). This does not mean, however, that the problem has no solution; it just means that some other combination of variables and a different product mix must be used to provide a solution that is meaningful.

REVIEW QUESTIONS

1. What is a shadow price?
2. Explain why a shadow price is valid only for a specified range of values of the right-hand side.
3. If a primal LP model has m constraints and n variables, how many constraints and variables will its dual have?
4. In what ways can sensitivity analysis be more valuable to management than the optimal solution alone?

5. For any nonbasic variable in an optimal LP solution, how much would its objective function coefficient have to change in order for it to enter the solution?
6. Explain whether each kind of change in (a), (b), and (c), below, prior to a change of basis can affect (1) solution, (2) solution value, (3) $c_j - z_j$ values, or (4) other entries in the tableau.
   a. Changes in the right-hand side
   b. Changes in the objective function coefficients
   c. Adding a new variable

PROBLEMS

5.1 Formulate the dual problem for the following linear programming model.

$$\text{Maximize} \quad 16x_1 + 10x_2 + 9x_3$$
$$\text{subject to} \quad 3x_1 - 4x_2 + 8x_3 \leq 52$$
$$14x_1 + 7x_2 + 4x_3 \leq 40$$
$$x_1, x_2, x_3 \geq 0$$

5.2 The LP problem following is the dual to a problem. Find the primal problem to which it corresponds.

$$\text{Minimize} \quad 3x_1 + x_2 + 5x_3$$
$$\text{subject to} \quad x_1 + x_2 + x_3 \geq 40$$
$$2x_1 + 3x_2 \geq 50$$
$$3x_1 + 2x_2 + 4x_3 \geq 20$$
$$x_1, x_2, x_3 \geq 0$$

5.3 Given the primal problem

$$\text{Minimize} \quad 15x_1 + 40x_2$$
$$\text{subject to} \quad x_1 \geq 13$$
$$x_2 \geq 10$$
$$3x_1 + 4x_2 \geq 15$$
$$-5x_1 + 17x_2 \geq 19$$
$$x_1, x_2 \geq 0$$

from a computational point of view, would you rather solve this primal or its associated dual? Why?

5.4 You are given the following product mix problem:

$$\text{Maximize} \quad 4x_1 + 5x_2$$

$$\text{subject to} \quad x_1 + 2x_2 \leq 8 \quad \text{(machine A hours)}$$

$$3x + 2x_2 \leq 12 \quad \text{(machine B hours)}$$

$$x_1, x_2 \geq 0$$

a. Write the dual of this problem.

b. Solve the primal and the dual.

c. Interpret the primal and the dual.

5.5 Solve Problem 5.4 (primal) graphically.

a. Show the new solution when the objective function changes to maximize $2x_1 + 5x_2$.

b. Show the new feasible region when the right-hand side changes from (8, 12) to (6, 8).

c. Describe in words what happens to the feasible region when an additional variable x_3 is added to the model.

5.6 Solve the following primal problem graphically, and solve its associated dual by inspection.

$$\text{Maximize} \quad 4x_1 + 8x_2$$

$$\text{subject to} \quad 8x_1 + 4x_2 \leq 8$$

$$x_1, x_2 \geq 0$$

5.7 Consider the model below that corresponds to a manufacturing problem with two products and three resources.

$$\text{Maximize} \quad 3x_1 + 8x_2$$

$$\text{subject to} \quad 2x_1 + 4x_2 \leq 1000 \quad \text{(resource 1)}$$

$$6x_1 + 2x_2 \leq 1200 \quad \text{(resource 2)}$$

$$x_2 \leq 200 \quad \text{(resource 3)}$$

$$x_1, x_2 \geq 0$$

The optimal simplex tableau is

c_B	Basic variables	c_j 3 x_1	8 x_2	0 s_1	0 s_2	0 s_3	Solution
3	x_1	1	0	$\frac{1}{2}$	0	-2	100
0	s_2	0	0	-3	1	10	200
8	x_2	0	1	0	0	1	200
	z_j	3	8	$\frac{3}{2}$	0	2	1900
	$c_j - z_j$	0	0	$-\frac{3}{2}$	0	-2	

a. What is the optimal solution?
b. What are the shadow prices?
c. Which resource has the highest marginal value at optimality?
d. Over what ranges in each of the RHS constants are these shadow prices valid?

5.8 For Problem 5.7,

a. Formulate the dual problem from the stated primal.
b. Obtain the optimal dual solution from the optimal primal tableau.
c. Compare the values of the optimal primal and dual objective functions.

5.9 Refer again to Problem 5.7:

a. Determine the permissible ranges over which the objective function coefficients can vary for variables s_1 and s_3.
b. Repeat part a for variables x_1, s_2, and x_2.
c. Consider the addition of a new variable x_3. This variable will require two units of each of the three resources. What must x_3's minimal profit contribution be in order for it to be profitable to produce?

5.10 The following primal problem has two variables and three constraints. Solve it indirectly by solving the dual problem using the simplex method.

$$\text{Maximize} \quad 2x_1 + x_2$$
$$\text{subject to} \quad x_2 \le 10$$
$$2x_1 + 5x_2 \le 60$$
$$2x_1 + 2x_2 \le 18$$
$$x_1, x_2 \ge 0$$

5.11 The optimal simplex tableau for a maximization problem with all $\leq$ constraints is as shown.

	c_j	4	2	0	0	0	
c_B	Basic variables	x_1	x_2	s_1	s_2	s_3	Solution
2	x_2	0	1	1	-1	0	4
4	x_1	1	0	$-\frac{1}{4}$	$\frac{3}{4}$	0	3
0	s_3	0	0	2	-4	1	8
	$c_j - z_j$	0	0	-1	-1	0	20

  a. Which of the three resources are being fully utilized?
  b. Suppose that the resources could be obtained at no cost. Which right-hand side would you recommend for expansion, and why?
  c. How much can each RHS value be increased before the basis changes?

5.12 Refer to the optimal tableau in Problem 5.11.

  a. How many variables are contained in the dual of this problem?
  b. What are the optimum dual variable values?
  c. How much can each RHS value be decreased before the basis changes?
  d. Without reworking the problem, predict the new objective function value and solution values for x_2, x_1, and s_3 when the first RHS value is increased by 6. *Hint:* Use the column of substitution coefficients under s_1.

5.13 Try to give an economic interpretation of the dual to the example concerning production distribution in Chapter 2.

5.14 Consider the diet problem example in Chapter 2. Try to give a possible economic interpretation of its dual. *Hint:* The dual variables can be thought of as values or "prices" associated with each nutrient.

5.15 Below you will find the optimal tableau of the diet problem example in Chapter 2.

c_B	c_j Basic variables	1.60 x_1	1.00 x_2	.65 x_3	.30 x_4	0 s_1	0 s_2	0 s_3	0 s_4	M A_1	M A_2	M A_3	M A_4	Solution
1.60	x_1	1	0	0	0	0	0	−.0018	0	0	0	.0018	0	.7407
0	s_1	0	−237	0	0	1	−47.89	23.62	0	−1	47.89	−23.62	0	28200.48
.30	x_4	0	0	0	1	0	−.014	.0010	0	0	.014	−.001	0	.6390
0	s_4	0	−7	−13	0	0	−.112	−.0435	1	0	.112	0.435	−1	13.8516
	$c_j - z_j$	0	1.00	.65	0	0	.0042	.0026	0	M	M − 0.042	M − .0026	M	$1.39

a. What is the optimal solution? Is it palatable to you? How much does it cost to feed each individual on a daily basis? Do you think the constraints covered everything that should be considered in a daily diet?

b. Which nutritional requirements are being met exactly? Which nutrients exceed the requirements?

c. Determine the range over which the vitamin C requirement can vary before the basis changes.

d. For all four foods, determine the range over which their prices can vary without changing the basis.

5.16 Given is the formulation and optimal computer solution to the Ace Manufacturing Company of Problem 2.1. Let

$$x_1 = \text{units of regular produced}$$
$$x_2 = \text{units of super produced}$$

$$\text{Maximize} \quad 50x_1 + 75x_2$$

$$\text{subject to} \quad 1.2x_1 + 1.6x_2 \leq 1600 \quad \text{assembly}$$
$$.8x_1 + .9x_2 \leq 700 \quad \text{paint}$$
$$.2x_1 + .2x_2 \leq 300 \quad \text{inspection}$$
$$x_1 \qquad\qquad \geq 150 \quad \text{regular demand}$$
$$x_2 \geq 90 \quad \text{super demand}$$

```
LP OPTIMUM FOUND AT STEP       3

        OBJECTIVE FUNCTION VALUE

    1)      55833.3400

    VARIABLE          VALUE          REDUCED COST
    REGULAR        150.000000           .000000
      SUPER        644.444500           .000000


      ROW     SLACK OR SURPLUS     DUAL PRICES
       2)       388.888900           .000000
       3)           .000000        83.333340
       4)       141.111100           .000000
       5)           .000000       -16.666670
       6)       554.444500           .000000

NO. ITERATIONS=        3

RANGES IN WHICH THE BASIS IS UNCHANGED:

                          OBJ COEFFICIENT RANGES
    VARIABLE        CURRENT       ALLOWABLE        ALLOWABLE
                      COEF        INCREASE         DECREASE
    REGULAR        50.000000      16.666670        INFINITY
      SUPER        75.000000       INFINITY       18.750000

                          RIGHTHAND SIDE RANGES
      ROW         CURRENT        ALLOWABLE        ALLOWABLE
                    RHS          INCREASE         DECREASE
       2        1600.000000       INFINITY       388.888900
       3         700.000000      218.750000      499.000000
       4         300.000000       INFINITY       141.111100
       5         150.000000      623.749900      150.000000
       6          90.000000      554.444500        INFINITY
```

a. What is the marginal value of the RHS value of the regular demand (fourth) constraint? Remember that this is a $\geq$ constraint!

b. Ace Manufacturing is faced with declining profit contribution in the face of inflation and would like to know the effect of declining profit on the optimal product mix. From the computer printout, determine the range over which the profit contributions of the regular and super products can vary before the current product mix is no longer optimal.

    c. Over what range can each of the RHS values vary while maintaining the optimality of the current product mix?

    d. Ace Manufacturing is considering the release of a regular demand contract for 50 units to produce more super product. How much should it be willing to pay to break the contract?

5.17 Consider the 2 × 2 example in Problem 5.4. Find three feasible solutions for the primal problem and three feasible solutions for the dual problem. Plug these feasible solutions into their respective objective functions and observe their respective solution values. Are the values of the objective function of the maximization problem (this is often called the *max* objective function) always less than or equal to those of the minimization (the *min*)? Observe their two optimal values.

dual theorem
    A fundamental result in duality theory is the *dual theorem*. It states that if both the primal and dual are feasible, then the solution value of any feasible solution of the max problem is always less than or equal to any feasible solution of the min problem. Furthermore, the optimal solution values of the two problems are equal.

complemen-
tary
slackness
5.18 Another fundamental property in duality theory is called *complementary slackness*. Basically, this is a statement of the fact that if a constraint in an LP problem is not tight (binding), its associated shadow price must be zero. A constraint is tight if the solution variable values equal the righthand side when they are substituted into the constraint. Thus, a nontight constraint is simply one in which some slack exists. Consider the optimal solution to the Faze Linear problem (Tableau 5.1). Which constraints are tight? Which shadow prices are zero?

    (Complementary slackness is intuitively reasonable, for if a constraint is not tight, some of the associated resource is left over and should have a marginal value (shadow price) of zero.)

5.19 Refer to Tableau 4.11, which is the optimal tableau for the minimization problem solved in Chapter 4.

    a. What are the shadow prices?

    b. What is the new minimum cost if the cost per gallon of crude oil B is dropped by $.02?

    c. How much can the RHS restriction of 20 on crude oil A change before the basis changes?

    d. Over what range can the cost for crude oil A vary without changing the basis?

5.20 Refer to the simplex solution of the solved problem at the end of Chapter 4.

    a. Perform a sensitivity analysis for both right-hand-side values.

    b. State the value of the shadow prices.

c. Perform a sensitivity analysis on the objective function coefficients of s_1, x_1, and x_2.

5.21 *Product mix.* The Southeastern Textile Mill produces four different styles of cotton cloth. The four basic materials are a bleached style, a printed style, and two dyed styles, red and blue. The profit contributions of these four products are $.80, $1.20, $1.50, and $1.60 per square yard, respectively. The company is committed to produce at least 6,000 square yards of the printed style for next week. The maximum possible sales for the bleached style is 100,000 square yards, and for the blue-dyed material it is 1,000,000 square yards in this particular week.

Southeastern's production involves five basic processes. These processes and their available capacity in millions of process hours are desizing, 15; bleaching, 150; printing, 180; dyeing, 15; and calendering, 45. The resource requirements of each of the four products are stipulated in Southeastern's LP model. Let

x_1 = number of square yards of bleached material to produce
x_2 = number of square yards of printed material to produce
x_3 = number of square yards of red-dyed material to produce
x_4 = number of square yards of blue-dyed material to produce

$$
\begin{aligned}
\text{Maximize} \quad & .80x_1 + 1.20x_2 + 1.50x_3 + 1.60x_4 \\
\text{subject to} \quad & 7.7x_1 + 11.1x_2 + 7.7x_3 + 8.3x_4 \leq 15,000,000 \\
& 100x_1 + 95x_2 + 91x_3 + 83x_4 \leq 150,000,000 \\
& 33x_2 \leq 180,000,000 \\
& 2.5x_3 + 2.9x_4 \leq 15,000,000 \\
& 2.5x_1 + 3.3x_2 + 3.1x_3 + 2.9x_4 \leq 45,000,000 \\
& x_1 \leq 100,000 \\
& x_2 \geq 6,000 \\
& x_4 \leq 1,000,000 \\
& x_1, x_2, x_3, x_4 \geq 0
\end{aligned}
$$

After adding the required slack and artificial variables, the optimal simplex tableau is as presented below.

a. What is the optimal solution and the total profit?

b. Is the solution degenerate? Are there alternative optima?

c. Which of the five departments appears to be most promising in terms of expansion? What else would you have to take into consideration?

d. What is the incremental profit associated with adding one more process hour of bleaching capacity? Over what range is this valid?

e. Consider another new printed style x_5 which requires 9.1 hours of printing and 4.0 hours of calendering. What does its profit contribution have to be in order for it to be profitably produced?

f. Suppose that an additional 10 hours of bleaching capacity is made available. What are the new values of x_1, x_2, x_3, and x_4? *Hint:* Use the appropriate substitution coefficients in the optimal tableau.

	c_j	.80	1.20	1.50	1.60	0	0	0	0	0	0	0	$-M$	0	
c_B	Basic Variables	x_1	x_2	x_3	x_4	s_7	s_1	s_2	s_3	s_4	s_5	s_6	A_7	s_8	Solution
0	s_1	$-.76$	0	0	0	3.06	1	$-.08$	0	0	0	0	-3.06	-1.28	1,012,400
1.50	x_3	1.10	0	1	0	1.04	0	.01	0	0	0	0	-1.04	$-.91$	730,000
0	s_3	0	0	0	0	33	0	0	1	0	0	0	-33	0	179,802,000
0	s_4	$-.91$	0	0	0	.06	0	$-.03$	0	1	0	0	$-.06$	$-.07$	39,817,200
0	s_5	-2.75	0	0	0	-2.61	0	$-.03$	0	0	1	0	2.61	$-.62$	10,275,000
0	s_6	1	0	0	0	0	0	0	0	0	0	1	0	0	100,000
1.20	x_2	0	1	0	0	-1	0	0	0	0	0	0	1	0	6,000
1.60	x_4	0	0	0	1	0	0	0	0	0	0	0	0	1	1,000,000
	$c_j - z_j$	$-.85$	0	0	0	$-.37$	0	$-.02$	0	0	0	0	$-M + .37$	$-.23$	2,702,200

5.22 Refer to the portfolio selection problem in the Solved Problem section at the end of Chapter 2. The United Credit Union has done an LP analysis of its model and has the following LP computer output with sensitivity analysis.

```
MAX      7.5 MBONDS + 6.5 GBONDS + 11.9 OIL + 8.8 COAL + 10 AUTO
SUBJECT TO
    2)    0.2 MBONDS + 6 OIL + 4.5 COAL + 5 AUTO <=   1500000
    3)    MBONDS + GBONDS >=   100000
    4) - 0.3 MBONDS + 0.7 GBONDS >=    0
    5)    COAL <=   250000
    6)    MBONDS + GBONDS + OIL + COAL + AUTO =      500000
```

```
LP OPTIMUM FOUND AT STEP        7

        OBJECTIVE FUNCTION VALUE

    1)      4746928.00

VARIABLE          VALUE          REDUCED COST
  MBONDS     179180.900000         .000000
  GBONDS      76791.810000         .000000
     OIL     244027.300000         .000000
    COAL          .000000        1.896928
    AUTO          .000000        1.097952


   ROW    SLACK OR SURPLUS      DUAL PRICES
    2)          .000000         .802048
    3)     155972.700000         .000000
    4)          .000000        -.839590
    5)     250000.000000         .000000
    6)          .000000        7.087713

NO. ITERATIONS=        7

RANGES IN WHICH THE BASIS IS UNCHANGED:

                         OBJ COEFFICIENT RANGES
VARIABLE        CURRENT        ALLOWABLE        ALLOWABLE
                COEF           INCREASE         DECREASE
  MBONDS       7.500000        6.714286          .819999
  GBONDS       6.500000         .848275        21.446660
     OIL      11.900000       24.599980         1.323868
    COAL       8.800000        1.896928         INFINITY
    AUTO      10.000000        1.097952         INFINITY

                         RIGHTHAND SIDE RANGES
   ROW        CURRENT         ALLOWABLE         ALLOWABLE
              RHS             INCREASE          DECREASE
    2  1500000.000000    914000.000000   1430000.000000
    3   100000.000000    155972.700000         INFINITY
    4        .000000     175000.000000      77586.210000
    5   250000.000000         INFINITY     250000.000000
    6   500000.000000  10214290.000000    152333.300000
```

a. What is the compostion of its optimal portfolio?

b. What is the average rate of return on its portfolio?

c. What is the marginal value of its capital?

d. Over what range can the expected yield for each investment vary without changing the optimal basis?

e. Over what range can the available capital vary without affecting the optimal basis?

5.23 Refer to the Akron Tire Co. (Problem 2.22). Solve this rather large problem (48 variables and 18 constraints) with an LP computer code that has a sensitivity analysis output report to answer the following questions.

a. During which months and which shifts is the marginal value of vulcanizing time the highest?

b. In the month of October, over what range can the cost of steel-belted radials and glass-belted tires vary before the production schedule is no longer optimal?

c. Suppose there was a 10 percent reduction in the level of forecasted demand for all tires in each of the three months. Would this invalidate the optimal basic feasible solution?

d. What would be the effect of an increase in the cost of inventory from $4 to $5 per month per tire?

5.24 Solve the multiperiod production planning problem (Problem 2.25) using an LP computer package that has a sensitivity analysis output report. Answer the following questions.

a. In each of the six months, what is the marginal value of additional capital for the operating budget?

b. In view of what you found in part (a), what would you recommend to management regarding the constant budget of $150,000 per month?

c. Over what range can the budget for the first month vary before the optimal basis would have to change?

d. What is the least amount the inventory carrying cost could vary before the basis was no larger optimal?

e. Suppose management states that the LP solution requires excessive manpower variation between months. How would you modify the model to produce a more acceptable solution?

5.25 Solve the multiperiod investment planning problem (Problem 2.26) using an LP computer package that has a sensitivity analysis output report.

a. Interpret the shadow price of the constraint involving the availability of the $2,000,000.

b. Over what range can the $2,000,000 vary before the basis changes?

c. Interpret the shadow price of the borrowing constraint in the third time period. Would you argue for the raising of the debt limit?

d. What is the effective cost of capital or rate i at which you would be willing to borrow in each period? You should compare the net worth (after three years) of an extra dollar available in period t versus paying $(1 + i)$ dollars back in period $t + 1$.

BIBLIOGRAPHY

Anderson, David R., Dennis J. Sweeney, and Thomas A. Williams, *An Introduction to Management Science,* 5th ed. St. Paul, Minn.: West Publishing Company, 1988.

Charnes, Abraham, and W. W. Cooper, *Management Models and Industrial Applications of Linear Programming.* New York: John Wiley & Sons, Inc., 1961.

Dantzig, George B., *Linear Programming and Extensions.* Princeton, N.J.: Princeton University Press, 1963.

Eppen, G. D., F. J. Gould, and C. P. Schmidt, *Introductory Management Science,* 2nd ed. Englewood Cliffs, N.J.: Prentice Hall, 1987.

Gass, Saul I., *Linear Programming,* 5th ed. New York: McGraw-Hill Book Company, 1985.

Taha, H. A., *Operations Research: An Introduction,* 4th ed. New York: Macmillan Publishing Company, 1987.

Wagner, Harvey M., *Principles of Management Science with Applications to Executive Decisions.* Englewood Cliffs, N.J.: Prentice-Hall, 1975.

6

Distribution and Assignment Problems

GENERAL MOTORS CORPORATION[1]

A company the size of General Motors would understandably have a very
large and complex production planning and distribution problem. To help
in the management of production planning and distribution, GM decided
to use a specialized network model. The objective of the analysis was to
determine the number and type of each model of car to produce at each
plant and then to determine the distribution center to which each model
should be shipped.

The type of network model used is called a transshipment model,
and Figure 6.5 illustrates a simplified network model of the problem. The
transshipment model can be used to incorporate the various production
costs at each plant, as well as the transportation costs from plant to distribution center. The model also reflects the bounded production capacities
at each plant and the limits for each type of car model at each plant.

A typical application for the Pontiac or Buick division involves a
transshipment model with approximately 4,000 network arcs and 1,200
network nodes. Recently developed network algorithms enable a network
model of this size to be solved on a computer in less than 10 seconds.
This kind of speed enabled GM to develop an on-line computer capability.
The network model is linked to a graphics display terminal and an English

[1] F. Glover and D. Klingman, "Network Application in Industry and Government,"
AIIE Transactions, 9, no. 4 (1977), 363–376.

language input processor. Thus, the manager need not be an OR/MS expert to use the system. Management can feed in relevant data using the English language and within seconds observe the optimal solution on the display terminal. The system is a successful decision support system that is currently being used for planning purposes. If the model is slightly modified for other settings, it can be used in production and distribution of products other than cars. The model can also be used to handle decisions relevant to various stages of a production process.

SPECIALIZED LP MODELS

In this chapter, we explore three very special LP models. These models have a special type of model structure that lend themselves to ease in computational analysis. These models—called transportation, transshipment, and assignment models—are widely used in OR/MS applications.

These three models fall into the category of network models. Network models are quite useful, and Chapters 7 and 8 are also concerned with network-type models. A network is a collection of nodes connected by arcs or links. Figure 6.1 depicts a simple network. The nodes represent places or points in time, and the arcs represent routes or means over which entities can flow. Figure 6.1 shows a portion of a physical distribution network which could be helpful determining least cost ways of distributing products from sources to destinations.

Transportation and transshipment models are particularly useful in determining the best distribution or allocation of a product from origin to destination. We have just learned how a transshipment network model was useful to General Motors in producing and distributing its automobiles. Other successful network applications discussed in this book include projects by Agrico (Chapter 1), Citgo (Chapter 5), and Du Pont (Chapter 7). The

FIGURE 6.1 **A simple network**

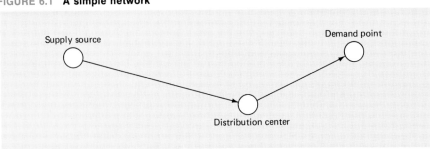

transportation and transshipment models are not limited to analyzing distribution systems. We shall also see how they are useful in production scheduling and the allocation of productive capacity over time.

special-
purpose
methods
The assignment problem is a special case of the transportation and transshipment models. It is concerned with the one-to-one assignment of one set of objects to another. The assignment model is useful in the matching of workers to jobs, jobs to machines, sales representatives to territories, and so on. It is often used as a submodel to more complex OR/MS models. Since transportation, transshipment, and assignment models can be solved by general-purpose LP codes, let us see why *special-purpose methods* have been developed and refined for solving this class of problems.

RATIONALE FOR SPECIAL-PURPOSE ALGORITHMS

algorithm
The transportation, transshipment, and assignment models we shall examine in this chapter are of the more common network models. They have many applications, both directly and as subproblems of even larger problems. They are LP models and thus can be solved by using a general-purpose LP computer code. However, these network models have a special mathematical structure that can be exploited to yield streamlined versions of the general simplex method. Taking advantage of special network structure can yield not only cost savings in terms of computation but also solutions to large-scale problems that are otherwise too large to be solved on contemporary computers by the general simplex method. These streamlined versions of the simplex method are special-purpose algorithms. An *algorithm* is a systematic procedure for arriving at a solution for a problem. The primary benefits of these special-purpose algorithms for transportation, transshipment, and assignment problems are as follows:

1. Computation time is generally 100 to 150 times faster than the general simplex method.
2. Significantly less computer memory is required, thus permitting even larger problems to be solved.
3. Transportation, transshipment, and assignment problems that have integer (whole-number) data yield integer solutions when solved by special-purpose algorithms.

This third factor is particularly important. Many real-world applications require whole-number solutions. For example, it is hard to ship half a car from Detroit or to build one-third of an airplane. Furthermore, general LP can yield noninteger solutions that deviate significantly from optimality when they are rounded off. Other general management science techniques that guarantee an integer solution, moreover, are usually inefficient and unable to solve large-scale problems.

In this chapter we emphasize the modeling and application of transportation, transshipment, and assignment problems. We present heuristics for solving the transportation problem in the next section. Specialized optimization methods for the transportation and assignment problems are presented in the supplement at the end of the chapter.

THE TRANSPORTATION PROBLEM

We begin our investigation of special LP models by looking at the Hitchcock-Koopman's transportation problem, named after its two formulators. The transportation model can be used to determine optimal shipping patterns. The model has many other applications, however; it is sometimes called the distribution problem.

EXAMPLE   The Faze Linear Company is very progressive and has already used LP to determine its optimal product mix (see Chapter 3). The company is now faced with the problem of how to distribute its electrical components from plants to regional warehouses. Faze Linear has plants located in Washington, D.C., Denver, and Los Angeles; regional warehouses are located in New York, Chicago, Dallas, and San Francisco (see Figure 6.2). This month, the company has available 50 units at Washington, 80 units at Denver, and 120 units at Los Angeles. To meet predicted demand, Faze Linear must ship 90 units to New York, 70 to Chicago, 40 to Dallas, and 50 to San Francisco. Relevant per unit transportation costs for each component as well as demand and supply data are given in Table 6.1. Faze Linear wants to determine the shipping pattern that meets all demand at minimum transportation cost.

TABLE 6.1   *Data for Faze Linear distribution problem*

	Shipping costs				
	To warehouse				
From plant	New York	Chicago	Dallas	San Francisco	*Supply*
Washington, D.C.	$ 8	$ 9	$11	$16	50
Denver	12	7	5	8	80
Los Angeles	14	10	6	7	120
Demand	90	70	40	50	

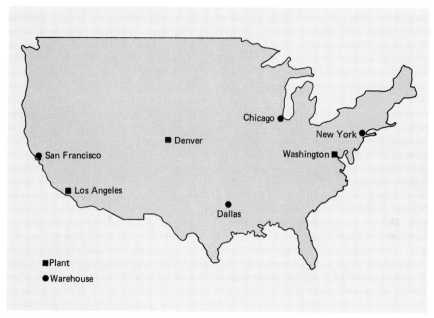

FIGURE 6.2 **Location of plants and warehouses for Faze Linear**

The network graph of the Faze Linear transportation problem is shown in Figure 6.3. The nodes of the network represent plants (origins) or warehouses (destinations). The numbers beside the nodes represent amount of supply available at the plant or the amount of demand at a warehouse. The numbers in the rectangles on the arcs represent per unit shipping costs from plant to warehouse. Network graphs are useful in modeling since they help the analyst to visualize the nature of the problem.

The Faze Linear distribution problem is actually an LP problem. To formulate it let x_{ij} denote the amount to be shipped from plant i to warehouse j, where $i = 1, 2, 3$ and $j = 1, 2, 3, 4$. In this notation, x_{23} represents the number of units to be shipped from Denver to Dallas. Notice that the first subscript refers to the row (plant) in Table 6.1 and the second subscript refers to the column (warehouse). Each of the x_{ij} decision variables also corresponds to an arc in the network graph. For example, variable x_{23} represents the amount of flow on the arc leading from plant 2 to warehouse 3 in Figure 6.3.

The LP formulation of the Faze Linear transportation problem is as follows:

Minimize $8x_{11} + 9x_{12} + 11x_{13} + 16x_{14} + 12x_{21} + 7x_{22} + 5x_{23} + 8x_{24}$
$+ 14x_{31} + 10x_{32} + 6x_{33} + 7x_{34}$

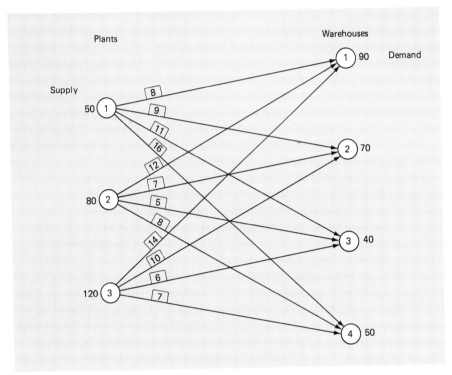

FIGURE 6.3 **Network graph of transportation problem**

$$\text{subject to} \quad x_{11} + x_{12} + x_{13} + x_{14} = 50$$

$$x_{21} + x_{22} + x_{23} + x_{24} = 80$$

$$x_{31} + x_{32} + x_{33} + x_{34} = 120$$

$$x_{11} + x_{21} + x_{31} = 90$$

$$x_{12} + x_{22} + x_{32} = 70$$

$$x_{13} + x_{23} + x_{33} = 40$$

$$x_{14} + x_{24} + x_{34} = 50$$

$$x_{ij} \geq 0; \; i = 1, 2, 3; \; j = 1, 2, 3, 4$$

modified distribution (MODI) method

The foregoing model can be solved directly using the general simplex method. However, streamlined procedures are available that offer the three benefits described earlier in this chapter. Charnes and Cooper developed the stepping-stone method, which was one of the first specialized simplex procedures for transportation problems. Later, Dantzig developed the *modified distribution,* or *MODI method,* which remains the best approach for solving transportation problems. Computational researchers have further refined the MODI method so that really significant computational savings can be achieved. For instance, transportation problems that have 1,000 plants and 1,000 warehouses (that is, 1 million decision variables) have been solved in 14 seconds or so on a CDC 6600 computer. Problems of this size are not even solvable without using special-purpose algorithms.

We can generalize transportation problems to include more than plants and warehouses. We may so interpret any situation in which a homogeneous product is available in the amounts $a_1, a_2, \ldots, a_m$ at m sources $1, 2, \ldots, m$, respectively. Furthermore, demands $b_1, b_2, \ldots, b_n$ are present at n destinations $1, 2, \ldots, n$, respectively. The transportation cost per unit from the ith source to the jth destination is a known constant, c_{ij}, and directly proportional to the amount shipped. Letting x_{ij} again represent the amount shipped from source i to destination j, we obtain the general transportation model

$$\text{Minimize} \quad \sum_{i=1}^{m} \sum_{j=1}^{n} c_{ij} x_{ij}$$

$$\text{subject to} \quad \sum_{j=1}^{n} x_{ij} = a_i, \quad i = 1, 2, \ldots, m,$$

$$\sum_{i=1}^{m} x_{ij} = b_j, \quad j = 1, 2, \ldots, n,$$

$$x_{ij} \geq 0 \text{ for } i = 1, 2, \ldots, m; j = 1, 2, \ldots, n$$

It is assumed that total supply equals total demand; that is,

$$\sum_{i=1}^{m} a_i = \sum_{j=1}^{n} b_j.$$

We shall find that this assumption can easily be circumvented by adding a dummy source or destination.

SOLVING TRANSPORTATION PROBLEMS HEURISTICALLY

In this section, we consider two heuristics for obtaining good but not necessarily optimal solutions for the transportation problem. Even though optimization methods such as the MODI method are usually used in real applications, heuristics are useful for two reasons. First, heuristics can provide an effective initial solution for optimization methods such as the MODI method. Second, heuristics are widely used in OR/MS practice since optimization is impossible or impractical in many applications. The emerging field of artificial intelligence also makes extensive use of heuristics. Heuristics usually reflect a human's insightful or intuitive approach to solving a problem.

heuristic   A *heuristic* is a rule-of-thumb procedure that determines a good, but not necessarily optimal, solution to a problem. The simplex method, for example, is not heuristic since it is an optimization technique that guarantees the optimal solution, provided one exists. Heuristic solutions are usually obtained much faster and thus at lower cost. These simple rules of thumb can also be performed by hand sometimes, thus eliminating the need to use a computer. On the other hand, heuristics cannot be considered as accurate as optimization techniques since an optimal solution is not guaranteed. A good heuristic is generally within 10 percent of optimality, but the great disadvantage of using a heuristic is that the amount of error is not known. That is, if you use a heuristic that has not been thoroughly tested, you do not know whether your answer is 5, 10, or even 30 percent from the optimal solution.

Row Minimum Method

The row minimum heuristic is a very quick way to obtain a feasible solution to the transportation problem. Computational investigations have shown that it is one of the best heuristics with which to start the MODI method for optimizing. That is, the row minimum heuristic coupled with the MODI method can solve transportation problems faster than other procedures.

To explain the row minimum procedure, we need a transportation tableau. A table of this type is helpful in solving transportation problems, just as the simplex tableau is helpful in solving LP problems. Tableau 6.1

TABLEAU 6.1   *Transportation tableau for Faze Linear*

From \ To	New York	Chicago	Dallas	San Francisco	Supply
Washington	8	9	11	16	50
Denver	12	7	5	8	80
Los Angeles	14	10	6	7	120
Demand	90	70	40	50	250

illustrates a transportation tableau for the Faze Linear problem. The usual practice in these tableaus is to list the sources as rows and the destinations as columns. The available supply for each source is listed in the far right column, and the required demands at each destination are summarized in the bottom row. The per unit transportation cost for shipping from source to destination is found in the upper left-hand corner of the square in the row associated with the source and the column associated with the destination. For example, the per unit transportation cost from the Los Angeles source to the Chicago destination is $10. The 12 squares (or *cells*) formed by the three sources and four destinations correspond to direct routes over which shipments can take place. In any feasible solution, the sum of the shipments across any row must not exceed the supply available, and the sum of the shipments down any column must satisfy the demand required.

cells

Unlike some other "quick and dirty" transportation heuristics, the row minimum rule does not ignore the costs for the various shipments. As the name implies, the row minimum heuristic proceeds by trying to assign shipments to the minimum-cost cell in each row. The process starts in row 1, continues to row 2, and so on, until all supply is exhausted and all demand is satisfied. To summarize the procedure,

1. Find the minimum-cost cell in row 1. If there is a tie, make an arbitrary choice. Allocate as much supply as possible to this cell. The maximum allocation is determined by the supply available and the demand required by the source and destination associated with this minimum-cost cell.
2. Delete the row (or column) whose supply (or demand) has just been exhausted by the allocation in the previous step.
3. Proceed to the next row that has not been deleted and find the minimum-cost cell. Again, make an allocation and delete the appropriate row or column.
4. Repeat step 3 until all supply is exhausted and all demand is satisfied. Whenever the last row in the tableau is reached, the process returns to the first row in the tableau for the next execution of step 3.

For the Faze Linear problem, the row minimum solution is shown in Tableau 6.2. The number added to a cell represents the shipment to be made from the associated source to destination. In this example, the row minimum procedure started in row 1 and made an allocation of 50 to the minimum-cost cell (1, 1). We shall use the notation (i, j) to denote the cell associated with source i and destination j. Row 1 has its supply exhausted and is deleted. Proceeding to the second row, we find that cell (2, 3), with a cost of 5, is minimal. Thus, 40 units is allocated to cell (2, 3), and column 3 is deleted. Proceeding to the third row, we find cell (3, 3), at a cost of 6, is minimal, but it is not available since column 3 has been deleted. Thus we allocate 50 units

TABLEAU 6.2 *Row minimum solution for Faze Linear*

To (j) / From (i)	New York	Chicago	Dallas	San Francisco	Supply
Washington	8 / 50	9	11	16	50
Denver	12	7 / 40	5 / 40	8	80
Los Angeles	14 / 40	10 / 30	6	7 / 50	120
Demand	90	70	40	50	250

to the next minimum-cost cell (3, 4). Since row 1 is deleted, we return to row 2 and allocate 40 units to cell (2, 2). This deletes row 2, and we again proceed to row 3, allocating 30 units to cell (3, 2) and then 40 units to cell (3, 1). This deletes all three rows and also satisfies all required demand. The cost of the row minimum solution is found by multiplying each shipment by its per unit transportation cost. The row minimum cost is $8(50) + 7(40) + 5(40) + 14(40) + 10(30) + 7(50) = \$2,090$.

Vogel's Approximation Method (VAM)

Vogel's approximation heuristic generally (though not always) yields a better solution than the row minimum rule. However, more calculations are involved, and thus, more total computation time is required when VAM is used with the MODI method to obtain an optimal solution. VAM can be used when the decision maker is satisfied with obtaining a good heuristic solution that is not necessarily optimal.

VAM is an interesting heuristic that can be applied to problems other than transportation problems. The basic idea in VAM is to avoid shipments that have a high cost. The row minimum method is somewhat shortsighted in that it simply assigns to the lowest-cost cell available *in a particular row;* this can cause high costs to be incurred in other rows. VAM looks at the opportu-

opportunity nity cost of not assigning to the minimum-cost cell in a row or column of the
loss transportation tableau. The *opportunity loss* is conservatively estimated to be the difference in cost between the lowest and next lowest-cost cells in that particular row or column. Then, assignment is made to the minimum-cost cell in the row or column that has the highest potential opportunity loss. If we view the opportunity loss as a possible penalty, the idea is to avoid a high penalty. This assignment then avoids incurring the highest opportunity loss.

The details of VAM are presented as follows:

1. For each row, calculate the potential opportunity loss as the difference between the minimum-cost cell and the next lowest-cost cell in that row.

2. For each column, calculate the potential opportunity loss as the difference between the minimum-cost cell and the next lowest-cost cell in that column.

3. Find the highest potential opportunity loss from among all rows and columns, and find the minimum-cost cell associated with that row or column. If a tie exists in opportunity losses among rows and columns, break the tie arbitrarily.

4. Allocate the maximum possible amount of supply to the minimum-cost cell in step 3; this will delete a row or column. Reduce the supplies and demands appropriately.

5. If a row has been deleted, recalculate the column opportunity losses. If a column has been deleted, recalculate the row opportunity losses.

6. If all allocations have been made, stop. Otherwise, begin another iteration by returning to step 3.

Let us apply the VAM procedure to the Faze Linear distribution problem. The VAM heuristic begins by calculating the potential opportunity losses of not assigning to the lowest-cost cell in each row and column. The beginning calculations are shown in Tableau 6.3. There you see that the

TABLEAU 6.3 *Initial VAM calculations for Faze Linear*

Row opportunity costs	Column opportunity costs		4	2	1	1	
	From	To	New York	Chicago	Dallas	San Francisco	Supply
1	Washington		8 50	9	11	16	50
2	Denver		12	7	5	8	80
1	Los Angeles		14	10	6	7	120
	Demand		90 40	70	40	50	250

TABLEAU 6.4   Second iteration for Faze Linear VAM

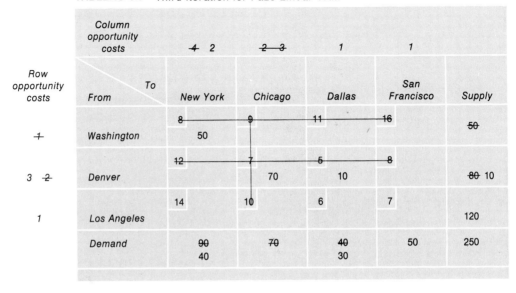

Column opportunity costs		4̶ 2	2̶ 3	1	1	
Row opportunity costs	From \ To	New York	Chicago	Dallas	San Francisco	Supply
1̶	Washington	8̶ 50	9̶	1̶1̶	1̶6̶	5̶0̶
2	Denver	12	7̶ 70	5	8	8̶0̶ 10
1	Los Angeles	14	1̶0	6	7	120
	Demand	9̶0̶ 40	7̶0̶	40	50	250

highest opportunity loss is 4, which is associated with column 1. This means that if we do not ship in the least-cost cell in this column ($8 per unit), we will have to ship in a cell that has a cost of at least $4 per unit more. In fact, the additional cost would be either $4 or $6, per unit. Thus, we allocate all the supply possible, which is 50 units, to cell (1, 1), which has the minimum cost

TABLEAU 6.5   Third iteration for Faze Linear VAM

Column opportunity costs		4̶ 2	2̶ 3̶	1	1	
Row opportunity costs	From \ To	New York	Chicago	Dallas	San Francisco	Supply
1̶	Washington	8̶ 50	9̶	1̶1̶	1̶6̶	5̶0̶
3̶ 2̶	Denver	1̶2̶	7̶ 70	5̶ 10	8̶	8̶0̶ 10
1	Los Angeles	14	1̶0	6	7	120
	Demand	9̶0̶ 40	7̶0̶	4̶0̶ 30	50	250

TABLEAU 6.6 *Final solution for Faze Linear VAM*

Column opportunity costs	~~4~~ ~~2~~ 0	~~2~~ ~~3~~	~~1~~ 0	~~1~~ 0	
Row opportunity costs / From \ To	New York	Chicago	Dallas	San Francisco	Supply
~~1~~ Washington	8 \ 50	9	11	16	~~50~~
~~3~~ ~~2~~ Denver	12	7 \ 70	5 \ 10	8	~~80~~ ~~10~~
~~7~~ ~~1~~ Los Angeles	14 \ 40	10	6 \ 30	7 \ 50	~~120~~ ~~80~~ 40
Demand	~~90~~ 40	~~70~~	~~40~~ ~~30~~	~~50~~	~~250~~

of $8. The supply for row 1 is exhausted; so we draw a line through the costs in row 1 as a reminder that these costs are no longer usable in calculating opportunity losses.

Tableau 6.4 shows the results we get when we recalculate the column opportunity losses for the next iteration. The highest opportunity loss is now 3 and is associated with column 2. Thus, we allocate all we can to the lowest-cost cell (2, 2); this allocation is 70 units, which is all the demand that is required in column 2. We adjust the supplies and demands, delete column 2 by drawing a line through its costs, and update the row opportunity losses in Tableau 6.5.

This time, the largest opportunity loss is the 3 associated with row 2. Allocating the available 10 units deletes row 2 and leaves only row 3 with available supply. Three more iterations are required to reach the final VAM solution. The final tableau is shown in Tableau 6.6.

The distribution cost of the VAM solution is 8(50) + 7(70) + 5(10) + 14(40) + 6(30) + 7(50) = $2,030, which is $60 lower than the row minimum solution. Usually, VAM provides at least as good a solution as row minimum, although not always.

FURTHER APPLICATIONS OF TRANSPORTATION MODELS

The utility of the transportation problem is that it may be applied to more than just transportation and distribution problems. Other fruitful areas of application are production scheduling and inventory storage problems. For illustrative purposes, let us consider the following case of the El Paso Slacks Company.

EXAMPLE   The El Paso Slacks Company produces a particular style of pants that is subject to demand fluctuations throughout the year. To smooth production costs, the company produces some excess during seasons when demand volume lessens and stores the pants as inventory for the season when demand is high. The production capacity is 120,000 pairs of pants per season except summer, when employee vacations reduce production capacity to 110,000 pairs. The marketing department has forecast sales for each season; figures are shown in Table 6.2. There are two types of costs; production and inventory storage. The per unit production cost is $5 per pair of pants during the first two seasons, but inflation is expected to raise production cost to $6 in fall and winter. As inventory, the pants can be stored for several months. However, it costs $1 per quarter to store them, and due to style changes, all pants should be delivered to retailers by the end of the year. No backlogging is allowed. The company is planning ahead and wants to know which production schedule minimizes combined production and inventory costs for the year.

The problem is legitimately modeled as a transportation problem, and the particulars are shown in Tableau 6.7. The rows of the tableau indicate quarterly production capacity, and the columns indicate quarterly demand. The costs in each cell indicate per unit production costs plus whatever unit storage costs apply. For instance, in cell (1, 4), which represents spring production for winter consumption, the cost is $8 = $5 production cost + $3 storage cost (for three quarters). Cell (3, 3) has a cost of $6 = $6 production cost + 0 storage cost. The crossed-out cells are impermissible cells because consumption cannot possibly precede production.

Solving this transportation model yields an optimum production and inventory storage schedule for the El Paso Slacks Company. The solution would be rendered in production and storage amounts rather than shipments from sources to destinations.

TABLE 6.2   *El Paso slacks sales forecast data (thousands)*

Season	Forecast demand	Production capacity
Spring	110	120
Summer	90	110
Fall	140	120
Winter	115	120
	455	470

TABLEAU 6.7 *El Paso Slacks Company problem*

Season	Spring	Summer	Fall	Winter	Excess capacity	Production capacity
Spring	5	6	7	8	0	120
Summer		5	6	7	0	110
Fall			6	7	0	120
Winter				6	0	120
Demand	110	90	140	115	15	470

THE TRANSSHIPMENT PROBLEM

The transshipment problem is sometimes called the minimum-cost network flow problem. It is the most general of the linear network models and contains transportation and assignment models as special cases. Its solution methodology is very similar to the transportation MODI method and hence will not be discussed.[2] Instead, we will focus on formulation and applications.

The transshipment model differs from the transportation model in that it allows nodes or points which are neither pure origins or pure destinations. In network terminology, a node that has all of its arcs leading away from the *source* node is called a *source*. A node that has all arcs leading into it is called a *sink* *sink*. The origins and destinations of a transportation problem are sources and sinks, respectively. Transshipment models allow another kind of node *transshipment* called a transshipment point. A *transshipment point* has arcs leading into *point* and out of the node. Source nodes can be thought of as having supply available; sink nodes typically represent demand points. Transshipment nodes can have a supply, or demand; they can also have a supply or demand of zero. In any case a transshipment node represents a point through which flow can pass on the way to other nodes in the network. Transshipment nodes allow us to model many interesting applications that can not be represented with only sources and sinks.

[2] In fact, any transshipment model can be reformulated as an equivalent transportation model and solved by the MODI method. However, transshipment algorithms are as efficient as the MODI method.

EXAMPLE: AGRICO DISTRIBUTION PROBLEM   To illustrate the transshipment model, let's consider a simplified version of the Agrico product distribution problem discussed in Chapter 1. (Recall that the actual problem had 4 production plants, 78 distribution centers, and approximately 2,000 customers.) In Figure 6.4, the nodes represent supply sites, distribution centers, and demand sites in the Agrico distribution system. The arcs (arrows) indicate the possible ways to ship goods from supply sites to distribution centers and from these to demand sites. The orientation of an arc (direction of the arrow) indicates the allowable direction of shipment.

In addition to nodes and arcs, transshipment models commonly have five data components: supplies, demands, costs, lower bounds, and upper bounds. Supplies and demands are associated with nodes, while costs, lower bounds, and upper bounds are associated with arcs. Supplies available are shown as positive numbers next to the source nodes. Thus, nodes 1 and 2 have supplies of 29 and 36, respectively. Demands are shown as negative numbers associated with nodes 5, 6, and 7, the sink nodes. The distribution centers (nodes 4 and 5) are transshipment nodes and in this case have no supply or demand.

The per unit shipping cost between a pair of nodes is given in the rectangle attached to the arc that connects the nodes. The upper and lower bounds are in parenthesis on an arc and indicate the allowable size of the shipment between a pair of nodes. For instance, the minimum shipment from node 1 to node 4 is 8 units, and the maximum shipment is 20 units.

The lower bound on an arc allows the network model to incorporate such features as contractual agreements to ship at least a certain amount of product between locations. The upper bound on an arc can be used to

FIGURE 6.4 **Network diagram of Agrico facilities**

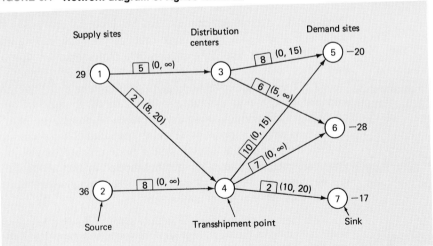

capture such things as management policies on shipment sizes or physical limitations such as vehicle or pipeline capacity.

LP Formulation of the Problem

The objective in any transshipment problem is to ship the available supply through the network to satisfy all demand at minimal cost. To formulate the transshipment problem shown in Figure 6.4 as an LP, define the following decision variables:

$$x_{ij} = \text{amount of flow from node } i \text{ to node } j$$

Each x_{ij} variable corresponds to an arc in the network. The constraints are similar to the transportation model constraints in that there is a constraint associated with each node. In the transshipment model, these node constraints are flow conservation or Kirchoff equations. These equations can be summarized as requiring that for each node

total flow out $-$ total flow in $=$ node supply (demand)

To illustrate, consider node 3 in Figure 6.4. Decision variables x_{35} and x_{36} represents total flow out of node 3. Variable x_{13} represents flow into node 3. Thus the flow conservation equation for node 3 is

$$x_{35} + x_{36} - x_{13} = 0$$

since node 3 has zero supply or demand.

Formulating the objective function and constraints we have the following LP model for the simplified Agrico network problem:

$$
\begin{aligned}
\text{Minimize} \quad & 5x_{13} + 2x_{14} + 8x_{24} + 8x_{35} + 6x_{36} + 10x_{45} + 7x_{46} + 2x_{47} \\
\text{subject to} \quad & x_{13} + x_{14} & = 29 \\
& x_{24} & = 36 \\
& -x_{13} + x_{35} + x_{36} & = 0 \\
& -x_{14} - x_{24} + x_{45} + x_{46} + x_{47} & = 0 \\
& -x_{35} - x_{45} & = -20 \\
& -x_{36} - x_{46} & = -28 \\
& -x_{47} & = -17
\end{aligned}
$$

$$0 \le x_{13}$$

$$8 \le x_{14} \le 20$$

$$0 \le x_{24}$$

$$0 \le x_{35} \le 15$$

$$5 \le x_{36}$$

$$0 \le x_{45} \le 15$$

$$0 \le x_{46}$$

$$10 \le x_{47} \le 20$$

The first seven constraints are the flow conservation constraints, and the last constraints are the upper- and lower-bound constraints. Optimization algorithms for the transshipment problem can handle the upper and lower bounds implicitly thereby treating the model as an LP with seven explicit constraints.

The special mathematical structure of the transshipment problem facilities very efficient solution algorithms. Some of the special structure is evident in examining the node-arc incidence matrix, which is simply the matrix of the model constraint coefficients. Table 6.3 shows the fact that each decision variable (arc) has precisely one $+1$ and one -1 coefficient in its column of the matrix. The $+1$ coefficient is in the row corresponding to the node in which the arc originates. The -1 coefficient is in the row corresponding to the node in which the arc terminates. All other entries in any column are zero. The fact that all coefficients are zero or ± 1 together with a "triangular basis property" allow the transshipment problem always to have an integer solution provided the RHS is all integer.

TABLE 6.3 *Node-arc incidence matrix*

Node	Arc								RHS
	x_{13}	x_{14}	x_{24}	x_{35}	x_{36}	x_{45}	x_{46}	x_{47}	
1	1	1	0	0	0	0	0	0	29
2	0	0	1	0	0	0	0	0	26
3	−1	0	0	1	1	0	0	0	0
4	0	−1	−1	0	0	1	1	1	0
5	0	0	0	−1	0	−1	0	0	−20
6	0	0	0	0	−1	0	−1	0	−28
7	0	0	0	0	0	0	0	−1	−17

General Formulation of the Transshipment Model

To formulate a general model for the transshipment problem, define the following:

$$N = \text{set of all arcs in the network}$$
$$n = \text{number of nodes in network}$$
$$x_{ij} = \text{amount of flow from node } i \text{ to node } j$$
$$c_{ij} = \text{per unit cost of flow from node } i \text{ to node } j$$
$$l_{ij} = \text{lower bound on flow from node } i \text{ to node } j$$
$$u_{ij} = \text{upper bound on flow from node } i \text{ to node } j$$
$$b_j = \text{supply (demand) at node } j$$

Additionally, let (i, j) denote an arc in the network.

The transshipment model can be stated as

$$\text{Minimize} \quad \sum_{(i, j) \in N} c_{ij} \, x_{ij} \tag{6.2}$$

$$\text{subject to} \quad \sum_{(j, k) \in N} x_{jk} - \sum_{(k, j) \in N} x_{kj} = b_j, \quad j = 1, \ldots, n$$

$$l_{ij} \leq x_{ij} \leq u_{ij}, \quad \text{all } (i, j) \in N$$

The general model assumes that $\sum_{j=1}^{n} b_j = 0$; that is, the total supply equals the total demand. If total supply and demand are not equal, a "dummy" source or sink must be added to the network to artificially balance supply and demand.

Production and Distribution Planning at GM

As a final application of the transshipment model, let us look at a simplified version of the General Motors production/distribution planning problem from the chapter's opening scenario. Figure 6.5 depicts the simplified transshipment model of the GM problem.

Standard transportation and transshipment models assume that there is a homogeneous commodity to be shipped. In the GM example, however, there are multiple car models to be distributed, and the problem is multicommodity in nature. A unique feature of the transshipment model in Figure 6.5 is that it handles multicommodities within a single-commodity problem structure.

Looking at Figure 6.5 the Oklahoma City and L.A. nodes are source nodes (plants) and the Pittsburgh and Chicago nodes are sink nodes (regional distribution centers). The other nodes are transshipment nodes and are la-

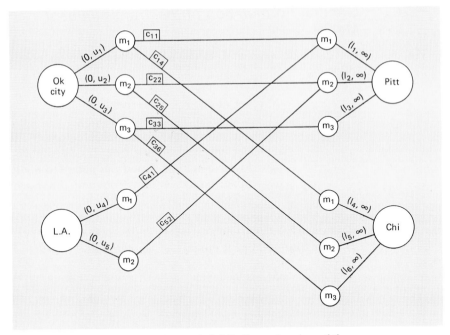

FIGURE 6.5 **Production planning and distribution network model**

beled m_1, m_2, or m_3 depending on the car model type they represent. Notice that m_1-type nodes connect only to other type m_1 nodes. The upper and lower bounds on the arcs leading out of the sources and into the sinks serve a useful purpose. For example, the upper bound of u_1 on the arc leading from Oklahoma City to m_1 represents the capacity of the Oklahoma City plant to produce m_1 type cars. Similarly, the lower bound of l_1 on the arc leading from m_1 to Pittsburgh represents the amount of demand for m_1-type cars at the Pittsburgh regional distribution center. Together the upper and lower bounds ensure that production capacities are not exceeded while demand levels are met.

THE ASSIGNMENT PROBLEM

The assignment problem is another special LP problem. It has a wide range of applications and, like the transportation and transshipment problems, is solvable by a special-purpose algorithm that is much more efficient than the regular simplex method.

The assignment problem is closely related to the transportation problem; in fact, it is a special case of the transportation problem. However, the

TABLE 6.4   *Cost data ($) for assigning jobs to machines*

	Machine		
Job	A	B	C
1	57	42	65
2	39	48	46
3	43	72	53

basic idea is to assign n single elements rather than many units from each source to destination. Some typical applications of the assignment problem include the least-cost or least-time assignment of jobs to machines, workers to tasks, salespersons to territories, and contracts to contractors. The assignment method is also used to solve subproblems of even larger and more involved management science models.

To illustrate the assignment problem, let us consider the Ace Machine Shop problem, whose data are presented in Table 6.4. Three jobs (1, 2, and 3) must be processed by the machine shop. Any of the three jobs can be processed on any of the three machines. However, each job is to be processed on only one machine, and each machine can be assigned only one job. Thus a solution will define a one-to-one correspondence between jobs and machines. The processing costs vary from machine to machine, as indicated in Table 6.4. The optimal solution is shown in Tableau 6.8. As indicated by the white, boldface numbers in Tableau 6.8, the least-cost solution is to assign job 1 to machine B, job 2 to machine C, and job 3 to machine A. The total cost of the assignment is $42 + 46 + 43 = $131. The Ace Machine Shop problem illustrates the characteristics of assignment problems. Notice in Tableau 6.8 that precisely one assignment occurs in each row and each

TABLEAU 6.8   *Optimal solution for Ace Machine Shop problem*

	Machine		
Job	A	B	C
1	57	42	65
2	39	48	46
3	43	72	53

column. Also, the problem is square in that there are an equal number of rows and columns. We can describe the assignment model as a transportation model with an equal number of sources and destinations and all supplies and demands equal to 1.

In general, if we have n jobs to be assigned to n machines, we can state the mathematical model of the assignment problem as

$$\text{Minimize} \quad \sum_{i=1}^{n} \sum_{j=1}^{n} c_{ij} x_{ij} \tag{6.3}$$

$$\text{subject to} \quad \sum_{j=1}^{n} x_{ij} = 1, \quad i = 1, 2, \ldots, n$$

$$\sum_{i=1}^{n} x_{ij} = 1, \quad j = 1, 2, \ldots, n$$

$$x_{ij} \geq 0 \quad \text{for all } i \text{ and } j$$

where c_{ij} equals the cost of assigning job i to machine j. In solving the assignment model, n of the x_{ij} variables are in solution at a value of 1 and all other x_{ij} equal 0.

The assignment model is a special case of the transportation model; this can be seen by comparing systems (6.1) and (6.3). The assignment problem can be solved by using a transportation method such as the MODI method. However, the resulting solution would be highly degenerate (it would contain $n - 1$ degenerate cells), and even faster and more efficient techniques are available for solving assignment problems. One of these optimization methods, called the Hungarian Method, is presented in the supplement at the end of the chapter.

COMPUTER IMPLICATIONS

Of all the mathematical programming models, linear network models are among the easiest to solve. Even though transportation, transshipment, and assignment models can be solved by the general simplex method, specialized algorithms can solve these models much more efficiently and with significantly less computer memory.

The implications of these efficiencies are far reaching. Large-scale problems which otherwise could not be solved are solvable using network algorithms. For example, the U.S. Department of the Treasury constructed a transportation model to merge population survey files. The resulting network had 62.5 million arcs (variables) and 50,000 nodes (constraints). Using a state-of-the-art transportation algorithm on a high-speed computer, the problem was solved in approximately one hour.

The efficiency of network algorithms also means that small and medium-sized problems can be solved in reasonable times on mini- and microcomputers. Thus, network models can be used to support on-line or real-time decision support systems in which a very fast response is required.

netform The computational efficiency of network models has led some re-
concept searchers to advocate a "netform concept," whose philosophy is to exploit network structure from a problem whenever possible. Some mathematical programming problems are not pure network problems, but have some network substructure. Exploiting the network substructure by embedding a network algorithm in the overall solution procedure can possibly yield significant computational efficiency and in some cases can yield solutions to previously unsolvable problems. This is especially true in integer programming where the integrality property of linear networks can help yield integer solutions.

SUMMARY

Network models are very important and have widespread applications. Transportation, transshipment, and assignment models are linear network models with a special structure that considerably simplifies their computation.

Transportation problems can be solved by heuristic methods, such as row minimum or VAM (Vogel's approximation method), that are fast and yield good, but not necessarily optimal, solutions. The MODI method can be used to take a starting feasible solution from row minimum or VAM and improve it to optimality. Transshipment models can be reformulated as a transportation problem and solved by the MODI method. However, transshipment optimization algorithms exist which are similar to and as efficient as the MODI method. An important characteristic of transportation and transshipment models is that integer parameters yield integer solutions. Applications other than physical distribution exist for transportation and transshipment models; among these are production scheduling and inventory planning problems.

The assignment problem is a special case of the transportation problem. It is concerned with the optimal assignment or 1–1 matching of one set of entities to another. The Hungarian method (presented in the supplement) is an efficient procedure for determining optimal solutions to assignment problems.

SOLVED PROBLEMS

PROBLEM STATEMENT

From warehouse	To city					
	1	2	3	4	5	Supply
1	1.50	1.65	2.05	1.40	1.35	800
2	1.60	2.10	1.80	1.65	2.00	1000
Demand	500	200	300	600	800	

The Burgraf Co. distributes its product from two warehouses to five major metropolitan areas. Next month's anticipated demand exceeds warehouse supplies and the management at Burgraf would like to know how to distribute its product to maximize revenue. Their distribution costs per unit are shown in the table. To be competitive Burgraf must charge a different price in the different cities. Selling prices are $9.95, $10.50, $9.50, $11.15, and $10.19 in cities 1, 2, 3, 4, and 5, respectively. The tableau of revenue = selling price − distribution cost is given as

From warehouse	To city					
	1	2	3	4	5	Supply
1	8.45	8.85	7.45	9.75	8.84	800
2	8.35	8.40	7.70	9.50	8.19	1000
Demand	500	200	300	600	800	

SOLUTION

Since this problem is a maximization rather than a minimization, we compute the opportunity costs for VAM as the difference between the most profitable cell and next most profitable cell in a row or column, and assign to the highest-profit cell in the row or column with the largest opportunity cost.

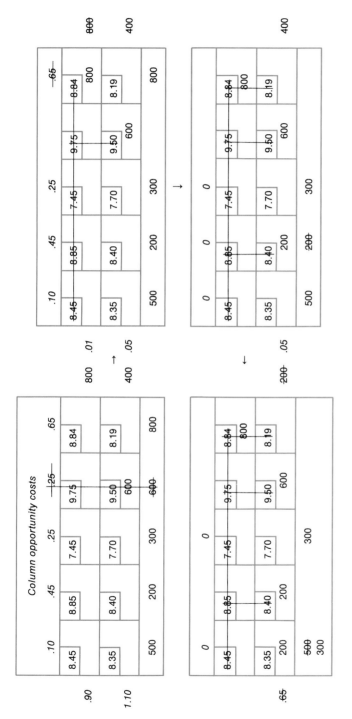

Summary of Results for Burgraf Co.   Page : 1

From	To	Shipment @ prft.	Opp.Ct.	From	To	Shipment @ prft.	Opp.Ct.
S1	D1	0	+8.4500	-.39000	S2	D4	+600.00	+9.5000	0
S1	D2	0	+8.8500	-.04000	S2	D5	0	+8.1900	-.16000
S1	D3	0	+7.4500	-1.3900	Dummy	D1	+300.00	0	0
S1	D4	0	+9.7500	-.24000	Dummy	D2	0	0	-.05000
S1	D5	+800.00	+8.4000	0	Dummy	D3	+300.00	0	0
S2	D1	+200.00	+8.3500	0	Dummy	D4	0	0	-1.1500
S2	D2	+200.00	+8.4000	0	Dummy	D5	0	0	0
S2	D3	0	+7.7000	-.65000					

Maximum value of OBJ = 16122 (multiple sols.)   Iterations = 3

The VAM solution in this example provides a feasible solution that is also optimal.

We can also verify the optimality of the solution by accessing a transportation computer package. The accompanying table shows the problem output from the transportation module of the QSB computer package. The total profit is $16,122. The S_i refer to sources and the D_i refer to the destinations. The "Dummy" represents the fictitious source that was added to balance supply and demand (for the optimization method).

PROBLEM STATEMENT

A distribution system consists of three plants, one warehouse, and four customer demand centers. Plants can ship directly to demand centers or transship through the warehouse. Supplies, demands, and shipping costs are

				Demand Center				
			Shipping Costs					
		Warehouse	1	2	3	4	Supply
Plants	1	$15	$22	$24	$27	$28	100 units
	2	10	25	23	26	27	150
	3	14	27	25	24	21	120
Demand (units)		0	80	100	90	100	

	Demand Center			
	1	2	3	4
Warehouse	$12	$11	$13	$14

The second table shows the shipping costs from the warehouse to the four demand centers. The following restrictions apply:

1. No single shipping link can handle more than 80 units.
2. The warehouse can handle no more than 90 units in total.

Draw the transshipment network graph representing the problem.

SOLUTION

The problem requires three plant nodes, four demand center nodes, one warehouse node, and one dummy node to limit the flow to 90 units from the warehouse. Arcs from plants to demand centers require an upper bound of 80. The upper bound on the arc from the warehouse node (*W*) to the dummy node is 90. Shipping costs are shown in the rectangles on the arcs.

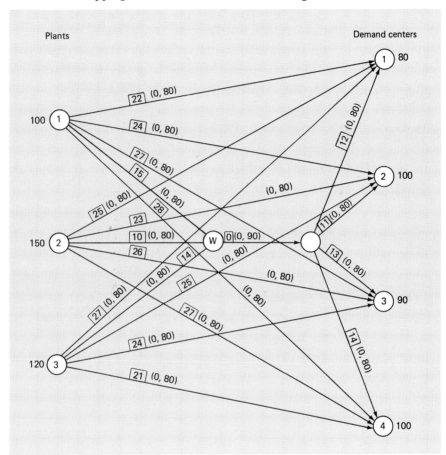

REVIEW QUESTIONS

1. Explain why transportation and assignment models are part of the category of network models.
2. What are the advantages of using special-purpose algorithms to solve transportation and assignment problems?
3. What are the advantages and disadvantages of using heuristics versus optimization techniques?
4. Why would you expect VAM usually to yield a better heuristic solution than the row minimum method?

5. Briefly discuss the theoretical basis of VAM.
6. List some applications of transportation models other than distribution of a commodity from plant to market.
7. Specifically, how does the assignment math model differ from the transportation math model?
8. What additional features of network flow problems can the transshipment model handle as compared to the transportation model?
9. List some applications of the assignment model.

PROBLEMS

6.1 *Product distribution.* The P & R Company distributes its product from three plants to four regional warehouses. The monthly supplies and demands along with per unit transportation costs are given in the table. Using the row minimum heuristic, find a feasible shipping pattern and total transportation cost.

	To warehouse				
From plant	1	2	3	4	Supply
1	2	12	6	10	20
2	14	6	2	12	10
3	18	8	10	8	25
Demand	11	13	17	14	55

6.2 Use VAM to solve Problem 6.1.

6.3 *Stock redistribution.* The Reasor Department Store chain has excess stock of a particular product at two stores and shortages at four others. The objective is to redistribute the stock at minimum transportation cost. Given the following stock and cost information, construct a network flow model to represent the problem and determine an effective solution.

Store	Excess	Shortage
1	50	
2	75	
3		20
4		30
5		45
6		30

	Cost data			
		To store		
From store	3	4	5	6
1	$7	$3	$5	$8
2	6	4	2	9

6.4 *Physical distribution.* Nationwide Distributors is trying to determine the most effective way to distribute its product to maximize profits. Its distribution costs from its three plants to their regional warehouses are shown in the table.

	To warehouse					
From plant	1	2	3	4	5	Supply
1	2.25	1.50	3.00	2.00	1.25	1000
2	3.15	2.75	1.00	1.95	1.60	1500
3	2.00	2.50	3.35	2.15	2.20	1200
Demand	800	600	1000	500	800	

The average selling price for the product at each warehouse is $9.75, $10.15, $9.95, $9.50, and $9.85, respectively. Determine the shipping pattern that maximizes revenue.

6.5 Solve the following transportation problem using VAM.

9	7	8	11	12	10	200
14	9	5	8	13	17	150
18	22	6	4	11	13	300
10	7	12	10	9	9	250
100	180	120	200	150	150	

6.6 *Court docket assignments.* A city government wants to improve the efficiency of the local court system. It has collected data on the average length of time a particular judge requires to handle each type of case. Given the composition of the types of cases scheduled on each docket, the times shown in the table were estimated for each judge to process each different docket. Determine the assignment of judges to dockets to minimize the time required to complete all dockets. Use QSB or another assignment software package.

		Docket			
		1	2	3	4
	1	13	20	17	18
Judge	2	15	19	18	13
	3	16	14	16	15
	4	14	15	18	17

6.7 *Production and distribution.* Consider a variation of the production/distribution example of Chapter 2. In this problem, it is necessary to address production, as well as transportation, costs in the transportation model. Assume that two plants have production capacities of 2,600 and 1,800, respectively. The three warehouses have demands of 1,500, 2,000, and 900. The product is produced at plant 1 at a per unit cost of $1.50, whereas the per unit cost at plant 2 is $2. Transportation costs are given in the table. Set up and solve a transportation model that determines the amount to produce at each plant and the resulting shipping pattern.

From plant	To warehouse			
	1	2	3	Supply
1	$.30	$.50	$.80	2,600
2	$.70	$.20	$.40	1,800
Demand	1,500	2,000	900	4,400

6.8 *Aggregate production planning.* The Yuba Manufacturing Co. is planning its aggregate production levels for the last quarter of the year and would like to minimize the combined cost of production and inventory. Production capacities for October, November, and December are 6,000, 6,000, and 4,000, respectively. The demand for the firm's product is expected to be 3,000, 7,000, and 5,000 during the last quarter. Given that per piece production cost is $3.00 and storage cost per month is $1.00, find a low-cost production/inventory schedule.

6.9 *Production scheduling.* The American Products Corporation must decide on its production schedule for the next four months. It has contracted to supply a special part for the months of October, November, December, and January at the rates of 12,000, 10,000, 15,000, and 17,000 units, respectively. American can produce each part at a cost of $6 during regular time or $9 during overtime. Each month, American has a production capacity of 10,000 units during regular time and 6,000 units during overtime. The part can be stored at a cost of $2 per month; however, there is zero inventory on hand at the beginning of October and there must be zero inventory at the end of January. American can thus overproduce in some months and store the excess to help meet future demand in other months. Construct a transportation model (tableau) to solve American's production scheduling and inventory storage problem. *Hint:* Define the sources as the modes of production in each month, and define the destinations as the demand required during each month.

6.10 *Least-time transportation model.* In the least-time transportation problem the objective is to minimize the maximum time required to complete any shipment. In a least-time transportation tableau the numbers in the cells represent times. The standard transportation objective function (6.1) is rewritten for the least-time model as minimize $z = \max \{t_{ij}\}$ such that $x_{ij} > 0$. The least-time problem corresponds, for example, to a military airlift operation in which it is desired to complete all operations as soon as possible.

Assume that the cost figures of the 4 × 6 tableau in Problem 6.5 corresponds to times. Devise your own procedure (heuristic or otherwise) to come up with a feasible solution that minimizes the maximum time of all cells with a positive shipment.

6.11 *Automobile distribution.* The Missan Sports Car Company produces several lines of automobiles, among which is its super racer, the 320ZX. These specialty cars are hand-assembled at each of four plants, in Boston, Cleveland, Denver, and Detroit. Missan currently has custom orders for one 320ZX at Chicago, Wichita, Tulsa, and Dallas. Each plant currently has one model ready for shipping. The transportation cost data are given in the table.

a. Which method is best for solving this problem?

b. Determine the optimal solution.

From \ To	Transportation cost per 320ZX			
	Chicago	Wichita	Tulsa	Dallas
Boston	$130	$240	$250	$300
Cleveland	40	210	220	270
Denver	150	110	115	125
Detroit	35	190	300	250

6.12 *Plant location.* The TDW Production Company is unable to meet its increased yearly demand because of production capacities. It is thinking about building a new factory to meet this new demand and also decrease transportation cost. The current production and distribution system is summarized below. The costs in the table indicate per unit transportation costs. The proposed new factory, *C*, would have a capacity of 2,000 and would have transportation costs of $3, $2.50, $4, and $2 to warehouses 1, 2, 3, and 4, respectively.

	Warehouse				
Factory	1	2	3	4	Factory capacity
A	$2.90	$2.60	$3.50	$4.00	2,500
B	3.10	3.30	3.70	3.00	1,500
Demand	1,000	1,500	2,000	500	4,000 / 5,000

The company is currently losing \$20 per unit on unsatisfied demand, since this is the profit it nets on each unit that is sold (not including transportation costs). However, the new factory would cost \$21,000 per year over the life of the factory. Evaluate TDW's proposal to add the new factory.

6.13 *Applicant selection.* The Psychological Testing Agency has recently tested seven applicants for five jobs that are available at the Coldman Company. Each job has a primary skill, and Coldman's objective is to pick the five applicants whose aptitude test scores will maximize total performance. Only one worker can be assigned to only one job. The aptitude test scores are listed below. Determine the five best applicants for the five jobs using QSB or another assignment package.

	Job				
Applicant	1	2	3	4	5
1	95	110	103	115	98
2	89	95	100	87	92
3	120	132	118	128	121
4	107	119	112	108	96
5	75	83	99	100	85
6	113	115	98	111	120
7	102	73	95	70	94

6.14 Construct the linear constraints of the transshipment model whose network diagram is shown in Solved Problem 2 at the end of the chapter.

6.15 Given the following transshipment model constraints, construct the associated node-arc incidence matrix and network diagram.

$$x_{12} + x_{13} = 20$$
$$-x_{12} - x_{42} + x_{23} = -10$$
$$-x_{13} - x_{23} - x_{53} = -8$$
$$x_{42} + x_{45} + x_{46} - x_{54} = 16$$
$$x_{53} + x_{54} + x_{57} - x_{45} = 0$$
$$-x_{46} - x_{76} = -12$$
$$x_{76} - x_{57} = -6$$

6.16 A company produces its product at two plant sites and distributes the product through three regional warehouses to four demand centers. The shipping costs per unit and the supply and demand data are as follows:

Plant \ Warehouse	Atlanta	Denver	Pittsburgh	Supply
Chicago	$26	$19	$20	1,500
Dallas	18	16	25	2,000

Warehouse \ Demand center	Miami	Kansas City	Houston	Philadelphia
Atlanta	$14	$22	$ 20	$16
Denver	32	17	21	28
Pittsburgh	19	18	23	8
Demand	800	950	1,000	750

Represent the distribution problem with a transshipment network graph. Solve the problem using QSB or any other transshipment software package.

6.17 A company has two manufacturing plants and three distribution centers. The company wishes to plan production, inventory, and distribution decisions over the next two planning periods. The unit shipping costs, production capacities, and production costs vary by time period and are given as follows:

Period 1

Capacity	Plant	Distribution center 1	2	3	
275	1	$25	$30	$22	
300	2	32	18	20	
		125	200	175	Demand

Period 2

Capacity	Plant	Distribution center 1	2	3	
250	1	$26	$30	$24	
270	2	33	19	21	
		175	240	150	Demand

Unit production cost

	Plant	
Period	1	2
1	$16	$14
2	18	15

The maximum that either plant can store in any period is 50 units, and the inventory holding cost is $1 per unit. Set up a network flow (transshipment) problem that can be used to minimize total production, distribution and inventory costs over the two-period planning horizon. *Hint:* Create a separate node for each location in each time period; inventory arcs are the only arcs to connect different time periods.

6.18 *Tire redistribution.* The Bottom Dollar Discount store chain has an excess supply of radial tires at some warehouses and a shortage at others. To get ready for its upcoming sale, it wants to redistribute its tire stock at minimum cost.

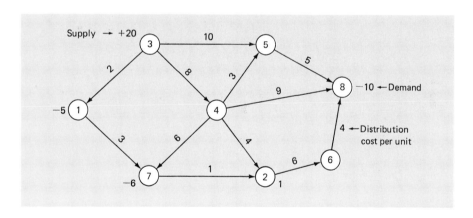

a. Use your ingenuity to determine an effective solution to the Bottom Dollar Discount distribution problem.

b. Use the QSB microcomputer package to determine the optimal solution.

BIBLIOGRAPHY

Bazaraa, Mokhtar S., and John J. Jarvis, *Linear Programming and Network Flows*. New York: John Wiley & Sons, Inc., 1977.

Charnes, Abraham, and W. W. Cooper, *Management Models and Industrial Applications of Linear Programming,* Vol. 1. New York: John Wiley and Sons, Inc., 1961.

Glover, F., and D. Klingman, "Network Application in Industry and Government," *AIIE Transactions,* 9, no. 4 (1977), 363–376.

Hillier, Frederick S., and Gerald J. Lieberman, *Introduction to Operations Research,* 4th ed. San Francisco: Holden-Day, Inc., 1986.

Hu, T. C., *Integer Programming and Network Flows.* Reading Mass.: Addison-Wesley Publishing Company, Inc., 1969.

Jensen, Paul A., *Students' Guide to Operations Research.* Oakland, Calif.: Holden-Day, Inc., 1986.

Kennington, Jeff L., and Richard V. Helgason, *Algorithms for Network Programming.* New York: John Wiley and Sons, Inc., 1980.

SUPPLEMENT: OPTIMIZING TRANSPORTATION AND ASSIGNMENT PROBLEMS

In this supplement we present the computational details of the MODI method for the transportation problem and the Hungarian method for the assignment problem.

SOLVING TRANSPORTATION PROBLEMS BY THE MODI METHOD

The heuristics that were covered earlier in the chapter provide a good but not necessarily optimal solution. The MODI method can be used to take any basic feasible solution to a transportation problem and determine an optimal solution from it. MODI is a streamlined version of the simplex method that takes advantage of the special mathematical structure of the transportation model.

One advantage of the MODI method is that it does not require the use of slack or artificial variables to get a starting feasible solution. It can also take advantage of the advanced starting feasible solutions provided by row minimum or VAM. The calculations in the MODI method are aimed at making successive improvements in a feasible solution until the optimal solution is reached. The method parallels the simplex method in that the following steps are executed:

1. A variable is found that can reduce transportation costs when brought into solution.
2. This variable's maximum allowable value is determined.
3. The variable that must leave the solution is determined; then all other variables in solution are updated.

Fortunately, it is not necessary to store and update a large number of entries in a transportation tableau as you must do in the general simplex method. The corresponding amount of storage space and computation is thus eliminated.

Consider the row minimum heuristic solution to the Faze Linear distribution problem that we restate in Tableau 6.9. Notice that there are six cells in which shipments occur. For a transportation problem that has m sources and n destinations, a basic feasible solution always involves $m + n - 1$ cells. Even though there are $m + n$ functional constraints, one of them is redundant since all the constraints are equalities and it is assumed that total supply

TABLEAU 6.9 *Row minimum solution for Faze Linear distribution problem*

From \ To	K_1 New York	K_2 Chicago	K_3 Dallas	K_4 San Francisco	Supply
R_1 Washington	8 50	9	11	16	50
R_2 Denver	12	7 40	5 40	8	80
R_3 Los Angeles	14 40	10 30	6	7 50	120
Demand	90	70	40	50	250

equals total demand. This can be illustrated by showing that a demand constraint equals the sum of all the supply constraints minus the sum of the remaining demand constraints. In using any starting solution from the row minimum or VAM heuristics, we must be sure that the solution contains $m + n - 1$ cells.

To improve any feasible transportation solution by means of the MODI method, we need to determine which cells need to have their shipments increased and which need to have their shipments decreased. As in the regular simplex method, we make these improvements one variable at a time. Thus, initially, we need to find a cell whose shipments we can increase and, by doing so, reduce transportation costs.

In the regular simplex method, cost-reducing variables are recognized by having a negative $c_j - z_j$ value. The same $c_j - z_j$ indicators are used in the MODI method but are calculated in a much easier way. The first step in determining $c_j - z_j$ values for all nonbasic cells (those that have no shipments) is to assign row and column indicators to each row and column of the transportation tableau. In our example, we let R_1, R_2, and R_3 represent row indicator values and K_1, K_2, K_3, and K_4 represent column indicators values. Refer to Tableau 6.9 to see these indicators associated with their appropriate rows or columns. For those of you who have already studied Chapter 5, these indicators are simply the dual variables of the dual problem.

In general, for an $m \times n$ transportation problem we let

$$R_i = \text{indicator value assigned to row } i, \ i = 1, 2, \ldots, m$$
$$K_j = \text{indicator value assigned to column } j, \ j = 1, 2, \ldots, n$$

As we have stated previously, x_{ij} represents the shipment from source i to destination j, and c_{ij} represents the associated per unit transportation cost.

To compute values for the R_i and K_j indicators, we use a result from duality theory that states

$$R_i + K_j = c_{ij} \qquad \text{whenever } x_{ij} > 0 \qquad (6.4)$$

Thus, $R_i + K_j = c_{ij}$ for any cell (i, j) in which a positive shipment occurs. Since we have m supply constraints and n demand constraints for a total of $m + n$ constraints, we might expect to have $m + n$ basic cells. However, since one constraint is always redundant in transportation models, we actually have $m + n - 1$ cells with positive shipments in any nondegenerate solution. Thus, condition (6.4) yields $m + n - 1$ equations, which we can solve to determine the R_i and K_j values. In Tableau 6.9, the cells (1, 1), (2, 2), (2, 3), (3, 1), (3, 2), and (3, 4) have positive shipments. Thus we obtain the following six equations:

$$R_1 + K_1 = c_{11} = 8 \qquad (6.5)$$
$$R_2 + K_2 = c_{22} = 7 \qquad (6.6)$$
$$R_2 + K_3 = c_{23} = 5 \qquad (6.7)$$
$$R_3 + K_1 = c_{31} = 14 \qquad (6.8)$$
$$R_3 + K_2 = c_{32} = 10 \qquad (6.9)$$
$$R_3 + K_4 = c_{34} = 7 \qquad (6.10)$$

Notice that we have six equations in seven unknowns. Since we have one more unknown than equation, we have one degree of freedom and can set any one of the R_i or K_j equal to an arbitrary value. It is simplest to set R_1 equal to zero and then to solve for the other indicator values. Solving such a system of equations may sound tedious, but the special structure of the transportation problem makes the system of equations trivial to solve. This system of equations is triangular once R_1 is set equal to zero, and the other R_i and K_j may be determined without any calculations.

For example, once $R_1 = 0$, then in equation (6.5) we have

$$R_1 + K_1 = 8 \qquad (6.5)$$
$$0 + K_1 = 8$$
$$K_1 = 8$$

Now that $K_1 = 8$, in (6.8) we have that

$$R_3 + K_1 = 14 \qquad (6.8)$$
$$R_3 + 8 = 14$$
$$R_3 = 6$$

And now that $R_3 = 6$, we have

$$R_3 + K_2 = 10 \qquad (6.9)$$
$$6 + K_2 = 10$$
$$K_2 = 4$$
$$R_3 + K_4 = 7 \qquad (6.10)$$
$$6 + K_4 = 7$$
$$K_4 = 1$$

With $K_2 = 4$, equation (6.6) becomes

$$R_2 + K_2 = 7 \qquad (6.6)$$
$$R_2 + 4 = 7$$
$$R_2 = 3$$

And finally, given $R_2 = 3$

$$R_2 + K_3 = 5 \qquad (6.7)$$
$$3 + K_2 = 5$$
$$K_3 = 2$$

We have solved the entire system of equations by merely setting $R_1 = 0$ and substituting for the remaining R_i and K_j values. Even though the R_i and K_j values are all nonnegative in this example, they may be positive, negative, or zero.

Recall that our purpose in calculating the R_i and K_j values was to determine which variables (cells), if any, can have their shipments increased and thereby reduce transportation costs. In the regular simplex method discussed in Chapter 4, we used the $c_j - z_j$ indicators to measure potential improvements. We can use precisely the same approach in the MODI method because the sum of $R_i + K_j = z_{ij}$ for any transportation variable x_{ij}. Thus, we can calculate the opportunity cost of increasing the shipments through any nonbasic cell (those with no shipments) as

$$c_{ij} - (R_i + K_j) \qquad (6.11)$$

Since we are trying to minimize costs, we achieve the optimal solution whenever all the $c_{ij} - (R_i + K_j)$ are zero or positive. We indicate the value of each $c_{ij} - (R_i + K_j)$ in the lower right-hand part of each nonbasic cell. See Tableau 6.10 for the R_i and K_j values for the initial row minimum solution of the Faze Linear distribution problem. Notice the $c_{ij} - (R_i + K_j)$ values in the enclosed portion of each empty nonbasic cell. (The $c_{ij} - (R_i + K_j)$ numbers were derived as shown in Table 6.5.) The only nonbasic cell that reduces transportation cost is cell (3, 3). This is so because it is the only cell that has

TABLEAU 6.10 *Initial transportation tableau with R_i and K_j values for Faze Linear*

		$K_1 = 8$ New York	$K_2 = 4$ Chicago	$K_3 = 2$ Dallas	$K_4 = 1$ San Francisco	Supply
	To **From**					
$R_1 = 0$	Washington	8 50	9 5	11 9	16 15	50
$R_2 = 3$	Denver	12 1	7 40	5 40	8 4	80
$R_3 = 6$	Los Angeles	14 40	10 30	6 −2	7 50	120
	Demand	90	70	40	50	

a negative opportunity cost. For each unit that we can ship through cell (3, 3) (that is, from Los Angeles to Dallas), we can reduce the total transportation cost by $2. This assumes that some of the existing shipment determinations we have made already will be reduced appropriately.

Increasing the shipments through cell (3, 3) actually causes a chain reaction in some of the other shipments from sources to destinations. For instance, if we increase the shipment through cell (3, 3) by, say, 10 units, then we must reduce the sum of the previous shipments out of source 3 by 10 units. This is true since source 3 (that is, Los Angeles) has only 120 units available. Likewise, if we ship 10 units through cell (3, 3) into destination 3 (Dallas), we must decrease the sum of the previous shipments into destination 3 by 10 units. The overall chain reaction is illustrated in Figure 6.6.

TABLE 6.5 $c_{ij} - (R_i + K_j)$ *values for Faze Linear second solution*

Nonbasic cell	$c_{ij} - (R_i + K_j)$		Opportunity cost
(1,2)	$9 - (0 + 4)$	=	$ 5
(1,3)	$11 - (0 + 2)$	=	9
(1,4)	$16 - (0 + 1)$	=	15
(2,1)	$12 - (3 + 8)$	=	1
(2,4)	$8 - (3 + 1)$	=	4
(3,3)	$6 - (6 + 2)$	=	−2

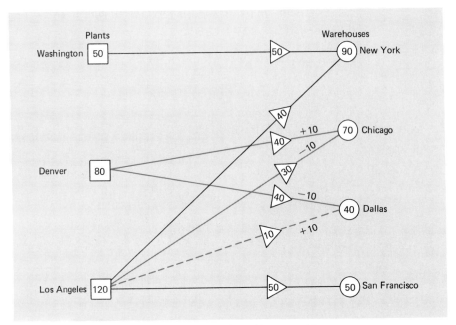

FIGURE 6.6 Graph of current solution for Faze Linear problem

The black lines in Figure 6.6 represent shipments that currently exist; the dashed blue line represents the upcoming shipment through cell (3, 3). The solid blue lines indicate the shipments that are affected by the chain reaction caused by increasing shipments through cell (3, 3). The blue lines, *closed loop* including the dashed one, form a *closed loop*. It is only around the closed loop that adjustments need to be made when the shipment from Los Angeles to Dallas is increased. Thus, if we increase the shipment through cell (3, 3), we must decrease the shipment through cell (2, 3), increase the shipment through cell (2, 2), and, finally, decrease the shipment through cell (3, 2). These adjustments meet all demands without exceeding any of the supply available.

It is easier to determine the chain reaction that occurs whenever a nonbasic cell's shipments are increased by finding the closed loop in the transportation tableau itself. This closed loop is established by a labeling process that assigns plus and minus signs to the appropriate cells. The general idea is to leave the nonbasic cell and make a rook's tour of the basic cells, creating a closed loop that returns to the nonbasic cell. For those of you who do not play chess, a rook's tour consists of only horizontal and vertical movements.

Only one closed loop exists in the tableau, and it can be determined and labeled by the following process: Begin by placing a plus sign (+) in the empty nonbasic cell that is to have its shipments increased. Trace a closed path consisting of basic cells (those with positive shipments) back to the nonbasic cell. The path may skip over some basic cells, but corners of the closed path must occur only at basic cells. After placing a plus sign in the nonbasic cell, alternate minus and plus signs in the basic cells that comprise the closed loop. Only label the basic cells necessary to complete the loop. Skip over any other basic cells. The number of labeled cells is always an even number.

To illustrate the process of identifying and labeling the closed loop, refer to Tableau 6.11, in which the closed loop for cell (3, 3) is shown. The loop was determined by placing a plus sign in cell (3, 3), a minus sign in cell (3, 2), a plus in cell (2, 2), and finally a minus in cell (2, 3). Notice that the plus and minus signs are placed only in basic cells.

Sometimes the closed loop is not immediately identifiable from looking at the transportation tableau. Fortunately, there is a systematic procedure for determining the cells in the loop. The procedure for finding the loop is as follows:

1. Place a plus sign (+) in the empty nonbasic cell that is to have its shipments increased.
2. Cross off any row or column that contains only one cell with a positive shipment. (*Note:* The plus sign counts as a "shipment.")
3. Successively cross out rows and columns until the only rows and columns left contain two shipments. The uncrossed cells define the closed loop.

TABLEAU 6.11 *Closed loop for cell (3, 3)*

		$K_1 = 8$ New York	$K_2 = 4$ Chicago	$K_3 = 2$ Dallas	$K_4 = 1$ San Francisco	Supply
$R_1 = 0$	Washington	8 50	9	11	16	50
$R_2 = 3$	Denver	12	7 40 +	5 40 −	8	80
$R_3 = 6$	Los Angeles	14 40	10 30 −	6 +	7 50	120
	Demand	90	70	40	50	250

The wide lines in Tableau 6.11 illustrate the crossed out rows and columns. Initially, row 1 and column 4 can be crossed out, since they contain only one positive shipment. Once the shipment of 50 is crossed out in row 1, the shipment of 40 is alone in column 1. We can then cross out column 1, but all other rows and columns contain two shipments and cannot be crossed out.

Once the closed loop has been traced, it is necessary to determine the amount of supply that can be shipped through cell (3, 3). The labels on the closed loop indicate the chain reaction caused by increasing the shipment through cell (3, 3). Thus, increasing shipments in cell (3, 3) also increases shipments in cell (2, 2) but decreases shipments through cells (2, 3) and (3, 2). Since no shipment can be negative, we can increase the shipment in cell (3, 3) no more than the minimum of shipments in the negatively labeled cells (2, 3) and (3, 2). The shipment of 30 units in cell (3, 2) is the smaller; thus, we can increase the shipment through cell (3, 3) by 30 units.

The new solution and adjustments in shipments is shown in Tableau 6.12. Notice how the shipments in the cell labeled with pluses have been increased by 30 and the shipments in the cells labeled with minuses have been decreased by 30. Effectively, variable x_{33} has entered the solution at a value of 30, and variable x_{32} has become a nonbasic variable and left the solution. The total cost of the original row minimum solution was $2,090. The total cost of the second solution obtained by the MODI method is calculated in Table 6.6. Its total cost, $2,030, represents a savings of $60.

TABLEAU 6.12   *Second solution for Faze Linear based on closed-loop adjustments*

From \ To		$K_1 = 1$ New York	$K_2 = 2$ Chicago	$K_3 = 0$ Dallas	$K_4 = 1$ San Francisco	Supply
$R_1 = 0$	Washington	8 — 50	9 — (7)	11 — (11)	16 — (15)	50
$R_2 = 5$	Denver	12 — (−1)	7 — 70	5 — 10	8 — (2)	80
$R_3 = 6$	Los Angeles	14 — 40	10 — (2)	6 — 30	7 — 50	120
	Demand	90	70	40	50	250

TABLE 6.6   *Total cost of second solution*

Route	Shipment	Cost per unit	Total cost
Washington/New York	50	$ 8	$ 400
Denver/Chicago	70	7	490
Denver/Dallas	10	5	50
Los Angeles/New York	40	14	560
Los Angeles/Dallas	30	6	180
Los Angeles/San Francisco	50	7	350
			$2,030

Coincidentally, this second solution is the same as the solution obtained by the VAM heuristic. This solution is not optimal; another iteration of the MODI method is required before optimality is achieved.

To see where further improvements can be made, we must calculate new values of the R_i and K_j indicators. These values must satisfy equations based on the general statement in (6.4) for the new solution. Since cells (1, 1), (2, 2), (2, 3), (3, 1), (3, 3), and (3, 4) are basic, we obtain the system

$$R_1 + K_1 = 8$$
$$R_2 + K_2 = 7$$
$$R_2 + K_3 = 5$$
$$R_3 + K_1 = 14$$
$$R_3 + K_3 = 6$$
$$R_3 + K_4 = 7$$

Setting R_1 equal to zero and substituting, we obtain $K_1 = 8$, $R_3 = 6$, $K_3 = 0$, $K_4 = 1$, $R_2 = 5$, and $K_2 = 2$ as the solution to the foregoing system of equations.

Now we can use the R_i and K_j values with expression (6.11) to calculate the opportunity cost of increasing the shipment in any nonbasic cell. The calculations of the $c_{ij} - (R_i + K_j)$ values are shown in Table 6.7 as are the R_i

TABLE 6.7 $c_{ij} - (R_i + K_j)$ *values for Faze Linear third solution*

Nonbasic cell	$c_{ij} - (R_i + K_j)$		Opportunity cost
(1,2)	9 − (0 + 2)	=	$ 7
(1,3)	11 − (0 + 0)	=	11
(1,4)	16 − (0 + 1)	=	15
(2,1)	12 − (5 + 8)	=	−1
(2,4)	8 − (5 + 1)	=	2
(3,2)	10 − (6 + 2)	=	2

TABLEAU 6.13 *Closed loop for cell (2, 1)*

12		7		5	
+				−	
			70		10
14		10		6	
−				+	
40					30

and K_j values and opportunity costs. Since nonbasic cell (2, 1) is the only cell with negative opportunity costs, we must increase shipments through it to make any improvements.

The next step is to determine the closed loop for cell (2, 1) so that the appropriate shipment adjustments can be made. Tableau 6.13 shows the part of the second-solution tableau that contains the closed loop. The loop was traced by assigning a plus to cell (2, 1), skipping basic cell (2, 2) because it is not needed, assigning a minus to cell (2, 3), a plus to cell (3, 3), and finally a minus to cell (3, 1). The smallest shipment in a cell with a minus label is 10 units in cell (2, 3). Thus, we adjust the labeled cells by 10 units and obtain the third solution in Tableau 6.14. To find out whether this third solution is optimal, again we calculate the R_i and K_j indicators. Since cells (1, 1), (2, 1),

TABLEAU 6.14 *Third solution (optimal) for Faze Liner problem*

		$K_1 = 8$	$K_2 = 3$	$K_3 = 0$	$K_4 = 1$	
	From \\ To	New York	Chicago	Dallas	San Francisco	Supply
$R_1 = 0$	Washington	8 50	9	11	16	50
$R_2 = 4$	Denver	12 10	7 70	5	8	80
$R_3 = 6$	Los Angeles	14 30	10	6 40	7 50	120
	Demand	90	70	40	50	250

TABLE 6.8 $c_{ij} - (R_i + K_j)$ values for Faze Linear optimal solution

Nonbasic cell	$c_{ij} - (R_i + K_j)$		Opportunity cost
(1,2)	$9 - (0 + 3)$	$=$	$ 6
(1,3)	$11 - (0 + 0)$	$=$	11
(1,4)	$16 - (0 + 1)$	$=$	15
(2,3)	$5 - (4 + 0)$	$=$	1
(2,4)	$8 - (4 + 1)$	$=$	3
(3,2)	$10 - (6 + 3)$	$=$	1

(2, 2), (3, 1), (3, 3), and (3, 4) are basic, we obtain the equations

$$R_1 + K_1 = 8$$
$$R_2 + K_1 = 12$$
$$R_2 + K_2 = 7$$
$$R_3 + K_1 = 14$$
$$R_3 + K_3 = 6$$
$$R_3 + K_4 = 7$$

Setting R_1 equal to zero and backsubstituting, we obtain $K_1 = 8$, $R_2 = 4$, $K_2 = 3$, $R_3 = 6$, $K_3 = 0$, and $K_4 = 1$.

FIGURE 6.7 **Optimal shipping pattern for Faze Linear**

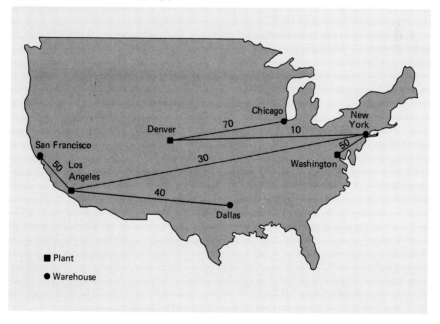

Again, we use expression (6.11) to determine the $c_{ij} - (R_i + K_j)$ opportunity costs (see Table 6.8). Since none of the opportunity costs are negative, no further improvement can be made and the third solution is optimal. Its minimum cost is calculated as $8(50) + 12(10) + 7(70) + 14(30) + 6(40) + 7(50) = \$2,020$. The optimal shipping pattern is shown in Figure 6.7.

SUMMARY OF MODI METHOD

1. Generate a starting feasible solution by using a heuristic such as the row minimum rule or VAM. Make sure that the starting feasible solution contains $m + n - 1$ basic cells.

2. Compute the R_i and K_j indicator values for the current solution by using the formula $R_i + K_j = c_{ij}$ for each basic cell (i, j). Solve the resulting $m + n$ equations by setting R_1 equal to zero and backsubstituting for the remaining R_i and K_j values.

3. Calculate the opportunity costs of increasing shipments through each nonbasic (unused) cell using the formula $c_{ij} - (R_i + K_j) =$ opportunity cost for nonbasic cell (i, j).

4. Select the nonbasic cell with the most negative $c_{ij} - (R_i + K_j)$ value. If no nonbasic cell has a negative $c_{ij} - (R_i + K_j)$, stop, for the solution is optimal.

5. Trace the closed path for the nonbasic cell that has the most negative $c_{ij} - (R_i + K_j)$ value. Place a plus sign in this nonbasic cell and subsequently alternate minus and plus signs in labeling the basic cells around the closed loop.

6. Determine the smallest shipment Δ (the capital delta symbol, Δ, usually represents amount of change) in all cells with a minus label. Adjust the shipments around the closed loop by subtracting Δ from minus-labeled cells and adding Δ to all plus-labeled cells.

7. Return to step 2.

It should be noted that the MODI method can be used to maximize transportation models as well as to minimize them. The modification is the same as in the simplex method for general LP. To maximize, we can change the signs of the objective function values and minimize, or we can choose the nonbasic cell with the most positive $c_{ij} - (R_i + K_j)$ to enter the solution; all other steps remain the same. A maximization example is solved in the solved problem section at the end of this chapter.

TOTAL SUPPLY AND DEMAND NOT EQUAL

In using the MODI method, we assume that total supply and demand are equal. This is generally not the case in real-world transportation applications. Usually, the problems are unbalanced in that supply exceeds demand, or vice versa. However, unbalanced transportation problems are easily balanced for the MODI method by simply adding a fictitious source or destination to absorb the excess demand or supply.

Supply Exceeds Demand

dummy *destination* Whenever supply exceeds demand, we simply add a fictitious, or *dummy, destination* whose demand equals the excess supply. Doing so artificially balances the transportation problem. To illustrate the technique, consider the Faze Linear problem with an additional 20 units of supply at the Washington plant. This makes total supply equal to 270 units, whereas total demand equals 250. Adding an additional destination is analogous to adding a slack variable in the simplex method. The cost of all shipments to the dummy destination must be zero. This is obviously the case since these shipments are never actually made. In developing a transportation tableau with excess supply, we add a dummy column with zero per unit transportation costs. The optimal tableau for the Faze Linear problem with excess supply is shown in Tableau 6.15.

The solution to a transportation problem that has a dummy destination is obtained by exactly the same MODI procedures. The only difference is in interpreting the optimal solution. In Tableau 6.15, we find that 20 units are

TABLEAU 6.15 *Balanced optimal tableau when supply exceeds demand*

From \ To	New York	Chicago	Dallas	San Francisco	Dummy	Supply
Washington	8 ·· 70	9	11	16	0	70
Denver	12 ·· 10	7 ·· 70	5	8	0	80
Los Angeles	14 ·· 10	10	6 ·· 40	7 ·· 50	0 ·· 20	120
Demand	90	70	40	50	20	270

allocated to cell (3, 5). This simply means that these 20 units are not shipped from Los Angeles. Thus, Los Angeles is the plant that stores the excess supply. We have determined not only the optimal shipping pattern but also which plant is not utilized at full capacity.

Demand Exceeds Supply

dummy source

Whenever demand exceeds supply, it is, of course, impossible to meet all demand requirements. The question becomes: Which destinations shall receive shipments to minimize the distribution cost of the supply that is available? The trick is similar to the case in which supply exceeds demand, except that a *dummy source* is added. Consider the Faze Linear problem with 20 additional units of demand at Dallas. Adding the dummy source to absorb the 20 extra units of demand requires an additional row in the transportation tableau. See Tableau 6.16 for the optimal tableau for the Faze Linear problem with excess demand.

In making accommodations for demand exceeding supply, more than one destination might fail to have all its demand requirements met. In this case, we can see in Tableau 6.16 that the 20 fictitious units at the dummy source are assigned to New York. This means that only 70 of the 90 units in demand at New York are shipped. However, the solution does allocate the 250 units of available supply at minimum transportation cost.

TABLEAU 6.16   *Balanced optimal tableau when demand exceeds supply*

From \ To	New York	Chicago	Dallas	San Francisco	Supply
Washington	8 \ 50	9	11	16	50
Denver	12 \ 10	7 \ 70	5	8	80
Los Angeles	14 \ 10	10	6 \ 60	7 \ 50	120
Dummy	0 \ 20	0	0	0	20
Demand	90	70	60	50	270

DEGENERACY

Recall from Chapter 4 that degeneracy occurs whenever a basic variable assumes a zero value. In the regular simplex method, degeneracy causes no problem, but it can in the MODI method if not handled properly. The MODI method, with m sources and n destinations, requires $m + n - 1$ basic cells. If fewer than $m + n - 1$ cells are designated as basic, then the R_i and K_j values cannot be calculated and closed loops do not exist. Degeneracy is easily handled by always maintaining $m + n - 1$ basic cells even though some may have zero shipment and be degenerate. Degeneracy can arise in the following situations:

1. In determining a feasible starting solution, fewer than $m + n - 1$ cells are used.
2. In working toward optimality, the MODI method may have more than one basic cell leave the solution at an iteration. This results in fewer than $m + n - 1$ cells being basic.

In the first situation, degeneracy is easily handled by never deleting a row and a column of the transportation tableau at the same time. For instance, in using either row minimum or VAM, we may assign to a cell whose associated source has 50 units of supply and associated destination has 50 units of demand. Allocating the maximum amount (50 units) to this cell would delete its row and column at the same time. However, $m + n - 1$ cells can be preserved if the associated row is not deleted but rather has its supply adjusted to be zero! That is, we delete the column but not the row and actually allocate the zero units of supply to another cell at another step in the heuristic. This results in some cell receiving a zero shipment, but the trick preserves the necessary number of $m + n - 1$ cells.

In the second case, degeneracy arises whenever there is more than one basic cell in the closed loop that is minus labeled and has the minimum

TABLEAU 6.17 *Degeneracy in the MODI method*

12		7		5	
+				−	
		70		10	
14		10		6	
−				+	
10				30	

$\rightarrow$

12		7		5	
10		70			
14		10		6	
0				40	

shipment amount. In this situation, care must be taken to delete only one of these cells. For example, consider Tableau 6.17, which is an altered version of Tableau 6.13. Both cells (2, 3) and (3, 1) have shipments of 10 units and are labeled with minus signs. In making the shipment adjustments, we can maintain $m + n - 1$ cells if we only delete one of these two cells, either (2, 3) or (3, 1). Arbitrarily deleting one and placing a zero shipment in the other maintains $m + n - 1$ basic cells. This same procedure extends to cases where more than two minus-labeled cells in the loop have the same minimal shipment.

The Hungarian Method

The Hungarian method for solving the assignment problem is named in honor of the Hungarian mathematician, D. König, who proved a theorem required for its development. Our version of this method can be calculated by hand, and it may seem rather simplistic. But properly executed, the Hungarian method yields optimal solutions to the assignment problem. The procedure is based on a mathematically proven algorithm for arriving at an optimal solution.

The method is founded upon the concept of opportunity losses. You have encountered opportunity losses before in calculations for the VAM heuristic. In the assignment method, the optimal solution incurs zero opportunity loss. Any other solution with a higher cost incurs an opportunity loss that is equal to its increase in cost over the minimum cost obtainable in the optimal solution. The basic idea in the Hungarian method is to avoid opportunity losses.

A fundamental principle underlying the Hungarian method is that a constant can be subtracted from any row or column in the assignment cost tableau without changing the optimal assignments. Changing the costs in such a manner changes the cost of the solution, of course, but not the actual assignments.

To develop the Hungarian method, let us consider the 4 × 4 assignment problem of the Research & Development Corporation, which is subcontracting four energy-related projects to four independent bidders. For political reasons, each of the bidders has been promised one project. The management at Research & Development wants to minimize the total expenditure for contracts. In Tableau 6.18, the bid amounts are indicated.

The Hungarian method has three basic steps: The first is to calculate an assignment tableau of opportunity losses; the second step is to determine whether an optimal assignment can be made. If an optimal assignment cannot be made, then we must revise the opportunity loss tableau and return to the second step. We repeat steps 2 and 3 until an optimum is achieved.

In solving the 4 × 4 assignment problem for the Research & Development Corporation, we must first calculate the opportunity loss tableau. We

TABLEAU 6.18   *Contract bid amounts (thousands of dollars) for Research & Development Corporation*

		Project		
Bidder	1	2	3	4
A	20	36	31	17
B	24	34	40	12
C	22	40	38	18
D	36	39	35	16

make use of the principle that subtracting a constant from any row or column does not change the location of the optimal assignments. In calculating the total opportunity loss tableau, we first calculate row opportunity losses, then column opportunity losses. The row opportunity losses are calculated by subtracting the least cost in each row from all other costs in that row. For instance, in Tableau 6.18, the lowest cost in row 1 is 17. Thus, making an assignment in cell $(1, 4)$ incurs zero opportunity loss. However, since cell $(1, 1)$ has a cost of 20, an assignment in cell $(1, 1)$ incurs an opportunity loss of $20 - 17 = 3$. Subtracting the lowest cost in a particular row from the other costs in that row yields at least one zero-cost cell in each row. This step is called a row reduction and is shown in Tableau 6.19. The row reduction does not change the solution to the problem, only the costs in the assignment tableau.

The next step is to perform a column reduction on the row-reduced tableau. This involves subtracting the lowest number in each column from all other numbers in that column. For example, Research & Development Corporation incurs a zero opportunity loss in assigning project 1 to bidder A. Referring to Tableau 6.19, we can see that the opportunity loss is $12 - 3 = 9$ if the assignment is made to cell $(2, 1)$ (that is, if project 1 is assigned to

TABLEAU 6.19   *Row reduction of Research & Development tableau*

		Project			Least cost subtracted from row
Bidder	1	2	3	4	
A	3	19	14	0	17
B	12	22	28	0	12
C	4	22	20	0	18
D	20	23	19	0	16

TABLEAU 6.20 *Total opportunity loss tableau for Research & Development Corporation*

Bidder			Project	
	1	2	3	4
A	0	0	0	0
B	9	3	14	0
C	1	3	6	0
D	17	4	5	0
	3	19	14	0

least cost subtracted from column ← of Tableau 6.19

bidder B). Performing the column reduction for each column from Tableau 6.19, we obtain the total opportunity loss tableau in Tableau 6.20.

The total opportunity loss tableau has the same assignment solution as the original problem, and it also has a zero in each row and each column. The zero-cost cells show where an assignment can be made that incurs no opportunity loss. An optimal solution is found whenever all assignments can be made in unique cells that have zero opportunity losses. Sometimes this is possible after determining the total opportunity loss tableau. However, this is not the case in Tableau 6.20, for only two assignments can be made in zero-cost cells.

We need a systematic procedure for determining whether an optimal solution has been found. One such procedure entails crossing out all zero costs by drawing as few horizontal and vertical lines as possible through the assignment tableau. If the number of lines necessary to accomplish this is

TABLEAU 6.21 *Crossing out all zero costs with only two lines*

Bidder			Project	
	1	2	3	4
A	0	0	0	0
B	9	3	14	0
C	1	3	6	0
D	17	4	5	0

TABLEAU 6.22   *Revised opportunity loss tableau*

Bidder	Project 1	2	3	4
A	0	0	0	1
B	8	2	13	0
C	0	2	5	0
D	16	3	4	0

less than the number of rows or columns in the assignment tableau, the problem is not optimal and the total opportunity cost tableau must be revised further. If, however, n lines in an $(n \times n)$ assignment problem are required to cross out all zero costs, then the problem is solved and optimal assignments can be made. The only weakness in this procedure is that it depends upon human judgment for determining the minimum number of lines.

This test for optimality is applied to the total opportunity loss tableau (Tableau 6.20). Only two lines are required (as is shown in Tableau 6.21) to cover all zero costs. Since the problem has four rows, an optimal assignment is not yet possible.

The next step is to revise the opportunity loss tableau to generate more zero-cost cells without altering the solution to the original problem. We do this in the following way: (1) we select the smallest number from each number not covered by a straight line, (2) we add this smallest number to each cost that lies at the intersection of two straight lines, and (3) we subtract it from each cost that is not covered by a line. Note that costs covered by only one line are unchanged by this procedure.

TABLEAU 6.23   *Optimal opportunity loss tableau*

Bidder	Project 1	2	3	4
A	0	0	0	3
B	6		11	0
C		2	5	2
D	14		2	

TABLE 6.9 *Cost (thousands of dollars) of Research & Development Corporation optimal solution*

Assignment	Cost
1 to C	$ 22
2 to B	34
3 to A	31
4 to D	16
Total cost	$103

In Tableau 6.21, we find that the smallest number not covered by a straight line is 1. Subtracting 1 from each cost not covered by a line and adding 1 to the point of intersection gives us the situation shown in Tableau 6.22. It is possible to cross out all zero costs in Tableau 6.22 with only three lines; thus, we must revise the opportunity loss tableau further. The smallest cost not covered in Tableau 6.22 is a 2; subtracting this from each cost not covered by a line and adding it to each point of intersection, we obtain Tableau 6.23.

Since four lines are required to cross out all zero costs, we can make an optimal assignment. The optimal assignment is to assign project 1 to bidder C, 2 to B, 3 to A, and 4 to D. The solution is indicated by the white, boldface numbers in Tableau 6.23. To calculate the total cost of the optimal solution, we refer to the original costs from Tableau 6.18 and calculate the data shown in Table 6.9.

Although we have determined that an optimal assignment can be made, it may not be obvious where these assignments should occur. A systematic approach to making the assignments is called for. One procedure is to find a row or column with only one zero-cost cell and no previous assignments. An assignment must be made in this cell. For example, column 3 in Tableau 6.23 has only one zero; it appears in cell (A, 3). Since no more assignments can be made in column 3 or row A, we draw a line through column 3 and row A. Then, we again seek a row or column with a single zero and find row D. We make an assignment in cell (D, 4) and draw lines through column 4 and row D. The procedure is repeated until all assignments are made. If the remaining rows or columns all have two or more zero-cost cells, an assignment can be made in any zero-cost cell that has not been covered by a straight line.

Summary of the Hungarian Method

1. Determine the total opportunity loss tableau:
    a. Select the least cost in each row and subtract it from each cost in that row.
    b. Using the row-reduced cost tableau that has been generated, select

the least cost in each column and subtract it from every cost in that column.

2. Determine whether an optimal assignment can be made by drawing the minimum number of horizontal and vertical lines through the total opportunity loss tableau that will cover all zero-cost cells. If the number of lines required is less than the number of rows (columns), go to step 3. Otherwise, stop and make the optimal assignments.

3. Revise the total opportunity loss tableau:
   a. Select the smallest number not covered by a line and subtract this number from every number not covered by a line.
   b. Add this same number to any number at the intersection of two lines. Go to step 3.

Note that the Hungarian method can also be used to maximize objectives in assignment problems. To accomplish this, we simply change the signs of the profit coefficients and minimize, or, alternatively, we may calculate the total opportunity loss tableau based on the largest profit, rather than the lowest cost, in each row or column.

SOLVED PROBLEMS

PROBLEM STATEMENT

Use the MODI method to verify the optimality of the VAM solution for the first solved problem at the end of Chapter 6.

SOLUTION

Adding a dummy row to balance supply and demand ensures that we have $m + n - 1$ or $3 + 5 - 1 = 7$ basic cells. Note that it was necessary to assign a zero amount to basic cell (3, 5).

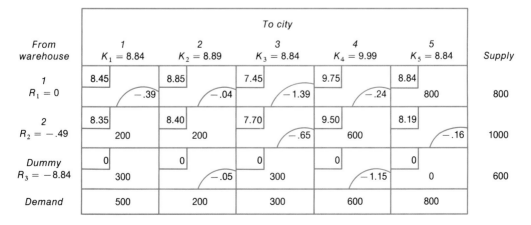

From warehouse	*To city*					Supply
	1 $K_1 = 8.84$	2 $K_2 = 8.89$	3 $K_3 = 8.84$	4 $K_4 = 9.99$	5 $K_5 = 8.84$	
1 $R_1 = 0$	8.45 $\diagdown -.39$	8.85 $\diagdown -.04$	7.45 $\diagdown -1.39$	9.75 $\diagdown -.24$	8.84 800	800
2 $R_2 = -.49$	8.35 200	8.40 200	7.70 $\diagdown -.65$	9.50 600	8.19 $\diagdown -.16$	1000
Dummy $R_3 = -8.84$	0 300	0 $\diagdown -.05$	0 300	0 $\diagdown -1.15$	0 0	600
Demand	500	200	300	600	800	

Since all $c_{ij} - (R_i + k_j)$ values are less than or equal to 0, the solution is optimal for the maximization problem.

PROBLEM STATEMENT

The assignment model is often used as a subproblem of more complex problems. It is useful in the solution of the well-known traveling salesman problem, which is a classical combinatorial problem that is very difficult to solve optimally. In the traveling salesman problem, a "salesman" must leave a home base, visit each of n locations once, and return to the home base. The objective is to determine the sequence of locations to minimize the distance traveled. For n locations there are $(n - 1)!$ possible sequences, called tours.

For an example, let us consider a delivery truck routing problem in which a truck must leave a warehouse and visit four customer delivery points and then return to the warehouse. The matrix of distances is shown below; point 1 is the warehouse.

			Distance (miles)			
From \ To		1	2	3	4	5
1		—	10	7	5	5
2		11	—	4	6	8
3		7	4	—	7	8
4		5	5	7	—	3
5		3	8	8	3	—

SOLUTION

In unusual cases, the solution of the distance matrix as an assignment problem yields an optimal sequence or tour for the traveling salesman problem. The vast majority of the time, however, the optimal assignment solution does not form a tour. It is possible to solve a sequence of properly constructed assignment problems that will eventually solve the traveling salesman problem. To illustrate, we solve the 5 × 5 distance problem as an assignment problem.

		Row reduction			
	1	2	3	4	5
1	—	5	2	0	0
2	7	—	0	2	4
3	3	0	—	3	4
4	2	2	4	—	0
5	0	5	5	0	—

After the row and column reduction, the optimal assignment is 1–4, 2–3, 3–2, 4–5, and 5–1. This assignment does not form a single connected tour, as shown in the graph.

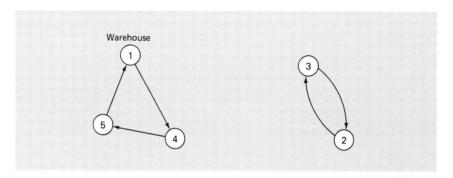

To preclude the infeasible subtour 3–2, 2–3, let us set the distance from 2 to 3 equal to infinity in the distance matrix. This will prevent 2 being assigned to 3.

	Row reduction				
	1	*2*	*3*	*4*	*5*
1	—	5	2	0	0
2	5	—	—	0	2
3	3	0	—	3	4
4	2	2	4	—	0
5	0	5	5	0	—

2 subtracted

	Column reduction				
	1	*2*	*3*	*4*	*5*
1	—	5	0	0	0
2	5	—	—	0	2
3	3	0	—	3	4
4	2	2	2	—	0
5	0	5	3	0	—
			2 subtracted		

After a row and column reduction, the total opportunity loss matrix yields a new optimal assignment. This time the assignment is 1–3, 3–2, 2–4, 4–5, and 5–1. This assignment yields the optimal tour of length $7 + 6 + 4 + 3 + 3 = 23$. The second graph shows the optimal tour.

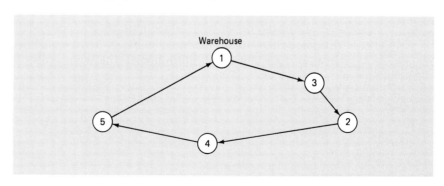

PROBLEMS

S6.1 Use the row minimum starting solution and the MODI method to determine an optimal solution to Problem 6.1.

S6.2 Solve the El Paso Slacks Company's production scheduling problem in Tableau 6.7 by the MODI method.

S6.3 Refer to Problem 2.12. Find an initial feasible solution using VAM and then solve by the MODI method.

S6.4 Determine the optimal solution to Problem 6.5 by using the MODI method.

S6.5 *Rental trailer relocation.* The Continental Trailer Rental Company has a problem in trying to relocate rented trailers. Currently, its supply exceeds the demand, and it is necessary to relocate trailers at minimum transportation cost. There are surplus trailers at locations 1, 2, 3, and 4, whereas trailers are in demand at locations 5, 6, and 7. The relevant data are given in the table. Determine the optimal relocation of trailers.

Trailer status	Location						
	1	2	3	4	5	6	7
Surplus	6	7	8	3			
Shortage					5	4	9

Cost per trailer transported			
From \ To	5	6	7
1	$ 8	$11	$8
2	12	10	6
3	15	7	9
4	12	12	7

S6.6 *Traveling salesman.* A salesman must fly from city to city to maintain his major accounts. This week he has to leave his home base and visit each of four cities and return home. The table shows the air fare between the various cities. The home city is city 1. Use the assignment method to determine the tour that will minimize the total air fare of visiting all cities and returning home.

To From	1	2	3	4	5
1	—	375	600	150	190
2	375	—	300	350	175
3	600	300	—	350	500
4	150	350	350	—	300
5	190	175	500	300	—

S6.7 *Job assignment.* Three jobs must be processed. There are three machines available, but each job must be done on only one machine. Jobs may not be split between machines. The cost of processing each job on each machine is given in the table. Determine the minimum-cost assignment for each job.

	Machine		
Job	X	Y	Z
1	10	16	8
2	8	6	4
3	16	12	8

S6.8 *More-for-less paradox.* Is it actually possible to ship more for less? Assuming no quantity discounts and the same transportation costs, is there ever a situation in which shipping more units will lower costs? Consider the following 3 × 4 transportation problem with optimal solution as shown in the first tableau. Suppose that we add an additional unit of supply to source 2 and an additional unit of demand to destination 1. The results are shown in the second tableau.

To destination

From source	$K_1 = -1$ 1	$K_2 = 3$ 2	$K_3 = 1$ 3	$K_4 = 3$ 4	Supply
$R_1 = 2$ 1	[1] 11	[6]	[3] 9	[5]	20
$R_2 = 0$ 2	[7]	[3] 2	[1] 8	[6]	10
$R_3 = 1$ 3	[9]	[4] 11	[5]	[4] 14	25
Demand	11	13	17	14	55

minimum cost $152

To destination

From source	1	2	3	4	Supply
1	[1]	[6]	[3]	[5]	20
2	[7]	[3]	[1]	[6]	11
3	[9]	[4]	[5]	[4]	25
Demand	12	13	17	14	56

minimum cost $151?

Obviously, shipping the additional unit through cell (2, 1) raises costs by $7. Without solving the problem from scratch, can you find an alternative shipping schedule that will lower costs.

S6.9 *Assignment of contracts.* The Concrete Construction Company has requested bids for subcontracts on five different projects. Five compa-

Bid amount

Bidder	Project 1	2	3	4	5
1	$41,000	$72,000	$39,000	$52,000	$25,000
2	22,000	29,000	49,000	65,000	81,000
3	27,000	39,000	60,000	51,000	40,000
4	45,000	50,000	48,000	52,000	37,000
5	29,000	40,000	45,000	26,000	30,000

nies have responded; their bids are represented below. Determine the minimum cost assignment of subcontracts to bidders, assuming that each bidder can receive only one contract. If each bidder could receive any number of contracts, then what would be the optimal assignment?

7

Network Models

REG. U.S. PAT. & TM. OFF

E. I. du PONT de NEMOURS AND COMPANY

The Clinical Systems Division of Du Pont markets a product called the aca discrete clinical analyzer to hospitals and other medical institutions.[1] The "aca" automates many of the routine tests made for patients in medical laboratories. Consumable chemical products are required to operate an "aca," and consumables are delivered to over 1,500 customers located in about 1,000 cities through the continental United States and Canada. New customers are being added at a rate of approximately 40 percent per year. The consumable delivery costs exceeded $1 million annually and were growing rapidly. Du Pont logistics management decided to launch a distribution system study.

The objective of the study was to reduce costs which primarily included fuel costs, truck depreciation, and driver wages. The distribution system consisted of two plants, four regional distribution centers, and a satellite terminal in Houston. The most typical mode of delivery involved the refrigerated trucks that drive weekly loops visiting twenty to fifty customers. A weekly loop typically begins early Monday at one of the five truck terminals and ends the following Friday or Saturday at the same

[1] M. L. Fisher, A. J. Greenfield, R. Jaikumar, and J. T. Lester III, "A Computerized Vehicle Routing Application," *Interfaces,* 12, no. 4 (August 1982), 42–52.

terminal. Customers are typically delivered once per month, so a driver and truck would handle four different loops in a month. Du Pont redesigns the routes twice a year and notifies the customers of any changes in delivery day.

Du Pont decided to use outside consultants and a computerized vehicle routing package called ROVER (Real-time Optimizer for Vehicle Routing) to redesign its routes. The ROVER computer program employs an embedded algorithm that solves linear generalized assignment problems to assign customers to routes and not exceed truck capacity. The actual sequence of stops is determined by a traveling salesman heuristic. Using the computer package, the analysts decided to replace the Houston satellite by one in Dallas and to transfer one route from the Atlanta region to the Wilmington region. The reduction in delivery costs as a result of the computerized route redesign was approximately 15 percent.

A color graphics interface was also developed to allow a scheduler to visualize the routes easily and to assess proposed changes and their effects on cost and feasibility. This is an effective way to deal with miscellaneous constraints and driver preferences that would be difficult to include in the optimization model.

INTRODUCTION

In this chapter we continue our study of network models. In Chapter 6 we looked at transportation, transshipment, and assignment models, and in Chapter 8 we will look at PERT/CPM, a network approach to project scheduling.

network   Recall that a *network* is a collection of nodes or points connected by arcs. Figure 7.1 depicts a simple network. Why are networks important and why are three chapters in this text related to network models? The answer is

FIGURE 7.1 **A simple network**

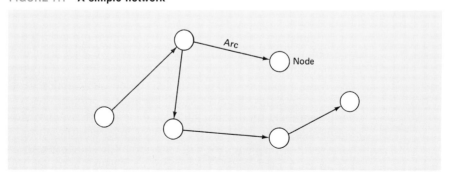

TABLE 7.1 *Examples of networks*

Physical distribution systems	City streets and traffic signals
Communication networks	Airline flight legs
Pipeline systems	Production assembly line systems

twofold. First, network models arise frequently in management science applications. Many real-world problems have a network structure or can be modeled in network form. Table 7.1 provides several common examples of systems that can be represented as networks. In addition to the physical systems listed in Table 7.1, there are some problems that do not appear physically to be a network but can be modeled as a network in the abstract. Some of these examples include scheduling problems, inventory problems, and even financial applications, including cash management.

A second reason for the importance of network models is their solution efficiency. Network models are at the problem-solving frontiers in terms of problem size and solution speed. In the previous chapter we discussed the netform concept of exploiting the underlying network substructure of a mathematical model whenever possible. The three network models examined in this chapter are the shortest-route problem, minimum spanning tree, and maximal flow problem. These network models have useful stand-alone applications, but also are found as subproblems embedded in larger more complex decision problems.

The shortest-route and maximal flow problems are special cases of the transshipment problem; however, both have simplified solution algorithms which offer gains in computational efficiency.

THE SHORTEST-ROUTE PROBLEM

shortest route The first model we consider is the shortest-route problem. In this problem the objective is to find the *shortest route* along arcs from one node to one or more other nodes in the network. The arcs usually represent distances, but can represent times or costs.

To illustrate the problem and an algorithm for solving it, let us consider the problem faced by a sales representative who has to visit each of her six main accounts each month. Figure 7.2 contains the network graph of the sales rep's problem. Node 1 is her home city, and the other six nodes represent the cities she must visit. The arcs represent the existing highways and the numbers on the arcs indicate distances between nodes. The arcs are *nondirected;* that is, they permit flow in either direction. In solving the shortest-route problem, we will determine the shortest route from the home base to each other city. The algorithm we use assumes that none of the distances are negative. In actual practice this is not a limiting assumption.

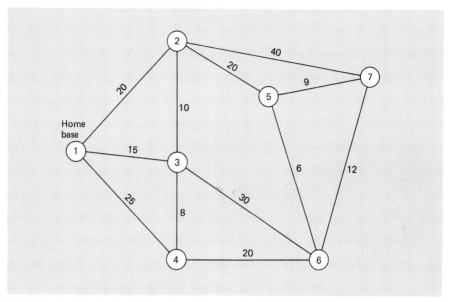

FIGURE 7.2 **Graph of sales rep's problem**

Shortest-Route Algorithm

The algorithm to solve the shortest-route problem is iterative. At each step the shortest distance to one node is determined; thus, after $n - 1$ steps the procedure is finished, where $n =$ number of nodes in the network.

The algorithm consists of two parts, a *labeling procedure* to determine the shortest distance from node 1 to every other node, and a *backtracking procedure* to determine the actual route from node 1 to any other node.

Labeling procedure   The labels for the nodes consist of an ordered pair of numbers, where the first number indicates the distance from node 1, and the second number indicates the preceding node on the route from node 1 to the node in question. The labels will initially be called temporary labels, but as the shortest distance is found, they will become permanent labels.

The labeling process begins by labeling all nodes that can be reached directly from node 1. In our example these are nodes 2, 3, and 4. We temporarily label each node with the direct distance from node 1 and the previous node on the route, which is node 1. These labels are shown in Figure 7.3. Notice that the first component of each label is simply the distance from node 1; these labels are 20, 15, and 25 for nodes 2, 3, and 4, respectively. Of these three nodes, node 3 is closest to node 1. Since all other arcs have positive distance, we can conclude that there is no shorter route to node 3 than directly from node 1. (Note that we cannot conclude this about node 4.) Thus, we can permanently label node 3 with the label (15,

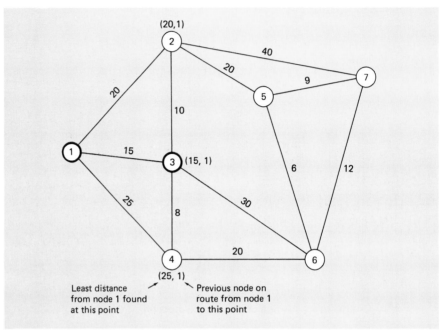

FIGURE 7.3 **Initial labels in shortest-route algorithm**

1). Permanently labeled nodes are indicated by a darker line around the node. Node 1 is permanently labeled at the beginning of the labeling process. We now have two classes of nodes: those that are permanently labeled and those that have temporary labels or no labels at all.

The next iteration in the algorithm begins by labeling "outward" from the newest permanently labeled node. We check all nodes that are reachable by a direct arc from node 3. These are nodes 2, 4, and 6. Passing through node 3 on the way from node 1 to node 2 offers no improvement to the direct route from node 1. Thus, node 2's label is unchanged. However, passing through node 3 does offer a distance reduction of 25 − (15 + 8) = 2 miles for node 4. Thus, we change node 4 label to (23, 3) to reflect the distance and previous node of the best route found so far in traveling from node 1 to node 4. Node 6 can also be labeled now with the label (45, 3). The 45 is obtained from the shortest distance to node 3 (15), plus 30, which is the length of the arc from node 3 to node 6. The updated labels are shown in Figure 7.4. Node 2, with a distance of 20, has the smallest distance from node 1 among all temporarily labeled nodes. Thus, the shortest distance from node 1 to node 2 is 20, and node 2 can be permanently labeled.

In the third iteration we can label nodes 5 and 7 from node 2. Node 4, however, has the smallest distance label and can be permanently labeled (see Figure 7.5).

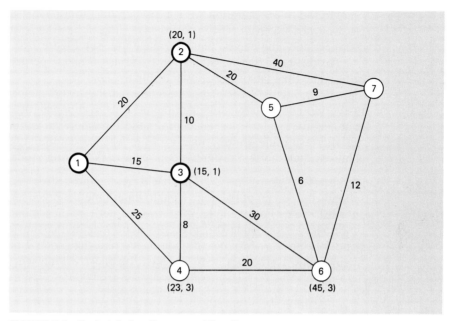

FIGURE 7.4   **Node labels after second iteration**

FIGURE 7.5   **Node labels after third iteration**

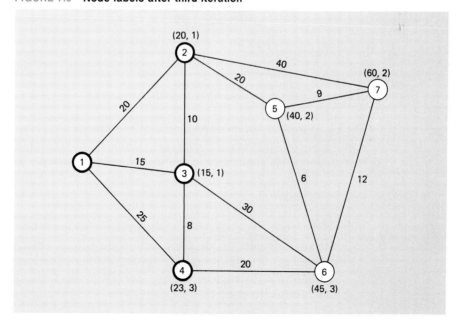

In the fourth iteration we can branch out from node 4 to improve the label on node 6 from (45, 3) to (43, 4). Node 5 has the lowest temporary distance label and can be fixed permanently (see Figure 7.6).

In the next two iterations we fix nodes 6 and 7 permanently in that order. The final labels are shown in Figure 7.7

From Figure 7.7 we can determine the shortest distances from node 1 to every other node by looking at the distance component of each label. For instance, we can look at the label for node 7 and determine that the length of the shortest route from 1 to 7 is 49 miles. To determine the route that achieves that shortest distance requires a backtracking process.

Backtracking procedure   The backtracking procedure simply uses the second component of the node label to determine the predecessors along the shortest route. For example, in starting at node 7, the second label tells us that node 5 is the node that precedes node 7 along the shortest route from node 1 to node 7. Moving to node 5, we find that node 2 precedes it and finally, node 1 precedes node 2. Thus, the backtracking sequence yields

$$7 \rightarrow 5 \rightarrow 2 \rightarrow 1$$

Using the same backtracking procedure, we can determine the shortest route from node 1 to all other nodes.

Node	Shortest route	Distance
2	1–2	20
3	1–3	15
4	1–3–4	23
5	1–2–5	40
6	1–3–4–6	43
7	1–2–5–7	49

The algorithm may seem to require a lot of steps for such a simple problem, which you can probably solve by inspection. However, for larger problems with hundreds or thousands of nodes and even more arcs, the algorithm is necessary and easily implemented on a computer. We summarize the shortest-route algorithm as follows:

LABELING

Step 1: Compute the distance from node 1 to all other nodes that are connected directly to node 1. Set the distance portion of their labels equal to the distance to node 1. Set the predecessor portion of their labels equal to node 1.

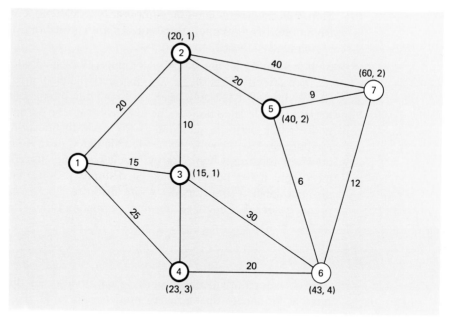

FIGURE 7.6 **Node labels after fourth iteration**

FIGURE 7.7 **Final labels for sales rep example**

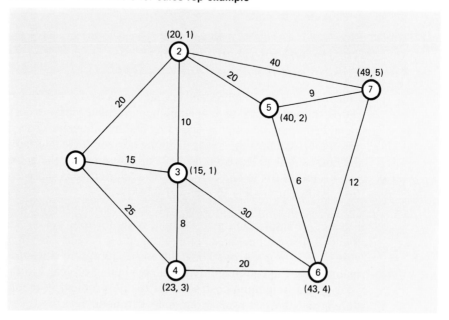

Step 2: Permanently label the temporarily labeled node whose distance from node 1 is minimum. Break ties (if any) arbitrarily. If all nodes are permanently labeled, go to step 4.

Step 3: Identify all unlabeled or temporarily labeled nodes that can be reached directly from the new permanently labeled node. Compute the new distance for the node reached by adding the distance label of the permanently labeled node to the distance from the permanently labeled node to the node in question. If the node in question is unlabeled, temporarily label it with the newly calculated distance. If the node in question is already temporarily labeled, update its current distance label only if the newly calculated distance is less than its previous distance label. For any node whose distance label is updated, set its predecessor label equal to the new permanently labeled node. Go to step 2.

BACKTRACKING

Step 4: After the labeling process, each node other than node 1 will have a permanent distance and predecessor label. To determine the shortest route from node 1 to any other node, say, node *j*, refer to the predecessor label for node *j*. Move to the node specified by the predecessor label and examine its predecessor label. Then move to the node specified and so on until node 1 is reached. The sequence of nodes traced in the backtracking process constitutes the shortest route from node 1 to node *j*.

Shortest-Route Application— Equipment Replacement Analysis

Consider a capital equipment leasing decision in which a company must choose between leasing new equipment at higher leasing costs or maintaining old equipment at higher operating and maintenance costs. For the example, let us assume a four-year planning horizon. One alternative available to the company is to lease a new piece of equipment at the beginning of year 1 and keep it until the end of year 4. The alternative is represented by the arc from node 1 to node 5 in Figure 7.8.

The cost c_{15} is associated with arc (1, 5) and represents the combined leasing, operating, and maintenance costs for four years. Another alternative is to lease a new piece of equipment each year. This alternative would cost $c_{12} + c_{23} + c_{34} + c_{45}$. Thus, the cost c_{ij} represents the cost of leasing and maintaining the equipment from the beginning of year *i* to the beginning of year *j*. The minimum-cost solution to the problem is obtained by simply finding the shortest route from node 1 to node 5.

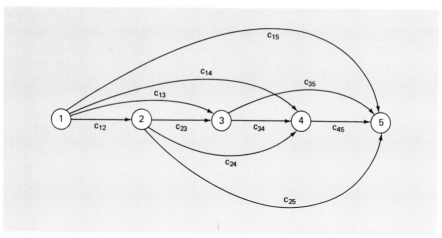

FIGURE 7.8   **Network for equipment replacement decision**

THE MINIMUM SPANNING TREE PROBLEM

The minimum spanning tree problem involves the selection of a set of arcs that will span (connect) all nodes of a network and will minimize the sum of the arc lengths. The problem differs from the shortest-route problem in that the arcs of the network do not yet exist and are to be selected.

The problem has applications in several areas. It is particularly useful in designing transportation systems in which the nodes of the network are *minimum* terminals and the arcs represent highways, pipelines, airways, and so on. *spanning tree* The *minimum spanning tree* is also applicable to communication and tele-processing systems, as we shall see later.

FIGURE 7.9   **A tree and a nontree**

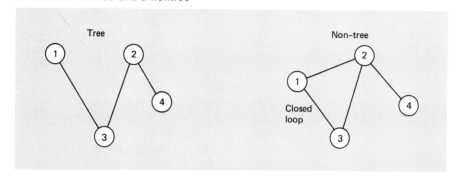

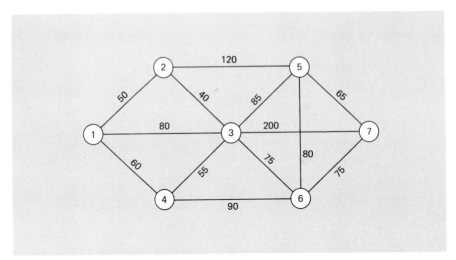

FIGURE 7.10 **Potential pipeline connections**

The type of structure that will connect all nodes in a network and be of minimal length is a tree. A *tree* is a graph in which the arcs connect all nodes (that is, provide paths along which one node can eventually reach any other node) and form no closed loops. A tree has the property that if it spans a network graph with n nodes, the tree will always contain $n - 1$ arcs. Figure 7.9 illustrates a tree and a graph that is not a tree.

To illustrate the minimum spanning tree problem, let us consider a pipeline design problem in which the objective is to lay as little pipe as possible to enable the terminals to send fluid to any other terminal. Figure 7.10 shows the seven terminals, their possible pipeline connections, and the length of the pipeline in miles.

Greedy Algorithm for Minimum Spanning Tree

Given the seven nodes in the pipeline network, we wish to select a tree consisting of six arcs that will connect all nodes and be of minimal length. The procedure for solving the problem is very straightforward and ranks among the simplest optimization techniques in all of OR/MS!

The minimum spanning tree algorithm is a type of *"greedy" algorithm* because at each step being greedy, that is, selecting the minimal-length arc, will lead to an optimal solution. To start the procedure simply begin at any node and select the shortest arc leading to another node. This forms a connected segment of two nodes and an unconnected segment of the remaining nodes. Next, select the shortest arc leading from a node in the connected segment to a node in the unconnected segment. Repeat this process until all nodes are connected. This procedure will construct the minimum spanning tree. We can summarize the greedy algorithm procedure as follows:

1. Start with any node and select the shortest arc leading to any other node. This forms a connected segment of two nodes.
2. Select the shortest arc leading from the connected segment to the unconnected segment of arcs.
3. Add the unconnected node of the newly selected arc to the list of connected nodes and delete it from the list of unconnected nodes. If all nodes are connected, STOP; otherwise, go to step 2.

The greedy algorithm can be executed using the matrix of distances between nodes of the network graph. Let us use the graph of the pipeline network to illustrate the greedy algorithm.

Since we can start with any node, let us start with node 1. The shortest arc leading out of node 1 is arc (1, 2), with a length of 50. Nodes 1 and 2 now become connected as indicated by the heavy line in Figure 7.11.

The shortest arc connecting node 1 or node 2 to the remaining arcs is arc (2, 3). Add arc (2, 3) to the tree (Figure 7.12).

The unconnected node closest to node 1, 2, or 3 is node 4. Connect 4 to 3 (Figure 7.13).

The next node to be connected is node 6, as it is closer than 5 or 7 (Figure 7.14).

Node 7 is closer than node 5 to the connected segment, so add arc (6, 7) to the tree (Figure 7.15).

Finally, connect node 5 to node 7, which is the closest node in the connected segment (Figure 7.16).

FIGURE 7.11   **Iteration 1: Select arc (1, 2)**

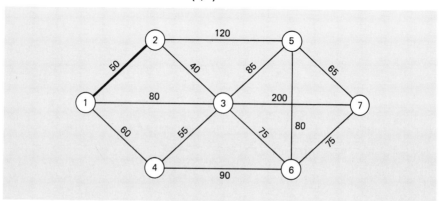

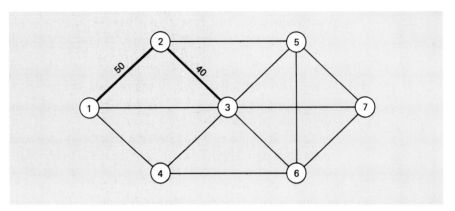

FIGURE 7.12   **Iteration 2: Select arc (2, 3)**

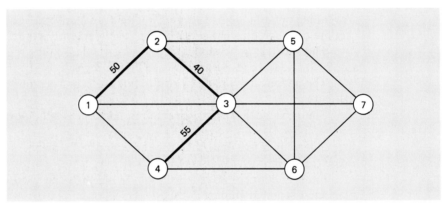

FIGURE 7.13   **Iteration 3: Select arc (3, 4)**

FIGURE 7.14   **Iteration 4: Select arc (3, 6)**

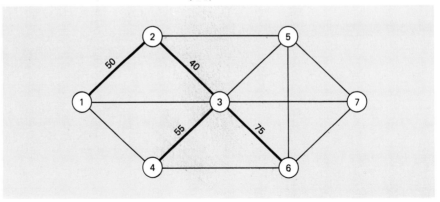

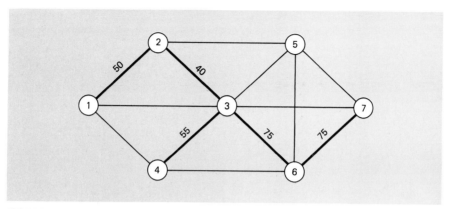

FIGURE 7.15   Iteration 5: Select arc (6, 7)

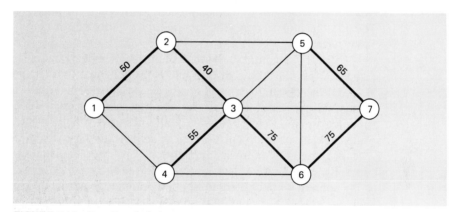

FIGURE 7.16   Iteration 6: Select arc (7, 5)

The spanning tree consists of the heavy arcs in the graph shown in Figure 7.16. Notice that the tree requires precisely six arcs, connects all nodes, and forms no closed loops. The total length of the minimal spanning tree is 360 miles.

Minimum Spanning Tree Application— Teleprocessing System Design

Consider the design of a teleprocessing system in which remote computer terminals must be connected to a data processing center and associated computer. The objective is to establish communication lines with sufficient capacity at minimal cost. The solution to this design problem is a tree if expensive switching equipment is not used to split signals passing through the nodes of the network. Figure 7.17 illustrates the relative locations of nine

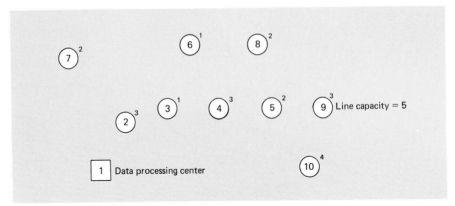

FIGURE 7.17 **Layout of teleprocessing design problem**

terminals which need to be connected to the central computer. The numbers beside the nodes represent the amount of information that is generated at that terminal.

Table 7.2 contains the matrix of distances between all pairs of the 10 nodes. Note that the cost of a line is proportional to its length.

If the communication lines to be established have no capacity limitations, the optimal solution to the teleprocessing design problem would be the minimal spanning tree. However, all lines have a finite capacity. Assume a line capacity of 5 in Figure 7.17. The solution to the problem then becomes a "capacitated minimum spanning tree." This problem is much more difficult to solve, but heuristic and optimization procedures do exist for solving it. One approach is a branch-and-bound optimization procedure (see Chapter 9) which utilizes the minimum spanning tree as a subproblem. We will not discuss the method here; however, the optimal capacitated minimum spanning tree is shown in Figure 7.18.

TABLE 7.2 *Matrix of distances*

		1	2	3	4	5	Node 6	7	8	9	10
	1	—	28	57	72	81	85	80	113	89	80
	2	28	—	28	45	54	57	63	85	63	63
	3	57	28	—	20	30	28	57	57	40	57
	4	72	45	20	—	10	20	72	45	20	45
Node	5	81	54	30	10	—	22	81	41	10	41
	6	85	57	28	20	22	—	63	20	28	63
	7	80	63	57	72	81	63	—	80	89	113
	8	113	85	57	45	41	20	80	—	40	80
	9	89	63	40	20	10	28	89	40	—	40
	10	80	63	57	45	41	63	113	80	40	—

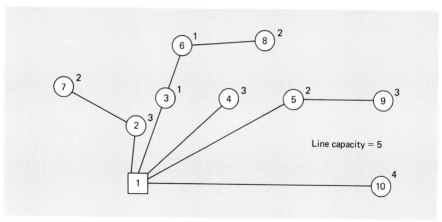

FIGURE 7.18 **Optimal solution to teleprocessing design problem**

THE MAXIMAL FLOW PROBLEM

In the maximal flow problem the objective is to determine the maximum amount of flow (fluid, traffic, information, etc.) that can be transmitted through the nodes and arcs of a network. We assume a single input node called the *source* and a single output node called the *sink;* all flows commence at the source and terminate at the sink. The problem has applications in such areas as the study of traffic flow, pipeline design, communication network design, and distribution systems. It is particularly helpful in capacity planning for these types of systems.

maximal The *maximal flow* problem is characterized by the arcs of the network
flow having finite capacities which limit the amount of flow that can pass through the arc in a given amount of time. The problem is to determine the amount of flow across each arc (subject to capacity restrictions) that will permit the maximal total flow from source to sink.

Let us return to the pipeline design problem of Figure 7.10 and assume
arc that all the pipelines indicated have been laid in order to meet demand
capacities requirements. The same pipeline network with *arc capacities* is shown in Figure 7.19. The numbers beside each arc specify the capacity in a particular direction. For example, looking at arc (1, 2), we have

The 3 by node 1 indicates a capacity of 3 in the direction of node 1 to node 2; the 0 on the arc indicates a 0 capacity in the reverse direction of node 2 to node 1.

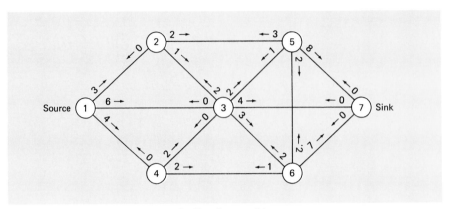

FIGURE 7.19 **Arc capacities for pipeline flow problem**

conservation of flow   Obviously, there are many possible ways to send various flow quantities along the paths from source to sink. One rule we must remember is the *conservation of flow,* which means that whatever flows into a node must flow out. Solving the maximal flow problem is almost as simple as repeatedly finding paths from source node to sink node with available capacity. For this procedure to work, there are two other guidelines that must be followed.

    The first guideline is that the maximum amount that can flow from source to sink along a given path is equal to the minimum available capacity on any arc in the path. (This is similar to the analogy of the weakest link in the chain.) Second, we need a way of changing flows along paths to achieve a better flow assignment. Our arbitrary assignment of flows along paths does not guarantee that we will achieve the optimal solution. The mechanism by which we can eventually achieve the optimal flow pattern is as follows: When assigning a flow to an arc, (1) reduce the capacity in the direction of the flow by the amount of the flow, and (2) increase the capacity in the opposite direction of the flow by the amount of the flow. Step 2 might seem strange, but it allows us to "undo" a flow that is not optimal.

FIGURE 7.20 **Before and after arc capacities**

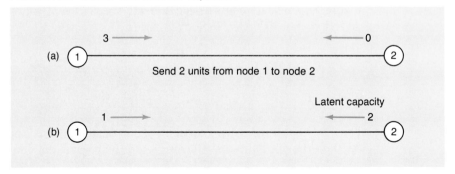

For example, consider arc (1, 2) in Figure 7.19. Before the assignment of any flows, the capacities of the arc are as shown in Figure 7.20(a). After an assigned flow of two units, the capacity of 3 is reduced by two units and the capacity of 0 is increased by two units in the opposite direction. This "artificial capacity" of two units is simply a latent capacity which gives us the opportunity to later "take back" the two units of flow from node 1 to node 2 and send them somewhere else to get more flow to the sink node.

A Maximal Flow Algorithm

Given the guidelines just described, we can now formalize a maximal flow algorithm.

1. Find a path from source node to sink node with positive flow capacity. If no paths with positive flow capacity exist, STOP, for the current flows are optimal.
2. Determine the arc in the path with minimum flow capacity, c_{min}. Increase the flow along the path by c_{min}.
3. Decrease the capacities in the direction of flow by c_{min} for all arcs in the path. Increase the capacities in the opposite direction by c_{min} for all arcs in the path. Go to step 1.

Step 1 leaves the choice of paths up to the decision maker; thus, different people might make different choices. However, if properly executed, the algorithm will provide an optimal solution. Let us apply the algorithm to the pipeline flow problem.

□ **Iteration 1:** Choosing path 1–2–5–7, the minimum capacity c_{min} is 2. Assigning a flow of 2 to the path and revising the network in Figure 7.19 yields the network shown in Figure 7.21.

FIGURE 7.21 **Iteration 1: Path 1–2–5–7, flow = 2**

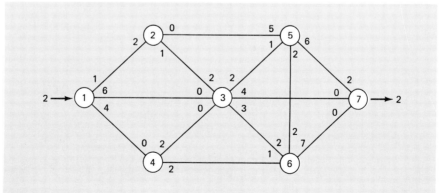

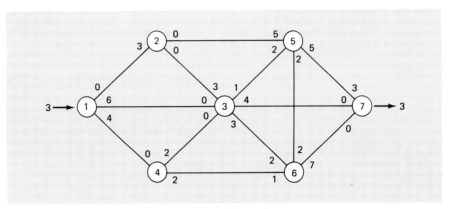

FIGURE 7.22 **Iteration 2: Path 1–2–3–5–7, flow = 1**

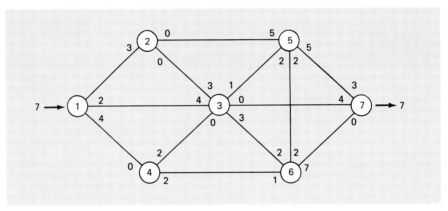

FIGURE 7.23 **Iteration 3: Path 1–3–7, flow = 4**

FIGURE 7.24 **Iteration 4: Path 1–3–6–7, flow = 2**

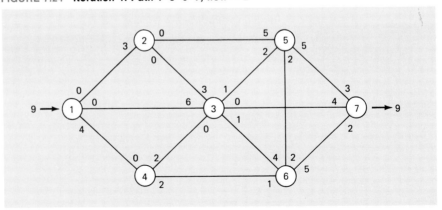

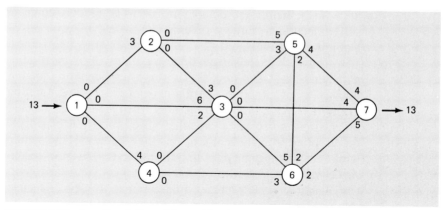

FIGURE 7.25   **Iteration 5, 7, and 7 combined, total additional flow = 4**

- □ **Iteration 2:** Selecting path 1–2–3–5–7 yields $c_{min} = 1$. Updating the network capacities, we have the network shown in Figure 7.22.
- □ **Iteration 3:** Select path 1–3–7. $c_{min} = 4$. The resulting network is shown in Figure 7.23.
- □ **Iteration 4:** Assign flow of 2 along path 1–3–6–7 as shown in Figure 7.24.
- □ **Iteration 5:** Assign flow of 1 along path 1–4–3–5–7.
- □ **Iteration 6:** Assign flow of 1 along path 1–4–3–6–7.
- □ **Iteration 7:** Assign flow of 2 along path 1–4–6–7.

The final network is shown in Figure 7.25.

The maximal flow through the network is 13 units. That no more flow is possible can be verified by observing that it is not possible to send any more flow along any route from node 1 to node 7. This is most evident by observing that there is no positive capacity in any of the arcs leading out of the source node. The actual flow quantities can be determined by keeping track of the flow assignments or by comparing the final arc capacities with the original capacities; the difference equals the flow.

COMPUTER IMPLICATIONS

As was discussed in the previous chapter, formulating mathematical programming problems using a network structure can transform an intractable problem into one that can be solved in a reasonable amount of computer time and computer memory. In other words, some problems without the efficiency introduced by a network formulation could not be solved even with today's largest and fastest computer. For those organizations that do not have large mainframe computers, network models could enable them to solve medium to large problems that would only be possible on a large mainframe if formulated as a general linear program or integer program.

Network models expand the capability of the management scientist in an additional dimension. With some applications, solving the problem quickly is crucial to the decision-making process. At American Airlines, for example, a major problem is created when flights are canceled or diverted to other airports because of weather. The problem is especially critical when the weather problem is at a major "hub" airport. The solution to the problem of reassigning and rerouting aircraft to get the airline back on schedule at the least cost to American and the least inconvenience to passengers can be formulated as an 0/1 integer programming problem. Because of the size of the potential problem, it could take up to 60 minutes to solve on a large computer. Because American must decide on the best course of action in real time and can't wait an hour for the computer to find an optimal solution, a straight integer linear programming approach is not feasible. Fortunately, the problem can be formulated as a shortest-path network problem, and optimal solutions can be generated in a manner of seconds.

In summary, because it is often crucial to the technical, economic, or environmental feasibility of a particular application, today's management scientist is well advised to adopt a "netform concept."

SUMMARY

In this chapter, we have continued our study of network models. They are important since many real-world problems can be modeled as a network. Even though two of the three network models discussed in the chapter can be solved by linear programming, this has been avoided in favor of special-purpose algorithms which are much easier, more intuitive, and much faster. Network models are currently at the frontiers of OR/MS in terms of the size of problems that can be solved optimally.

Each of the three models—the shortest route, minimum spanning tree, and maximal flow—is applicable to specialized kinds of problems. They are, in general, however, applicable to physical distribution problems, scheduling problems, and design problems such as pipeline or teleprocessing systems design.

The shortest-route and maximal flow problems are part of the family of linear network flow problems. They are special cases of the more general transshipment model presented in Chapter 6. The "netform concept" applies to the three network models presented since they yield integer solutions and are efficiently solved. Thus, they are sometimes exploited as subproblems of more complex problems to make them easier to solve.

SOLVED PROBLEMS

PROBLEM STATEMENT

Given the network shown, find the shortest distance to all nodes from node 1 and the shortest route to node 6.

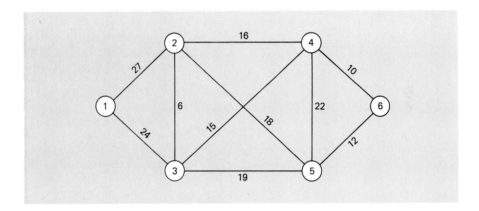

SOLUTION

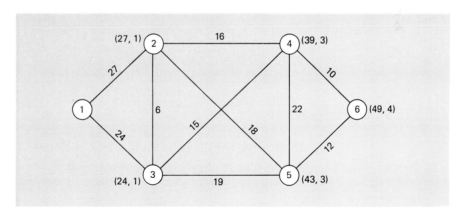

The shortest route from node 1 to node 6 is 1–3–4–6.

Listed below is output from the shortest-route module of the QSB microcomputer package. The B_i are the default names that the program assigns to the arcs in the network.

	The Final Shortest Routes for Solved Problem		
Node	Distance	Shortest Route from Node 1	
2	27	1- 2 (B1)	
3	24	1- 3 (B2)	
4	39	1- 3- 4 (B2-B6)	
5	43	1- 3- 5 (B2-B7)	
6	49	1- 3- 4- 6 (B2-B6-B9)	

PROBLEM STATEMENT

Determine the minimum spanning tree for the network in the preceding problem.

SOLUTION

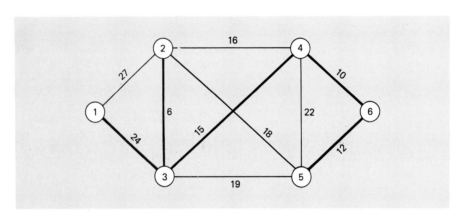

REVIEW QUESTIONS

1. Why are network models an important part of OR/MS?
2. List three specific applications of network models.
3. What determines whether a model is a linear network model?
4. Explain what is meant by a greedy algorithm.
5. Why won't the shortest-route algorithm always work if we allow negative arc lengths?
6. The maximal flow algorithm assumed a single source and sink. How might you handle the case of multiple sources or multiple sinks?
7. Are any of the three network algorithms in this chapter a heuristic?

PROBLEMS

7.1 Find the shortest route from node 1 to all other nodes in the network shown.

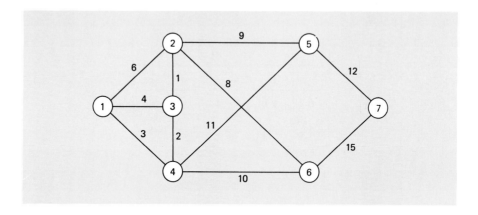

7.2 Find the minimum spanning tree for the network in Problem 7.1.

7.3 Given the following arc capacities on the network from Problem 7.1, determine the maximum flow from node 1 to node 7. Specify the flows on each arc.

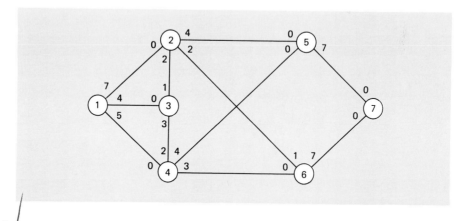

7.4 *Equipment replacement strategy.* An enterprising marketing student has decided to operate a single-plane commuter service between a major city and a resort area during his four years of college. Having limited funds, he is trying to determine the optimal replacement strategy. Assuming that year 0 is now, the following table gives the total net discounted cost (in thousands) associated with purchasing an airplane (purchase price minus trade-in allowance, plus running and mainte-nance costs) at the end of year i and trading it in at the end of year j.

a. Formulate a shortest-route model to determine at which times the airplane should be replaced to minimize total cost over four years.

b. Solve the problem.

	j			
i	*1*	*2*	*3*	*4*
0	8	15	20	30
1		9	17	22
2			10	18
3				12

7.5 *Air-conditioning system design.* A contractor is trying to plan the air-conditioning system for a new single-level office building. The required air-conditioning outlets are shown in the diagram. The arcs represent feasible runs for the air-conditioning ducts. The numbers on the arcs represent linear feet. What duct layout will service all outlets and use the least amount of duct length?

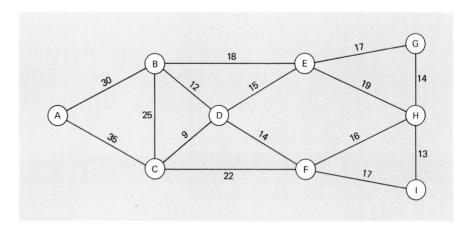

7.6 *Traffic flow.* The east-west freeway system passing through a metro-politan area can accommodate traffic flows with capacities in thou-sands of vehicles per hour as shown. What is the peak traffic load in vehicles per hour that the freeway system could handle?

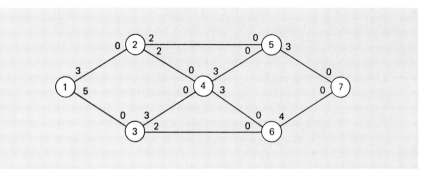

7.7 *Telephone cable layout.* The Rural Telephone Co. is developing plans to connect six outlying towns with underground cable in order that any one town can communicate with another. The matrix of distances between towns is given below. Determine the cable connections that will result in minimal total length.

	To Town					
From town	A	B	C	D	E	F
A	—	10	9	30	27	20
B	10	—	15	18	17	20
C	9	15	—	25	21	16
D	30	18	25	—	8	17
E	27	17	21	8	—	13
F	20	20	16	17	13	—

7.8 *Telecommunication system design.* In a telecommunication network, reliability is sometimes defined as the maximum number of users to be "down" due to a single telecommunication cable failure. Given the seven terminals and one computer center shown, draw the network tree that is most reliable. Is it likely to be a minimum spanning tree?

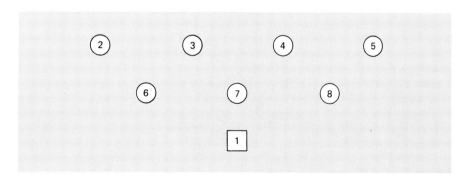

7.9   In the sales rep's routing problem of Figure 7.2, suppose that a new turnpike has been developed to connect node 1 to node 5 at a distance of 35 miles. Does this change the shortest route from node 1 to node 7? Determine the new shortest routes to all nodes.

7.10   *Parts routing.* Reliable Airlines maintenance base has a state-of-the-art materials handling system for their shop. Computerized "auto pickers," computer terminals, and a pneumatic tube system enable mechanics to obtain parts through the tube system from another building, where the warehouse is located. Assuming that time is proportional to distance, specify the pneumatic tube routings from each department to the warehouse to minimize parts travel time.

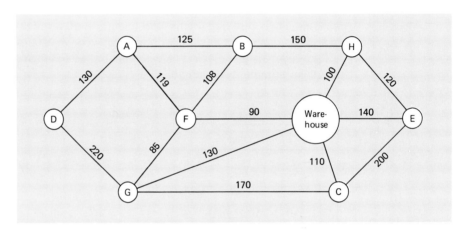

7.11   *Max flow/min cut theorem.* Suppose that we partition the set of network nodes into two sets, c and its complement $\bar{c}$. Those arcs that have one node in c and the other node in $\bar{c}$ comprise a network cut. Removing the cut arcs from the network completely disconnects the sink node

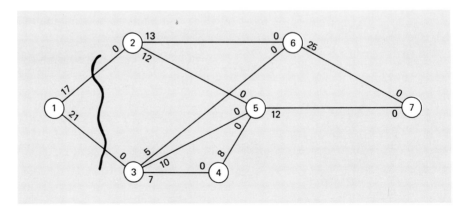

from the source node and thus eliminates any flow. The capacity of the cut equals the sum of the arc capacities in the cut. A cut is illustrated below and is comprised of arcs (1, 2) and (1, 3). The cut capacity is 38.

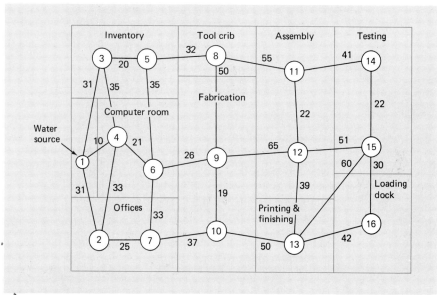

The max flow/min cut theorem states that the maximal flow from source to sink is equal to the minimal cut capacity. That is, of all possible cuts, the one with minimal capacity yields the value of the maximal flow. Find the minimum cut in the network shown and verify its minimal cut capacity by determining the maximal flow.

7.12 *Sprinkler system design.* Reba Manufacturing will have to install a sprinkler system in its plant to get fire insurance. The plant manager has sketched possible pipe routings, distances, and the required outlets in the various departments. He would like to use as little piping as possible in servicing the various areas. Design the optimal sprinkler system for Reba.

7.13 *Crude oil shipping.* Far Eastern Freight Lines has an opportunity to ship crude oil from a Middle Eastern country to the United States. The contract would be lucrative, but Far Eastern has made previous freight commitments of other commodities in other ports. The freighter will have some capacity to ship oil, but the question is, how much? The available cargo capacities in barrels between various ports are shown on the following page. What is the maximum amount of crude oil that Far Eastern can ship from port A to the United States.

				Capacities (1000 bbl)				
From \ To		A	B	C	D	E	F	U.S.
A		—	—	30	25	10	—	—
B		—	—	15	8	—	12	15
C		—	5	—	25	18	13	—
D		—	—	12	—	17	9	—
E		—	14	—	15	—	16	—
F		—	—	—	6	11	—	16

7.14 *Purchasing.* A private refuse collection company must purchase a front-end-loading truck to meet demand on its newly acquired routes. The truck has an economic life of four years. A new truck costs $48,000 now but will cost $54,000 two years from now. The operating costs and salvage values are shown in the table. Determine the optimum purchase plan for providing a truck for four years. Consider both new and used truck options.

Can't buy a used truck.

Numbers of years used	Salvage value end of year	Annual operating and maintenance costs
1	$30,000	$ 6,000
2	22,000	8,000
3	15,000	12,000
4	8,000	15,000

7.15 Assume an arbitrary network with a single source, a single sink, and costs and capacities associated with each arc. Describe how you would set up the problem as a transshipment problem to

a. Determine the shortest route from source to sink.

b. Determine the maximal flow from source to sink through the network.

BIBLIOGRAPHY

Bazaraa, M. S., and J. J. Jarvis, *Linear Programming and Network Flows.* New York: John Wiley & Sons, Inc., 1977.

Ford, L. R., Jr., and D. R. Fulkerson, *Flows in Networks.* Princeton, N.J.: Princeton University Press, 1962.

Glover, F., and D. Klingman, "Network Application in Industry and Government," *AIIE Transactions,* 9, no. 4 (1977), 363–376.

Hillier, F. S., and G. J. Lieberman, *Introduction to Operations Research,* 4th ed. San Francisco: Holden-Day, Inc., 1986.

Hu, T. C., *Integer Programming and Network Flows.* Reading, Mass.: Addison-Wesley Publishing Company, Inc., 1969.

Kennington, Jeff L., and Richard V. Helgason, *"Algorithms for Network Programming."* New York: John Wiley and Sons, Inc., 1980.

Wagner, H. M., *Principles of Operations Research,* 2nd ed. Englewood Cliffs, N.J.: Prentice Hall, 1975.

8

Project Scheduling

LTV AEROSPACE
AND DEFENSE COMPANY[1]

When a large manufacturing corporation with advanced data processing application systems decides to restructure its organization into separate operating divisions, the impact on the production computer systems can be immense. Such was the case with LTV Aerospace and Defense Company, a subsidiary of the LTV Corporation. In 1983, the Sierra Research Corporation, a high-technology electronics firm, and the AM General Corporation, a subsidiary of American Motors Corporation which manufactures vehicles for the armed services, were acquired by LTV. The decision was made to form four operating divisions. The newly acquired companies would form two divisions. The existing structure previously had been split into an Aero Products Division supporting the large aircraft subcontract business base and a Missiles and Advanced Programs Division which would include the company's highly successful Multiple Launch Rocket System contract.

The reorganization affected 39 computer systems in all phases of corporate operation, including the finance, manufacturing, materials, engineering, administration, and human resources departments. With concur-

[1] Scenario prepared by John Porter and David Walton, both employed by LTV: Aerospace and Defense Company.

rent year-end processing activities and the requirement that all of the changes to these interrelated systems dovetail properly, the management and coordination of the more than 600 tasks with more than 2,000 precedence relationships would have been a nightmare without a computerized project management system. IBM's Project Management System software and Systonetics' EZPERT graphics support software were used to schedule the activities.

The transition from data processing for one company to processing for multiple companies involved some tasks which had to be completed from start to finish within 24-hour "windows," while others could have their activities spread over months. PERT (program evaluation and review technique) was valuable in determining those tasks which demanded immediate attention and ensured that a mandatory predecessor activity was not overlooked. Another feature of the Project Management System which proved valuable was the resource allocation processor. This subsystem identified those tasks which could not be completed on time because the programmer/analyst who normally would have done the task was working on another critical activity. Lists by day identified other programmer/analysts who were available to help during peak periods.

PERT's capability of incorporating completions and partial completions of tasks provided a dynamic control system in which problems were quickly identified and feasible alternatives evaluated in a matter of minutes. Leaders were able to manage the project effectively and assure that the objectives of the conversion were successfully met.

INTRODUCTION

Project scheduling is one of the few applications of management science that is widely used among both large and small organizations. Project managers must know how long a specific project will take to finish, what the critical tasks are, and, very often, what the probability is of completing the project within a given time span. In addition, it is often important to know the effect on the total project of delays at individual stages. For these and other reasons, several techniques have been created upon which project managers rely. This chapter examines how the manager can integrate the use of a work breakdown structure (WBS), Gantt charts, and program evaluation and review technique (PERT) to solve the problems of scheduling and controlling projects.

The scheduling techniques we discuss in this chapter can be applied to a wide variety of projects. Government contractors are almost always required to use scheduling techniques such as PERT for projects of even moderate size. Construction companies often use these techniques for scheduling moderate to large-scale projects. One construction company, for example, applies PERT to all projects with a cost greater than $150,000. Designers of computerized information systems are using analytical scheduling techniques more and more. In short, almost any project is a likely candidate because the cost of using these techniques is often outweighed by the benefit.

WORK BREAKDOWN STRUCTURE

When confronted with the task of scheduling and controlling a project of significant size and scope, you must identify each of the tasks involved. In addition, time estimates for each task must be developed, and the necessary resources, both human and nonhuman, must be identified. To accomplish this primary task, it is often desirable to use a work breakdown structure (WBS). WBS is a graphical representation of the tasks involved in a particular project. The technique constitutes a way to classify individual tasks by a natural breakdown of the project in a manner analogous to an organization chart. Indeed, WBS is the organizational structure of the project. It starts with a word description of the project and then breaks the project down into *work* major tasks. These major tasks are reduced to tasks, then to minor tasks, *package* and so on. Finally, the smallest element in the WBS, the *work package,* is defined in detail. Each work package identifies the resources and time it

FIGURE 8.1 **General form of work breakdown structure (WBS)**

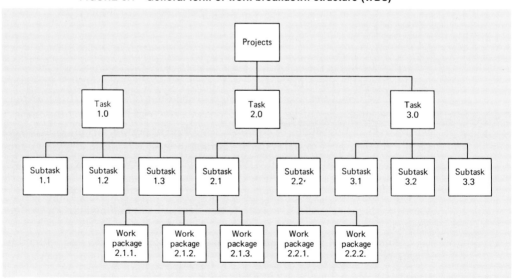

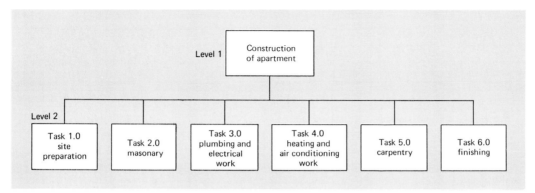

FIGURE 8.2 **Second-level WBS**

requires, all important precedence relationships, and the individual who is responsible for that work package. When all work packages are completed, the project is complete. Figure 8.1 illustrates the general form of the WBS.

Let us use the construction of an apartment building to illustrate the use of WBS. As you can see in Figure 8.2, the entire project can be broken down into six major tasks. These major tasks can then be broken into subtasks, as shown in Figure 8.3. Finally, these subtasks can be broken into work packages, as shown in Figure 8.4. It should be emphasized that WBS is not a solution to the project scheduling problem but rather a preliminary, structured approach to collecting the data necessary for use with one of the more sophisticated techniques, such as PERT. Once the project has been

FIGURE 8.3 **Third-level WBS**

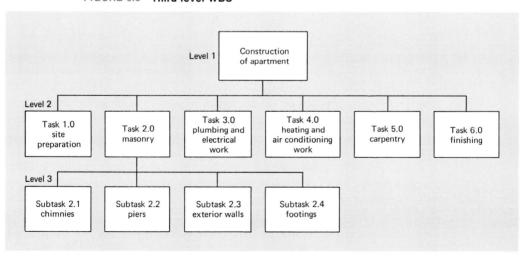

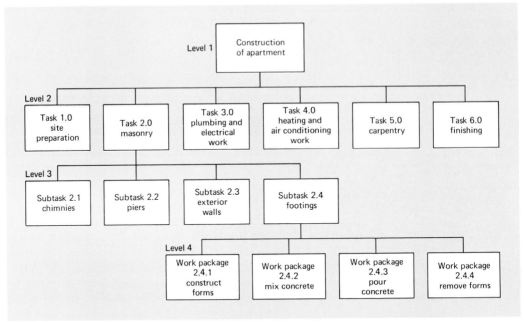

FIGURE 8.4 **Fourth-level WBS**

broken down using WBS, the next step is to choose a way to schedule and control the project.

GANTT CHARTS

For relatively small projects, a simple Gantt milestone chart, or a series of them, may be the best scheduling tool. A Gantt chart is simply a bar chart that plots tasks against time. Once the project manager has created the WBS for a project, the *begin* and *finish* dates for the various tasks, subtasks, and work packages can then be scheduled. A single Gantt chart for major tasks and subtasks might be designed for management review, but any real scheduling must be done at the lowest level in the WBS. Each work package must have beginning and ending dates.

A relatively small project, such as building a house, might be effectively scheduled and controlled by means of a Gantt chart. Ordinarily, however, Gantt charts are primarily record-keeping tools for monitoring projects. They are limited in that they cannot generate information about the interrelationships among various tasks nor about the minimum possible completion times for various tasks. Figure 8.5 shows a Gantt chart for an actual consulting project.

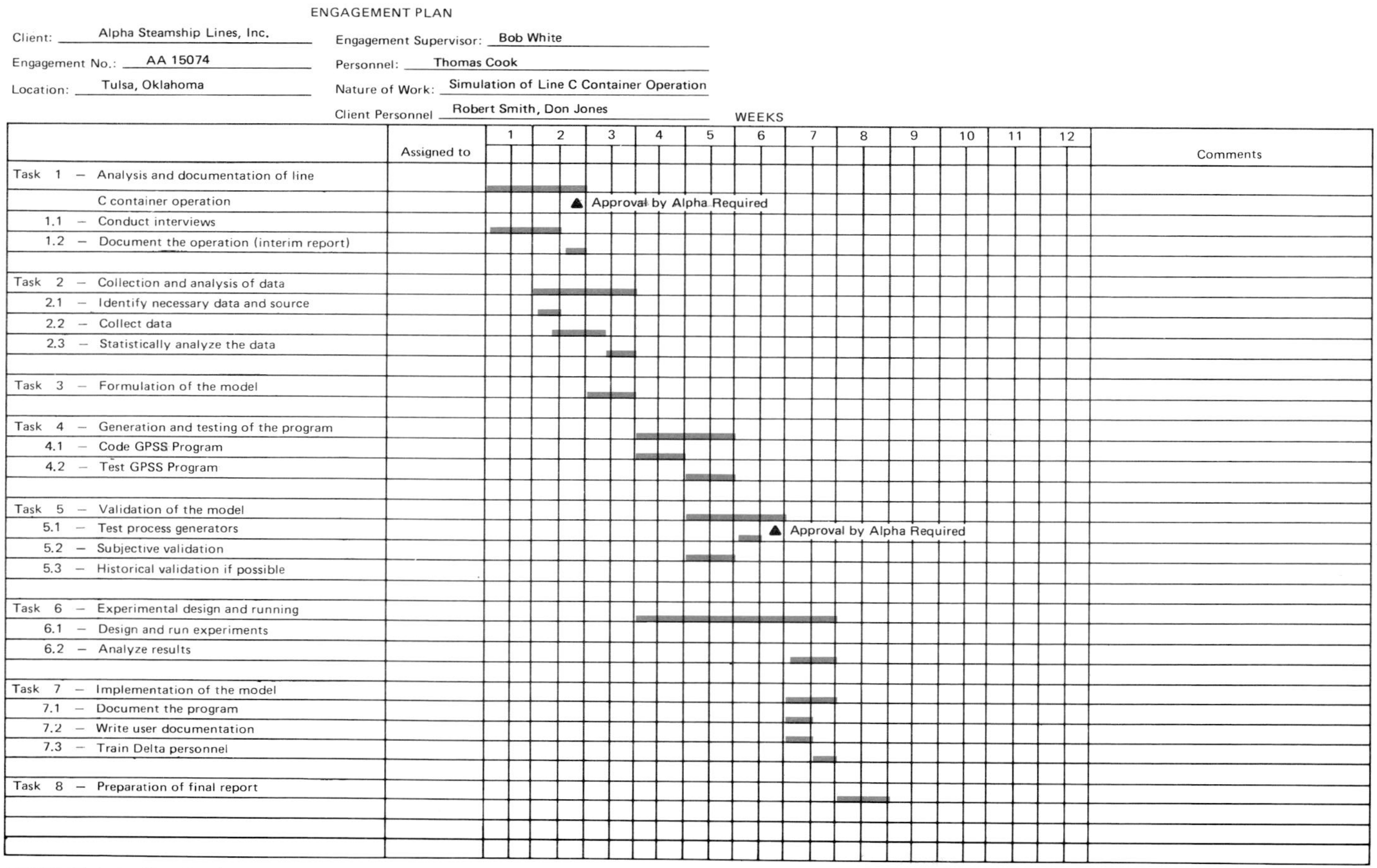

ENGAGEMENT PLAN

Client: Alpha Steamship Lines, Inc.

Engagement Supervisor: Bob White

Engagement No.: AA 15074

Personnel: Thomas Cook

Location: Tulsa, Oklahoma

Nature of Work: Simulation of Line C Container Operation

Client Personnel: Robert Smith, Don Jones

	Assigned to	1	2	3	4	5	6	7	8	9	10	11	12	Comments
Task 1 — Analysis and documentation of line														
C container operation			◄ Approval by Alpha Required											
1.1 — Conduct interviews														
1.2 — Document the operation (interim report)														
Task 2 — Collection and analysis of data														
2.1 — Identify necessary data and source														
2.2 — Collect data														
2.3 — Statistically analyze the data														
Task 3 — Formulation of the model														
Task 4 — Generation and testing of the program														
4.1 — Code GPSS Program														
4.2 — Test GPSS Program														
Task 5 — Validation of the model														
5.1 — Test process generators							◄ Approval by Alpha Required							
5.2 — Subjective validation														
5.3 — Historical validation if possible														
Task 6 — Experimental design and running														
6.1 — Design and run experiments														
6.2 — Analyze results														
Task 7 — Implementation of the model														
7.1 — Document the program														
7.2 — Write user documentation														
7.3 — Train Delta personnel														
Task 8 — Preparation of final report														

WEEKS

FIGURE 8.5   Gantt chart

DETERMINISTIC PERT

PERT evolved from Gantt charts in the late 1950s and was first applied to the U.S. Navy's Polaris submarine project. This project was so large that it was actually a necessity to create a planning and control technique such as PERT. The Polaris project, for instance, had more than 3,000 contractors, many of whom were performing multiple functions. Because of PERT's success in this and subsequent programs, major federal contracting agencies, such as the Department of Defense and NASA, require contractors to utilize PERT in scheduling and controlling their projects.

What, specifically, can PERT do for the project manager? PERT can be used as a planning tool as well as a controlling tool. In its planning function, PERT can be used to compute the total expected time needed to complete a project, and it can identify ''bottleneck'' activities that have a critical effect on the project completion date. Stochastic PERT, to be discussed later in this chapter, allows the project manager to estimate the probability of meeting project deadlines. One of PERT's greatest benefits is that it forces the project manager to plan the project in explicit detail.

Once a project has been scheduled using PERT, you might think that the technique is of no further use. This is not the case; PERT is typically used throughout the project as a control technique. Used periodically during the project, PERT monitors progress and calls attention to any delays that threaten the success of the project as a whole. In addition, PERT and similar techniques such as the critical path method (CPM) can be used to evaluate and make decisions concerning time and cost trade-offs of specific project activities.

Before we examine PERT as a methodology for scheduling and controlling a project, it is important for you to know certain terminology that we shall relate to a specific example.

activity   An *activity* is a task the project requires. Because of the nature of PERT, an activity corresponds to the smallest task in the WBS, namely, the *time estimate* work package. Each activity must have associated with it a *time estimate*, *precedence* and any *precedence relationships* must be defined. Table 8.1 depicts this *relationships* pertinent information for a small project.

TABLE 8.1 *Project table*

Activity	Immediate predecessor	Time estimate (days)
A	—	3
B	A	4
C	A	5
D	B, C, F	7
E	—	3
F	E	6

As these data show, work on activities A and E can begin immediately. Activities B and C cannot be started until activity A has been completed. Activities B, C, and F must be completed before activity D can be started.

network diagram or PERT chart

One of the problems that PERT addresses is the determination of the minimum time required to complete the project. To analyze our project more completely, a *network diagram,* or *PERT chart,* is introduced. The PERT chart (Figure 8.6) is a graphical representation of the entire project. An

event arrow represents an activity, and a circle represents an, *event,* which is defined as the beginning or completion of an activity. The network depicts the precedence relationships involved in the project. As the project table

dummy activity states, the PERT chart shows graphically that it is necessary to finish activity A before beginning activities B and C. The *dummy activity* depicted in Figure 8.6 is a way to indicate diagrammatically that both B and C must be

path finished before D can be started. A *path* through a PERT network is a sequence of connected activities. In our example, there are three paths, A–B–D, A–C–D, and E–F–D. The length of each path can be computed by adding the times for each activity on the path. Thus, the length of path A–B–D is 3 + 4 + 7 = 14 days, and the lengths of paths A–C–D and E–F–D are 15 and 16 days, respectively. The longest path through the network is

critical path called the *critical path.* The length of the critical path corresponds to the minimum time required to complete the project—thus the critical nature of

critical activities the longest path. The activities on the critical path are *critical activities* because a delay in any of these results in a delay of the entire project. In

slack time other words, there is no slack time in the activities on the critical path. *Slack time* is defined as the latest time an activity can be completed without delaying the project minus the earliest time the activity can be completed. In other words, slack time is the amount of time an activity can be delayed without delaying the entire project.

FIGURE 8.6 **PERT chart showing critical path E–F–D**

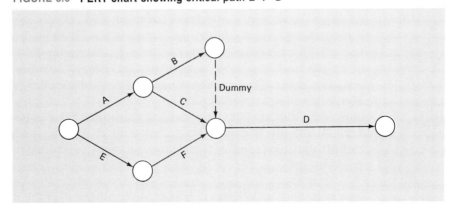

Returning to our example, it is a simple process to identify the critical path by comparing the lengths of each path. Path E–F–D has a length of 16 days. Hence, the minimum time in which the project can be completed is 16 days from the start of the project; delay of activities E, F, or D will delay the entire project. Path A–B–D has a total 2 days of slack time, and path A–C–D has 1 day of slack time.

As the number of activities increases, drawing a chart and finding the critical path by inspection or complete enumeration becomes more and more impractical. Therefore, we need an algorithm (a systematic approach) to find the critical path. To explain the algorithm, four variables must be defined. Let

ES_i = earliest start time for activity i assuming all predecessor activities started at their earliest start time
EF_i = earliest finish time for activity i
  = $ES_i + t_i$ where t_i is the time estimated for activity i
LF_i = latest finish time for activity i without delaying the project
LS_i = latest start time for activity i without delaying the project
  = $LF_i - t_i$

Let us return to our example to illustrate how these four variables are calculated and how the critical path is identified. The algorithm to find the critical path is basically a three-step process. The first step is to calculate the earliest start time (ES_i) and the earliest finish time (EF_i). The second step is to calculate the latest start time (LS_i) and the latest finish time (LF_i) for each activity. Finally, the slack time is calculated for each activity, and the critical path is the sequence of activities that has zero slack time.

To calculate the earliest start time, let all activities that don't have any predecessors start at time zero. To calculate the earliest finish time for these initial activities, merely add the time it takes to complete the activities. Hence, the earliest start time for activities A and E of our example is zero, and the earliest finish time for both activities is $ES_i + t_i$, or $0 + 3$. To calculate the earliest start and earliest finish times for the other activities, it is necessary to add the largest earliest finish time of all immediate predecessor activities to the time for that activity. In our example, activity A has to be finished before B and C are started. Therefore, the earliest start time for activities B and C is 3 (which is the earliest finish time for predecessor A). The earliest finish time for B is $ES_B + t_B$, or $3 + 4 = 7$. Similarly, the earliest finish time for C is 8, and the earliest finish time for F is 9. Consequently, because activity D cannot be started until B, C, and F are finished, the earliest start time for D is 9 (the largest earliest finish time of all immediate predecessors).

Calculating the latest finish times and latest start times is a similar procedure, but to do it we must start at the other end of the PERT network. For all ending activities, set the latest finish time equal to the largest earliest finish time. In our example, there is only one ending activity; hence, the latest finish time is equal to the earliest finish time for activity D. Subtracting the end activity's time from its latest finish time yields the latest start time. The latest finish time for the other activities is equal to the smallest latest start time for all immediate successor activities. Therefore, the latest finish time for activities B, C, and F is 9. The latest start time for activity B is $9 - 4 = 5$.

The latest start time for activity C is $9 - 5 = 4$. Activity A has two successor activities, B and C. Remember, activity A's latest finish time is the minimum latest start time for its successor activities. Hence, the latest time activity A can finish is 4. If activity A finishes after the fourth day, the project will be delayed.

Once the four times have been calculated for each activity, it is a simple procedure to identify the critical path. Slack time is calculated by subtracting the earliest finish time from the latest finish time. Activities with zero slack time are on the critical path. In other words, a delay in any activity on the critical path results in a delay of the entire project. Table 8.2

TABLE 8.2   *Data for PERT algorithm*

Activity	Immediate predecessor	Time	ES	EF	LS	LF	Slack
A	—	3	0	3	1	4	1
B	A	4	3	7	5	9	2
C	A	5	3	8	4	9	1
D	B, C, F	7	9	16	9	16	0
E	—	3	0	3	0	3	0
F	E	6	3	9	3	9	0

FIGURE 8.7   Evaluated PERT chart

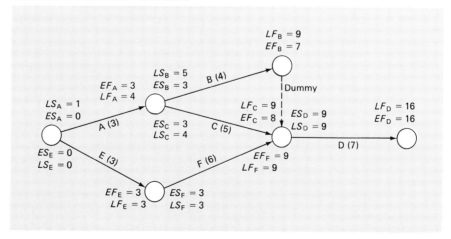

indicates that the critical path is comprised of activities E–F–D. (See Figure 8.7 for the graphical representation of this situation.) Any activity that has a nonzero slack time is not critical and can be delayed as much as the slack time without delaying the project.

We can formalize the initial path calculations that were described in the preceding example. The critical path algorithm consists of two parts. In the forward pass we calculate the ES and EF times for each activity and in the backward pass we calculate the LS and LF times.

FORWARD PASS

1. For all beginning activities i, set

$$ES_i = 0$$

2. In general, $ES_j = \max \{EF_i\}$, where i indexes all predecessors and $EF_j = ES_j + t_j$.

BACKWARD PASS

3. For all ending activities j, set

$$LF_j = \text{largest } EF_j \text{ found in forward pass}$$

4. In general, $LF_i = \min \{LS_j\}$ where j indexes all successors and $LS_i = LF_i - t_i$.

STOCHASTIC PERT

Until now, we have treated PERT as a deterministic technique in which all activity times are known with certainty. It is obvious that for most projects these activity times are random variables. If these random times take on values significantly different from those point estimates used in the PERT analysis, the output from PERT (that is, the critical path, project completion time, and so on) is rendered invalid. To compensate for the lack of certainty in many of the time estimates, the project manager is often asked to give three subjective time estimates for each activity. These time estimates are

$a_i = $ most optimistic time required for activity i
$m_i = $ most likely time required for activity i
$b_i = $ most pessimistic time required for activity i

These three time estimates are used to define a probability distribution of *beta* time for each activity. The distribution used almost exclusively is the *beta* *distribution* *distribution*. There is no rigorous mathematical proof that the beta distribu-

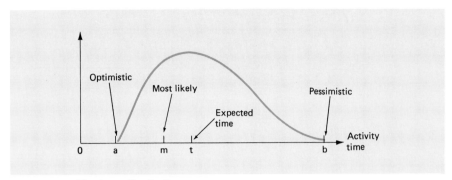

FIGURE 8.8 **The beta distribution**

tion is most appropriate, but three properties make the beta a logical choice. First, it is a continuous probability distribution; second, it is unimodel and not necessarily symmetrical; and finally, it has a bounded range of values. In addition, empirical investigations support the use of the beta distribution for PERT activity times. Figure 8.8 depicts a beta-distributed activity time.

The mean of the distribution, the expected time for an activity, is estimated using the following function,

$$\bar{t}_i = \frac{a_i + 4m_i + b_i}{6}$$

where $\bar{t}_i$ = the expected time for activity i.

The standard deviation of the beta distribution can be approximated using

$$\sigma_i = \frac{b_i - a_i}{6}$$

Suppose, for example, the three time estimates for activity 5 are $a_5 = 2$ days, $m_5 = 6$ days, and $b_5 = 10$ days. Then the expected time for activity 5 is $\bar{t}_5 = (2 + 24 + 10)/6 = 6$ days. The standard deviation of time required for activity 5 is $\sigma_5 = (10 - 2)/6 = 8/6 = 1.33$.

The reason for calculating the standard deviation is to provide a means of computing the probability of completing the project on or before the scheduled completion date. To explain how this probability is computed, let us look at a stochastic version of our original problem. The first step is to estimate the expected time and standard deviation for each activity using the *expected* formulas specified. This is accomplished in Table 8.3. The next step is to find *critical path* the *expected critical path*. (Since the calculated critical path may not, in fact, be the actual critical path, we can only refer to it as an expected critical path.) Finding the expected critical path is done by using the algorithm previously developed for deterministic PERT. The only difference is that in

TABLE 8.3 *Stochastic PERT table*

Activity	Immediate predecessor	a_i	m_i	b_i	$\bar{t}_i$	σ_i	σ_i^2
A	—	1	3	5	3.00	.67	.45
B	A	1	4	5	3.67	.67	.45
C	A	3	5	7	5.00	.67	.45
D	B, C, F	3	7	12	7.17	1.50	2.25
E	—	2	3	4	3.00	.33	.11
F	E	2	6	9	5.83	1.17	1.37

this situation you use the expected activity time instead of the single time estimate. As you can see in Table 8.4, the expected critical path is E–F–D.

Once the expected critical path has been identified, it is often useful to know the probability of completing the expected critical path within a given length of time. For example, what is the probability that the tasks on the expected critical path will all be completed by the end of the project's seventeenth day? To compute a probability of this type, it is necessary to calculate the variance (σ_i^2) for each activity's time. This is done by simply squaring the standard deviation. If we assume that the activities on a given path are independent (that is, that the duration of one task has no effect on the length of time necessary to complete another task), then the variance related to an entire path's length is the sum of the variances of the individual activities on that path. Therefore, assuming independence, the variance for path E–F–D is .11 + 1.37 + 2.25 = 3.73. In addition, if there are many activities on a given path, the distribution of the total time of the path is often assumed (using the central limit theorem) to be normally distributed.

Given the mean and variance of a normally distributed random variable (path length), it is possible to determine the probability of completing that path within a certain length of time. For example, what is the probability of completing path E–F–D within 17 days? The standard deviation of the total time that it takes to complete path E–F–D is $\sqrt{3.73}$, or 1.93, and the mean is

TABLE 8.4 *Data for stochastic PERT algorithm*

Activity	Immediate predecessor	Expected time	ES	EF	LS	LF	Slack
A	—	3.00	0	3.00	0.83	3.83	0.83
B	A	3.67	3.00	6.67	5.16	8.83	2.16
C	A	5.00	3.00	8.00	3.83	8.83	0.83
D	B, C, F	7.17	8.83	16.00	8.83	16.00	0
E	—	3.00	0	3.00	0	3.00	0
F	E	5.83	3.00	8.83	3.00	8.83	0

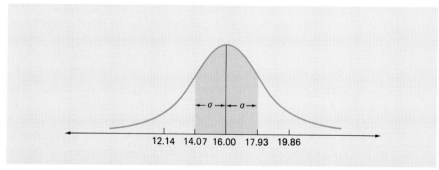

FIGURE 8.9 **Normal distribution of days necessary to complete path E–F–D**

16.00. Given these facts, the theoretical distribution of times necessary to complete path E–F–D is shown in Figure 8.9. The probability of completing path E–F–D within 17 days is represented by the shaded portion of the normal curve in Figure 8.10.

To compute this probability, it is necessary to transform our normal distribution into the standard normal with a mean of 0 and a standard deviation of 1. This is done by using the following transformation:

$$Z = (x - \mu)/\sigma$$

where

μ = mean of the nonstandard normal
σ = standard deviation of the nonstandard normal
x = nonstandardized normal variate

Therefore, the probability of completing path E–F–D is calculated by first calculating Z. Thus, $Z = (17 - 16.00)/1.93 = .5181$. Once Z has been com-

FIGURE 8.10 **Normal distribution showing probability of completing E–F–D within 17 days**

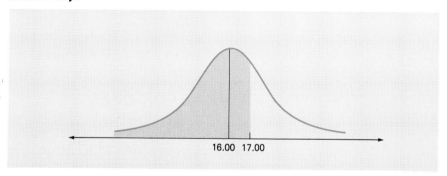

puted, finding the probability of $Z \leq .5181$ is accomplished by using a standard normal table such as Appendix C at the back of this book. The probability that path E–F–D will be finished within 17 days is approximately .6985. (To find this, you look up $Z \leq .5181$ in the table. Be sure to verify it for yourself.) In other words, $P(x \leq 17) = P(Z \leq .5181) = .6985$. It is important to remember that the normality assumption postulates the existence of a large number of random variables (that is, activities on a path). For rough approximations, 30 random variables is usually acceptable; for more rigorous applications, however, an n closer to 100 is preferable.

Having computed the probability of completing the expected critical path within 17 days, can you then conclude that this probability is the probability of completing the project in 17 days or less? The answer is no. Since activity times are random variables, it is possible that a path different from the expected critical path might cause the project to last longer than 17 days. To illustrate this idea, let us consider path A–C–D. The expected time for path A–C–D (t_{A-C-D}) is $3 + 5 + 7.17 = 15.17$, and the standard deviation for path A–C–D is $\sqrt{.45 + .45 + 2.25} = 1.775$. Thus, $Z = (17 - 15.17)/1.775 = 1.031$. Therefore, $P(t_{A-C-D} \leq 17) = P(Z \leq 1.031) \cong .8485$. Similarly, the probability of completing path A–B–D within 17 days is approximately .9625. Now, if we assume that the length of the paths are independent random variables, we can compute the probability of completing the project within 17 days as the joint probability of completing each path within 17 days. In other words, P (project time ≤ 17 days) $= P$ (path A–B–D ≤ 17 and path A–C–D ≤ 17 and path E–F–D ≤ 17). If independence is assumed, P (project time ≤ 17) $= (.9625)(.8485)(.6985) = .5705$. In this example, since the paths have activities in common and the number of activities is small, it would be inappropriate to multiply the individual probabilities.

If the various assumptions necessary to compute the probability of project completion cannot be made (that is, if the individual paths are not independent or do not have a large number of activities), *discrete digital simulation* can be used to estimate the probability of project completion within a specific time period. For each activity, the computer merely samples from a beta distribution for which the parameters have been estimated as previously described. On each iteration, a project completion time is computed and is added to a frequency distribution of project lengths. Given enough iterations, it is reasonable to use this frequency distribution to describe the probabilities of various project durations.

EVALUATING TIME-COST TRADE-OFFS

So far, we have discussed two variations of PERT that emphasize time factors in project evaluation. Deterministic PERT is useful when a project's time parameters are known with a large degree of certainty. Stochastic *critical path method (CPM)* PERT, on the other hand, allows uncertain times to be estimated so that probabilities concerning such activities' duration and completion can be computed. In a third technique, the *critical path method (CPM)*, cost was introduced, as a companion factor to time, for project evaluation.

In their early use, PERT and CPM actually differed in two ways. First, PERT allowed for stochastic times, using the three-point estimate discussed in the preceding section. CPM, however, assumed that times are known with certainty. This distinction is still valid to some extent. When a project is rather uncertain in nature (as, for example, a research project or an out-of-the ordinary undertaking), PERT is the logical technique to use for planning and control. For more common projects, such as certain construction projects in which the times necessary to complete individual tasks can be closely estimated, deterministic PERT or CPM may be more desirable.

As we have mentioned, the second distinction between PERT and CPM is in the area of project costs. CPM made use of a dual perspective: time and cost. You should realize, however, that this difference between PERT and CPM has faded as both techniques have evolved. In fact, most PERT software packages now include provisions for evaluating time-cost trade-offs. For that reason, the discussion of time and cost factors that follows refers to using "versions of PERT and CPM" because, in fact, both methods have been used to make valid analyses of the kind to be discussed.

Until now, we have talked about these project-evaluating techniques primarily as descriptive and predictive tools. Versions of PERT and CPM, however, are used to make decisions concerning how best to shorten a project's completion time. A project manager often has the prerogative of increasing resource allocation to specific tasks so that the project can be finished at an earlier date. In other words, a project manager may have such options as hiring additional workers or working personnel overtime to expedite the completion of a task. To give you an idea of how these time-cost trade-off decisions are made, let us consider our previous deterministic example. Table 8.5 reflects the costs of feasible reductions in each activity's completion time.

TABLE 8.5 *Time-cost trade-off data*

Activity	Normal time estimate (days)	Crash time estimate (days)	Incremental cost of crash time
A	3	2	$150
B	4	3.5	100
C	5	4	200
D	7	5	300
E	3	3	—
F	6	5	75

The crash time estimate in Table 8.5 represents the amount of time it would take to complete an activity if management wished to allocate additional resources to that activity. The incremental cost of crashing an activity is also reflected in Table 8.5. Remember that there were three paths in the PERT network of our original problem. These paths are summarized in Table 8.6. In terms of shortening the total project, it is clear that to shorten paths A–B–D or A–C–D without shortening path E–F–D does no good. Remember, the minimum length of the project is the length of the longest individual path. Therefore, we must look at path E–F–D to determine how to expedite the completion of the total project. Table 8.7 indicates that we have two alternatives for shortening path E–F–D. Because of the lower per day cost, it seems logical to add resources to activity F (that is, activity F is crashed), so that the length of the project is reduced from 16 days to 15 days at a cost of $75.

To shorten the project further, paths A–C–D and E–F–D must both be shortened. Since D is the only activity that can still be shortened on path E–F–D, there is no alternative. Fortunately, D is common to all three paths, and a reduction in D results in shortening all three paths. For $300, D can be reduced from 7 days to 5 days, and each path can be reduced 2 days. Therefore, paths E–F–D and A–C–D would take 13 days and path A–B–D would take 12 days. Further reduction in paths A–B–D or A–C–D would not be fruitful because the length of path E–F–D cannot be reduced. To summarize, we can reduce the project schedule from 16 days to 13 days at a cost of $375. The crashing procedure described can be summarized in the following three steps

Step 1: Consider only activities on the critical path.

Step 2: Shorten the critical path (or paths) until another path becomes critical and go to step 1.

Step 3: Stop when any critical path can no longer be shortened.

TABLE 8.6   *PERT paths*

Path	Length (days)
A–B–D	14
A–C–D	15
E–F–D	16

TABLE 8.7   *Alternatives for shortening E–F–D*

Activity	Days saved by crashing	Cost of crash per day	Cost of crash
E	0	—	—
F	1	$ 75	$ 75
D	2	150	300

PERT/COST

Every project manager has two major problems when managing a large project. First, he or she must be concerned with the time and schedule aspect of the project. We have seen that PERT/CPM can be a very useful tool for scheduling the project and continually monitoring the schedule. A second major problem the project manager is concerned with is that of cost budgets. PERT/Cost can be used to aid in planning, scheduling, and controlling the cost of the project. Specifically, once the various work packages have been identified in the WBS and their costs have been estimated, the project manager must predict the cash flow for the project. In addition, the project manager must periodically review expenditures to determine if actual costs are exceeding budgeted cost so that he or she can take the necessary corrective action to reduce or eliminate cost overruns. Our discussion of PERT/Cost is divided into two sections, the prediction of cash flows and the monitoring and control of project costs.

The estimation of a project's cash flow using PERT/Cost is a five-step process. This five-step process is depicted in the flow chart in Figure 8.11.

FIGURE 8.11 Steps in project cash flow analysis

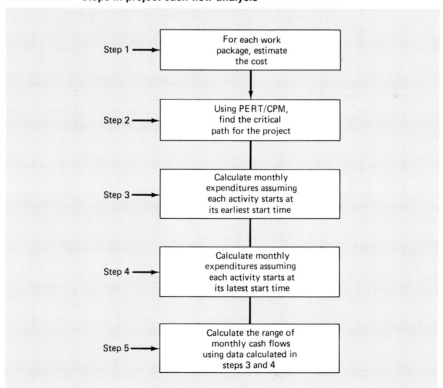

TABLE 8.8 Project table

Activity	Time (months)	Immediate predecessors
A	2	—
B	3	—
C	3	A
D	2	A
E	2	B
F	7	B
G	4	C
H	3	D, E
I	2	H
J	4	G, I

Let us illustrate how PERT/Cost estimates monthly cash flows by using the example shown in Table 8.8. The first step in the cash flow analysis is
to estimate or budget each activity. In many applications, the cost of a work
package or individual task is assumed to be linear (constant). Thus, if activity A is estimated to cost $10,000, the per month cost is assumed to be $5,000
($10,000/ 2 months). With many PERT/Cost software packages, this simpli-
fying assumption is not necessary; in our example, however, costs are
assumed to be linear. The estimated costs for each activity are shown in
Table 8.9.

The next step is to find the critical path for the network depicted in
Figure 8.12. Using the PERT algorithm discussed earlier in this chapter, we
can identify the critical path as path B–E–H–I–J. See Table 8.10 for the
necessary results.

Step 3 is to calculate expected monthly expenditures based on the
assumptions that each activity starts as soon as possible and that cost expen-

TABLE 8.9 Project budget

Activity	Total estimated cost	Estimated monthly cost
A	$ 10,000	$ 5,000
B	24,000	8,000
C	30,000	10,000
D	20,000	10,000
E	40,000	20,000
F	140,000	20,000
G	160,000	40,000
H	90,000	30,000
I	100,000	50,000
J	100,000	25,000
	$714,000	

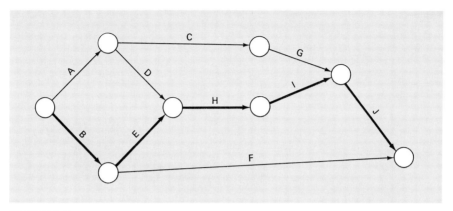

FIGURE 8.12 **PERT network**

ditures are at a uniform rate. Given these two assumptions, the monthly expenditures are calculated in Table 8.11.

The next step is to calculate the expected monthly cash outflows based on the assumption that activities start at their latest starting times. These outflows are calculated in Table 8.12.

The final step in predicting the monthly cumulative cash requirements for a project is to examine the range between the expected monthly cumulative cash outflow assuming an earliest start time and the expected cumulative cash outflow assuming a latest start time. This information is summarized in Table 8.13. The feasible region of cumulative expected cash outflows is graphed in Figure 8.13.

From our example, it should be obvious that the project manager faces a dilemma in scheduling activity starting times when he or she considers project costs as well as project schedules. If activity times are not known with certainty, then starting at the earliest possible times provides the pro-

TABLE 8.10 *Data for the PERT algorithm*

Activity	Time	ES_i	EF_i	LS_i	LF_i	Slack
A	2	0	2	1	3	1
B	3	0	3	0	3	0
C	3	2	5	3	6	1
D	2	2	4	3	5	1
E	2	3	5	3	5	0
F	7	3	10	7	14	4
G	4	5	9	6	10	1
H	3	5	8	5	8	0
I	2	8	10	8	10	0
J	4	10	14	10	14	0

TABLE 8.11 Budgeted monthly cash expenditures assuming earliest start time

Activity	1	2	3	4	5	6	7	8	9	10	11	12	13	14
A	5,000	5,000												
B	8,000-	8,000	8,000											
C			10,000	10,000	10,000									
D			10,000	10,000										
E				20,000	20,000	20,000	20,000	20,000	20,000	20,000				
F				20,000	20,000									
G						30,000	30,000	30,000						
H									50,000	50,000				
I						40,000	40,000	40,000	40,000					
J											25,000	25,000	25,000	25,000
Monthly cost	13,000	13,000	28,000	60,000	50,000	90,000	90,000	90,000	110,000	70,000	25,000	25,000	25,000	25,000
Accumulated project cost	13,000	26,000	54,000	114,000	164,000	254,000	344,000	434,000	544,000	614,000	639,000	664,000	689,000	714,000

TABLE 8.12 Budgeted monthly cash expenditures outflows assuming latest start time

Activity	1	2	3	4	5	6	7	8	9	10	11	12	13	14
A		5,000	5,000											
B	8,000	8,000	8,000											
C				10,000	10,000	10,000								
D				10,000	10,000									
E								20,000	20,000	20,000	20,000	20,000	20,000	20,000
F				20,000	20,000									
G						30,000	30,000	30,000						
H									50,000	50,000				
I							40,000	40,000	40,000	40,000				
J											25,000	25,000	25,000	25,000
Monthly cost	8,000	13,000	13,000	40,000	40,000	40,000	70,000	90,000	110,000	110,000	45,000	45,000	45,000	45,000
Accumulated project cost	8,000	21,000	34,000	74,000	114,000	154,000	224,000	314,000	424,000	534,000	579,000	624,000	669,000	714,000

TABLE 8.13   *Range of expected cash requirements by month*

Month	Cumulative expected cash outflows assuming LS_i	Cumulative expected cash outflows assuming ES_i
1	$ 8,000	$ 13,000
2	21,000	26,000
3	34,000	54,000
4	74,000	114,000
5	114,000	164,000
6	154,000	254,000
7	224,000	344,000
8	314,000	434,000
9	424,000	544,000
10	534,000	614,000
11	579,000	639,000
12	624,000	664,000
13	669,000	689,000
14	714,000	714,000

ject manager with a hedge. This hedge, however, is not without a cost. The cost is derived from the time value of money. In other words, in addition to the direct budgeted cost of the project, the cost of financing the project must be considered. This cost of financing can be a significant factor in persuading a project manager to delay the start of a task as long as is possible.

In addition to predicting the monthly cash needs for a project, a primary responsibility of the project manager is to monitor and control costs. It is extremely important for a project manager to identify cost overruns and

FIGURE 8.13   **Feasible region for cumulative expected cash outflows**

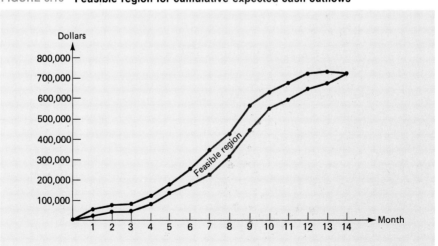

cost underruns so that appropriate action can be taken. Typically, monitoring of project costs is facilitated by a PERT/Cost report produced periodically (monthly or biweekly), which identifies activities that are projected to have a cost overrun or underrun. Let us examine how this critical report is produced. Periodically, a project manager reviews the status of the various work packages to ascertain the actual expenditure to date and the work package's percentage completion. This information, together with the original detailed budget for the project, allows the project manager to identify cost overruns and underruns. Let us illustrate the process of producing a PERT/Cost report by using our previous example. If we assume that we are at the end of the sixth month and the expenditures and activity completion percentages are as shown in Table 8.14, it is possible to calculate a value of work completed for each activity using the formula

$$V_i = \frac{P_i}{100} B_i$$

where

V_i = value of the work completed
P_i = percentage of work completed for activity i
B_i = budget for activity i

Once V_i has been calculated for each activity, it is possible to calculate the amount of the cost overrun or underrun by subtracting the value of the work completed from the actual cost of the work completed using the formula

$$D_i = C_i - V_i$$

TABLE 8.14 *Activity cost and completion data after six months*

Activity	Expenditures to date	Percent completion
A	$12,000	100
B	24,000	100
C	30,000	80
D	18,000	100
E	45,000	95
F	60,000	50
G	40,000	25
H	30,000	25
I	0	0
J	0	0

where

D_i = difference between the actual cost and the value of the work on activity i; if this difference is positive we have a cost overrun, and if it is negative we have a cost underrun

C_i = actual cost of activity i

TABLE 8.15 *PERT/Cost report*

Activity	Budget, B_i	Expenditures to date, C_i	Value V_i	Differences, D_i
A	$ 10,000	$12,000	$10,000	$ 2,000
B	24,000	24,000	24,000	0
C	30,000	30,000	24,000	6,000
D	20,000	18,000	20,000	−2,000
E	40,000	45,000	38,000	7,000
F	140,000	60,000	70,000	−10,000
G	160,000	40,000	40,000	0
H	90,000	30,000	22,500	7,500
I	100,000	0	0	0
J	100,000	0	0	0

It is apparent from the PERT/Cost report in Table 8.15 that several activities have overruns and several have underruns and that these overruns and underruns nearly balance each other. The prudent project manager, however, would look closely at activities C, E, and H to determine the cause of the overrun and see if some type of corrective action might be appropriate.

Resource-Constrained PERT

The project scheduling methods that we have examined up to this point have assumed that resources are unlimited or at least have no impact on the scheduling of activities. However, in many applications there might be a limited staff of skilled personnel, a fixed number of machines, or budget restrictions. As a result, activities can be scheduled only as required resources become available. The net effect on project scheduling is to delay certain activities and possibly the project completion date.

To illustrate the effects of resource constraints, consider the PERT problem from Figure 8.6 at the beginning of this chapter. Suppose that a certain number of people are required to complete each task. Figure 8.14 shows the resource requirements on the associated PERT chart. Notice that activities A and E require three and five people, respectively. If eight people are available, then both activities can be scheduled simultaneously. However, if less than eight people are available, then either A or E must be delayed.

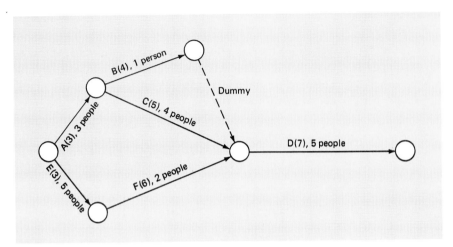

FIGURE 8.14 **PERT chart showing resource requirements**

Figure 8.15 shows the resource requirements over the 16-day planning horizon assuming that activities begin at their earliest start times. Figure 8.15 is different in that the duration of each activity is represented by the length of that activity's arrow. The number on the arrow represents the number of people required. Thus, adding the manpower requirement of all activities in progress on each day gives the total manpower requirements as shown at the bottom of Figure 8.15. The manpower requirement varies from a low of two people to a high of eight people over the 16-day planning horizon. Suppose, however, that only six people are available for the project on any one day?

FIGURE 8.15 **Schedule graph for earliest start times and resource requirements**

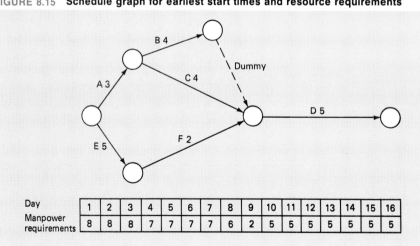

Day	1	2	3	4	5	6	7	8	9	10	11	12	13	14	15	16
Manpower requirements	8	8	8	7	7	7	7	6	2	5	5	5	5	5	5	5

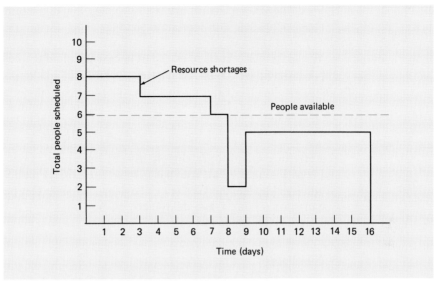

FIGURE 8.16 **Resource requirements chart**

Figure 8.16 shows the resource requirements profile over the 16-day scheduling period. Notice that personnel shortages occur on days 1–7. It is possible to delay some activities with slack to try to reduce peak resource requirements and not extend project duration beyond the earliest finish time *resource* of 16 days. This process of rescheduling activities with slack to smooth peak *leveling* resource requirements is called *resource leveling.*

In this problem it is not possible to reduce peak resource requirements below 8 people and finish the project within 16 days. A more realistic objec *resource-* tive is to schedule the project so as to not exceed resource constraints but *constrained* still to complete the project as soon as possible. These are the objectives in *PERT* *resource-constrained PERT.* Solution methods for resource-constrained PERT include integer programming models and heuristics. Heuristic scheduling rules are widely used since they are easy to apply and yield reasonably good solutions.

MINIMUM SLACK TIME SCHEDULING RULE (MINSLK)

In this section we focus on a simple but effective scheduling rule that prioritizes competing activities so that the activity with the least amount of slack receives the resource allocation. The heuristic can be summarized as follows:

1. Allocate resources serially in time. Begin on the first day and schedule all jobs possible; then do the same for the next day, and so on.

2. When several activities are ready to begin, give preference to starting those activities with minimum slack.

The MINSLK heuristic does not necessarily find the best solution, but research has shown it to be among the most effective heuristics. Let's apply the heuristic to the PERT problem in Figure 8.14. Assuming that only six people are available, the MINSLK rule results in the following decisions:

DAY 1

▫ Activities A and E are eligible to start but only 6 people are available. From Figure 8.7, we see that E is on the critical path with zero slack while A has one day of slack. Therefore, allocate five people to E so E can start on day 1 and delay activity A.

Day 2 and 3

▫ No change.

Day 4

▫ Activity E is finished and activities A and F are now eligible for scheduling. It is necessary to update earliest start and latest start calculations to recalculate slack. Figure 8.17 shows the updated calculations. Activity F now has two days of slack whereas A now has none. Thus, A is

FIGURE 8.17   Updated ES, EF, LS, and LF calculations after three days

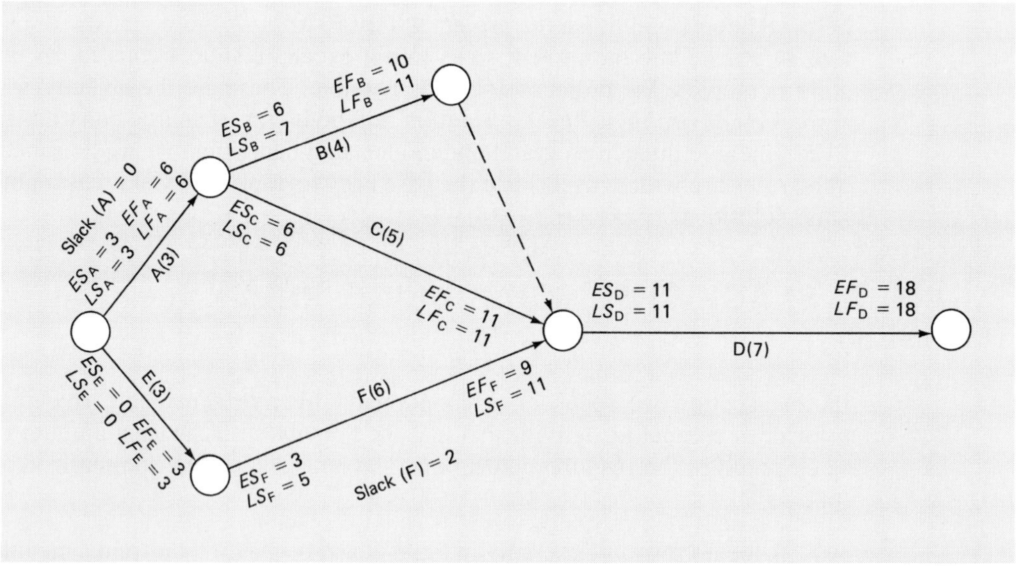

TABLE 8.16 *MINSLK scheduling decisions*

Day	Activities eligible to start	Slack	Start time	Finish time
1	A	1	—	—
	E	0	0	3
4	A	0	3	6
	F	2	3	9
7	B	1	—	—
	C	0	6	11
10	B	0	9	13
14	D	0	13	20

scheduled first and three people are allocated. Since activity F requires only two people, it can also be started at this time.

DAY 5 and 6

□ No change.

DAY 7

□ Activity A has been completed and activities B and C are eligible for scheduling concurrent with activity F. Since C has less slack than B, it is scheduled to start. Activity B is further delayed.

Continuing to schedule the project using the MINSLK heuristic results in a project duration of 20 days. Thus, staying within the resource limitations results in a 4-day delay for the total project duration. Table 8.16 summarizes all the MINSLK scheduling decisions.

For simplicity, the example has dealt with only one resource. However, some PERT applications involve multiple resources. The MINSLK heuristic is directly extended to the multiple-resource case: Those activities having minimum slack are allocated resources and started first. Many software packages are now available to handle project scheduling with resource constraints. The less powerful packages display resource profiles and allow user manipulation of schedules. The more powerful packages have the capability to develop their own schedules in response to tight resource constraints.

COMPUTER IMPLICATIONS

Because of the widespread use of network techniques for controlling large projects of all types, a large number of software packages are available. The computer programs vary widely with respect to their cost, functionality, and the type and size of computer for which they are programmed. In an article for *Project Management Quarterly*,[2] Smith and Mills describe 40 different project management software packages. Some of the packages are available at virtually no cost ($30 for a magnetic tape) whereas some cost as much as $110,000 to buy. Many packages can be leased by the month and some can be accessed for a royalty charge through national time-sharing networks.

In their article, Smith and Mills report that over 85 percent of the packages evaluated had the following features:

- Gantt chart presentation capability
- Ability to use calendar dates
- A flexible report generator where the project manager could specify the type and format of the reports he or she wanted
- Updating capability
- Cost control and cost reporting
- Resource allocation which allows the user to balance resources and simultaneously adjust the schedule
- Plotter-created network diagrams

As indicated by the foregoing listed features, it is apparent the state of the art of available project scheduling software has reached an advanced stage.

The computer hardware that these packages are available for range from Microsoft Project for small microcomputers to a program marketed by Accuratech, Inc., which runs on one of the world's fastest computers, the Cray 1.

In short, use of a PERT/CPM type of methodology is very common not only because the methodology has great potential for aiding the project manager control the cost and schedule of a large project, but also because of the availability of a large variety of "user-friendly" software packages.

SUMMARY

The management of large complex projects is a significant problem in today's modern industrial society. Fortunately, management science has pro-

---

[2] Larry A. Smith and Joan Mills, "Project Management Network Programs," *Project Management Quarterly*, June 1982, pp. 18–29.

vided several tools such as PERT/CPM, PERT/Cost, and resource-constrained PERT, that greatly aid the project manager in scheduling and controlling large projects. WBS is a necessary first step in organizing any project, as it represents the organizational structure of the project in hierarchical form. Once the WBS has been completed, PERT or CPM can be used to schedule the project, identify critical tasks, and estimate project completion times with various degrees of confidence. PERT is typically used during the life of the project for schedule monitoring and control purposes. This monitoring function is necessary so that the consequences of various delays can be predicted and corrective action in the form of additional resources can be applied to keep the project on schedule. In addition, PERT/Cost enables the project manager to estimate cash outflows and monitor the project's cost to identify cost overruns early enough to take the appropriate action. Resource-constrained PERT enables the project manager to better schedule a project in which human or other resources are in limited supply.

SOLVED PROBLEMS

PROBLEM STATEMENT

Consider the project information in the accompanying table.

Task	Immediate predecessor	Time estimate (days)
A	—	5
B	—	4
C	A	6
D	A	3
E	B	3
F	B	6
G	E	2
H	F	5
I	C, D	8
J	G, H	5

1. Draw the PERT network for the project.
2. Use the PERT algorithm to find the critical path.
3. What is the minimum project completion time?

SOLUTION

1. The PERT chart is

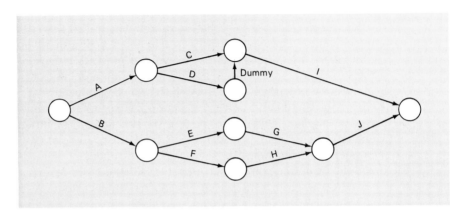

2. To find the critical path, it is necessary to compute the slack time for each task. This is done below using the PERT algorithm. The critical path consists of those activities that have zero slack time. Therefore, the critical path is B–F–H–J.

Task	Time	ES	EF	LS	LF	Slack time
A	5	0	5	1	6	1
B	4	0	4	0	4	0
C	6	5	11	6	12	1
D	3	5	8	9	12	4
E	3	4	7	10	13	6
F	6	4	10	4	10	0
G	2	7	9	13	15	6
H	5	10	15	10	15	0
I	8	11	19	12	20	1
J	5	15	20	15	20	0

3. The minimum project completion time is the length of the critical path. The length of the critical path is the latest finish time for activity J, which is 20 days.

COMPUTER SOLUTION

The following computer solution was obtained by using the PERT module of the QSB microcomputer package on an IBM personal computer.

```
┌─────────────────────────────────────────────────────────────────────────┐
│                  PERT Analysis for PROJ     Page   1                      │
├──────────┬──────────────┬─────────┬─────────┬─────────┬─────────┬─────────┤
│Activity  │  Activity    │Earliest │ Latest  │Earliest │ Latest  │  Slack  │
│No. Name  │Exp.Tm. Var.  │ Start   │ Start   │ Finish  │ Finish  │  LS-ES  │
├──────────┼──────────────┼─────────┼─────────┼─────────┼─────────┼─────────┤
│ 1   A    │5.0000  0     │  0      │ 1.0000  │ 5.0000  │ 6.0000  │ 1.0000  │
│ 2   B    │4.0000  0     │  0      │ 0       │ 4.0000  │ 4.0000  │Critical │
│ 3   D    │3.0000  0     │ 5.0000  │ 9.0000  │ 8.0000  │ 12.000  │ 4.0000  │
│ 4   C    │6.0000  0     │ 5.0000  │ 6.0000  │ 11.000  │ 12.000  │ 1.0000  │
│ 5   E    │3.0000  0     │ 4.0000  │ 10.000  │ 7.0000  │ 13.000  │ 6.0000  │
│ 6   F    │6.0000  0     │ 4.0000  │ 4.0000  │ 10.000  │ 10.000  │Critical │
│ 7   DUMMY│0       0     │ 8.0000  │ 12.000  │ 8.0000  │ 12.000  │ 4.0000  │
│ 8   I    │8.0000  0     │ 11.000  │ 12.000  │ 19.000  │ 20.000  │ 1.0000  │
│ 9   G    │2.0000  0     │ 7.0000  │ 13.000  │ 9.0000  │ 15.000  │ 6.0000  │
│10   H    │5.0000  0     │ 10.000  │ 10.000  │ 15.000  │ 15.000  │Critical │
│11   J    │5.0000  0     │ 15.000  │ 15.000  │ 20.000  │ 20.000  │Critical │
├──────────┴──────────────┴─────────┴─────────┴─────────┴─────────┴─────────┤
│               Expected completion time = 20                               │
└─────────────────────────────────────────────────────────────────────────┘

Critical paths for PROJ  with completion time =  20

CP # 1   : (with variance = 0 )
    B           F           H           J
  1=======>  3========>  7========>  8========>  9
```

PROBLEM STATEMENT

Consider the project information in the table on the following page.

1. Draw the PERT network for this project.
2. Compute the mean and variance in time for each activity.
3. Find the expected critical path.
4. What is the expected length of the critical path?
5. Assuming normality and path independence, what is the probability of completing the project in less than 22 days?

Task	Immediate predecessor	a_i	m_i	b_i
		Time estimates		
A	—	4	5	7
B	A	2	3	5
C	A	5	7	11
D	B	2	2	2
E	B	3	4	6
F	D	3	5	6
G	C	3	3	3
H	C	2	2	2
I	G, H	3	4	6
J	E, F	4	6	7

SOLUTION

1. The PERT network is

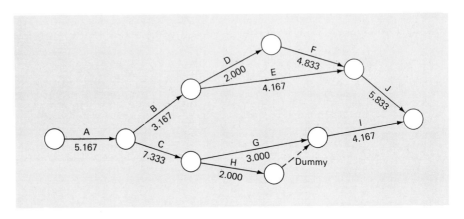

2. The mean time for task A is computed as follows.

$$\bar{t}_A = \frac{4 + 4(5) + 7}{6}$$

$$= \frac{31}{6} = 5.167$$

The standard deviation for task A is computed:

$$\sigma_A = \frac{7 - 4}{6} = \frac{3}{6} = \frac{1}{2}$$

Therefore, the variance for task A is

$$\sigma_A^2 = \left(\frac{1}{2}\right)^2 = \frac{1}{4} = .25$$

The mean time and variances for the remaining tasks are shown in the table.

Task	Mean time	Variance
A	5.167	.25
B	3.167	.25
C	7.333	1.00
D	2.000	.00
E	4.167	.25
F	4.833	.25
G	3.000	.00
H	2.000	.00
I	4.167	.25
J	5.833	.25

3. The expected critical path is composed of all those activities whose slack time is zero. Slack times are computed in the table.

Task	Expected time	ES	EF	LS	LF	Slack time
A	5.167	0	5.167	0	5.167	0
B	3.167	5.167	8.334	5.167	8.334	0
C	7.333	5.167	12.500	6.500	13.833	1.333
D	2.000	8.334	10.334	8.334	10.334	0
E	4.167	8.334	12.501	11.000	15.167	2.667
F	4.833	10.334	15.167	10.334	15.167	0
G	3.000	12.500	15.500	13.833	16.833	1.333
H	2.000	12.500	14.500	14.833	16.833	2.333
I	4.167	15.500	19.667	16.833	21.000	1.333
J	5.833	15.167	21.000	15.167	21.000	0

Therefore, the expected critical path is A–B–D–F–J.

4. The expected length of the critical path is the latest finish time of the ending activity (activity J), which is 21 days.

5. The probability of completing the project in 22 days is the probability completing all paths within 22 days. To illustrate, let us make the necessary but unrealistic assumption concerning the independence of the various paths. The probability of completing A–B–D–F–J in 22 days can be computed as follows:

$$Z = \frac{X - \mu}{\sigma}$$

$$= \frac{22 - 21}{\sqrt{.25 + .25 + 0 + .25 + .25}}$$

$$= \frac{1}{1} = 1$$

$$P(\text{path A–B–D–F–J} \leq 22) = P(Z \leq 1) = .8413$$

Similarly, $P(\text{path A–B–E–J})$ is computed as

$$Z = \frac{22 - 18.334}{\sqrt{.25 + .25 + .25 + .25}} = 3.667$$

$$P(\text{path A–B–E–J} \leq 22) \cong 1.0$$

$P(\text{path A–C–G–I} \leq 22)$ is

$$Z = \frac{22 - 19.667}{\sqrt{.25 + 1.0 + 0 + .25}}$$

$$= 1.905$$

$$P(\text{path A–C–G–I} \leq 22) = P(Z \leq 1.905)$$

$$= .9713$$

P(path A–C–H–I $\leq$ 22) is

$$Z = \frac{22 - 18.667}{\sqrt{.25 + 1.0 + 0 + .25}}$$
$$= 2.72$$
$$P(\text{path A–C–H–I} \leq 22) = P(Z \leq 2.72)$$
$$= .9967$$

The probability of all paths being complete in 22 days, assuming independence of paths and normality, is the product of the individual probabilities, or

$$P(\text{project time} \leq 22) = (.8413)(1)(.9713)(.9967)$$
$$= .814$$

COMPUTER SOLUTION

```
            PERT Analysis for PROJ    Page  1

Activity      Activity       Earliest   Latest   Earliest   Latest    Slack
No. Name     Exp.Tm. Var.    Start      Start    Finish     Finish    LS-ES

1    A       5.1667  0.2500   0          0        5.1667     5.1667    Critical
2    B       3.1667  0.2500   5.1667     5.1667   8.3333     8.3333    Critical
3    C       7.3333  1.0000   5.1667     6.5000   12.500     13.833    1.3333
4    D       2.0000  0        8.3333     8.3333   10.333     10.333    Critical
5    E       4.1667  0.2500   8.3333     11.000   12.500     15.167    2.6667
6    H       2.0000  0        12.500     14.833   14.500     16.833    2.3333
7    G       3.0000  0        12.500     13.833   15.500     16.833    1.3333
8    F       4.8333  0.2500   10.333     10.333   15.167     15.167    Critical
9    DUMMY   0       0        14.500     16.833   14.500     16.833    2.3333
10   I       4.1667  0.2500   15.500     16.833   19.667     21.000    1.3333
11   J       5.8333  0.2500   15.167     15.167   21.000     21.000    Critical

            Expected completion time = 21
```

```
Critical paths for PROJ  with completion time = 21

CP # 1   : (with variance = 1 )
     A             B             D             F          J
  1========>   2========>   3========>   5========>   8========>  9
```

```
                    Probability Analysis for PROJ

    The following probability calculations assume that activities are
independent and that all paths are also independent.  It also assumes that
your network has a large enough number of activities so as to enable use of
the normal distribution.  Therefore, when the activities are not independent
or the number of activities is not large, the following analysis may be
highly biased.

Expected completion time = 21

What is your project schedule time (type 0 to end analysis) ? 22

    On CP # 1 :  Variance = 1   Standard deviation = 1
        Probability of finishing within 22 is  .8413513

The probability of finishing the whole project within 22 is  .8413513

Do you want to enter a new scheduled completion time (Y/N)?
```

PROBLEM STATEMENT

Consider the project information in the accompanying table. Given the maximum number of workers that are available for the project is five, develop a project plan utilizing the MINSLK heuristic.

Task	Immediate predecessor	Time estimate (no. days)	Labor requirement (people)
A		5	3
B		7	5
C	B	10	2
D	B	12	4
E	A, B	11	4
F	C, D, E	14	3

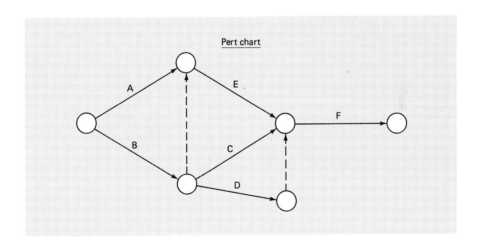

Pert chart

ITERATION 1

Task	Time	ES	EF	LS	LF	Slack time
A	5	0	5	3	8	3
B	7	0	7	0	7	0
C	10	7	17	9	19	2
D	12	7	19	7	19	0
E	11	7	18	8	19	1
F	14	19	33	19	33	0

The initial critical path is B–D–F. Therefore, start task B immediately utilizing all five people.

ITERATION 2

Task	Time	ES	EF	LS	LF	Slack time
A	5	7	12	7	12	0
B	7		— Complete —			
C	10	7	17	13	23	6
D	12	7	19	11	23	4
E	11	12	23	12	23	0
F	14	23	37	23	37	0

The new critical path is A–E–F. Therefore, start task A at the end of the seventh day utilizing three people. Also, start activity C using the remaining two people.

ITERATION 3

Task	Time	ES	EF	LS	LF	Slack time
A	5			— Complete —		
B	7			— Complete —		
C	10			— In progress —		
D	12	7	19	11	23	4
E	11	12	23	12	23	0
F	14	23	37	23	37	0

At the end of day 12, three people become available to be assigned. Two tasks (D and E) are eligible to be initiated at this time; however, both require four people and therefore cannot be started. Thus, we must wait for task C to complete before starting the next task.

ITERATION 4

Task	Time	ES	EF	LS	LF	Slack time
A	5			— Complete —		
B	7			— Complete —		
C	10			— Complete —		
D	12	17	29	17	29	0
E	11	17	28	18	29	1
F	14	29	43	29	43	0

At the end of day 17, start activity D using four people.

ITERATION 5

Task	Time	ES	EF	LS	LF	Slack time
A	5		— Complete —			
B	7		— Complete —			
C	10		— Complete —			
D	12		— Complete —			
E	11	29	40	29	40	0
F	14	40	54	40	54	0

At the end of day 29, assign four people to task E, and when task E is complete on day 40, assign four people to task F.

Given the plan developed here the project should be completed in 54 days.

REVIEW QUESTIONS

1. Distinguish between Gantt charts and PERT.
2. What are the basic elements in a work package?
3. What is the basic purpose of using WBS?
4. On what kinds of projects would you use deterministic PERT rather than stochastic PERT?
5. What can PERT do for the project manager?
6. Define "critical path."
7. How is slack time computed?
8. Why is the beta distribution used for PERT times?
9. Why compute σ_i?
10. What assumptions are made to make probabilistic statements about project completion schedules?
11. Explain in your own words how and why simulation is used with PERT.
12. What does PERT/cost do for the project manager?
13. What is the objective of resource-constrained PERT?
14. In your own words describe the MINSLK heuristic.

PROBLEMS

8.1 Prepare the WBS for a project with which you are familiar. In addition to identifying each task and subtask, prepare the necessary work packages.

8.2 Draw Gantt charts for the various task levels of the WBS prepared for Problem 8.1.

8.3 Consider the information in the table.

Task	Immediate predecessor	Estimated time (days)	No. of people required
A	—	5	2
B	—	4	3
C	A	3	1
D	B	7	3
E	C	2	3
F	D, E	1	1

a. Draw the PERT network diagram for this project.

b. Use the PERT algorithm for finding the critical path.

c. What is the minimum project completion time ignoring resource constraints?

d. Would the critical path change if F were to take five days rather than one? Explain.

e. Develop the project plan using the MINSLK heuristic. Assume 4 people are available.

8.4 Consider the project information in the table.

Task	Immediate predecessor	Estimated time (weeks)	No. of people required
A	—	5	3
B	—	6	2
C	A	4	3
D	B	3	3
E	B	5	1
F	C, D	2	1
G	E	2	2
H	E	4	4
I	F, G	3	5
J	H	2	3
K	I, J	5	2

a. Draw the PERT network diagram for the project.

b. Use the PERT algorithm for finding the critical path.

c. What is the minimum project completion time ignoring resource constraints?

d. Develop the project plan using the MINSLK heuristic. Assume 5 people are available.

8.5   Consider the project information in the table.

Task	Immediate predecessor	Estimated time (weeks)		
		a_i	m_i	b_i
A	—	3	5	6
B	A	3	4	7
C	A	1	3	5
D	B	2	4	7
E	C	2	5	8
F	D	1	2	4
G	E	2	3	4

a. Draw the PERT network diagram for this project.

b. Compute the mean and variance in time for each activity.

c. Find the critical path by inspection.

d. What is the expected length of the expected critical path?

e. Assume that the time required to complete a path is normally distributed. What is the probability of completing the critical path in less than or equal to 15 weeks?

f. Again assuming normality and path independence, what is the probability of completing the entire project in less than or equal to 15 weeks?

g. If you wanted to be at least 95 percent sure of completing the project on time, what schedule would you quote?

8.6   Consider the information in the table.

a. Draw the PERT network diagram for this project.

b. Compute the mean and variance in time for each activity.

c. Find the critical path using the PERT algorithm.

d. What is the expected length of the expected critical path?

e. Assuming that the time required to complete a path is normally distributed, what is the probability of completing the critical path in less than or equal to 50 weeks?

f. Again assuming normality and path independence, what is the probability of completing the entire project in less than or equal to 50 weeks?

g. If you wanted to be at least 95 percent sure of completing the project on time, what schedule would you quote?

		Estimated time (weeks)		
Task	Immediate predecessor	a_i	m_i	b_i
A	—	4	5	7
B	—	5	9	11
C	A	5	10	15
D	A	4	5	8
E	A	5	7	12
F	D, C	3	4	7
G	D, C	2	3	4
H	D	7	12	18
I	B, E	6	11	14
J	F	5	6	9
K	G	5	7	9
L	H, I	2	3	5
M	J, K	7	8	9
N	L	1	3	4
O	M, N	15	17	22

8.7 *Sports scheduling*. State University is planning a holiday basketball tournament and has decided to use PERT to schedule the project. The tasks and time estimates have been identified as set forth in the table.

			Estimated time (days)		
Task	Description	Immediate predecessors	a_i	m_i	b_i
A	Team selection	—	1	3	5
B	Mail out invitations and receive acceptances	A	4	5	10
C	Arrange accommodations	—	8	10	15
D	Plan promotional strategy	B	2	3	5
E	Print tickets	B	4	5	8
F	Sell tickets	E	15	15	15
G	Complete arrangements	B, C	7	8	10
H	Develop practice schedules	C	2	3	4
I	Practice sessions	H	2	2	2
J	Conduct tournament	F, I	3	3	3

a. Draw the PERT diagram and identify the expected critical path.

b. If the tournament is to be held starting December 27, when should team selection begin to assure 98 percent certainty that the tournament will be held as scheduled?

8.8 Consider the project in Problem 8.3. Assume crash times and crash costs as set forth in the table.

Activity	Normal time estimate (days)	Crash time estimate (days)	Incremental cost of crash time
A	5	4	$100
B	4	3.5	100
C	3	2.5	150
D	7	5	400
E	2	2	—
F	1	1	—

a. What is the shortest time in which the project can be completed?

b. What is the total incremental cost of achieving the shortest completion time?

c. What is the minimum incremental cost of completing the project in 10 days?

8.9 Consider the project in Problem 8.4. Assume the crash times set forth in the table.

Activity	Normal time estimate (weeks)	Crash time estimate (weeks)	Incremental cost of crash time
A	5	4	$100
B	6	4	400
C	4	3.5	100
D	3	3	—
E	5	4	100
F	2	1.5	150
G	2	2	—
H	4	3	175
I	3	2	125
J	2	2	—
K	5	2	550

a. What is the shortest time in which the project can be completed?

b. What is the total incremental cost of achieving the shortest completion time?

c. What is the incremental cost of completing the project in 18 weeks?

8.10 Consider the information in the table.

Task	Immediate predecessor	Time estimates (days)		
		a_i	m_i	b_i
A	—	3	4	7
B	—	4	9	12
C	A	5	11	15
D	A	3	5	8
E	B	5	7	12
F	D, C	3	4	7
G	D, C	2	3	4
H	E	7	11	18
I	E	7	10	14
J	F	4	6	9
K	G	5	7	9
L	H, I	2	3	5
M	J, K	7	8	9
N	L	1	3	4
O	M, N	14	17	23

a. Draw the PERT network diagram for this project.

b. Compute the mean and variance in time for each activity.

c. Find the critical path using the PERT algorithm.

d. What is the expected length of the expected critical path?

e. Assuming the time required to complete a path is normally distributed, what is the probability of completing the critical path in 50 days or less?

f. Again assuming normality and path independence, what is the probability of completing the entire project in 50 days or less?

g. If you wanted to be at least 95 percent sure of completing the project on time, what schedule would you quote?

8.11 Consider the project in Problem 8.4, assuming the normal times and the crash times set forth in the table.

Activity	Normal time estimate	Crash time estimate	Incremental cost of crash time
A	5	4	$100
B	6	4	400
C	3	2.5	100
D	5	5	—
E	4	3	100
F	2	1.5	150
G	1	1	—
H	4	3	175
I	3	2	125
J	1	1	—
K	7	4	500

a. What is the shortest time in which the project can be completed?

b. What is the total incremental cost of part (a)?

c. What is the incremental cost of completing the project in 18 weeks?

8.12 Apply PERT to the project described in your WBS for Problem 8.1.

8.13 Consider the project in Problem 8.4. The budgeted costs for the various activities are shown in the table. Develop a total cost budget based on both an earliest start time and a latest start time schedule.

Activity	Budgeted cost
A	$70,000
B	85,000
C	27,000
D	43,000
E	45,000
F	50,000
G	15,000
H	25,000
I	32,000
J	48,000
K	79,000

8.14 Again using the project in Problems 8.4 and 8.13, prepare a cost report that reflects overruns and underruns at the end of 6 weeks. Progress on the project and actual costs incurred through 6 weeks are shown in the table.

Activity	Cost incurred	Percentage complete
A	$75,000	100
B	77,000	90
C	20,000	10
D	10,000	5
E	0	0
F	0	0
G	0	0
H	0	0
I	0	0
J	0	0
K	0	0

8.15 Consider the following project. After 6 weeks of working on the project, top management has requested a detailed cost report that would reflect total cost overruns and cost overruns by various tasks or work packages. To comply, the data shown in the table have been collected. You are to prepare a report that reflects the total cost overruns or underruns and the individual work package overruns and underruns.

Activity	Cost incurred to date	Budget	Percentage complete
A	$ 22,000	$ 25,000	100
B	48,000	45,000	90
C	75,000	100,000	100
D	20,000	20,000	95
E	14,000	20,000	50
F	94,000	85,000	100
G	47,000	40,000	100
H	125,000	120,000	100
I	109,000	100,000	100
J	97,000	100,000	100
K	87,000	100,000	70
L	0	25,000	0
M	0	75,000	0
N	0	73,000	0
O	0	197,000	0

8.16 AMTRAK, the public corporation that operates the national passenger train service, was in need of a system to help their space and equipment controllers (SECs) assemble the trains that operated each day. For example, each configuration or ''consist'' of train 9 from Los Angeles to Chicago needed to contain the correct number of sleepers, day coaches, diners, and club cars to handle the expected number of travelers—as well as the locomotives needed to pull it. Since

AMTRAK's fleet of passenger and service cars is limited, the "consist" of any one train is sure to impact the "consists" required for other trains running that week. The system that AMTRAK employed required the SEC to assemble each train manually by using physical location and status reports on all available cars. Each SEC relies on a set of heuristics and his own experience to assemble the trains such that the resulting schedule allocation is feasible and that the "consists" can handle the expected traffic.

Experience has shown that while the first condition is always met, the trains, especially during peak travel periods, frequently failed to handle the number of travelers wanting space. Realizing that the present system was costing the railroad significant revenue, AMTRAK's management contacted several consulting firms, including American Airline Decision Technologies (AADT), to develop a fully automated system of car allocation which would not only provide feasible assignments and routings for each car type, but would also optimize the revenue to be realized from traffic projections.

In preparing their proposal, the AA group felt that the project for the fleet allocation system (FAS) should be completed in four phases:

I. Development of detailed system design
II. Development of system prototype
III. Development and installation of production version of FAS
IV. Integration of FAS with AMTRAK's real-time reservation system

The planning and costing of phase I was critical to the success of the project: AMTRAK, being accountable to Congress, did not want to spend a lot of money prior to the development of the prototype system. In fact, AMTRAK's request for proposal required that tangible results (i.e., phase II start-up) must be seen within 70 days of the beginning contract date at a cost of no more than $75,000. The consultant group also received word that a competing group was going to submit a bid of $72,000 for its system design work.

The AADT consultants analyzed the work activities of phase I, and their results are shown in Table 1. The cost figures are based upon the group's normal charges for consulting work. The crash cost figures represent additional analysts being assigned to the project.

1. What timing and pricing strategy should the AADT group use in its phase 1 proposal to AMTRAK? Specifically, develop a Gantt chart of the phase I work, and derive a cost schedule by activity suitable for submission to Amtrak.

TABLE 1

Task	Activity	Previous activity	Likely effort	Best effort	Worst effort	Cost per person-day	Days saved by crashing	Total cost of crash
A	Review SEC operating environment	—	14	12	15	$640	4	3200
B	Review system environment sources	A	6	6	7	640	0	—
C	Review system data sources	A	5	5	7	570	0	—
D	Determine functional requirements	B, C	16	14	19	640	4	3200
E	Determine system operating requirements	A	6	6	8	580	0	—
F	Formulate mathematical model	D	24	22	30	670	2	1600
G	Develop system design document	E, F	18	16	19	520	3	2400
H	Prepare phase II work plan	F	10	9	11	640	2	1600

2. Structure the analysis of your proposal by using PERT and CPM so that your management will be convinced that the proposal as submitted will be profitable.

BIBLIOGRAPHY

Bierman, Harold, Jr., Charles P. Bonini, and Warren H. Hausman, *Quantitative Analysis for Business Decisions,* 7th ed. Homewood, Ill. Richard D. Irwin, Inc., 1986.

Moder, Joseph J., and Cecil R. Phillips, *Project Management with CPM, PERT, and PRECEDENCE Diagramming,* 3rd ed. New York: Van Nostrand Reinhold, 1983.

Murdick, Robert G., and Joel E. Ross, *Information Systems for Modern Management,* 3rd ed. Englewood Cliffs, N.J.: Prentice Hall, 1984.

Wiest, J., and F. K. Levy, *Management Guide to PERT/CPM: with GERT/PDM/DCPM and Other Networks,* 2nd ed, Englewood Cliffs, N.J.: Prentice Hall, 1977.

9

Integer and Goal Programming

MOBIL OIL CORPORATION[1]

Mobil Oil Corporation has annual sales of approximately $4 billion for its light petroleum products. These products include gasoline, diesel, heating oil, and so forth. Mobil receives 50,000 customer orders per month for these products and must dispatch a fleet of more than 430 vehicles from 120 bulk terminals.

Prior to the spring of 1985, Mobil used four light products control centers, where order entry and dispatching were performed manually. The objectives of the dispatching process are to minimize the cost of the delivered product, to balance the work load among the company trucks, and to load the maximum weight on a truck while adhering to all laws and proper loading rules. All these constraints must be met while maintaining acceptable customer service levels.

To achieve an acceptable dispatch the following four sets of decisions must be made:

□ From which terminal to supply each order
□ Assignment of orders to delivery trucks

[1] G. G. Brown, C. J. Ellis, G. W. Graves, and D. Ronen, "Real Time, Wide Area Dispatch of Mobil Tank Trucks," *Interfaces* 17 (January–February 1987): 107–120.

□ Gallonization of order quantities to fit truck compartments, loading vehicles to their maximum legal weight

□ Routing the trucks and sequencing deliveries

Due to the complexity of the decisions and the interaction among them, human dispatchers are usually looking for acceptable feasible solutions. They cannot be expected to optimize or consistently achieve low-cost solutions.

To automate the order-entry and dispatch process. Mobil first automated the order-taking process by developing the Mobil order response center (MORC). To automate the dispatching process, Mobil contracted to develop the computer-assisted dispatching (CAD) system. The CAD system required more than two years to develop. At the heart of the system is a collection of integer programming methods used within a real-time, transaction-driven information management system, which allots approximately one second per dispatch for optimization.

Usage of the MORC and CAD systems has enabled Mobil to consolidate three manual control centers into one automated center. The productivity of dispatching personnel has increased more than twofold. According to Mobil's manager of operation services, the more important benefits of the new system include:

□ Savings of approximately $3,000,000 per year in operating expenses associated with delivering light products

□ Better service to customers through improved utilization of assets and resources and consistency of performance

□ Assurance that all shipments are within legal weight limits, regardless of volume differences due to local temperatures or specific gravities

□ Greater capability to evaluate fleet productivity

INTRODUCTION

Even though linear programming is a very useful technique, there are many business decision problems that do not satisfy the LP linearity or certainty assumptions. Many of these same decision problems, however, can generally be represented as another type of mathematical programming model. These other types of mathematical models are classified as integer, goal, dynamic, or nonlinear programming problems.

Just how do these mathematical models differ from linear programming models? Integer programming models differ only in that they require some or all decision variable values to be integer (whole numbers). Recall the divisibility assumption of LP, which allows LP solutions to be fractional or noninteger. Goal programming is different in that it addresses the existence of more than one objective or goal. The objective in goal programming is to develop a solution that satisfies as many goals as possible. However, these goals are often incompatible, so that the goals must be ranked in order of importance. Dynamic programming is significantly different from LP in that it takes a serial approach to solving the problem. It breaks the main problem into a series of smaller subproblems. Additionally, dynamic programming can be applied to stochastic problems and problems whose parameters change over time. Finally, nonlinear programming addresses all models whose objective function or constraints contain a nonlinear expression. This is an area of mathematical programming in which special cases have been solved, but no general procedure exists for solving all types of nonlinear problems. In this chapter we will explore the nature of integer and goal programming, and in the following chapter we will look at dynamic programming.

INTEGER PROGRAMMING

integer programming *Integer programming* has grown in importance for two basic reasons. One reason is that many real-world problems require whole-number solutions. The other reason is that integer programming enables us to formulate or structure problems that otherwise could not be modeled. That is, certain modeling "tricks" can be employed using integer-valued variables.

Most mathematical models do not yield integer solutions, naturally. However, we should point out again that certain network models, such as transportation, assignment, and transshipment, do yield integer solutions.

Types of Integer Models

All integer models require some or all of the decision variables to be integer.
all integer The *pure-integer* or *all-integer* model requires all variables to be integer. If all other relationships in the model are linear, the problem is called an integer linear program, or ILP. *Mixed-integer,* or MILP, models require some vari-
mixed integer ables to be integer but allow the remaining variables to be continuous (noninteger).
0-1 integer teger). Finally, *0-1 integer* models require all variables to assume a value of either 0 or 1. To illustrate these three types of models, consider these three models:

$$\text{Maximize} \quad 35x_1 + 20x_2$$

$$\text{subject to} \quad 4x_1 + 7x_2 \leq 28$$

$$9x_1 + 12x_2 \leq 50 \qquad \text{all-integer model}$$

$$x_1, x_2 \text{ integers}$$

$$\text{Maximize} \quad 35x_1 + 20x_2$$

$$\text{subject to} \quad 4x_1 + 7x_2 \leq 28$$
$$9x_1 + 12x_2 \leq 50$$
$$x_1 \geq 0$$
$$x_2 \text{ integer}$$

mixed-integer model

$$\text{Maximize} \quad 35x_1 + 20x_2$$

$$\text{subject to} \quad 4x_1 + 7x_2 \leq 28$$
$$9x_1 + 12x_2 \leq 50$$
$$x_1, x_2 = 0 \text{ or } 1$$

0–1-integer model

The three models differ only in the nature of the integer requirements on the decision variables. However, the solution of each type of integer model benefits by the use of different solution procedures. The 0–1 models are easiest to solve because they present fewer combinations of decision-variable values.

Solution of Integer Programming Models

Of all the approaches to integer programming, none is nearly as efficient as the simplex method for linear programming. Thus, the size of the integer models that can be solved optimally is generally much smaller. The primary approaches to obtaining integer solutions to otherwise linear models are:

1. Linear programming with rounding
2. Complete enumeration
3. Cutting-plane techniques
4. Partial enumeration via branch and bound

Rounding off LP solutions to linear models with integer restrictions is probably the most common or practical approach. It is convenient and often results in optimal or near-optimal solutions. However, the approach has two pitfalls. First, the rounded solution can be far from optimal. Examples have been contrived to show that this is true, although in most real-world problems the rounded solutions are close to optimal. Second, and more seriously, it may be impossible, or at least extremely difficult, to round off the variables and satisfy all the constraints.

Complete enumeration involves the evaluation of all possible combinations of decision-variable values. As you can imagine, the number of combinations can grow astronomically large for even medium-sized problems. Even though complete enumeration will provide an optimal solution, it is a viable approach only for relatively small problems.

Cutting-plane techniques were the focus of early attempts to derive

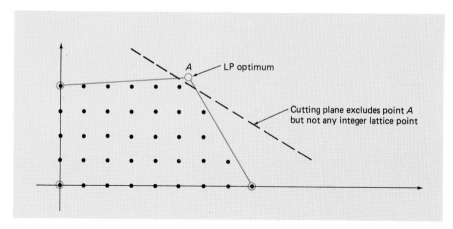

FIGURE 9.1 **A cutting plane**

integer solutions. The basic idea was to ignore the integer restrictions and solve the model as an LP. Noninteger optimal solutions were "cut off" by adding an additional constraint to the model which would exclude the noninteger point, but would not exclude any integer points. Figure 9.1 shows a *cut* that defines a new feasible region and excludes the previous LP optimum. In actual practice, cutting-plane methods worked but required the successive solution of many LP solutions before an integer extreme point was generated. The slowness of cutting-plane methods encouraged research in the direction of partial enumeration procedures.

cut

partial enumeration

    Partial enumeration determines the optimal solution by examining only a portion of all possible combinations of integer values. The procedure basically divides the set of all solutions into subclasses and searches only among promising subclasses of solutions. One means of performing partial enumeration is called branch and bound. This procedure appears to be the most promising of the four approaches. One of its disadvantages is that it must be tailored for the specific problem to be solved; it is unlike the simplex method, which is a general method applicable without modification to all LP models.

GRAPHICAL EXAMPLE   To illustrate the nature of integer programming problems, let us look at a two-variable graphical example. Consider the maximization problem

$$\text{Maximize} \quad 6x_1 + 4x_2$$

$$\text{subject to} \qquad\qquad x_2 \leq 3$$

$$4x_1 + 1.5x_2 \leq 12$$

$$2x_1 + 2x_2 \leq 8$$

$$x_1, x_2 \geq 0 \text{ and integer}$$

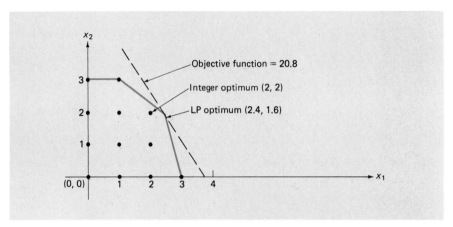

FIGURE 9.2 **Feasible integer points**

The feasible region for the foregoing problem consists of the integer (lattice) points shown in Figure 9.2. Notice that the feasible region consists of 12 points, not an infinite number as in the LP case. The LP optimal solution to the model ignoring the integer restriction is $x_1 = 2.4$ and $x_2 = 1.6$. Rounding down this solution yields (2, 1), which is not the optimal integer solution. Evaluating all the integer points yields $x_1 = 2$, $x_2 = 2$ as the optimal integer solution. Evaluating all integer points is not difficult for this small problem, but it becomes impossible with large problems. We turn now to a systematic procedure for evaluating integer points more efficiently.

Branch-and-Bound Method

The simplex method is an adjacent-extreme-point procedure that moves along extreme points successively, making improvements until an optimum is found. Unfortunately, in integer programming the optimum is not necessarily at an extreme point of the convex hull of the feasible region. Furthermore, we have no systematic procedure such as the simplex method that will take us directly to the optimum. Thus, we are restricted to intelligent search-type procedures.

branch-and-bound *Branch-and-bound* procedures partition the set of all solutions into smaller subsets and search among promising subsets. Initially, the method breaks the set of all solutions into two mutually exclusive subsets. Subsequently, these two subsets are partitioned into two smaller subsets and so on. Fortunately, not all subsets are further subdivided, as some are deter-

bounding mined not to contain an optimal solution. The *bounding* aspect of branch and bound determines upper and/or lower bounds on the best solution contained in any subset of solutions. In a maximization problem, a subset whose upper bound is less than the value of a known feasible solution will be excluded from further consideration. It is in this manner that partial enumeration is achieved. The process of determining how to partition the subsets is called *branching* *branching*. Branch and bound is a general approach rather than a specific procedure for a given problem. The branching-and-bounding rules will differ for each type of problem. We now look at how the rules are developed for a 0–1-integer programming problem called the knapsack problem.

Branch and bound applied to the knapsack problem   We first encountered a knapsack-type problem in Table 1.1. Recall that the objective is to choose, from among a set of items, the subset that maximizes the value of the subset subject to a capacity constraint. Consider the following 0–1-integer programming formulation of a five-item knapsack problem:

$$\text{Maximize}\quad 60x_1 + 54x_2 + 32x_3 + 18x_4 + 13x_5$$

$$\text{subject to}\quad 30x_1 + 36x_2 + 32x_3 + 24x_4 + 26x_5 \leq 90$$

$$x_i = 0 \text{ or } 1, \qquad i = 1, 2, \ldots, 5$$

The coefficients in the objective function represent utility values, the coefficients in the constraint represent weights, and the right-hand-side (RHS) value, 90, represents a weight capacity. Each item must be selected in its entirety or not at all; fractional parts are not allowed. If fractional parts were allowed, the problem would have a trivial solution via linear programming.

The bounding part of branch-and-bound algorithms is often accomplished by model relaxation. Before you go to sleep solving the problem, however, we should point out that relaxation in this context refers to loosen-*LP* ing or dropping restrictive assumptions. The most common relaxation is the *relaxation* *LP relaxation*, in which the integer restriction is dropped and the variables are treated as continuous. The LP relaxation of this knapsack problem is accomplished by replacing

$$x_i = 0 \text{ or } 1$$

with $0 \leq x_i \leq 1$. Solving the relaxed problem yields an objective function value that is greater than or equal to (less than or equal to for a minimization problem) the optimal integer objective function value. This principle is illustrated in Figure 9.3, in which the set of integer programming solutions is contained within the set of linear programming solutions. Thus, if the optimal LP solution to the relaxed problem happens to be integer, it will be the optimal solution to the integer problem. The reverse is not generally true; that is, the optimal integer solution is not generally optimal for the relaxed LP.

Solving the relaxed knapsack problem (sometimes called the cheesecake problem because we can now take fractional pieces) is particularly

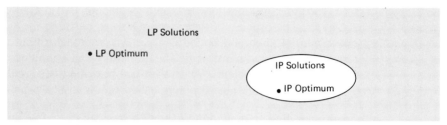

FIGURE 9.3   Set of IP solutions as a subset of LP solutions

simple and does not require the simplex method. If we form the ratio of value to weight, the optimal LP solution is obtained by simply loading the knapsack with highest-ratio items first until the capacity is depleted. Using this "biggest bang for the buck" approach, the last item placed in the knapsack might be fractional. Listing the items in order of value/weight, we have

Item	Value/weight
1	2.0
2	1.5
3	1.0
4	0.75
5	0.50

Thus, the optimal LP solution to the relaxed LP is to enter item 1, item 2, and $\frac{24}{32}$ of item 3. We cannot place all of item 3 in the 90-pound knapsack, since it weighs 32 pounds and items 1 and 2 together weigh 66 pounds. Substituting $x_1 = 1$, $x_2 = 1$, and $x_3 = \frac{24}{32}$ into the objective function yields an upper bound $= 60 + 54 + 24 = 138$ on the value of the optimal integer solution.

We now need to implement a branching process to partition the set of all solutions into the smaller subsets. Since the knapsack problem involves 0–1 variables, the partitioning process will create a binary tree. The first partition is shown in Figure 9.4. Since the decision variable with a fractional value is the one in question, we will partition the set of all solutions into two classes: those in which the fractional variable $=0$ and those in which the fractional variable $=1$. In Figure 9.4 we have created two nodes in the tree— one representing the set of all solutions in which $x_3 = 0$ and the other representing the set of all solutions in which $x_3 = 1$. Fixing $x_3 = 0$ in the relaxed LP and solving for the remaining variables, we obtain $x_1 = 1$, $x_2 = 1$, and $x_4 = 1$; the bound is shown in the node as 132. Fixing $x_3 = 1$ and solving the relaxed LP, we obtain $x_1 = 1$, $x_3 = 1$, and $x_2 = \frac{28}{36}$; the bound is 134.

Notice in the $x_3 = 0$ node of the branch-and-bound tree that the LP solution is integer. This means that we found the optimal solution in the $x_3 =$

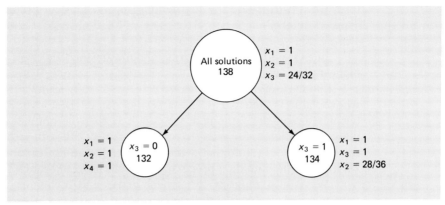

FIGURE 9.4 **First level in branch-and-bound tree**

0 class of solutions. Since the $x_1 = 1$, $x_2 = 1$, $x_4 = 1$ solution is feasible, its *lower bound* value of 132 constitutes a *lower bound* on the optimal solution to the knapsack problem. Thus, given the *upper bound* of 134 in the $x_3 = 1$ node, we can *upper bound* conclude that the value of the optimal solution is bounded within 132 to 134. Also, there is no further need to branch from the $x_3 = 0$ node in the branch-and-bound tree; we say that this node is fathomed. In the $x_3 = 1$ node, however, we have a decision to make regarding the value of x_2; hence, we will branch from this node. Normally, when there are several nodes from which we could branch, we choose the node with the highest upper bound.

Branching from the $x_3 = 1$ node yields the binary tree shown in Figure 9.5. In solving the cheesecake problem for the second-level nodes of the

FIGURE 9.5 **Second level in branch-and-bound tree**

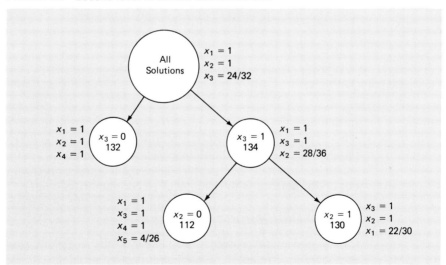

tree, we must include the restrictions specified by all predecessor nodes. Thus, in determining a bound for the $x_2 = 1$ node, we must fix $x_3 = 1$ and $x_2 = 1$ in the relaxed LP.

In examining the three terminal nodes of the tree, we can see that the highest upper bound is associated with the $x_3 = 0$ node. Thus, the $x_2 = 0$ and *fathomed* $x_2 = 1$ nodes are *fathomed* because we have already found a feasible solution whose value is higher than the upper bounds of these two nodes. Since all terminal nodes are fathomed, we conclude that the optimal solution is the integer solution $x_1 = 1$, $x_2 = 1$, $x_3 = 0$, $x_4 = 1$, $x_5 = 0$ with value 132 found at the $x_3 = 0$ node. (Note that if the $x_3 = 0$ node had not generated an integer solution in the bounding process, we would have to branch from it.)

We can summarize the branch-and-bound technique for an integer maximization problem as follows:

1. Establish an upper bound on the set of all solutions by using LP relaxation or some other bounding procedure.
2. Branch from the unfathomed terminal node in the branch and bound tree that has the largest upper bound. (This will create two more nodes in 0–1-integer problems.)
3. Calculate an upper bound for each new node created in step 2.
4. Consider a node to be fathomed if its upper bound is lower than a known feasible solution, the node contains no feasible solution, or the bounding process generated an integer solution whose value equals the upper bound of the node.
5. Stop only if all nodes have been fathomed; otherwise, go to step 2.

The general procedure for a minimization problem is identical except that lower bounds are used in place of upper bounds.

APPLICATIONS AND FORMULATION POSSIBILITIES

In addition to knapsack-type problems, integer programming has several other types of interesting applications; many of these will be covered in the problems at the end of the chapter. The nature of the 0–1 or integer variables enables us to model decision problems using integer programming that could not be formulated with noninteger or continuous variables.

Capital-Budgeting Problems

Capital-budgeting problems are similar to the knapsack problem that was presented in Chapter 1. In capital-budgeting problems, however, there are usually several constraints and the objective is to allocate capital or development funds to various projects. These projects can involve a wide range of possibilities and might include capital equipment, financial investments, research and development, new business ventures, or real estate projects. In any case, considerable amounts of money are often involved in capital-budgeting problems. If projects can be partially funded then linear programming can be used to model the budgeting problem. (See Problem 2.15 in Chapter 2.) However, integer programming is required whenever projects must be funded in total or not at all. We can use 0–1-integer variables to model the project-selection decision.

We can formulate the capital budgeting problem as

$$\text{Maximize} \quad c_1 x_1 + c_2 x_2 + c_3 x_3 + \cdots + c_n x_n$$

$$\text{subject to} \quad a_{11} x_1 + a_{12} x_2 + a_{13} x_3 + \cdots + a_{1n} x_n \leq b_1$$

$$a_{21} x_1 + a_{22} x_2 + a_{23} x_3 + \cdots + a_{2n} x_n \leq b_2$$

$$\vdots \qquad\qquad\qquad\qquad \vdots$$

$$a_{m1} x_1 + a_{m2} x_2 + a_{m3} x_3 + \cdots + a_{mn} x_n \leq b_m$$

$$x_j = 0 \text{ or } 1, \quad j = 1, 2, \ldots, n$$

where

$c_j =$ the profit contribution from project j
$b_i =$ the amount of capital or resource of type i available
$a_{ij} =$ the amount of capital or resource of type i required to support project j

The various types of capital can refer to monies available at different periods of time or the availability of resources such as manpower or capital equipment.

SET-COVERING AND SET-PARTITIONING PROBLEMS

Set-covering problems are a class of integer programming problems in which the objective is to "cover" or provide a set of conditions at minimum cost. Applications include crew scheduling, facility location, assembly-line balancing, and vehicle routing. The best known application is probably the airline crew scheduling problem. In this problem, the requirements to be covered are the crew requirements of the flights which the airline is committed to fly during the next schedule period. A specific crew will typically fly a number of flights on a given day, but not necessarily on the same aircraft.

The problem is to determine which flights should comprise a crew's trip. A trip can comprise 1, 2, 3, or more days of work. For example, a crew might start in Dallas, fly four flights that day, overnight in Boston, then fly three flights the next day, overnight in San Diego and fly four flights the third day ending back up in Dallas, the home base. The flights flown during this three day round trip comprise what is called a *pairing*.

The 0–1-integer model for the set-partitioning problem is of the form:

$$\text{Minimize} \quad \sum_{j=1}^{n} c_j x_j$$

$$\text{subject to} \quad \sum_{j=1}^{n} a_{ij} x_j = 1, \quad \text{for } i = 1, 2, \ldots, m$$

$$x_j = 0 \text{ or } 1, \quad \text{for } j = 1, 2, \ldots, n$$

where each a_{ij} coefficient is either 0 or 1 and the objective function coefficients c_j are nonnegative. The set-partitioning problem is a special case of the set-covering problem. In the set covering problem the constraint relationships are greater than or equal to rather than equations.

The interpretation of the set-partitioning problem in terms of airline crew scheduling is as follows. The rows ($i = 1, \ldots, m$) represent flight legs that must be flown. The columns ($j = 1, \ldots, n$) represent possible pairings that a crew might fly. The objective function coefficient c_j is the cost associated with pairing j, and

$$a_{ij} = \begin{cases} 1, & \text{if flight leg } i \text{ is on pairing } j \\ 0, & \text{otherwise} \end{cases}$$

The 0–1 decision variable for each pairing and the partitioning equations mean that each flight leg must be covered by exactly one of the selected ($x_j = 1$) pairings. The 0–1 optimization problem is then to select a minimum cost set of pairings that satisfies the partitioning equations.

In the case of some of the larger airlines (e.g., American, United, and Delta), the size of the set-partitioning problem is so large for their large fleets (hundreds of rows and billions of columns) that the problem must be decomposed into subproblems that are solved using special-purpose set-partitioning algorithms. By solving a large number of subproblems the best pairing optimization models do an excellent job of reducing crew costs. For the smaller fleets in the large airlines (less than 50 aircraft) and for smaller airlines like Braniff or Air Canada, it is possible to find global solutions to the crew pairing problem using special-purpose set-partitioning solution soft-

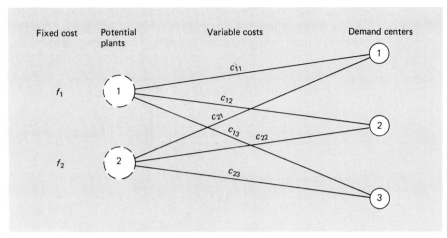

FIGURE 9.6   A fixed-charge problem

ware.[2] The cost reductions as compared to manual solutions range from 5 to 30 percent and amount to millions of dollars in annual savings. At American Airlines the benefit of its pairing optimization program has been estimated at $18 million per year. A simplified example of the crew scheduling problem is presented in the Problems section at the end of the chapter.

Fixed-Charge Problems

fixed charge   *Fixed-charge* problems arise frequently in business applications where a fixed cost must be incurred to obtain a product or service. Consider, for example, the simple plant location problem shown in Figure 9.6. The graph resembles the standard transportation problem of Chapter 6, but there is one important difference: the plants, indicated by the dashed nodes, are not yet open. The problem is to decide which plants to open to minimize the combined costs of transportation and the fixed costs required to operate and maintain the plant. It is assumed that each plant has enough capacity to supply all demand requirements. To formulate the problem, let

c_{ij} = unit transportation cost from plant i to demand center j
b_j = demand at demand center j
x_{ij} = amount shipped from plant i to demand center j
f_i = fixed cost of plant i
$y_i = \begin{cases} 1 & \text{if plant } i \text{ is opened} \\ 0 & \text{otherwise} \end{cases}$

[2] Roy Marsten and Fred Shepardson, "Exact Solution of Crew Scheduling Problems Using the Set Partitioning Model: Recent Successful Applications," *Networks*, 11 (Summer 1981), 165–177.

We can formulate the simple plant location problem shown in Figure 9.6 as a mixed-integer programming problem in which the x_{ij} variables are continuous and the y_i variables are 0–1 integer variables. The formulation is

Minimize
$$c_{11}x_{11} + c_{12}x_{12} + c_{13}x_{13} + c_{21}x_{21} + c_{22}x_{22} + c_{23}x_{23}$$
$$+ f_1y_1 + f_2y_2$$

subject to
$$\left.\begin{array}{l} x_{11} + x_{21} = b_1 \\ x_{12} + x_{22} = b_2 \\ x_{13} + x_{23} = b_3 \end{array}\right\} \quad \text{demand constraints}$$

$$\left.\begin{array}{l} x_{11} + x_{12} + x_{13} \leq My_1 \\ x_{21} + x_{22} + x_{23} \leq My_2 \end{array}\right\} \quad \begin{array}{l} \text{constraints that force plant } i \\ \text{closed unless } y_i = 1 \end{array}$$

$$x_{ij} \geq 0 \quad \text{all } i \text{ and } j; \quad y_1, y_2 = 0 \text{ or } 1$$

In the last set of constraints, the M denotes an arbitrarily large number. These constraints do not allow plant i to be opened unless y_i equals 1, in which case the fixed cost of f_i is incurred in the objective function. When y_i equals 1, the M essentially allows the shipments out of plant i to be as large as necessary to satisfy all demand.

The presence of fixed costs destroys the linearity of the objective function. As shown in Figure 9.7, the fixed cost introduces a jump discontinuity in the total cost function and makes the problem much harder to solve than a linear problem.

Multiple-choice constraints   In addition to fixed charges, integer variables can be used to limit choices among competing alternatives. Suppose that in

FIGURE 9.7   **Cost function with fixed-cost component**

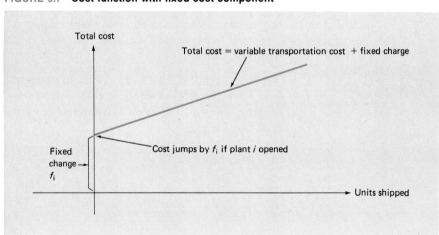

the simple plant location problem, we again let

$$y_i = \begin{cases} 1 & \text{if plant } i \text{ is opened} \\ 0 & \text{otherwise} \end{cases}$$

Suppose that we are considering five plant locations but have decided that only one plant will be opened. We can accomplish this by adding the following constraint to the simple plant location model:

$$y_1 + y_2 + y_3 + y_4 + y_5 = 1$$

Since the y_i are 0–1 variables, only one of the y_i can be 1; the others must be zero. Note that in linear programming, the variables can assume fractional values; thus the foregoing constraint forces multiple choices only if 0–1 variables are used.

***K* out of *N*-alternatives constraints**   Suppose that instead of selecting just one alternative, we are interested in selecting K out of N. For example, suppose that we want to open precisely three out of five possible plants. Extending the multiple-choice constraint idea, we have

$$y_1 + y_2 + y_3 + y_4 + y_5 = 3$$

Furthermore, we can model the opening of at most two plants by

$$y_1 + y_2 + y_3 + y_4 + y_5 \leq 2$$

and the opening of at least two plants with

$$y_1 + y_2 + y_3 + y_4 + y_5 \geq 2$$

These constraints all assume that the y_i are restricted to values of 0 or 1.

If-then constraints   Sometimes it is necessary to tie together certain projects or alternatives. Dependency requirements can be met by requiring certain 0–1 variables to be dependent. For example, suppose in the example above that plant 2 can be opened only if plant 5 is opened. We can enforce this by

$$y_2 - y_5 \leq 0$$

If plants 2 and 5 are corequisite, that is, plant 2 is open when plant 5 is open, and vice versa, we must equate the two by

$$y_2 - y_5 = 0$$

Other formulation possibilities exist through the use of integer variables. We have presented some of the more useful formulation "tricks." The price that is paid for these formulation conveniences (relative to linear programming) is an increase in the difficulty of solving the problem. However, in many instances the use of integer variables is the only way to represent the problem as a mathematical model.

MULTIPLE-CRITERIA DECISION MAKING

Up to this point we have discussed models and techniques that can be applied to problems that have a single objective. For example, both linear and integer programming address problems that have a single objective such as cost minimization, profit maximization, or some other unidimensional objective. However, many decision problems involve multiple objectives, some of which are incompatible or conflicting. For example, a company might want to maximize profits, minimize costs, improve its quality of service, and increase its warehouse inventories. Some of these objectives are incompatible in that one can be accomplished only at the expense of another. However, these kinds of conflicts are common in the realm of real-world decision making. In fact, decision making has been loosely defined as a struggle to resolve the dilemma of conflicting objectives.

PARETO OPTIMALITY

To investigate systematic ways of aiding multiple-criteria decision making, we must abandon the single-objective notion of a unique optimal solution that is clearly superior to all other solutions. Given multiple and conflicting objectives, we will have to evaluate trade-offs between improving one ob-
pareto jective at the expense of another. There is an extremely useful concept
optimality from traditional economic theory that can help in searching for solutions to
principle multiple-objective problems. This is the *pareto optimality principle* and it states:

> A state of the world A is preferable to a state of the world B if at least one person is better off in A and nobody is worse off.

The pareto optimality principle when applied to multiple-criteria decision making results in the notion of nondominance of solutions. To illustrate the nondominance concept let's consider a portfolio selection problem. Suppose there are two criteria for the investment decision: expected return and

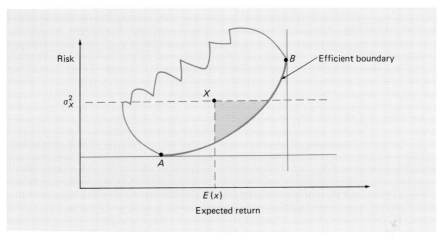

FIGURE 9.8   **Pareto optimality**

risk. If we measure the risk of a portfolio by the variance of the probability distribution of returns, then one criterion in the portfolio selection process is to minimize σ_x^2 for a given portfolio X. Similarly we can use $E(x)$, the expected value of the return, as a measure for the criterion involving portfolio return.

Figure 9.8 graphically illustrates the concept of nondominance of solutions. The graph shows the set of all portfolios under consideration assuming finite mean and variance. Note that all portfolios in the shaded area have returns equal to or greater than the return of portfolio X; all portfolios in the shaded region also have risk that is less than or equal to portfolio X. Portfolio X is dominated by all portfolios in the shaded region. Note also that all portfolios on the interior of the feasible region are dominated by the portfolios lying on the boundary. The points lying on the darkened boundary are *efficient set* called the *efficient set* or *nondominated solutions*. In searching for an effective portfolio, we need only search among the nondominated solutions. Of course there are an infinite number of points on the efficient boundary in Figure 9.8. Risk takers would tend to favor points closer to point B, whereas risk averters would tend to prefer points closer to point A. There is no absolute optimal solution, however; a given decision maker could choose among the nondominated points to find a portfolio that best meets his or her multiple objectives.

One approach to multiple objective decision making is actually to search among all nondominated solutions to find one most satisfactory to the decision maker. This approach, however, can be computationally infeasible for problems having a large number of points in the efficient set. What is needed are quantitative techniques that help the decision maker consider a reasonable number of alternatives. Some of the primary approaches to multiple-criteria decision making include goal programming, multiple-objective linear programming, and interactive computer-based methods. We turn now to what is probably the most widely applied multiple-criteria approach, namely, goal programming.

GOAL PROGRAMMING

goal programming Goal programming is generally applied to linear problems and is a variation of linear programming. *Goal programming,* as the name implies, is concerned with the achievement of prespecified goals or targets. It was first identified by Charnes and Cooper in the early 1960s and later extended by Ignizio and Lee.[3] The original approach by Charnes and Cooper is nonpreemptive in that goals are comparable and differ by numerical weights. More recent approaches are preemptive in that the goals are ranked by order of importance. A higher-priority goal is assumed to be infinitely more important than a lower-priority goal. The preemptive approach is more common and is the one we will study in this chapter.

The preemptive approach to goal programming requires the decision maker to assign priorities to the goals of the decision problem. There can be several goals with the same priority; however, the solution algorithm sequentially satisfies the goals, starting with the highest-priority goals. Obviously, if two goals are truly incompatible, both cannot be achieved to the fullest extent. Goal programming achieves as many higher-priority goals as possible and then attempts to "get as close as possible" to satisfying the remaining goals. Since not all goals are always achieved, this is sometimes *satisficing* called *satisficing,* or the achieving of a satisfactory solution.

Goal programming was originally developed as a linear programming extension. It has since been developed for integer and nonlinear models. In this chapter we limit our focus to linear goal programming models. In this case, goal programming is a straightforward generalization of linear programming.

A Two-Goal Model

deviational variables One basic difference between goal programming and linear programming is that the goals are expressed as constraints of the model rather than directly in the objective function. In each constraint that represents a goal, *deviational variables* are defined which measure the extent to which the goals are achieved. These deviational variables are equivalent to positive or negative slack variables in linear programming. In goal programming, however, they

---

[3] A. Charnes and W. W. Cooper, *Management Models and Industrial Applications of Linear Programming* (New York: John Wiley and Sons, Inc., 1961); James P. Ignizio, *Goal Programming and Extensions* (Lexington, Mass.: D. C. Heath and Company, 1976); and Sang Lee, *Goal Programming for Decision Analysis* (Philadelphia: Auerbach Publishers, Inc., 1972).

are placed in the objective function with priority rankings. These deviational variables represent positive or negative deviations from a goal; hence, these deviations are to be minimized.

To illustrate the goal programming formulation procedure, let us return to the familiar Faze Linear product mix problem of Chapters 2 to 6. Recall the LP formulation as

$$
\begin{array}{lllll}
\text{Maximize} & 200x_1 + 500x_2 & & \text{profit} \\
\text{subject to} & & x_2 \leq 40 & & \text{transistor availability} \\
& 1.2x_1 + & 4x_2 \leq 240 & & \text{assembly time} \\
& .5x_1 + & 1x_2 \leq 81 & & \text{inspection time} \\
& x_1, x_2 \geq 0 & & &
\end{array}
$$

where x_1 and x_2 represent the number of amplifiers and preamplifiers to produce, respectively. The optimal LP solution is to produce 28.5 preamps and 105 amps, for a total profit of $35,250.

Now let us assume that the Faze Linear management would like to achieve two goals:

> priority 1: achieve profit of $40,000
> priority 2: limit overtime of inspectors

Looking first at the highest-priority goal, introduce two deviational variables:

d_1^- = amount by which the target profit of $40,000 is underachieved
d_1^+ = amount by which the target profit of $40,000 is overachieved

We can now write the profit goal as a constraint:

$$
200x_1 + 500x_2 + d_1^- - d_1^+ = 40{,}000
$$

Notice that the $40,000 profit goal need not be met exactly. If d_1^- has a positive solution value, we will fall short of 40,000, and if d_1^+ has a positive solution value, we will exceed 40,000.

Assuming that the 81 hours of inspection time is regular time (not overtime), we can formulate the second goal by defining deviational variables

d_2^- = amount by which inspection time is underutilized (i.e., short of 81 hours)
d_2^+ = amount by which inspection time is overutilized (i.e., more than 81 hours requires overtime)

We formulate the overtime goal as

$$.5x_1 + 1x_2 + d_2^- - d_2^+ = 81$$

Incorporating these goals as constraints in the LP formulation, we obtain the goal programming formulation:

Minimize $\quad P_1 d_1^- + P_2 d_2^+$

$$
\begin{array}{lrll}
\text{subject to} & x_2 \le & 40 \text{ transistors} & \left.\vphantom{\begin{array}{c}a\\b\end{array}}\right\} \text{ resource constraints} \\
& 1.2x_1 + \quad 4x_2 \le 240 \text{ assembly} & \\
& 200x_1 + \quad 500x_2 + d_1^- - d_1^+ = 40{,}000 & \left.\vphantom{\begin{array}{c}a\\b\end{array}}\right\} \text{ goal} \\
& .5x_1 + \quad 1x_2 + d_2^- - d_2^+ = \quad 81 & \text{constraints}
\end{array}
$$

$$x_1, x_2, d_1^-, d_1^+, d_2^-, d_2^+ \ge 0$$

hard or soft constraints The first two constraints are system constraints or *hard constraints*. They cannot be violated if the problem is to have a feasible solution. The last two constraints are goal constraints or *soft constraints* that can be violated if necessary. The first goal constraint concerns the achievement of the $40,000 *min under-achievement goal* profit goal. Since the company is concerned with achieving less than $40,000 but is not dissatisfied if it exceeds this goal, this constraint is a *minimize underachievement* type of goal. The underachievement deviational variable d_1^- is in the objective function. The second goal constraint concerns the *min over-achievement goal* overutilization of inspection time. The company is concerned with using more than 81 hours of inspection time but does not care if less than 81 hours are used. This constraint is a *minimize overachievement* constraint, and the deviational variable d_2^+ is in the objective function.

The example illustrates goal constraints that minimize underachievement and overachievement of a specific goal. Two other types of goal con*target goal* straints are possible. A *target goal* constraint attempts to minimize both the underachievement and overachievement of a specific goal. Thus, if Faze Linear were interested in using exactly 81 hours of inspection time (i.e., minimize underachievement as well as overachievement), they would place both d_2^- and d_2^+ in the objective function. Another type of goal is represented *goal interval* by a *goal interval* constraint. Suppose that Faze Linear wanted to limit inspection time to between 75 and 85 hours. This goal could be represented by two soft constraints:

$$.5x_1 + 1x_2 + d_i^- \ge 75$$

and

$$.5x_1 + 1x_2 - d_i^+ \le 85$$

Both d_i^- and d_i^+ would appear in the objective function together with the slack variables to convert the inequalities to equations.

The P_1 and P_2 symbols in the objective function reflect the fact that d_1^- and d_2^+ represent priority 1 and 2 goals, respectively. Priorities of a higher rank are infinitely more important than are those of a lower rank. Thus, the priority relationship is often expressed as

$$P_1 \ggg P_2$$

where $\ggg$ means "very much greater than." Note that the deviational variables are to be minimized, since they represent the amount by which the goals are not satisfied.

The result of the ordinal priority rankings is that the profit goal will be achieved to the greatest extent possible before the overtime goal is considered. If satisfying any part of the overtime goal causes any reduction in the higher-ranking profit goal, the overtime goal will not be satisfied at all.

Graphical Solution of Goal Programming

The graphical solution of the Faze Linear goal programming problem is shown in Figure 9.9. The solid lines define the fixed feasible region as bounded by the two resource constraints of the model. The two dashed lines represent the two goal constraints and are flexible, as they can be moved closer to or away from the feasible region. In satisfying the first-priority goal of profit maximization, we want to minimize profit underachievement by making variable d_1^- as small as possible by finding an extreme point that is on the profit constraint or on the d_1^+ side of the constraint. Examining the region

FIGURE 9.9 **Graphical solution of a goal programming problem**

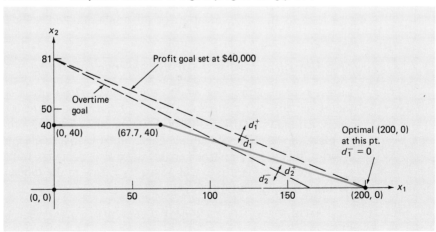

we see that point (200, 0) is on the $40,000 profit line and achieves a d_1^- value of 0. This solution of $x_1 = 200$, $x_2 = 0$ achieves the first-priority goal to the fullest extent with a profit of $40,000.

Turning to the overtime goal, however, we find that minimizing overtime through the d_2^+ variable requires us to move toward the "southwest," away from point (200, 0). Since lower-priority goals are never satisfied at the expense of higher-priority goals, no attempt is made to achieve the second goal, and the point (200, 0) is accepted as the optimum. Notice that Faze Linear is able to achieve an even higher profit than in the LP formulation, although it is at the expense of undesirable overtime. If the priorities were reversed and the overtime goal had priority 1, how would you argue the fact that the point (105, 28.5) would become optimal?

In addition to handling multiple objectives, goal programming offers another advantage over the ordinary linear programming approach. The addition of deviational variables to the constraints allows the constraint requirement to be "soft." In other words the constraint does not have to be met exactly. If an LP model had a constraint to meet demand of 500 units but did not have the capacity to so, the end result would be no feasible solution. However, in goal programming the use of deviational variables will enable the model to produce a solution; it might not meet the demand of 500 units, but it would produce a feasible solution showing what could be accomplished. Additionally, the model could be used to show what capacity or overtime increases would be needed to meet the demand of 500 units.

Goal programming is potentially very useful and probably the most widely used approach to multiple-criteria decision making. However, as Zeleny[4] points out, a goal programming solution can (under certain circumstances) turn out to be a dominated solution; that is, not the best one with respect to currently available alternatives. This suboptimizing possibility of goal programming is implied by the fact that the goals are set a priori. Later in the chapter we will look at multiple-objective linear programming, which can lead to the determination of all nondominated solutions of a linear problem.

The Simplex Method for Goal Programming

Larger goal programming models will obviously require a solution method that is solvable on a computer. The simplex method of linear programming is easily extended to the goal programming case. The only real modification involves the handling of multiple goals rather than a single goal. In a simplex tableau, this is accomplished by having a $c_j - z_j$ matrix rather than a single $c_j - z_j$ row. That is, there will be a $c_j - z_j$ row in the tableau for each goal having a different priority level.

[4] Milan Zeleny, *Multiple Criteria Decision Making* (New York: McGraw-Hill Book Company, 1982).

TABLEAU 9.1 *Initial simplex tableau for goal programming problem*

c_j		0	0	0	0	P_1	0	0	P_2		
c_B	Basic variables	x_1	x_2	s_1	s_2	d_1^-	d_1^+	d_2^-	d_2^+	Solution	Minimum ratio
0	s_1	0	1	1	0	0	0	0	0	40	$\frac{40}{1} = 40$
0	s_2	1.2	4	0	1	0	0	0	0	240	$\frac{240}{4} = 60$
P_1	d_1^-	200	500	0	0	1	−1	0	0	40,000	$\frac{40,000}{500} = 80$
0	d_2^-	.5	1	0	0	0	0	1	−1	81	$\frac{81}{1} = 81$
P_2	$c_j - z_j$	0	0	0	0	0	0	0	1	0	
P_1	$c_j - z_j$	−200	−500	0	0	0	1	0	0	40,000	

↑

Consider again the Faze Linear goal programming problem. Adding two slack variables to convert the problem to standard form, we have

Minimize $\quad P_1 d_1^- + P_2 d_2^+$

subject to

$$x_2 + s_1 \qquad\qquad\qquad\qquad = \quad 40$$
$$1.2x_1 + 4x_2 \quad + s_2 \qquad\qquad\qquad = \quad 240$$
$$200x_1 + 500x_2 \qquad\qquad + d_1^- - d_1^+ \qquad\qquad = 40,000$$
$$.5x_1 + 1x_2 \qquad\qquad\qquad\qquad + d_2^- - d_2^+ = \quad 81$$

$$x_j, s_j, d_i^+, d_i^- \geq 0$$

The initial tableau for the Faze Linear goal programming problem is shown in Tableau 9.1. There are several facts to notice in Tableau 9.1.

1. As usual, there are as many basic variables as there are constraints.
2. Those dummy variables (slack or deviational) with a positive 1 coefficient in the original constraints are basic in the initial tableau.
3. All c_j objective function coefficients are zero except for those deviational variables having a priority (P_i) ranking.
4. Since there are two levels of goal priorities, there are two $c_j - z_j$ rows; one for priority 1 (P_1) and one for priority 2 (P_2).

The $c_j - z_j$ for a given priority level is calculated precisely the same as in the linear programming case. Thus, for the P_1 $c_j - z_j$ row, we calculate z_1 in the column for x_1 by taking the product of the c_B column times the substitution coefficients in the x_1 column. This yields

$$z_1 = 0(0) + 0(1.2) + P_1(200) + 0(.5) = 200P_1$$

Since $c_1 = 0$, the final $c_1 - z_1$ calculation for the P_1 $c_j - z_j$ row is

$$c_1 - z_1 = 0 - 200 = -200$$

The remaining $c_j - z_j$ for the P_1 and P_2 rows are calculated similarly.

Since we are minimizing, we will look for negative entries in the $c_j - z_j$ row to improve the solution. Going first to the higher-priority P_1 row, we find that the most negative entry is a -500. Thus, we will bring x_2 into the solution to help satisfy the P_1 goal. Notice the last two numbers in the solution column in the P_1 and P_2 rows. These numbers, 0 and 40,000, represent the unattained portion of goals P_2 and P_1, respectively.

Having chosen the entering variable, we need to determine the variable leaving the basis. This is accomplished in exactly the same way as in the LP case, by calculating the minimum ratio. Here we find that variable s_1 leaves the solution.

The simplex procedure continues the pivoting process by bringing in variables having a negative $c_j - z_j$ in the highest-priority row. If there are no negative entries in the highest-priority row, we move to the next-highest-priority row and again search for negative entries. One difference, however, is that we must never bring in a variable x_j if it has a positive $c_j - z_j$ entry in a higher-priority $c_j - z_j$ row. That is, we must never improve a lower-priority goal at the expense of a higher-priority goal. The simplex method terminates with an optimal solution when all $c_j - z_j$ rows have nonnegative entries, or the satisfaction of a lower-priority goal can be accomplished only at the expense of a higher-priority goal.

After bringing x_2 into the solution, the simplex method continues through four iterations, achieving the optimal solution shown in Tableau 9.2. Notice that there are no negative entries in the P_1 $c_j - z_i$ row. There is, however, a $-.004$ in the second priority P_2 $c_j - z_j$ row. Nevertheless, we

TABLEAU 9.2 *Optimal simplex solution to goal programming problem*

	c_j	0	0	0	0	P_1	0	0	P_2	
c_B	Basic variables	x_1	x_2	s_1	s_2	d_1^-	d_1^+	d_2^-	d_2^+	Solution
0	x_2	0	1	0	1	$-.006$	.006	0	0	0
0	x_1	1	0	0	-2.5	.02	$-.02$	0	0	200
P_2	d_2^+	0	0	0	$-.25$	.004	$-.004$	-1	1	19
0	s_1	0	0	1	-1	.006	$-.006$	0	0	40
P_2	$c_j - z_j$	0	0	0	.25	$-.004$	.004	1	0	19
P_1	$c_j - z_j$	0	0	0	0	1	0	0	0	0

cannot bring d_1^- into the solution since d_1^- has a 1 in the $P_1 c_j - z_j$ row; this would negatively affect the attainment of the P_1 profit goal. Thus, no further improvements can be made and the solution is optimal. It is the same solution that we obtained in the graphical method with $x_1 = 200$, $x_2 = 0$. The last two numbers in the solution column indicate that the unattained portions of goals P_1 and P_2 are 0 and 19, respectively.

A Goal Programming Application[5]

The Lord Corporation in Erie, Pennsylvania, established ten goals in its research and development process:

1. No program may consume more than 10 percent of the resources.
2. Sales growth should exceed 15 percent per year.
3. Discounted cash-flow rate of return should exceed 30 percent.
4. Projects must have five-year capital limits.
5. Projects must promote constructive change in the industry.
6. Company should develop leadership role.
7. Company should develop new technology.
8. Advanced technology is interrelated.
9. Project must provide diversification of product and market.
10. Current balance of allocations between units is to be maintained.

Goal 1 is insurance against a disastrous project, goals 2–4 are financial in nature, goals 5–9 relate to corporate purpose and image, and goal 10 prevents dislocations of competent technical personnel.

Faced with 25 potential R & D projects, the top management at Lord Corporation decided to use goal programming to assist in allocating funds to the projects. A goal programming model was developed, and four separate computer runs were made under a variety of assumptions. As a check, an integer programming model was also employed, but it proved to be not nearly as satisfactory as the goal programming approach. Fifteen projects were selected that were suggested by the majority of the goal programming runs. Three projects were also added by top management; two of these three were suggested by the integer programming solution.

Goal programming was of definite value to the Lord Corporation in the funding of R & D projects. It appeared to offer advantages over other math programming approaches in that a variety of variable types could be accommodated. It also helped management to assess the nature of the conflict between financial goals and goals relating to corporate purpose; it did this in

[5] Anthony A. Salvia and William R. Ludwig, "An Application of Goal Programming at Lord Corporation," *Interfaces,* 9 (August 1979), 129–133.

a scientific manner—a departure from the often subjective or ad hoc top-management decision process.

MULTIPLE-OBJECTIVE LINEAR PROGRAMMING

In this section we consider multiple-objective linear programming, an alternative to goal programming. Multiple-objective linear programming (MOLP) differs from goal programming in that objectives are stated in terms of a linear objective function rather than a prespecified goal. An objective function represents an unbounded, directionally specified requirement which is to be followed to the greatest extent possible. Only the constraints limit the achievement of the best possible objective value. In some cases MOLP has an advantage over goal programming in which the goals are stipulated before the problem is solved.

An MOLP model looks like an LP model with more than one objective function. There are no goals or deviational variables in the constraints. To illustrate the MOLP approach, let's reconsider the Faze Linear product mix problem. Suppose that the profit contribution of power amps has increased from 200 to 300.

The objective function representing short-term profit can be expressed as

$$\text{Maximize} \quad 300x_1 + 500x_2$$

Suppose further that Faze Linear is planning to introduce a compact digital disk player that will require the Faze Linear preamp to operate. Since Faze Linear expects compact disk players to be a significant product in the current decade, it would like to sell as many of its preamps as possible to accommodate the future introduction of the disk player. In terms of long-range profits the company estimates that preamps will contribute four times as much profit as power amps.

Thus, its long-term profit function looks like

$$\text{Maximize} \quad 1x_1 + 4x_2$$

The complete multiple-objective formulation of the Faze Linear problem can be expressed as

$$\text{Maximize} \quad z_1 = 300x_1 + 500x_2 \qquad \text{subject to} \qquad x_2 \leq 40$$
$$\text{Maximize} \quad z_2 = 1x_1 + 4x_2 \qquad\qquad\qquad 1.2x_1 + 4x_2 \leq 240$$
$$.5x_1 + 1x_2 \leq 81$$
$$x_1, x_2 \geq 0$$

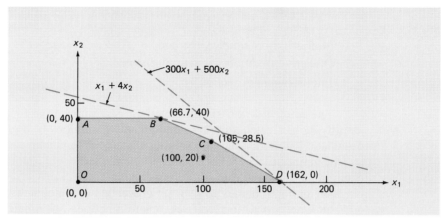

FIGURE 9.10   **MOLP solution to Faze Linear problem**

The formulation is identical to the original formulation except that we now have two objective functions, whose values are represented by z_1 and z_2, respectively.

The graphical solution to the MOLP Faze Linear problem is shown in Figure 9.10. If we consider only the first objective function, its value z_1 is maximized at the point (162, 0). The second objective function's value z_2 is maximized at the point (66.7, 40). Observe that point (100, 20) is a dominated point. The only points that are not dominated are the points along the darkened boundary from point (66.7, 40) to point (162, 0). This boundary is the efficient set or set of nondominated solutions. Given this set, what is the optimal solution? The answer is . . . it just depends. The most desirable solution in the set of nondominated solutions depends on the personal biases of the decision maker. In Table 9.1 we have summarized the extreme point solutions in the nondominated set. The choice of the best solution by Faze Linear would depend on the relative trade-offs between the advantages and disadvantages of each of the three nondominated extreme points.

In attacking real problems, the graphical method is no more useful in MOLP than it is in ordinary linear programming. We need systematic procedures that can determine all or at least part of the set of nondominated solutions.

TABLE 9.1   *Nondominated extreme points*

Point	Objective z_1	Function value z_2
(66.7,40)	40,000	226.7
(105,28.5)	45,750	219
(162,0)	48,600	162

The primary approaches to solving MOLP include the following:

1. Multicriterion simplex method
2. Objective function weighting schemes
3. Interactive approaches

The multicriterion simplex method is a simplex-based procedure for identifying and calculating all nondominated solutions of a given problem. Calculating all nondominated solutions is a complex technical task and one that is impractical for all but small problems. However, the method can be used to generate a subset of the nondominated solutions.

Weighting schemes apply a set of weights to the objective functions to add the functions to form one aggregate function. The single function can then be solved to yield an efficient solution. However, there is a great deal of difficulty in assigning the weights a priori. Let $\lambda_i, i = 1, \ldots, n$ be the weight assigned to objective function i. The weights are required to be greater than or equal to zero and form a convex combination; that is,

$$\sum_{i=1}^{n} \lambda_i = 1$$

The problem with a priori weighting schemes is that the decision maker may be unable to specify a precise set of weights. Another problem that has been discovered in actual practice is that the prespecified set of weights do not always yield a solution that is acceptable to the decision maker. Steuer and Schuler[6] report on the problems with the weighting approach in an actual application involving forest management.

Interactive approaches seem to offer the most flexibility and success in handling real applications. Steuer and Schuler's interactive approach to the forest management problem does not require the decision maker to specify any weights for the objectives. At each iteration the decision maker is presented with a small number of candidate solutions. The decision maker then selects his or her most preferred solutions from this small set. A technical analyst uses a vector-maximum algorithm and a gradient cone contraction technique to develop the next set of nondominated solutions. In the forest management application, there were 5 objective functions, 13 constraints, and 31 variables in the problem. The time required between iterations involving the decision maker and analyst was one to two weeks. The procedure converges to a final solution after a fixed number of iterations.

---

[6] Ralph E. Steuer and Albert T. Schuler, "An Interactive Multiple-Objective Linear Programming Approach to a Problem in Forest Management," *Operations Research*, 26 (March–April 1978), 254–269.

The area of MOLP and multiple-criteria decision making remains an active area of research. No single method is generally accepted in the way that the simplex method is for single-objective linear programming. Given the complexity of multiple-criteria decision making we cannot expect an all-encompassing solution procedure to be developed soon, if ever. However, several approaches do exist that can aid significantly in addressing multiple-criteria problems and we can expect ongoing research to yield more refined approaches in the near future.

COMPUTER IMPLICATIONS

There are several computer software packages available to solve integer and goal programming types of problems. However, the quantity and availability of these is limited compared to packages available for general LP and PERT applications which we have examined in previous chapters. Perhaps the most widely available integer programming package is the IBM MPSX-MIP/370 system, which is available for most IBM mainframe computers. Another package is the LINDO system that is illustrated in this text.

The problem size that can be tackled in integer programming is significantly smaller than the size that can be solved by linear programming. Thus, computer memory requirements and computer time become more significant issues in addressing integer problems. It is possible to formulate a large-scale integer model which is not solvable to optimality. In these cases we have recourse to heuristic methods or efforts to obtain good feasible solutions prior to the achievement of optimality. There has been more progress in solving large-scale integer problems with a special structure, such as plant location or set covering, than in solving the general integer programming problem. Recently, researchers have been able to solve significantly larger ILP models than in the past. Future research will undoubtedly lead to the ability to solve larger problems and to handle new applications.

The multiple-criteria methods are relatively new and not commonly available as software packages. Nonpreemptive goal programming problems are solvable by the readily accessible ordinary simplex method. There are several independently developed codes for solving the preemptive case such as the one by Ignizio.[7] In terms of computer resources, goal programming would be very comparable to linear programming. Other multiple-criteria methods are available on a limited basis. For a list of published and commercially available multiple-criteria packages the interested reader should refer to Zeleny.[8]

[7] Ignizio, *Goal Programming and Extensions.*
[8] Zeleny, *Multiple Criteria Decision Making.*

SUMMARY

Many real-world problems must be modeled as mathematical programming models that do not satisfy all the requirements of pure LP models. In this chapter, we have examined two of the more widely used mathematical programming approaches (not including LP).

Integer programming extends LP by allowing the requirements of whole-number solutions. The types of integer models include pure, mixed, and 0–1. The branch-and-bound partial enumeration procedure is generally the most successful approach to achieving integer solutions. Using integer-valued variables permits the formulation of many interesting problems, such as the fixed-charge problem and the crew scheduling problem.

Goal programming extends linear programming by accommodating multiple objectives. These objectives can be preemptive or nonpreemptive. In the preemptive case, the objectives must be ordinally ranked and are satisfied (if possible) in order of priority. Often, a final solution satisfices rather than completely achieves all goals. Linear goal programming models can be solved by a modified version of the simplex method. Many applications exist for goal programming, particularly in the public sector.

Another approach to multiple-objective decision making is MOLP, or multiple objective linear programming. This approach can determine the set of all nondominated solutions to a problem. The most promising approach to solving MOLP problems appears to be the interactive approach, although future research should yield even more effective methodologies.

SOLVED PROBLEMS

PROBLEM STATEMENT

Consider the following 0–1 integer programming model:

$$\text{Maximize} \quad 35x_1 + 40x_2 + 42x_3$$
$$\text{subject to} \quad 7x_1 + 6x_2 + 13x_3 \leq 75$$
$$2x_1 - x_2 + x_3 \leq 30$$
$$x_1, x_2, x_3 = 0 \text{ or } 1$$

Reformulate the problem so that no more than two decision variables are nonzero, and if $x_2 = 1$ then $x_3 = 1$, and vice versa. Then solve the model using an ILP computer code.

SOLUTION

The solution is presented in the context of the LINDO computer package. LINDO is capable of solving all-integer, mixed-integer, or 0–1-integer models. To obtain an integer solution, the user simply specifies which variables are required to be integer.

What follows is the reformulation of the 0–1 model and the resulting LINDO output. The first n variables in the model can be specified as 0–1 by using the INTEGER n command. (If there are more than n decision variables, the remaining variables are assumed to be noninteger.) The output indicates that x_2 and x_3 have a value of 1 in the optimal solution. The optimal objective function value is 82.

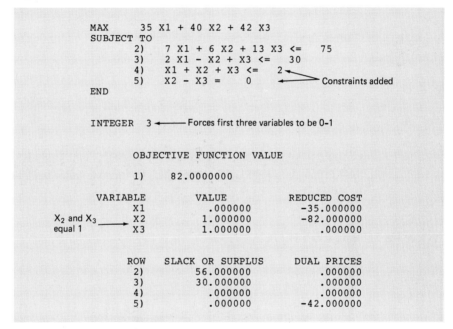

```
MAX       35 X1 + 40 X2 + 42 X3
SUBJECT TO
        2)    7 X1 + 6 X2 + 13 X3 <=    75
        3)    2 X1 - X2 + X3 <=    30
        4)    X1 + X2 + X3 <=    2
        5)    X2 - X3 =    0          ← Constraints added
END


INTEGER   3  ← Forces first three variables to be 0-1


            OBJECTIVE FUNCTION VALUE

        1)    82.0000000

        VARIABLE        VALUE        REDUCED COST
                 X1      .000000      -35.000000
X2 and X3 →      X2     1.000000      -82.000000
equal 1          X3     1.000000       .000000


            ROW    SLACK OR SURPLUS    DUAL PRICES
            2)      56.000000          .000000
            3)      30.000000          .000000
            4)       .000000           .000000
            5)       .000000          -42.000000
```

PROBLEM STATEMENT

Recall the Faze Linear LP model of the goal programming section of this chapter. Its LP formulation is as follows:

$$\text{Maximize} \quad 200x_1 + 500x_2$$

$$\text{subject to} \qquad\qquad\quad x_2 \leq\ 40$$

$$1.2x_1 +\quad 4x_2 \leq 240$$

$$.5x_1 +\quad 1x_2 \leq\ 81$$

$$x_1, x_2 \geq 0$$

Reformulate the Faze Linear model as a goal programming model with the following goals:

- Priority 1: Produce at least 10 preamps and 150 amps.
- Priority 2: Maximize profit.
- Priority 3: Limit assembly overtime to 10 hours.

SOLUTION

$$\text{Minimize} \quad P_1(d_1^- + d_2^-) + P_2 d_3^- + P_3 d_4^+$$

subject to

$$\left. \begin{array}{r} x_2 \le 40 \\ .5x_1 + 1x_2 \le 81 \end{array} \right\} \quad \text{resource constraints}$$

$$\left. \begin{array}{r} x_1 + d_1^- - d_1^+ = 150 \\ x_2 + d_2^- - d_2^+ = 10 \end{array} \right\} \quad \text{priority 1}$$

$$200x_1 + 500x_2 + d_3^- - d_3^+ = 999{,}999 \qquad \text{priority 2}$$

$$1.2x_1 + 4x_2 + d_4^- - d_4^+ = 250 \qquad \text{priority 3}$$

$$x_j, \, d_i \ge 0$$

In the priority 2 goal constraint, the 999,999 represents an unrealistically high profit. It is simply used as a target, that is, to get as close as possible to this profit.

REVIEW QUESTIONS

1. Explain how each of the following differs from LP.
   a. Integer programming
   b. Goal programming
   c. Multiple objective linear programming
2. How does branch and bound avoid complete enumeration?
3. What is the efficient set in multiple-criteria decision making?
4. List three types of formulation possibilities that can be modeled through integer programming.
5. What is meant by the ordinal ranking of goals in goal programming?
6. What is one possible theoretical advantage of MOLP compared to goal programming?
7. In what way is the simplex method modified for the goal programming approach?
8. Contrast the state of the art in the solution capabilities of linear versus integer programming.

9. Explain the difficulties in using LP with rounding to obtain integer solutions.

10. Under what conditions is a node fathomed in the branch and bound process?

11. In selecting R & D projects, the Lord Corporation did not use just one computer run. What did it do?

PROBLEMS

9.1 *Research and development project selection.* The Kleber Corporation is considering six R & D projects for the next fiscal year. It has allocated $250,000 for research and development projects. All projects must be completely funded or not funded at all. Given the expected rate of return for the six projects in the table, formulate a mathematical model to maximize return from the R & D projects.

Project	Rate of return	Cost
1	20%	$80,000
2	23	50,000
3	30	40,000
4	15	70,000
5	18	80,000
6	25	60,000

Maximize $20X_1 +$

S.T. $80,000X_1$

9.2 In Problem 9.1, let $x_i = 1$ if project i is selected and 0 otherwise. Specify the appropriate constraints for each of the following conditions:

a. At most five projects are to be selected.

b. If project 1 is selected then project 5 is not selected.

c. Exactly four projects are to be selected.

d. If project 2 is selected then project 4 is also selected.

e. Either condition (a) or (b) applies, but not both.

9.3 Solve the following knapsack problem by branch and bound.

$$\text{Maximize} \quad 180x_1 + 80x_2 + 130x_3 + 110x_4$$

$$\text{subject to} \quad 7x_1 + 2x_2 + 6x_3 + 5x_4 \le 15$$

$$x_i = 0 \text{ or } 1$$

9.4 Specify whether each of the following models is pure integer, mixed integer, 0–1 integer, or linear.

a. Maximize $\quad x_1 + x_2$

$\quad$ subject to $\quad 3x_1 + 2x_2 \le 20$

$\qquad\qquad\quad 4x_1 + x_2 \le 50$

$\qquad\qquad\qquad x_i = 0 \text{ or } 1$

b. Minimize $\quad 3x_1 + 4x_2 + 6x_3$

$\quad$ subject to $\quad x_1 + x_2 + x_3 \ge 3$

$\qquad\qquad\quad 2x_1 - x_2 + 3x_3 = 18$

$\qquad\qquad\qquad x_1 \text{ integer}$

$\qquad\qquad\qquad x_2, x_3 \ge 0$

c. Minimize $\quad 4x_1 + 5x_2$

$\quad$ subject to $\quad 2x_1 + 3x_2 \ge 40$

$\qquad\qquad\quad 6x_1 + 2x_2 \ge 30$

$\qquad\qquad\qquad x_1, x_2 \ge 0$

d. Maximize $\quad 3x_1 + 7x_2$

$\quad$ subject to $\quad x_1 + x_2 \le 10$

$\qquad\qquad\quad 8x_1 + 9x_2 \le 100$

$\qquad\qquad\qquad x_1, x_2 \text{ integer}$

9.5 *Personnel recruiting.* Midwestern University must fill 30 faculty and 10 staff positions for next year. To control costs and better satisfy EEOC requirements, Midwestern has the following goals:

☐ Priority 1: at least 30 percent of new hirings are to be minorities
$\qquad\qquad\qquad$ at least 20 percent of new hirings are to be women
☐ Priority 2: stay within recruiting budget of $40,000
☐ Priority 3: limit budget overrun to $10,000

Assume that it costs $1,100 to recruit a faculty member and $300 to recruit a staff member. Furthermore, it costs 20 percent more to recruit a minority or female faculty member. Formulate the problem as a goal programming model.

9.6 Solve the following goal programming problem graphically.

$$\text{Minimize} \quad P_1(d_1^- + d_1^+) + P_2 d_2^-$$
$$\text{subject to} \quad 2x_1 + 3x_2 \quad\qquad\qquad \geq 12$$
$$x_1 \qquad\qquad\qquad\qquad \geq 3$$
$$x_1 + x_2 + d_1^- - d_1^+ = 6$$
$$x_2 + d_2^- - d_2^+ = 3$$
$$x_1, x_2, d_1^-, d_1^+, d_2^-, d_2^+ \geq 0$$

9.7 Solve Problem 9.6 by the modified simplex method.

9.8 Given a knapsack problem with five items, what is the maximum number of nodes that could possibly comprise the branch and bound tree?

9.9 Consider the pure integer problem given.

$$\text{Maximize} \quad 3x_1 + 4x_2$$
$$\text{subject to} \quad x_1 \qquad\quad \leq 4$$
$$x_2 \leq 3$$
$$3x_1 + 4x_2 \leq 22$$
$$x_1, x_2 \geq 0 \text{ and integer}$$

a. Graph the constraints and plot all feasible lattice points.

b. Ignore the integer restrictions, and solve the LP relaxation of the problem graphically.

c. Specify an upper and lower bound on the value of the optimal integer solution.

d. Determine the optimal integer solution.

9.10 *Production planning.* The Crosby Co. has contracted to produce 500 fittings next week for one of its customers. Crosby has three machines in its machine shop that can produce the fitting, but at different variable and fixed costs. These costs and weekly production limits are shown in the table. The fixed cost is incurred only if the machine is set up to produce the fitting.

Machine	Per unit production cost	Fixed set-up cost	Weekly production limit
1	$1.12	$60	300
2	1.40	55	250
3	1.23	50	270

Formulate an integer programming model to determine how to produce the 500 fittings at minimal cost.

9.11 *Investment decision problem.* Assume one of your friends has just inherited $100,000 after taxes. He has several ideas for the money, but is unable to do them all. He would like to invest in gold, with an expected return of 20 percent but a risk factor of .15. He would also like to invest in an uninsured money market CD yielding 11.5 percent with a risk factor of .10. His other ideas are to invest in an insured passbook account yielding 7 percent with risk factor .02 and to invest in a mutual fund yielding 9.5 percent with risk .07. Finally, he would like to loan you $25,000 (at 0 interest and risk .10) to start your own business upon graduation. Since not all these ideas are simultaneously possible, he has specified the following priorities:

P_1: total investments must absolutely not exceed $100,000
P_2: achieve an average yield of 10 percent
P_3: achieve an average risk of no more than .06
P_4: loan you $25,000

Formulate the investment decision problem as a goal programming model.

9.12 *Advertising strategy.* A major sporting goods manufacturer is bringing out a new line of graphite golf clubs and wants to accomplish several goals in its new advertising campaign. The campaign will focus on ads in the leading golf magazine and television ads during coverage of PGA tournaments. A magazine ad costs $12,000 and has a "reach" of 350,000 effective exposure units. A television ad costs $20,000 and achieves 1,400,000 effective exposure units. The company has allocated $500,000 for advertising the new line of clubs. Formulate a goal programming model to incorporate the following goals:

P_1: stay within advertising budget of $500,000
P_2: maximize the audience "reach," that is, the number of effective exposure units
P_3: run at least 10 television ads
P_4: run at least 8 magazine ads

9.13 Solve Problem 9.12 by the graphical goal programming method.

9.14 *Cargo loading.* An independent trucker makes a weekly trip from Los Angeles to New Orleans. To make his trip more profitable he has decided to be more selective in how he loads his truck. His truck has a volume capacity of 2,500 cubic feet and a weight capacity of 40,000 pounds. The following table lists each type of item and its weight, boxed volume, and profitability.

	Weight (lbs.)	Volume	Profit contribution
Electric ranges	180	20	$17
Washing machine	250	24	20
Refrigerator	380	54	25
Dishwasher	120	19	9
Television	100	18	13
Stereo speakers	99	15	10

Formulate the cargo loading problem as an integer programming problem, assuming profit maximization as the goal.

9.15 *Staff shift scheduling.* Northern Airlines is in the process of finalizing an on-line reservations system. To staff the system, telephone reservationists will need to be available in the following quantities:

Period	Time	Reservationists needed
1	6 A.M.–8 A.M.	3
2	8 A.M.–10 A.M.	12
3	10 A.M.–12 noon	13
4	12 noon–2 P.M.	10
5	2 P.M.–4 P.M.	12
6	4 P.M.–6 P.M.	10
7	6 P.M.–8 P.M.	6
8	8 P.M.–10 P.M.	5
9	10 P.M.–12 midnight	4
10	12 midnight–2 A.M.	3

Northern plans to have six work shifts, of which two are split shifts. The shift times are as follows:

Shift	Time
1	6 A.M.–2 P.M.
2	8 A.M.–4 P.M.
3	10 A.M.–6 P.M.
4	6 P.M.–2 A.M.
5	10 A.M.–1 P.M. and 4 P.M.–8 P.M.
6	8 A.M.–11 A.M. and 5 P.M.–9 P.M.

The airline wants to assign reservationists to shifts in order to meet demand. However, they want to hire the minimal number of people to meet demand. Formulate an integer programming model to determine the minimum number of reservationists required for each shift.

9.16 *Curve fitting via goal programming.* Several factors are used to predict graduate school performance. For MBAs, their GMAT test scores are often used together with other information. The development of prediction equations that regress one variable against another is usually done by the method of least squares. However, the least squares method develops a predicting equation that minimizes the sum of the squares of the residuals or differences between actual and predicted dependent variable values. Unfortunately, extreme or outlying cases can bias the resulting equation to an undesirable extent. The use of goal programming can reduce the effect of "outliers" by minimizing the sum of the absolute value of residuals rather than the squared value.

Returning to the prediction of GPA given GMAT test scores, we want an equation

$$\text{predicted GPA} = ax + b$$

where x = the student's GMAT score and a and b are to be determined. Goal programming can be used by applying the equation

$$\text{predicted GPA}_i + r_i = \text{actual GPA}_i$$

where the residual r_i = actual GPA_i − predicted GPA_i for the ith observation.

For n observations, the goal programming objective function would be

$$\text{Minimize} \sum_{i=1}^{n} (d_i^- + d_i^+)$$

where $r_i = d_i^- - d_i^+$.

Listed next are 10 real GMAT scores and GPAs for 10 randomly selected MBAs at a Southwestern University.

GMAT	GPA
665	3.20
629	3.63
588	3.00
523	3.60
513	3.00
483	3.00
452	3.10
442	3.00
441	3.15
388	2.50

a. Formulate a goal programming model that will predict the GPA given GMAT scores based on the sample given.

b. If you have access to an LP computer package, solve the model on the computer to determine the predicting equation.

9.17 Consider the following multiple-objective linear programming problem:

$$\text{Maximize} \quad z_1 = 4x_1 + x_2$$

$$\text{Maximize} \quad z_2 = \qquad x_2$$

$$\text{subject to} \qquad 2x_1 + x_2 \le 16$$

$$\tfrac{5}{6}x_1 + x_2 \le 10$$

$$x_1 + x_2 \ge \; 5$$

$$x_1, x_2 \ge 0$$

a. Graph the feasible region and the efficient set of solutions.

b. Determine the nondominated extreme point solutions.

9.18 *Airline crew scheduling problem.* Stochastic Airlines is in the process of determining its crew assignment schedule. Stochastic Airlines is a very small airline and currently operates the following set of flights:

Flight no.	Origin	Destination	Time
75	Chicago	LA	afternoon
450	New York	Chicago	afternoon
210	New York	Dallas	night
27	LA	Chicago	afternoon
93	Chicago	New York	night
120	Dallas	New York	morning

The basic problem is to determine the next flight, if any, that a crew operates after it completes one flight. This process consists of determining the appropriate tours or rotations for a crew. A tour consists of from one to three connecting flights. A tour which requires "deadheading," that is, termination in a city other than the origin city, incurs additional expense. In its simple problem, Stochastic has specified six possible one-flight tours, four two-flight tours, and two three-flight tours. Listed next are the tours and their costs.

One-flight tours	Cost	Two-flight tours	Cost	Three-flight tours	Cost
1. 75	4100	7. 450, 93	3100	11. 210, 120, 450	2900
2. 450	3700	8. 210, 120	3200	12. 120, 450, 93	3000
3. 210	3800	9. 27, 93	3500		
4. 27	4100	10. 120, 450	3400		
5. 93	3700				
6. 120	3800				

Formulate a 0–1 integer programming model to select the appropriate tours for Stochastic Airlines to cover all required flights at minimum cost.

9.19 *Multifamily aggregate production planning with fixed changeover costs.* The Westerbeck Co. manufactures several models of washers and dryers. The projected demand requirements over the next year for its automatic washers are:

Month	Family 1 requirement	Family 2 requirement
January	800	900
February	1,030	900
March	810	900
April	900	900
May	950	900
June	1,340	900
July	1,100	900
August	1,210	900
September	600	900
October	580	900
November	890	900
December	1,000	900

Beginning inventory is 100 units for family 1 and 2 washers. The firm's current capacity is 1800 units per month in terms of family 1 washers. Family 1 washers require only 80 percent of the production capacity of family 2 washers. The average salary of production workers is $1,300 per month. Overtime is paid at time and one-half up to 20 percent additional time. Each production worker can produce 30 units per month of family 1 washers. Additional labor can be hired for a training cost of $250, and existing workers can be laid off at a cost of $500. Any increase or decrease in the production rate costs $2,000 for tooling, setup, and line changes. This does not apply, however, to overtime. Inventory-holding costs are $25 per unit per month. Backorders cost $75 per unit short. Model the problem as a mixed-integer program to minimize total costs over the one-year planning horizon. Assume that only the production changeover decisions are subject to integer restrictions. Solve the model using LINDO or any other MIP computer code.

BIBLIOGRAPHY

Charnes, Abraham, and William W. Cooper, *Management Models and Industrial Applications of Linear Programming*. New York: John Wiley & Sons, Inc., 1961.

Garfinkel, R. S., and G. L. Nemhauser, *Integer Programming*. New York: John Wiley & Sons, Inc., 1972.

Hu, T. C., *Integer Programming and Network Flows*. Reading, Mass.: Addison-Wesley Publishing Company, Inc., 1969.

Ignizio, James P., *Goal Programming and Extensions*. Lexington, Mass.: D. C. Heath and Company, 1976.

Lee, Sang M., *Goal Programming for Decision Analysis*. Philadelphia: Auerbach Publishers, Inc., 1972 (New York: Petrocelli Books, 1973).

Loomba, Narendra P., and Efrian Turban, *Applied Programming for Management*. New York: Holt, Rinehart and Winston, Inc., 1974.

Nemhauser, G. L., and L. A. Wolsey, *Integer and Combinatorial Optimization*. New York: John Wiley & Sons, Inc., 1988.

Plane, Donald R., and Claude McMillan, Jr., *Discrete Optimization*. Englewood Cliffs, N.J.: Prentice Hall, 1971.

Salkin, H. M., *Integer Programming*. Reading, Mass.: Addison-Wesley Publishing Company, Inc., 1975.

Taha, Hamdy A., *Integer Programming.: Theory, Applications and Computations*. New York: Academic Press, 1975.

Zeleny, Milan, *Multiple Criteria Decision Making*. New York: McGraw-Hill Book Company, 1982.

Zionts, Stanley, *Linear and Integer Programming*. Englewood Cliffs, N.J.: Prentice Hall, 1974.

10

Dynamic Programming

PHILLIPS PETROLEUM COMPANY

The Phillips Petroleum Company manages approximately 1,500 passenger cars and 3,800 trucks in its U.S. fleet.[1] The fleet includes a large number of passenger cars and light trucks used for oil well maintenance and service and for pipeline maintenance. The fleet also includes large highway tractors used to transport petroleum and petrochemical products.

To analyze equipment replacement decisions, Phillips has been using an OR model that used the policy to replace after n months of service or m miles, whichever comes first. However, this model ignored some important financial and time-related questions dealing with tax laws and depreciation schedules, license tags, and improved fuel efficiency of newer models.

To make replacement decisions easier and more complete, a more comprehensive model was developed. The new model was to answer the questions: Should this particular vehicle be replaced? If not now, then when? A network model was constructed to represent all the retain-replace decisions that could occur over the duration of the activity. The resulting network is suitable for solution by using the mathematical programming technique of dynamic programming. The interval from one replacement opportunity to the next was defined as a stage in the model.

[1] R. Waddell, "A Model for Equipment Replacement Decisions and Policies," *Interfaces,* 13, no. 4 (August 1983), 1–7.

The states of the dynamic programming model are represented by the equipment age. Each arc in the network has an assigned DOCF (discounted outgoing cash flow). The dynamic programming model determines the path from start to termination that minimizes the sum of the DOCFs. The DOCFs consist of several components including maintenance and operating costs such as fuel, oil, and salaries. The model also links decisions to the age of the vehicle and incorporates the tax laws of the Economic Recovery Act of 1981.

The model is implemented via a batch processing computer program. The program was designed so that replacement opportunities occur at the end of each month. The program yields two solutions. One solution is optimal assuming an initial replace decision; the other solution is optimal assuming an initial retain decision.

The program is used only as a tool in decision making. Its suggested solution is recognized as a qualified "best solution." Phillips management also considers factors such as safety, driver comfort, and morale. The model has been used for several years in making decisions for highway tractor replacement decisions. The program has also been used for some preliminary lease versus buy studies. Phillips is now using the program to establish replacement policies for company passenger cars and light trucks. Cost savings are expected to exceed $90,000 annually.

INTRODUCTION

Mathematical programming methods involving linear programming, integer programming, and goal programming are concerned primarily with single-period or static decision problems. In these math programming approaches, the entire solution is determined "all at once" by a specific solution procedure such as the simplex method. By contrast, dynamic programming is best suited for multiperiod or multistage decision problems in which a sequence of decisions is required and where the problem parameters change from period to period. Dynamic programming is also very flexible and is applicable to stochastic problems in which some parameters are probablistic. Many multistage decision problems exist in business and engineering applications. Some of these applications include production and distribution problems, scheduling, inventory control, resource allocation, employment decisions, replacement and maintenance problems, and chemical engineering processes.

Dynamic programming would perhaps be better named serial or recursive optimization. It proceeds by breaking the problem into smaller subproblems, called stages, and develops optimal policies or decisions for each stage. The stages are tied together through recursive relationships, so that when the last stage is calculated, the solution to the overall problem is determined. You will find that dynamic programming is a rather unique approach to optimization. It is a solution approach and not a specific technique such as the simplex method for LP. It is similar to the branch and bound method for integer programming in that each different application requires a tailor-made solution algorithm. In this chapter, we will present the basic principles and concepts of dynamic programming through not only discussion but several popular examples.

THE SHORTEST-ROUTE PROBLEM REVISITED

We examined the network approach to the shortest-route problems in Chapter 7. The labeling algorithm we learned in Chapter 7 is one of the best methods for solving shortest-route problems. We reconsider the shortest-route problem here since it is an excellent vehicle through which to illustrate the basics of dynamic programming.

To illustrate the dynamic programming approach let's consider the shortest-route problem shown in Figure 10.1. The number associated with each arc represents the distance between the two associated nodes, and the objective is to find the shortest route from node 1 to node 7.

In the next section of this chapter we delve into the formal theory of dynamic programming. At this point let's take a simple approach and focus on only two principles, namely, decomposition and the principle of optimality. Decomposition involves breaking the problem into subproblems or stages. Each stage of a dynamic programming problem is smaller and easier to solve than the overall original problem. Figure 10.2 illustrates one way in which the given shortest-route problem can be decomposed into stages. The

FIGURE 10.1 **Shortest-route network**

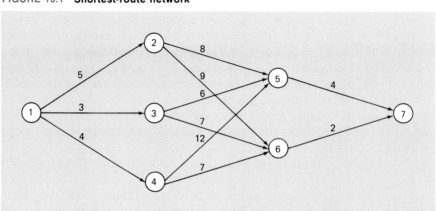

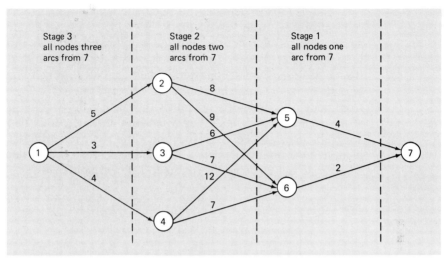

FIGURE 10.2 **Shortest-route problem broken into stages**

dynamic programming approach proceeds sequentially from one stage to another. It begins at stage 1 and determines the shortest route from nodes 5 and 6 to node 7. It then moves to stage 2 and uses the information from stage 1 to determine the shortest route from each node in stage 2 to node 7. Finally, in stage 3 it uses the information from stage 2 to determine the shortest route from node 1 to node 7.

If we follow the serial stage-by-stage approach to the shortest-route problem, how can we be certain of achieving the optimal solution? The principle of optimality is a fundamental precept that can guarantee our success. Adapted to the shortest-route problem, the principle of optimality states that:

> If a given node is on the shortest route, the shortest path from the given node to the end node is also on the shortest route.

Applying the principle of optimality to the shortest-route problem in Figure 10.2 implies a backward calculation process. We assume each node is possibly on the shortest route and calculate the shortest path from it to every node in the next stage. Thus, knowing the shortest route to node 7 from nodes 5 and 6 in stage 1, we can proceed to nodes 2, 3, and 4 in stage 2 to determine easily the shortest path from each of those nodes to node 7. These dynamic programming calculations may seem like complete enumeration of all possible routes, but they are not, since at each stage we use only the output or information from the immediately preceding stage.

Let us look in detail at the calculations required to solve the shortest-route problem. Note first in Figure 10.2 that we have defined the stage 1 subproblem as all nodes that are one arc from end node 7. Similarly, stage 2 is comprised of all nodes that are 2 arcs from end node 7 and so on. We begin the calculations by first considering the nodes in stage 1. If you are at node 5 or node 6 you have no choice but to go directly to node 7. The shortest route from node 5 to node 7 is obviously 5–7 with a distance of 4. The shortest route from node 6 to node 7 is 6–7 with a distance of 2. Thus, the stage 1 subproblem is solved by inspection. For each node in stage 1 we have identified the optimal decision, that is, the shortest route to node 7. We can summarize our calculations for stage 1 in the table below:

Stage 1

Node	Shortest route to next stage	Shortest distance to node 7
5	5–7	4
6	6–7	2

We use the output from stage 1 as the input to stage 2. We must find the shortest route from each of the stage 2 nodes 2, 3, and 4 to the end node 7. It does not matter which node is selected first. Starting with node 2 a decision must be made concerning the successor node in stage 1. There are only 2 choices, node 5 or node 6. The total distance from node 2 to node 7 is 8 + 4 = 12 if node 5 is chosen as the successor to node 2. The total distance is 9 + 2 = 11 if node 6 is chosen as the successor node. Thus, the shortest distance from node 2 to node 7 is 11. The calculations for the shortest distance from node 3 can be expressed as:

$$\text{Minimum} \quad \{6 + 4, 7 + 2\} = 9$$

The calculation for the shortest distance from node 4 can be expressed as:

$$\text{Minimum} \quad \{12 + 4, 7 + 2\} = 9$$

We can summarize the stage 2 calculations as:

Stage 2

Node	Shortest route to next stage	Shortest distance to node 7
2	2–6	11
3	3–6	9
4	4–6	9

Since stage 3 is the last stage, we will have solved the shortest-route problem when we have completed the stage 3 calculations. We use the output from the stage 2 calculations to calculate the shortest route from node 1. The choices for the successor node for node 1 are nodes 2, 3, and 4. If we choose node 2, the distance to node 7 is the distance from node 1 to node 2 plus the shortest distance from node 2 to node 7. These distances are 5 + 11 = 16. Notice that by using the shortest distance found in the stage 2 calculations, we have avoided making those calculations again.

Considering the alternative successor nodes 3 and 4 we have the following calculations:

$$\text{Minimum} \quad \{5 + 11, 3 + 9, 4 + 9\} = 12$$

Thus, the optimal successor node for node 1 is node 3 yielding a total distance of 12. The stage 3 calculations can be summarized as

Stage 3

Node	Shortest route to next stage	Shortest distance to node 7
1	1–3	12

We now know that the shortest distance from node 1 to node 7 is 12 and can determine the sequence of arcs comprising the shortest route by working backward from stage 3 through stage 1.

Stage	Shortest route to next stage
3	1–3
2	3–6
1	6–7

The shortest route is 1–3–6–7 and is obtained directly from the summary information of the stage calculations. The final solution to the shortest-route problem is shown in Figure 10.3. The colored numbers above each node represent the shortest distance to the end node.

The previous calculations may seem like complete enumeration of all paths. In small examples such as this one the computational effort can approach that of complete enumeration. However, our calculations were actually less than complete enumeration and for larger problems the computational effort would be drastically reduced. Dynamic programming is a powerful approach to many types of problems. We turn now to the formal structure and underlying principles of dynamic programming.

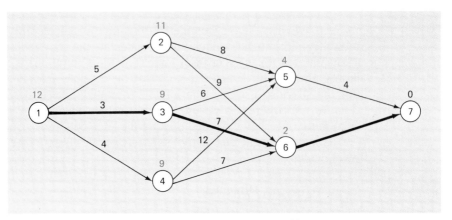

FIGURE 10.3 **Optimal solution to the shortest-route problem**

FUNDAMENTAL CONCEPTS AND NOTATION

The foregoing example illustrates the basic ideas in dynamic programming, but it is necessary to formalize these procedures to develop a systematic and precise approach. Let us look at the terminology and underlying structure of dynamic programming. You should not expect all of the dynamic programming terminology and relationships to be perfectly clear upon first reading. Plan to read through the material more than once and try to relate the concepts to the examples presented in the chapter. Your familiarity with the examples will facilitate your understanding of dynamic programming.

In every dynamic programming formulation, we have the following concepts:

stage 1. *Stage.* Each problem is broken into subproblems or stages. A stage corresponds to a point in time or a situation where a decision must be made.

state 2. *State.* States are associated with each stage and represent the various possible conditions of the system. Usually, state variables are used to describe the status of the system.

policy decision 3. *Policy.* A decision rule or set of decisions which, at any stage, determines the decision for each possible state. The effect of the policy decision at each stage is to transform the current stage into a state associated with the next stage.

return 4. *Return.* The return at any stage is the net reward that occurs at that stage due to the decision policy and the state of the system. A return function is a measure of contribution analogous to the objective function in linear programming.

recursive relationship

5. *Recursive relationship.* A mathematical relationship that identifies the optimal decision policy for each state at stage n, given the optimal decision policy for each state at stage $(n - 1)$. The recursive relationship is the mechanism by which decisions and states are related between stages.

Additionally, we now have the formal statement of the principle of optimality which is a fundamental principle of dynamic programming.

principle of optimality

> An optimal policy (set of decisions) has the property that whatever the initial state and initial decision are, the remaining decisions must constitute an optimal policy with regard to the state resulting from the first decision.

The principle of optimality implies that given the current system state, an optimal policy for the remaining stages is independent of the policy adopted in previous stages. Relating this to the shortest-route problem, the implication is that given our position at a particular node, the shortest route to the end node is independent of how we got to the particular node. For dynamic programming problems in general, knowledge of the current state of the system conveys all the information about its previous behavior necessary for determining the optimal policy henceforth.

Given the fundamental concepts of stages, states, policy decisions, returns, and recursive relationships, how do these fit together in dynamic programming? In terms of the shortest-route problem, the stages of the problem consisted of groups of nodes that had the common property of being a specific number of arcs away from the destination. Within each stage, a state simply consists of your location at a particular node. For each possible state (node), we had to determine the optimal policy decision, which consisted of the choice of the best arc leading to the next stage. The criterion or return function consisted of the measure of the distance to the end node. Figure 10.4 further illustrates the relationships among policy decisions, states, stages, and returns.

To describe the dynamic programming approach in more precise terms, let us define the following:

$$x_n = \text{decision variable at stage } n$$
$$s_n = \text{state variable input to stage } n$$
$$r_n = \text{return at stage } n$$

We can symbolically represent the relationship of the components of a dynamic programming formulation as shown in Figure 10.5. The return func-

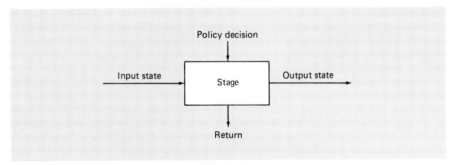

FIGURE 10.4 Model components in dynamic programming

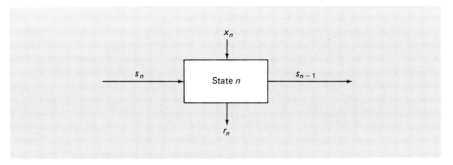

FIGURE 10.5 Symbolic representation of model components in dynamic programming

tion r_n is actually a function of the state variable s_n and the decision variable x_n. The return is therefore expressed as

$$r_n(s_n,x_n)$$

and represents the return associated with a particular state–decision combination (s_n,x_n) in stage n.

To tie the various stages together, we need a return function that represents not only the return in stage n, but also the total return from stage $n - 1$ given the input state to stage $n - 1$ and the decision at stage $n - 1$. We refer to the function as the total return function and denote it by

$$f_n(s_n,x_n)$$

Figure 10.6 shows the decomposed dynamic programming problem and the relationships among return functions, states, and stages.

The total return function $f_n(s_n,x_n)$ in stage n is defined in terms of the

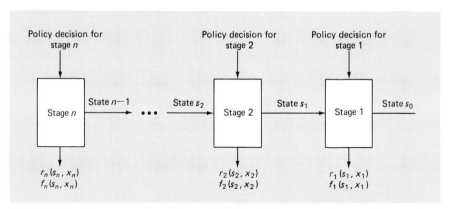

FIGURE 10.6 **Decomposed problem and relationships among stages, states, and return functions**

total return function $f_{n-1}(s_{n-1}, x_{n-1})$ in stage $n - 1$. This type of relationship is called a recursive relationship and exists whenever the current value of a function or variable is redefined in terms of the previous value. Thus, $f_2(s_2, x_2)$ is defined in terms of $f_1(s_1, x_1)$, $f_3(s_3, x_3)$ is defined in terms of $f_2(s_2, x_2)$ and so on. Notice that when functional relationships are defined recursively, the returns in one stage depend only on the returns from the previous stage. The recursive calculations offer significant computational efficiency compared to complete enumeration.

The general form of the recursive return function of dynamic programming is:

$$f_n(s_n, x_n) = r_n(s_n, x_n) + f_{n-1}(s_{n-1}, x_{n-1})$$

Thus, the total return at stage n is equal to the stage n return plus the total return at stage $n - 1$. Since we have already made the stage $n - 1$ calculations before moving to stage n, we can use the optimal returns in stage $n - 1$ given the possible states and decisions input to stage $n - 1$. Letting $f_n^*(s_n, x_n)$ denote the optimal return function value for a given s_n and x_n, we can restate the dynamic programming recursive relationship as:

$$f_n(s_n, x_n) = r_n(s_n, x_n) + f_{n-1}^*(s_{n-1}, x_{n-1})$$

Each dynamic programming problem will have its own specific types of functions that substitute for $f_n(s_n, x_n)$ and $r_n(s_n, x_n)$. It is the modeler's responsibility to specify the functions and recursive relationships accurately. We turn now to some specific examples to illustrate the formulation and calculation of dynamic programming problems.

A Purchasing-Inventory Problem

To present a more formalized look at the dynamic programming approach, let us consider a multiple-period purchasing and inventory decision problem. A heating and air-conditioning distributor must make quarterly purchasing decisions for a special type of compressor. Data for the three-month purchasing and storage problem are as follows:

Month	Demand	Cost per compressor at beginning of month	Storage cost for inventoried compressors
October	3	$150	$12
November	4	160	10
December	2	175	10

At the beginning of each month the company must purchase enough compressors to satisfy demand. Excess purchases are carried over as inventory for the next month. The company has zero units on hand October 1 and wants no inventory after December.

To present the dynamic programming formulation of this problem, let us use the following terms:

x_n = decision variable for stage n; the purchase quantity for month $n = 1, 2, 3$

s_n = state variable representing the amount of inventory on hand at the beginning of month n

d_n = demand in month n

$r_n(s_n, x_n)$ = the sum of purchasing and storage costs in stage n

$f_n(s_n, x_n)$ = the overall return function that accounts for the cost of the preceding time periods as well as the current one

The problem breaks into natural stages, with each month representing a stage. We will let December represent stage 1, with November and October representing stages 2 and 3. In any month the cost will be comprised of purchasing plus storage costs. At any stage n (month n) we need a return function that will account for the purchase costs in the current stage as well as storage costs for the inventory left over from the preceding stage. If we let $r_n(s_n, x_n)$ = the cost of the purchasing and storage costs in stage n, then

$$r_n(s_n, x_n) = p_n x_n + c_n(s_n + x_n - d_n)$$

where p_n and c_n represent purchase and storage costs per unit in stage n. Note also that $s_n + x_n - d_n$ represents the amount by which beginning inventory plus purchases exceed current demand; hence, $s_n + x_n - d_n$ equals inventory at the beginning of the succeeding month. Notice that the inventory level in month $i - 1$ is defined by

$$s_{i-1} = s_i + x_i - d_i$$

or the previous month's inventory plus purchases minus demand. This particular expression represents the stage transformation for the purchasing-inventory problem. The stage transformation describes how the states and stages of a dynamic programming problem are interconnected. The stage transformation function "transforms" the input to a stage into the output. Thus, it functionally defines the value a state variable will have at each stage. If we denote the stage transformation function as

$$t(s_n, x_n)$$

then for the purchasing-inventory problem the stage transformation is expressed as

$$s_{i-1} = t(s_i, x_i) = s_i + x_i - d_i$$

In Figure 10.7 we illustrate the stage transformations for the purchasing-inventory problem. In this purchasing-inventory problem the stage transformation can be described mathematically by the expression $s_{i-1} = s_i + x_i - d_i$. Other dynamic programming problems will be different. For example, the stage transformation in the shortest-route problem is not determined by a mathematical expression, but by the arc that leads from one node in one stage to another node in the next stage.

Finally, to begin our formal calculations we need the expression for the overall return function and the recursive relationship. The overall return

FIGURE 10.7 The stage transformation function describes the relationship of the stages in the purchasing-inventory problem

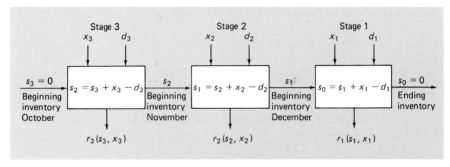

function in stage n, $f_n(s_n, x_n)$, is described by

$$f_n(s_n, x_n) = r_n(s_n, x_n) + f^*_{n-1}(s_n + x_n - d_n)$$

Notice the recursive nature of this function and how $f_n(s_n, x_n)$ depends on $f^*_{n-1}(s_n, x_n)$. By relating the impact of current-time-period decisions with succeeding-time-period decisions, we can arrive at an overall optimum.

In beginning the computation, let us examine how many possible states exist for December = stage 1. Since no inventory is desired at the end of the month and the December demand is only 2, we can have at most 2 units in inventory at the beginning of December; the least we can have is 0. Thus, state variable s_1 can be 0, 1, or 2. For each possible state we will need to compute total purchasing and inventory costs. This is conveniently done in the following table.

Stage 1. Minimize $f_1(s_1, x_1) = 175x_1 = 10(s_1 + x_1 - d_1)$

Possible states, s_1	$f_1(s_1, x_1)$ for:			Optimal solution	
	$x_1 = 0$	$x_1 = 1$	$x_1 = 2$	$f^*_1(s_1, x_1)$	x^*_1
0	—	—	350	350	2
1		175	—	175	1
2	0	—	—	0	0

The table shows the optimal decision given each possible inventory state. For example, if we enter December with $s_1 = 1$ units in inventory, the optimal decision is to purchase $x_1 = 1$ compressor. The overall return function is defined as

$$
\begin{aligned}
f_1(s_1, x_1) &= r_1(s_1, x_1) + f^*_0(s_0, x_0) \\
&= 175x_1 + 10(s_1 + x_1 - d_1)
\end{aligned}
$$

since $f_0(s_0, x_0)$ is zero and since ending inventory must equal zero, we have $s_1 + x_1 - d_1 = 0$, and the total return function simplifies to $f_1(s_1, x_1) = 175x_1$. Notice that the two columns on the far right represent the optimal cost and optimal purchase quantity for each possible state (beginning inventory level for December). We will use this information in the next stage.

In stage 2 there are seven possible states, since we can have as much as 6 units to cover the demand in November and December; we can also have a beginning inventory of 0. In the table, the dashes indicate decision variable values that are too small to satisfy demand or too large and exceed stage 2 plus stage 1 demand. Performing a simple return function calculation for

Stage 2.   Minimize $f_2^*(s_2,x_2) = 160x_2 + 10(s_2 + x_2 - d_2) + f_1^*(s_2 + x_2 - d_2)$.

Possible states, s_2	$f_2(s_2, x_2)$ for:							Optimal solution	
	$x_2 = 0$	$x_2 = 1$	$x_2 = 2$	$x_2 = 3$	$x_2 = 4$	$x_2 = 5$	$x_2 = 6$	$f_2^*(s_2,x_2)$	x_2^*
0	—	—	—	—	990	985	980	980	6
1	—	—	—	830	825	820	—	820	5
2	—	—	670	665	660	—	—	660	4
3	—	510	505	500	—	—	—	500	3
4	350	345	340	—	—	—	—	340	2
5	185	180	—	—	—	—	—	180	1
6	20	—	—	—	—	—	—	20	0

$s_2 = 2$ and $x_2 = 3$, we have

$$f_2(2, 3) = 160(3) + 10(2 + 3 - 4) + f_1^*(2 + 3 - 4)$$
$$= 480 + 10 + 175$$
$$= 665$$

Notice how the $f_1^*(1) = 175$ value is retrieved from the stage 1 calculations. This shows how we tie in optimal decisions from the previous stage; it also shows that in computerized dynamic programming with discrete variables, the optimal decision for each stage must be stored in memory.

In stage 3 we have only one state variable value $s_3 = 0$, since we know that the beginning October inventory is zero. However, the purchase quantity can range from 3 to 9 units.

Stage 3.   Minimize $f_3(s_3,x_3) = 150x_3 + 12(s_3 + x_3 - d_3) + f_2^*(s_3 + x_3 - d_3)$.

Possible states, s_3	$f_3(s_3,x_3)$ for:							Optimal solution	
	$x_3 = 3$	$x_3 = 4$	$x_3 = 5$	$x_3 = 6$	$x_3 = 7$	$x_3 = 8$	$x_3 = 9$	$f_3^*(s_3,x_3)$	x_3^*
0	1430	1432	1434	1436	1438	1440	1442	1430	3

Given the optimal decision of $x_3 = 3$ for zero beginning inventory, we can determine the optimal decision in the previous two stages by a simple stage *transformation.*

$$s_2 = s_3 + x_3 - d_3 = 0 + 3 - 3 = 0$$

Thus, $x_2 = 6$ for $s_2 = 0$ (from the table of stage 2 calculations),

$$s_1 = s_2 + x_2 - d_2 = 0 + 6 - 4 = 2$$

and $x_1 = 0$ for $s_1 = 2$. The optimal decision is to purchase 3, 6, and 0 compressors in October, November, and December, respectively; the minimum purchasing and inventory cost is $1,430.

A Capital-Budgeting Problem

Consider the Amdeck Co., which is planning its capital improvement projects for the upcoming year. The company has budgeted $10 million and is reviewing four possible projects for funding. Listed are the projects, together with their costs and net present values of returns:

Project	Cost (millions)	Return
1	$5	$ 5
2	7	10
3	3	6
4	3	3

Amdeck will not partially fund a project; thus a project will be funded entirely or not at all. Amdeck's objective is to maximize the return on the projects.

We can formulate the Amdeck capital-budgeting problem as a 0–1-integer model as follows:

$$\text{Maximize} \quad 5x_1 + 10x_2 + 6x_3 + 3x_4$$

$$\text{subject to} \quad 5x_1 + 7x_2 + 3x_3 + 3x_4 \leq 10$$

$$x_i = 0 \text{ or } 1$$

This model is a specific application of the knapsack type of problem and could be solved by the branch and bound methodology of Chapter 9. However, let us solve the capital-budgeting problem using dynamic programming.

In any dynamic programming problem we must answer the following questions:

1. What are the stages?
2. What are the possible system states?
3. What are the policy decisions to be made?
4. What is the nature of the stage transformation?

5. What is the form of the total return function and the recursive relationship?

Let us try to answer these questions one at a time for the capital-budgeting problem.

There is no time element to suggest time-related stages for this problem. However, the problem breaks naturally into stages if we consider each individual project as a stage. We thus have a four-stage problem.

The relevant state of the system is the state that affects our decision to select a project. In this case the relevant state is the amount of capital available. Thus, the state variable s_i is defined by

$$s_i = \text{the capital available at stage } i$$

The policy decision to be made at each stage i is whether to fund project i or not. Thus, $x_i = 0$ or 1 at each stage.

If we let c_i denote the cost of project i, then we can define the stage transformation as

$$s_{i-1} = s_i - c_i x_i$$

The amount of capital available in stage $i - 1$ depends on how much was spent in previous stages.

Finally, if we let r_i denote the return from project i we can define the single stage return function as

$$r_i(s_i, x_i) = r_i x_i$$

and we can define the total return function as

$$f_i(s_i, x_i) = \text{Max } \{r_i x_i + f^*_{i-1}(s_i - c_i x_i)]$$
$$x_i = 0 \text{ or } 1$$

Before we begin the computations we can observe that $10 million of capital will be available for stage 4. The available capital (s_1) in stage 1 is not known. However, depending on what was funded in stages 2–4, the available capital can range from $0 to 10 million. Assuming that the Amdeck managers are rational people, we can conclude that they will fund at least one project prior to stage 1. The resulting states will therefore be $0, $3, $4, or $7 million.

Stage 1: $f_1(s_1,x_1) = \text{Max} \{5x_1\}$
$x_1 = 0 \text{ or } 1$

Possible states s_1	$f_1(s_1,x_1)$ for: $x_1 = 0$	$x_1 = 1$	Optimal solution $f_1^*(s_1,x_1)$	x_1^*
0	0	—	0	0
3	0	—	0	0
4	0	—	0	0
7	0	5	5	1

In stage 2 the states will be 4, 7, or 10 depending on whether projects 3 and 4 were both funded, only one funded, or not funded at all.

Stage 2: $f_2(s_2,x_2) = \text{Max} \{10x_2 + f_1^*(s_2 - 7x_2)\}$
$x_2 = 0 \text{ or } 1$

Possible states s_2	$f_2(s_2,x_2)$ for: $x_2 = 0$	$x_2 = 1$	Optimal solution $f_2^*(s_2,x_2)$	x_2^*
4	0	—	0	0
7	5	10	10	1
10	5	10	10	1

The colored line connecting the two stages emphasizes the fact that if $7 million is available in stage 2 and project 2 is not funded, then project 1 can be funded and will yield $5 million.

Stage 3: $f_3(s_3,x_3) = \text{Max} \{6x_3 + f_2^*(s_3 - 3x_3)\}$
$x_3 = 0 \text{ or } 1$

Possible states s_3	$f_3(s_3,x_3)$ for: $x_3 = 0$	$x_3 = 1$	Optimal solution $f_3^*(s_3,x_3)$	x_3^*
7	10	6	10	0
10	10	16	16	1

Stage 4: $f_4(s_4,x_4) = \text{Max} \{3x_4 + f_3^*(s_4, 3x_4)\}$
$x_4 = 0 \text{ or } 1$

Possible states s_4	$f_4(s_4,x_4)$ for: $x_4 = 0$	$x_4 = 1$	Optimal solution $f_4^*(s_4,x_4)$	x_4^*
10	16	13	16	0

The optimal return is \$16 million. We can determine the projects to fund by observing that $x_4 = 0$; for $s_3 = 10$, $x_3 = 1$; for $s_2 = 7$, $x_2 = 1$; and for $s_1 = 0$, $x_1 = 0$. Thus, the projects to be funded are projects 2 and 3.

Dynamic programming has the capability for some built-in sensitivity analysis. If we had included other possible states such as 8, 9, or 11 for values of s_4, then we could have determined the optimal return and associated projects under these budget levels as well as the \$10 million level. The price of this additional information is not only an increased number of states in stage 4, but also in stages 1, 2, and 3. Thus, the sensitivity analysis would require a corresponding increase in calculations and computer memory (if solved on a computer). In some cases the additional information generated would be well worth the extra computational effort.

Advantages and Disadvantages of Dynamic Programming

In our two example problems we have focused on problems having discrete variables. Dynamic programming is also applicable to continuous-variable decision problems. In these problems, the decision variables can assume an infinite number of possible values. Continuous decision problems can be linear, but are often nonlinear in nature. The solution of nonlinear problems usually requires the use of classical optimization techniques and differential calculus. While these techniques are beyond the scope of this introductory text, it is interesting to note that dynamic programming has application in the engineering and physical sciences as well as business. In fact dynamic programming is a powerful broad-based technique that can be applied to a wide range of problems, including complex stochastic problems. However, what it gains in breadth it sometimes sacrifices in efficiency. We turn now to the major advantages and disadvantages of the technique.

ADVANTAGES

1. For some problems in such areas as inventory management, control theory, or chemical engineering design, dynamic programming is the only technique that can solve the problems.
2. It is particularly well suited for multistage, multiperiod, or sequential decision processes.
3. Dynamic programming is very broad in scope and is applicable to linear or nonlinear problems, discrete or continuous variables, and deterministic or stochastic problems.
4. It is readily adapted to the computer and can provide some degree of sensitivity analysis.

DISADVANTAGES

1. No general formulation of the dynamic programming problem exists, and each problem must be modeled uniquely. This requires ingenuity, experience, and insight.

2. The *curse of dimensionality* requires that the number of state variables be kept relatively low to prevent excessive computational requirements.

3. In general, the dynamic programming approach is not particularly efficient when compared to other math programming algorithms, such as the simplex method.

COMPUTER IMPLICATIONS

There are two important computer implications of dynamic programming. The first involves the fact that dynamic programming is an approach rather than a technique. For this reason there is no general computer software package (such as the IBM MPSX/370 system for LP) for solving dynamic programming problems. Software packages do exist for solving specific applications, but new applications will usually require a dynamic programming model with its own stages and recursive relationships to be developed from scratch.

curse of dimension- ality   The second implication involves the *curse of dimensionality*. This refers to the fact that the number of calculations and computer memory requirements can increase dramatically as the number of states increase in each stage. For example, let us reconsider the capital-budgeting problem of the Amdeck Co. They had a $10 million budget and wanted to allocate the capital to the projects in $1 million increments. The maximum number of possible states is therefore 11 for any stage. However, if Amdeck wanted to consider allocation increments in multiples of $10,000 the number of possible states would explode to 1001. Another increase in the number of possible states occurs when there is more than one state variable. In our simple examples we have considered only one state variable. Consider, for example, a knapsack problem with limitations on both weight and volume. The dynamic programming formulation will require two state variables, one for weight and one for volume. If there are 100 possible states for weight and 100 possible states for volume, there will be $100 \times 100 = 10,000$ possible states for the two-dimensional problem. This will require significantly more computation time and computer memory, and is one example of the curse of dimensionality in dynamic programming.

SUMMARY

In this chapter we have presented the fundamental concepts of dynamic programming. It is a mathematical programming approach that is particularly appropriate for multistage or sequential decision problems. Unlike LP, integer, or goal programming, it can be more easily applied to probabilistic and nonlinear problems. However, it requires a unique formulation in terms of stages, states, and recursive relationships for each different type of decision problem.

We have focused on discrete dynamic programming problems in which the calculations are carried out in a tabular form. Dynamic programming can also be applied to continuous problems in which calculus-based methods can be used to express mathematically the optimal policy decision at each stage.

The basic idea in any dynamic programming formulation is to break a larger problem into more easily solved subproblems. Dynamic programming formulations often require a great deal more modeling insight and expertise than the other methods that we have studied in this text. Dynamic programming is not always a very efficient solution procedure, but it is sometimes the only viable optimization approach to a real-world problem.

SOLVED PROBLEM

A RELIABILITY PROBLEM

Reliability is an important design factor in many business and engineering systems. Consider the telecommunication design problem as shown in Figure 10.8.

FIGURE 10.8 Reliability of lines in a telecommunication network

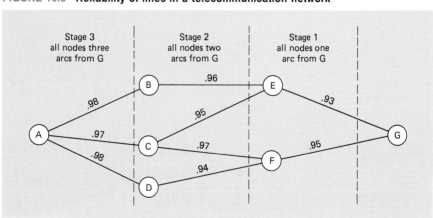

The numbers on each arc of the network represent probabilities that the line will not have a failure or incur random noise during data transmission from one point to another. The objective is to determine the most reliable path of lines from node A to node G. The problem is much like the shortest-route problem of this chapter except that the probabilities must be multiplied rather than added to obtain the probability of a successful transmission from A to G. That is, the probability of a successful transmission from A to G along path A–B–E–G is $.98 \times .96 \times .93 = .8749$.

The reliability problem has three stages as depicted in Figure 10.8. The states s_i correspond to the node locations at a given stage, and the decision variables x_i represent the arcs to be chosen to reach the next stage. The total return function is based on a multiplicative rather than an additive relationship. If $r(s_i, x_i)$ represents the return function (measure of reliability) at a given stage, then the total return function can be expressed as

$$f_n(s_n, x_n) = r_n(s_n, x_n) \cdot f^*_{n-1}(s_{n-1}, x_{n-1})$$

The calculations are as follows:

Stage 1:   Maximize $f_1(s_1, x_1) = r_1(s_1, x_1)$

Possible states s_1	Possible successor nodes G	Optimal solution $f^*_1(s_1,x_1)$	x^*_1
E	G	.93	E–G
F	G	.95	F–G

Stage 2:   Maximize $f_2(s_2, x_2) = r_2(s_2, x_2) \cdot f^*_1(s_1, x_1)$

Possible states s_2	Possible successor nodes E	F	Optimal solution $f^*_2(s_2,x_2)$	x^*_2
B	$.96 \times .93 = .8928$	—	.8928	B–E
C	$.95 \times .93 = .8835$	$.97 \times .95 = .9215$	.9215	C–F
D	—	$.94 \times .95 = .8930$	.8930	D–F

Stage 3:   Maximize $f_3(s_3, x_3) = r_3(s_3, x_3) \cdot f^*_2(s_2, x_2)$

Possible states s_3	Possible successor nodes B	C	D	Optimal Solution $f^*_3(s_3,x_3)$	x^*_3
A	$.98 \times .8928 = .8749$	$.97 \times .9215 = .8939$	$.98 \times .8930 = .8751$	.8939	A–C

The best achievable reliability factor is.8939 and is obtained by transmitting along path A–C–F–G.

REVIEW QUESTIONS

1. In what way does dynamic programming offer flexibility in attacking optimization problems?
2. List two advantages and two disadvantages of dynamic programming.
3. Why is there no general software package for solving all types of dynamic programming problems?
4. Explain the "curse of dimensionality" in dynamic programming.
5. If both LP and dynamic programming could be used to model and solve a decision problem, which method would you prefer to use and why?
6. State the principle of optimality in your own words.
7. Explain the relationship between stages and states in dynamic programming.

PROBLEMS

10.1 Use dynamic programming to find the shortest route from node 1 to node 7 in the following network:

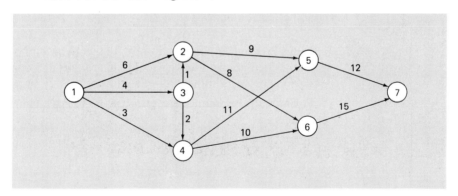

10.2 Consider the following three-item knapsack problem:

Item	Weight, w_i	Value, v_i
1	5	5
2	8	10
3	3	6

capacity $= 10$

a. Identify the dynamic programming structure for this problem; that is, determine the stages and states, and specify the recursive relationship between stages through the return function.

b. Solve the problem.

10.3 *Project management.* A construction contractor has four construction projects under way and wants to minimize the time required to complete all projects. The following table reflects the estimated time required to complete the project for a specified number of foremen assigned to the project.

Project	Number of foremen assigned		
	1	2	3
A	5	3	2
B	7	5	3
C	9	8	7
D	11	8	8

Given that the contractor has only six foremen and he wishes to minimize the sum of the project completion times (assuming each project is assigned at least one foreman):

a. Formulate the problem as a dynamic programming problem. Identify the stages, states, and return function.

b. Solve the problem.

10.4 Consider Problem 10.3 with a different objective. Suppose the contractor wants to minimize the maximum time required to complete any one of the four projects rather than the sum of project times.

a. Formulate the mini-max problem as a dynamic programming problem.

b. Solve the problem.

10.5 Solve the knapsack Problem 9.3 in Chapter 9 using dynamic programming.

10.6 *Purchase and storage cost minimization.* Sound Waves, Inc., plans to stock the new Tofler amplifier kit. The kit is aimed at the high-end market and demand of 2, 5, and 3 units is anticipated for the next three months. The following table indicates the purchase and storage costs during each month.

Month	Cost per kit at beginning of month	Storage cost per kit per month
Nov.	$385	$20
Dec.	435	21
Jan.	450	22

No inventory is desired at the end of January. Use dynamic programming to determine the optimal purchasing and storage strategy to minimize costs, assuming no beginning inventory.

10.7 *System reliability design.* A subsystem for the automatic pilot function on an aircraft consists of four electronic components, each of which has a specified probability of failure. To reduce the probability of failure, it is possible to install parallel backup components that will take over whenever its predecessor component fails. The following table gives the probability of failure of each component function for a given number of backup units.

| Number of backup units | Probability of failure of individual components | | | |
	Component 1	Component 2	Component 3	Component 4
0	.01	.015	.01	.02
1	.0001	.000225	.0001	.0004
2	.000001	.000003375	.000001	.000008

The probability that the total subsystem will function is the product of the probabilities that each individual component will function. The success probability is the complement of the failure probability. Thus, the probability of the subsystem functioning with no backup units is $.99 \times .985 \times .99 \times .98 = .946$.

The material and installation costs of the components are $30, $40, $35, and $45 for components 1, 2, 3, and 4, respectively. Given a budget of $350, use dynamic programming to determine the optimal number of backup units for each component to maximize the probability that the subsystem will function.

10.8 Refer to the cargo loading problem (Problem 9.14) of Chapter 9. It is similar to the knapsack problem except that it involves both a weight and a volume capacity limitation.

a. Formulate the cargo loading problem as a dynamic programming problem. Do not solve.

b. Comment on the relative desirability of solving the problem through integer or dynamic programming.

10.9   *Police beat design.* Planners for the police department of a city are trying to allocate new patrol cars to precincts to minimize crime. The number of patrol cars assigned to a precinct has an effect on the crime rate as estimated in the following table. The planners have six cars to allocate and have decided that no precinct should have more than three cars.

	Crime rate per day			
	Number of patrol cars per precinct			
Precinct	0	1	2	3
1	3	2.5	2.0	1.7
2	6	4.2	3.5	2.9
3	4	3.6	3.1	2.5

a. Identify the dynamic programming components of this problem including the recursive relationship for the total return function.

b. Determine the optimal allocation of police cars by solving the dynamic programming model.

10.10   Solve the equipment replacement Problem 7.4 of Chapter 7 using dynamic programming.

10.11   *Production and inventory control.* The ABC Co. has estimated the following demand levels for the next four months:

Month	Demand
June	4
July	6
August	3
September	7

The company would like to determine a minimum-cost production schedule. The setup cost for production is $10, the variable production cost is $3, and the inventory carrying cost is $2 per unit per month. ABC has a maximum production capacity of 5 units a month. At the beginning of June they have one unit in inventory from the previous month. Use dynamic programming to determine the optimum production schedule.

10.12   *Nonlinear integer programming problem.* Consider the following mathematical programming problem:

$$\text{Maximize}\quad 2x_1^2 + 3x_1x_2 + 6x_3^2$$

$$\text{subject to}\quad x_1 + x_2 + 2x_3 \le 4$$

$$x_1, x_2, x_3 \ge 0 \text{ and integer}$$

Use dynamic programming to solve this problem. *Hint:* Let each decision variable x_j be a stage and let the state be the amount of right-hand side available to be allocated.

10.13 *Advertising expenditures.* A manufacturer of golf balls is trying to determine the most effective advertising and promotional strategy for the introduction of its new line of golf balls. It is considering advertising in four media: radio, television, a golf magazine, and a direct-mail promotional campaign in which a free golf ball is distributed. The company has budgeted $500,000 for the advertising campaign. All expenditures will be in increments of $100,000. The following table presents an estimate of the potential sales revenue per $100,000 spent.

Medium	*Expenditure (in $100,000's)*				
	1	*2*	*3*	*4*	*5*
Radio	.90	1.80	2.70	3.60	4.80
Television	1.05	2.10	3.15	4.25	5.50
Magazine	1.10	2.05	3.20	4.20	5.10
Direct Mail	.85	1.95	3.50	4.40	5.60

a. Model the advertising expenditure problem as a dynamic programming model.

b. Solve the model to determine the most effective advertising strategy.

10.14 *Capital investment.* Suppose you have $100,000 to invest in three possible ventures. You have decided to invest a minimum of $20,000 in each of the three alternatives. The ventures and their returns are listed as follows:

Alternative 1		*Alternative 2*		*Alternative 3*	
Investment	*Expected return*	*Investment*	*Expected return*	*Investment*	*Expected return*
$20,000	$1,900	$20,000	$1,800	$20,000	$2,500
30,000	2,800	30,000	2,400	30,000	4,000
40,000	3,700	40,000	4,200	40,000	4,900
50,000	5,000	50,000	5,300	50,000	5,500
60,000	5,900	60,000	6,700	60,000	5,800

You also have the opportunity to invest any unallocated monies in a CD yielding 9 percent. Use dynamic programming to determine your optimal investment strategy. Assume any investment is in increments of $10,000.

10.15 *Equipment replacement.* An oil company uses its fleet of light trucks to maintain and service oil wells. The company would like to develop a replacement policy based on the minimization of capital and operating costs. A new truck costs $15,000. Maintenance and operating costs for a five-year period as well as salvage values are shown in the table below. For $4,000 the company can perform a major overhaul on a truck which will cause the maintenance costs and salvage value to be equivalent to a two-year-old truck. The company will not keep any truck longer than five years without an overhaul or replacement. Formulate a dynamic programming model to determine the optimal maintenance-replacement policy for the trucks. Assume that the trucks in the current fleet are two years old, and that the trucks can be sold at the end of the last period.

Age of truck at beginning of year	Operating and maintenance costs	Salvage value at end of year
New	$500	$8,000
1	1,500	6,000
2	2,500	4,000
3	4,000	2,000
4	5,000	0

BIBLIOGRAPHY

Bellman, R., *Dynamic Programming*. Princeton, N.J.: Princeton University Press, 1957.

Bellman, R., and S. E., Dreyfus, *Applied Dynamic Programming*. Princeton, N.J.: Princeton University Press, 1962.

Dernardo, E. V., *Dynamic Programming: Theory and Application*. Englewood Cliffs, N.J.: Prentice Hall, 1975.

Dreyfus, S., and A. M. Law, *The Art and Theory of Dynamic Programming*. New York: Academic Press, Inc., 1977.

Hillier, F. S., and G. J. Lieberman, *Operations Research*, 4th ed. San Francisco: Holden-Day, Inc., 1986.

Loomba, Narendra P., and Efrian Turban, *Applied Programming for Management*. New York: Holt, Rinehart & Winston, Inc., 1974.

Nemhauser, George L., *Introduction to Dynamic Programming*. New York: John Wiley & Sons, Inc., 1966.

11

Probability Concepts and Distributions

Amtrak®

AMTRAK—THE NATIONAL PASSENGER RAILROAD

Until recently, Amtrak management had resisted overbooking its trains, but because of last-minute cancellations and "no shows" and increased emphasis on profitability, Amtrak is being forced to adopt more aggressive policies such as overbooking, more discount classes, and improved allocation of the seat inventory similar to those policies that the airlines have used for years.

Amtrak is in the process of implementing a sophisticated revenue-maximization system that attempts to optimize the overbooking of reserved trains and also allocate the seat and compartment inventory on a specific train in such a way that will maximize the revenue on that train. Each day Amtrak's new revenue maximization system must decide how many reservations of each type to accept on each train up to more than 300 days into the future. The system must forecast demand for that train, city pair, and type of accommodation. In addition, cancellations and "no shows" have to be forecasted. Once these forecasts have been generated, the system must balance accepting a short-haul discount reservation (a sure thing) against the probability of being able to sell a longer haul or full-fare seat with more profitability at a later date.

The new system is projected to be worth millions of dollars in incremental revenue to Amtrak. The models that drive Amtrak's new revenue-maximization system are based on the probability concepts introduced in this chapter.

INTRODUCTION

Earlier, you learned that there are three states in which decisions are made: certainty, in which all relevant information is known; stochastic, or risk, conditions, in which limited information (usually in terms of probabilities) is available; and total uncertainty, in which little or nothing is known. Decisions under certainty are, of course, the easiest to make. When information is certain, a systematic analysis of even large-scale decision problems can usually be made. However, most real-world decision problems are made under conditions that are neither completely certain nor completely uncertain. The decision maker usually has some information to work with but is uncertain to a degree about what will happen after the decision is made.

The use of probability theory can be of great help in making decisions under risk conditions. By organizing relevant information, assessing the likelihood of various alternatives, and systematically analyzing the problem, the decision maker can usually reach a more effective decision than by a seat-of-the-pants, or intuitive, approach. Overall goals or objectives can best be met when probabilistic information is considered in a systems context. For example, probability theory can be useful in helping a contractor decide whether or not to bid on a $100,000 contract that costs $5,000 in bidding expenses. Or a production manager might use probability theory to decide how much inventory to stock in order to avoid large stockouts and provide an adequate level of service to the customer.

Founded in mathematics, probability theory is rigorous and well-defined. In this chapter, we shall develop only the aspects you will need for the material in the rest of this book. In effect, then, this is a brief and specialized review. If you have not studied probability theory before, you will find an elementary introduction to the subject here.

In simple terms, a probability is a measure of the likelihood that an event will occur. If we reach into a deck of cards, we can say that the likelihood of getting a card that is a club is $\frac{13}{52}$, or .25. The .25 is a quantification of the likelihood that we will draw a club. Thus, a probability is actually a measure of chance. Probability is the mathematical expression of uncertainty; modern probability has its foundations in mathematical measure theory.

objective We shall be concerned with probabilities as they pertain to decision *probability* making. Probabilities of two types are used in decision making. *Objective probabilities* are those for which there is definitive historical information or rigorous analysis to support the assignment of probabilities. For instance, the .25 probability of drawing a club from a deck of cards is an objective probability. The probability of getting a head in tossing a fair coin is .50 and is an objective probability. Past experience has shown that this statement of likelihood is true, and it can easily be argued mathematically.

subjective Frequently, a decision maker is confronted with a situation in which an exact objective probability is not available. For example, the exact probabil-ity of receiving a contract is not known, or the probability of next month's *probability* sales exceeding $50,000 is not known with certainty. A *subjective probabil-ity* is based on the personal experience of the decision maker. It may rely in part on previous records or outside information, but it represents the deci-sion maker's degree of belief that a particular event will occur. The odds a bookie gives for major sports events are subjective probabilities, but they are based also on past records, outside information, and so on. A retail clothing buyer's sales estimates also qualify as subjective probabilities. The buyer must consider the desirability of various lines and then subjectively estimate potential sales. In deciding how much to order, the buyer may subjectively assess the probabilities that sales will be at or below different volumes.

Subjective probabilities are essentially educated guesses, and some people feel that subjective probabilities should not be included as input to formal analysis of a decision problem. These objectivists feel that subjective input should be considered only after a formal analysis is accomplished with the available objective information. Subjectivists, on the other hand, believe in using subjective estimates and probabilities in analyzing a decision prob-lem. They argue that people who run businesses and others who make con-sequential decisions do so based on their experience, intuition, and hunches. Subjectivists feel that the decision process is more likely to be correct if subjective estimates and probabilities are used in a formal or systematic analysis.

BASIC CONCEPTS

event In probability applications, we often want to determine the likelihood of a particular random phenomenon or occurrence. In probability theory, we call a specified outcome of a random phenomenon an *event*. If we perform a statistical experiment in coin tossing, we may ask what the probability is of the event *getting two heads in a row*. An inventory manager may want to determine the probability of the event *incurring a stockout next month*.

simple event Events may be classified as simple or compound. A *simple event* con-sists of a single possible outcome of a random phenomenon. For example, *compound* suppose we toss three coins and consider the event getting three heads, or *event* HHH. This is a simple event. A *compound event,* on the other hand, con-

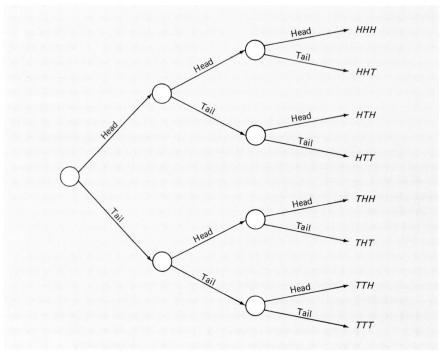

FIGURE 11.1 **Counting tree**

sists of two or more simple events. The event of getting two heads when we toss three coins is a compound event since it consists of the three simple events HHT, THH, and HTH.

In assessing probabilities for a particular problem, it is necessary to specify the universe of all possible outcomes. A simple event is called a *sample point,* and the collection of all possible sample points is called the *sample space.* We denote the sample space by the letter S. Thus, in the example of tossing three coins, the sample space S consists of all possible outcomes. As shown in Figure 11.1, the sample space consists of eight sample points. In other words,

sample point
sample space

$$S = \{HHH, HHT, HTH, HTT, THH, THT, TTH, TTT\}$$

Assuming that the coins are fair, each of the sample points in S is equally likely to occur; thus, the probability of each sample point is $\frac{1}{8}$.

Let us consider another random experiment in which a single die is cast. The six-sided cube will show from one to six dots. If we let the simple events be defined by the number of dots showing, then $S = \{1, 2, 3, 4, 5, 6\}$.

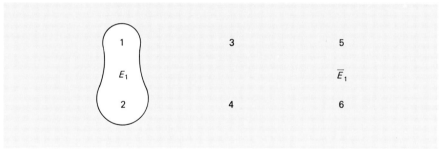

FIGURE 11.2 **The sample space S**

In Figure 11.2 we represent S with a Venn diagram. Consider the event E_1, which is defined as getting a one or a two. E_1 is the outlined area in Figure 11.2. Event E_1 is a compound event, and its probability is equal to the probability of the simple events of which it is composed. If we denote $P(E_1)$ as the probability of E_1, we have $P(E_1) = \frac{1}{6} + \frac{1}{6} = \frac{1}{3}$.

complemen-   For every event E there exists a *complementary event* $\overline{E}$. The comple-
tary event ment $\overline{E}$ consists of all the sample points in S that are not in E. Thus, in Figure 11.2, $\overline{E}_1 = \{3, 4, 5, 6\}$. Together, an event and its complement must comprise the entire sample space. By knowing the probability of each sample point, we can calculate the probability of each event in S. Thus, $P(\overline{E}_1) = \frac{1}{6} + \frac{1}{6} + \frac{1}{6} + \frac{1}{6} = \frac{2}{3}$. However, this counting process is not convenient for large or infinite sample spaces. Fortunately, basic probability laws can be used to help determine probabilities in more general situations.

Probability Axioms

Certain properties of probability are fundamental to the understanding and application of probability theory. For example, the probability of any event being between 0 and 1 is a fundamental property. Let E_i represent any event in the sample space $S;$ then we have the following three axioms.

Nonnegativity   The probability of any event in S is greater than or equal to 0 and less than or equal to 1.

$$0 \leq P(E_i) \leq 1 \qquad \text{for any } E_i \text{ in } S$$

Additivity   If two events E_i and E_j are both in S but have no sample points in common, the probability that at least one of these events occurs is the sum of $P(E_i)$ and $P(E_j)$.

$$P(E_i \text{ or } E_j) = P(E_i) + P(E_j)$$

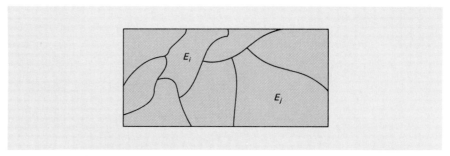

FIGURE 11.3 **Mutually exclusive events E_i and E_j**

Completeness of sample space   The probability of the entire sample space is 1.

$$P(S) = 1$$

mutually exclusive events The additivity property of the second axiom refers to events that are mutually exclusive. *Mutually exclusive events* cannot occur at the same time and are characterized by not having any sample points in common. Figure 11.3 graphically illustrates two mutually exclusive events E_i and E_j. In Figure 11.2, E_1 and $\overline{E}_1$ are also mutually exclusive events. An event and its complement are always mutually exclusive. But an event and its complement are also collectively exhaustive. A group of events is *collectively exhaustive* if together they include all the sample points in the sample space. Thus, $E_1 = \{1, 2\}$ and $\overline{E}_1 = \{3, 4, 5, 6\}$ are collectively exhaustive in $S = \{1, 2, 3, 4, 5, 6\}$.

collectively exhaustive events

Marginal, Conditional, and Joint Probabilities

So far, we have only considered the probabilities of events that are unaffected by the outcome of other events. Unconditional probabilities that do not depend on other events are sometimes called *marginal probabilities*. The term *marginal* applies since these probabilities (as we shall see) can be found in the margin of a probability table.

marginal probability

If we roll a die and ask what the probability of a 5 is, then we are asking for a marginal probability since it does not depend on other events or outside information. For a fair die, the probability of a 5 is $\frac{1}{6}$. But suppose we consider another event that constitutes additional information concerning the outcome of the die. Suppose you cannot see the die at first and someone tells you that it does not show a 3. Now what is the probability of a 5? The probability is now $\frac{1}{5}$ rather than $\frac{1}{6}$ since one of the six possibilities has been eliminated. This is an example of a *conditional probability*, a probability that depends on the outcome of another event.

conditional probability

Conditional probabilities are important in the business world, for there are many instances in which decisions under uncertainty depend on the outcome of other factors. For instance, we might want to know the probability of small car sales given new government fuel-efficiency regulations, or we might want to estimate the chances of success for a new product given a nationwide advertising effort.

We denote conditional probability as $P(A|B)$, which is read, "the probability of A, given B." If we roll a die and let A equal the event of getting a 5, and B the event a 3 or 4 does not show, then we have $P(A) = \frac{1}{6}$ but $P(A|B) = \frac{1}{4}$. If we let C equal the event that a 4 or 5 does not show, then $P(A|C) = 0$.

We determined the foregoing probabilities by logical reasoning, but there exists a formula for conditional probability:

$$P(A|B) = \frac{P(A \text{ and } B)}{P(B)} \qquad \text{provided that } P(B) > 0 \qquad (11.1)$$

We only consider conditional probabilities when $P(B) > 0$, because it makes little sense to consider the probability of A given B if B never occurs. By $P(A$ and $B)$, we mean the probability that both A and B occur. To understand this and the concept of conditional probability, consider the Venn diagram in Figure 11.4. Notice that the shaded area A and B is the intersection of event A and event B. We can intuitively explain formula (11.1) for conditional probability by assuming that the areas A, B, and A and B correspond to actual probabilities. Thus, if a sample point falls in B, the probability that it also falls in A is equal to the ratio of the area of A and B to the area of B. Thus we get $P(A|B) = [P(A$ and $B)]/[P(B)]$.

joint
probability   The probability of two or more events occurring is called a *joint probability*. Thus $P(A$ and $B)$ is a joint probability.

EXAMPLE   Let us illustrate some of these conditional and joint probabilities with an example. For a graduate thesis, a student is attempting to determine the relationship between the success of OR/MS projects and the

FIGURE 11.4   **Venn diagram of conditional probability**

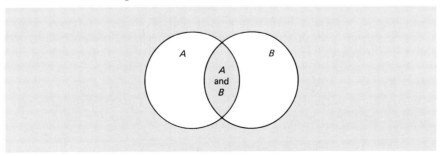

TABLE 11.1   *Probabilities revealed by 100-company survey*

		Formalized	Not formalized	
	Event	*C*	*D*	*Marginal probability*
Success	*A*	.40	.30	.70
Failure	*B*	.10	.20	.30
Marginal probability		.50	.50	

formalization of OR/MS procedures within the company. To gather information, 100 companies are surveyed about their OR/MS operations. The student finds that 70 of the companies report that their OR/MS projects are successful, and 50 report formalization of OR/MS procedures. Let us define four different events:

> *A* = company reports success
> *B* = company reports failure
> *C* = company has formalized OR/MS procedures
> *D* = company does not have formalized OR/MS procedures

Based on the 100-company sample, the student calculated the probabilities shown in Table 11.1. We shall use these data for insight into the nature of various probabilities by posing some pertinent questions, then showing you how to find the answers.

Regardless of whether the company formalized procedures or not, what is the probability that the company had successful OR/MS applications? The required probability is $P(A)$, which is an unconditional or marginal probability found in the margin of Table 11.1. There you see that $P(A) = .70$.

If you were to pick one of the companies surveyed at random, what is the probability that it would report both formalized procedures and project success? This probability is a joint probability involving both events A and C. From Table 11.1 we can see that the graduate student has calculated $P(A \text{ and } C)$ and found it to be .40.

What is the probability that a company surveyed had not formalized OR/ MS procedures? This is another marginal probability, this time represented by $P(D)$. We can read that $P(D) = .50$ from the bottom margin of the table.

What is the probability that a company reported OR/MS success given that it had formalized procedures? This question requires a conditional probability. Specifically, we seek $P(A|C)$. From formula (11.1) we have

$$P(A|C) = [P(A \text{ and } C)]/[P(C)] = \frac{.40}{.50} = .80$$

What is the probability that a company reported OR/MS success given that it had not formalized procedures? Again we seek a conditional probability, $P(A|D) = [P(A \text{ and } D)]/[P(D)] = \frac{.30}{.50} = .60$.

Notice the probabilities of success of .80 and .60, respectively, given formalized and nonformalized procedures. If the foregoing survey were actual and had been carefully performed, these probabilities would lead you to some reasonable conclusions about formalized versus nonformalized OR/MS procedures. You could then make decisions that would significantly improve the probability of project success.

The Additive and Multiplicative Laws

additive law   In addition to the axioms of probability, two other rules are helpful in calculating probabilities. The *additive law* pertains to the union of two events; we read $P(A \text{ or } B)$ as the probability that either A or B (or both) occurs. The additive law states that

$$P(A \text{ or } B) = P(A \cup B) = P(A) + P(B) - P(A \text{ and } B) \qquad (11.2)$$

This formula makes sense intuitively if you look again at Figure 11.4. The sum $P(A) + P(B)$ includes $P(A \text{ and } B)$ twice. Thus $P(A \text{ or } B) = P(A) + P(B) - P(A \text{ and } B)$. In the special case where A and B are mutually exclusive events, the additive rule is equivalent to the additivity axiom, yielding $P(A \text{ or } B) = P(A) + P(B) - 0 = P(A) + P(B)$.

multiplicative   The *multiplicative law* pertains to the intersection of events; it can be *law* derived directly from the conditional probability formula (11.1). In fact, the multiplicative law is merely another statement of the definition of conditional probability. The multiplicative law states that

$$P(A \text{ and } B) = P(A \cap B) = P(A) \cdot P(B|A) \qquad (11.3)$$

The multiplicative and additive rules are useful in determining probabilities of compound events. Compound events, you will recall, consist of two or more simple events. Let us explore some examples.

EXAMPLE   The Bugle Company (a newspaper publisher) conducted a survey to determine the readership of the various newspapers within the city. The company publishes both a morning and an evening paper. The survey indicated that 60 percent of subscribers to any newspaper read the morning *Bugle,* 30 percent read the evening *Bugle,* and 10 percent read both.

What is the probability that a subscriber in the city received either the morning or the evening paper from the Bugle Company? We define two events. Let

$$A = \text{a subscriber reads the morning } Bugle$$
$$B = \text{a subscriber reads the evening } Bugle$$

The desired probability is $P(A$ or $B)$. From the additive law, we have $P(A$ or $B) = P(A) + P(B) - P(A$ and $B)$. Since $P(A$ and $B)$ is given in the problem as .10, we have $P(A$ or $B) = .60 + .30 - .10 = .80$.

What is the probability that a subscriber receives neither a morning nor an evening paper from the Bugle Company? This probability is the complement of $(A$ or $B)$ that we found in the preceding question. Thus, the probability that a subscriber takes neither paper is $1 - P(A$ or $B) = 1 - .80 = .20$. Clearly, the Bugle Company has a lion's share of the market.

EXAMPLE   The Medalist Golf Ball Company sells its products in boxes of a dozen balls. Quality control consists of testing two balls taken randomly from each box. The box is rejected only if both balls tested prove to be defective. Suppose that a box actually has two defective balls. What is the probability that it will be rejected?

First, define the events:

$$A = \text{first ball is defective}$$
$$B = \text{second ball is defective}$$

Then, we want $P(A$ and $B)$. From the multiplicative law we have that $P(A$ and $B) = P(A) \cdot P(B|A)$. Since there are 2 defectives out of 12 balls, $P(A) = \frac{2}{12}$. However, $P(B|A) = \frac{1}{11}$ since if A occurs there are only 11 balls in the box and only 1 is defective. Thus, $P(A$ and $B) = (\frac{2}{12})(\frac{1}{11}) = (\frac{2}{132}) = .0152$. The probability that the box would be rejected is quite small.

Independent and Dependent Events

We have already defined three relationships between events; we have discussed complementary, mutually exclusive, and collectively exhaustive events. The meaning of independent events is easy to perceive. Two events A and B are independent if the outcome of one has no effect on the probability of the outcome of the other. More formally, events A and B are *independent* if

$$P(A|B) = P(A) \text{ or } P(B|A) = P(B)$$

If these conditions do not hold, then the events are *dependent*.

Imagine flipping a coin in your left hand and another in your right hand. Does the outcome of one coin affect the outcome of the other? It does not. The probability of a head is $\frac{1}{2}$ for each hand regardless of the outcome in the other hand. In the golf balls example, however, we had a case of dependence. The probability of drawing a defective golf ball on the second draw did depend on the outcome of the first draw.

For independent events, the multiplicative law simplifies since $P(A|B)$ = $P(A)$. Thus, for independent events, we have

$$P(A \text{ and } B) = P(A) \cdot P(B) \qquad (11.4)$$

Formula 11.4 extends to more than two events, as the following example illustrates.

EXAMPLE   Consider a coin-tossing experiment in which we toss a fair coin five times.

If a head has appeared four times in a row, what is the probability of a head on the fifth trial? Since each trial is an independent event, the probability of a head on the fifth trial is still $\frac{1}{2}$.

What is the probability of tossing five straight heads? Each trial is an independent event, but in this case we are asking for the probability that all five events will happen. Thus, the multiplicative law yields the probability $(\frac{1}{2})(\frac{1}{2})(\frac{1}{2})(\frac{1}{2})(\frac{1}{2}) = \frac{1}{32}$.

EXAMPLE   Consider a playing card problem in which we have an ordinary deck of 52 cards composed of four suits of 13 cards each. Suppose we randomly draw 1 card and then another without replacing the first.

What is the probability that both cards are clubs? Define the events:

$$A = \text{first card is a club}$$
$$B = \text{second card is a club}$$

Then, it is straightforward to find that $P(A \text{ and } B) = P(A) \cdot P(B|A) = \frac{13}{52}(\frac{12}{51}) = \frac{156}{2,652} = .059$. In this case, the second draw is dependent on the first.

What is the probability of drawing two clubs if the first is replaced? Since the events are now independent, we have $P(A \text{ and } B) = P(A)P(B) = \frac{13}{52}(\frac{13}{52}) = \frac{169}{2,704} = .063$.

Bayes' Theorem

Bayes' law is often helpful in computing conditional probabilities. In fact, Bayes' law is so important to statistical and business decision theory that decision theory is often called Bayesian decision theory. Bayes' law or Bayes' theorem, as it is sometimes called, is

$$P(A_i|B) = \frac{P(A_i)P(B|A_i)}{\sum\limits_{j=1}^{k} P(A_j)P(B|A_j)}$$

where A_j represents mutually exclusive and collectively exhaustive events.

To give you an intuitive justification for Bayes' law, consider two events A and B. We know from the general law of multiplication that

$$P(A \cap B) = P(A|B)P(B)$$

If we divide both sides of the foregoing equation by $P(B)$, we get

$$P(A|B) = \frac{P(A \cap B)}{P(B)}$$

Now, since $P(A \cap B) = P(B|A)P(A)$, we have

$$P(A|B) = \frac{P(B|A)P(A)}{P(B)}$$

Since A and $\overline{A}$ are mutually exclusive and are the only events that jointly occur with B, we know

$$\begin{aligned} P(B) &= P(A \cap B) + P(\overline{A} \cap B) \\ &= P(B|A)P(A) + P(B|\overline{A})P(\overline{A}) \end{aligned}$$

Therefore,

$$P(A|B) = \frac{P(B|A)P(A)}{P(B|A)P(A) + P(B|\overline{A})P(\overline{A})}$$

The expression can be generalized for more than two events jointly occurring with B to give Bayes' law.

EXAMPLE   Consider the following problem. There are 100 opaque urns, each filled with 10 balls. There are two different kinds of urns. Type I holds 5 black balls and 5 white balls. Type II urn has 8 black balls and 2 white balls. There are 70 type I urns and 30 type II urns. An urn is picked at random from the 100 urns, and you are asked to guess whether it is type I or type II urn. If you are allowed to take one ball from the urn and it is black, what is the probability that the urn is type I? What is the probability that the urn is type II given drawing a black ball?

Let A be the event that the urn chosen is of type I. Let C be the event that the urn chosen is of type II. Let B be the event of choosing a black ball and W be the event of choosing a white ball, The probability of a type I urn given a black ball is denoted by

$$P(A|B)$$

and Bayes' law says

$$P(A|B) = \frac{P(B|A)P(A)}{P(B|A)P(A) + P(B|C)P(C)}$$

Since there are 5 black and 5 white balls in type I urns,

$$P(B|A) = .5$$

Since there are 70 type I urns out of a total of 100,

$$P(A) = .7$$

Similarly, $P(B|C) = .8$ and $P(C) = .3$.

Therefore, the probability of a type I urn given a draw of a black ball is

$$P(A|B) = \frac{(.5)(.7)}{(.5)(.7) + (.8)(.3)} = \frac{.35}{.59}$$
$$= .593$$

The probability of an urn of type II given a black ball is

$$P(C|B) = \frac{P(B|C)P(C)}{P(B|C)P(C) + P(B|A)P(A)}$$
$$= \frac{(.8)(.3)}{.59} = \frac{.24}{.59}$$
$$= .407$$

In a similar fashion, we can calculate the probability of each type of urn given the draw of a white ball.

$$P(A|W) = \frac{P(W|A)P(A)}{P(W|A)P(A) + P(W|C)P(C)}$$
$$= \frac{(.5)(.7)}{(.5)(.7) + (.2)(.3)}$$
$$= \frac{.35}{.41} = .854$$
$$P(C|W) = \frac{P(W|C)P(C)}{P(W|C)P(C) + P(W|A)P(A)}$$
$$= \frac{(.2)(.3)}{.41} = \frac{.06}{.41}$$
$$= .146$$

PROBABILITY DISTRIBUTIONS

In this section, we shall define a random variable and examine the concept of a probability distribution. In addition, we shall describe several discrete probability distributions and several continuous probability distributions.

random variable
You learned earlier that an event is a specified outcome of an experiment or a random phenomenon. An example is the toss of a coin. The outcomes associated with the experiment are the displays of a head or of a tail. Now, if a numerical value, such as 0 or 1, is attached to each of the two possible outcomes, then the elementary, or individual, outcomes of the experiment can be termed a random variable. More specifically, a *random variable* is a function whose numerical value depends on the outcome of some experiment. For example, the roll of one die can be thought of as an experiment with the outcomes being the spots on the face of the die. The random variable could then be defined as the number of spots on the face of the die or any other similar function, such as those described in Table 11.2. Remember, a random variable is a function that assigns a numerical value to an elementary outcome of an experiment.

probability distribution
A *probability distribution* relates a probability to the values a random variable can take on. These values of the random variable represent an exhaustive and mutually exclusive set of values. Consequently, the probabilities of a probability distribution must add to 1.

Discrete Probability Distributions

discrete probability distribution
Discrete probability distributions are probability distributions in which the random variables are discrete. That is, the random variable takes on specific and discontinuous values. In other words, there are gaps between values that the random variable can take on. In a *continuous probability distribution,* on the other hand, the random variable can take on the value of any real number between the limits of the distribution. An example of a discrete probability distribution is a simple toss of a coin where a head is assigned the

continuous probability distribution

TABLE 11.2   *Random variables*

Number of spots on face of the die	Possible value of the random variable	Possible value of the random variable
1	1	25
2	2	50
3	3	75
4	4	100
5	5	200
6	6	35

TABLE 11.3   *Probability distribution of a coin toss*

Random variable	Probability
0	.50
1	.50
	1.00

TABLE 11.4   *Discrete probability distribution*

Random variable	Probability
0	$\frac{1}{16}$
1	$\frac{4}{16}$
2	$\frac{6}{16}$
3	$\frac{4}{16}$
4	$\frac{1}{16}$

value of 0 and a tail is assigned the value of 1. Table 11.3 defines this probability distribution.

If the example is expanded to the toss of four coins and the random variable is defined as the number of heads, then the probability distribution in Table 11.4 is defined. You can verify the probability reflected in Table 11.4 by listing all the possible outcomes and adding those outcomes that yield a specific number of heads. There are 2^4, or 16, possible outcomes. The probability distribution in Table 11.4 is graphed in Figure 11.5.

cumulative probability distribution   A *cumulative probability distribution* is a function of some random variable that defines the probability of the random variable's being less than

FIGURE 11.5   **Discrete probability distribution for number of heads in four tosses of a fair coin**

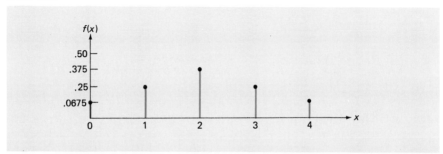

TABLE 11.5 *Cumulative probability distribution for four coin tosses*

x	Probability	Cumulative probability
0	$\frac{1}{16}$	$\frac{1}{16}$
1	$\frac{4}{16}$	$\frac{5}{16}$
2	$\frac{6}{16}$	$\frac{11}{16}$
3	$\frac{4}{16}$	$\frac{15}{16}$
4	$\frac{1}{16}$	1.0

or equal to a specific value of the random variable. In other words,

$$F(x) = P(X \leq x) \tag{11.5}$$

where X = random variable and x = value of the random variable. In the discrete case,

$$F(x) = \sum_{x_i \leq x} P(x_i) \tag{11.6}$$

Given our previous example of four coin tosses, the cumulative probability function is shown in Table 11.5 and Figure 11.6.

Binomial distribution   One of the most common discrete probability distributions is the binomial distribution. For you to make sense of the binomial *Bernoulli* distribution, you must first understand what is meant by a Bernoulli trial. A *trial* *Bernoulli trial,* sometimes called a Bernoulli *process,* is a random phenomenon involving two mutually exclusive and exhaustive events. A flip of a coin is a Bernoulli trial. An acceptance or rejection of a shipment of parts is a

FIGURE 11.6 Cumulative probability distribution for four coin tosses

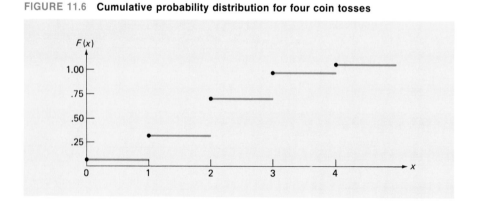

TABLE 11.6 *Binomial distribution with p = .5, n = 4*

x	P(x)
0	.0625
1	.2500
2	.3750
3	.2500
4	.0625

Bernoulli trial. Typically, the two events are referred to as success and failure. The probability of a success is denoted by p, and the probability of a failure is $1 - p$, which is denoted by q. Suppose that there are 100 balls in an urn, 5 gold and 95 silver. We draw 1 ball from the urn at random. If a gold ball is considered a successful draw and a silver ball is considered a failure, $p = .05$ and $q = .95$.

The random variable of a binomial distribution is the number of successes in n *independent* Bernoulli trials where the probability of a success remains constant. In the case of drawing balls from an urn, the ball must be placed back in the urn for independence to be maintained. Let us return to our example of tossing a coin four times. The random variable is the number of heads. What we have is four independent Bernoulli trials with a head defined as a success and a tail defined as a failure. In this case, p is equal to .50, and q is equal to .50. If the random variable is the number of heads in four tosses, then that random variable is binomially distributed, as shown in Table 11.6.

To assess probabilities for binomial random variables with any number of Bernoulli trials and any probability of success, the following probability function can be used.

$$P(x) = ({}_nC_x)(p^x q^{n-x}) \tag{11.7}$$

where

$$x = \text{number of successes}$$
$${}_nC_x = \text{number of combinations of } n \text{ things taken } x \text{ at a time}$$
$$p = \text{probability of success}$$
$$q = \text{probability of failure}$$

and

$$_nC_x = \frac{n!}{x!(n-x)!}$$

where

$$n! = (n)(n - 1)(n - 2) \cdots (1)$$
$$0! = 1$$

To illustrate the use of this function, consider the following problem. A shipment of 20 light bulbs has just been received. Historically, 10 percent of the light bulbs received from the supplier have been defective. If each bulb is tested and a defective bulb is designated as a success, then the probability distribution of the number of defective bulbs in a random shipment of 20 is as shown in Table 11.7. As you can see from Table 11.7, the probability that there would be more than 9 defective bulbs is virtually zero.

Let us illustrate the use of the probability function to calculate one of these discrete probabilities.

$$P(x = 2) = [20!/2!(20 - 2)!](.1)^2(.9)^{18}$$
$$= (20 \cdot 19/2)(.1)^2(.9)^{18}$$
$$= (190)(.01)(.1501)$$
$$\cong .2852$$

As you can easily see, the computation of binomial probabilities can get very laborious, even using an electronic calculator. For this reason, binomial tables are included as Appendix D. To illustrate the use of the binomial table, let us find one of the probabilities reflected in Table 11.7. The probability of having three or fewer defective bulbs can be found by looking in the table for $n = 20$, $p = .1$, and $c = 3$. From the table, then, $P(x \leq 3) = .8670$.

TABLE 11.7 *Binomial distribution
with p = .1, n = 20*

Number of defective bulbs	Probability
0	.1216
1	.2702
2	.2852
3	.1901
4	.0898
5	.0319
6	.0089
7	.0020
8	.0004
9	.0001
10	.0000
11	.0000
⋮	⋮
20	.0000

Now, to find the probability that there are exactly three defective bulbs, we must find the probability of having two or fewer defective bulbs and subtract that probability from the probability of having three or fewer. In other words,

$$P(x = 3) = P(x \leq 3) - P(x \leq 2)$$

From the table, $P(x \leq 2) = .6769$. Therefore, $P(x = 3) = .8670 - .6769 = .1901$. You should verify the values in Table 11.7 by using the binomial table.

Poisson distribution   The other discrete probability distribution we shall discuss in this chapter is the Poisson distribution, derived by Siméon Poisson in 1837. We examine the Poisson distribution because of its significant application in queuing theory (the subject of Chapter 14). Let us define a random variable as the number of events that occur during a certain interval of time or space. The random variable could be the number of telephone calls in an hour, the number of arrivals at a toll gate in 15 minutes, or the number of customers to shop at a store in a day. If the following three conditions are present, the random variable is said to be Poisson distributed.

1. During some interval Δt, the probability of an occurrence of an event (such as an arrival) is constant, regardless of when Δt starts.
2. The occurrence of an event is independent of any other occurrence of the event.
3. If Δt is chosen such that the probability of the occurrence of an event within Δt is small, then the probability that the event will occur is approximately proportional to the width of the interval. For example, let $\Delta t = 1$ second. If P (occurrence in Δt) = .005, then P (occurrence in $2 \Delta t$) = .01.

probability mass function   If a random variable is distributed in a Poisson manner, the probability that the random variable will take on any value k is given in equation (11.8). This function is called a *probability mass function*.

$$P(X = k) = e^{-m} m^k / k! \qquad \text{for } m > 0; \, k = 0, 1, 2, \ldots \qquad (11.8)$$

where

e = the base of natural logarithms, with a value approximately equal to 2.71828

m = mean number of events occurring in a given time interval

k = number of events

Consider the following example. An average of three cars per minute arrives at a toll gate according to a Poisson process. The probability distribution of

TABLE 11.8 *Poisson distribution with m = 3*

Arrivals to toll gate in 1 minute	Probability
0	.0498
1	.1494
2	.2240
3	.2240
4	.1680
5	.1008
6	.0504
7	.0216
8	.0081
9	.0027
10	.0008
11	.0002
12	.0001

the number of cars arriving at the toll gate per minute is contained in Table 11.8. To illustrate how these probabilities are calculated, let us find the probability of four cars arriving during 1 minute.

$$
\begin{aligned}
P(X = 4) &= e^{-3}3^4/4! \\
&= 3^4/[(2.71828^3)(4)(3)(2)(1)] \\
&= 81/[(20.0855)(24)] \\
&= .1680
\end{aligned}
$$

Poisson tables are included at the end of the book so that you won't have to work probability calculations out for yourself. To illustrate how to use the Poisson table, Appendix E, let us find $P(x = 4)$ in the table. Since the table reflects cumulative probabilities, it is necessary to look up $P(x \le 4)$ and the $P(x \le 3)$ to calculate $P(x = 4)$. The probability that $x \le 4$ is found by looking in the row $\mu = 3.0$ and the column $r_o = 4$. Therefore, $P(x \le 4) = .815$. Similarly, $P(x \le 3) = .647$. Since $P(x = 4) = P(x \le 4) - P(x \le 3)$, $P(x = 4) = .815 - .647 = .168$.

Continuous Probability Distributions

Continuous probability distributions are analogous to discrete probability distributions. The only difference is in the nature of the random variable. If a random variable can take on all values of the real number system between two limits, then it is said to be *continuous*. For example, the number of customers arriving at a supermarket is a discrete random variable, but the time between customer arrivals is continuous because time can be measured on a continuous scale.

Continuous probability distributions can be hard to understand if you have not been exposed to the integral calculus because these probabilities can no longer be calculated by a simple counting procedure. With continuous random variables, it is not appropriate to define the probability of the random variable taking on some specific value. The probability that the random variable equals some value k is zero, or, notationally, $P(X = k) = 0$. It is only appropriate to ascertain the probability that the random variable will fall within some range of values. For example, the probability that a randomly selected 35-year-old man will weigh between 175 and 200 pounds can be calculated given certain assumptions about the probability distribution of the weight of 35-year-old men. The probability of a man weighing 175 pounds exactly, and not the most minute fraction more or less, is theoretically zero. A *probability density function* (*pdf*) describes a continuous probability distribution. On a graph, the pdf is represented by a curve. The total area under the curve defined by a pdf is equal to 1.

probability density function (pdf)

This all becomes easier to understand if you look at Figure 11.7. The probability that the random variable x falls between 0 and 3 equals the ratio of the area under the curve between 0 and 3 to the total area under the curve, which by definition must equal 1. By merely looking at the graph in Figure 11.7, you might estimate that the probability that x will fall between 0 and 3 is approximately .60. To calculate $P(0 < x < 3)$ exactly, the calculus must be used. Fortunately, the tables at the end of the book relieve you of the necessity of calculating probabilities directly for several of the most common probability distributions. In actuality, the exact probability is found by taking the definite integral from 0 to 3 of $f(x)$. In the following sections, we are going to examine the two continuous probability distributions most commonly used in management science.

FIGURE 11.7 **Probability density function (pfd)**

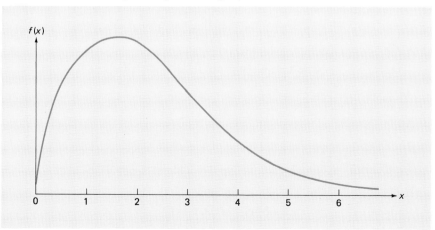

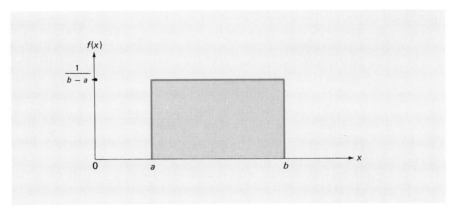

FIGURE 11.8 **Uniform distribution**

Uniform distribution   As you will see in Chapter 15, the uniform distribution is basic to computer simulation and understanding it is essential to your understanding of simulation. If b is the upper limit that the random variable x can take on and a is the lower limit, then the pdf for the uniform distribution is

$$f(x) = \begin{cases} \dfrac{1}{b - a} & \text{for } a \leq x \leq b \\ 0 & \text{elsewhere} \end{cases} \qquad (11.9)$$

The graph of the pdf in equation (11.9) is shown in Figure 11.8.

The key to understanding the uniform distribution is this: You must realize that the probability of a uniformly distributed random variable's falling within a certain range is merely the ratio of the width of that interval to the entire width of the uniform distribution. For example, suppose that a random variable x is uniformly distributed between 2 and 10. The pdf for this distribution is $f(x) = 1/(10 - 2)$ for $2 \leq x \leq 10$, and zero elsewhere; so the $P(2 \leq x \leq 4)$ is merely $\frac{2}{8}$, or .25. Figure 11.9 shows graphically that the area under the curve from 2 to 4 is 25 percent of the area under the curve.

The cumulative probability distribution function is expressed as follows:

$$F(x) = \begin{cases} 0 & \text{for } x < a \\ \dfrac{x - a}{b - a} & \text{for } a \leq x \leq b \\ 1 & \text{for } x > b \end{cases}$$

where

$$F(x) = P(X \leq x)$$
$$X = \text{a uniformly distributed random variable}$$

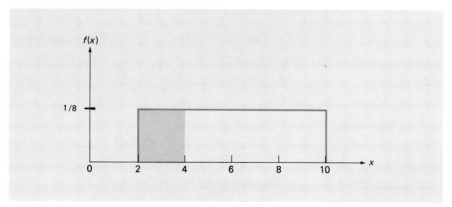

FIGURE 11.9   **Uniform distribution with a = 2, b = 10**

If we apply it to the preceding example, the probability that x will be ≤ 6 is $F(6) = (6 - 2)/(10 - 2) = \frac{4}{8} = .50$.

Normal distribution   Perhaps the most useful of the continuous probability distributions is the normal, also referred to as the *Gaussian* distribution. Reasons for the normal distribution's utility include the following:

1. The normal can be used under certain conditions to approximate both the binomial distribution and the Poisson distribution.
2. Many random phenomena behave according to a normal distribution, including such examples as height of adult females, IQ scores, classroom performances of students, and so on.
3. Due to the central limit theorem, if x is a random variable with mean μ and variance σ^2, then the mean of random samples of size n is normally distributed with mean μ and variance σ^2/n, irrespective of the distribution of the random variable x, if n is sufficiently large.

The pdf of the normal distribution is

$$f(x) = \left(\frac{1}{\sigma\sqrt{2\pi}}\right) e^{-(x-\mu)^2/2\sigma^2} \qquad \text{for } -\infty < x < \infty \qquad (11.10)$$

where

$$\mu = \text{mean}$$
$$\sigma = \text{standard deviation}$$

Because the foregoing function [equation 11.10] cannot be integrated directly, probabilities associated with the normal distribution are calculated by using a table of probabilities for a standard normal distribution with a mean

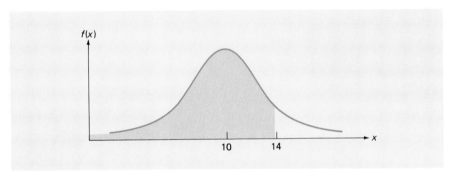

FIGURE 11.10   **Normal distribution with $\mu = 10$, $\sigma = 2$**

of zero and a standard deviation of one. To use this table for a normal distribution with mean μ and variance σ^2, the following transformation is necessary,

$$Z = \frac{x - \mu}{\sigma} \qquad (11.11)$$

where Z = a normally distributed random variable with mean 0 and standard deviation 1. Once Z is calculated, it is easy to look the probability up in the normal tables at the end of the book.

To illustrate the use of the normal table, let us assume that a random variable is normally distributed with mean 10 and standard deviation 2. What is the probability that random variable x is less than 14? First, when we calculate Z, we get $Z = (14 - 10)/2 = 2$. The normal distribution table in Appendix C gives the probability that the random variable Z is less than or equal to some specific value z_i, $P(Z \leq z_i)$; in other words, the table gives the area under the standard normal curve from $-\infty$ to z_i.

FIGURE 11.11   **Normal distribution with $\mu = 0$, $\sigma = 1$**

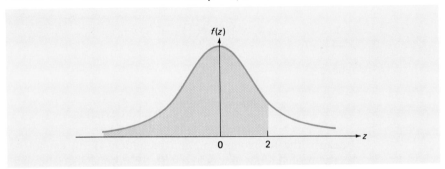

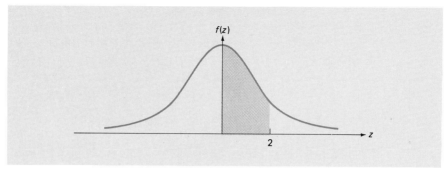

FIGURE 11.12   **Normal distribution with $\mu = 0$, $\sigma = 1$**

To find $P(x \leq 14)$, which is the shaded area in Figure 11.10, we merely look in the normal table for $P(Z \leq 2)$, which is the shaded area in Figure 11.11, because $P(x \leq 14) = P(Z \leq 2)$.

The standard normal table gives the probability that the random variable Z will be less than or equal to some specific value. If it is necessary to find $P(a \leq x \leq b)$ or $P(x \geq b)$, you must use the symmetry properties of the normal distribution. For example, suppose you had $P(10 \leq x \leq 14) = P(0 < Z < 2)$ (see Figure 11.12). We know that half the distribution lies to the left of $Z = 0$; therefore, $P(0 \leq Z \leq 2) = .9772 - .5 = .4772$. Similarly,

$$P(x > 14) = 1 - P(x < 14)$$
$$= 1 - .9772$$
$$= .0228$$

One final example: What is the probability that x will fall between 12 and 14? Looking at Figure 11.13, it is easy to see that $P(12 < x < 14) = P(x \leq 14) -$

FIGURE 11.13   **Normal distribution with $\mu = 10$, $\sigma = 2$**

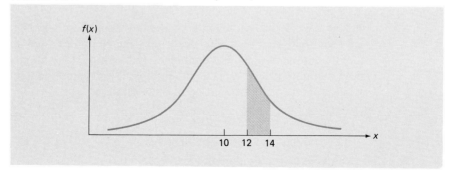

$P(x \leq 12)$. Remember that

$$P(x \leq 14) = P[Z \leq (14 - 10)/2]$$
$$= P(Z \leq 2)$$
$$= .9772$$
$$P(x \leq 12) = P[Z \leq (12 - 10)/2]$$
$$= P(Z \leq 1)$$
$$= .8413$$

Therefore, $P(12 \leq x \leq 14) = .9772 - .8413 = .1359$.

SUMMARY

The real world is a world in which events do not occur with absolute certainty. Demand for products and services are not known with certainty. The amount of oil to be recovered in a field is not known. Even internal costs and the availability of resources are often only estimated. In short, we live in a stochastic world. Management science models can be classified as deterministic models or stochastic models. Thus far, we have discussed only those types of models in which the parameters of the problem were assumed to be known. In the remainder of this text, we examine stochastic models. To understand these probabilistic models, it is necessary for you to have at least a rudimentary background in probability theory. In this chapter, we have attempted to introduce those concepts which are most important for an understanding of the various stochastic models that are examined in the following chapters.

SOLVED PROBLEMS

PROBLEM STATEMENT

A country club has three kinds of memberships: golf, tennis, and swimming. Of the 1,000 members, 300 have golf memberships, 400 have swimming memberships, and 300 have tennis memberships. One hundred golfers also have swimming and tennis memberships. If a member is selected at random, what is the probability that he or she will have

a. A tennis membership?
b. A tennis or golf membership?
c. A tennis or swimming membership?
d. A tennis and golf membership?

SOLUTION

a. Let A be the event of a member having a tennis membership only and B be the event of a member having both a golf and a tennis membership. Since A and B are mutually exclusive,

$$P(\text{tennis membership}) = \frac{300}{1{,}000} + \frac{100}{1{,}000} = \frac{4}{10} = .4$$

b. Let A = tennis membership and B = golf membership. Then

$$P(A \cup B) = P(A) + P(B) - P(A \cap B)$$
$$= .4 + .3 - .1$$
$$= .6$$

c. Let A = tennis membership and B = swimming membership. Since A and B are mutually exclusive,

$$P(A \cup B) = P(A) + P(B)$$
$$= .4 + .3$$
$$= .7$$

d. Let A = tennis membership and B = golf membership. Then

$$P(A \cap B) = P(A|B)P(B)$$
$$= \frac{1}{3} \cdot \frac{3}{10}$$
$$= .1$$

PROBLEM STATEMENT

Two ocean liners are crossing the Atlantic Ocean at the same time. From past history, ship A has a 75 percent chance of arriving on schedule and ship B a 95 percent chance of arriving on schedule.

a. What is the probability of both ships arriving on schedule?
b. What is the probability of either ship A or ship B arriving on schedule?
c. What is the probability of both ships being late?

SOLUTION

Let A = ship A arriving on schedule and B = ship B arriving on schedule.

a. Since A and B are independent events,

$$P(A \cap B) = P(A) \cdot P(B)$$
$$= (.75)(.95)$$
$$= .7125$$

b. $P(A \cup B) = P(A) + P(B) - P(A \cap B)$
$$= .75 + .95 - .7125$$
$$= .9875$$

c. $P(\overline{A} \cap \overline{B}) = P(\overline{A}) \cdot P(\overline{B})$
$$= (.25)(.05)$$
$$= .0125$$

PROBLEM STATEMENT

A soccer team has a six-game season. At the beginning of the season the coach estimates the probability of winning any single game as .6, or slightly better than 50–50.

   a. What is the probability of an undefeated season?
   b. What is the probability of a winless season?
   c. What is the probability of winning at least one game?
   d. What is the probability of winning only one game?

SOLUTION

   a. Let A_i = the event of winning game i. Then

$$P(\text{undefeated season}) = P(A_1) \cdot P(A_2) \cdots P(A_6)$$

Assuming independence,

$$P(\text{undefeated season}) = P(A_1) \cdot P(A_2) \cdots P(A_6)$$
$$= .6^6$$
$$= .0467$$

   b. $P(\text{winless season}) = P(\overline{A}_1) \cdot P(\overline{A}_2) \cdots P(\overline{A}_6)$
$$= .4^6$$
$$= .004096$$

   c. $P(\text{at least one game}) = 1 - P(\text{no games})$
$$= 1 - .004096$$
$$= .9959$$

   d. $P(\text{winning only one game}) = P(A_1)P(\overline{A}_2) \cdots P(\overline{A}_6)$
$$+ P(\overline{A}_1 \cap A_2 \cap \overline{A}_3 \cap \overline{A}_4 \cap \overline{A}_5 \cap \overline{A}_6)$$
$$+ P(\overline{A}_1 \cap \overline{A}_2 \cap A_3 \cap \overline{A}_4 \cap \overline{A}_5 \cap \overline{A}_6)$$
$$+ P(\overline{A}_1 \cap \overline{A}_2 \cap \overline{A}_3 \cap A_4 \cap \overline{A}_5 \cap \overline{A}_6)$$
$$+ P(\overline{A}_1 \cap \overline{A}_2 \cap \overline{A}_3 \cap \overline{A}_4 \cap A_5 \cap \overline{A}_6)$$
$$+ P(\overline{A}_1 \cap \overline{A}_2 \cap \overline{A}_3 \cap \overline{A}_4 \cap \overline{A}_5 \cap A_6)$$
$$= (6)(.6)(.4)^5$$
$$= .036864$$

PROBLEM STATEMENT

A medical laboratory has taken blood samples from 10 adult males between the ages of 45 and 50. Nationwide, it has been found that 20 percent of men in this age group have dangerously high cholesterol in their blood. For our group, what is the probability of

   a. Two people having high cholesterol?
   b. More than 8 having high cholesterol?
   c. None of the men in the sample having a cholesterol problem?

SOLUTION

Since each blood test can be defined as an independent Bernoulli trial and a positive test classified as a success, the number of high-cholesterol samples in 10 is a binomially distributed random variable:

$$n = 10$$
$$p = .2$$

   a. $P(x = 2) = \dfrac{10!}{2!8!} \cdot 2^2 \cdot 8^8$

$$= .3020$$

   b. $P(x > 8) = .0000$
   c. $P(x \cong 0) = .1074$

PROBLEM STATEMENT

Arrivals at an ice cream store are distributed in a Poisson manner, at an average rate of 10 per hour. What is the probability that there will be

   a. Exactly 4 arrivals?
   b. Less than 5 arrivals?
   c. More than 7 arrivals?

SOLUTION

   a. $P(x = 4) = \dfrac{e^{-10} \cdot 10^4}{4!}$

$$= .019$$

   b. $P(x < 5) = P(x \le 4) = .029$ (table look-up)
   c. $P(x > 7) = 1 - P(x \le 7) = 1 - .220$
$$= .780$$

PROBLEM STATEMENT

A train consistently runs between 0 and 5 minutes late. Late time is uniformly distributed. What is the probability that the train will be

a. Less than 2 minutes late?
b. More than 3 minutes late?
c. Between 2 and 3 minutes late?

SOLUTION

a. $P(x < 2) = \dfrac{2 - 0}{5 - 0} = .4$

b. $P(x > 3) = \dfrac{5 - 3}{5 - 0} = .4$

c. $P(2 < x < 3) = \dfrac{3 - 2}{5 - 0} = .2$

PROBLEM STATEMENT

Scores on college entrance exams are normally distributed with a mean of 450 and a standard deviation of 50. What is the probability that a score selected at random is

a. Greater than 550?
b. Less than 400?
c. Between 400 and 500?

SOLUTION

a. $Z = \dfrac{550 - 450}{50} = 2$

$P(x > 550) = P(Z > 2) = .0228$

b. $Z = \dfrac{400 - 450}{50} = -1$

$P(x < 400) = P(Z < -1) = .1587$

c. $Z_{400} = \dfrac{400 - 450}{50} = -1$

$Z_{500} = \dfrac{500 - 450}{50} = 1$

$P(400 < x < 500) = P(-1 < Z < 1)$
$\qquad\qquad\qquad\quad = .6826$

REVIEW QUESTIONS

1. Why is an understanding of probability important for making business decisions?
2. Explain the difference between objective and subjective probabilities. Give an example of each.
3. An event and its complement have no points in common. Are they independent or dependent? Explain.
4. What is conditional probability?
5. Distinguish between mutually exclusive events and independent events.
6. If a collection of events is mutually exclusive and collectively exhaustive, what is the sum of their probabilities?
7. Define and give an example of a random variable.
8. What is a probability distribution?
9. Distinguish between a discrete probability distribution and a continuous probability distribution.
10. Define and give an example of a cumulative probability distribution.
11. What is a Bernoulli trial? Give an example.
12. Why is the Poisson distribution important to management science?

PROBLEMS

11.1 Suppose that you flip a fair coin four times:
   a. What is the probability that you will obtain the outcome HTHT?
   b. What is the probability of getting four heads in a row?
   c. What is the probability of getting a tail in the fourth trial given that the results the first three times were heads?

11.2 Consider an urn that has six black and four white balls:
   a. Suppose that after each ball is drawn it is replaced. What is the probability of drawing a white ball?
   b. What is the probability of drawing three white balls in a row?
   c. Suppose now that the balls are not replaced after drawing. What is the probability of drawing a white on the second trial given that the first trial resulted in a black ball?

11.3 *Project management.* A project manager is currently supervising four projects. The probabilities that each one will be completed on time are .70, .90, .80, and .60, respectively. Assuming that the project times are independent, what is the probability that all four projects will be completed on time?

11.4   *Sales management.* A marketing executive is going on a short trip to attempt to close two important deals. His subjective probability is .7 that he will be successful with the first deal and .5 that he will be successful with the second deal. What is the probability that

a. He will successfully close both deals?

b. He will close one or the other?

c. He will close the first deal but be unsuccessful on the second?

11.5   *Retail sales.* Daily demand for a particular TV model runs from 0 to 4, with the following respective probabilities: .1, .2, .35, .2, .15.

a. What is the probability of two or more TV sets being demanded?

b. What is the probability of fewer than two TV sets being demanded?

11.6   *Market research.* A market survey conducted in four cities pertained to preference for brand A soap. The responses are shown by city in the table.

	Dallas	Atlanta	Chicago	New York
Yes	45	55	60	50
No	35	45	35	45
No opinion	5	5	5	5

a. What is the probability that a consumer selected at random preferred brand A?

b. What is the probability that a consumer preferred brand A and was from Chicago?

c. What is the probability that a consumer preferred brand A given that he was from Chicago?

d. Given that a consumer preferred brand A, what is the probability that he was from New York?

11.7   *Recreation.* Membership at a local tennis facility is divided on the issue of facility maintenance. Some members favor a low-cost, do-your-own-cleaning policy, whereas others prefer to pay to have the maintenance done. There are 1,000 members, 800 men and 200 women. During a recent referendum, 100 women voted to pay for maintenance and only 25 voted against. Five hundred men voted against paying and 100 men voted for paying.

a. If we choose a member at random and ask his or her opinion, what is the probability of that person favoring low-cost maintenance? High-cost maintenance?

b. If we randomly choose a man and a woman, what is the probability that they will both favor low-cost maintenance?

c. If we randomly choose two members regardless of sex, what is the probability of at least one of them favoring the high-cost solution to the maintenance problem?

11.8 *Manufacturing quality control.* An electronic firm purchases a particular transistor from three different sources. Source A supplies 30 percent, source B, 50 percent, and source C, 20 percent. Based on historical data, the probability of a defective transistor is as shown in the table.

Supplier	Probability of defective transistor
A	.02
B	.01
C	.03

a. What percentage of transistors purchased will be defective?

b. If the transistor is found to be defective, what is the probability that it came from supplier B? supplier C?

c. If the transistor is good, what is the probability that it came from supplier A?

11.9 *University administration.* Eight out of 10 professors at State University have a Ph.D., whereas only 1 out of 10 have a Ph.D. at City College. If 1 professor is chosen from each institution at random, what is the probability that

a. Both hold a Ph.D.?

b. State University's professor does not hold a Ph.D. and City College's professor does?

c. Both professors have earned doctorates?

d. Neither professor has a Ph.D.?

11.10 *Retail sales.* The owner of a ski shop has observed closely the buying habits of his female customers. Fifty percent of the women coming in the store buy ski outfits; 30 percent buy ski boots and skis.

a. What is the probability that a female customer will buy skis, boots, and clothes?

b. What is the probability that she won't buy anything?

c. What is the probability that she will buy either clothes or equipment?

11.11 *Aerospace engineering.* The NASA space shuttle has two oxygen systems. If the probability of the primary system failing is .01 and the probability of the secondary system failing is .03:

a. What is the probability of both systems failing?

b. What is the probability that either the primary system or the secondary system is defective?

11.12 *University administration.* The ages of students in the freshman class at a certain university vary from 16 to 23. The ages of 2,000 incoming freshmen are distributed as shown in the table.

Age	Frequency
16	50
17	800
18	900
19	50
20	45
21	55
22	60
23	40

a. Using the relative frequency, plot the probability mass function and cumulative density function.

b. What is the probability of a randomly selected student being less than 20 years old?

c. What is the probability that the student selected will be either 17 or 18?

11.13 *University administration.* The College of Business at a large university has 15 scholarships to offer to potential business majors. In the past, about 75 percent of those students who were offered scholarships accepted them. Compute the following probabilities.

a. The probability of fewer than 5 acceptances.

b. The probability of between 5 and 10 acceptances.

c. The probability of 100 percent acceptance.

11.14 *Forecasting demand.* A production manager has studied past daily demand for widgets and has arrived at the following probability distribution for demand shown in the table. What is the probability of 2 or more units of demand during any day?

Demand	Probability
0	.10
1	.20
2	.30
3	.25
4	.15

11.15 *Auditing.* An accountant has to audit 20 accounts of a firm. Fifteen of these accounts are high volume and 5 are low volume. If the account-ant randomly selects 4 accounts, what is the probability that not one is a low-volume account?

11.16 *Market research.* A market survey conducted in four cities pertained to preference for Flagrant soap. The responses are shown by city in the table.

	Los Angeles	Chicago	Boston	Miami
Yes	47	50	63	45
No	33	50	30	48
No opinion	10	8	7	7

a. What is the probability that a consumer selected at random pre-ferred Flagrant?

b. What is the probability that a consumer preferred Flagrant and was from Chicago?

c. What is the probability that a consumer preferred Flagrant given that he was from Chicago?

d. Given that a consumer preferred Flagrant, what is the probability that she was from Miami?

11.17 *Insurance sales.* An insurance broker estimates that there is a 30 per-cent chance of a sale upon initial contact with a client. However, on a callback, there is a 60 percent chance of a sale. If the broker is limited to one callback per prospective customer, what is the probability that any prospect will buy?

11.18 *Accounting.* Suppose that the failure rate for candidates initially sitting for the C.P.A. exam is 70 percent. If four candidates sit for the exam for the first time, what is the probability that only three will pass?

11.19 *Construction.* Sturdy Construction has submitted a bid on a project. If Sturdy's leading competitor submits a bid, then the management at Sturdy feels its chance of getting the contract is .50. However, if the leading competitor does not submit a bid, Sturdy's chances increase to .80. If there is a .90 chance that the leading competitor will submit a bid, what are Sturdy's chances of receiving the contract?

11.20 *Medical research.* A new procedure has been developed to test for the presence of a rare disease. The procedure is accurate 95 percent of the time in diagnosing a patient who has the disease. The procedure is accurate 90 percent of the time in diagnosing a patient who does not have the disease. Given a positive test result, what is the actual probability that the patient has the disease? Assume that roughly 20 percent of those who take the test have the disease.

11.21 *University administration.* An M.B.A. class has 35 students, whose ages are distributed as shown in the table.

Age	Number of students
21	15
22	5
23	5
24	4
25	3
28	2
40	1

a. Define the probability distribution of the ages of the students.

b. Define the cumulative probability distribution of the ages of the students.

c. If a student is picked out of the class at random, what is the probability that the student will be less than 24 years old?

d. What is the probability that a student randomly chosen will be 22 or 23 years old?

11.22 *Sales.* A door-to-door salesman has a 10 percent chance of making a sale at any one house.

a. If he makes 10 calls during 1 day, what is the probability of making 2 sales?

b. If he makes 15 calls during 1 day, what is the probability of making 2 sales?

c. If he makes 10 calls, what is the probability of his making more than 3 sales?

d. If he makes 12 calls during the day, define the probability distribution of the number of sales during the day.

11.23 *University administration.* A prestigious university accepts approximately 25 percent of applicants applying for admission to its Ph.D.

program in English. The program is quite small and this year had only 25 applicants.

a. What is the probability that the first-year Ph.D. class in English will exceed 10 students?

b. What is the probability of fewer than 2 students being admitted to the program?

11.24 *Quality control.* Upon receiving a shipment of valves, a company inspects a random sample of 15 valves. Historically, 10 percent of the inspected valves have been defective. If management has decided that the entire shipment should be rejected if 2 or more bad valves are found in the sample, what is the probability that the shipment will be accepted?

11.25 *Demand forecasting.* Demand at a TV store for the 25-inch color TV set has been about 2 sets per week.

a. What is the probability that 10 sets will be sold in the next 4 weeks?

b. What is the probability that fewer than 10 sets will be sold in the next 4 weeks?

c. What is the probability that between 7 and 14 sets will be sold in the next 4 weeks?

11.26 *Professional football.* A professional football team has a firm policy of drafting defensive linemen that have certain attributes. One attribute is height. If a college prospect is less than 6 feet 3 inches tall, the policy states that he cannot be drafted. The height of college defensive linemen is normally distributed, with a mean of 6 feet 5 inches and a standard deviation of 3 inches.

a. What proportion of defensive linemen will be rejected due to height?

b. What is the probability that a college defensive lineman will be between 6 feet 2 inches and 6 feet 9 inches tall?

11.27 *Dairy industry.* A local dairy has a machine that fills gallon cartons of milk automatically. State regulations allow a tolerance of ± 1 ounce for a gallon of milk. The amount the machine automatically puts in the carton is normally distributed, with a mean of 128 ounces and a standard deviation of .5 ounce.

a. What percentage of the gallon cartons are in violation of state regulations?

b. What is the probability that a carton chosen at random will contain less than 126 ounces?

c. What is the probability that a carton chosen at random will contain between 126 and 130 ounces?

11.28 *Education.* Assume that IQ scores are normally distributed, with a mean of 100 and a standard deviation of 10.

  a. What is the minimum score that would put a person in the top 10 percent?

  b. What is the probability of a person's scoring between 90 and 110?

  c. If people scoring over 140 are classified as geniuses, what percentage of the population is in this category?

11.29 *Computer operations.* If we assume that computer runtime is normally distributed with a mean of 30 seconds and a standard deviation of 10 seconds, what is the probability

  a. That the job will run longer than 1 minute?

  b. That the job will take less than 5 seconds?

11.30 *Computer operations.* If we assume that computer run time is uniformally distributed with parameters $a = 0$ seconds and $b = 60$ seconds, what is the probability that

  a. The job will run longer than $\frac{1}{2}$ minute?

  b. The job will run between 20 and 40 seconds?

11.31 *Manufacturing.* Jobs arrive at a machine center in a Poisson fashion at an average rate of 5 per day. Show the probability distribution for the number of arrivals in 1 day.

11.32 *Quality control.* Metal tennis rackets are tested by X-raying the welds. Historically, 5 percent of the rackets tested have been rejected due to faulty welds. A sample of 10 rackets is drawn. What is the probability that

  a. No rackets will fail the X-ray test?

  b. Fewer than 2 rackets will fail?

  c. Exactly 1 racket out of 10 will be found defective?

11.33 *Professional football.* A professional football team chooses its running backs based on several criteria, one of which is speed in the 40-yard dash. The head coach has ruled out any back slower than 4.6 in the 40-yard dash. It has been determined that the mean speed of major college running backs is 4.5 and the standard deviation is .2 second. What is the percentage of running backs that do not meet the head coach's criterion?

11.34 *Water department forecast.* The mean water demand for a certain town is 60,000 gallons and the standard deviation is 8,000 gallons. Demand has been found to be normally distributed.

  a. What demand level will be exceeded 75 percent of the time?

  b. What is the probability that demand will exceed 75,000 gallons?

11.35 *Inventory control.* The food concession at a local soccer stadium has the capacity to sell 10,000 hot dogs. Hot-dog demand is estimated by a normal distribution with a mean of 7,000 and a standard deviation of 2,500. What is the probability of a sellout of hot dogs?

11.36 *University administration.* Students arrive at a professor's office at an average rate of 5 per hour, according to a Poisson distribution. Compute the probability that

a. No student will arrive.

b. Exactly 5 students will arrive.

c. More than 8 students will arrive.

BIBLIOGRAPHY

Clark, Charles T., and Eleanor W. Jordan, *Introduction to Business and Economic Statistics,* 7th ed. Cincinnati, Ohio: South-Western Publishing Company, 1985.

Feller, William, *An Introduction to Probability Theory and Its Applications,* Vol. I, 3rd ed., 1968; Vol. II, 2nd ed., 1971. New York: John Wiley & Sons, Inc.

Hoel, Paul G., *Introduction to Mathematical Statistics,* 5th ed. New York: John Wiley & Sons, Inc., 1984.

Mendenhall, William, and James E. Reinmuth, *Statistics for Management and Economics.* 4th ed. North Scituate, Mass.: Duxbury Press, 1982.

12

Decision Theory

OHIO**EDISON**
The Energy Makers

OHIO EDISON COMPANY[1]

Coal will likely play an increasingly important part in America's energy future. The United States has abundant supplies of coal. But companies that burn coal, especially electric companies, must meet a number of air quality requirements set by the Environmental Protection Agency (EPA). Ohio Edison Company faced a decision of what type of pollution control equipment to retrofit on units 5, 6, and 7 of their W. H. Sammis coal-fired power plant located on the Ohio River in eastern Ohio. Because the decision was a multimillion-dollar capital-budgeting decision and because of the uncertain nature of many of the different costs that could occur during the life of the pollution control equipment, Ohio Edison management decided that a decision theory approach to the problem was appropriate.

Because of physical and legal constraints, the decision analysis was limited to a choice between fabric filters and electrostatic precipitators. The fabric filters utilize thousands of fiberglass bags to collect fly ash from the flue gas in a way similar to the way home vacuum cleaners use paper bags to collect dust. Electrostatic precipitators use strong electric fields to remove particles from the flue gas.

[1] Thomas J. Madden, Michael S. Hyrnick, and James Hodde, "Decision Analysis Used to Evaluate Air Quality Control Equipment for Ohio Edison Company," *Interfaces,* 13, no. 1 (February 1983), 66–84.

Associated with each alternative were a number of uncertain variables. These include:

- Capital cost
- Maintenance cost
- Operating power cost
- Catastrophic equipment failure cost
- Sulfur percentage
- Filter failure cost
- Noncompliance cost

Based on the type of analysis described in this chapter, Ohio Edison decided to invest in electrostatic precipitators at the plant. The equipment was all in place by 1984. Management at Ohio Edison found the use of decision analysis extremely useful for the following reasons.

- The methodology helped to define the decision problem and management objectives.
- The methodology required a careful search for alternatives.
- The evaluation criteria had to be defined.
- Decision trees aided in identifying possible scenarios and in communicating those scenarios to management.
- The methodology forced management to gather detailed information on important uncertainties.

In short, management at Ohio Edison believe that decision analysis enabled them to choose the type of pollution control equipment that will yield both lower expected revenue requirements and lower risk over the life of the equipment.

INTRODUCTION

Earlier, we said that management science is a rational methodology for making management decisions. Decision theory fits the same generic definition; in fact, decision theory constitutes a particular branch of management science. Most complex executive decisions are decisions that must be made in an environment of uncertainty. For example, capital expansion decisions must be made even though such important factors as product demand, cost of materials, and cost of labor are not known with certainty. Often, the manager must choose among several different courses of action in an attempt to optimize his decision process. Decision theory helps the decision maker address the problem of making complex choices under uncertain conditions. It must be noted that decision theory does not generate alternative courses of action; it merely provides a rational way of choosing among several alternative strategies.

For example, a marketing vice-president of a cosmetic firm may need to make the decision to introduce or not to introduce a particular new product. What does this decision depend on? The potential payoff or profit generated from the new product would have to be considered. This payoff would depend on a number of factors, such as demand for the product, the actions of competitors, price, and promotional strategy. Obviously, the "simple" product development problem is much more complicated than it appears on the surface. It is further complicated by the uncertain nature of factors such as levels of demand and actions of competitors. Some risk or uncertainty might be reduced by spending money on market research. (Whether to do so involves another potentially difficult decision.) Decision theory can be very helpful in confronting a multifaceted decision such as this.

Decision theory can be used for a wide range of problems. These problems generally involve discrete choices and probabilistic events that have a bearing on the desirability of the various actions the decision maker can take. The following applications indicate the flexibility of decision theory.

□ *Natural resources development*   Should an oil or gas well be drilled? What set of seismic experiments should be run? What is the expected payoff of the investment in exploration?

□ *Agricultural applications*   What crops should be planted? Should excess acreage be planted? What actions should be taken to fight pests?

□ *Financial applications*   What is the proper investment portfolio? What capital investments should be made this year?

□ *Marketing applications*   Which new product should be introduced? What is the best distribution channel to use? What is the best inventory strategy?

□ *Production applications*   Which of several different types of machine should be purchased? What maintenance schedules should be used?

□ *Personal decisions*   What college should you go to? What should you major in? Should you go to graduate school or to work? If to work, which job offer should you accept? Should you get married?

To illustrate the general approach of decision theory, let us look at the following example.

EXAMPLE   Imagine yourself as the president of a small manufacturing firm. One of your bright young engineers has developed a new household gadget for roasting hot dogs and has obtained a U.S. patent on the device. Since she developed the hot-dog roaster on her own time, she is offering to sell the patent rights for $50,000, or $25,000 plus a 2 percent royalty on total revenue. From your experience, you surmise that demand for the roaster will be one of three levels. One, the roaster will find no acceptance by the consuming public, in which case your total investment in the patent will be lost, as will the $100,000 needed to develop and promote the product. The second demand level possible is one of 20,000 units. The selling price of the roaster is expected to be $20, and the variable cost (not including patent cost and developmental cost) is estimated to be approximately $12.00. The third level of demand is estimated to be 100,000 units. Now that you have the parameters of the problem, what is the correct decision? If you do not have a decision off the top of your head, let us try to analyze the problem systematically using a decision theory approach. First, we must identify the alternative decisions we could make. There are three conceivable decisions. Let

d_1 = buy patent rights outright for $50,000
d_2 = buy patent rights for $25,000 and agree to pay a 2 percent royalty
d_3 = refuse to get involved in the hot-dog roaster product

Second, we must define the various events or states of nature that affect the quality of the decision. In this problem, the states of nature correspond to the different levels of demand. Let

s_1 = no demand for the hot-dog roaster
s_2 = demand of 20,000 units
s_3 = demand of 100,000 units

Since our decision is a financial one, it is necessary to compute the payoffs given the different decisions we can make and the different states of nature. It is convenient to depict these payoffs in tabular form, called a payoff table or payoff matrix. The payoff table for the hot-dog roaster is depicted in Table 12.1. The dollar values in the table represent the net profit

TABLE 12.1 *Payoff table for hot-dog roaster*

Alternative decision	State of nature		
	s_1	s_2	s_3
d_1	−$150,000	$10,000	$650,000
d_2	−125,000	27,000	635,000
d_3	0	0	0

to the firm for each combination of decision and state of nature. For example, if you decide to buy the patent outright (d_1) and the demand is for 20,000 units (s_2), the payoff or profit would be $10,000. These payoffs are computed using the following formula: payoff = revenue − patent cost − royalty − variable cost − developmental cost.

To illustrate, let us calculate the payoff for paying $25,000 for the patent plus 2 percent royalty if the demand is for 100,000 units ($d_2|s_3$).

$$\underset{\text{revenue}}{\text{payoff}} = [(\$20.00)(100,000) - \underset{\text{patent cost}}{\$25,000} - [(\$20.00)(100,000)(.02)]$$
$$- [(\$12.00)(100,000)] - \$100,000$$

$$= 2,000,000 - 25,000 - 40,000 - 1,200,000 - 100,000$$
$$= \$635,000$$

Given the payoff matrix in Table 12.1, you should be able to make a more rational decision concerning the hot-dog roaster simply because you have organized the pertinent information in a rational way. The rest of this chapter discusses methodology helpful in determining the best decision given various criteria for decision making. As you have probably already guessed, much of the utility of decision theory is that it forces a systematic and rational structuring of the pertinent information for making a given decision.

CRITERIA FOR DECISION MAKING WHEN STATE-OF-NATURE PROBABILITIES ARE UNKNOWN

Often, a decision maker is faced with making a decision in which he or she can identify the possible alternative decisions, can define the various states of nature, and can reasonably calculate the relevant payoffs, but is unable to ascertain or subjectively estimate the probabilities of the various states of nature. If the probabilities of the states of nature are unknown, there are various criteria that can be used to rationally make a decision. Let us examine several criteria briefly and apply each to the hot-dog roaster problem.

The Maximin Criterion

The maximin criterion simply maximizes the minimum payoffs given the various decisions that are possible. It is a simple two-step process once the payoff table has been formulated. The first step is to identify the minimum

TABLE 12.2 *Payoff table for hot-dog roaster*

	Alternative decision	State of nature		
		s_1	s_2	s_3
maximin decision	d_1	$\$-150,000$	$\$10,000$	$\$650,000$
	d_2	$-125,000$	$27,000$	$635,000$
	d_3	0	0	0

payoff for each decision. The second step is to pick the largest minimum payoff. Let us illustrate by applying the maximin criterion to the hot-dog roaster problem. Table 12.2 shows the payoff table with minimum payoffs for each decision circled. Since d_3 has the maximum minimum payoff of the three decision alternatives, the maximin criterion would dictate that you should not buy the patent rights for the roaster. Obviously, the maximin rule is a very conservative one that takes a pessimistic view of the various states of nature.

The Maximax Criterion

The maximax criterion maximizes the maximum payoffs for the different decisions. We start by identifying the maximum payoffs for each alternative decision. Then the maximax decision is that decision which yields the largest maximum payoff. As shown in Table 12.3 the maximax decision for the hot-dog roaster problem is to buy the patent rights outright for $50,000 ($d_1$).

It should be obvious that the maximax rule is an extremely optimistic criterion for choosing alternative decisions.

The Minimax Regret Criterion

The minimax regret criterion involves the construction of an opportunity loss or regret matrix prior to applying the minimax rule. To construct an opportunity loss table, we must transform each element in the payoff table to

TABLE 12.3 *Hot-dog roaster payoff table*

	Alternative decision	State of nature		
		s_1	s_2	s_3
(maximax decision)	d_1	$\$-150,000$	$\$10,000$	$\$650,000$
	d_2	$-125,000$	$27,000$	$635,000$
	d_3	0	0	0

TABLE 12.4   Opportunity loss table

	State of nature		
Alternative decision	s_1	s_2	s_3
d_1	$150,000	$17,000	$ 0
d_2	125,000	0	15,000
d_3	0	27,000	650,000

an opportunity loss. The magnitude of the opportunity loss for a given element is the loss incurred by not selecting the optimal alternative decision given a state of nature. To convert a payoff table to an opportunity loss table is a two-step iterative process. The first step is to find the largest element in the first column. This element represents the best decision given a particular state of nature. The second step is to subtract each element in the column from the largest element to compute the opportunity loss. This two-step process is repeated for each state of nature (each column in the payoff table). The opportunity loss table for the hot-dog roaster problem is given in Table 12.4.

Now that we have constructed the opportunity loss table, it is possible to apply the minimax regret criterion to determine the appropriate decision. The minimax regret rule says to identify the maximum regret (opportunity loss) for each decision and then choose that decision with the smallest maximum regret. Table 12.5 reflects the minimax regret decision for the hot-dog roaster problem.

It should be clear that once you have organized a given decision problem into a payoff table, the decision you make is going to depend on the criterion you use for decision making. We have examined three criteria, and when applied to the hot-dog roaster problem, each decision rule indicated that a different decision should be made. Other decision criteria exist and you could possibly devise your own rules. Which rule is best depends on the decision parameters, the decision environment, and the attitude of the deci-

TABLE 12.5   Regret table

		State of nature		
	Alternative decision	s_1	s_2	s_3
	d_1	($150,000)	$17,000	0
minimax → regret decision	d_2	(125,000)	0	$ 15,000
	d_3	0	27,000	(650,000)

sion maker. In the rest of the chapter, we introduce probabilities to the decision process which will facilitate the decision-making process by giving the decision maker more information upon which to base decisions.

CRITERIA FOR DECISION MAKING WHEN STATE-OF-NATURE PROBABILITIES ARE KNOWN

It is a rare occasion when the decision maker has no estimate of the relative likelihood of the various states of nature. If the probabilities of the states of nature can be estimated, we can calculate expected values of various decisions. Let us illustrate this concept with the following problem.

A Basic Decision Problem

There are 100 opaque urns, each filled with 10 balls. There are two different kinds of urn. Type 1 urn holds 5 black balls and 5 white balls. Type II urn has 8 black balls and 2 white balls. There are 70 type I urns and 30 type II urns. An urn is picked at random from the 100 urns, and you are asked to guess whether it is type I or type II. If you guess that it is a type I urn and it is, you win $500; if it is a type II urn, you lose $200. If you guess that it is an urn of type II and it is, you win $1,000; but if it is a type I urn, you lose $150. Remember that the urn in front of you, the decision maker, is either a type I or type II urn. In other words, there are two states of nature, s_1 and s_2, corresponding to the urns of type I and type II. You have three alternatives: You can guess either type I or type II or refuse to take the gamble. Which action would you take? What could you expect to gain or lose from your decision? These are the kinds of questions decision theory can answer.

The facts of this decision problem are summarized in Table 12.6. If you

TABLE 12.6 *Payoff table for the urn problem*

Alternative decision	State of nature		EMV
	s_1	s_2	
d_1	$500	$-$200	$290
d_2	$-150	1,000	195
d_3	0	0	0
Probability of state of nature	.7	.3	

expected monetary value (EMV) know the expected value of each of the three alternative actions, you can simply choose the alternative with the highest expected value. The *expected monetary value (EMV)* of d_1 (the first alternative, namely, guessing that the urn is type I), is simply

$$\text{EMV}[d_i] = \sum_{i=1}^{2} p(s_i)x_i$$

where

$p(s_i)$ = probability that the true state of nature is s_i
x_i = payoff for the alternative action, given s_i is the true state of nature

Hence,

$$\begin{aligned}
\text{EMV}[d_1] &= (.7)(500) + (.3)(-200) \\
&= 350 - 60 \\
&= \$290 \\
\text{EMV}[d_2] &= (.7)(-150) + (.3)(1,000) \\
&= -105 + 300 \\
&= \$195 \\
\text{EMV}[d_3] &= (.7)(0) + (.3)(0) \\
&= 0
\end{aligned}$$

Therefore, if your objective is to maximize the expected monetary value of the urn decision problem, you would guess that the urn in front of you is type I. You can feel confident that if you were allowed to take this gamble a large number of times, on the average you could expect to gain $290. However, if you are allowed only one chance to guess, you stand a good chance of losing $200.

Decision Trees

decision tree A *decision tree* presents another way to visualize the typical decision theory problem. Figure 12.1, for example, shows an unevaluated decision tree for the urn problem. There are four didactic, or instructive, parts to a decision tree: decision nodes (shown as squares in the illustrations), chance nodes (shown as circles), alternative branches (straight lines that represent alternatives), and probabilistic branches (straight lines that represent probabilities).

decision node A *decision node* represents the choice between alternatives. From it come *alternative branches* that show, or name, the choices. These branches often lead to *chance nodes,* which represent factors in the decision situation over which the decision maker has no control. From these chance nodes

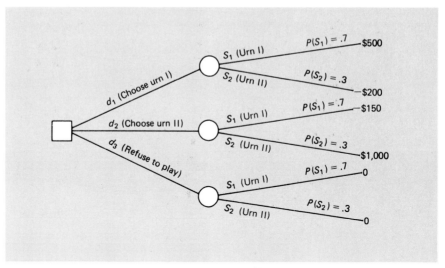

FIGURE 12.1 **Decision tree for the basic urn problem**

probabilistic come *probabilistic branches* that represent the actual or estimated numerical
branch likelihood of various chances. Since the events, or states of nature, are
mutually exclusive and exhaustive, the probabilities associated with each
event must add to 1.

A decision must be made among several alternatives. One or more
alternatives are associated with chance factors. These chances, however, can
be assessed probabilistically. On the basis of evaluation at several stages,
therefore, the decision maker can regard the alternatives rationally and
choose the one most compatible with his or her ultimate goals.

How to Evaluate Decision Trees

To evaluate a decision tree, it is necessary to evaluate each chance node and
each decision node. These two types of nodes are evaluated differently.
Chance nodes are evaluated using the expected value, and the value of a
decision node is the expected value of the most desirable alternative action.
Nodes 2, 3, and 4 in the decision tree in Figure 12.2 are chance nodes, and
consequently their values are equal to the expected values calculated earlier.
Node 1 is a decision node where the decision maker is asked to choose
among d_1, d_2, and d_3. Since the highest EMV of the alternative actions is
$290, the value of node 1 is $290. Given that the decision maker wishes to
maximize EMV, d_1 is the appropriate choice, rather than d_2 or d_3.

In the urn problem, the probabilities associated with the two states of
nature were known because the total number of each type of urn was known
and the urn was chosen randomly (each urn had an equal chance of being

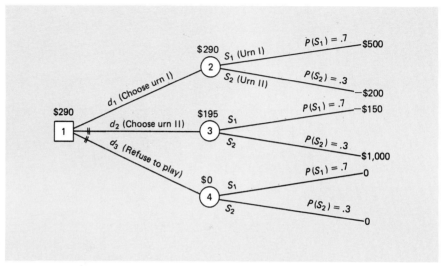

FIGURE 12.2   **Evaluated decision tree for the urn problem**

chosen). In real problems, these probabilities are rarely known with certainty, and usually the decision maker is forced to estimate the various probabilities subjectively. The quality of the decision, therefore, can depend greatly upon reliable subjective probabilities.

EXAMPLE   Fred Fudd is graduating from high school this year and must decide first which college to attend and then which course of study to pursue. Because of parental pressure, Fred must go to college, but he is free to select which college to attend. He has narrowed his choice to two very dissimilar schools. He has been accepted at State University and his hometown university, Wood. In addition to choosing between schools, Fred must decide whether to major in engineering or business. Because of the nature of the two schools, Fred has a different probability of success (that is, of graduating) depending on which college he attends and which field he majors in.

1. If he goes to State University and chooses business, his probability of graduating is .60.
2. If he chooses State University and chooses engineering, his probability of success is .70.
3. If he goes to Wood and chooses business, his probability of success is .90.
4. If he goes to Wood and chooses engineering, his probability of success is .95.

5. A State University graduate in business averages $35,000 per year for the first five years of full-time employment.
6. A State University graduate in engineering averages $30,000 per year for the first five years of full-time employment.
7. A Wood graduate in business averages $24,000 per year for the first five years of full-time employment.
8. A Wood graduate in engineering averages $25,000 per year for the first five years of full-time employment.
9. If Fred doesn't graduate, he will average $18,000 per year for the first five years of full-time employment.

In approaching Fred's problem, let us assume that his sole criterion for making a decision is to maximize average expected income over the first five years of his career. Having made that assumption, it is fairly easy to solve Fred's problem using decision theory. What decisions must Fred make? First, he must decide which university to attend; then, he must decide what to major in. So he has two decisions to make. What are the states of nature associated with the alternatives? No matter what school or discipline Fred chooses, he will either graduate or flunk out. Let

S_1 = graduate from State University Business School
S_2 = fail to graduate from State University Business School
S_3 = graduate from State University Engineering School
S_4 = fail to graduate from State University Engineering School
S_5 = graduate from Wood Business School
S_6 = fail to graduate from Wood Business School
S_7 = graduate from Wood Engineering School
S_8 = fail to graduate from Wood Engineering School
d_1 = choose to go to State University
d_2 = choose to go to Wood
d_3 = choose to major in business
d_4 = choose to major in engineering

Figure 12.3 shows the decision tree presenting Fred's problem. To show more clearly how to evaluate a decision tree, let us evaluate each node in Figure 12.3 individually. Nodes 4 to 7 are chance nodes and are, therefore, evaluated by finding the expected value. Nodes 1 to 3 are decision nodes whose value is the expected value of the most desirable alternative action.

the value of node 7 denoted by $N_7 = (.95)(25,000) + (.05)(18,000)$
$= \$24,650$
the value of node 6 denoted by $N_6 = (.9)(+24,000) + (.1)(18,000)$
$= \$23,400$

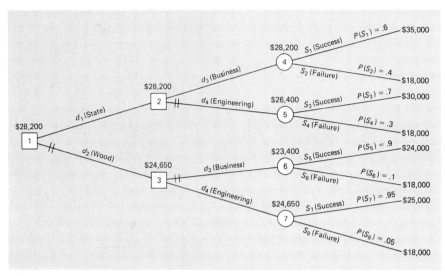

FIGURE 12.3 **Decision tree for the college problem**

the value of node 5 denoted by $N_5 = (.7)(30,000) + (.3)(18,000)$
$$= \$26,400$$
the value of node 4 denoted by $N_4 = (.6)(35,000) + (.4)(18,000)$
$$= \$28,200$$

The value of node 3 denoted by N_3 is determined as follows: Since $N_7 > N_6$, $N_3 = N_7$ and action d_4 is preferable to d_3, $N_3 = \$24,650$.

The value of node 2 denoted N_2 is determined as follows: Since $N_4 > N_5$, $N_2 = N_4$ and action d_3 is preferable to d_4, $N_2 = \$28,200$.

The value of node 1 denoted by N_1 is determined as follows: Since $N_2 > N_3$, $N_1 = N_2$ and action d_1 is preferable to d_2, $N_1 = \$28,200$.

You should verify each number on the decision tree and work through the process of arriving at the decision.

THE DECISION PROBLEM WITH AN OPPORTUNITY TO OBTAIN ADDITIONAL INFORMATION

So far, we have considered a basic, and the least complex, decision theory problem. Actually, however, real-world problems are seldom so simple. Now, we will complicate the basic decision problem so that you will see how more complex problems can be solved.

Often, the decision maker has an opportunity to gather or purchase additional information that may have a bearing on the decision process. Most decision problems in the real world include the option of obtaining additional information. For example, as the urn chooser in our first problem, it would certainly be beneficial if you had the opportunity to sample a ball from the urn in front of you to better guess the real state of nature. The question is, how does the additional information change the basic decision problem? The answer is that the *probabilities* of the various states of nature are actually changed. If the probabilities are changed, then obviously the EMVs of the various actions are also changed. What might have been the optimal decision before the additional information was obtained might now be least desirable.

Let us change the original urn problem by allowing you, as the decision maker, to draw one ball out of the urn. Let us further assume that the cost of drawing the ball from the urn is $50. You now have two decisions to make: First, you must decide whether or not to buy the information, and second, you must guess which type of urn has been placed in front of you. If you

FIGURE 12.4 Urn decision tree when sampling is possible

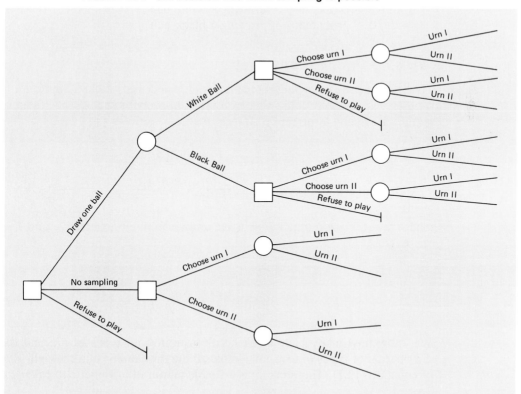

elect to pay for the opportunity to sample from the urn, either of two outcomes is possible: You will select a white ball or a black ball. Based on this
limited information, you must decide on the type of urn.

A decision tree helps to clarify the decision process when additional
information is obtainable. Notice that the lower part of the decision tree in
Figure 12.4 has not changed from the original problem. However, if you
choose to pay $50 to sample a ball from the urn, the decision tree becomes
considerably larger; that is, the changing situation is reflected by new
branches. To evaluate the top of the decision tree, we must assess new
probabilities, such as the probability of S_1 given that a white ball is chosen
from the urn [$P(S_1|W)$]. There are two types of chance node in the Figure
12.4 decision tree. Chance determines what color ball is drawn, and chance
determines which kind of urn is on the table. It is necessary to assess the
following probabilities:

$P(S_1|W)$ = probability of urn type I given that a white ball is drawn
$P(S_1|B)$ = probability of urn type I given that a black ball is drawn
$P(S_2|W)$ = probability of urn type II given that a white ball is drawn
$P(S_2|B)$ = probability of urn type II given that a black ball is drawn
$P(W)$ = probability of drawing a white ball
$P(B)$ = probability of drawing a black ball

Revising Prior Probabilities

Bayes' To determine the foregoing probabilities, it is necessary to use *Bayes' theo-*
theorem *rem.* Bayes' theorem allows us to revise the probabilities of the states of
nature given new information. Bayes' theorem states

$$P(A_i|B) = \frac{P(A_i)P(B|A_i)}{\sum_{i=1}^{k} P(A_i)P(B|A_i)} \tag{12.1}$$

where the A_i's are mutually exclusive and collectively exhaustive and B is
any event.

If we apply Bayes' theorem to our example, we have

$$P(S_1|W) = \frac{P(W|S_1)P(S_1)}{P(W|S_1)P(S_1) + P(W|S_2)P(S_2)} \tag{12.2}$$

We know how many balls of each color are in both types of urn and the
distribution of types of urns. We know all the probabilities on the right side
of equation (12.2). Therefore, it is a simple matter of arithmetic to calculate

$P(S_1|W)$:

$$P(S_1|W) = [(.5)(.7)]/[(.5)(.7) + (.2)(.3)]$$
$$= .35/.41$$
$$= .854$$

Similarly,

$$P(S_2|W) = [P(W|S_2)P(S_2)]/[P(W|S_2)P(S_2) + P(W|S_1) \cdot P(S_1)]$$
$$= [(.2)(.3)]/[(.2)(.3) + (.5)(.7)]$$
$$= .06/.41$$
$$= .146$$
$$P(S_1|B) = [P(B|S_1)P(S_1)]/[P(B|S_1)P(S_1) + P(B|S_2)P(S_2)]$$
$$= [(.5)(.7)]/[(.5)(.7) + (.8)(.3)]$$
$$= .35/.59$$
$$= .593$$
$$P(S_2|B) = [P(B|S_2)P(S_2)]/[P(B|S_1)P(S_1) + P(B|S_2)P(S_2)]$$
$$= [(.8)(.3)]/.59$$
$$= .24/.59$$
$$= .407$$

a posteriori
probabilities   These conditional probabilities are called *a posteriori probabilities* because they cannot be established exclusive of some other property of the problem. In this example, we cannot determine the a posteriori probabilities until after the sampling is completed. Since S_1 and S_2 are mutually exclusive and exhaustive, $P(W$ and $S_1) + P(W$ and $S_2) = P(W)$, and since $P(W$ and $S_1) = P(W|S_1)P(S_1)$, then

$$P(W) = P(W|S_1)P(S_1) + P(W|S_2)P(S_2)$$
$$= (.5)(.7) + (.2)(.3)$$
$$= .41$$

Similarly,

$$P(B) = P(B|S_1)P(S_1) + P(B|S_2)P(S_2)$$
$$= (.5)(.7) + (.8)(.3)$$
$$= .59$$

Obviously, since the ball that is drawn in the sample must be either a white or a black ball, $P(W) + P(B)$ must equal 1. Remember: the probabilities at any chance node must add to 1. Now that we have calculated the necessary probabilities, it is a fairly mechanical procedure to evaluate the tree. Notice in Figure 12.5 that the cost of the additional information is subtracted from

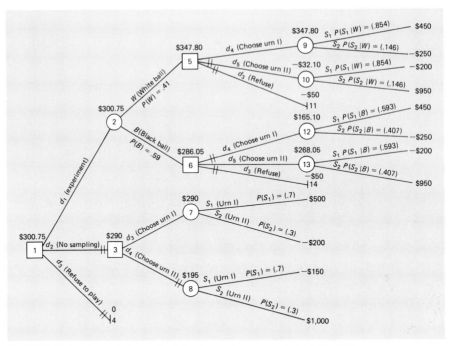

FIGURE 12.5 **Expanded urn decision tree when sampling is possible**

each applicable payoff at the ends of the decision tree. The same adjustment can be achieved if we leave the payoffs the same and charge a tariff of $50 at branch d_1.

Let us evaluate the decision tree in Figure 12.5 node by node where the value of node i is denoted by N_i:

Node 14: $N_{14} = -\$50$

Node 13: $N_{13} = (.593)(-200) + (.407)(950)$
$= -118.60 + 386.65$
$= \$268.05$

Node 12: $N_{12} = (.593)(450) + (.407)(-250)$
$= 266.85 - 101.75$
$= \$165.10$

Node 11: $N_{11} = (.854)(-50) + (.146)(-50)$
$= -\$50$

Node 10: $N_{10} = (.854)(-200) + (.146)(950)$
$= -170.80 + 138.70$
$= -\$32.10$

Node 9: $N_9 = (.854)(450) + (.146)(-250)$
$$= 384.30 - 36.50$$
$$= \$347.80$$

Node 8: $N_8 = (.7)(-150) + (.3)(1,000)$
$$= -105 + 300$$
$$= \$195$$

Node 7: $N_7 = (.7)(500) + (.3)(-200)$
$$= 350 - 60$$
$$= \$290$$

Node 6: Since $N_{13} > N_{12} > N_{14}$, d_5 is the most attractive alternative and
$N_6 = \$268.05$

Node 5: Since $N_9 > N_{10} > N_{11}$, d_4 is the best alternative and
$N_5 = \$347.80$

Node 4: $N_4 = 0$

Node 3: Since $N_7 > N_8$, d_3 is the best alternative and $N_3 = \$290$

Node 2: $N_2 = (.41)(347.80) + (.59)(268.05)$
$$= 142.60 + 158.15$$
$$= 300.75$$

Node 1: Since $N_2 > N_3 > N_4$, it seems wise to experiment and
$N_1 = \$300.75$

optimal, or
Bayesian,
strategy
According to our evaluation of this decision tree, the *optimal strategy* (sometimes referred to as the *Bayesian strategy*) would be to sample one ball and if it is white, guess that the urn is type I. If the sampled ball is black, then you should guess that the urn is type II. The expected monetary value of the urn decision is $300.75.

The Value of Information

expected
value of
sample
information
(EVSI)
To make the decision whether or not to buy additional information, it is often helpful to ascertain the expected value of sample information (EVSI) and the expected value of perfect information (EVPI). Clearly, most information is imperfect; hence, the upper bound on the amount you would be willing to pay for information is the expected value of perfect information. The *expected value of sample information* is merely the EMV with the information minus the EMV without any information. Therefore, in our urn example, the EVSI = $350.75 - $290, or $60.75.

expected
value of
perfect
information
(EVPI)
The value of perfect information is a legitimate issue when you are deciding whether or not to buy information. Clearly, if the expected value of a market research project is $10,000, it would be foolish to pay $15,000 for the study. The *expected value of perfect information* can be calculated by

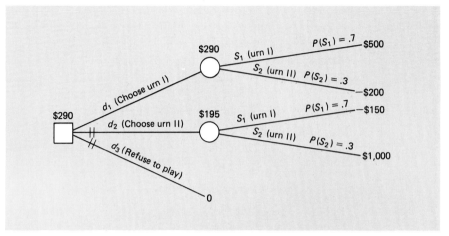

FIGURE 12.6 **Urn decision tree when perfect information is not available**

subtracting the EMV without information from the EMV with perfect information.

Let us take the urn example (see Figure 12.6). The EMV without information is $290. The EMV with perfect information is

$$\sum_{i=1}^{N} P(S_i)P_i$$

where

$$P(S_i) = \text{probability that } S_i \text{ is the true state of nature}$$
$$P_i = \text{optimal payoff if } S_i \text{ is the true state of nature}$$
$$N = \text{number of states of nature}$$

Therefore,

$$\text{EMV with perfect information} = (.7)(500) + (.3)(1,000)$$
$$= 350 + 300$$
$$= \$650$$

Consequently,

$$\text{EVPI} = 650 - 290$$
$$= \$360$$

If you are one who makes decisions by maximizing EMV (an *EMVer*), then you would pay up to $360 for perfect knowledge of the type of urn that is sitting on the table.

EXAMPLE   A contractor has been invited to bid on a construction job. The value of the contract depends on the length of time it takes to complete the project. If the project is finished on time, there is profit of $50,000. If the contractor is late finishing the project, he will lose $10,000. Weather is the sole determinant of whether the project will be late. If the weather is good, the project will be completed on time; if it is bad, the project will not be completed on schedule. Based on his past experience the contractor's subjective probability of good weather is 20 percent. The contractor, however, has the opportunity to buy a long-range forecast from an independent weather-forecasting company. The weather-forecasting company has a fairly good track record for these long-range forecasts. Its files indicate that 70 percent of the time it successfully predicted good weather, and 80 percent of the time it was able to predict bad weather. In other words,

$$P(I_1|S_1) = .7 \qquad P(I_1|S_2) = .20$$
$$P(I_2|S_1) = .3 \qquad P(I_2|S_2) = .80$$

where

I_1 = prediction of good weather
I_2 = prediction of bad weather
S_1 = good weather
S_2 = bad weather

The cost of the weather-forecasting service is $5,000.

In developing the decision tree for the contractor's problem, it is helpful to identify what decisions the contractor must make and in what sequence those decisions must be made. First, he must make the decision whether to buy the weather forecast information. If the decision is made to buy the information, the contractor must make the bid decision based on the forecast. The decision tree in Figure 12.7 is fairly straightforward.

To evaluate the decision tree in Figure 12.7, it is necessary to calculate the a posteriori probabilities.

$$P(S_1|I_1) = [P(I_1|S_1)P(S_1)]/[P(I_1|S_1)P(S_1) + P(I_1|S_2)P(S_2)]$$
$$= [(.7)(.2)]/[(.7)(.2) + (.2)(.8)]$$
$$= .14/(.14 + .16)$$
$$= .14/.30$$
$$= .467$$
$$P(S_2|I_1) = [(.2)(.8)]/.30$$
$$= .16/.30$$
$$= .533$$
$$P(S_1|I_2) = [(.3)(.2)]/[(.3)(.2) + (.8)(.8)]$$
$$= .06/.70$$
$$= .086$$

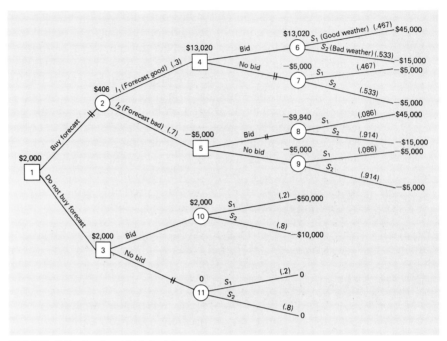

FIGURE 12.7 **Contract bid decision tree**

$$P(S_2|I_2) = [(.8)(.8)]/.7$$
$$= .64/.70$$
$$= .914$$
$$P(I_1) = P(I_1|S_1)P(S_1) + P(I_1|S_2)P(S_2)$$
$$= (.7)(.2) + (.2)(.8)$$
$$= .30$$
$$P(I_2) = .70$$

Once the probabilities have been calculated, the tree is evaluated by assessing the value of each chance node and each decision node.

$$\text{Node 11:} \quad N_{11} = (0)(.2) + (0)(.8)$$
$$= 0$$
$$\text{Node 10:} \quad N_{10} = (.2)(50,000) + (.8)(-10,000)$$
$$= 10,000 - 8,000$$
$$= \$2,000$$
$$\text{Node 9:} \quad N_9 = (.086)(-5,000) + (.914)(-5,000)$$
$$= -\$5,000$$

Node 8: $N_8 = (.086)(45,000) + (.914)(-15,000)$
$= 3,870 - 13,710$
$= -9,840$

Node 7: $N_7 = (.467)(-5,000) + (.533)(-5,000)$
$= -\$5,000$

Node 6: $N_6 = (.467)(45,000) + (.533)(-15,000)$
$= 21,015 - 7,995$
$= \$13,020$

Node 5: Since $N_9 > N_8$, the value of node 5 is $-\$5,000$

Node 4: Since $N_6 > N_7$, the value of node 4 is $13,020$

Node 3: Since $N_{10} > N_{11}$, the value of node 3 is $2,000$

Node 2: $N_2 = (.3)(13,020) + (.7)(-5,000)$
$= \$406$

Node 1: Since $N_3 > N_2$, the value of node 1 is $2,000$

Therefore, the Bayesian, or optimal, strategy is to bid on the project without buying the forecast. This strategy has an expected value of $2,000.

If the price of the weather forecast is negotiable, the next step in the analysis would be to calculate the expected value of the weather forecast, which is denoted by EVSI. Since we subtracted $5,000 from the payoffs in the upper part of the decision tree, it is necessary to add back this $5,000 when computing EVSI. Remember that the expected value of sample information is the EMV with information minus the EMV without the information. Therefore, the expected value of the weather information is

$$\begin{array}{cc} \text{EMV with} & \text{EMV without} \\ \text{information} & \text{information} \end{array}$$
$$\text{EVSI} = (\$406 + \$5,000) - \$2,000$$
$$= \$3,406$$

The expected value of a perfect weather forecast remember is defined as the EMV with perfect information minus the EMV without any information. Consequently, the value of a perfect weather forecast is calculated as follows:

$$\begin{array}{cc} \text{EMV with} & \text{EMV without} \\ \text{perfect information} & \text{any information} \end{array}$$
$$\text{EVPI} = [(.2)(\$50,000) + (.8)(\$0)] - \$2,000$$
$$= \$8,000$$

DECISION PROBLEM FOR NON-EMVers

Decision makers can be classified in three categories:

1. Risk takers
2. EMVers
3. Risk averters

A risk taker might choose a gamble that has a negative EMV. People who gamble in Nevada know that the expected value of their gamble is negative, but because they enjoy the excitement or the thrill of winning they are willing to play against the odds. A risk taker might take the gamble pictured in Figure 12.8 even though the EMV is −$20.

People who take action strictly on the basis of the EMV of the decision probably constitute the smallest category of decision maker. Later in this section, we shall discuss methodology to deal with decisions under uncertainty for the non-EMVer.

The last category of decision maker is that of risk avoiders, or risk averters. Most people fit into this category when they are confronted with decisions that entail significant monetary payoffs. Would you pay $250 to be allowed to gamble on the flip of a coin that has a payoff of $1,000 if you win and −$500 if you lose? If not, what would you pay for the chance pictured in Figure 12.9? If you would not pay $250 or more for the gamble, you are a risk avoider. If you would pay more than $250 for the chance to play the coin flip gamble, you are a risk taker.

FIGURE 12.8 **Negative EMV gamble**

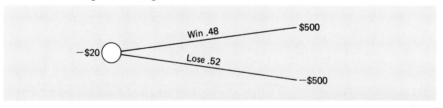

FIGURE 12.9 **Simple coin flip gamble**

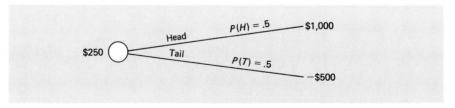

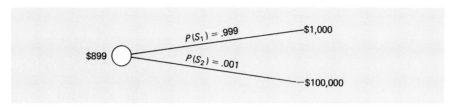

FIGURE 12.10 Simple gamble

If you have decided you would pay up to $250 for the Figure 12.9 gamble, what about the gamble pictured in Figure 12.10? An EMVer would be willing to pay up to $899 to take this gamble. Would you? Would you take the gamble for nothing? By now, you probably realize that at least for some ranges of monetary payoffs, many people are not EMVers.

Let us reconsider the urn problem without any experimental options. One way to proceed is to determine the value of each chance node subjec-*certainty* tively instead of computing the expected value. This value is known as the *equivalent* *certainty equivalent* of a gamble. In other words, ask yourself the question, What is the gamble at node 2 in Figure 12.11 worth? If, after some delibera-tion, you determine that you would pay $100 for the gamble, assign a value of $100 to node 2. Similarly, suppose you decide the certainty equivalent of the node 3 gamble is $25; then you would choose urn I. If you had an extreme aversion to risk, you might not assign positive values to nodes 2 and 3. That is, someone might have to pay you to take either of these gambles.

It becomes less feasible to assign a certainty equivalent to each chance node in a decision process as the number and complexity of the chance nodes increase. In other words, what if the chance node has more than two

FIGURE 12.11 Urn decision tree

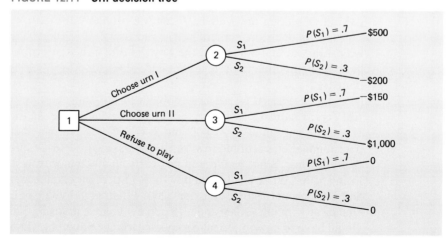

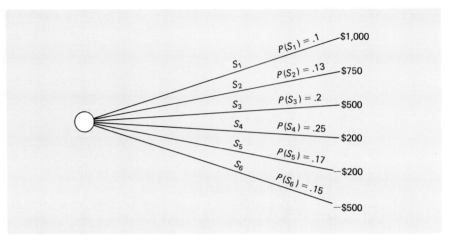

FIGURE 12.12 **Complex gamble**

or three states of nature and its probabilities are difficult to assess subjectively? For example, what would your certainty equivalent be for the gamble pictured in Figure 12.12?

Fortunately, there is a procedure for dealing with the psychology of the non-EMVer. The basic idea is to measure the decision maker's attitude toward risk and then to substitute payoffs modified by the decision maker's risk attitude for the original monetary payoffs. The substitute payoffs can be thought of as specially designed lottery tickets that entitle the owner to a p chance at winning W and a $1 - p$ chance at winning L. (Usually, L is a negative dollar amount.) The only requirements are that W be clearly preferable to L and that the decision maker be a rational person. If W and L are monetary values, then the monetary value of a lottery ticket with $p = 1$ is W, and a lottery ticket with $p = 0$ has a dollar value of L. Since attitudes toward risk differ among individuals, these are probably the only two points that a group of decision makers can agree upon. If W and L are sufficiently wide apart to encompass all the payoffs of a decision problem, then intermediate points relating relevant dollar values to lottery tickets can be determined.

Let us return to the urn problem to illustrate how to adjust for non-EMVers. Figure 12.13 shows the original decision tree. In the urn problem, W can be set equal to $1,000 and L to $-$200. We can then measure the decision maker's attitude toward risk by asking a series of questions such as the following: What would you pay for a 50-50 chance at winning $1,000 or losing $200? What would you pay for a 75 percent chance at winning $1,000 and a 25 percent chance at losing $200? What would you pay for a 25 percent chance at winning $1,000 and a 75 percent chance at losing $200? If someone would have to pay you to take a specific lottery ticket, how much would they

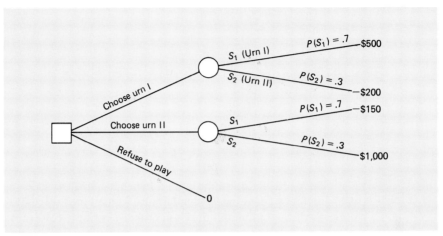

FIGURE 12.13 **Decision tree for the basic urn problem**

have to pay you? (Remember, lottery tickets represent various gamble parameters.)

Let us assume that a decision maker has answered a series of these kinds of questions and the answers are summarized in Table 12.7. These values can be plotted and a smooth, concave curve fitted to them. (We have done so in Figure 12.14.) This curve represents the locus of points where a particular decision maker professes indifference between the choices of taking a precisely defined gamble and a certain amount of money. You will note that the illustration contrasts the non-EMVer's indifference curve with an EMVer's.

FIGURE 12.14 **Non-EMVer's indifference curve contrasted with EMVer's**

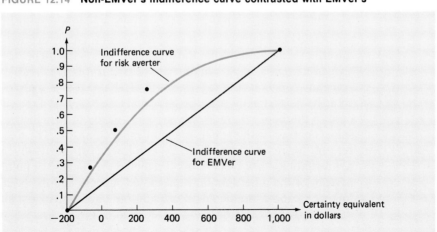

TABLE 12.7 *Lottery ticket dollar equivalence*

p	Certainty equivalent
0.00	$-200
.25	-50
.50	50
.75	200
1.00	1,000

Once the indifference curve has been drawn, it is easy to use the decision theory developed thus far in this chapter to solve decision problems in terms of the individual decision maker's attitude toward risk. The simple procedure is based upon one very reasonable principle: If a gamble is modified by substituting a different payoff and if the decision maker is indifferent between the original payoff and the new payoff, then that same decision maker should be indifferent between the original gamble and the modified gamble if all else remains unchanged.

Therefore, if a decision maker is indifferent between x dollars and a lottery ticket with a specific value for p, it is reasonable to substitute the lottery ticket for the monetary payoff. If lottery tickets with different values of p are substituted for each monetary payoff, and the decision tree is evaluated in terms of expected p values, then the strategy that optimizes expected p values is the optimal strategy for that decision maker's particular attitude toward risk. Obviously, this optimal strategy may differ from the optimal strategy of an EMVer or even of another risk averter. To further understand the use of decision theory for a non-EMVer, consider the next example.

EXAMPLE   An editor of a large publishing company has just received a prospectus and four chapters of a manuscript. After reviewing the material, the editor's intuition is that the proposed book has a 40 percent chance to be successful and a 60 percent chance to fail. If it is successful, the publishing company can expect to make a profit of $100,000 over a period of five years. If the book is a failure, the company will lose $50,000. If the editor decides to publish the book, there is only a 50-50 chance of convincing the authors to sign a contract with the editor's publishing company. The manuscript can be sent off for review by outside experts for a cost of $1,000. In the past, this review process has successfully predicted the success or failure of a book 80 percent of the time; that is, *P*(predicted success and the book was successful) = .80 and *P*(predicted failure and the book failed) = .80. An EMVer's decision tree for this problem is depicted in Figure 12.15.

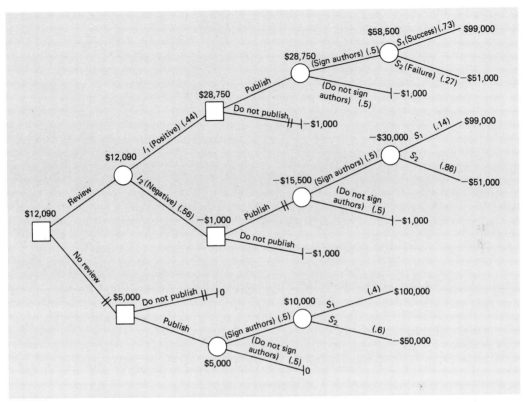

FIGURE 12.15 **Editor's decision tree**

If the editor were an EMVer, the manuscript should be sent out for review and the project signed if the reviews are positive or abandoned if the reviews are negative. This particular editor, however, has an aversion to risk and wonders whether the strategy of an EMVer is consistent with this attitude toward risk. Using $100,000 as W and $-\$51,000$ as L, the editor has

TABLE 12.8 *Indifference table*

p	Certainty equivalent
0.00	$\$-51,000$
.10	$-45,000$
.25	$-35,000$
.50	$-10,000$
.75	$15,000$
.90	$55,000$
1.00	$100,000$

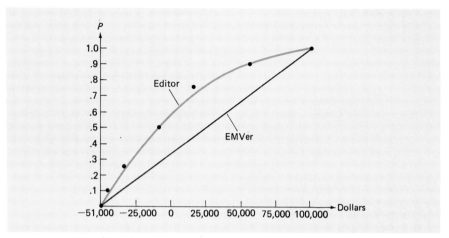

FIGURE 12.16 **Editor's indifference curve**

decided after considerable deliberation that the indifference parameters are established by p chance at winning \$100,000 and $1 - p$ chance at losing \$51,000 (the publishing company's money) and the dollar amounts shown in Table 12.8.

FIGURE 12.17 **Editor's decision tree with p values as payoffs**

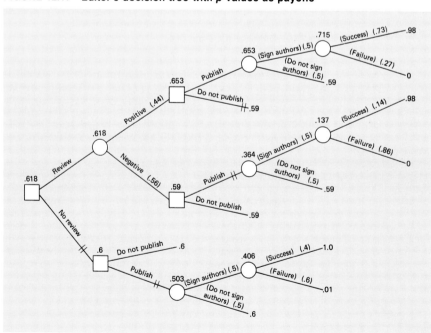

Figure 12.16 fits an indifference curve to the points in Table 12.8. With the function graphed in Figure 12.16, it is now possible to substitute (from the indifference curve) lottery tickets with specific p values for monetary payoffs in the editor's original decision tree (Figure 12.15). Once the substitution is made, it is simply a mechanical procedure to evaluate the tree in terms of p values and thus find the optimal strategy for the editor's individual attitude toward risk. This is done in Figure 12.17.

As you can see by comparing Figure 12.15 and 12.17, an EMVer would not act differently from an individual with an attitude toward risk similar to the editor's as graphed in Figure 12.16. Why?

COMPUTER IMPLICATIONS

The application of decision theory to real-world problems does not require the use of the computer because the computational burden is relatively light. However, for complex decision problems the computer can be useful in calculating the payoffs, the a posteriori probabilities, and evaluating the decision tree. If the decision maker is risk averse, several software packages have been developed that will, through an interactive session between the decision maker and the computer, estimate the decision maker's attitude toward risk and develop his or her personal indifference function. In short, software packages that support the decision analysis described in this chapter can be useful and are available on microcomputers and large mainframes.

There are many decisions in which the chance nodes do not contain discrete states of nature. The Ohio Edison investment decision discussed at the beginning of this chapter is a good example. Some of the probabilistic events in that decision, such as the cost of a catastrophic failure or the percent of sulfur in the coal, could be better modeled as a continuous probability distribution. An appropriate way of handling a decision problem with continuous states of nature is by using the power of the computer to simulate the decision tree. Instead of calculating the expected value of each chance node as described earlier in this chapter, a value for each chance node is generated using the assumed probability distribution for that node. These generated values are used to evaluate the decision tree. The evaluation of the decision tree is repeated a large number of times until the decision stabilizes. The key point to remember is that for complex decisions with nondiscrete states of nature it may be desirable to simulate the decision tree instead of evaluating it using expected values. If this is the case, the computer becomes a necessity, not merely a useful tool. More will be said about the simulation approach to decision analysis in Chapter 15.

SUMMARY

A great many decision problems exist in which a decision must be made among several alternative actions. The consequences of those alternatives depend upon the existence of one or more states of nature, each of which has some probability of being the true state of nature. Critics of decision theory contend, however, that because probability estimates are subjective in nature, the theory is of little practical value. The fact that subjective probabilities are imperfect should make you cautious in your use of decision theory, but it should not prevent you from using it. A decision maker should, however, be aware of the sensitivity of a basic decision made using decision theory to plausible changes in the probabilities. These can be considered by perturbing the various probabilities and reevaluating the decision tree.

SOLVED PROBLEMS

PROBLEM STATEMENT

The president of a large oil company must decide how to invest the company's $10 million of excess profits. He could invest the entire sum in solar energy research, or he could use the money to research better ways of processing coal so that it will burn more cleanly. His only other option is to put half of this R&D money into solar research and half into coal research. The president estimates 1,000 percent return on investment if the solar research is successful and a 500 percent return on investment if the coal research is successful.

a. Construct a payoff table for the president's R&D investment problem.
b. Based on the maximin criterion, what decision should the president make?
c. Based on the maximax criterion, what decision should the president make?
d. Based on the minimax regret criterion, what decision should the president make?

Let

S_1 = neither coal nor solar research is successful
S_2 = solar research is successful and coal research is not
S_3 = coal research is successful and solar research is not

S_4 = both coal and solar research are successful
d_1 = invest in solar R&D only
d_2 = invest in coal R&D only
d_3 = invest 50 percent in coal and 50 percent in solar R&D

SOLUTION

a. TABLE 12.9 *Payoff table for the R&D problem*

Alternative decision	State of nature (all payoffs are in millions)			
	S_1	S_2	S_3	S_4
d_1	−$10	$100	−$10	$100
d_2	− 10	− 10	50	50
d_3	− 10	45	20	75

b. Since the maximin loss for each of the three decisions is the same ($10 million), the maximin criterion indicates that the president could choose any of the three options he has identified.

c. The maximax criterion dictates the choice of d_1 (solar research only) because it has a potential return of $100 million.

d. The opportunity loss table for this problem is reflected in Table 12.10.

TABLE 12.10 *Opportunity loss table for the R&D problem*

Alternative decision	State of (all payoffs are in millions) nature			
	S_1	S_2	S_3	S_4
d_1	0	0	$60	0
d_2	0	$110	0	$50
d_3	0	55	30	25

The minimax regret criterion would choose d_3 (invest in both types of research).

PROBLEM STATEMENT

Given the previous R&D decision problem, the president estimates that the probability of the solar research being successful is .25 and the probability of successful research on coal is .50. If the president is an EMVer, what is his optimal strategy?

SOLUTION

The decision tree is shown as follows:

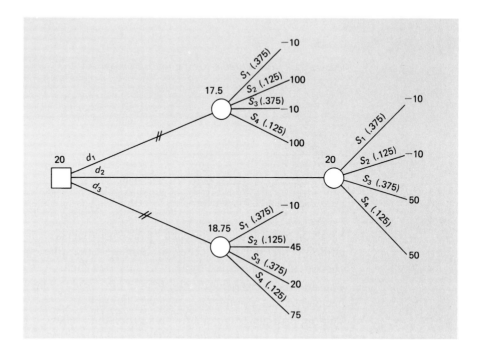

The calculation of the probabilities of the states of nature might require some explanation. If we assume success in solar research is independent of success in coal research, and let

A = event that solar research is successful
B = event that coal research is successful

We can then describe the states of nature as composite events of A and B, and show their complements.

$S_1 = \overline{A \cup B}$ = neither solar nor coal research is successful
$S_2 = A \cap \overline{B}$ = solar research is successful and coal research is unsuccessful
$S_3 = B \cap \overline{A}$ = coal research is successful and solar research is not
$S_4 = A \cap B$ = both solar and coal research are successful

$$P(S_1) = P(\overline{A \cup B}) = 1 - P(A \cup B)$$
$$= 1 - P(A) + P(B) - P(A \cap B)$$
$$= 1 - .25 + .50 - .125$$
$$= .375$$
$$P(S_2) = P(A \cap \overline{B})$$
$$= P(A) \cdot P(\overline{B})$$
$$= (.25)(.5)$$
$$= .125$$
$$P(S_3) = P(B \cap \overline{A})$$
$$= P(B) \cdot P(\overline{A})$$
$$= (.5)(.75)$$
$$= .375$$
$$P(S_4) = P(A \cap B)$$
$$= P(A) \cdot P(B)$$
$$= (.25)(.5)$$
$$= .125$$

As the decision tree indicates, the optimal strategy for an EMVer is to invest in coal research only (d_2). This strategy yields an EMV of $20 million.

COMPUTER SOLUTION

As you have learned in this chapter, the major benefit of a decision theory approach to a decision is the structure that it affords. The evaluation of a decision tree is a mechanical process that can easily be programmed. However, specifying the structure of the decision tree to the computer and inputting the necessary data is time consuming and often it is easier to evaluate the decision tree manually. In other words, the utility of the computer is often mitigated by the effort involved in supplying the necessary information to the computer. In the following case, evaluating the decision tree took longer using a microcomputer than using a $5.00 calculator. See Figure 12.18 for the microcomputer output.

PROBLEM STATEMENT

The Ace Trucking Co. of Chicago has a request to haul two shipments, one to St. Louis and one to Pittsburgh. Because of scheduling problems, Ace cannot accept both assignments. The St. Louis customer has guaranteed a return shipment, but the Pittsburgh customer indicates that the odds of a return shipment is 50-50. The value of the St. Louis contract is $2,500. The value of the Pittsburgh contract is $2,000 without return shipment and $4,000 with return.

```
              Input Data of The Problem SOLAR--Decision Tree Page 1

Branch    Branch        Start    End      Start node     Probability      Payoff/cost
number    name          node     node       type
  1      <D1    >     <1 >     <2  >    <1    >       <        0>      <         0>
  2      <D2    >     <1 >     <4  >    <1    >       <        0>      <         0>
  3      <D3    >     <1 >     <3  >    <1    >       <        0>      <         0>
  4      <S1    >     <2 >     <5  >    <1    >       <0.375000>      <-10.0000>
  5      <S2    >     <2 >     <6  >    <2    >       <0.125000>      < 100.000>
  6      <S3    >     <2 >     <7  >    <2    >       <0.375000>      <-10.0000>
  7      <S4    >     <2 >     <8  >    <2    >       <0.125000>      < 100.000>
  8      <S1    >     <3 >     <9  >    <2    >       <0.375000>      <-10.0000>
  9      <S2    >     <3 >     <10 >    <2    >       <0.125000>      < 45.0000>
 10      <S3    >     <3 >     <11 >    <2    >       <0.375000>      < 20.0000>
 11      <S4    >     <3 >     <12 >    <2    >       <0.125000>      < 75.0000>
 12      <S1    >     <4 >     <13 >    <2    >       <0.375000>      <-10.0000>
 13      <S2    >     <4 >     <14 >    <2    >       <0.125000>      <-10.0000>
 14      <S3    >     <4 >     <15 >    <2    >       <0.375000>      < 50.0000>
 15      <S4    >     <4 >     <16 >    <2    >       <0.125000>      < 50.0000>



                           Decision Tree Analysis


        Node        Type of node      Expected value      Decision


         1           decision              20                D2
         2           chance               17.5
         3           chance              18.75
         4           chance               20
```

FIGURE 12.18   QSB Decision theory computer output

The Ace Trucking Co. can phone a Pittsburgh dispatcher and can ask whether shipping activity is busy or slow. If the report is busy, the chances of obtaining a return shipment are increased. If I_1 is a busy report, I_2 is a slow report, S_1 is getting a return shipment, and S_2 is failure to get a return shipment, the prior conditional probabilities are

$$P(I_1|S_1) = .8 \qquad P(I_2|S_1) = .2$$
$$P(I_1|S_2) = .3 \qquad P(I_2|S_2) = .7$$

a. Construct the decision tree for this problem.

b. Assume that you are an EMVer; what is the optimal strategy?

c. What is the EMV?

d. What is the EVSI?

SOLUTION

a.

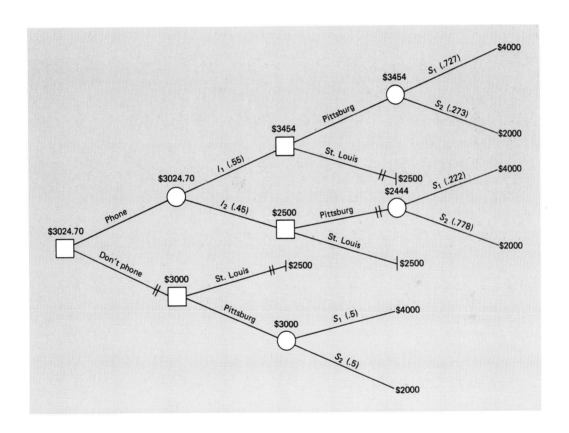

b. The optimal strategy is to phone, and if the dispatcher indicates that shipping activity is busy in Pittsburgh (I_1), accept the Pittsburgh assignment. If the dispatcher says that business is slow, take the St. Louis shipment.

c. $3,024.70

d. EVSI = $3,024.70 − $3,000 = $24.70

```
              Input Data of The Problem TRUCK--Decision Tree Page 1

Branch    Branch       Start     End      Start node    Probability      Payoff/cost
number    name         node      node        type
  1     <Phone    >    <1  >    <2   >    <1    >      <        0>      <        0>
  2     <NoPhone  >    <1  >    <3   >    <1    >      <        0>      <        0>
  3     <I1       >    <2  >    <4   >    <2    >      <0.550000>      <        0>
  4     <I2       >    <2  >    <5   >    <2    >      <0.450000>      <        0>
  5     <StLouis  >    <3  >    <6   >    <1    >      <        0>      <     2500>
  6     <Pitts    >    <3  >    <7   >    <1    >      <        0>      <        0>
  7     <Pitts    >    <4  >    <8   >    <1    >      <        0>      <        0>
  8     <StLouis  >    <4  >    <17  >    <1    >      <        0>      <     2500>
  9     <Pitts    >    <5  >    <9   >    <1    >      <        0>      <        0>
 10     <StLouis  >    <5  >    <10  >    <1    >      <        0>      <     2500>
 11     <S1       >    <7  >    <11  >    <2    >      <0.500000>      <     4000>
 12     <S2       >    <7  >    <12  >    <2    >      <0.500000>      <     2000>
 13     <S1       >    <8  >    <13  >    <2    >      <0.727000>      <     4000>
 14     <S2       >    <8  >    <14  >    <2    >      <0.273000>      <     2000>
 15     <S1       >    <9  >    <15  >    <2    >      <0.222000>      <     4000>
 16     <s2       >    <9  >    <16  >    <2    >      <0.778000>      <     2000>
```

```
                        Decision Tree Analysis

         Node       Type of node    Expected value    Decision


          1          decision          3024.7          Phone
          2          chance            3024.7
          3          decision          3000            Pitts
          4          decision          3454            Pitts
          5          decision          2500            StLouis
          7          chance            3000
          8          chance            3454
          9          chance            2444
```

REVIEW QUESTIONS

1. Define *decision theory*.
2. Distinguish among the maximin, maximax, and minimax regret criteria for decision making.
3. When is decision theory most helpful?
4. Does decision theory generate answers to problems? Explain.
5. Describe several decisions that you often make where decision theory could be applied.
6. Distinguish between subjective probabilities and objective probabilities.

7. What does EMV stand for? How is EMV calculated?
8. In your own words, how is a decision tree evaluated?
9. What does EVSI stand for? How is EVSI calculated?
10. Why is it sometimes important to know the expected value of perfect information?
11. In your own words, how is EVPI calculated?
12. What does Bayes' theorem contribute to decision theory?
13. State Bayes' theorem algebraically.
14. Distinguish between EMVers and risk averters.
15. What are the major criticisms of decision theory?

PROBLEMS

12.1 Given the following payoff table, what is the recommended decision under each of the following criteria?

  a. Maximin

  b. Maximax

  c. Minimax regret

Payoff table

	State of nature			
Alternative decision	S_1	S_2	S_3	S_4
d_1	$500	$ 400	$450	$300
d_2	425	400	350	375
d_3	200	450	300	250
d_4	− 100	1,000	200	100

12.2 *Stock market investment.* You are trying to determine what stock to invest in. The wisdom of your decision depends on the state of the stock market in one year. There are three possible states of nature: the market could go down, stay about the same, or it could go up. You have narrowed your investment choices to four stocks. The payoffs for the various combinations of investment choices and market conditions are shown in the table.

Payoff table

Alternative decision—	State of nature		
	Market is up	Market is unchanged	Market is down
Stock A	$ 20,000	$5,000	$ – 15,000
Stock B	10,000	8,000	6,000
Stock C	100,000	0	– 50,000
Stock D	15,000	5,000	– 10,000

What are the correct investment choices given the following decision making criteria?

a. Maximin

b. Maximax

c. Minimax regret

12.3 *Stock market investment.* If the probabilities of the various stock market conditions in Problem 12.2 were each $\frac{1}{3}$, what would the optimal strategy of an EMVer be?

a. Draw and label the decision tree.

b. Evaluate the decision tree.

c. What is the EMV of the optimal decision?

12.4 *Construction industry.* The Ace Construction Company has been asked to make a sealed bid on building 40 lighted tennis courts for State University. It costs $10,000 to build each court, and just to bid costs $5,000. The company is considering five bids and, based on previous experience, each bid has a different subjective probability of being the winning bid. The bids and probabilities are summarized in the table.

Bid number	Amount of bid	Probability of winning
1	Cost + 5%	.90
2	Cost + 10%	.75
3	Cost + 15%	.60
4	Cost + 20%	.40
5	Cost + 25%	.10

a. Draw the decision tree for this problem.

b. Assuming that Ace Construction Company wants to maximize the EMV, what bid should it submit to State University?

12.5 *Personal decision making.* You have a trip to make next week, and you are trying to decide whether to make the trip by air, automobile, or train. The weather is the primary determinant of your enjoyment of the trip. The weather bureau has forecast an 80 percent chance of good weather next week. Your trip enjoyment in case of good and bad weather is measured in utiles in the table.

Weather	Airplane	Auto	Train
Good	100	65	50
Bad	0	20	50

a. Draw the decision tree for this problem, labeling all branches, states of nature, payoffs, and probabilities.

b. If you wish to maximize expected utiles, which mode of transportation would you choose?

12.6 *Retail sales.* You are the owner of a local sporting goods shop, and you have an opportunity to buy leather soccer balls at a special price if you buy the balls sometime before July 31. You must, however, buy in even dozens. If you buy early, you can buy the balls for $10 each. If you buy during the soccer season, the balls will cost $12 each. If you overstock and must sell the balls after the soccer season, you feel you will have to sell them for $8 each. The balls retail for $18 and the level of demand shown in the table is predicted. Notice that sales are also in even dozens.

Demand (dozen)	Probability
2	.25
3	.30
4	.30
5	.15

a. Draw the decision tree, labeling properly.

b. Evaluate the tree.

c. How many soccer balls would an EMVer order early?

12.7 *Personal decision making.* You are an engineering student and are trying to decide whether, upon graduation, to go to work as an engineer or spend another year in school getting an M.B.A. Since you are an EMVer, all you really care about is your expected income. Presently, the market for engineers is depressed, and the probability of getting an engineering job is only .50. Your subjective probability of getting a job requiring an M.B.A. in one year is .70. However, you can do some research into expected strength of the market for M.B.A.s. You feel that this research will be correct with a probability of .70. The states of nature are that you will be able to get a job utilizing your education or you will not; that is, $P(I_1|S_1) = .7$. The average M.B.A. earns $36,000 per year to start, and the average engineering student makes $28,000 at the start. If you can't get a job utilizing your education, you can always drive a taxi for $19,000 per year. Use five-year earnings to determine the optimal strategy.

a. Draw the decision tree and label it.

b. What is the optimal strategy of an EMVer?

c. What is the optimal EMV?

d. What is the expected value of sample information?

12.8 *Gambling decisions.* You are a betting person and wish to bet on the State University varsity/alumni game. You have no information on the odds for either team's winning. The only information you have is that the varsity has won 12 and the alumni have won 8. Ties are broken by sudden death playoffs. You have an opportunity to do some research into the strengths and weaknesses of the two teams; the outcome of this research will predict a winner. The only bet you can make is an even $100.

I_1 = research indicates varsity will win
I_2 = research indicates the alumni will win
S_1 = varsity will win
S_2 = alumni will win
$P(I_1|S_1) = .70$
$P(I_2|S_1) = .30$
$P(I_1|S_2) = .40$
$P(I_2|S_2) = .60$

a. Draw the decision tree.

b. Indicate the optimal strategy for an EMVer.

c. Interpret the decision tree in your own words.

d. Would your decision strategy be the same as an EMVer's strategy? Explain.

12.9 *Drilling decision.* An oil company is trying to decide on its bidding policy for the purchase of some offshore drilling rights. Based on the history of other areas with similar characteristics, the management of the oil company thinks that there are three possible levels of oil in the offshore area in question, with the probabilities reflected in the table.

State of nature	Payoff	Probability
1	Not enough recoverable oil to cover drilling and production costs (i.e., total loss of $25 million)	.40
2	Total oil production of 50 million barrels	.50
3	Total oil production of 100 million barrels	.10

Drilling costs and production costs are estimated at $100 million for the life of the area. The current market price of oil is $31 per barrel. The problem is that management does not know whether to bid or how much to bid for the oil rights. Its policy is that management should select one of the three bidding strategies and bid $22, $23, or $24 per expected barrel of oil based on its supposition of what the competition will bid. Management's subjective probabilities on this aspect of the problem of getting the drilling rights are summarized in the following table.

Bid ($)	Probability of outbidding the competition
22	.10
23	.30
24	.60

a. Draw the decision tree and label it properly.

b. Evaluate the decision tree from the point of view of an EMVer.

c. What is the optimal strategy, and what is the EMV of the oil company's drilling rights problem?

12.10 *Product development.* A small firm has developed a new machine to manufacture printed circuit boards. The machine is a considerable improvement over machines currently on the market. If management decides to manufacture this new machine, it is almost certain that the larger firms in the industry will copy the design and take the majority of the market through price competition. Therefore, management feels that the decision of whether or not to manufacture depends solely on expected profit in the first year of production. The costs of setting up the production lines and marketing the new machine are estimated to be $250,000. The variable cost of the machine is about $10,000 per machine, and the firm plans to sell the machine for $15,000. To simplify the problem, let us assume that the market demand will be either 50 or

75 machines. Assume that demand and production are evenly distributed throughout the year. Management believes that these two levels of demand are equally likely. Market research can be done at a cost of $10,000. In the past, this market research has successfully predicted demand level 75 percent of the time; that is, *P*(research indicates demand will be for 50 machines given the demand is for 50 machines) = .75.

a. Draw and label the decision tree.

b. Evaluate the decision tree.

c. What is the optimal strategy of an EMVer?

d. Interpret the decision tree.

e. What is the expected value of sample information?

f. What is the expected value of perfect information?

12.11 *Oil drilling.* An oil company must decide whether or not to drill an oil well in a particular area. The decision maker believes that the area could be dry, reasonably good, or a bonanza, with the respective probabilities of .40, .40, and .20. If the well is dry, no revenue is generated. If the well is reasonably good, the expected revenue is $75,000. If the well is a bonanza, the expected revenue is $200,000. In any case, the cost of drilling the well is $40,000. At a cost of $15,000, the company can take a series of seismic soundings determining the underlying geological structure at the site. These experiments will disclose whether there is no structure, open structure, or closed structure. Let us denote these experimental outcomes as I_1, I_2, and I_3, respectively. Let

$$S_1 = \text{dry hole}$$
$$S_2 = \text{reasonably good potential}$$
$$S_3 = \text{bonanza}$$

Past experience has indicated the following conditional probabilities:

$$P(I_1|S_1) = .60 \qquad P(I_1|S_2) = .40 \qquad P(I_1|S_3) = .10$$
$$P(I_2|S_1) = .30 \qquad P(I_2|S_2) = .40 \qquad P(I_2|S_3) = .40$$
$$P(I_3|S_1) = .10 \qquad P(I_3|S_2) = .20 \qquad P(I_3|S_3) = .50$$

a. Draw and label the decision tree for this problem.

b. Evaluate the decision tree.

c. What is the optimal strategy for an EMVer?

d. What is the EMV of the optimal strategy?

e. What is the EVSI?

f. What is the EVPI?

12.12 *Capital investment.* XYZ Manufacturing Company has made a bid to supply a major piece of industrial equipment to another company. If XYZ Company gets the contract, a capital investment of $300,000 would be justified to enable XYZ Company to economically build the equipment. The problem is that the lead time on the capital investment is too long, and consequently a decision concerning capital expenditure must be made now. If XYZ Company gets the contract and buys the capital equipment, it will net $600,000 on the deal. If XYZ Company does not get the contract, the entire capital investment is lost. If the company gets the contract and uses existing facilities (that is, there is no capital investment), it will lose $100,000 on the contract. Marketing has estimated that XYZ Company has a 50-50 chance of winning the contract.

a. Draw and evaluate the decision tree and label it properly.

b. What should XYZ Company do?

c. What is the EMV of the decision?

12.13 *Capital investment.* The XYZ Company in Problem 12.12 could spend $25,000 to obtain information concerning the probability of getting the contract. In the past, this type of information proved accurate about 80 percent of the time.

a. Draw and evaluate the decision tree for this new problem.

b. What is the Bayesian strategy?

c. What is the EVSI?

12.14 *Personal.* You are presently taking a course on a pass/fail basis and want to decide whether or not to drop the course. If you drop before the first test, all your tuition will be refunded. If you drop after the first test, no tuition will be refunded. At present, you believe you have a 75 percent chance of passing the course. The following are your subjective estimates of the prior conditional probabilities.

$$P(I_1|S_1) = .9 \qquad P(I_1|S_2) = .3$$
$$P(I_2|S_1) = .1 \qquad P(I_2|S_2) = .7$$

where

$S_1 = $ passing the course
$S_2 = $ failing the course
$I_1 = $ passing the test (first test)
$I_2 = $ failing the test (first test)

The payoffs are in utiles and are the following:

$$\begin{aligned}
\text{pass} &= 100 \text{ utiles} \\
\text{fail} &= 0 \text{ utiles} \\
\text{drop before test} &= 50 \text{ utiles} \\
\text{drop after test} &= 25 \text{ utiles}
\end{aligned}$$

a. Draw the decision tree.

b. Evaluate the decision tree.

c. What is the Bayesian strategy?

12.15 Design a series of questions and try to find a friend's indifference curve for various levels of dollar investment.

12.16 Assume that you are the president of Ace Construction Company in Problem 12.4. What would your optimal strategy be, given your personal attitude toward risk?

12.17 Measure your personal attitude toward the risk involved in Problem 12.11. Substitute p values for monetary payoffs, and then find your optimal strategy. Discuss and interpret your answer.

12.18 *Flight planning.* The Operations Research Group at American Airlines has recently developed a very promising model to generate flight plans for each of its more than 2,000 flights per day. A flight plan is a plan that tells the pilot and the air traffic control system how the aircraft will get from its origin to its destination. It specifies the track along the ground that the aircraft will follow, when it will climb, what altitudes to fly at, and how fast to fly. The quality of the flight plan can be measured by the length of the flight and how much fuel is consumed.

The new prototype flight planning model utilizes a dynamic programming approach to the problem, and therefore if it is implemented properly it can optimize individual flight plans. To estimate the value of the new approach, the OR project team "benchmarked" the model against the old fixed route and profile model for a wide variety of flights. The results of the benchmark demonstrated that the new dynamic programming approach resulted in an average of 2.3 percent fuel-burn savings over the old methodology.

This fuel-burn savings translates to more than $30 million per year for American Airlines.

Shortly after the benchmark was complete, results were reviewed with senior management and an intensive effort was undertaken by Data Processing Department to improve the existing methodology based on the benchmark results. Unfortunately, due to the computing environment a dynamic programming approach was considered infeasible.

The head of the Operations Research group has a difficult problem. Should he go along with Data Processing and hope that most of the savings that were demonstrated can be effected by the changes the DP project leader has proposed or should he try to impose a dynamic programming approach on Data Processing. Another alternative is to do another benchmark after Data Processing has finished its enhancements to the existing flight planning system. If he decides to do the benchmark, his project team has estimated the likelihood of the various outcomes as shown:

Benchmark outcomes

Fuel-burn savings	Probability
.0%	.05
.2	.2
.4	.4
.6	.2
.8	.1
1.0	.05

If the head of the OR Department decides to develop an entirely new flight planning system without the involvement of Data Processing, it will cost approximately 250 person-months (at a cost of $800 per person-month) and have only a 75 percent chance of success. If successful, there is only a 10 percent chance that Data Processing will accept the system without their involvement. By waiting to do the benchmarking, the probability of DP acceptance is a function of projected fuel savings as shown in the following table.

Probability of acceptance per projected level of fuel-burn savings

Fuel-burn savings	Probability of DP acceptance
.0	.0
.2	.05
.4	.1
.6	.15
.8	.3
1.0	.4

Develop the decision tree for this decision problem. Document the assumptions that were necessary to do the analysis and make a recommendation to the head of the OR Department.

12.19 *Capital investment.* BelchFire Motor Company makes a wide variety of large gas-guzzling luxury automobiles. Recently, several prestigious European manufacturers have established dealerships in the United States, and BelchFire's sales have suffered due to the sharper prices of the Europeans. To counter this, BelchFire's senior management is seriously considering the introduction of two new luxury "motor cars" with European styling and performance ratings. BelchFire also plans to automate part or all of its production process to price the new cars competitively. Each of the proposed new cars, the "Czecho" and the "South Wales," will have different production standards and consumer markets. Management must decide whether to automate or semiautomate; which, if any, of the two new cars to produce; or do nothing and review again in two years. BelchFire's research department came up with estimates of net return on investment for each of the various alternatives:

Production	Market demand	Likelihood	Return on investment
Automatic "Czecho"	High	.25	$7,500,000
	Average	.45	4,000,000
	Low	.30	1,500,000
Semiauto "Czecho"	High	.25	6,200,000
	Average	.45	3,700,000
	Low	.30	1,600,000
Automatic "S. Wales"	High	.15	9,200,000
	Average	.45	4,600,000
	Low	.40	1,200,000
Semiauto "S. Wales"	High	.15	7,000,000
	Average	.45	3,500,000
	Low	.40	1,900,000

Management's third alternative is to liquidate the business in two years and retire to Buenos Aires. The estimated value of the liquidation is

Likelihood	Value
.10	$5,600,000
.35	4,700,000
.25	4,300,000
.15	3,800,000
.10	3,300,000
.05	2,000,000

Use decision tree analysis and make the decision for BelchFire. (Assume all return amounts are in present value dollars.)

BIBLIOGRAPHY

Baird, Bruce F., *Introduction to Decision Analysis*. North Scituate, Mass.: Duxbury Press, 1978.

Bunn, Derek W., *Applied Decision Analysis*. New York: McGraw-Hill Book Company, 1984.

Felson, Jerry, *Decision Making Under Uncertainty*. New York: CDS Publishing Co., 1976.

Holloway, Charles A., *Decision Making Under Uncertainty; Models and Choices*. Englewood Cliffs, N.J.: Prentice Hall, 1979.

Radford, K. J., *Managerial Decision Making*. Reston, Va.: Reston Publishing Company, 1981.

Raiffa, Howard, *Decision Analysis: Introductory Lectures on Choices Under Uncertainty*. Reading, Mass.: Addison-Wesley Publishing Co., 1968.

Schlaifer, R., *Analysis of Decisions Under Uncertainty*. New York: McGraw-Hill Book Company, 1978.

Simon, H. A., *The New Science of Management Decisions*. New York: Harper and Row, 1977.

Vatter, Paul A., Stephen P. Bradley, Sherwood C. Frey, Jr., and Barbara B. Jackson, *Quantitative Methods in Management: Text and Cases*. Homewood, Ill.: Richard D. Irwin, 1978.

13

Forecasting

THE MANITOBA TELEPHONE SYSTEM[1]

The Manitoba Telephone System (MTS) provides telephones and telecommunications to individuals and businesses in the province of Manitoba, Canada. In 1982, management decided to install a control system to minimize telephone inventory in its retail phone centers. The inventory model was designed to determine the number of each type of telephone a phone center should order from the MTS warehouse and when that order should be placed, while maintaining a goal of meeting 95 percent of customer demand.

To implement the system, MTS needed forecasts of customer demand and returns for 62 telephone types at each phone center. However, in the process of acquiring data for the forecasting model, MTS discovered that each phone center collected different types of data over different periods of time. To get around this problem, and to simplify the forecasting process, MTS did a study on one phone center and aggregated the 62 product types into three categories using standard ABC analysis (see Chapter 16). But because of the scarcity of the data, sophisticated forecasting techniques such as time-series and regression analysis did not work.

---

[1] Rochele Cohen and Fraser Dunford, ''Forecasting for Inventory Control: An Example of When 'Simple' Means Better,''' *Interfaces,* 16, no. 6 (November–December 1986), 95–99.

Faced with the problem of insufficient data, MTS took a simple, commonsense approach: it produced frequency tables for each of the 62 telephone types in the various phone centers. Since telephone demand had been fairly constant for several years, these tables provided a simple but satisfactory estimate of demand for the inventory system. In a five-month test period, service level was consistently above 95 percent while stock levels in most phone centers were reduced by 45 percent. Incidentally, the computer program used to generate the frequency tables cost $1.00 to run.

INTRODUCTION

Regardless of whether an organization's role in society is to provide medical care, police protection, safe streets, consumer goods, or consumer services, it needs accurate and timely forecasts. Hospitals need to predict the demand for resources such as X-ray facilities, surgical rooms, special nursing stations, and so on. Computer organizations must predict demand so that the appropriate hardware and software can be acquired. Farmers need weather forecasts for making planting and harvesting decisions. Automobile manufacturers need demand forecasts to develop the master schedules that are a necessary input to materials requirements planning and aggregate scheduling. In short, many planning decisions are based on various forecasts, and it is becoming increasingly important for the competitive firm to perform the forecasting function accurately and efficiently.

To emphasize this point, let us demonstrate the effect of a 10 percent error in the demand forecast for automobiles. Let us assume that demand for September is estimated at 100,000 automobiles. Based on this forecast, workforce planning, production schedules, inventory policies, and many other important planning decisions are made. Now assume that sales for September are 90,000 units rather than the 100,000 projected. If we oversimplify the consequences of the forecasting error by using the cost of holding additional inventory to measure the cost of that error, we can compute it in the following manner:

cost of forecast error
   = (cost of auto)(number of excess autos produced)(cost of capital)

For illustrative purposes, let the per unit cost of the automobile be $5,000 and the cost of capital be 12 percent per year, or 1 percent per month. Then the cost of the forecast error for September is

$$(\$5{,}000)(10{,}000)(.01) = \$500{,}000$$

It ought to be obvious from this oversimplified example that accurate demand forecasts are not only important to the typical organization but are possibly the difference between surviving and not surviving in a competitive marketplace.

short-range forecasts

medium-range forecasts

long-range forecasts

Regardless of whether the subject of the forecast is sales, cash flow, GNP, or the weather, forecasts can be categorized by their time horizon. As depicted in Figure 13.1, *short-range forecasts* (up to one year, but typically a quarter) help the management make current operational decisions such as production scheduling and short-term financing. *Medium-range forecasts* (one to three years) aid in making planning decisions that have a longer lead time. For example, a computer installation may use a three-year forecast of demand to make decisions concerning hardware acquisitions necessary to satisfy that demand. *Long-range forecasts* (three or more years) are used to make decisions that affect the organization further in the future. A utility company must make long-range forecasts concerning both its demand and the availability and cost of various fuels, in order to make decisions concerning new plant and equipment.

qualitative techniques

time-series analysis

Forecasting techniques can be grouped into one of three categories: qualitative techniques, time-series analysis, and causal methods. *Qualitative techniques* use qualitative data such as the aggregate opinion of the sales force to forecast the future. *Time-series analysis* relies entirely on historical data, focusing on seasonal and cyclical variations and trend extrapolations.

FIGURE 13.1 **Forecasting time horizon**

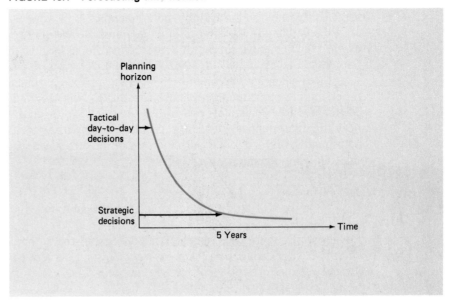

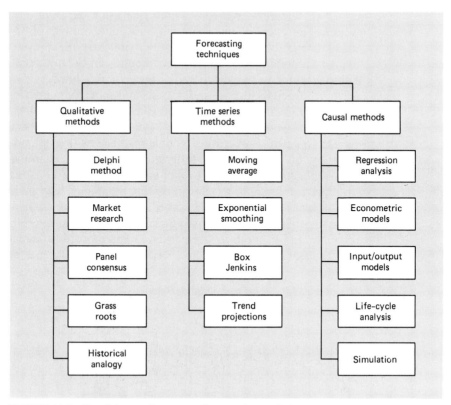

FIGURE 13.2 **Breakdown of common forecasting techniques**

causal methods *Causal methods* attempt to define relationships among independent and dependent variables in a system of related equations. Each of these three general categories can be further subdivided into individual forecasting techniques. See Figure 13.2 for a breakdown of commonly used forecasting methods. Obviously, the decision of which technique to use is dependent on the parameters of the individual forecasting problem. In this chapter, however, we attempt to indicate the comparative advantages, costs, and logical applications of the various techniques.

When selecting a forecasting technique, a decision maker must keep two types of costs in mind: cost of inaccuracy and cost of the forecast itself. The objective should be to minimize the total costs. In other words, it makes little sense to spend a large amount for a forecast of little significance to the organization. A "gut-feeling" forecast from the sales manager might be adequate. Alternatively, an important decision that is very sensitive to future conditions may warrant the expenditure of thousands of dollars to improve the forecast by only a small amount.

The selection of a forecasting technique depends on a multitude of factors. Many techniques require a substantial amount of historical data. If adequate and relevant historical data do not exist or are prohibitively expensive to accumulate, then many techniques can be automatically ruled out. Another factor to be considered is the planning horizon. Some techniques are more suited to short-term forecasts and some to long-term forecasts. The time available to make the forecast is an important consideration. If a manager needs a forecast for a current decision, he may not be able to wait six months to get it. Forecasting techniques vary as to cost and accuracy, and therefore it is important to identify the accuracy needed in the forecast and a reasonable cost for a given level of accuracy. Figure 13.3 gives some logical structure for deciding which forecasting technique is appropriate.

The first question to be asked concerns the availability of historical data. All quantitative forecasting techniques depend upon the existence of adequate and accurate historical data. Therefore, if adequate data do not exist, causal methods and time-series analysis techniques are not feasible

FIGURE 13.3 **Forecast technique decision**

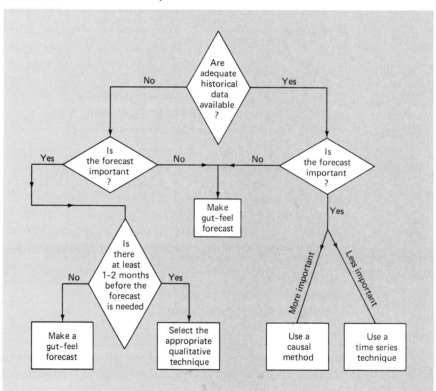

alternatives. However, even if adequate data do not exist but the forecast is important, there are qualitative techniques that can be employed that generally yield better results than a ''gut-feeling'' or ''seat-of-the-pants'' forecast. The more sophisticated qualitative techniques, however, usually take several months to implement, and therefore if the decision maker cannot wait several months, a ''gut-feeling'' forecast is the forecaster's only alternative.

If adequate historical data do exist and the forecast is an important one, a wide variety of forecasting techniques are available. These methods range from quick-and-dirty time-series techniques to very sophisticated econometric models containing hundreds of equations and hundreds of variables. The cruder and simpler methods require very little time and involve little cost. The more commonly used time-series techniques are described later in this chapter. Some causal methods can require months and even years of development and hundreds of thousands of dollars. The automobile demand forecast mentioned earlier in this chapter would be a likely candidate for a causal forecasting method such as multiple regression or econometric modeling.

QUALITATIVE TECHNIQUES

Often, data necessary to generate a forecast using either time-series analysis or some type of causal model are not available, and the manager is forced to use some kind of qualitative technique that substitutes human judgment for historical data. This situation frequently arises with the introduction of new products or services. The qualitative forecasting methods discussed in this chapter can be and often are formalized, technical procedures designed to incorporate human judgment into the forecasting process.

In this chapter, we describe five commonly used qualitative techniques:

1. The Delphi method
2. Market research
3. Panel consensus
4. Grass-roots forecasting
5. Historical analogy

Delphi method The *Delphi method* establishes a panel of experts. This panel is interrogated, using a series of questionnaires in which the answers to each questionnaire are used as input to designing the next. In this way, information is shared among the experts without the disadvantage of having individual

TABLE 13.1 *Qualitative forecasting methods*

	Delphi method	Market research	Panel consensus	Grass roots	Historical analogy
Accuracy					
Short-term	Fair to very good	Excellent	Poor to fair	Fair	Poor
Medium-term	Fair to very good	Good	Poor to fair	Poor to fair	Good to fair
Long-term	Fair to very good	Fair to good	Poor	Poor	Good to fair
Cost	$4,000 +	$10,000 +	$2,000 +	$2,000 +	$2,000 +
Time required	2 months +	3 months +	2 weeks +	2 months +	1 month +

Source: Adapted from J. S. Chambers, S. K. Mullich, and D. D. Smith, "How to Choose the Right Forecasting Technique," *Harvard Business Review*, July–August 1971. Cost figures have been arbitrarily adjusted for inflation.

experts influencing each other; in other words, the bandwagon effect of majority opinion is eliminated. As indicated in Table 13.1, the Delphi method is effective regardless of the forecast's planning horizon. The cost, however, can be rather high.

market research *Market research* is probably the most sophisticated of the qualitative techniques and also the most quantitative. "Market research" encompasses an entire family of techniques that are helpful in revealing predictions about the size, structure, and configuration of markets for various goods and services. Market researchers obtain information about markets of interest through the use of mail questionnaires, telephone surveys, panels, and personal interviews. The data obtained are then subjected to various statistical tests so that hypotheses about the market can be tested. Market research techniques are generally the most expensive form of qualitative forecasting, take the longest to implement, and if properly applied are often the most accurate.

panel consensus *Panel consensus* is a technique based on the assumption that several heads are better than one. With this technique, a panel of experts is assembled for the purpose of jointly developing a forecast. Free communication is encouraged, and the job is finished when a consensus opinion is arrived at. Obviously, the relative merit of this approach depends heavily on the configuration of the panel of experts, but it is generally considered inferior to most other qualitative methods with respect to accuracy. It can, however, be accomplished in a relatively short amount of time at a modest cost.

grass-root forecasting *Grass-roots forecasting* refers to asking the people closest to the problem to make individual forecasts for their territory. These individual forecasts are then aggregated to form the overall forecast. Sales forecasts are frequently accomplished in this way. This type of approach depends on the quality of the individual forecasts coming from the field. If done conscientiously, grass-roots forecasting can be very effective.

There are several weaknesses associated with grass-roots forecasting. These weaknesses include:

- **Opportunity cost**—It is often argued that the sales force should spend its time selling and administrative duties should be minimized. The cost of the forecast could be lost sales.
- **Lack of motivation**—If salespeople are working on a commission basis, many will lack the motivation necessary to develop a thoughtful forecast.
- **Lack of forecasting expertise**—Accurate forecasting often requires market information and specialized educational training that many salespersons lack.

historical analogy The final qualitative forecasting tool to be discussed is the *historical analogy* approach. Like other qualitative methods, this approach is used when specific data are scarce. For example, if a firm is introducing a new product that has strong similarities to an established product, it may use sales data relevant to the established product to predict the relative success or failure of the new product for which no data exist. This technique, while having a modest cost, is dependent on the availability of several years of data on the model product or service. Historical analogy forecasts seem to perform better for medium- and long-range planning horizons than for short range.

TIME-SERIES ANALYSIS

A time series is a set of raw data arranged chronologically; monthly sales is a good example. Time-series analysis is commonly used when several years of data exist and when trends are both clear and relatively stable. Because time-series analysis is totally dependent upon historical data, its implicit assumption is that the past is a good guide to the future. Consequently, time-series analysis performs better in the short-term than in the long-term forecast. In addition, time-series analysis cannot predict turning points in trend. For example, typical seasonally adjusted sales for a textbook like this one over a four-year period might behave as shown in Figure 13.4. If our historical data were limited to 1986 and 1987 sales data, we might project sales to be 8,000 copies per quarter by 1989 when in fact sales dropped to 2,000. A turning point in sales was caused by the existence of the used-book market, and mere time-series analysis does an extremely poor job of predicting turning points in trend. If the data exist, however, most time-series analysis techniques are extremely inexpensive, and projections can be produced on a computer in a matter of seconds.

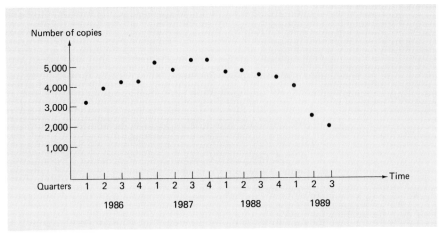

FIGURE 13.4 **Sales time series**

A time series is composed of four basic elements: *a trend component, a seasonal component, a cyclical component,* and *an erratic or random component.* Trend refers to long-term growth or decay. A seasonal fluctuation in the forecasted variable recurs regularly at periodic intervals. Many products experience seasonal fluctuations with respect to demand. Cyclical fluctuations about trend are explainable fluctuations but differ from seasonal fluctuations in that their length of time and amplitude are not as constant. Finally, if a forecaster could precisely measure trend, seasonality, and the cyclical factor, there would still be an unexplained variation between the forecast and reality. This unexplained variation is usually referred to as the erratic or random component in a time series.

In this chapter, we discuss four common types of time-series forecasting techniques:

1. Moving average
2. Exponential smoothing
3. Trend projection
4. Box-Jenkins method

Simple Moving Average

The simple-moving-average forecasting method simply eliminates the effects of seasonal, cyclical, and erratic fluctuations by averaging the historical data points. Therefore, if seasonality, trend, and cyclical factors are not critical in the variable being forecast, the moving-average method is of some value. The effect of the simple-moving-average technique can be seen in Figure 13.5.

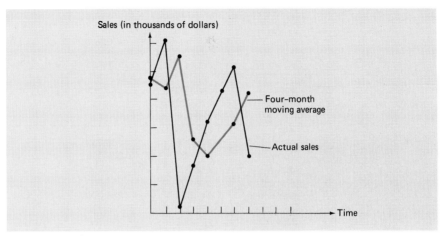

FIGURE 13.5 **Sales forecast using simple moving average**

To compute a simple moving average, simply choose the number of points in the time-series data to include in the average. Then, as each time period evolves, add the new time-period data and subtract the oldest time-period data, and calculate a new average.

Mathematically, then,

$$F_t = \frac{\sum\limits_{i=1}^{N} S_{t-i}}{N} \qquad (13.1)$$

where

$$F_t = \text{forecast for time period } t$$
$$S_{t-i} = \text{actual sales for period } t - i$$
$$N = \text{number of time periods used in the averaging process}$$

For example, let us calculate the moving average for the sales data contained in Table 13.2, using a four-month moving average.

Since our data go back only to January 1987, our first possible sales forecast using a four-month moving average is for May 1987. The forecast for May 1987 can be computed as follows:

$$F_5 = \frac{S_1 + S_2 + S_3 + S_4}{4}$$
$$= \$238,250$$

TABLE 13.2 *Sales data for time-series analysis*

Year	Month	Sales	Simple four-month moving-average forecast
1987	January	$250,000	
	February	210,000	
	March	223,000	
	April	270,000	
	May	245,000	$238,250
	June	261,000	237,000
	July	212,000	249,750
	August	226,000	247,000
	September	241,000	236,000
	October	252,000	235,000
	November	261,000	232,750
	December	229,000	245,000
1988	January	247,000	245,750
	February	255,000	247,250
	March	271,000	248,000
	April	261,000	250,500
	May	258,000	258,500
	June	265,000	261,250
	July	250,000	263,750
	August	275,000	258,500
	September	245,000	262,000
	October	260,000	258,750
	November	255,000	257,500
	December	263,000	258,750

Once May sales data are available, the forecast for June can be computed:

$$F_6 = \frac{S_2 + S_3 + S_4 + S_5}{4}$$

$$= \$237,000$$

It is obvious from Figure 13.6 that the longer the period over which the averaging takes place, the smoother the forecast function.

Weighted Moving Average

Often, it is desirable to vary the weights given to historical data to forecast future demand or sales. Past history may show that a significantly better forecast is computed when the more recent data are given heavier weight.

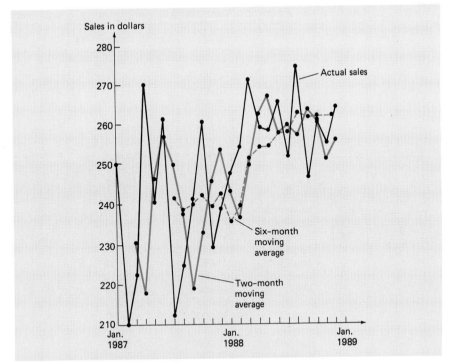

FIGURE 13.6 **Sales forecast using simple moving average**

Mathematically, the weighted moving average is computed as follows:

$$F_t = \frac{\displaystyle\sum_{i=1}^{N} W_{t-i} S_{t-i}}{\displaystyle\sum_{i=1}^{N} W_{t-i}} \qquad (13.2)$$

where

F_t = forecast for time period t
S_{t-i} = actual sales for time period $t - i$
N = number of time periods used in the averaging process
W_{t-i} = weight given to the $t - i$th period in the averaging process

For example, assume that a weight of 50 is assigned to the most recent month, a weight of 25 to the next most recent month, and weights of 15 and 10 to the next two months, respectively. Using the data in Table 13.2, the four-month weighted moving average for May 1987 is computed (in thou-

TABLE 13.3 *Four-month weighted moving average*

Year	Month	Actual sales	Four-month weighted moving-average
1987	January	$250,000	
	February	210,000	
	March	223,000	
	April	270,000	
	May	245,000	$247,250
	June	261,000	244,450
	July	212,000	254,550
	August	226,000	235,000
	September	241,000	229,650
	October	252,000	234,900
	November	261,000	241,350
	December	229,000	252,250
1988	January	247,000	241,650
	February	255,000	245,100
	March	271,000	249,700
	April	261,000	259,200
	May	258,000	261,200
	June	265,000	260,400
	July	250,000	263,250
	August	275,000	256,050
	September	245,000	265,550
	October	260,000	255,250
	November	255,000	257,500
	December	263,000	256,750

FIGURE 13.7 **Simple moving average versus weighted moving average**

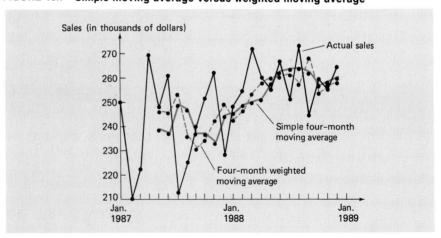

sands) as follows:

$$F_5 = \frac{(50)(270) + (25)(223) + (15)(210) + (10)(250)}{100}$$

$$= \$247,250$$

The data shown in Table 13.3 are plotted in Figure 13.7.

The major advantages of the moving-average technique are its simplicity, low cost, and the little time necessary to implement. In general, however, the moving-average technique does a poor job for long-range and medium-range forecasts. For "quick-and-dirty" short-term forecasts that do not require a great deal of accuracy, a moving-average forecast may be a workable alternative to other forecasting methods.

Exponential Smoothing

Exponential smoothing refers to a family of forecasting models that are very similar to the weighted moving average. The simplest exponential smoothing model is of the following form:

$$F_t = F_{t-1} + \alpha(A_{t-1} - F_{t-1}) \tag{13.3}$$

where

$$F_t = \text{forecast for time period } t$$
$$A_{t-1} = \text{actual value of variable being forecast in period } t - 1$$
$$\alpha = \text{smoothing constant}$$

The value of α, which can range from 0 to 1, determines the degree of smoothing that takes place and how responsive the model is to fluctuation in the forecast variable. The setting of α is typically not a scientific process and is usually done by trial and error. Let us assume an α of .15 and a January 1988 forecast of 250 units. The actual January demand turned out to be 260 units. The forecast for February could be computed as follows:

$$F_t = 250 + (.15)(260 - 250)$$
$$= 250 + 1.5$$
$$= 251.5 \text{ units}$$

Given the forecasts in Table 13.4, let us compare the effect of different smoothing constants by looking at Figure 13.8.

Other exponential smoothing models exist that compensate for the various components of a times series such as the seasonal or trend compo-

TABLE 13.4 *Effects of various smoothing constants*

	Actual demand	*Forecast: $\alpha = .05$*	*Forecast: $\alpha = .25$*	*Forecast: $\alpha = .4$*
January	250	250	250	250
February	210	250.500	252.500	254.000
March	223	248.475	241.875	236.400
April	270	247.201	237.156	231.040
May	245	248.341	245.367	246.624
June	261	248.174	245.275	245.974
July	212	248.815	249.207	251.985
August	226	246.975	239.905	235.991
September	241	245.926	236.429	231.994
October	252	245.680	237.572	235.597
November	261	245.996	241.179	242.158
December	229	246.746	246.134	249.695

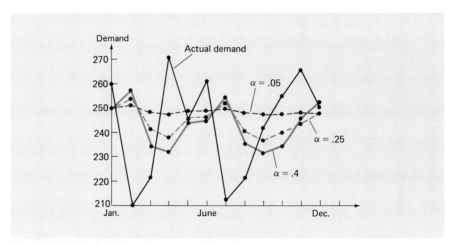

FIGURE 13.8 **Effect of various smoothing constants**

nent. To illustrate more complex exponential smoothing models, let us consider a model that has an adjustment for trend built into it. If trend exists in either a positive or a negative form, there will be a lag using the simple exponential smoothing model just described (see Figure 13.9). The basic idea behind the trend-adjusted model is to calculate a simple, exponentially smoothed forecast as described above and adjust the forecast for a trend lag.

Mathematically, the trend-adjusted model can be described as follows:

$$F'_t = F_t + \frac{1 - \beta}{\beta} T_t \tag{13.4}$$

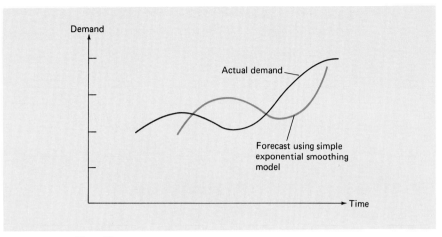

FIGURE 13.9 Trend lag

where

F'_t = trend-adjusted forecast for time period t
F_t = simple exponential smoothing forecast for time period t
β = trend smoothing factor
T_t = exponentially smoothed trend for time period t

T_t is computed using the formula

$$T_t = T_{t-1} + \beta(t_t - T_{t-1}) \qquad (13.5)$$

where $t_t = F_t - F_{t-1}$.

To compute a trend-adjusted forecast is a four-step process:

1. Compute a simple forecast for time period t (F_t).
2. Compute t_t by finding the difference between F_t and F_{t-1}.

$$t_t = F_t - F_{t-1}$$

3. Calculate the exponentially smoothed trend.

$$T_t = T_{t-1} + \beta(t_t - T_{t-1})$$

4. Finally, calculate a trend-adjusted forecast by using the formula

$$F'_t = F_t + \frac{1 - \beta}{\beta} T_t$$

TABLE 13.5 *Time-series data in which trend is present*

Period	Demand
1	12
2	17
3	19
4	16
5	22
6	24
7	30
8	29
9	33
10	34
11	37
12	38

Let us illustrate how to compute a trend-adjusted, exponentially smoothed forecast using the demand data in Table 13.5 and smoothing constants α and β, equal to .3 and .25, respectively. Let the initial forecast be 11.5. The trend-adjusted forecast for period 2 is computed as follows:

The first step is to compute F_2:

$$
\begin{aligned}
F_2 &= F_1 + \alpha(A_1 - F_1) \\
&= 11.5 + .3(12 - 11.5) \\
&= 11.65
\end{aligned}
$$

The next step is to calculate t_2:

$$
\begin{aligned}
t_2 &= F_2 - F_1 \\
&= 11.65 - 11.50 \\
&= .15
\end{aligned}
$$

T_2 can now be calculated, assuming the initial trend adjustment is 0:

$$
\begin{aligned}
T_2 &= T_1 + \beta(t_2 - T_1) \\
&= 0 + .25(.15) \\
&= .0375
\end{aligned}
$$

Finally, the trend-adjusted forecast for time period 2 can be computed:

$$
\begin{aligned}
F'_2 &= F_2 + \frac{1 - .25}{.25} T_2 \\
&= 11.65 + 3(.0375) \\
&= 11.7625
\end{aligned}
$$

TABLE 13.6 *Trend-adjusted forecasts*

Time period	Actual demand	F_t	t_t	T_t	F_t'
1	12	11.5000	0	0	11.5000
2	17	11.6500	.15000	.03750	11.7625
3	19	13.2550	1.60500	.42938	14.5431
4	16	14.9785	1.72350	.75291	17.2372
5	22	15.2850	3.06450	.64130	17.2089
6	24	17.2995	2.01450	.98460	20.2533
7	30	19.3096	2.01010	1.24098	23.0325
8	29	22.5167	3.20710	1.73251	27.7142
9	33	24.4617	1.94500	1.78563	29.8186
10	34	27.0232	2.56150	1.97960	32.9620
11	37	29.1162	2.09300	2.00795	35.1401
12	38	31.4814	2.36520	2.09726	37.7732

Doing the same calculations for the remaining time periods for the time-series data shown in Table 13.5 results in the trend-adjusted forecasts reflected in Table 13.6. Figure 13.10 graphically contrasts the unadjusted and adjusted forecasts for the time series in Table 13.6.

Generally, exponential smoothing is considered superior to the moving-average methods previously discussed. Its cost is equivalent and its accuracy, especially in the short term, is usually better. Owing to their relatively small computational cost and computer storage requirements, exponential-smoothing models are probably the most widely used of the time-series techniques. For longer-term forecasts, however, exponential smoothing is considered a poor technique.

FIGURE 13.10 **Time-series forecast with and without trend adjustment**

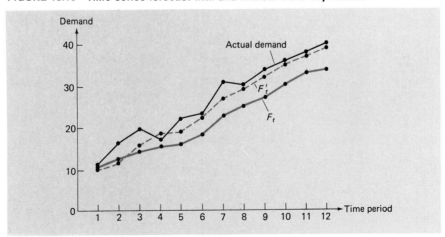

In addition to providing a more accurate forecast when trend exists in the data, the trend-adjusted exponential-smoothing model has the advantage of providing a forecast for more than one time period into the future. To calculate a forecast for n periods into the future use the following formula:

$$F'_{t+n} = F_t + nT_t$$

To illustrate, let us calculate a demand for time period 18 using the data in Table 13.6,

$$F'_{18} = F_{12} + nT_{12} = 31.4814 + 6(2.09726)$$
$$= 44.0650$$

Trend Projection

Trend projection using a technique called least squares is a special case of a category of causal forecasting methods called regression analysis. The basic idea in trend projection using least squares is to fit a function to a set of time-series data in which the independent variable is time and the dependent variable is the variable to be forecasted, such as demand. This function can be linear or nonlinear and the basic idea and methodology are the same. In this chapter, however, we consider only linear trend projection.

Consider the scatter diagram in Figure 13.11. It is easy to imagine a straight line running through the data such that the sum of the differences between the data points and the trend line is minimized. If the equation of the trend line is a function of time, then it is a simple matter to "substitute" a future time period into the function and calculate a forecast.

Recall that the general equation for a straight line is

$$y = mx + b \qquad (13.6)$$

FIGURE 13.11   Scatter diagram

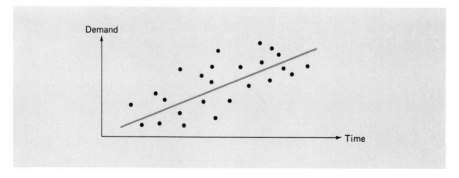

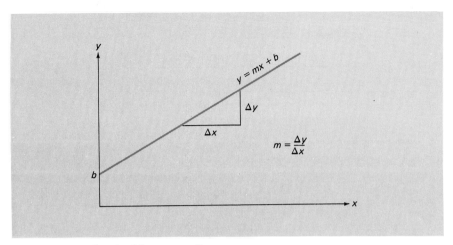

FIGURE 13.12 **Graph of linear equation**

where

$$y = \text{dependent variable}$$
$$b = y \text{ intercept}$$
$$m = \text{slope of the line}$$
$$x = \text{independent variable}$$

See Figure 13.12 for a graphical interpretation of a straight line.

Now, if we define x as time and y as demand, and b (the y intercept) and m (slope of the line) are known, demand can be computed by merely letting x assume a value. For example, assume that the linear function is

$$y = 150x + 5{,}000$$

If 1989 is the tenth time period in the time series, the demand forecast for 1989 can be forecast, substituting 10 into the equation:

$$y = 150(10) + 5{,}000$$
$$= 6{,}500 \text{ units}$$

Now let us turn to the method of deriving the "best fit" linear equation for a set of time-series data. It is possible to find a line that provides a good fit of the data by merely "eyeballing" the scatter diagram and superimposing a line on it. Then, relying on the accuracy of the graph, a y intercept (b) can be read, and the slope of the line can be calculated as $\Delta y / \Delta x$.

TABLE 13.7 *Historical demand data*

x Time period	y Demand (units)
1	1,200
2	1,700
3	1,900
4	1,600
5	2,200
6	2,400
7	3,000
8	2,900
9	3,300
10	3,400
11	3,700
12	3,800

A more accurate way to find the linear equation that best fits the data is to solve the following equations simultaneously for b and m.

$$\sum_{i=1}^{n} y_i = nb + m \sum_{i=1}^{n} x_i \tag{13.7}$$

$$\sum_{i=1}^{n} x_i y_i = b \sum_{i=1}^{n} x_i + m \sum_{i=1}^{n} x_i^2 \tag{13.8}$$

where

y_i = dependent variable for the ith time period
n = number of historical time periods
x_i = independent variable for the ith time period

normal Equations 13.7 and 13.8 are called *normal equations* and are derived using
equation the differential calculus. To illustrate how the simple linear regression equation is found, let us use the data in Table 13.7.

dependent/ The *dependent variable* (y) is demand, whereas the time period is the
independent *independent variable.* Looking at equations (13.7) and (13.8), it is clear that
variable several sums are required. These values are computed in Table 13.8.

Substituting the appropriate sums into the two normal equations, we have the following two equations with two unknowns, b and m:

$$31,100 = 12b + 78m \tag{13.9}$$
$$236,300 = 78b + 650m \tag{13.10}$$

TABLE 13.8 *Least-squares calculations*

x_i	y_i	x_iy_i	x_i^2
1	1,200	1,200	1
2	1,700	3,400	4
3	1,900	5,700	9
4	1,600	6,400	16
5	2,200	11,000	25
6	2,400	14,400	36
7	3,000	21,000	49
8	2,900	23,200	64
9	3,300	29,700	81
10	3,400	34,000	100
11	3,700	40,700	121
12	3,800	45,600	144
$\sum_{i=1}^{12} x_i = 78$	$\sum_{i=1}^{12} y_i = 31{,}000$	$\sum_{i=1}^{12} x_iy_i = 236{,}300$	$\sum_{i=1}^{12} x_i^2 = 650$

If we multiply both sides of equation (13.9) by 6.5 and subtract it from equation (13.10), the b terms will be eliminated:

$$
\begin{aligned}
236{,}300 &= 78b + 650m \\
-202{,}150 &= -78b - 507m \\
\hline
34{,}150 &= 143m \\
m &= 238.811
\end{aligned}
$$

Solving for b by substituting m into equation (13.9), we find

$$31{,}100 = 12b + 78(238.811)$$
$$b = 1{,}039.4$$

Therefore, the "best fit" linear forecasting equation is

$$y = 238.811x + 1{,}039.4 \qquad (13.11)$$

trend extrapolation Once this equation has been derived, *trend extrapolation* is a mechanical procedure. If a prediction for the fourteenth time period is desired, simply set x equal to 14 and solve for y using equation (13.11). The forecast for time period 14 is therefore

$$
\begin{aligned}
y_{14} &= 238.811(14) + 1{,}039.4 \\
&= 4{,}382.754
\end{aligned}
$$

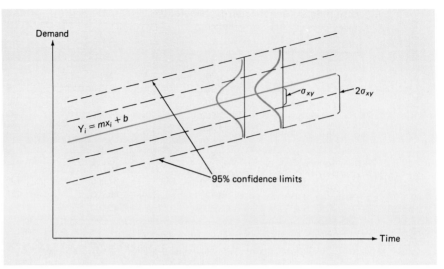

FIGURE 13.13   **Least-squares differences**

standard If we compute a *standard error of estimate* to determine how well the
error of regression line fits the data, it is possible that more information about a
estimate forecast can be obtained (see Figure 13.13). The standard error can be defined mathematically as

$$s_{yx} = \sqrt{\dfrac{\sum\limits_{i=1}^{n} (y_i - Y_i)^2}{n - 2}}$$

where

y_i = dependent variable for time period i (in our example, demand)
Y_i = value for the dependent variable obtained from the regression equation
n = number of historical time periods

To compute the standard error of estimate, we merely do the computation necessary to complete Table 13.9, using the data in Table 13.7 and the regression equation (13.11).

If we assume that demand is normally distributed around the regression line as depicted in Figure 13.13 and want 95.5 percent of the demand values to fall within our prediction interval, the prediction interval can be calculated as follows:

$$\text{prediction interval for } Y_i = Y_i \pm 2s_{yx}$$

TABLE 13.9 *Standard error computation*

x_i	y_i	Y_i	$y_i - Y_i$	$(y_i - Y_i)^2$
1	1,200	1,278.21	−78.211	6,116.96
2	1,700	1,517.02	182.978	33,480.90
3	1,900	1,755.83	144.167	20,784.10
4	1,600	1,994.64	−394.644	15,743.88
5	2,200	2,233.45	−33.455	1,119.24
6	2,400	2,472.27	−72.266	5,222.37
7	3,000	2,711.08	288.923	83,476.50
8	2,900	2,949.89	−49.888	2,488.81
9	3,300	3,188.70	111.301	12,387.90
10	3,400	3,427.51	−27.510	756.80
11	3,700	3,666.32	33.679	1,134.28
12	3,800	3,905.13	−105.132	11,052.70
				333,765.00

$$s_{yx} = \sqrt{\frac{333,765}{10}}$$
$$= 182.692$$

where

$$Y_i = \text{regression equation value}$$
$$s_{yx} = \text{standard error of estimate}$$

In our example,

$$\text{prediction interval for } Y_{14} = 4,382.754 \pm 2(182.692)$$
$$= 4,382.754 \pm 365.384$$

or

$$4,017.37 \le Y_{14} \le 4,748.14$$

Remember that we calculated Y_i and s_{yx} using historical data, and to say we are 95.5 percent confident that demand for time period 14 will fall between 4,017 and 4,748 units is to assume that the future is going to behave like the past. Also, a sample size of 12 is too small to assume normality, and a student's t distribution should be used when the sample size is small.

Simple linear regression using time period as the independent variable often outperforms both moving-average and exponential-smoothing techniques with regard to forecast accuracy. Usually, very good short-term forecasts can be derived using trend projections, and occasionally, good long-term forecasts can be based on least-squares trend projections. If the historical data are available, the cost of the forecast is minimal and the time required to derive the forecast is often less than one day.

Box-Jenkins Method

You should be aware that there is another widely used time-series technique available referred to as the Box-Jenkins method. Box-Jenkins is often the most accurate time-series forecasting technique available. Unfortunately, it is a more expensive technique to develop and requires at least 50 data points and a computer to implement. Because of its mathematical sophistication, it requires considerable expertise and the proper computer software to build forecasting models using the Box-Jenkins method. However, some relatively inexpensive expert systems versions of the Box-Jenkins method are available for usage on a personal computer. Because the quality of Box-Jenkins forecast is often superior to other time-series methods, the methodology should be considered for those forecasts that are considered important.

Adaptive Forecasting

In general, time-series methods such as those discussed in this section provide fairly accurate and very inexpensive short-term forecasts. It is therefore very common for one or more of these techniques to be integrated into computerized multiproduct inventory systems such as IBM's IMPACT system. In automated multiproduct inventory systems in which forecasts are automatically generated using a time-series technique such as exponential smoothing, it is necessary to consistently monitor the forecasting process to report to management when the forecast and actual demand for a time period differ significantly. This discrepancy may be due to keypunch errors, extraordinary market conditions, or the unsatisfactory performance of the forecasting technique. Whatever the reason, management must be alerted through some type of exception reporting that there is a need to investigate a product's forecast versus its demand and take the appropriate corrective action.

Later in this chapter we will describe the measurement of forecast error and the commonly used methods for tracking the forecast accuracy so that management can be notified when the forecast error for a particular forecast exceeds specified limits.

In this section we have explored only a small subset of the time-series forecasting techniques that have been developed and are currently being used in practice. In fact, there are so many time-series techniques available that many computer-based systems that have forecasting modules imbedded in them do not rely on any single technique. Rather, the system might have 10 to 20 different time-series forecasting techniques, and the system analyzes the accuracy of each technique and chooses that technique with the

adaptive smallest forecast error. When such flexibility is built into a computer-based
forecasting system, the forecasting is referred to as *adaptive forecasting*. Adaptive forecasting is especially useful in large-scale inventory control systems where
demand must be forecast for each inventory item before a reorder decision
can be made. If an item has reached its reorder point, the adaptive forecasting module typically forecasts historical demand using a variety of techniques, calculates the forecast error for each technique, and picks the technique with the smallest forecast error. The chosen technique is used to
forecast demand for the future time period in question. Naturally, adaptive
forecasting takes more CPU runtime, and those designing these types of
systems must weigh this increased computer cost against the benefits of the
more accurate forecasts that adaptive forecasting generally provides. As the
cost of computers continues to decline, adaptive forecasting will become
increasingly cost effective.

CAUSAL METHODS

When a particular forecast is of vital importance to an organization and
adequate historical data exist, it is often advisable to develop a causal forecasting model in which the variable to be forecast is a function of several or
many causal variables. Sales may be a function of price, advertising budget,
competitors' actions, quality-control budget, disposable personal income, or
other independent variables. If the relationship between these independent
variables can be adequately defined mathematically, superior forecasts can
result. Causal models are the most sophisticated type of forecasting model
and generally require more data, more time, and substantially more money
than the time series approaches discussed earlier.

There are three predominant causal forecasting methods:

◻ Multiple regression models
◻ Econometric models
◻ Computer simulation

Multiple Regression Models

According to a number of surveys, multiple regression is one of the most
widely used of all quantitative techniques. In addition, its use is spreading
very rapidly because of advances made in computer software and the increased emphasis being placed on quantitative techniques in business school
curricula.

Multiple linear regression analysis is a simple extension of simple linear regression. The difference is that instead of one independent variable in
the regression equation, there are several or many independent variables.

The general form of a multiple linear regression equation is

$$Y = \sum_{i=1}^{n} a_i x_i + b$$

where

a_i = coefficient of independent variable x_i
b = constant
x_i = independent variable
Y = forecast variable
n = number of independent variables

As indicated earlier, the proper application of multiple regression requires a strong statistical background, which is beyond the scope of this text. You are directed to the bibliography at the end of this chapter for texts that provide comprehensive coverage of regression analysis.

To gain an appreciation for this important forecasting technique, let us look at the following example.

EXAMPLE   A typewriter manufacturing firm wishes to forecast demand for 2 years' maintenance contracts for its most popular typewriter. It is felt that demand is a function of the advertising budget, the premium for a 1-year contract, the premium for a 2-year contract, and trend. Historical data for the last 10 years are available; they are shown in Table 13.10. These data were used to derive the following regression equation:

$$Y = .05085x_1 + 4.01746x_2 - 7.26361x_3 + 433.17578x_4 + 5{,}226.50$$

TABLE 13.10   *Maintenance contracts sales data*

Year	Number of two-year contracts sold	Annual advertising budget	Premium for one-year contract	Premium for two-year contract
1978	5,000	$50,000	$250	$550
1979	6,000	50,000	250	500
1980	6,500	55,000	250	550
1981	7,000	55,000	300	600
1982	6,000	45,000	300	650
1983	7,500	60,000	350	650
1984	8,000	60,000	300	650
1985	9,000	70,000	300	600
1986	10,000	75,000	325	550
1987	10,500	75,000	325	550
1988	12,000	80,000	325	500

where

Y = demand for two-year maintenance contracts
x_1 = annual advertising budget
x_2 = premium for one-year contract
x_3 = premium for two-year contract
x_4 = time period, using 1978 as time period one

To calculate a forecast for 1989, values for x_1, x_2, x_3, and x_4 must be set. If the advertising budget for 1989 is set at \$90,000, the premium for a one-year contract at \$325, and the premium for two-year contract at \$550, then forecast demand can be calculated as

$$Y = (.05085)(90{,}000) + (4.01746)(325) - (7.26361)(550) + (433.17578)(12)$$
$$+ 5{,}226.50$$
$$= 12{,}311.80 \text{ contracts}$$

FIGURE 13.14 **Steps in a regression study**

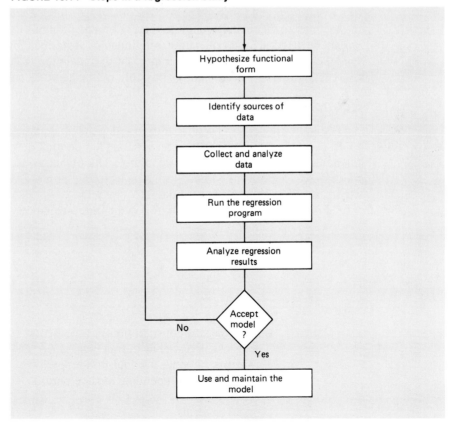

To give you a better understanding of regression analysis without developing the statistical methodology, we will describe the steps in a typical regression study. As depicted in Figure 13.14, the first step is for the analyst to hypothesize a functional form for the regression equation by specifying the independent variables he or she thinks are important in predicting the dependent variable. It should be noted that the analyst doing the regression analysis must hypothesize not only which variables should be included but should also decide whether the function is linear or nonlinear and, if nonlinear, what form it is likely to take.

Next, sources of the data necessary to estimate the equation must be identified. Third, the data have to be collected and analyzed. Often at this step "bad" data are eliminated from the data to be used in the analysis. The fourth step is to perform the regression analysis using a computer software package such as SAS or SPSS. Once the regression has been run, the analyst must use the statistical output from the run to assess the predictive quality of the regression equation and the strength of the relationship among the model's variables. If after analyzing the regression results the analyst feels that the model is not good enough, he or she can hypothesize new variables or a new functional form and repeat the analysis or turn to another forecasting technique. Once an acceptable regression equation has been developed, it can be used. However, many relationships described by a regression model change over time and it is important to update the model periodically by reestimating its parameters or possibly by changing its functional form.

Econometric Models

An econometric model is a system of interdependent equations that attempt to describe the complex relationships among factors that describe some real phenomenon such as a nation's economy. The objective of these types of models is to measure the impact of changes to one or more variables on the other variables present in the model.

For example, consider the following three-equation, eight-variable macroeconomic model:

$$C_t = x_1 I_t + x_3 Y_t + x_4 C_{t-1} + x_5 R_t + U_1$$
$$I_t = \beta_1 + \beta_2 Y_t + \beta_3 R_t + U_2$$
$$Y_t = C_t + I_t + G_t$$

where

C_t = aggregate consumption in time period t
I_t = gross investment in time period t
Y_t = gross national product in time period t
G_t = government spending in time period t
R_t = short-term interest rate
U_t = error terms

x_i = parameter estimates for first equation
β_i = parameter estimates for second equation

These equations are solved simultaneously to find the values for unknown variables C_t, I_t, and Y_t. If government economists are considering changing the level and timing of fiscal expenditure, the model could be used to estimate the effect on other key economic variables.

Econometric models are extremely expensive to develop, use, and maintain. Development cost can range from $100,000 and up because of the necessity of having highly trained model builders and large-scale computing. To run a sophisticated econometric model is expensive because of the data bases that must be maintained to run the model and the necessity to augment model results with expert judgments. Because most of the real phenomena being modeled econometrically are dynamic, constant model maintenance from highly skilled people is an absolute necessity. Because of the expense associated with econometric models, only governments and a few large companies are utilizing this extremely powerful class of forecasting model.

Simulation Models

Computer simulation is often used to forecast a variety of phenomena. Simulation is very common for predicting cash flows, operating income and balance sheet performance. These types of simulation result in pro forma financial statements. Other types of system behavior can be predicted with the use of digital simulation. A good example of such an application was developed by the Federal Aviation Administration (FAA). The FAA developed, with the help of several contractors, a large-scale simulation model that successfully models the airspace and groundside of an airport. When properly applied, the model successfully predicts arrival rates of aircraft, taxi times, and on-time performance for each airline operating at an airport. The model has been used to design the airspace for the air traffic control system and runway and taxi way configurations for the airport board at a number of airports. It has also been used to forecast on-time performance of different proposed airline schedules.

Of all the forecasting tools described in this chapter, simulation and econometric modeling are the most expensive to use, and consequently both tools are often considered tools of last resort. Computer simulation will be treated in more detail in Chapter 15.

FORECAST ERROR

By their inherent nature all forecasts are wrong, and it should be obvious that building a forecast model devoid of error is impossible regardless of the sophistication of the technique being used. The objective of any forecasting activity should be to provide a forecast with a sufficient degree of accuracy at the least possible cost. It is often more important to measure and track the forecast error than to maximize the accuracy of the forecast. This section describes the most commonly used methods for measuring and tracking forecast error.

Measurement of Forecast Error

The two most common methods for measuring the error in a forecast are the mean absolute deviation (MAD) and the mean squared error (MSE). The mean absolute deviation is simply the average of the absolute differences between the forecast and the actual variable (see Table 13.11). Mathematically,

$$\text{MAD} = \frac{\sum_{t=1}^{n} |A_t - F_t|}{n} \tag{13.11}$$

where

$$A_t = \text{actual for time period } t$$
$$F_t = \text{forecast for time period } t$$
$$n = \text{number of time periods}$$

Let us illustrate how to calculate the MAD using the data in Table 13.11. The MAD for Table 13.11 data is:

$$\text{MAD} = 2{,}452/6$$
$$= 408.7$$

If we assume that the MAD of a forecast is normally distributed, then we can estimate the probability that the MAD will fall within a specific

TABLE 13.11   *MAD calculation*

Month	Actual demand	Forecast demand	$|A_t - F_t|$
1	2150	2500	350
2	3210	2465	745
3	2622	2540	82
4	2475	2548	73
5	2910	2541	369
6	3412	2579	833
			2452

TABLE 13.12 *Confidence interval for MADs*

Range of MAD	Relative frequency of MADs falling within the range
±1	.5705
±2	.8895
±3	.9833
±4	.9986

confidence interval. It can be shown that 1 MAD = .8 standard deviations. Using the foregoing relationship, we can compute the relative frequency of MADs falling within specified ranges. See Table 13.12.

The mean squared error is defined as the average of the squared forecast errors. Mathematically,

$$MSE = \frac{\sum\limits_{t=1}^{n} (A_t - F_t)^2}{n}$$

where

$$A_t = \text{actual for time period } t$$
$$F_t = \text{forecast for time period t}$$
$$n = \text{number of time periods}$$

Using the same data we used for the MAD calculation seen in Table 13.11, we find

$$MSE = \frac{1,519,628}{6}$$
$$= 253,271$$

TABLE 13.13 *MSE calculation*

Month	Actual demand	Forecast demand	$(A_t - F_t)$	$(A_t - F_t)^2$
1	2,150	2,500	−350	122,500
2	3,250	2,465	745	555,025
3	2,622	2,540	82	6,724
4	2,475	2,548	−73	5,329
5	2,910	2,541	369	136,161
6	3,412	2,579	833	693,889
				1,519,628

When analyzing the comparative merits of several different forecasting models, both measures (MAD and MSE) are often used. The choice of which measure to use is up to the user of the forecast. It is possible that model A could outperform model B as measured by MAD and underperform model B if measured by MSE. Large forecast errors are magnified using MSE, and therefore, if the decision maker wants to avoid large forecast errors he or she may choose MSE as the measure of forecast error when comparing models.

Tracking of Forecast Error

A tracking signal is often used to identify those forecasts which are failing to keep pace with either a positive or negative trend. A tracking signal is defined mathematically in equation (13.12).

$$TS_n = \frac{\sum_{t=1}^{n} d_t}{\text{MAD}_n} \qquad (13.12)$$

where

$$TS_n = \text{tracking signal for time period } n$$
$$d_t = \text{forecast error } (A_t - F_t) \text{ in time period } t$$
$$\text{MAD}_n = \text{mean absolute deviation as of time period } n$$

To illustrate the calculation of the tracking signal, let us calculate the tracking signal for the fifth month in Table 13.14.

$$TS_5 = \frac{(-350 + 745 + 82 - 73 + 369)}{323.8}$$
$$= 2.39$$

Most automated forecasting systems have a tracking signal designed into the system. This tracking signal is used by those responsible for the forecast to signal when the forecasting technique is not keeping up with growth or delay in the forecasted variable. If management were to choose a critical level of 3.0 for the tracking signal, then the system would flag the item in Table 13.14 in June (month 6). If the critical value were set at 4.0, then the item would be included in an exception report for the month of July. Where to set the critical value for a tracking signal depends on the importance of the forecast. If the forecast is important management may want to establish a fairly low critical level (e.g., 2 or 3). However, if it is of little importance a low critical level would be inappropriate because it would indicate a need for investigation and corrective action which may not be cost justified.

TABLE 13.14 *Tracking signal calculation*

Month	Actual demand	Forecast demand	Actual deviation $A_t - F_t$	Absolute deviation $|A_t - F_t|$	MAD	Tracking signal
1	2150	2500	−350	350	350.0	−1.00
2	3210	2465	745	745	547.5	.72
3	2622	2540	82	82	392.3	1.22
4	2475	2548	−73	73	312.5	1.29
5	2910	2541	369	369	323.8	2.39
6	3412	2579	833	833	408.7	3.93
7	3310	2662	648	648	442.9	5.09
8	3570	2727	843	843	492.9	6.28
9	3771	2811	960	960	544.8	7.45
10	3621	2907	714	714	561.7	8.49
11	3924	2978	946	946	596.6	9.58
12	4150	3073	1077	1077	636.7	10.67

COMPUTER IMPLICATIONS

The computer is extremely important when it comes to forecasting. With time-series models the computer can be useful in evaluating the type of model that best fits the data and in finding the model parameters such as the smoothing constant that provides the best model. Once the time-series model has been chosen and its parameters are set, the model is usually imbedded into some type of computer-based system. In some progressive computer-based systems, several models are available for the system to choose from based on minimizing an approproate measure for forecast error.

The computer is even more essential when forecasting with causal models. In fact, the computer is a necessary tool in developing the three types of causal models discussed in this chapter, regression analysis, econometric models and simulation models. Fortunately, high-level computer languages such as those reflected in Table 13.15 have been developed to facilitate the development of these types of models. Once a causal model has been developed, the computer (with the possible exception of some regression equations) is a necessary vehicle for solving the forecasting model.

TABLE 13.15 *Causal forecasting tools*

Type of causal model	Software package/language
Regression models	SAS, SPSS, BMD
Econometric models	Chase model, Wharton model
Simulation models	GPSS, IFPS, SLAM II, SIMSCRIPT II.5, Lotus 1-2-3

SUMMARY

Surveys have shown that forecasting techniques are the most widely used of all quantitative techniques in business. This is not surprising when one looks at the importance of a good forecast to the health of an organization in business or the public sector. Almost all managerial decisions are based on forecasted information. In a business firm, financial decisions, marketing decisions, production decisions, and personnel decisions are all based on the firm's outlook of the future. Policy decisions of governments and nonprofit organizations are equally dependent on quality forecasts.

In this chapter, we have described the major forecasting methods and indicated areas of applicability. We divided forecasting methods into three categories: qualitative methods, time-series analysis techniques, and causal methods. In general, qualitative techniques are used when quantitative historical data are not available. Time-series analysis techniques are used when the importance of the forecast is not great enough to justify the use of more expensive causal methods. Causal methods are used when their extra cost and time of implementation can be justified by the importance to the organization of the forecast accuracy. To be effective, a forecasting system needs a way to track forecast errors so that management can be alerted when a forecast error starts to exceed acceptable limits. In automated systems, this tracking signal is usually calculated using the MAD or MSE.

SOLVED PROBLEMS

PROBLEM STATEMENT

For the demand data in Table 13.16, calculate the four-quarter moving average for the fourth quarter of 1988 and the first quarter of 1989.

SOLUTION

$$\frac{\text{forecast for the}}{\text{fourth quarter of 1988}} = \frac{50,000 + 65,000 + 75,000 + 80,000}{4}$$

$$= 67,500 \text{ units}$$

$$\frac{\text{forecast for the}}{\text{first quarter of 1989}} = \frac{65,000 + 75,000 + 80,000 + 100,000}{4}$$

$$= 80,000 \text{ units}$$

TABLE 13.16 *Calculator demand*

Time period	TI-53 calculator demand (units)
1st quarter 1985	1,000
2nd quarter 1985	2,500
3rd quarter 1985	3,000
4th quarter 1985	4,000
1st quarter 1986	10,000
2nd quarter 1986	12,000
3rd quarter 1986	15,000
4th quarter 1986	14,000
1st quarter 1987	20,000
2nd quarter 1987	25,000
3rd quarter 1987	40,000
4th quarter 1987	50,000
1st quarter 1988	65,000
2nd quarter 1988	75,000
3rd quarter 1988	80,000
4th quarter 1988	100,000

PROBLEM STATEMENT

Using a weighted five-quarter moving average with the weights as shown, calculate the forecast for the first quarter of 1989 for Table 13.16 data.

	Period	Weight
Oldest data	1	.05
	2	.10
	3	.15
	4	.25
Most recent data	5	.45

SOLUTION

The forecast for the first quarter of 1989 is computed as follows:

$$F = \frac{\begin{array}{c}(.05)(50,000) + (.1)(65,000) + (.15)(75,000) \\ + (.25)(80,000) + (.45)(100,000)\end{array}}{1.00}$$

$$= 85,250 \text{ units}$$

PROBLEM STATEMENT

Using a simple exponential smoothing model, calculate the forecast for the first quarter of 1989, given that the forecast for the last quarter of 1988 was 80,250 units. Use $\alpha = .15$.

SOLUTION

The exponentially smoothed forecast for the first quarter of 1989 is computed as follows:

$$F_t = F_{t-1} + \alpha(A_{t-1} - F_{t-1})$$
$$= 80,250 + .15(100,000 - 80,250)$$
$$= 83,212.5 \text{ units}$$

PROBLEM STATEMENT

Using a trend-adjusted exponential smoothing model, calculate the forecast for the first quarter of 1989. Use a smoothing factor of .15 for the simple model forecast and a smoothing factor of .1 for the trend-smoothing factor.

SOLUTION

The first step is to calculate the simple exponential-smoothing forecast for the first quarter of 1989. This was accomplished in the preceding example:

$$F_t = 80,250 + .15(100,000 - 80,250)$$
$$= 83,212.5 \text{ units}$$

The next step is to calculate t_t:

$$t_t = F_t - F_{t-1}$$
$$t_t = 83,212.5 - 80,250$$
$$= 2,962.5$$

Now we must calculate T_t, assuming that the initial trend adjustment is 0.

$$T_t = T_{t-1} + \beta(t_t - T_{t-1})$$
$$= 0 + .1(2,962.5)$$
$$= 296.25$$

Finally, the trend-adjusted forecast for the first quarter of 1989 can be computed as follows:

$$F'_t = F_t + \frac{1 - \beta}{\beta} T_t$$

$$= 83{,}212.5 + \left(\frac{1 - .1}{.1}\right) 296.25$$

$$= 83{,}212.5 + 2{,}666.25$$

$$= 85{,}878.75 \text{ units}$$

PROBLEM STATEMENT

Using the least-squares method, find the regression line for the data in Table 13.16 and calculate the forecast for the first quarter of 1989.

SOLUTION

To derive the regression equation, it is necessary to solve the following two normal equations simultaneously:

$$\sum_{i=1}^{n} y_i = nb + m \sum_{i=1}^{n} x_i$$

$$\sum_{i=1}^{n} x_i y_i = b \sum_{i=1}^{n} x_i + m \sum_{i=1}^{n} x_i^2$$

To solve the two equations simultaneously, the four sums in the two equations must first be found. This is done in Table 13.17.

Substituting these sums into the two normal equations, we get

$$516{,}500 = 16b + 136m$$
$$6{,}535{,}000 = 136b + 1{,}496m$$

To find what factor to multiply the first equation by to add it to the second to eliminate the b terms, we divide 136 by 16, getting 8.5. Therefore, if we multiply the first equation by -8.5 and add it to the second equation, we get

$$6{,}535{,}000 = 136b + 1{,}496m$$
$$\underline{-4{,}390{,}250 = -136b - 1{,}156m}$$
$$2{,}144{,}750 = 340m$$

TABLE 13.17

x_i	y_i	$x_i y_i$	y_i^2
1	1,000	1,000	1
2	2,500	5,000	4
3	3,000	9,000	9
4	4,000	16,000	16
5	10,000	50,000	25
6	12,000	72,000	36
7	15,000	105,000	49
8	14,000	112,000	64
9	20,000	180,000	81
10	25,000	250,000	100
11	40,000	440,000	121
12	50,000	600,000	144
13	65,000	845,000	169
14	75,000	1,050,000	196
15	80,000	1,200,000	225
16	100,000	1,600,000	256
136	516,500	6,535,000	1,496

Therefore,

$$m = \frac{2,144,750}{340}$$
$$= 6,308.0882$$

Once we have the value of one unknown, we can substitute it into either normal equation to find the other unknown. Hence,

$$6,535,000 = 136b + (1,496)(6,308.0882)$$
$$6,535,000 = 136b + 9,436,900$$
$$136b = -2,901,900$$
$$b = -21,337.5$$

We can now write the regression equation:

$$Y = 6,308.0882x - 21,337.5$$

To calculate first quarter 1989 demand, we merely substitute the x value corresponding to the first quarter 1989 which is 17.

$$\text{demand for first quarter 1989} = Y_{17} = (6,308.0882)(17) - 21,337.5$$
$$= 85,900 \text{ units}$$

COMPUTER SOLUTION

Regression analysis is similar to linear programming with respect to the use of the computer for a number of reasons, which include the following:

- ☐ Real problems are almost always solved using a computer because of the amount of calculations necessary.
- ☐ A number of "user-friendly" software packages are available for solving both types of problems.

This simple regression problem took less than 1 minute to input the necessary data, and the problem was solved instantaneously using a hand-held calculator.

PROBLEM STATEMENT

Management of the calculator manufacturing firm feels that in addition to time period, the demand for calculators is also a function of price. After price data for the 16 time periods were fed into a multiple regression software package on the company computer, the following regression equation was produced:

$$Y = 8,121x_1 - 1,045x_2 - 5,525$$

where

$$x_1 = \text{time period}$$
$$x_2 = \text{price}$$
$$Y = \text{demand}$$

What is the forecast for the first quarter of 1989 if the price of the TI-53 calculator is $14.95?

SOLUTION

Forecasting demand for first quarter 1989 is a mechanical procedure of substituting the multiple regression equation with values of the independent variables:

$$Y = 8,121(17) - 1,045(14.95) - 5,525$$
$$= 116,909.25 \text{ units}$$

REVIEW QUESTIONS

1. Define the three basic time horizons for forecasts.
2. List the three categories of forecasting techniques described in this chapter.
3. When are qualitative forecasting techniques most useful?
4. What is the major advantage of time-series analysis?
5. How do causal methods differ from time-series analysis?
6. What is the major disadvantage of time-series analysis?
7. Which category of forecasting technique performs best for long-term forecasts?
8. List four factors to consider in selecting the proper forecasting techniques.
9. List five commonly used qualitative forecasting techniques.
10. Define the Delphi method.
11. Which of the qualitative forecasting techniques discussed in this chapter is the most sophisticated and the most expensive?
12. Which qualitative forecasting technique is generally considered to yield the most accurate forecasts?
13. How does panel consensus differ from a "grass-roots" approach?
14. Using a historical analogy approach depends on what?
15. List three weaknesses of grass-roots forecasting.
16. What is a time series?
17. What are the four major components of a time series?
18. To what planning horizon is time-series analysis best suited?
19. Distinguish among moving average, exponential smoothing, and trend projection.
20. What is the effect of changing the smoothing constant?
21. Why is simple exponential smoothing inadequate when trend exists in time-series data?
22. Write the equation of a straight line and define each parameter and variable.
23. Why is it desirable to calculate the standard error of estimate?
24. Distinguish between simple linear regression and multiple linear regression.
25. Define adaptive forecasting.
26. What is the primary advantage and disadvantage of adaptive forecasting?
27. What are the two most common measures of forecast error?
28. What is the basic purpose of a tracking signal?

PROBLEMS

13.1 Calculate the four-year simple moving average for 1989 using the time-series data in Table 13.18.

13.2 For the data in Table 13.18, calculate a six-year weighted moving average for 1989, using the following weights:. 1, .1, .1, .2, .2, and .3 from the oldest to the most recent year.

13.3 Using an α of .25, calculate the 1989 forecast using the simple exponential-smoothing model. Use the data in Table 13.18 and assume a 1988 forecast of $500,000.

13.4 Using trial-and-error techniques, determine the best α, .10 or .25, for the data in Table 13.18. Assume a 1970 forecast of 250,000.

13.5 Again using Table 13.18 data, calculate the 1989 forecast using the trend-adjusted exponential-smoothing model. Assume $\alpha = .15$, $\beta = .20$, and a 1988 forecast of $500,000.

13.6 For Problem 13.5 find an α and β that you think do a good job of forecasting sales by using the QSB software package or by writing and running a computer search program.

13.7 Draw a scatter diagram for the time-series data of Table 13.18.

13.8 Using the method of least squares, find the regression equation for the time-series data in Table 13.18. Use the regression equation to forecast sales for 1990.

TABLE 13.18 *Time-series data*

Year	Sales
1970	$250,000
1971	262,000
1972	300,000
1973	351,000
1974	364,000
1975	365,000
1976	377,000
1977	402,000
1978	393,000
1979	400,000
1980	425,000
1981	415,000
1982	430,000
1983	440,000
1984	455,000
1985	457,000
1986	481,000
1987	492,000
1988	505,000

13.9 Find the interval estimate for the regression equation derived in Problem 13.8 corresponding to a 95.5 percent confidence level. Assume normality.

13.10 Given the data in Table 13.19, compare a 6-month moving-average forecast and a 3-month moving average forecast for the 12 months of 1988.

13.11 Choose weights for a 6-month moving average that do a better job of forecasting demand than the simple 6-month moving average calculated in Problem 13.10.

13.12 Which is the better smoothing constant for the 1988 data in Table 13.19, $\alpha = .05$ or $\alpha = .25$? Justify your answer.

13.13 By a limited search procedure, define a good trend-adjusted exponential-smoothing model for the 1988 time-series data in Table 13.19.

13.14 Use the QSB software package or write a computer program that will accomplish the search required by Problem 13.13.

TABLE 13.19 *Time-series data for Part No. 215-22000*

Year	Month	Demand
1987	January	25,450
	February	25,000
	March	25,150
	April	24,950
	May	24,500
	June	24,600
	July	24,250
	August	23,000
	September	23,100
	October	22,900
	November	22,000
	December	19,500
1988	January	19,750
	February	18,950
	March	19,150
	April	18,740
	May	18,500
	June	18,250
	July	17,475
	August	17,500
	September	17,650
	October	17,250
	November	17,100
	December	16,550

13.15 Draw a scatter diagram of the time-series data of Table 13.19 on graph paper and "eyeball" a regression line. Read the slope and intercept off the graph to construct the regression equation.

13.16 Find the simple linear regression equation for the Table 13.19 data using the least-squares method.

13.17 How do the January 1989 demand forecasts differ using the "eye-balled" equation and the least-squares equation derived in Problem 13.16?

13.18 Given a confidence level of 90 percent, what is the prediction interval for demand for February 1989?

13.19 The number of pediatric admissions for one month can be forecasted using the following regression equation:

$$Y = 5.1 + 5.72x_1 + .002x_2 + 4.16x_3$$

where

$$Y = \text{number of pediatric admissions for one month}$$
$$x_1 = \text{number of pediatricians on the hospital staff}$$
$$x_2 = \text{city population of people under age 20}$$
$$x_3 = \text{number of obstetricians on the hospital staff}$$

If the hospital has seven pediatricians and nine obstetricians and the under-20 population is 14,000, what is the monthly forecast for pediatrics admissions?

13.20 Calculate a MAD and MSE for each month of 1988 in Table 13.19 using a simple exponential-smoothing model with an α of .25. Which months during 1988 would the tracking signal alert management if the critical level were set at 3.0?

13.21 *Sales forecast.* The ACME Corporation has experienced steady growth in annual sales in its 19-year history. The firm has traditionally used a 4-year moving average to predict sales for the coming year. The new vice-president of marketing feels that a simple 4-year moving average is too "simple minded" and results in extremely poor sales forecasts. Because these inaccuracies affect many important managerial decisions, the vice-president of marketing has asked you to determine the best time-series technique for estimating sales by comparing

a. The 4-year moving average.

b. A weighted 6-year moving average using the following weights: .1, .1, .1, .2, .2, .3 from the oldest to the most recent year.

c. A simple exponential-smoothing model using an α of .25. Assume a 1971 forecast of $247,000.

    d. A trend-adjusted exponential-smoothing model using an $\alpha = .15$ and $\beta = .20$.

    e. A least-squares regression equation.

Acme Corporation annual sales

1971	$247,000
1972	251,000
1973	257,000
1974	259,000
1975	271,000
1976	275,000
1977	295,000
1978	289,000
1979	287,000
1980	305,000
1981	328,000
1982	345,000
1983	370,000
1984	387,000
1985	404,000
1986	405,000
1987	419,000
1988	417,000

13.22 *Market price forecast.* The price of ACME Corporation has varied over the past year. The price at the end of each month is reflected in the table.

Month	Price per share	Month	Price per share
1	$55\frac{1}{8}$	7	$68\frac{3}{4}$
2	$57\frac{1}{4}$	8	$69\frac{1}{8}$
3	$57\frac{1}{2}$	9	$72\frac{1}{8}$
4	$59\frac{3}{8}$	10	$72\frac{3}{8}$
5	65	11	$72\frac{1}{8}$
6	$63\frac{1}{4}$	12	$75\frac{1}{5}$

    a. Draw a scatter diagram for these data.

    b. Forecast the next month's price per share using simple linear regression.

    c. Forecast next month's price per share using a trend-adjusted exponential smoothing model with $\alpha = .2$ and $\beta = .3$. Assume $F_{12} = \$74.00$ per share and $T_{12} = 0$.

    d. Forecast price per share for month 16 using the trend-adjusted model used in part (c).

13.23 *Business failures.* The small computer service bureau business is a very volatile and risk-ridden sector of the economy. In a large southwestern city the number of service bureaus going out of business in the last three years has been extremely high. The number of failures for each quarter of the previous three years is reflected in the table.

	1986		1987		1988
Quarter	Number of failures	Quarter	Number of failures	Quarter	Number of failures
1	27	1	30	1	35
2	29	2	35	1	42
3	40	3	49	3	57
4	35	4	40	4	47

a. What is your forecast for each quarter of 1989 using only the time-series data given and a trend-adjusted exponential smoothing model with an $\alpha = .25$ and a $\beta = .15$?

b. If the data were available, what other factors do you think would have an effect on service bureau bankruptcies?

13.24 *Crime.* Crime in the streets has been increasing in the last three years at a dramatic rate, and the mayor and the city council are trying to decide on what action to take to alleviate the situation. The police chief contends that if something isn't done soon, the number of violent crimes reported in a month will reach epidemic proportions. Using simple linear regression, predict the number of violent crimes that will be committed for January, June, and December of 1989.

	Number of violent crimes		
Month	1986	1987	1988
January	12	19	35
February	11	22	32
March	14	21	37
April	13	25	38
May	13	23	41
June	15	25	40
July	16	24	45
August	15	27	38
September	18	26	47
October	17	18	49
November	18	23	48
December	20	30	55

13.25 *University enrollment.* Enrollment in the College of Business Administration at State University has been increasing in the last few years. The dean of the college is preparing a five-year plan in which he is asking the university's central administration for significant increases in human and other resources. These requested resources are based on the dean's forecast of future enrollments in the College of Business. Given semester enrollment for the last five years, what is your best estimate of full-time equivalent enrollment at the end of the next five years? Use simple linear regression. What is wrong with using a simple time-series forecast to predict enrollment at the end of 1993?

	Full-time equivalent enrollment	
Year	Semester 1	Semester 2
1984	1,077	998
1985	1,117	1,103
1986	1,353	1,297
1987	1,471	1,419
1988	1,503	1,475

13.26 For the sales data in Table 13.18, find an α and β that you think do a good job of forecasting sales by using the QSB software package or by writing and running a computer search program. Does this trend-adjusted model outperform the least-squares regression equation found in Problem 13.8?

13.27 *Demand.* ZUKON manufacturing company held a patent on its number one selling product until two years ago. Since that time, demand has been decreasing. Monthly demand for the last two years is reflected in the table.

	Demand (units)	
Month	1987	1988
January	12,150	10,002
February	12,043	10,041
March	12,220	9,679
April	11,980	9,683
May	11,570	9,555
June	11,245	9,145
July	11,247	8,512
August	11,050	8,672
September	10,550	8,444
October	10,600	8,554
November	10,243	8,312
December	10,076	8,001

a. Use the least-squares method to develop a simple linear regression equation.

b. Draw a scatter diagram and visually fit a straight line to the data.

c. Using the regression equation in part (a), forecast demand for April 1989.

d. What is your forecast for the total demand for 1989?

e. Calculate the MAD, MSE, and the tracking signal for all months of 1987 and 1988. Use the regression equation developed in part (a).

f. Fit a trend-adjusted exponential-smoothing model to the data and project June 1989 demand.

g. Compare the accuracy of the trend projection model [part (a)] and the smoothing model [part (f)] using the MAD and MSE.

13.28 Imagine that the unemployment rate in the United States for the years 1986, 1987, and 1988 has fluctuated as shown in the table. Which, if any, times-series techniques would you apply to the data to predict unemployment levels for 1989? How would you improve your forecast?

Hypothetical unemployment rates in the United States			
Quarter	1986	1987	1988
1st	7.46	10.20	10.73
2nd	8.10	11.00	10.73
3rd	8.90	11.96	10.10
4th	9.63	11.83	9.21

13.29 *Retail.* Outtasight Stores is having its quarterly buyers' planning meeting next month, and its research department must estimate the company's sales for the next three months. Research has summarized the historical data in the table on the next page.

Keeping in mind the seasonal nature of the retail clothing business, Research must select an appropriate forecasting system and then present its forecast of the first three months of 1989 to management.

1. Adjust the data for seasonal variation by first calculating a seasonal index (SI) for each month:

$$\text{SI for month } j = \frac{\text{average for month } j \text{ for the three years}}{\text{average for all months for the three years}}$$

2. Divide each month by its SI to get the seasonally adjusted sales figures.

1986	Sales (in millions of dollars)	1987	Sales (in millions of dollars)	1988	Sales (in millions of dollars)
Jan.	5.8	Jan.	6.1	Jan.	6.3
Feb.	7.0	Feb.	7.2	Feb.	8.4
Mar.	8.5	Mar.	8.8	Mar.	8.1
Apr.	8.4	Apr.	9.1	Apr.	9.6
May	6.1	May	6.7	May	6.6
Jun.	6.4	Jun.	7.0	Jun.	7.4
Jul.	6.4	Jul.	7.5	Jul.	7.8
Aug.	8.0	Aug.	8.8	Aug.	9.3
Sep.	9.1	Sep.	9.5	Sep.	9.9
Oct.	7.8	Oct.	8.3	Oct.	9.2
Nov.	9.1	Nov.	9.7	Nov.	11.1
Dec.	8.4	Dec.	9.9	Dec.	10.8

3. Find, by analytical means, the appropriate forecasting method and calculate the required projections.

4. Convert the seasonally adjusted projections back to actual projections and graph the results.

BIBLIOGRAPHY

Adam, Everett E., and Ronald J. Ebert, *Production and Operations Management,* 3rd ed. Englewood Cliffs, N.J.: Prentice Hall, 1986.

Armstrong, J. Scott, "The Ombudsman: Research on Forecasting—A Quarter Century Review, 1960–1984," *Interfaces,* 16 (January–February 1986), 89–103.

Chambers, I. S., S. K. Mullich, and D. D. Smith, "How to Choose the Right Forecasting Technique," *Harvard Business Review,* July–August 1971.

Chase, Richard B., and Nicholas J. Aquilano, *Production and Operations Management,* 4th ed. Homewood, Ill.: Richard D. Irwin, Inc., 1981.

Gaither, Norman. *Production and Operations Management,* 3rd ed. New York: Dryden Press, 1987.

Hoel, Paul G., and Raymond J. Jessen, *Basic Statistics for Business and Economics,* 3rd ed. New York: John Wiley & Sons, Inc., 1982.

Monks, Joseph G., *Operations Management: Theory and Problems,* 2nd ed. New York: McGraw-Hill Book Company, 1982.

Sullivan, William G., and W. Wayne Claycombe, *Fundamentals of Forecasting.* Reston, Va.: Reston Publishing Co., 1977.

Queuing Models

THE XEROX CORPORATION[1]

"Run off a Xerox copy . . ." is evidence of the dominant role the Xerox Corporation plays in the office copier and duplicator marketplace. A major reason for this dominance has been attributed to the service that Xerox provides to its customers. In a recent application of queuing theory, Xerox has implemented a new service strategy for the 9200 duplicator which provides better customer service at less cost to Xerox.

Until the announcement of the Model 9200 duplicating system, Xerox copying machines were "convenience" machines, which dictated a certain level of service. Because the Model 9200 is directed at the offset printing market, it was designed as a revenue-generating system. Downtime changed from being an inconvenience to the customer to a genuine loss of revenue. Because of the increased impact of an inoperable machine, Xerox found it necessary to reorganize its service organization. Prior to the Model 9200 introduction, the National Service Department of Xerox was organized according to one-person territories. Because of the change brought about by the Model 9200 introduction, the one-person territory strategy was uneconomical and had to be discarded. It was decided that miniteams of technical representatives should replace the one-person territory strategy. The critical question was: How many technical

[1] W. H. Bleuel, "Management Science's Impact on Service Strategy," *Interfaces*, 6, Part 2 (November 1975), 1–12.

representatives should comprise one team? Using analytical queuing models such as those described in this chapter, Xerox found that three-person miniteams yield the best balance between customer response times and tech rep utilization. By using queuing analysis, Xerox was able to reduce service cost for the Model 9200 duplicating system by almost 50 percent and at the same time improve customer service so that response times for customer-initiated service calls could be specified to prospective customers.

INTRODUCTION

queuing system *Queue* is another name for a waiting line, and a *queuing system* is simply a system that involves a waiting line. *Queuing theory* is a branch of management science that enables the analyst to describe the behavior of queuing systems.

queuing theory

It is clear that each of us comes in contact with many queuing systems everyday. If you have ever taken a trip by airplane, you have been a member of many queues by the time the trip is over. First, you waited to obtain the services of a ticket agent. Then, the agent joined a queue to find out if the flight you wanted was full. After buying your ticket, you had to wait in line to check in at the gate where the flight was boarding. Next, you waited to board; and once on board, your plane became a member of the queue of planes waiting to use the runway for takeoff. Eventually, the plane was circling the destination airport, waiting to land. Once on the ground, the plane may have had to wait for an unloading gate; and then, you had to wait to deplane. Finally, there was the wait for luggage and, possibly, a taxi.

The point is that the occasions for applying queuing theory are numerous and varied. When people who design systems that contain queues use queuing theory or digital simulation to estimate expected waiting times, *calling units* queue lengths, and so on, members of the queue (or *calling units*) usually spend less time waiting in line.

For a sample list of queuing applications, see Table 14.1. The queuing analysis we undertake in this chapter is different in nature from some of the optimization techniques, such as linear programming, that you have already studied. Queuing theory does not address optimization problems directly. Rather, it uses elements of statistics and mathematics for the construction of models that describe the important descriptive statistics of a queuing system. This statistical description of the operation of the queuing system then becomes part of the data upon which optimization decisions are based. The queuing system descriptive statistics include such factors as the expected *service* waiting time of the calling units, the expected length of the line, and the *facility* percentage of idle time for the *service facility* (the source of goods or services for which the calling units wait).

TABLE 14.1 *Queuing applications*

System	Calling units	Servers
Toll road	Automobiles, trucks, etc.	Toll booth
Machine shop	Jobs	Machine centers
Machine shop	Machines	Repairmen
Doctor's office	Patients	Nurse, doctor, lab, etc.
Computer system	Jobs, programs, messages	Computer
Class registration	Students	Student advisers
Ski resort	Skiers	Ski lifts
Harbor	Ships	Tugs, port facilities
Criminal court	Cases	Trial
Restaurant	Customers, orders	Tables, waiters, kitchen
Telephone	Callers	Switching equipment
Auto body shop	Wrecked automobiles	Body repair area, painting area
Professor's office	Students	Professor

When queuing theory is applied, management's objective is usually to minimize two kinds of costs: those associated with providing service and those associated with waiting time. After queuing theory has generated its statistical interpretation of the queuing system, the analyst assesses the various costs of providing service versus the costs of customers waiting to design the system that best meets the objectives of the organization.

THE QUEUING SYSTEM

As you can see in Figure 14.1, there are four parts of any queuing system: the calling population, the queue, the service facility, and the served calling units. Three of these entities have certain properties and characteristics that

FIGURE 14.1 **Queuing system**

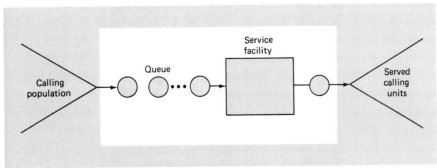

must be considered before appropriate modeling schemes can be formulated. We shall describe the calling population, the queue, and the service facility in some detail. In general, served calling units merely leave, or exit, the system.

Characteristics of the Calling Population

As shown in Figure 14.2, the calling population, often referred to as the *input source,* has three characteristics that are important to consider when deciding on what type of queuing model to apply:

- The size of the calling population
- The pattern of arrivals at the queuing system
- The attitude of the calling units

infinite calling population

Size of the calling population   This factor has a dramatic effect on the choice of queuing models. (Compare the number of alternatives associated with infinite versus finite calling populations in Figure 14.3.) Queuing systems in which the calling population can be considered *infinite* in size are generally more likely to be amenable to analytical solution. Examples of infinite calling populations in queuing systems are cars on a toll road and patients at the emergency room of a hospital. It is much more difficult to derive queuing models that can be applied to systems in which the calling populations are very limited. Examples of *finite,* or *limited-source, queuing systems* include three in-house computers that must be serviced by a cus-

finite calling population

FIGURE 14.2   **Calling population characteristics**

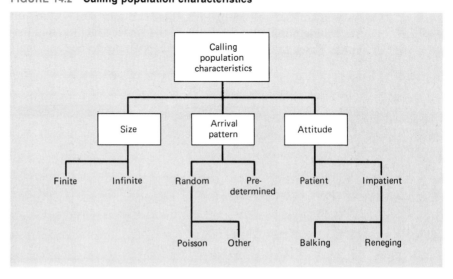

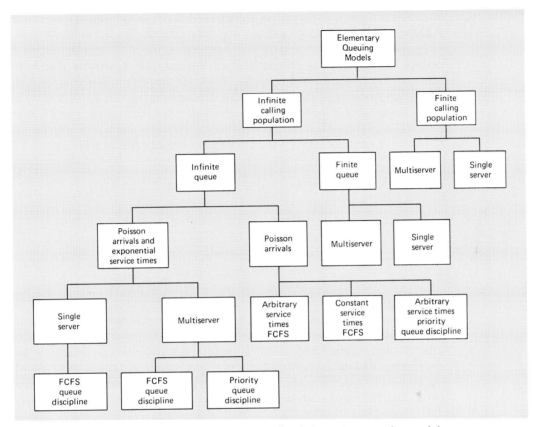

FIGURE 14.3 **A representative sample of elementary queuing models**

tomer engineer if they break down and students who may take advantage of a professor's office hours for help in a specific course.

The key to determining whether you can assume an infinite calling population is whether the probability of an arrival is significantly changed when a member or members of the population are receiving service and thus cannot arrive to the system. If there are only three calling units in a calling population and one is receiving service, the probability of another arrival is significantly reduced because the size of the calling population is cut by 33.3 percent.

random **Pattern of arrivals**   Calling units arrive at the queuing system either ac-
arrivals cording to some predetermined schedule or in a *random* fashion. If arrivals are scheduled, such as patients at a dentist's office, analytical queuing models are usually inappropriate. If arrivals are random, it is necessary to determine the probability distribution of the time between arrivals. It has been shown mathematically that if the probability density function of the

Poisson interarrival times is exponential, calling units arrive according to a so-called
process *Poisson process*. Poisson arrivals are very common in queuing systems.
They generally exist in situations where the number of arrivals during a
certain time interval is independent of the number of arrivals that have
Poisson occurred in previous time intervals. This basic property states that the con-
probability ditional probability of any future event depends only on the present state of
density the system and is independent of previous states of the system. The *Poisson*
function the system and is independent of previous states of the system. The *Poisson*
probability density function gives the probability of *n* arrivals in time period
t. The mathematical form of the Poisson probability function is

$$P_n(t) = \frac{e^{-\lambda t}(\lambda t)^n}{n!} \qquad n = 0, 1, 2, \ldots$$

where

n = number of arrivals
t = size of the time interval
λ = mean arrival rate per unit of time

Although many queuing systems have random arrivals that behave according to a Poisson process, it is possible for the interarrival times to be distributed in a nonexponential fashion. Therefore, it is necessary to determine the
distribution and parameters of the interarrival time statistically before deciding on how to approach any queuing problem. How to determine the probability distribution of a random variable such as interarrival time is discussed
in Chapter 15.

Attitude of the calling units The final characteristic of the calling population that must be considered is the attitude of the calling unit. Calling units
can be classified as being patient or impatient. A patient customer or calling
unit is one that will enter the queuing system and stay regardless of the state
of the system. An impatient calling unit may balk (refuse to enter the system)
or renege (leave the system before receiving service). Generally, most analytical queuing models assume a very patient calling unit.

The Property of Queue Length

This characteristic of queues is related in a sense to calling population size
and, sometimes, to calling population attitude. In applying models, the
queue is characterized by its maximum length, which can be *limited* or
unlimited. Limitation is usually attributable either to customer attitude or to
the space available for the queue. There are few analytical choices for queuing systems that have finite queues. Generally, if you can assume that calling
units join the queue regardless of its length, the probability of applying an
analytical queuing model is greatly increased.

Characteristics of the Service Facility

As depicted in Figure 14.4, the three basic properties of the service facility are:

- ☐ The structure of the queuing system
- ☐ The distribution of service times
- ☐ The service discipline

single
channel

multichannel

Queuing system structure   Service facilities can be described as single channel or multichannel. A *single-channel* system is a system with only one server. A *multichannel* system, on the other hand, has more than one server performing the same service. A drive-in bank facility is a single-channel system when there is only one teller on duty and a multichannel system when more than one teller is working.

single phase

multiphase

In addition to multichannel versus single channel, the service facility can be classified as single or multiphase. A *single-phase* system is one in which the calling unit receives service from only one type of server. A pay telephone, for example, is a single-phase queuing system. A *multiphase* system exists when the calling unit must obtain the services of several different types of server. Imagine a freighter pulling into the harbor to unload its cargo: First, that freighter must obtain the services of a tugboat; then, it must obtain a berth; then be unloaded; and after having been unloaded, the tug's services are needed again for the freighter's return to the open water. (Obviously, queuing systems can represent any combination of phases and channels.) An example of a multiphase, multichannel system is a harbor that

FIGURE 14.4 **Characteristics of the service facility**

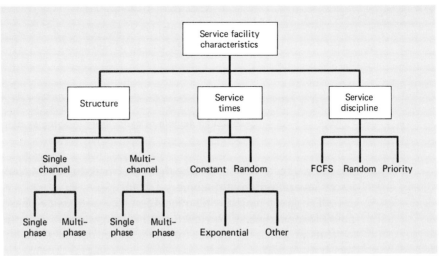

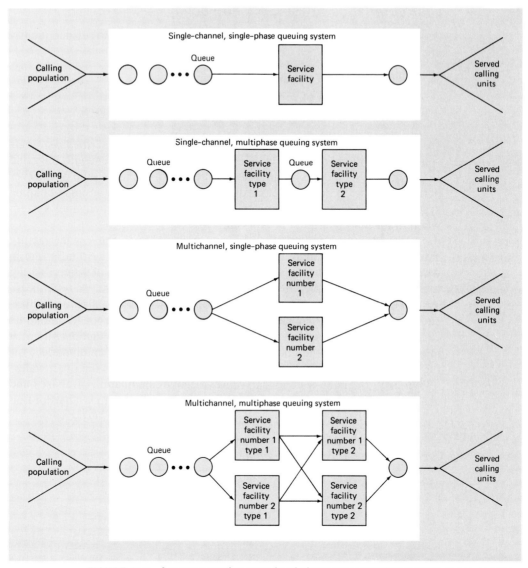

FIGURE 14.5 **A representative sample of elementary queuing system characteristics**

has more than one tug and more than one berth. Figure 14.5 depicts schematics of several different queuing structures.

The great majority of queuing models are single-phase models. It is possible, nonetheless, to view a multiphase system as separate, single-phase systems in which the output from one server becomes the input for another server.

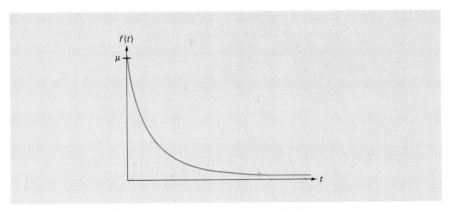

FIGURE 14.6 **Graph of f(t) = $\mu e^{-\mu t}$ (exponential distribution)**

constant **Distribution of service times**   Service times can be *constant* or random in
nature. If service time is a *random* variable, it is necessary for the analyst to
random determine how that random variable is distributed. In many cases, service
times are exponentially distributed; when this is the case, the probability of
finding an applicable model is increased.
exponential   As you can see in Figure 14.6, if service times are *exponentially distributed,* the probability of relatively long service times is small. The length of
telephone calls has been shown to be exponentially distributed.
The important point is that you should not make assumptions concerning either the service times of the various servers in the system or, equally
important, about the arrival pattern of calling units, without using the appropriate nonparametric statistical tests.

Service discipline   This characteristic is the decision rule that determines
which calling unit in the queuing system receives service. A service discipline (or *queue discipline,* as it is sometimes called) can be classified in one
of three ways:

- First come, first served (FCFS)
- Priority
- Random

Most queuing systems that involve people operate with FCFS service discipline, even though it has been shown to be somewhat inefficient, simply
because people usually do not tolerate other systems. Priority disciplines
preemptive can be divided into two categories: preemptive priority and nonpreemptive
priority priority. *Preemptive priority* disciplines allow calling units that arrive at the
queuing system to replace units already receiving service. For example,
consider an emergency room of a hospital when only one doctor is on duty.

Obviously, if that doctor is treating a patient whose condition is not critical at the time a critically ill patient arrives, the patient who was being served is preempted because a calling unit has arrived to the system with a higher priority.

non-preemptive priority   *Nonpreemptiue priority* simply causes the units in the queue to be arranged so that, when a service facility becomes available, the calling unit with the highest priority receives service first. There is no displacement of units in service. Computer systems frequently use priority scheduling.

random selection   It is also possible for a queuing system to have no formal queue discipline, in which case the server selects calling units at random. *Random selection* sometimes exists at the candy and popcorn counter in a movie theater.

Descriptive Statistics of a Queuing System

Now that we have described the important properties of a queuing system's major components, the calling population, the queue, and the service facility, you should have a good notion of the nature of the queuing system itself. Before we go on to the specific subject of queuing models, you should be aware that almost all such mathematical models reveal information about the

steady state   operating characteristics of a queuing system at *steady state*. As depicted in Figure 14.7, steady-state conditions exist when a system's behavior is not a function of time. Typically, a queuing system goes through a stage, called the transient stage, in which queuing statistics do not reflect the long-term expected values. This stage often occurs at a system's "start." For example, when a grocery store opens its doors in the morning, no customers are present in the system; therefore, there is a period of time when a statistic such as the expected time spent waiting in line would be understated. Fol-

FIGURE 14.7   **Transient versus steady-state conditioning**

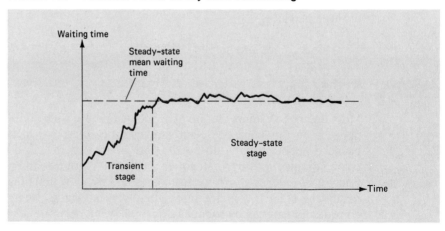

lowing the transient stage is the steady-state stage, in which system behavior is not affected by time.

Many queuing systems never reach a steady state because of the dynamic nature of the system. Consider a system in which arrivals to the system are a function of some other event. For example, airline reservations calls may surge shortly after a TV commercial or at half-time of a football game. In this case, steady-state statistics based on an average arrival rate will not be very accurate. A better example might be arrivals to an airline ticket counter. Arrivals are dependent on the airline's flight schedule and may never reach a steady state. Consequently, steady state queuing statistics may not be appropriate when deciding how many agents to schedule.

ELEMENTARY QUEUING MODELS

In this section, we define some of the queuing models you first saw in Figure 14.3 and show the functions that describe various queuing statistics. Because the mathematics necessary to derive most queuing models is beyond the scope of this text, we have omitted model derivations. The emphasis, instead, is on identifying the assumptions of each model and on explaining how these models are used.

Notation and Definitions

To help you understand the specific queuing statistics that are available from most queuing models, we must first define certain queuing terms and introduce a limited amount of notation. You should become familiar with the following list of notations and definitions before you read further in this chapter.

L_q = expected or mean length of the queue (number of calling units in the queue)

L_s = expected number of calling units in the system (number in the queue plus number being served)

W_q = expected or mean time spent waiting in line

W_s = expected or mean time spent in the system (including waiting time and service time)

λ = mean arrival rate (number of calling units per unit of time)

μ = mean service rate (number of calling units served per unit of time)

$1/\mu$ = mean service time for a calling unit

s = number of parallel (equivalent) service facilities in the system

$P(n)$ = probability of having n units in the system

ρ = server utilization factor (that is, the proportion of time the server can be expected to be busy)

Models That Have an Infinite Calling Population

All queuing models can be classified as either infinite source models or finite source models. Infinite source models are much more numerous and varied than models with finite calling populations. All models described in this text assume that μ (mean service rate) is independent of the number of calling units in the system. Moreover, all queuing statistics given are steady-state statistics.

The basic single-server model   The assumptions of this model are

- Poisson arrival process
- Exponential service times
- Single server
- FCFS service discipline
- Infinite source
- Infinite queue

The steady-state queuing statistics for the basic single-server model are given by the following formulas:

the probability of 0 calling units in the system: $P(0) = 1 - (\lambda/\mu)$
the probability of n calling units in the system: $P(n) = P(0)(\lambda/\mu)^n$
the proportion of time the server is busy: $\rho = \lambda/\mu$
expected number of calling units in the system: $L_s = \lambda/(\mu - \lambda)$
expected number of calling units in the queue: $L_q = \lambda^2/[\mu(\mu - \lambda)]$
expected time in the system: $W_s = 1/(\mu - \lambda)$
expected time waiting in line: $W_q = \lambda/[\mu(\mu - \lambda)]$

EXAMPLE   To illustrate these results consider the following application. A particular toll road has one attendant at an exit lane. Cars arrive at that toll gate in a Poisson fashion at a rate of 120 cars per hour, and it takes the attendant, on the average, 15 seconds to service a car. Service times are exponentially distributed. Assumptions of an infinite calling population and an infinite queue are reasonable. What are the basic queuing statistics for this very simple system?

First, it is necessary to determine the units of time for λ and μ. Obviously, λ and μ must be expressed in the same time units. Let's choose minutes. Therefore, $\lambda = 2$ cars per minute and $\mu = 4$ cars per minute. Thus, we have

$$P(0) = 1 - (\lambda/\mu) = 1 - (2/4)$$
$$= .5 \quad \text{(probability of an empty system)}$$
$$\rho = \lambda/\mu = 2/4 = .5 \quad \text{(proportion of time the server is busy)}$$
$$L_s = \lambda/(\mu - \lambda) = 2/(4 - 2)$$
$$= 1 \quad \text{(expected number of cars in the system)}$$
$$L_q = \lambda^2/[(\mu(\mu - \lambda)] = 2^2/[4(4 - 2)] = 4/8$$
$$= .5 \quad \text{(expected number of cars waiting in the queue)}$$
$$W_s = 1/(\mu - \lambda) = 1/(4 - 2) = .5 \text{ minutes}$$
$$= 30 \text{ seconds} \quad \text{(expected total time in the system for each customer)}$$
$$W_q = \lambda/[\mu(\mu - \lambda)] = 2/[4(4 - 2)] = 2/8 = .25 \text{ minutes}$$
$$= 15 \text{ seconds} \quad \text{(expected waiting time for each customer)}$$

Given these steady-state queuing statistics, it appears unnecessary to employ two attendants at the toll gate. In other words, a half-minute wait is probably not unreasonable, and therefore, the cost of another attendant could not be justified.

Multiserver model with Poisson arrivals and exponential service times The assumptions of this model are identical to those of the basic single-server model described previously except that the number of servers is assumed to be greater than one. There is an additional assumption: All servers have the same rate of service.

The steady-state queuing statistics are

$$P(0) = \frac{1}{\sum_{n=0}^{s-1} \frac{(\lambda/\mu)^n}{n!} + \frac{(\lambda/\mu)^s}{s!}\left(1 - \frac{\lambda}{s\mu}\right)^{-1}}$$

$$P(n) = \frac{(\lambda/\mu)^n}{n!} P(0) \quad \text{for } 0 \leq n \leq s$$

$$= \frac{(\lambda/\mu)^n}{s! s^{n-s}} P(0) \quad \text{for } n \geq s$$

$$\rho = \lambda/s\mu \quad \begin{array}{l}\text{(assuming each server has the same mean service} \\ \text{rate of } \mu \text{ units per time period)}\end{array}$$

$$L_q = \frac{P(0)(\lambda/\mu)^s \rho}{s!(1 - \rho)^2}$$

$$W_q = L_q/\lambda$$
$$W_s = W_q + (1/\mu)$$
$$L_s = L_q + (\lambda/\mu)$$

For computational convenience, a table of $P(0)$ can be found in Appendix H at the end of the book.

EXAMPLE   Consider the toll road example again, but let us assume that the arrival rate has increased to 600 cars per hour and that three attendants are on duty rather than one.

$$\lambda = 10 \text{ cars per minute}$$
$$\mu = 4 \text{ cars per minute}$$
$$s = 3$$

$$P(0) = \cfrac{1}{\displaystyle\sum_{n=0}^{2} \frac{(10/4)^n}{n!} + \frac{(10/4)^3}{3!} \cdot \left(\frac{1}{1 - (10/12)}\right)}$$

$$= \cfrac{1}{1 + \dfrac{10}{4} + \dfrac{25/4}{2} + \dfrac{1,000/64}{6} \cdot \dfrac{12}{2}}$$

$$= 64/1,424 = .045$$

$$L_q = \frac{.045(10/4)^3(10/12)}{3![1 - (10/12)]^2}$$

$$= 3.5 \text{ cars}$$

$$W_q = 3.5/10 = .35 \text{ minutes per car}$$

$$W_s = .35 + .25 = .60 \text{ minutes per car}$$

$$L_s = 3.5 + (10/4) = 6.0 \text{ cars}$$

Given these queuing statistics, three attendants would constitute a very tolerable service facility from a driver's point of view. However, for a more complete analysis, queuing statistics for two attendants should be computed to see if the degradation in service with fewer attendants is worth the decrease in cost. Since the value of driver waiting time is unspecified, a value judgment must be made. The utility of the queuing model is that the value judgment you make after using it is more informed and generally should result in a better decision.

Single-server model with arbitrary service times   If the analyst has determined that arrivals to the system are Poisson-distributed but cannot accept the hypothesis that service times are exponentially distributed, it is quite possible that a valid model does exist. Specifically, the assumptions of this model are

- ☐ Poisson arrival process.
- ☐ Infinite calling population.
- ☐ Infinite queue.

- FCFS queue discipline.
- Single server.
- The distribution of service time is unknown, but it has a mean, $1/\mu$, and a variance, σ^2. These parameters are known.

The steady-state results are

$$
\begin{aligned}
L_q &= (\lambda^2\sigma^2 + \rho^2)/[2(1 - \rho)] \\
\rho &= \lambda/\mu \\
L_s &= \rho + L_q \\
W_q &= L_q/\lambda \\
W_s &= W_q + (1/\mu) \\
P(0) &= 1 - \rho
\end{aligned}
$$

It is interesting to note that as σ^2 increases L_q, L_s, W_q, and W_s all increase. This means that the performance of the queuing system is not solely dependent on mean service time but on the variance in service time as well. Consequently, a server with a longer mean service time may still be the more productive if it is also the more consistent.

When service times are constant, as might be the case in a process such as a car wash, the same model can be applied. The only difference is that the variance σ^2 is equal to zero. Therefore, $L_q = \rho^2/[2(1 - \rho)]$. The other relationships remain unchanged.

EXAMPLE   A savings and loan association is opening a branch in a nearby suburb. This branch is expected to need one savings counselor, but management wants to have descriptive queuing statistics to confirm an intuition that only one savings counselor is actually necessary. Plans are to transfer one savings counselor from the main office. Data concerning this particular counselor's time spent with a customer have been collected, but goodness-of-fit tests indicate that these service times are not exponentially distributed. It is further estimated that the mean service time is $\frac{1}{4}$ hour and variance is $\frac{1}{6}$ hour^2. Customers are expected to arrive in a Poisson manner at a rate of two per hour.

$$
\begin{aligned}
\lambda &= 2 \text{ customers per hour} \\
\mu &= 4 \text{ customers per hour} \\
\sigma^2 &= 1/6 \text{ (hour)}^2 \\
\rho &= 2/4 = 1/2 \\
L_q &= \frac{4(1/6) + (1/2)^2}{2[1 - (1/2)]} \\
&= \frac{11/12}{1} = 11/12 = .92 \text{ customer}
\end{aligned}
$$

$$L_s = 1/2 + 11/12 = 17/12 = 1.42 \text{ customers}$$

$$W_q = \frac{11/12}{2} = 11/24 \text{ hour} = 27.5 \text{ minutes}$$

$$W_s = 11/24 + 6/24 + 17/24 \text{ hour} = 42.5 \text{ minutes}$$

$$P(0) = 1 - 1/2 = 1/2$$

The foregoing queuing statistics suggest that either the savings and loan customers are going to have to be very patient or the firm will lose savings customers if it carries out its plan to have only one savings counselor.

EXAMPLE   The manager of a small, coin-operated car wash is thinking about adding a vacuum to the business so that customers can vacuum the inside of their automobiles. Service time for the vacuum is constant at 5 minutes, and arrivals are Poisson at a rate of 10 per hour. For this example, assume an infinite queue and calling population. Before investing in the vacuum, the manager wishes to know what to expect with respect to customers waiting for the vacuum.

$$\lambda = 10 \text{ customers per hour}$$

$$1/\mu = 1/12 \text{ hour per customer}$$

$$\sigma^2 = 0$$

$$\mu = 12 \text{ customers per hour}$$

$$\rho = 5/6 = .833$$

$$L_q = \frac{(5/6)^2}{2(1/6)} = 2.08 \text{ customers}$$

$$L_s = 5/6 + 25/12 = 2.92 \text{ customers}$$

$$W_q = \frac{25/12}{10} = .208 \text{ hour} = 12.5 \text{ minutes}$$

$$W_s = 12.5 + 5 = 17.5 \text{ minutes}$$

With these results, the manager might want seriously to consider two vacuums since the probability of a customer's joining the queue when there are two or more cars waiting is low.

Single-server model with arbitrary service times and a priority queue discipline   Limited results exist for queuing models that do not have a FCFS queue discipline. The model described in this section uses a nonpreemptive priority queue discipline and makes no assumption about the service time distribution. The explicit assumptions of this model are the following:

- Poisson arrival process.
- Infinite calling population.

□ Infinite queue.

□ The queue discipline divides calling units into classes, and service is FCFS within each priority class.

□ Single server.

□ The service time distribution for each priority class is unknown, but the mean service time and variance are known for each priority class.

The steady-state queuing statistics are given by the following expressions:

$$W_q^k = \frac{\sum_{i=1}^{m} \lambda_i [(1/\mu_i)^2 + \sigma_i^2]}{2(1 - S_{k-1})(1 - S_k)}$$

where

W_q^k = the expected waiting time for a calling unit in priority class k

λ_i = arrival rate of priority class i

μ_i = service rate of priority class i

σ_i^2 = variance in service time of priority class i

$S_k = \sum_{i=1}^{k} \rho_i < 1, \ k = 1, 2, \ldots, m$

$S_0 = 0$

m = number of priority classes

$\rho_k = \lambda_k/\mu_k$

$L_q^k = \lambda_k W_q^k$

$W_s^k = W_q^k + (1/\mu_k)$

$L_s^k = L_q^k + \rho_k$

$W_q = \sum_{k=1}^{m} \frac{\lambda_k}{\lambda} W_q^k \qquad$ where $\lambda = \sum_{k=1}^{m} \lambda_k$

   = expected waiting time for any customer

$W_s = \sum_{k=1}^{m} \frac{\lambda_k}{\lambda} W_s^k$

   = expected time spent in the system for any customer

EXAMPLE   Jobs to be run on a computer system are of two types and hence two different priorities. Only one job can run at one time. Both types of jobs arrive according to a Poisson process, but service time distributions are normal, with means of 1/12 hour and 1/4 hour. Variances for the two priority classes are 1/12 (hour)^2 and 1/24 (hour)^2, respectively. Type I jobs arrive at a rate of three per hour, and type II jobs arrive at a rate of two per hour. What are the steady-state queuing statistics?

$$\rho_1 = 3/12 = .25$$
$$\rho_2 = 2/4 = .50$$
$$S_1 = .25$$
$$S_2 = .25 + .50 = .75$$
$$\lambda_1 = 3 \text{ jobs per hour}$$
$$\lambda_2 = 2 \text{ jobs per hour}$$
$$\mu_1 = 12 \text{ jobs per hour}$$
$$\mu_2 = 4 \text{ jobs per hour}$$
$$\sigma_1^2 = 1/12 \ (\text{hour})^2$$
$$\sigma_2^2 = 1/24 \ (\text{hour})^2$$
$$W_q^1 = \frac{3[(1/12)^2 + (1/12)] + 2[(1/4)^2 + (1/24)]}{2(1 - 0)[1 - (3/12)]}$$
$$= .47916/1.5 \text{ hour} = .31944 \text{ hour} = 19.17 \text{ minutes}$$
$$W_q^2 = \frac{3[(1/12)^2 + (1/12)] + 2[(1/4)^2 + (1/24)]}{2[1 - (3/12)][1 - (3/12 + 2/4)]}$$
$$= \frac{(39/144) + (30/144)}{(18/12)(3/12)} = 23/18 \text{ hours} = 1.278 \text{ hours}$$
$$= 76.6 \text{ minutes}$$
$$L_q^1 = 3(.31944) = .96 \text{ job}$$
$$L_q^2 = 2(1.278) = 2.56 \text{ jobs}$$
$$W_s^1 = 19.17 + 5 = 24.17 \text{ minutes}$$
$$W_s^2 = 76.6 + 15 = 91.6 \text{ minutes}$$
$$L_s^1 = .96 + .25 = 1.21 \text{ jobs}$$
$$L_s^2 = 2.56 + .5 = 3.06 \text{ jobs}$$
$$W_q = (3/5)(19.17) + (2/5)(76.6) = 42.14 \text{ minutes}$$
$$W_s = (3/5)(24.17) + (2/5)(91.6) = 51.14 \text{ minutes}$$

This model might be used to evaluate the desirability of a priority queue discipline as opposed to a FCFS queue discipline. How might you accomplish such a comparison?

Single-server model with a finite queue   Often, queue length constitutes a constraint on the queuing system. If queue length is limited either by customer attitude or the physical facilities, it is not desirable to use any of the models previously described. The model we present in this section has assumptions identical to the first basic single-server model we defined in this chapter *except that* the assumption of an infinite queue capacity no longer applies. The steady-state results that have been derived are as follows:

$$P(0) = \frac{1 - (\lambda/\mu)}{1 - (\lambda/\mu)^{M+1}}$$

where M = maximum number of calling units in the system and the maximum queue length is $M - 1$:

$$P(n) = P(0)(\lambda/\mu)^n \quad \text{for } n = 0, 1, \ldots, M$$

$$L_s = \frac{\lambda/\mu}{1 - (\lambda/\mu)} - \frac{(M + 1)(\lambda/\mu)^{M+1}}{1 - (\lambda/\mu)^{M+1}}$$

$$L_q = L_s + P(0) - 1$$

$$W_q = \frac{L_q}{\lambda[1 - P(M)]}$$

$$W_s = W_q + 1/\mu$$

The foregoing results require that $\lambda < \mu$.

EXAMPLE   A basic programming course includes a lab at which a student "consultant" is on duty to help students debug their programs. It can be assumed that no student will get in line for help if there are more than three other students waiting. Students arrive at the lab according to a Poisson process at an average rate of four per hour. Service times are exponential, and the mean service time is 10 minutes. Because the class is large, an infinite calling population can be assumed. What are the steady-state queuing statistics?

$$M = 4$$
$$\lambda = 4$$
$$\mu = 6$$
$$P(0) = \frac{1 - (2/3)}{1 - (2/3)^5} = .384$$
$$P(4) = .384(2/3)^4$$
$$\quad = \text{probability of a full system so that}$$
$$\quad \quad \text{a student refuses to join the queue}$$
$$\quad = .076$$
$$L_s = \frac{2/3}{1 - (2/3)} - \frac{5(2/3)^5}{1 - (2/3)^5}$$
$$\quad = 2 - .758 = 1.242 \text{ students}$$
$$L_q = 1.242 + .384 - 1 = .626 \text{ student}$$
$$W_q = .626/[4(1 - .076)] = .17 \text{ hour, or 10.2 minutes}$$
$$W_s = .17 + 1/6 = .337 \text{ hour, or 20.2 minutes}$$

Given these queuing statistics, it is probable that university administrators are quite satisfied with the lab system because there is only a 7.6 percent chance of a student's not being serviced, and those who choose to wait must wait only 10.2 minutes, on the average. The students might not agree with the university administration.

There is a multiserver extension of this model, which is beyond the scope of this text.

Models that have a finite calling population   In some queuing systems, the size of the calling population is so small that to assume it to be infinite would seriously degrade the usefulness of a queuing model. Some results that have been derived for a limited-source model are presented in this section. The model described next assumes a Poisson arrival process and exponentially distributed service times. It can be applied to a multiserver queuing system or a single-server system whose queue discipline is FCFS. The steady-state descriptive statistics are

$$P(0) = \cfrac{1}{\left[\sum_{n=0}^{s-1} \cfrac{N!}{(N-n)!n!} \left(\cfrac{\lambda}{\mu}\right)^n + \sum_{n=s}^{N} \cfrac{N!}{(N-n)!s!s^{n-s}} \left(\cfrac{\lambda}{\mu}\right)^n \right]}$$

where

N = number of calling units in the calling population
λ = mean arrival rate for *each* individual unit
s = number of servers

$$P(n) = \begin{cases} P(0) \cfrac{N!}{(N-n)!n!} \left(\cfrac{\lambda}{\mu}\right)^n & \text{for } 0 \le n \le s \\[2ex] P(0) \cfrac{N!}{(N-n)!s!s^{n-s}} \left(\cfrac{\lambda}{\mu}\right)^n & \text{for } s \le n \le N \\[2ex] 0 & \text{for } n > N \end{cases}$$

$$L_s = \sum_{n=1}^{N} nP(n)$$

$$W_s = L_s/\lambda_e \quad \text{where } \lambda_e = \lambda(N - L_s)$$

$$W_q = W_s - (1/\mu)$$

$$L_q = \lambda_e W_q$$

EXAMPLE   In a certain computer facility, three central processing units (CPUs) are serviced by two customer engineers. Each CPU breaks down in a Poisson manner on the average of every 24 hours. Repair times are exponentially distributed, with a mean of 1 hour. Determine the steady-state queuing statistics.

$$\lambda = .04167 \text{ per hour}$$
$$\mu = .1 \text{ per hour}$$

$$P(0) = 1 \Bigg/ \Bigg[\frac{3!}{(3-0)!0!} \cdot \left(\frac{.04167}{1}\right)^0 + \frac{3!}{(3-1)!1!} \cdot \left(\frac{.04167}{1}\right)^1$$

$$+ \frac{3!}{(3-2)!2!2^0} \cdot \left(\frac{.04167}{1}\right)^2 + \frac{3!}{(3-3)!2!2^1} \cdot \left(\frac{0.4167}{1}\right)^3 \Bigg]$$

$$= .8847$$

$$P(1) = .8847 \cdot \left(\frac{3!}{2!1!}\right)\left(\frac{.04167}{1}\right)^1 = .1106$$

$$P(2) = .8847 \cdot \left(\frac{3!}{1!2!}\right)\left(\frac{.04167}{1}\right)^2 = .0046$$

$$P(3) = .8847 \cdot \left(\frac{3!}{0!2!2^1}\right)\left(\frac{.04167}{1}\right)^3 = .0001$$

$$L_s = .1106 + 2(.0046) + 3(.0001) = .1201 \text{ CPUs}$$
$$\lambda_e = .04167(3 - .1201) = .12$$
$$W_s = .1201/.12 = 1.0008 \text{ hours}$$
$$W_q = 1.0008 - 1.0 = .0008 \text{ hours or .05 minutes}$$
$$L_q = (.12)(.0008) = .000096 \text{ CPU}$$

An economic analysis of this queuing system would be possible, since the cost of waiting could conceivably be computed, as could the cost of additional repairmen. Consequently, the queuing model could be used to make a very rational decision regarding the optimal number of repairmen.

For a concise summary of the models presented in this chapter, see Table 14.2.

APPLICATION OF QUEUING THEORY

So far in this chapter, we have described the structure and characteristics of queuing systems and have defined several representative queuing models. In this section we discuss the application of queuing theory to solving real-world problems.

As shown in Figure 14.8, the first step in the application of queuing theory is to analyze carefully the real queuing system that needs to be modeled. This analysis includes determining the attributes of the calling

TABLE 14.2 *Summary of basic queuing models*

Model name	Model assumptions	P(0)
Basic single server	Poisson arrivals Exponential service times Single server FCFS Infinite source Infinite queue	$1 - (\lambda/\mu)$
Basic multi-server	Poisson arrivals Exponential service times Multiserver FCFS Infinite source Infinite queue	$\dfrac{1}{\displaystyle\sum_{n=0}^{s-1} \dfrac{(\lambda/\mu)^n}{n!} + \dfrac{(\lambda/\mu)^s}{s!}\left(1 - \dfrac{\lambda}{s\mu}\right)^{-1}}$
Single server with arbitrary service times	Poisson arrivals Service time distribution unknown Infinite source Infinite queue FCFS Single server	$1 - \rho$
Single server with priority queue discipline	Poisson arrivals Infinite source Infinite queue FCFS within priority class Single server Unknown service distribution with known mean and variance	
Single server, finite queue	Poisson arrivals Exponential service times Single server FCFS Infinite source Finite queue	$\dfrac{1 - (\lambda/\mu)}{1 - (\lambda/\mu)^{M+1}}$
Limited source	Poisson arrivals Exponential service times Single or multiserver FCFS Limited input source Infinite queue	$\dfrac{1}{\left[\displaystyle\sum_{n=0}^{s-1} \dfrac{N!}{(N-n)!n!}\left(\dfrac{\lambda}{\mu}\right)^n + \sum_{n=s}^{N} \dfrac{N!}{(N-n)!s!s^{n-s}}\left(\dfrac{\lambda}{\mu}\right)^n\right]}$

$P(n)$	L_q	L_s	W_q	W_s
$P(0)(\lambda/\mu)^n$	$\lambda^2/[\mu(\mu-\lambda)]$	$\lambda/(\mu-\lambda)$	$\lambda/[\mu(\mu-\lambda)]$	$1/(\mu-\lambda)$
$\dfrac{(\lambda/\mu)^n}{n!}P(0)$ for $0\le n\le s$ $\dfrac{(\lambda/\mu)^n}{s!s^{n-s}}P(0)$ for $n\ge s$	$\dfrac{P(0)(\lambda/\mu)^s\rho}{s!(1-\rho)^2}$	$L_q+(\lambda/\mu)$	L_q/λ	$W_q+(1/\mu)$
	$\dfrac{(\lambda^2\sigma^2+\rho^2)}{[2(1-\rho)]}$	$\rho+L_q$	L_q/λ	$W_q+(1/\mu)$
	$L_q^k=\lambda_k W_q^k$	$L_s^k=L_q^k+\rho_k$	$\displaystyle\sum_{k=1}^m \frac{\lambda_k}{\lambda}W_q^k$ where $$W_q^k=\frac{\displaystyle\sum_{i=1}^m \lambda_i[(1/\mu_i)^2+\sigma_i^2]}{2(1-S_{k-1})(1-S_k)}$$	$\displaystyle\sum_{k=1}^m \frac{\lambda_k}{\lambda}W_s^k$ where $W_s^k=W_q^k+(1/\mu_k)$
$P(0)(\lambda/\mu)^n$ for $n=0,1,\ldots M$	$L_s+P(0)-1$	$\dfrac{\lambda/\mu}{1-(\lambda/\mu)}-\dfrac{(M+1)(\lambda/\mu)^{M+1}}{1-(\lambda/\mu)^{M+1}}$	$\dfrac{L_q}{\lambda[1-P(M)]}$	W_q+1/μ
$P(0)\dfrac{N!}{(N-n)!n!}\left(\dfrac{\lambda}{\mu}\right)^n$ for $0\le n\le s$ $P(0)\dfrac{N!}{(N-n)!s!s^{n-s}}\left(\dfrac{\lambda}{\mu}\right)^n$ for $s\le n\le N$ $0\quad$ for $n\ge N$	$\lambda_e W_q$	$\displaystyle\sum_{n=1}^N nP(n)$	$W_s-(1/\mu)$	L_s/λ_e

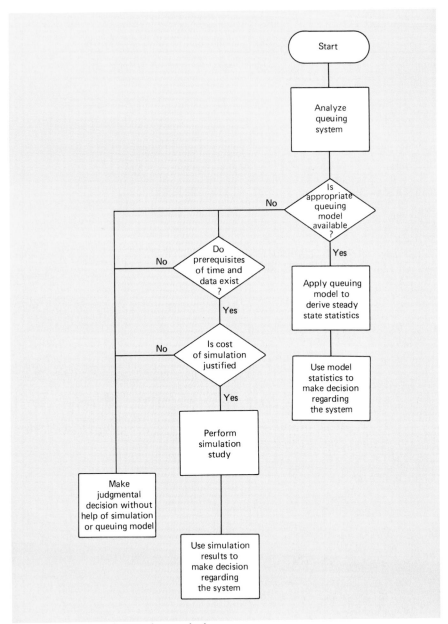

FIGURE 14.8 **Steps in queuing analysis**

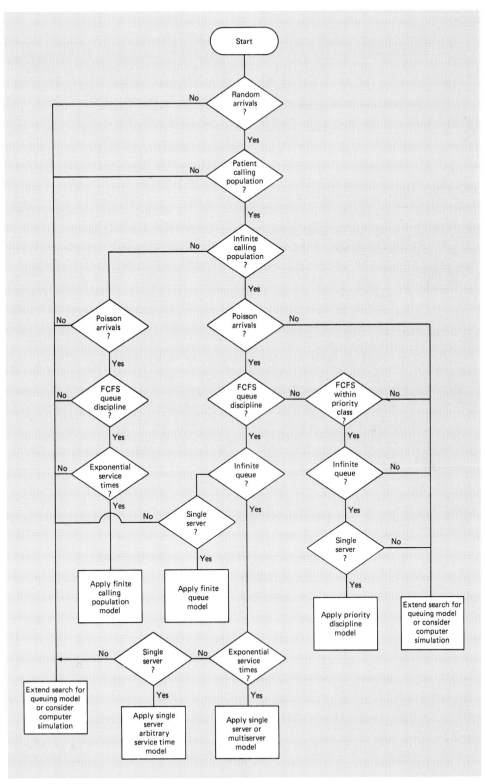

FIGURE 14.9 **Model selection decision**

population, the service facility, and the queue itself. If the queuing models introduced in this text were the only analytical models available, this first step could be described by the flow chart in Figure 14.9. After the analyst goes through a decision process similar to that depicted in Figure 14.9, he or she must make the decision of whether an appropriate analytical model exists.

If he or she is unable to find an appropriate model, then a decision must be made of whether to resort to computer simulation to model the queuing system in question. The decision of whether to use simulation hinges on several factors. First, are the data necessary to build and validate the model available? Second, is the time necessary to develop the simulation model too long to affect the decision process? If management must make a decision as to the design of the system within a week, simulation analysis is probably not a viable alternative. Finally, does the importance of the decision affecting the queuing system justify employment of a more costly simulation approach? If the problem justifies the additional cost of simulation and the data and time are available, the analyst should perform the simulation study. For a summary of the comparative advantages of simulation and queuing theory, see Table 14.3.

The major advantage of queuing theory is that it is generally less costly to develop, run, and maintain a queuing model and takes less time to develop. Simulation's major advantage is that it can be used to model a much wider variety of queuing systems simply because it is not limited by the complexity of the mathematics. It has been said that a queuing theory solution to a queuing problem is an elegant solution as opposed to the brute force method of discrete digital simulation. Unfortunately, "elegant" solutions don't always exist.

Regardless of whether a queuing model or a simulation model is used to perform the analysis, the analyst must use the model to assist in making a decision or a set of decisions that will affect the performance and cost of the

TABLE 14.3 *Comparative strengths of queuing theory and simulation*

Queuing theory	Simulation
Less expensive to 　Develop 　Run 　Maintain Takes less time to develop Contains no sampling error More easily imbedded in 　decision support systems	More flexible More robust Output is more descriptive

real queuing system. The first step in using the model to analyze the decision problem is to identify relevant decision variables. These variables can include:

- The number of servers
- The type and speed of the servers
- The queue discipline
- The physical arrangement of the system facilities

Having identified decision variables, each of which is generally discrete in nature, the analyst must determine the criteria for an effective decision. These criteria are usually economic in nature.

Two approaches to the problem of applying a queuing model to making decisions are common. One approach is to define explicitly the cost of implementing and operating the queuing system and then minimize an objective function such as

$$Z = C_q + C_w$$

where

$$C_q = \text{cost of the queuing system}$$
$$C_w = \text{cost of waiting}$$

As shown in Figure 14.10 the cost of operating the queuing system and the cost of waiting are in direct opposition to each other. As the cost of the

FIGURE 14.10 **Queuing system costs**

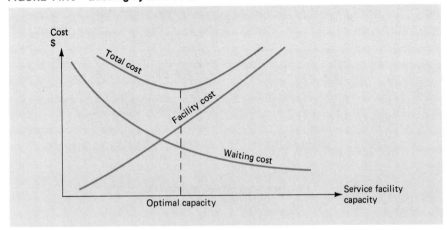

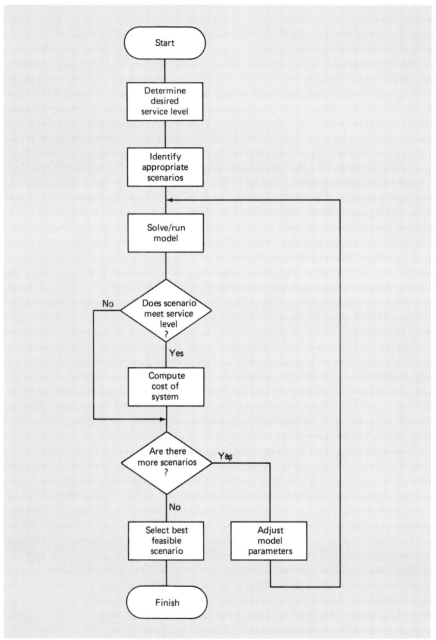

FIGURE 14.11 **Queuing model application**

system increases, the waiting time is typically decreased. If the cost functions depicted in Figure 14.10 can be explicitly defined, then finding the best solution to the queuing problem is fairly easy.

If you are trying to decide on how many teller windows to have open in a bank or how many checkout counters to have open in a supermarket, the loss of goodwill caused by long lines and long waits is difficult to measure. If, however, you are trying to decide on the number of repairmen to have available to fix your productive machinery, these costs can be reasonably estimated.

A second and more common approach to applying queuing theory is to seek to minimize the cost of the queuing system subject to some realistic service-level constraint as measured by model outputs such as expected waiting time and expected length of the waiting line. This approach is more common simply because of the difficulty in measuring the cost of waiting. With this approach, management usually provides service-level standards based on their knowledge of the customer's attitude and the level of service provided by competitors.

Regardless of whether the analyst uses an analytical model or a simulation model and regardless of which method is used to minimize cost, you should realize that determining the best set of decision variables is a trial-and-error process in which the model is used to predict the performance of the queuing system under a variety of scenarios. The typical decision process is summarized in Figure 14.11.

The first step is for management to provide guidance as to the desired service level. Once the desired service level has been determined and the relevant decision variables identified, the analyst creates a number of scenarios that reflect a variety of combinations of decision variables. Then these scenarios are run through the model sequentially, and model output is checked to determine if that particular scenario met the desired service level. If the scenario's service level is satisfactory the cost of that option is analyzed. The process is continued until all scenarios have been analyzed. Finally, the best system configuration is chosen from those that met minimal service levels. As you can see the decision process is typically not purely a quantitative one which the computer can make without human judgment. Rather the model provides a "what if" tool which assists management in making a more informed and, hopefully, better decision.

COMPUTER IMPLICATIONS

Because of the closed form of analytical queuing models, most models are easily adapted to a computer. Because these types of models have a reasonably modest appetite for input data and require relatively few computer resources, they can be solved manually or with the use of a microcomputer.

However, large-scale queuing systems are often installed on larger computers because they require more data or because they are searching for an optimal server configuration for a large number of multichannel/multiphase systems. For example, American Airlines has developed and is using a system called the Trunk Planning and Analysis System (TAPS) that is implemented on a large mainframe computer. The objective of TAPS is to provide a planning tool for communications management to determine the "optimal" voice network configuration. In other words, TAPS seeks to determine the least-cost configuration given a minimum service level that has been dictated by senior management. The system is a large queuing-based decision support system that utilizes models similar to those described in this chapter. With a communications budget in excess of $200 million per year, it is not surprising that TAPS saves American several millions of dollars annually.

SUMMARY

Queuing systems exist everywhere in the real world, and queuing theory can play an important role in the design of systems involving waiting lines and the scheduling of many services. The importance of properly applying analytical queuing models cannot be overstated. To avoid misapplication, system properties must be carefully analyzed before an appropriate model can be selected.

We have examined only a subset of the queuing models that have been derived, but you should realize that there is a large probability that an analytical queuing model that fits the real-world system you are interested in may not exist and may be impossible to derive mathematically. If such is the case, simulation is often used to analyze queuing systems that are too complex to be described using an analytical queuing model.

When analyzing queuing systems it is important to understand that queuing theory, like computer simulation, is a descriptive tool that yields expected operating characteristics of the queuing system under differing configurations. Decision variables such as queue discipline, number of servers, speed of the server, and so on, must be supplied to the model and are not output from the model. Typically, the output from queuing models becomes an input to a judgmental decision concerning the configuration of the queuing system.

SOLVED PROBLEMS

PROBLEM STATEMENT

The city council of a small town has decided to build a tennis court in the central park. Players are expected to arrive on the average of 10 sets of players per 12-hour day. Playing time is exponentially distributed with a mean of 1 hour. Arrivals are Poisson. What are the expected queuing statistics assuming the basic single-server model?

SOLUTION

If we let hours be the time unit,

$$\lambda = \tfrac{10}{12} \text{ arrival per hour}$$
$$\mu = 1 \text{ departure per hour}$$

The probability of no one using the tennis court is

$$P(0) = 1 - \frac{\lambda}{\mu} = 2/12 = .1667$$

The expected utilization of the tennis court is

$$\rho = \frac{\lambda}{\mu} = 10/12 = .8333$$

The number of groups expected to be waiting for a court is

$$L_q = \frac{\lambda^2}{\mu(\mu - \lambda)} = \frac{(10/12)^2}{1(1 - 10/12)} = 4.167 \text{ groups}$$

The number of groups expected to be waiting and playing tennis is

$$L_s = \frac{\lambda}{\mu - \lambda} = 5 \text{ groups.}$$

The expected waiting time is

$$W_q = \frac{\lambda}{\mu(\mu - \lambda)} = 5 \text{ hours.}$$

The expected time waiting and playing is

$$W_s = \frac{1}{\mu - \lambda} = 6 \text{ hours.}$$

PROBLEM STATEMENT

Given the steady-state queuing statistics found in the previous example, the city council wants to investigate the effect of building two tennis courts rather than one.

SOLUTION

$$\lambda = \frac{10}{12} \qquad \mu = 1 \qquad s = 2$$

The probability of empty tennis courts is

$$
\begin{aligned}
P(0) &= \frac{1}{\displaystyle\sum_{n=0}^{s-1} (\lambda/\mu)^n/n! + (\lambda/\mu)^s/s! \, (1 - \lambda/s\mu)^{-1}} \\
&= \frac{1}{(10/12)^0/0! + (10/12)^1/1! + (10/12)^2/2! \, (1 - 10/12/2)^{-1}} \\
&= \frac{1}{1.83 + .59524} \\
&= \frac{1}{2.425} = .4123
\end{aligned}
$$

The average utilization of the tennis courts is

$$\rho = \frac{\lambda}{s\mu} = \frac{10/12}{2} = .4167$$

The number of groups expected to be waiting for a court is

$$
\begin{aligned}
L_q &= \frac{P(0)(\lambda/\mu)^s \rho}{s!(1 - \rho)^2} \\
&= \frac{(.4123)(10/12)^2(.4167)}{2!(1 - .4167)^2} \\
&= \frac{.1193}{.6805} \\
&= .1753 \text{ group}
\end{aligned}
$$

The number of groups expected to be waiting and playing is

$$L_s = L_q + \frac{\lambda}{\mu}$$
$$= .1753 + 10/12$$
$$= 1.009 \text{ groups}$$

The expected waiting time is

$$W_q = \frac{L_q}{\lambda}$$
$$= \frac{.1753}{10/12}$$
$$= .21 \text{ hour or } 12.6 \text{ minutes}$$

The average time spent playing and waiting is

$$W_s = W_q + \frac{1}{\mu}$$
$$= 12.6 \text{ minutes} + 60 \text{ minutes}$$
$$= 72.6 \text{ minutes}$$

PROBLEM STATEMENT

If the assumption about exponential service times is dropped from the single-tennis court problem and the variance is 1/2 (hour)^2, what would the queuing statistics be? Remember: λ = .8333 group per hour and μ = 1 group per hour.

SOLUTION

The expected length of the queue is

$$L_q = \frac{\lambda^2 \sigma^2 + \rho^2}{2(1 - \rho)}$$
$$= \frac{(.8333)^2(\frac{1}{2}) + .8333^2}{2(1 - .8333)}$$
$$= 3.1241 \text{ groups waiting}$$

The expected utilization of the tennis courts is

$$\rho = \frac{\lambda}{\mu}$$
$$= \frac{10/12}{1} = .8333$$

The average number of groups playing and waiting is

$$L_s = \rho + L_q$$
$$= .8333 + 3.1241$$
$$= 3.9574 \text{ groups}$$

The average waiting time is

$$W_q = \frac{L_q}{\lambda}$$
$$= 3.1241/.8333$$
$$= 3.7491 \text{ hours}$$

The average time spent waiting and playing is

$$W_s = W_q + \frac{1}{\mu}$$
$$= 3.7491 + 1$$
$$= 4.7491 \text{ hours}$$

Finally, the probability of the court not being used is

$$P(0) = 1 - \rho$$
$$= 1 - .8333$$
$$= .1667$$

PROBLEM STATEMENT

Because of budgetary restrictions, city managers feel that only 1 tennis court can be built at the present time. Someone has suggested limiting play to 1 hour for each group to reduce waiting time and lines. How would this suggestion change the queuing statistics?

SOLUTION

By prescribing 1 hour of playing time, the problem reduces to a single-server model with constant service times. The expected queuing statistics are as follows:

The expected utilization of the court remains

$$\rho = \frac{\lambda}{\mu} = .8333$$

The average number of groups waiting to play is

$$L_q = \frac{\rho^2}{2(1 - \rho)}$$
$$= \frac{.8333^2}{2(1 - .8333)}$$
$$= 2.08 \text{ groups}$$

The average number of groups playing and waiting is

$$L_s = \rho + L_q$$
$$= .8333 + 2.08$$
$$= 2.9133 \text{ groups}$$

The average waiting time is

$$W_q = \frac{L_q}{\lambda}$$
$$= 2.08/.8333$$
$$= 2.496 \text{ hours}$$

The average time spent playing and waiting is

$$W_s = W_q + \frac{1}{\mu}$$
$$= 2.496 + 1$$
$$= 3.496 \text{ hours}$$

Therefore, it looks as though some improvement can be made by restricting play to 1 hour.

PROBLEM STATEMENT

One member of the city council has challenged the validity of the assumption of an infinite queue. He contends that people will not wait on a court if two groups are already waiting. What effect does the omission of the infinite queue have on the queuing statistics?

SOLUTION

The maximum number of calling units in the system is three. The probability of the tennis courts being idle is

$$P(0) = \frac{1 - \lambda/\mu}{1 - (\lambda/\mu)^{M+1}}$$
$$= \frac{1 - .8333}{1 - (.8333)^4}$$
$$= .3219.$$

The probability of the court being used but no line is

$$P(1) = P(0)\left(\frac{\lambda}{\mu}\right)^1$$
$$= (.3219)(.8333)$$
$$= .2682.$$

The probability of one group waiting is

$$P(2) = (.3219)(.8333)^2$$
$$= .2235.$$

The probability of two groups waiting or probability of a group arriving and not staying is

$$P(3) = (.3219)(.8333)^3$$
$$= .1863.$$

The expected number of groups playing and waiting is

$$L_s = \frac{\lambda/\mu}{(1 - \lambda/\mu)} - \frac{(M + 1)(\lambda/\mu)^{M+1}}{1 - (\lambda/\mu)^{M+1}}$$
$$= \frac{.8333}{1 - .8333} - \frac{(3 + 1)(.8333)^4}{1 - (.8333)^4}$$
$$= 4.9988 - 3.7246$$
$$= 1.2742 \text{ groups}$$

The expected number of groups waiting is

$$L_q = L_s + P(0) - 1$$
$$= 1.2742 + .3219 - 1$$
$$= .5961$$

The expected time spent waiting is

$$W_q = \frac{L_q}{\lambda[1 - P(M)]}$$
$$= \frac{.5961}{.8333(1 - .1863)}$$
$$= .8791 \text{ hours.}$$

The expected time spent waiting and playing is

$$W_s = W_q + \frac{1}{\mu}$$
$$= .8791 + 1$$
$$= 1.8791 \text{ hours.}$$

COMPUTER SOLUTION

Using the QSB queuing theory module, this problem required only 5 input numbers and the solution shown was generated instantaneously.

```
                Input Data of The Problem COURT

            M/M/1 with finite queue

     Customer arrival rate (lambda)    =    0.833

                    Distribution       :    Poisson

              Number of servers        =    1

         Service rate per server       =    1.000

                    Distribution       :    Poisson

              Mean service time        =    1.000   HOUR

              Standard deviation       =    1.000   HOUR

                    Queue limit        =       3

          Customer population          =    Infinity




                Solving the Model for COURT

                M/M/1 with finite queue
   With lamda = .8333 customers per HOUR    and μ = 1 customers per HOUR

                        Utilization factor (p) =   .8333
        Average number of customers in the system (L) =   1.27417
        Average number of customers in the queue (Lq) =   .5960937
          Average time a customer in the system (W) =   1.879096
          Average time a customer in the queue (Wq) =   .8790957
        The probability that all servers are idle (Po)=   .321924
        The probability an arriving customer waits(Pw)=   .678076

   P(1) =0.26826   P(2) =0.22354   P(3) =0.18628   P(4) =0.00000   P(5) =0.00000
   P(6) =0.00000   P(7) =0.00000   P(8) =0.00000   P(9) =0.00000   P(10) =0.00000

                    10
                    Σ  P(i) =0.678076
                    i=1
```

REVIEW QUESTIONS

1. Define what is meant by the term "queuing theory."
2. How does queuing theory differ from linear programming?
3. What are the two major costs involved in any queuing system?
4. What are the basic elements of a queuing system?
5. What characteristics of the calling population must be analyzed when applying a queuing model to a real queuing system?
6. What three basic properties of the service facility must be analyzed when applying queuing models?
7. What is meant by "steady-state queuing statistics"?
8. Explain two basic approaches used in applying queuing theory to decision making.
9. How would you classify the structure of a hospital's emergency room?
10. What is meant by "queue discipline"?
11. What is meant by "customers arrive according to a Poisson process"?
12. Distinguish between preemptive and nonpreemptive priority queue disciplines.
13. What is meant by the statement that queuing theory is *not* an optimization technique?
14. List two reasons you might choose to use digital simulation rather than queuing theory.
15. Why is simulation referred to as the technique of last resort when applied to queuing systems?

PROBLEMS

14.1 Analyze the following queuing systems by describing their various system properties:
  a. Barber shop
  b. Bank
  c. Machine repairman
  d. Traffic light
  e. Grocery store checkout counter
  f. Tugs in a harbor
  g. Airport runway
  h. Computer system
  i. Hospital emergency room

j. Gas station

k. Car wash

l. Tool crib

m. Laundromat

14.2 *Retail.* A large department store is preparing for the Christmas season. Last year, the store had two Santas for the children to talk to. Lines were long, and the store is trying to decide how many Santas to employ this year. Describe this problem as a queuing problem. Be sure to identify all pertinent characteristics. Include a representative schematic of the system.

14.3 *Manufacturing.* Consider a tool crib in a large factory. At the present time, one worker operates the tool crib, but the vice-president of production has noticed rather long lines of workers waiting for tools. Factory employees arrive at the tool crib at a rate of 25 per hour. Service times are exponential, with a mean of 2 minutes. The arrival process is Poisson. Analyze the desirability of adding a second tool-crib clerk.

14.4 *State government.* The Toll Road Authority wants to know how many toll booths to design into its Main Road exit. Naturally, an objective is to minimize cost, but there is also a stipulation that the expected line length during peak hours should not exceed 5 cars. From data taken from other toll road exits, it has been determined that interarrival times and service times are exponentially distributed. The peak arrival rate is expected to be 10 cars per minute. The average service time is 15 seconds. How many toll booths should be designed into the system?

14.5 *Amusement park.* At Disneyland, plans are being made to install a new ride. Management would like to get a feel for the length of lines and the expected waiting times for this ride so that a decision can be made whether to have one or two such installations. People arrive in a Poisson manner, but the time the ride takes is constant. Estimates are that people will arrive at a rate of one every 2 minutes. The ride takes 1.75 minutes. Analyze the queuing system.

14.6 *Barber shop.* Consider a one-chair barbershop. At the present location a barber has, on the average, 10 customers per day. The average haircut takes 20 minutes. Cutting time has been shown to be exponentially distributed. It has been this barber's experience that customers do not wait for a haircut if two people are already waiting. A move to a new location is possible. The new location would probably increase the number of customers per day to 15. Analyze the present system and the proposed system by computing the queuing statistics for each system. Make a recommendation concerning the proposed move.

14.7   *University*. A certain professor holds office hours 2 hours each day. Three types of people need to see this professor: female students, other faculty, and male students. Many students complain that the queue discipline is not FCFS but a priority discipline with the priority scheme as follows: (1) female students, (2) other faculty members, and (3) male students. The conference time has been analyzed using historical data and has been found to be normally distributed, with a mean of .08 hours and a variance of .0667 (hours)^2. People arrive at the professor's office in a Poisson manner (that is, no appointments are allowed during office hours). The arrival rate for female students is three per hour. The arrival rates for faculty members and male students are two and four per hour, respectively. What would be the effect on the queuing statistics if the professor changed to a FCFS queue discipline? Assume an infinite queue and calling population.

14.8   *Supermarket*. The local supermarket has the policy that checks are cashed by the store manager only. Customers wishing to cash checks arrive in a Poisson manner at an average rate of 45 customers per hour. The manager takes, on the average, 1 minute to cash a check. This service time has been shown to be exponentially distributed. Accomplish the following:

   a. Compute the percentage of time that the manager spends cashing checks.

   b. Compute the average time a customer is expected to wait.

   c. Compute the number of customers waiting to get checks cashed.

   d. Compute the probability of the manager attending to some other function, assuming that check cashing is the manager's first priority.

   e. Explain to the manager how you would analyze the effect of adding the assistant manager to the check-cashing function.

14.9   *Legal practice*. Two lawyers are in partnership. Each lawyer has a secretary. Jobs arrive to each secretary in a Poisson manner at a rate of three per hour, on the average. It takes either secretary an average of 15 minutes to accomplish each individual job. This service time is exponentially distributed.

   a. Assuming that each secretary does only the work of one lawyer, what is the expected waiting time for each job?

   b. What would be the effect of pooling the secretaries?

14.10   *Aerospace manufacturing*. A certain aerospace company has five identical numerically controlled milling machines. Each machine fails on the average of three times per week, and it takes a technician on the average 2.5 hours to fix the machine. Historical data indicate a Poisson arrival process and exponential service times. Because of serious scheduling consequences, management does not want a machine down for more than 3 hours. For this reason, it has been decided that expected waiting time should not exceed $\frac{1}{2}$ hour. Assume that the plant operates the equipment only during the prime shift.

a. What are the expected times a machine will have to wait with one technician on duty? With two technicians on duty?

b. What is your recommendation to management?

c. What options do you think management has in addition to the number of technicians?

14.11 *Airline industry.* A national travel agency employs one agent in a local office during the day. The agent has suggested that another agent be hired so that calling customers will not have to wait an inordinate amount of time. Management has decided that on the average, a customer should not have to wait more than 2 minutes. To study the desirability of adding another agent, a study was done to determine the distribution of arrival times and service times. Calls arrived in a Poisson manner on the average of 30 per hour. The time it takes to make a reservation is exponentially distributed with a mean of 1.5 minutes. Given the company's policy of an average waiting time of less than 2 minutes, what should be done with regard to hiring additional agents?

14.12 *Hospital administration.* An administrator at a small hospital is contemplating a relocation of the hospital's X-ray facility. Currently, the X-ray department is located such that only two patients can be waiting for the X-ray machine at one time. This has resulted in emergency patients being sent back to emergency and other in-patients being sent back to their rooms. The potential new location would double the amount of waiting space available. Arrivals to X-ray occur in a Poisson manner at a rate of six per hour. On the average, it takes about 8 minutes to service an X-ray request. These service times have been shown to be exponential. Analyze the administrator's decision problem using queuing theory.

14.13 *Port administration.* Ships arrive at a harbor in a Poisson fashion at a rate of five per 8-hour day. It takes the one tug servicing the harbor on the average of 1 hour per ship. Tugging has been shown to be normally distributed with a variance of .0333 (days)^2. Compute the steady-state queuing statistics for the harbor tug operation.

14.14 *Hospital administration.* A free one-doctor outpatient clinic of a hospital takes patients without appointments from 1:00 to 5:00 in the afternoon. Patients arrive according to a Poisson process at a rate of five per hour. Service times are exponential with a mean of 10 minutes. Patients are taken on a first come, first-served basis. Apply the appropriate queuing model and calculate pertinent queuing statistics. What assumptions did you make about the outpatient clinic?

14.15 Can two doctors be justified in your judgment for the outpatient clinic described in Problem 14.14?

14.16 *Service station.* A one-pump service station has room for only 2 cars waiting. Cars arrive at the station in a Poisson manner at a rate of 10 cars per hour. It takes on the average 4 minutes to service a customer. These times are thought to be exponential. What are the expected queuing statistics for the service station? What, specifically, are the assumptions of your queuing model?

14.17 *Flying club.* A flying club is contemplating the construction of its own private airport. Plans are to build one landing strip. Demand for the landing strip is estimated by club members to be seven planes per hour. Landing times are known to be normally distributed with a mean of .0833 hours and a variance of .0011 (hours)^2. If arrivals are assumed to be Poisson, what are the expected queuing statistics?

14.18 *Department store.* The manager of a large department store has noticed long customer lines in the catalog sales department. At present the department has two clerks. The manager has asked you to do a study and recommend changes in the system to decrease customer waiting time and the length of the lines. You have collected arrival and service-time data and have found that arrivals are Poisson-distributed and that service times are exponentially distributed. Customers arrive at an average rate of 20 per hour and the average catalog sale takes 5 minutes. Analyze the problem and make your recommendation to the store manager.

14.19 *Catalog sales.* A entrepreneurial friend of yours is thinking about building a catalog sales business and wants your advice on how many telephone lines and sales agents she should plan on for when she initiates the business. Because of the line installation costs and the way rental space is leased, she wants to be fairly sure she has adequate lines and space to allow for some growth. Her start-up and recurring costs are summarized as follows:

Cost summary

Item	Nonrecurring cost	Recurring cost
Telephone	$500 per line	$200 per month
Space	$1,000 per workstation	$10 per square foot per year
Agents	$500 hiring cost	$7.50 per hour

By sampling the response time of her competitors, your friend has determined that a minimum service level of an average wait time of 20 seconds is reasonable. Your friend's best estimates of demand and expected talk time are summarized as follows:

Arrival rate/service time estimates

Subjective probability	Mean arrival rate (per hour)	Subjective probability	Mean service time (minutes)
.1	40	.2	5
.4	60	.5	10
.3	80	.3	15
.2	100		

Analyze your friend's decision problem and recommend the most attractive queuing system for her consideration.

14.20 *Car wash.* The owner of the local coin-operated car wash has been getting complaints from his customers that the time that $.50 buys (4 minutes) is not quite adequate. It has been his experience that if two cars are waiting, other customers will not join the line. Arrivals to the three-stall car wash arrive at an average rate of 30 per hour. Variable operating cost for each stall is approximately $2 per hour. What additional information if any would be required to analyze the problem? How would you structure the analysis? What type of model would you use and why?

BIBLIOGRAPHY

Bhat, U. Narayan, *Elements of Applied Stochastic Processes,* 2nd ed. New York: John Wiley & Sons, Inc., 1984.

Cooper, Robert B., *Introduction to Queuing Theory,* 2nd ed. New York: North-Holland, 1981.

Gross, Donald, and Carl M. Harris, *Fundamentals of Queuing Theory,* 2nd ed. New York: John Wiley & Sons, Inc., 1985.

Hillier, Frederick S., and Gerald J. Lieberman, *Introduction to Operations Research,* 4th ed. San Francisco: Holden-Day Inc., 1986.

Saaty, Thomas L., *Elements of Queueing Theory: With Applications.* New York: Dover Publications, 1983.

Taha, Hamdy A., *Operations Research: An Introduction,* 4th ed. New York: Macmillan Publishing Company, 1987.

15

Discrete Digital Simulation

UNITED AIRLINES[1]

Good advertising slogans, such as "Fly the Friendly Skies of United," have helped United Airlines become America's largest domestic airline. Having a management team progressive enough to use management science tools such as discrete digital simulation aggressively has also played a critical role.

Because "congestion at the major airports results in over 25,000 hours of delay per month, inconvenience to the traveling public, and increases the direct operating costs by more than $10 million per month for the domestic airline industry," a management science team consisting of representatives from the Federal Aviation Administration, O'Hare Airport, and the major airlines operating out of O'Hare was organized. The goal of the O'Hare Delay Task Force was to find ways of relieving the congestion at O'Hare Airport and thus reduce costly delays. With the use of the O'Hare simulation model, various decision strategies were evaluated and analyzed. Because of the complex nature of the problem, no other management science tool was appropriate for attacking the airport congestion problem and, consequently, the only alternative to using simulation would have been to implement various strategies at O'Hare and measure their relative effectiveness on the real system.

[1] Herbert B. Hubbard, "Terminal Airspace/Airport Congestion Delays," *Interfaces*, 8 (February 1978), 1–14.

On the basis of the study, three strategies appeared to have the greatest short-term payoff:

1. Selecting the best runway configurations for the existing wind and weather conditions.
2. Installing equipment to determine the minimum safe separation of airplanes.
3. Improving the systems for controlling the traffic demand during peak periods.

The results of the study were dramatic. The average inbound holding delays at O'Hare were reduced by 2 to 3 minutes. A conservative estimate of United Airlines' annual savings at O'Hare Airport alone is in excess of $1.2 million. In addition to the dollars that can be saved using a simulation approach to the airport congestion problem, the domestic airline industry can conserve up to 5 million barrels of jet fuel annually by minimizing traffic delays due to airport congestion.

INTRODUCTION

Simulation was used in the United Airlines application as a method of last resort, because no other tool in the management scientist's bag could have been applied successfully to the airport congestion problem. Because simulation is often the technique of last resort, and because of its flexibility, it is also the most widely used management science technique.'' According to recent surveys, only linear programming rivals simulation as the most useful MS/OR technique.

Monte Carlo simulation   In this chapter, we describe discrete digital simulation, which is often referred to as *Monte Carlo simulation*. In general, simulation is a descriptive, rather than an optimization technique that involves developing a model of some real phenomenon and then performing experiments on that model. This broad definition applies to types of simulation other than discrete digital simulation. A spacecraft simulator, a wind tunnel, a model airplane, and an analog simulation of some continuous process are all examples of simulations that differ fundamentally from the discrete digital simulation used in management science. To be more specific, discrete digital simulation is a numerical technique that involves modeling a system on a digital computer with the intention of predicting the system's behavior.

A simulation model serves the management scientist in much the same way that a laboratory serves the physical scientist. By making changes in the various parameters of a simulation model, the management scientist can observe the results of the simulation and infer how different configurations of the real system would behave under various circumstances.

REASONS FOR USING SIMULATION

The many reasons why a manager uses simulation to solve a problem can be clustered into two major categories.

☐ Experimentation with the real system may be impractical or impossible. A hospital administrator may have difficulty justifying experimenting with the real coronary care unit to determine the optimal number of beds and the best medical team configuration, whereas experimentation on a surrogate system, a computer simulation model, would be totally acceptable.

☐ The real system may be too complex to permit mathematical representation or model solution.

Often, if experimentation with the real system is impractical, an alternative would be to develop a mathematical model of the system or problem in question. As was the case with O'Hare Airport, the real system is often too complex to model or solve mathematically, and simulation is used as the tool of last resort.

SIMULATION APPLICATIONS

The literature contains a wealth of diverse applications of discrete digital simulation. The list that follows represents a small sample of successful applications.

Health care applications   Simulation has been used to predict the effect of various physician mixes on the utilization of hospital resources, and to plan the configuration of emergency rooms, coronary care units, and other hospital facilities. Staffing of nursing stations and primary care teams, and scheduling operations and admissions are all problems that have been attacked using computer simulation. Even the optimal location of ambulances has been examined using simulation.

Urban applications   Cities have used simulation to solve some of their most pressing problems. Problems such as police dispatching and beat design, the planning and design of transit systems, evaluating operating alternatives at airports, planning for snow emergencies, garbage collection, the location of emergency vehicles, long-range financial planning, and many more urban problems have been solved using computer simulation.

Industrial applications   Manufacturing organizations have used simulation to schedule their production process, make inventory policy decisions, design production systems, determine machine maintenance schedules, design distribution systems, and even to test the effects of increased production on the operation of an overhead crane.

Financial applications   The rapid growth in the use of simulation as a financial planning tool is evidenced by the more than 25 financial modeling software packages currently available commercially. All kinds of pro forma statements are produced using financial simulation packages. Portfolio selection models are common, as are capital budgeting models.

Military applications   Large-scale military battles as well as individual weapon systems have been simulated to aid in the design both of weapon systems and of strategic and tactical operations.

Agricultural applications   Simulation has been used to make decisions concerning equipment on a sugar plantation, to predict the effects of various policy alternatives on the Venezuelan cattle industry, and to aid in the design of regional grain collection, handling, and distribution in Canada.

Table 15.1 is a sample listing of real-world applications of simulation.

TABLE 15.1   *Real-world applications of simulation*

Air Traffic Control	Maintenance Scheduling
Aircraft Ground Traffic Control	Facility Layout
Airport Design	Financial Forecasting
Emergency Vehicle Location	Pro Forma Financial Statements
Assembly Line Balancing	Harbor Design
Bank Teller Scheduling	Factory Design
Grocery Store Clerk Scheduling	Parking Facility Design
Inventory Control	Baggage Handling
Data Network Design	Airport Manning
Voice Network Design	Railroad Scheduling
Computer System Design	Traffic Control
Job Shop Scheduling	Water Resource Development
Distribution System Design	Petrochemical Process Design
Warehouse Location	Library Design
Vehicle Routing	Information System Design
Emergency Room Design	Airline Passenger Demand
Hospital Design	Tool Crib Manning
Bus Scheduling	Flight Crew Scheduling
Airline Operations	Union Contract Negotiations

MANUAL SIMULATION

To give you some understanding of computer simulation, let us analyze a very simple problem. Two new ship docking facilities are being finished this year and a decision of how many tugs will be necessary to service ships wishing to dock must be made. Data from similar ports were used to estimate the time between ship arrivals distribution shown in Table 15.2.

Using data from similar ports and a great deal of subjective judgment, the time between ship arrivals is distributed as shown in Table 15.2. Time spent at the dock was estimated in similar manner. That probability distribution is reflected in Table 15.3. Tugging time is fairly constant at 1 hour per tug, and ships are taken on a first-come, first-served basis, with ships being tugged to sea having priority over those being tugged to port. The flow of a ship through the port facility is shown in Figure 15.1. Notice that a tug is needed initially to tow the ship to the berth and it is then released while the ship is unloaded. Once the ship is ready to leave the berth, a tug is needed to tow the ship into the open water.

The first step in developing the simulation is to develop a way of generating the two stochastic variables in the system: ship arrival times and

TABLE 15.2 *Ship interarrival time distribution*

Time between ship arrivals (hrs)	Probability
1	.30
2	.25
3	.15
4	.15
5	.05
6	.05
7	.05
	1.00

TABLE 15.3 *Unloading time distribution*

Unloading time (hrs)	Probability
1	.05
2	.15
3	.20
4	.25
5	.30
6	.05
	1.00

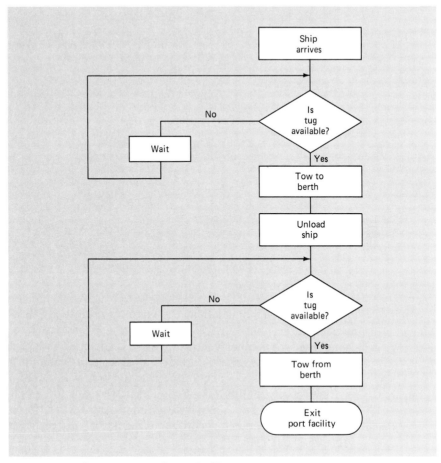

FIGURE 15.1   Ship flow through port facility

process unloading times. This is done using a function called a *process generator,*
generator which takes numbers from a uniform distribution and converts them to the
appropriate stochastic variable. This process of creating stochastic variables
from a particular probability distribution is the fundamental process underlying Monte Carlo simulation. Figure 15.2 illustrates this basic concept. Notice
in Figure 15.2 that the random variate *r* which is uniformly distributed[2]
between 0 and 1 is converted to a random variate *x* that is distributed according to the desired distribution. In the example in Figure 15.2 we are interested in generating a random variate that is distributed according to the
interarrival time distribution shown in Table 15.2.

The basic simulation process typically requires a random number as

[2] For a review of the uniform distribution, see Chapter 11.

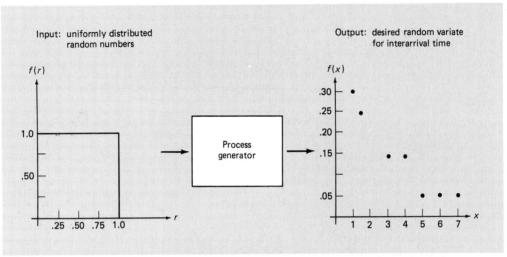

FIGURE 15.2 **Illustration of fundamental process in Monte Carlo simulation**

input. For manual simulations the numbers are usually found in a random number table, but for real simulation applications a computer-based pseudorandom number generator is used. Given a random number, a process generator converts the random number to a nonuniformly distributed random variate. The process generator function is different for each different type of probability distribution that we want to sample from. In the tugboat simulation problem, we want to generate two different random variates that are distributed according to the probability distributions shown in Table 15.2 and Table 15.3.

In this example, the stochastic interarrival times and unloading times are treated as discrete variables for the sake of simplicity. In a real simulation of the harbor problem, these variables would be continuous in nature. The function describing arrival times and unloading times can be found by defining the cumulative probability distributions of the two variables and relating that distribution to a uniform random variable between 0 and 1. Because a number chosen from a uniform distribution with parameters 0 and 1 will fall in the 0 to .3 range 30 percent of the time, 30 percent of the ships generated according to the function described in Table 15.4 will arrive 1 hour after the preceding ship. Similarly, 15 percent of the arrivals will come just 4 hours after the preceding ship.

The generation of unloading times is accomplished in a similar manner. If a random number is chosen between 0 and .05, the generated unloading time is 1 hour. If the random number is between .4 and .65, the generated unloading time is 4 hours. See Table 15.5 for the unloading-time generating function.

TABLE 15.4   *Ship interarrival time generating function*

Uniform random variable	Time between arrivals (hrs)
0–.30	1
.30–.55	2
.55–.70	3
.70–.85	4
.85–.90	5
.90–.95	6
.95–1.0	7

TABLE 15.5   *Unloading-time generating function*

Uniform random variable	Unloading time (hrs)
0–.05	1
.05–.20	2
.20–.40	3
.40–.65	4
.65–.95	5
.95–1.0	6

You must remember, however, that we are describing a random process, and it would take a large number of ship arrivals for these proportions to be considered very accurate. In other words, if only 50 arrivals were generated, it would not be unreasonable for 12 or 13 ships to take 3 hours to unload, even though the expected number of ships taking 3 hours to unload is 10 (.2 times 50).

Having defined the system and the process generators, we are now ready to simulate the harbor operation. First, we must decide on what experiments we are interested in running. For illustration, let us run two experiments, one with one tug and the other with two tugs. The critical output variable from the simulator is the average time spent by a ship waiting on a tug. Let us simulate 48 hours and assume an around-the-clock operation. Let us also assume that the random numbers needed to generate ship arrivals are chosen from the random numbers in Table 15.6, starting in the upper left-hand corner. Random numbers to generate unloading times are chosen from the same table, starting in the upper right-hand corner. In a computer simulation, these random numbers would be generated by a random number generating function, not chosen from a table.

Looking at Table 15.7, because the random number .445282 falls between .3 and .55, the first ship is simulated to arrive 2 hours into the simulated time period. The next ship arrives only 1 hour later, because its random number, .066257, falls between 0 and .3. Since a tug is available at 2 hours

TABLE 15.6 *Random number table*

.445282	.353333	.112460	.494758	.956412	.285648	.106182
.066257	.441906	.055118	.353555	.625270	.569627	.790333
.615352	.579120	.936548	.407208	.014319	.421038	.397360
.594821	.992685	.602720	.682154	.668440	.871255	.211575
.428152	.664736	.135047	.827656	.750516	.054190	.570499
.935282	.477204	.445679	.379244	.264349	.172899	.658255
.393437	.436322	.077000	.535109	.517650	.289920	.080668
.874724	.522334	.261491	.867939	.854214	.313831	.195065
.345906	.319852	.805962	.957102	.488950	.319787	.518168
.230927	.722047	.253941	.025220	.865850	.968126	.016103
.383484	.155976	.484498	.503207	.658759	.423696	.613343
.866792	.680668	.282878	.571261	.881661	.148613	.956734
.402887	.806714	.214300	.025378	.223563	.112981	.665817
.978072	.876081	.453834	.838279	.945164	.126478	.252390
.376035	.984704	.523906	.281099	.971441	.298754	.049552
.608526	.205187	.754386	.679630	.288311	.613193	.084362
.987430	.165323	.105069	.142509	.909431	.174001	.859131
.588776	.800478	.503880	.818984	.378979	.903020	.007307
.916667	.434235	.355410	.224342	.147361	.865086	.864270
.399848	.620655	.125302	.165914	.867769	.713384	.470383
.401840	.177596	.449017	.095737	.533275	.338016	.228617
.329558	.919797	.552755	.038363	.255378	.187000	.823605
.258627	.139314	.508244	.795636	.199622	.037007	.425445
.219602	.488609	.955238	.333945	.406528	.433665	.943236
.756436	.049489	.489014	.488679	.530948	.787576	.946926
.593372	.037899	.887044	.981170	.903624	.591212	.414656
.167034	.270299	.118483	.278210	.602910	.113570	.255230
.509250	.758433	.967347	.978183	.162974	.174195	.578402
.902657	.210320	.138008	.935174	.368968	.797242	.462741
.601267	.442931	.246182	.490711	.728634	.955403	.174712
.449643	.125448	.705902	.106384	.285185	.753657	.955278
.948750	.094997	.031238	.332454	.713580	.289390	.314123
.280228	.854264	.603533	.932821	.165132	.595403	.086226
.158733	.176363	.629582	.190230	.475139	.138766	.556342
.089161	.527890	.364889	.438324	.345949	.130772	.671094
.849617	.057854	.700570	.682735	.791279	.603053	.496812
.553393	.849053	.113780	.041200	.223180	.968275	.801036
.091737	.341098	.220956	.255856	.546529	.976471	.940064
.852144	.652287	.244428	.595987	.376065	.892506	.970457
.790186	.007002	.930339	.519015	.741036	.775080	.981155
.911208	.636852	.620241	.989783	.356524	.231102	.177894
.987448	.323640	.054813	.416119	.003391	.275281	.621161
.249438	.906181	.192145	.997242	.254147	.549703	.010896
.118046	.610211	.598851	.101210	.217602	.394718	.409892
.906891	.752321	.351903	.340528	.876046	.191524	.264726
.864643	.805323	.050154	.053020	.866732	.723211	.538683
.723195	.491027	.437407	.205195	.294510	.920305	.871236
.944672	.826904	.459380	.314145	.750449	.675389	.298291
.711250	.582876	.096009	.330172	.116949	.730150	.328360
.398807	.437603	.036349	.279671	.350884	.588266	.371640

into the simulation, it is assigned immediately to the first ship, and 1 hour later the ship is ready for unloading. Unloading time for ship 1 is generated at 2 hours because .106182 is between .05 and .20. The one tug is assigned to ship 2 immediately after servicing ship 1 but is idle for an hour waiting for ship 1 to be loaded. To make sure you understand how the simulation is working, you should verify the numbers in Tables 15.7 and 15.8.

Upon examination of Tables 15.7 and 15.8, it is apparent that if the object were to minimize ship waiting time, two tugs should be employed, since the average wait time is reduced from .5 hours (hours spent waiting/ number of ships) to 0 hours. If, however, the objective is to minimize the cost of waiting plus the cost of operating the port, then costs of waiting and the cost of operating a tug would have to be determined.

Figure 15.3 is a listing of a GPSS computer program that simulates the harbor problem. The experiments described in Tables 15.7 and 15.8 were run on the computer for a simulated time of 4,800 hours instead of 48 hours. It took just a few seconds to run the simulation on a small desktop microcomputer. The GPSS program took less than 1 hour to write and debug. During that simulated time, 1,745 ships arrived to the port facility. The results of the two experiments are summarized in Table 15.9.

Although the correlation between the manual and computer simulations is quite close for the two-tug configuration, the computer simulation of the one-tug configuration gives an average waiting time of more than twice

FIGURE 15.3 **GPSS simulation model—harbor problem**

```
1         FUNCTION   RN1,C7
.3, 1/.55, 2/.7, 3/.85, 4/.9, 5/.95, 6/1.0,7
2         FUNCTION   RN1, C6
.05, 1/.2, 2/.4, 3/.65, 4/.95, 5/1.0, 6
TUG       STORAGE    1
BERTH     STORAGE    2
          GENERATE   FN1
          QUEUE      TUGLN
          ENTER      TUG
          DEPART     TUGLN
          ADVANCE    1
          LEAVE      TUG
          ENTER      BERTH
          ADVANCE    FN2
          LEAVE      BERTH
          QUEUE      TUGLN
          ENTER      TUG
          DEPART     TUGLN
          ADVANCE    1
          LEAVE      TUG
          TERMINATE
          GENERATE   4800
          TERMINATE  1
          START      1
          END
```

TABLE 15.7 Harbor simulation—one-tug configuration (all time in hours)

Ship number	Random number	Arrival time	Time when tug was engaged (to berth)	Arrival time at berth	Random number	Time unloading is finished	Time when tug was engaged (from berth)	Time tug was released	Time spent waiting
1	.445282	2	2	3	.106182	5	5	6	0
2	.066257	3	3	4	.790333	9	9	10	0
3	.615352	6	6	7	.397360	10	10	11	0
4	.594821	9	11	12	.211575	15	15	16	2
5	.428152	11	12	13	.570499	17	17	18	1
6	.935282	17	18	19	.658255	24	24	25	1
7	.393437	19	19	20	.080668	22	22	23	0
8	.874724	24	25	26	.195065	28	28	29	1
9	.345906	26	26	27	.518168	31	31	32	0
10	.230927	27	27	28	.016103	29	29	30	0
11	.383484	29	30	31	.613343	35	35	36	1
12	.866792	34	34	35	.956734	41	41	42	0
13	.402887	36	36	37	.665817	42	42	43	0
14	.978072	43	43	44	.252390	47	47	48	0
15	.376035	45	45	46	.049552	47	48	49	1
16	.608526	48	49	50	.084362	52	52	53	1

TABLE 15.8 Harbor simulation—two-tug configuration (all time in hours)

Ship number	Random number	Arrival time	Time when tug was engaged (to berth)	Arrival time at berth	Random number	Time unloading is finished	Time when tug was engaged (from berth)	Time tug was released	Time spent waiting
1	.445282	2	2	3	.106182	5	5	6	0
2	.066257	3	3	4	.790333	9	9	10	0
3	.615352	6	6	7	.397360	10	10	11	0
4	.594821	9	9	10	.211575	13	13	14	0
5	.428152	11	11	12	.570499	16	16	17	0
6	.935282	17	17	18	.658255	23	23	24	0
7	.393437	19	19	20	.080668	22	22	23	0
8	.874724	24	24	25	.195065	27	27	28	0
9	.345906	26	26	27	.518168	31	31	32	0
10	.230927	27	27	28	.016103	29	29	30	0
11	.383484	29	29	30	.613343	34	34	36	0
12	.866792	34	34	35	.956734	41	41	42	0
13	.402887	36	36	37	.665817	42	42	43	0
14	.978072	43	43	44	.252390	47	47	48	0
15	.376035	45	45	46	.049552	47	47	48	0
16	.608526	48	48	49	.084362	51	51	52	0

TABLE 15.9 *Harbor simulation results*

Configuration	Total number of ships generated	Average tug utilization	Average berth utilization	Average time spent waiting on a tug (hr)
One-tug	1,745	.727	.676	1.172
Two-tug	1,745	.363	.671	.030

that given by the manual simulation. It should be clear that the reason we include an example of a manual simulation in this chapter is to give you a more in-depth understanding of what computer simulation is—not to suggest that real problems are solved using manual simulation.

STEPS IN A SIMULATION STUDY

The harbor situation introduced you to simulation as an idea and a technique. In the rest of this chapter, we reinforce this intuitive understanding by describing the various stages or tasks in a simulation study. Figure 15.4 depicts the steps or phases of a simulation study.

Problem Formulation

It's difficult to arrive at the right answer if you are working on the wrong problem. Therefore, the first step is to formulate the problem properly. Often, the manager has only a vague idea of what the problem is. It is the job of the management scientist to translate this vague idea into an explicit, written statement of the objectives of the study. The explicit original statement of the problem should not be considered sacrosanct, however, for this reason: As the simulation study progresses, the management scientist becomes more knowledgeable about the system being simulated and about the objectives of the organization. Consequently, it is sometimes necessary to modify the objectives as the nature of the problem becomes clearer. Usually, the statement of objectives takes the form of questions to be answered, hypotheses to be tested, and effects to be estimated. Obviously, it is also necessary to identify the criteria to be used to evaluate these questions.

Data Collection

The second task, and possibly the most time-consuming step in a simulation study, is the job of collecting data. Quantitative data are necessary for several reasons. First, data are required to describe the system being simulated. If you do not understand the real system thoroughly, it is not very likely that you will simulate the system properly. Second, data must be gathered as the

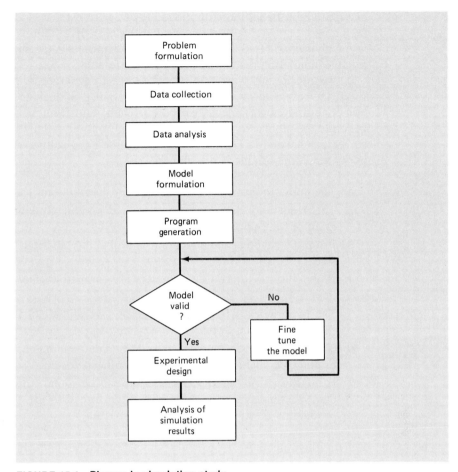

FIGURE 15.4 **Phases in simulation study**

foundation for generating the various stochastic variables in the system. For example, in a simple queuing system, real data concerning arrivals and service times must be gathered and analyzed to determine the proper probability distributions and their parameters. Finally, data are necessary to test and validate the model. To use a simulation model to make decisions, the decision maker must be confident that the real-world phenomenon has been adequately and accurately represented. Often, the best way to accomplish this validation is to compare simulator output with historical data.

Data Analysis

Once the data have been collected, they must be analyzed and the proper generating functions must be developed. In the harbor example, the stochastic variables—ship arrival times and unloading times—were generated using cumulative probability distributions. These were estimated subjectively using limited data. Actually, subjective probability distributions are somewhat atypical; probability distributions based on empirical data usually yield more reliable simulation results and thus are preferable.

Two basic tasks must be accomplished to generate random variables. First, the raw data of a stochastic variable must be analyzed to determine how that random variable is distributed. Then, a function must be derived to generate the stochastic variable using a uniformly distributed random number between 0 and 1. The following procedure is typically used to determine how a random variable is distributed:

1. The data are grouped into a frequency distribution.
2. This frequency distribution is depicted graphically either as a histogram or a frequency polygon.
3. From the shape of the histogram, a probability distribution is hypothesized.
4. Probability distribution parameters are estimated using sample statistics.

chi-square and Kolmogorov-Smirnov tests

5. The hypothesis is tested using one of several statistical tests such as the *chi-square* or *Kolmogorov-Smirnov test*.
6. If the hypothesis is rejected, distribution parameters can be perturbed, or changed slightly, and the new hypothesis tested.
7. If no known probability distribution can be found to fit the sampled data, the management scientist is often forced to use the cumulative probability distribution of the sample data.

Let us illustrate these steps by a simple example. The following service times at a gas station were collected during one day: 3.4, 5.4, 4.2, 5.5, 7.9, 0.6, 9.5, 0.0, 9.5, 5.1, 6.7, 1.6, 6.2, 0.5, 1.9, 9.6, 7.9, 6.9, 4.2, 2.7, 5.5, 4.8, 1.8, 9.0, 3.5, 3.9, 6.5, 0.5, 8.8, 3.6, 8.9, 2.4, 0.4, 4.7, 0.8. The frequency distribution for these raw data is reflected in Table 15.10 and a graphical representation is shown in Figure 15.5.

TABLE 15.10 *Frequency distribution*

Class	Frequency of observations
0–2	9
2–4	6
4–6	8
6–8	6
8–10	6

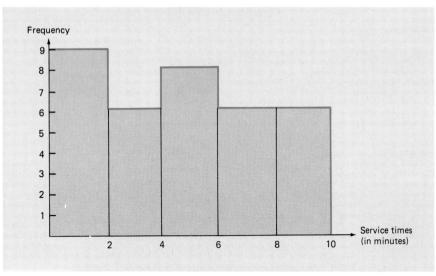

FIGURE 15.5 **Histogram of frequency distribution of gas station service times**

From the shape of the histogram in Figure 15.5, let us hypothesize that the random variable (gas station service times) is uniformly distributed with parameters 0 and 10. Therefore,

H_0: sample is drawn from a uniformly distributed population with $a = 0$ and $b = 10$

H_α: population is not uniformly distributed with $a = 0$ and $b = 10$

To test this null hypothesis, either a standard chi-square test or the Kolmogorov-Smirnov, a generally more powerful test, can be used. The latter entails the following steps:

1. Formulate the null hypothesis and the alternative hypothesis.
2. Establish the theoretical probability for each class by taking the definite integral of the hypothesized probability density function.
3. Calculate the relative frequency for each class by dividing the number of observations in a class by the sample size.
4. Compute the cumulative probability distribution of the sample data by successively adding the relative frequencies of each class. (This is also called the *observed cumulative distribution,* or *OCD.*)
5. Establish the cumulative probability distribution of the theoretical distribution that has been hypothesized by successively adding the theoretical probabilities of each class. (This is also called the *theoretical cumulative distribution,* or *TCD.*)

TABLE 15.11 *Kolmogorov–Smirnov test applied to gas station data*

Class	Theoretical probability	Relative frequency	Theoretical cumulative distribution	Observed cumulative distribution	Absolute difference
0–2	.2	.257	.2	.257	.057
2–4	.2	.171	.4	.428	.028
4–6	.2	.229	.6	.657	.057
6–8	.2	.171	.8	.828	.028
8–10	.2	.171	1.0	.999*	.001
	1.0	.999*			

* Failure to sum to 1.0 is due to truncation error.

6. Compute the absolute difference between the observed cumulative distribution and the theoretical cumulative distribution for each class in the frequency distribution by subtracting the TCD from the OCD. This operation gives you the absolute difference.

7. Compare the absolute difference for each class interval with the critical value found in a standard Kolmogorov-Smirnov table. If the critical value exceeds every absolute difference then the null hypothesis cannot be rejected.

The results of submitting the gas station data to this procedure are shown in Table 15.11. Because the critical Kolmogorov-Smirnov value with a level of significance of .05 is equal to .23, the null hypothesis cannot be rejected. (Verify these values in the Kolmogorov-Smirnov table in Appendix G.)

The next step in analyzing the data is to develop the functions necessary to generate a nonuniformly distributed random variable from a uniform random number between 0 and 1. If the random variable is discrete, it is easy to use the cumulative probability distribution, as we did in the manual simulation of the harbor.

For example, let x be the number of arrivals at an emergency room in 1 hour. Let us assume that this random variable, x, is distributed in a Poisson manner with a mean of 1. This probability distribution is shown in Table 15.12. It is then a simple matter to generate a uniform random number between 0 and 1 and use this random number to determine the value of x. For example, if the random number is between .3679 and .7358, x takes on the value of 1. If the random number is less than .3679, no arrivals occurred during that hour. The generating function is as shown in Table 15.13.

To derive a generating function for continuous random variables, you must use the integral calculus, but the basic idea is the same. The object is to define the stochastic variable in terms of a uniformly distributed random number. For example, the process generator for a random variable

TABLE 15.12   *Poisson distribution with mean = 1*

Number of arrivals	Probability	Cumulative probability
0	.3679	.3679
1	.3679	.7358
2	.1839	.9197
3	.0613	.9810
4	.0153	.9963
5	.0031	.9994
6	.0005	.9999
7	.0001	1.0000

TABLE 15.13   *Poisson generating function*

Random number	x
0–.3679	0
.3679–.7358	1
.7358–.9197	2
.9197–.9810	3
.9810–.9963	4
.9963–.9994	5
.9994–.9999	6
.9999–1.000	7

distributed according to a negative exponential distribution is

$$x = -\frac{1}{\lambda} \ln{(r)}$$

where

x = exponentially distributed random variable
r = uniform random number between 0 and 1
$1/\lambda$ = mean
$\ln(r)$ = the natural logarithm of r

Model Formulation

A simulation model is an abstraction of some real phenomenon or system. Model building is a very difficult step in the simulation process, because the model builder must strike a balance between model realism and the cost of developing that model. If a crucial variable or functional relationship is omitted, the model will not accurately predict the behavior of the real system. If the model is too close to the real-world system, it can easily be too expensive to collect data for or to program and execute. The goal of the model builder is to build a model that adequately describes the real system at a minimum cost of human and computer resources. You can imagine that model building is an art rather than a science.

Program Generation

Most management science studies require the use of the computer, but for simulation the management scientist has no alternative. The computer is an absolute necessity. The computer language you use is, therefore, a matter of some consequence.

Computer programming languages can actually be thought of in a hierarchy. The assembler languages of the various computer manufacturers are at the lowest level, and they are almost never used in simulation studies. For one thing, they are machine-dependent, which means that an assembler language program will not run on a machine other than the model for which it was created. An IBM assembler language program, for example, cannot run on a Honeywell computer. Also, it is excessively complex to write a simulation program in assembler language. A simple, single-channel queuing simulator might take as many as 5,000 assembler language instructions.

Compiler languages, the next level of programming languages, are used for simulation. FORTRAN, BASIC, PL/1, and PASCAL are the most popular of these for simulation. Compiler languages are machine-independent, and because they are more sophisticated than assembler languages, a programmer has far less detail to be concerned with; so the programming effort is reduced.

Special-purpose simulation languages, such as SIMSCRIPT II.5, GPSS, SLAM II, and SIMNET simplify programming even more. This advantage is graphically demonstrated in Figures 15.6 and 15.3. The manual simulation we performed in the harbor problem is coded in FORTRAN in Figure 15.6 and in GPSS in Figure 15.3.

In view of these illustrations, you can readily see why the management scientist should use a special-purpose simulation language to write a simulation program. The reason for the obvious reduction in programming effort with a simulation language such as GPSS is that each GPSS statement or block can be thought of as a FORTRAN subroutine (a small program in itself), and such things as the simulation clock and next-event logic are preprogrammed into the GPSS software. An additional benefit is that the probability of creating a valid program is increased.

Why, then, are many simulators written in compiler languages such as FORTRAN and BASIC? One reason is that special-purpose simulation languages such as GPSS and SIMSCRIPT are not as widely available as the

```
      FORTRAN BY    SHARON WILSON
      DIMENSION X(15),Y(15),A(16),B(16),EVENT(15,20),ITEMP(20)
      DIMENSION C(15),D(15),E(20),F(20),IT(20)
    1 READ(5,10,END=1000)NUMBER,ISET,ITIME,IFREQ,N
   10 FORMAT(10I5)
      WRITE(6,11)NUMBER,ITIME,IFREQ,N
   11 FORMAT('1',////,'    * * * * THIS PROGRAM WILL CALCULATE',I5,' SIMUL
     1ATIONS STARTING AT',I5,' HOURS',/,3X,'WITH ONE ARRIVAL EVERY',I5,
     2' MINUTES AND',I5,' TOTAL NUMBER OF ARRIVALS.',////)
      READ(5,20)(X(I),I=1,15)
   20 FORMAT(15F5.0)
      DO 21 I=1,15
      IF(X(I).EQ.0.0)GO TO 22
   21 CONTINUE
   22 LX=I-1
      WRITE(6,23)(X(I),I=1,LX)
   23 FORMAT('0 PROBABILITIES FOR INCOMING EVENTS',/,15F8.4)
      IF(ISET.EQ.0)GO TO 40

      READ(5,20)(Y(I),I=1,15)
      DO 31 I=1,15
      IF(Y(I).EQ.0.0)GO TO 32
   31 CONTINUE
   32 LY=I-1
      WRITE(6,33)(Y(I),I=1,LY)
   33 FORMAT('0 PROBABILITIES FOR OUT GOING EVENTS',/,15F8.4)
   40 CONTINUE
      SUM=0.0
      DO 41 I=1,LX
   41 SUM=SUM+X(I)
   50 IF(ISET.EQ.0)GO TO 55
      SUM=0.0
      DO 51 I=1,LY
   51 SUM=SUM+Y(I)
   55 IX=9
      LXX=LX
      LYY=LY
      LX=LX+1
      LY=LY+1
      TIME = ITIME
      READ(5,20)(C(I),I=1,LXX)
      WRITE(6,24)(C(I),I=1,LXX)
   24 FORMAT('0 EARLY TIME ARRIVALS',/,15F8.1)
      IF(ISET.EQ.0) GO TO 54
      READ(5,20)(D(I),I=1,LYY)
      WRITE(6,25)(D(I),I=1,LYY)
   25 FORMAT('0 DURATION TIME',/,15F8.1)
   54 CONTINUE
      A(1)=0.0
      DO 57 I=1,LX
   57 A(I+1)=A(I)+X(I)
      IF(ISET.EQ.0)GO TO 60
      B(1)=0.0
      DO 56 I=1,LY
   56 B(I+1)=B(I)+Y(I)
   60 DO 500 IJ=1,NUMBER
      WRITE(6,61)IJ
   61 FORMAT('1',29X,'* * * * * * * * * * * * * * * *',/,' ',
     129X,'* * * S I M U L A T I O N ',I5,' * * *',/,' ',29X,
     2'* * * * * * * * * * * * * * * *',////)
      CALL MOVE(0,EVENT,0,1200)
      DO 70 J=1,N
      CALL RANDNO(IX,IY,RAND)
      RAND=ABS(RAND)
      IX=IY
      IF      (RAND.LT.0.0.OR.RAND.GT.1.0)RAND=0.0
      DO 71 I=1,LX
      IF(A(I).LE.RAND.AND.RAND.LE.A(I+1))GO TO 73
   71 CONTINUE
      GO TO 70
   73 EVENT(I,J)=1.
   70 CONTINUE
      IF(ISET.EQ.0)GO TO 100
      DO 80 J=1,N
      CALL RANDNO(IX,IY,RAND)
      RAND=ABS(RAND)
      IX=IY
      IF(RAND.LT.0.0.OR.RAND.GT.1.0)RAND=0.0
      DO 81 I=1,LY
      IF(B(I).LE.RAND.AND.RAND.LE.B(I+1))GO TO 83
   81 CONTINUE
      GO TO 80
   83 EVENT(I,J)=EVENT(I,J)+2.
   80 CONTINUE
  100 CONTINUE
      DO 110 I=1,N
  110 E(I)=IFREQ*(I-1)
      WRITE(6,150)
  150 FORMAT(12X,'PROBABILITY',14X,'ARRIVAL NUMBER',/,11X,74('-'))
      DO 175 I=1,LXX
      K=1
      DO 160 J=1,N
      IF(EVENT(I,J).EQ.1.0.OR.EVENT(I,J).EQ.3.0)GO TO 159
      GO TO 160
  159 ITEMP(K)=J
      K=K+1
  160 CONTINUE
      K=K-1
      IF(K.EQ.0) GO TO 170
      WRITE(6,165)I,A(I),A(I+1),(ITEMP(KK),KK=1,K)
```

```
  165 FORMAT(' EVENT ',I2,2X,'!',F5.3,'-',F5.3,'!',20(I2,'/'))
      GO TO 175
  170 WRITE(6,165)I,A(I),A(I+1)
  175 CONTINUE
      WRITE(6,180)
  180 FORMAT(11X,74('-'))
      IF(ISET.EQ.0) GO TO 300
      WRITE(6,250)
  250 FORMAT(///,12X,'PROBABILITY',14X,'DEPARTURE NUMBER',/,11X,74('-'))
      DO 275 I=1,LYY
      K=1
      DO 260 J=1,N
      IF(EVENT(I,J).EQ.2.0.OR.EVENT(I,J).EQ.3.0) GO TO 259
      GO TO 260
  259 ITEMP(K)=J
      K=K+1
  260 CONTINUE
      K=K-1
      IF(K.EQ.0) GO TO 270
      WRITE(6,165)I,B(I),B(I+1),(ITEMP(KK),KK=1,K)
      GO TO 275
  270 WRITE(6,165)I,B(I),B(I+1)
  275 CONTINUE
      WRITE(6,180)
  300 CONTINUE
      WRITE(6,600)
  600 FORMAT(///,24X,'**************',/,24X,'***SCHEDULE***',/,24X,
     1'**************')
      WRITE(6,601)
  601 FORMAT('0',12X,'   ARRIVAL      ARRIVAL      DEPARTURE',/,14X,
     1'  NUMBER        TIME         TIME   ',/,12X,
     2'                IN HOURS     IN HOURS',/,12X,40('-'))
      DO 650 J=1,N
      DO 640 I=1,LXX
      IF(EVENT(I,J).EQ.1.0.OR.EVENT(I,J).EQ.3.0) GO TO 639
      GO TO 640
  639 IT(J)=J
      E(J)=E(J)-C(I)
  640 CONTINUE
  650 CONTINUE
      CALL ORDER(N,E,IT)
      IF(ISET.EQ.0) GO TO 775
      DO 750 J=1,N
      DO 740 I=1,LYY
      IF(EVENT(I,J).EQ.2.0.OR.EVENT(I,J).EQ.3.0) GO   TO 739
      GO TO 740
  739 F(J)=D(I)
  740 CONTINUE
  750 CONTINUE
  775 CONTINUE
      INDEX=IT(1)
      IF(ISET.EQ.0) GO TO 780
      TEMPO=((E(1)+F(INDEX))/60.)+TIME
  780 TEMP1=(E(1)/60.)+TIME
      IF(ISET.EQ.0) WRITE(6,800) INDEX,TEMP1
      WRITE(6,800)INDEX,TEMP1,TEMPO
  800 FORMAT(12X,I7,6X,2(F10.3,3X))
      DO 900 ICHEAT=2,N
      INDEX=IT(ICHEAT-1)
      IF(ISET.EQ.0) F(INDEX)=0.
      IF(E(ICHEAT).GE.(E(ICHEAT-1)+F(INDEX)))GO TO 875
      FUDGE=E(ICHEAT-1)+F(INDEX)-E(ICHEAT)
      E(ICHEAT)=E(ICHEAT)+FUDGE
      INDEX=IT(ICHEAT)
      IF(ISET.EQ.0) GO TO 850
      TEMPO=((E(ICHEAT)+F(INDEX))/60.)+TIME
  850 TEMP1=(E(ICHEAT)/60.)+TIME
      IF(ISET.EQ.0) WRITE(6,800) INDEX,TEMP1
      WRITE(6,800)INDEX,TEMP1,TEMPO
      GO TO 900
  875 INDEX=IT(ICHEAT)
      IF(ISET.EQ.0) GO TO 880
      TEMPO=((E(ICHEAT)+F(INDEX))/60.)+TIME
  880 TEMP1=(E(ICHEAT)/60.)+TIME
      IF(ISET.EQ.0) WRITE(6,800) INDEX,TEMP1
      WRITE(6,800)INDEX,TEMP1,TEMPO
  900 CONTINUE
  500 CONTINUE
      GO TO 1
 1000 CONTINUE
      CALL END
      STOP
      END
      SUBROUTINE ORDER(LX,X,IT)
      DIMENSION X(2),IT(2)
      K=0
      DO 20 J=1,LX
      K=K+1
      INDEX=K
      DO 10 I=K,LX
   10 IF(X(INDEX).GT.X(I))INDEX=I
      XMIN=X(INDEX)
      IMIN=IT(INDEX)
      X(INDEX)=X(J)
      IT(INDEX)=IT(J)
      IT(J)=IMIN
   20 X(J)=XMIN
      RETURN
      END
      SUBROUTINE RANDNO(IX,IY,YFL)
      IY=IX*65539
      IF(IY)5,6,6
```

FIGURE 15.6 FORTRAN source listing for harbor problem

compiler languages. All but the very smallest computers have FORTRAN, COBOL, or BASIC compilers in their software packages. Often, a simulation language is not used because the management scientist conducting the simulation study may not know a special-purpose language and may be unwilling to invest the time needed to learn one. Clearly, an organization that uses management science techniques to aid in its decision process should consider acquiring a simulation processor such as SLAM II or SIMSCRIPT II.5, and then train its staff in the use of the simulation language.

Model Validation

Perhaps the most difficult step in a simulation study is validating the simulation model. It is foolish to use simulation results in the decision-making process unless you are quite confident that the simulation model represents the real-world situation accurately. Absolute validation is probably unattainable, but it is possible to gain confidence in a simulation model by making certain verifications. These validation steps include the following:

Program testing One aspect of a simulation that must be validated is whether the programmer has instructed the computer properly. It is possible that a simulation model is valid as designed but invalid as implemented on the computer. Standard program-testing techniques should be employed to ensure congruence between simulator design and simulator program. These techniques include manual calculations, program traces, and so on. It is necessary to verify the absence of programming errors when you are validating a simulation, but this step alone is not sufficient. The program can be perfect and the simulation model may still be totally invalid.

Variable generation test Earlier in this chapter we applied nonparametric goodness-of-fit tests to hypotheses concerning the distributions of the various stochastic variables. These same tests should be applied to the output from the various process generators to ensure that the real-world variables and simulated variables are distributed in the same manner. For example, if the interarrival time in a real queuing system is normally distributed with a mean of 5 minutes and a standard deviation of 2 minutes, then the random variable of interarrival times being generated in the simulation program should also be normally distributed with $\mu = 5$ and $\sigma = 2$.

Subjective validation The design as well as the output of the simulation model ought to be reviewed by the people who are most familiar with the real system. This subjective validation should properly be done by people not directly involved in the simulation study.

Historical validation If the simulator is designed to simulate an existing system, it is often possible to simulate the system as it is presently configured and then compare actual historical data with simulation output. For example, if the real system is a harbor operation, vital statistics such as the average wait time of a vessel and the average time a vessel spends in the harbor should be compared to the distribution of various output variables. The absence of significant differences between simulated results and historical results may tend to validate the simulator, but it does not guarantee that the simulator will accurately predict the behavior of the real system under different conditions.

Confidence in the validity of a simulation model is crucial to the successful use of simulation. For this reason, the management scientist should leave no stone unturned when performing the validation step of a simulation study.

Experimental Design

Once a simulation model has been implemented and validated, it can be used for its original purpose, experimentation. Simulation, you will recall, is a means of providing information necessary for decision making when a real-world system cannot be sufficiently manipulated. A simulation model synthetically gathers the information necessary to describe the system under study. The object is to gather the information necessary for decision making—at the lowest possible cost. Usually, real-world experiments are more costly than simulation experiments, and thus the management scientist can experiment with a greater number of alternatives when using a simulation model. For example, if the system under study is a harbor and the decision variables are the number of tugs, the number of berths, and the queue discipline, by means of simulation the management scientist can experiment with many combinations of decision variables to determine the optimal harbor configuration. If, however, experiments were made on the real system, far fewer alternatives could be evaluated.

Defining alternative scenarios to be run is the joint responsibility of the management science analyst and the relevant decision makers who are relying on the simulation results. Typically, these scenarios present management with a variety of system configurations and input parameters. For example, in the O'Hare Airport example at the beginning of this chapter, the Chicago Airport Board, the major airlines operating at O'Hare, the FAA and the model builders specified a variety of airspace and airport configurations and air traffic control procedures to be tested in conjunction with a variety of airline schedules.

Once the scenarios have been identified the management scientist must deal with questions of the length of simulation runs, initialization periods, sample sizes, and optimization procedures that are beyond the scope of this text. Many of the answers are contained in the traditional literature concerning experimental design.

Analysis of Simulation Results

If the simulation model is valid and the simulation experiments have been designed properly, analysis of simulation output is fairly straightforward. It is the function of the management scientist to interpret simulation results and make the appropriate inferences necessary for rational decision making. Often, certain statistical techniques, such as analysis of variance, can be helpful in analyzing simulation results.

DETERMINISTIC SIMULATION

deterministic simulation

Thus far in this chapter, the discussion of simulation has been limited to those types of models which involve stochastic or probabilistic events. A *deterministic simulation* model is a descriptive model that has no stochastic events. The major reason for creating a deterministic simulation model is to provide a vehicle for changing the parameters of the model and predicting the behavior of the system under a variety of scenarios.

Let us illustrate the difference between stochastic and deterministic simulation with a real-world application which utilized both types of simulation. In January 1983 American Airlines was in the midst of a major expansion at their main hub in Dallas, Texas (DFW Airport). With the new terminal that was scheduled for operation in April 1983, management had to decide on how many of the 34 gates they could actually schedule airplanes into without seriously degrading schedule dependability. The number of spare gates was known to have a significant impact on dependability but because of the revenue potential of "scheduling" a gate, management wanted to minimize the number of gates to be designated as spares without degrading schedule performance. Because the new terminal was still under construction in January 1983, arrivals of aircraft and the time necessary to service them had to be generated using historical probability distributions. The resulting model was a stochastic simulation model that indicated that the appropriate number of spare gates was 3 during most of the day and possibly 4 during several busy hours of the day.

In August 1983, after 4 months of operation with 4 spare gates, senior management at American decided to revisit the spare gate issue. This time, however, the Operations Research Department had the advantage of using a deterministic (or data driven) simulation approach. Instead of generating arrivals, taxi times, and gate times from historical probability distributions, the OR analyst was able to use operational data that records every significant movement of each aircraft. This deterministic simulator was used to analyze the spare gate issue by varying the number of spare gates and changing the gate assignment procedures. The deterministic model allowed management to alter the spare gate configuration and answer questions about the opera-

		NET	PMTS/		
	INTEREST	OPERATING	PROCEEDS	INCOME	CASH
YEAR	PAYMENTS	INCOME	ON HOUSE	TAX	FLOW
1987	$3,970	$6,000	$14,632	$59	($8,691)
1988	3,901	6,300	4,632	163	1,505
1989	3,824	6,615	4,632	272	1,711
1990	3,740	6,946	4,632	389	1,925
1991	3,646	7,293	4,632	512	2,149
1992	3,543	7,658	4,632	643	2,383
1993	3,429	8,041	4,632	782	2,626
1994	3,303	8,443	4,632	930	2,881
1995	3,164	8,865	4,632	1,087	3,145
1996	3,010	9,308	(26,158)	14,745	20,721
Net Present Value:					$7,577

Purchase Price: 50,000   Monthly Payment: 386.01
Loan Amount: 40,000   Annual Depreciation: 1818.18
Interest Rate: 10.0%   Sale Price: 60,000
Marginal Tax Rate: 28%   Adjusted tax basis: 31,818
Cost of Capital: 14%

FIGURE 15.7 **Deterministic simulation of financial planning problem**

tional effects during the period being modeled. After the second study, senior management decided to reduce the number of spare gates at DFW from 4 to 3. This decision was especially important because of an additional long-term construction project at DFW that necessitated removing several gates from service during the span of the construction.

The point is computer simulation can be applied to a decision without having to generate stochastic events. These types of deterministic models are a very common approach to financial problems. In fact, the majority of financial models are descriptive models that are devoid of stochastic variables and hence, can be classified as deterministic simulation models. Many of the popular spreadsheet packages such as Lotus 1-2-3 are a convenient means of performing deterministic financial simulations on a microcomputer.

Figure 15.7 illustrates a Lotus 1-2-3 spreadsheet analysis of a financial planning problem. The key deterministic parameters are purchase price, loan amount, interest rate, marginal tax rate, and cost of capital. Varying any one of the parameters allows the financial planner to view the net effect on the overall net present value of the investment.

WHEN TO SIMULATE

Once a problem has been formulated, the management scientist must decide whether or not to attempt to solve the problem using discrete digital simulation. This decision process is depicted in Figure 15.8.

As we said earlier in this chapter, the problem should be formulated

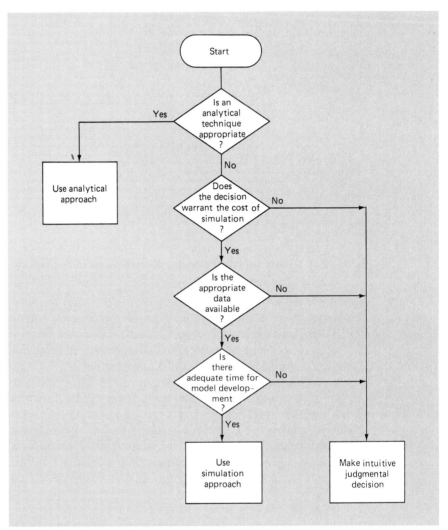

FIGURE 15.8 **When to simulate**

explicitly in terms of hypotheses to be tested and questions to be answered. After the problem has been formulated, a solution technique other than simulation is often judged to be more appropriate. The important point is that choosing a solution methodology must succeed, not precede, the problem formulation phase of any management science study. If an analytical technique or model is available or can be adapted to the problem, it should probably be used. If an analytical technique such as classical inventory theory or queuing theory cannot be applied, then the management scientist must often make the decision between simulating and making an intuitive, seat-of-the-pants decision. This judgment, in turn, depends on the nature of the individual decision. In other words, is the decision important enough to justify the estimated cost of developing, validating, and experimenting with a simulation model?

Even though the cost of developing and using a simulation model to support a decision is outweighed by the potential benefit it still may not be a feasible approach. As we have indicated, simulation models have a large appetite for data, and if the data are not available, decision support using simulation would be ill advised. Another important issue concerns the time window of the decision process. If a decision must be made in a short time frame and is not likely to reoccur, simulation is probably not a viable approach. Even fairly simplistic simulation models take several months to build and validate. In summary, a simulation approach should be considered for important decisions when more efficient analytical approaches aren't appropriate and when the data and development time are available.

Advantages of Simulation

In deciding whether or not to simulate, the management scientist must weigh the advantages and disadvantages of the technique.

- The greatest advantage is that simulation allows the management scientist to model complex and dynamic phenomena that otherwise could not be dealt with in a scientific way.
- Simulation permits experimentation that might be impossible or infeasible otherwise. "What if" questions can be asked using simulation.
- By simulating the system, the management scientist gains valuable insight into the system and into the relative importance of the different variables.
- Simulation allows for the compression of real time. To predict the behavior of a system over the period of a year may take only a few seconds or minutes using computer simulation.
- To comprehend the basic concept of simulation does not require a sophisticated mathematical background and, consequently, managers are more likely to use simulation as a decision-making tool.

Disadvantages of Simulation

Naturally, there are some significant disadvantages to using discrete digital simulation to solve management decision-making problems.

- Simulation is not an optimization technique. Typically, different system configurations are experimented with to find a good, but *not* guaranteed best, solution.

□ Simulation is an expensive way to solve a problem. In addition to the cost of building and validating a simulation model, experimentation using computer simulation can be quite costly.

□ Because of the nature of simulation, sampling error exists in all output from stochastic simulation models. Of course, this sampling error can be reduced by increasing the sample size and by lengthening the computer runtime.

□ A real disadvantage is that simulation is often misused because many people who are qualified to write a simulation program are not qualified to perform a total simulation study. In other words, many programmers do not possess the necessary statistical background.

□ Another serious shortcoming of simulation is that it is a tool of solution evaluation and thus does not generate problem solutions. Therefore, the decision maker has to develop proposed solutions; then, simulation can be used to test the relative desirability of those solutions.

COMPUTER IMPLICATIONS

Simulating a complex system without a computer is like playing major league baseball without a glove. The computer is an absolute necessity for all but the most simple applications.

Because simulation can be used to assist decision making in a wide variety of application areas, it is one of the most widely used management science techniques. Developments in computer hardware and software have increased and will continue to increase the application of simulation dramatically. These developments include

□ **The decrease in the cost of computing** In the past, the cost of running a large-scale simulation often prohibited the use of simulation because arriving at the appropriate answer was not cost effective. With the rapid decrease in the cost of computing fewer applications of simulation are not cost effective.

□ **The increase in corporate data bases** As you learned in this chapter, adequate data are necessary to building a simulation model. The appropriate data are becoming increasingly available in machine-readable form in corporate data bases. Existence of the appropriate data reduces the cost of developing a simulation model, increases its validity and helps reduce the time needed to develop the model.

□ **The increase in the quantity and quality of simulation languages** Simulation languages will continue to evolve and, indeed, be invented, thus reducing the cost and the elapsed time necessary to develop a simulation model.

In short, the computer is a necessary ingredient in a simulation study and trends in computer hardware and software are predicted to combine to significantly increase the use of simulation as a tool for management decision making.

SUMMARY

Discrete digital simulation is probably the most potent, most flexible, and consequently, one of the most commonly used tools in the tool kit of the management scientist. Simulation's major contribution is that it allows the decision maker to predict the behavior of a complex system under various circumstances and configurations.

The application of simulation to solving management problems is on a steep growth trend. Simulation is being applied to a rapidly increasing variety of problems mainly because of its ability to model complex and dynamic systems that could not otherwise be modeled. Another reason for the recent explosion in simulation applications is that the major disadvantages of simulation—cost and the unavailability of data necessary to build and validate the model—are being mitigated by the rapid advances that have been made and are being made in computer hardware and software technology.

SOLVED PROBLEM

PROBLEM STATEMENT

A car wash chain is planning to build another car wash facility and is trying to decide how many stalls to build. Past experience has shown that the time between arriving customers is exponentially distributed. The mean of the distribution depends on the traffic count per hour going by the facility. Based on city traffic engineering data, the mean time between arrivals is estimated to be 10 minutes. The time required to wash a car is 10 minutes and constant. Also, it has been established that people generally do not get in line if there are more than 2 cars waiting. If management wants to build a facility such that there is a low probability of losing customers due to the length of the line but at the same time does not want to overbuild, how many stalls should be built? Simulate for 8 hours, or 480 minutes.

SOLUTION

The process generator for the exponential distribution is

$$x = -\frac{1}{\lambda} \ln (r)$$

			One stall		
Random no.	Time of arrival	Time in	Time out	No. in line (excluding new arrival)	Lost customer?
.494	7	7	17	0	No
.353	17	17	27	0	No
.407	26	27	37	0	No
.682	30	37	47	0	No
.827	32	47	57	1	No
.379	42	57	67	1	No
.535	48	67	77	1	No
.867	49	—	—	2	Yes
.957	49	—	—	2	Yes
.025	86	86	96	0	No
.503	93	96	106	0	No
.571	99	106	116	0	No
.025	136	136	146	0	No
.838	138	146	156	0	No
.281	151	156	166	0	No
.679	155	166	176	1	No
.142	175	176	186	0	No
.818	177	186	196	0	No
.224	192	196	206	0	No
.165	210	210	220	0	No
.095	234	234	244	0	No
.038	267	267	277	0	No
.795	269	277	287	0	No
.333	280	287	297	0	No
.488	287	297	307	0	No
.911	288	307	317	0	No
.278	301	317	327	1	No
.978	301	—	—	2	Yes
.935	302	—	—	2	Yes
.490	309	327	337	1	No
.106	331	337	347	0	No
.332	342	347	357	0	No
.932	343	357	367	1	No
.190	360	367	377	0	No
.438	368	377	387	0	No
.682	372	387	397	1	No
.041	404	404	414	0	No
.255	418	418	428	0	No
.595	423	428	438	0	No
.519	430	438	448	0	No
.989	430	448	458	1	No
.416	439	458	468	1	No
.997	439	—	—	2	Yes
.101	462	468	478	0	No
.340	473	478	488	0	No
.053	502	—	—		

			Two stalls			
Random no.	Time of arrival	Stall no.	Time in	Time out	No. in line (excluding new arrival)	Lost customer?
.494	7	1	7	17	0	No
.353	17	1	17	27	0	No
.407	26	2	26	36	0	No
.682	30	1	30	40	0	No
.827	32	2	36	46	0	No
.379	42	1	42	52	0	No
.535	48	2	48	58	0	No
.867	49	1	52	62	0	No
.957	49	2	58	68	0	No
.025	86	1	86	96	0	No
.503	93	2	93	103	0	No
.571	99	1	99	109	0	No
.025	136	1	136	146	0	No
.838	138	2	138	148	0	No
.281	151	1	151	161	0	No
.679	155	2	155	165	0	No
.142	175	1	175	185	0	No
.818	177	2	177	187	0	No
.224	192	1	192	202	0	No
.165	210	1	210	220	0	No
.095	234	1	234	244	0	No
.038	267	1	267	277	0	No
.795	269	2	269	279	0	No
.333	280	1	280	290	0	No
.488	287	2	287	297	0	No
.911	288	1	290	300	0	No
.278	301	1	301	311	0	No
.978	301	2	301	311	0	No
.935	302	1	311	321	0	No
.490	309	2	311	321	1	No
.106	331	1	331	341	0	No
.332	342	1	342	352	0	No
.932	343	2	343	353	0	No
.190	360	1	360	370	0	No
.438	368	2	368	378	0	No
.682	372	1	372	382	0	No
.041	404	1	404	414	0	No
.255	418	1	418	428	0	No
.595	423	2	423	433	0	No
.519	430	1	430	440	0	No
.989	430	2	433	443	0	Lost
.416	439	1	440	450	0	No
.997	439	2	443	453	0	No
.101	462	1	463	473	0	No
.340	473	1	474	484	0	No
.053	502					

To calculate the time between arrivals, merely substitute the random number into the function shown. For example,

$$r = .494$$
$$x = -10 \ln (.494)$$
$$= (-10)(-.7052)$$
$$= 7.052 \quad \text{(rounded to 7 minutes)}$$

The time until the next arrival is $7 + x$, where

$$x = -10 \ln (.353)$$
$$= (-10)(-1.04)$$
$$= 10 \text{ minutes} \quad \text{(rounded)}$$

Therefore, the second customer arrives at 17 minutes into the simulation. The rest of the solution tables merely keep track of the system as simulated time progresses.

If management were to use the simulation to make a decision concerning the number of stalls, the profit lost from customers not stopping would

```
BLOCK
NUMBER    *LOC   OPERATION      A,B,C,D,E,F,G,H,I              COMMENTS
          *
          *    FUNCTION DEFINITIONS(S):
          *
          EXPON FUNCTION    RN2,C24
          0,0/.1,.104/.2,.222/.3,.355/.4,.509/.5,.69/.6,.915
          .7,1.2/.75,1.38/.8,1.6/.84,1.83/.88,2.12/.9,2.3
          .92,2.52/.94,2.81/.95,2.99/.96,3.2/.97,3.5/.98,3.9
          .99,4.6/.995,5.3/.998,6.2/.999,7/.9998,8
          *
          *    STORAGE CAPACITY DEFINITIONS(S):
          *
          WASH   STORAGE        1
          *
          *    SIMULATION LOGIC:
          *
                 SIMULATE
    1            GENERATE       10,FN$EXPON
    2            TEST LE        Q$WASHQ,2,BALK
    3            QUEUE          WASHQ
    4            ENTER          WASH
    5            DEPART         WASHQ
    6            ADVANCE        10
    7            LEAVE          WASH
    8            TERMINATE
          *
    9     BALK   QUEUE          BALKQ
   10            DEPART         BALKQ
   11            TERMINATE
          *
   12            GENERATE       1440
   13            TERMINATE      1
                 START          5
                 END
```

PARTIAL COMPUTER OUTPUT   1 STALL

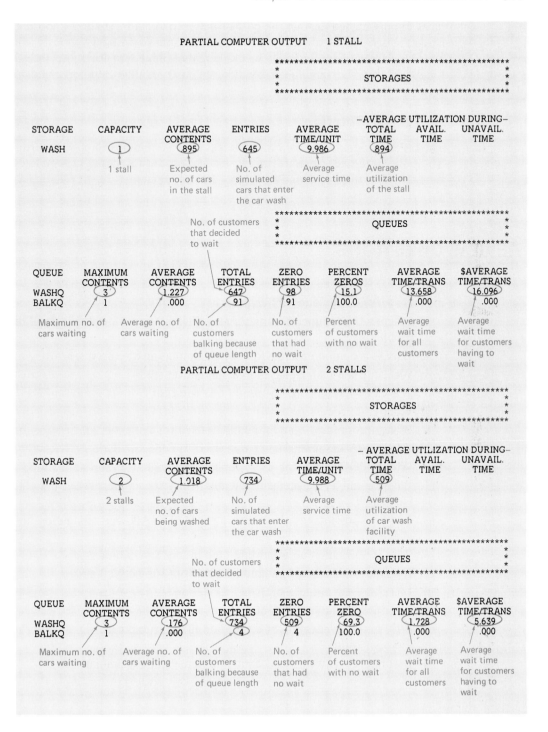

****
*   *
*   STORAGES   *
*   *
****

STORAGE	CAPACITY	AVERAGE CONTENTS	ENTRIES	AVERAGE TIME/UNIT	–AVERAGE UTILIZATION DURING–		
					TOTAL TIME	AVAIL. TIME	UNAVAIL. TIME
WASH	1	.895	645	9.986	.894		
	1 stall	Expected no. of cars in the stall	No. of simulated cars that enter the car wash	Average service time	Average utilization of the stall		

No. of customers that decided to wait

****
*   *
*   QUEUES   *
*   *
****

QUEUE	MAXIMUM CONTENTS	AVERAGE CONTENTS	TOTAL ENTRIES	ZERO ENTRIES	PERCENT ZEROS	AVERAGE TIME/TRANS	$AVERAGE TIME/TRANS
WASHQ	3	1.227	647	98	15.1	13.658	16.096
BALKQ	1	.000	91	91	100.0	.000	.000
	Maximum no. of cars waiting	Average no. of cars waiting	No. of customers balking because of queue length	No. of customers that had no wait	Percent of customers with no wait	Average wait time for all customers	Average wait time for customers having to wait

PARTIAL COMPUTER OUTPUT   2 STALLS

****
*   *
*   STORAGES   *
*   *
****

STORAGE	CAPACITY	AVERAGE CONTENTS	ENTRIES	AVERAGE TIME/UNIT	– AVERAGE UTILIZATION DURING–		
					TOTAL TIME	AVAIL. TIME	UNAVAIL. TIME
WASH	2	1.018	734	9.988	.509		
	2 stalls	Expected no. of cars being washed	No. of simulated cars that enter the car wash	Average service time	Average utilization of car wash facility		

No. of customers that decided to wait

****
*   *
*   QUEUES   *
*   *
****

QUEUE	MAXIMUM CONTENTS	AVERAGE CONTENTS	TOTAL ENTRIES	ZERO ENTRIES	PERCENT ZERO	AVERAGE TIME/TRANS	$AVERAGE TIME/TRANS
WASHQ	3	.176	734	509	69.3	1.728	5.639
BALKQ	1	.000	4	4	100.0	.000	.000
	Maximum no. of cars waiting	Average no. of cars waiting	No. of customers balking because of queue length	No. of customers that had no wait	Percent of customers with no wait	Average wait time for all customers	Average wait time for customers having to wait

have to be weighed against the cost of the second stall. Another important statistic might be the average time a customer spent waiting. Obviously, the prudent management scientist would run the simulation for more than 8 hours, so that the sampling error inherent in simulation studies could be significantly reduced.

Computer Solution

The GPSS program that follows took less than 30 minutes to code and run. The CPU time necessary to run the simulation for 120 hours of simulated time was less than a second on a large IBM computer.

REVIEW QUESTIONS

1. Define "discrete digital simulation."
2. How does simulation differ from LP?
3. Discuss two major reasons for using simulation for solving decision problems.
4. Why is a computer necessary when simulating a real system?
5. What are the major phases in a simulation study?
6. What is a Kolmogorov-Smirnov test used for?
7. What is a process generator?
8. What are uniform random numbers used for in simulation?
9. Why aren't assembler languages used to code simulation models?
10. Why is FORTRAN the most popular language used for simulation?
11. Why should a management scientist use a special-purpose simulation language?
12. List two advantages GPSS has over FORTRAN as a simulation language.
13. Why is validation an important step in any simulation study?
14. How does historical validation differ from subjective validation?
15. List three advantages of using simulation.
16. List three disadvantages of using simulation.
17. Why is the application of simulation likely to increase significantly in the near future?
18. Distinguish between stochastic and deterministic simulation.

PROBLEMS

15.1 *Milk company.* The Page Milk Company has a large, gallon-bottling machine that occasionally breaks down due to bearing failure. The machine has two bearings of this type. To replace one of the bearings, the machine must be shut down. This machine shutdown costs the company approximately $30 per hour. The bearings are relatively inexpensive, at $5 per bearing. At the present, a bearing is replaced only when it fails. The time between bearing failures is distributed as shown in the first table. The time it takes to replace a bearing is fairly constant

Hours between bearing failures	Probability
20	.05
40	.07
60	.13
70	.35
80	.30
90	.07
100	.03

at 1 hour. An employee has suggested that, since it is as easy to replace both bearings as one, the company should try a new policy of replacing both bearings when either one fails. Limited experience with similar bearings has yielded the following probability distribution of bearing failures when both bearings are replaced:

Hours between bearing failures	Probability
40	.05
75	.10
100	.15
125	.25
150	.20
180	.15
200	.10

Use manual or computer simulation to solve this policy problem. If you simulate manually, simulate for the period of 1 month. Assume a 24-hour workday and a 7-day workweek.

15.2 *Port administration.* The following times have been collected at the local harbor. How are these two random variables distributed?

Docking times (min)				Unloading times (min)			
8.59	9.62	9.29	11.34	47.78	17.55	23.82	5.58
13.84	12.89	13.52	12.02	11.93	4.40	18.06	11.16
13.59	13.99	14.87	11.03	48.10	53.61	45.82	12.32
9.29	8.79	13.13	13.86	54.90	43.57	29.43	7.61
12.79	11.03	10.00	13.41	56.65	3.25	36.63	11.24
9.89	13.32	11.62	13.98	23.00	38.50	27.78	58.47
14.14	9.44	13.58	9.57	25.65	15.94	9.77	12.15
13.08	13.89	12.29	8.69	29.76	103.05	7.92	9.88
10.86	13.86	16.66	13.38	27.62	3.00	66.32	34.73
11.39	12.62	14.23	10.73	88.40	59.47	8.79	26.62
12.71	12.03	11.67	8.73	9.40	11.36	21.46	13.29
10.70	9.63	9.56	12.47	2.75	4.21	45.32	57.50
9.20	10.12	13.71	12.78	3.28	89.12	2.38	67.63
11.49	11.24	10.66	11.18	53.67	21.62	17.70	35.54
14.90	15.95	11.76	11.22	1.97	23.51	128.14	3.48
10.09	13.06	11.43	12.27	65.01	30.41	70.32	15.82
12.62	10.21	11.96	13.53	40.49	80.90	23.95	19.19
10.92	9.21	12.56	12.57	19.32	59.24	5.36	4.76
12.70	9.77	12.86	10.17	6.03	44.61	.97	29.71
7.77	12.88	10.75	13.54	51.45	67.02	37.99	17.87
12.26	13.14	12.63	11.91	9.86	14.91	.64	1.08
10.01	14.44	9.98	10.54	10.73	11.32	32.70	5.68
16.45	13.03	10.36	11.03	9.97	13.42	47.02	37.98
15.85	13.26	8.75	12.09	136.41	12.20	44.65	42.04
9.68	13.99	13.28	11.53	14.89	42.75	22.21	1.85

15.3 *Barber shop.* The Checkmate Barbershop presently has only one barber. Business is quite good, and the proprietor is trying to decide whether to hire an additional barber. Customers arrive at the barbershop in a Poisson manner at a rate of 3 per hour (interarrival times are distributed exponentially, with a mean of 20 minutes). The time it takes to give a haircut is exponentially distributed, with a mean of 15 minutes. The barber has noticed that when 2 customers are waiting for a haircut, a new customer generally will not join the queue. Haircuts cost $4, and a new barber would cost the shop $100 per week plus $1 for each haircut. Use simulation to help in the decision of whether or not to hire the additional barber.

15.4 *Doctor schedule.* Dr. Williams has the appointment schedule reflected in the following table. Based on his past experiences, Dr. Williams's estimate of arrival times is:

  □ 10 percent chance of a patient arriving 15 minutes early
  □ 20 percent chance of a patient arriving 5 minutes early

Dr. Williams's appointment schedule

Appointment time	Patient	Expected appointment duration (min)
9:00	Dupont	30
9:15	Austin	20
9:45	Stratman	20
10:00	Rief	30
10:30	Hoffer	20
11:00	Stoltz	30
11:30	Gilbert	20
11:45	Collins	30

- □ 45 percent chance of a patient arriving on time
- □ 15 percent chance of a patient arriving 10 minutes late
- □ 5 percent chance of a patient arriving 20 minutes late
- □ 5 percent chance of a patient failing to arrive

The duration of each patient's appointment is a stochastic variable that, from past experience, is estimated to be distributed as follows:

- □ 10 percent chance that it will take 80 percent of the expected time
- □ 15 percent chance that it will take 90 percent of the expected time
- □ 40 percent chance that it will take 100 percent of the expected time
- □ 25 percent chance that it will take 110 percent of the expected time
- □ 5 percent chance that it will take 120 percent of the expected time
- □ 5 percent chance that it will take 130 percent of the expected time

Dr. Williams is due in surgery at 1:30 P.M. and must leave the office by 12:15 to make it. Dr. Williams would like to know the probability of not canceling any appointments and being on time for surgery. Assume that Dr. Williams gets to the office at 9:00 and sees patients on a first-come, first-served basis. Use manual or computer simulation to answer Dr. Williams's question. If you simulate manually, simulate five mornings.

15.5 *Inventory control.* A ski shop carries a particularly popular pair of skis that sells for $150 and wishes to know how many pairs to order and when to order. Demand is not known with certainty (see the first table). The lead time is 7 days. The cost of the skis, which depends on the quantity ordered, is reflected in the second table. It costs $25 to place an order and a stockout is assumed to cost $25 per unit. The cost of

Historical frequency of demand

Demand per day	Number of observations
0	20
1	26
2	41
3	50
4	38
5	13
6	8
7	3
8	1
	200

Price schedule

Order	Price per pair of skis
Less than 25	$100
25 but < 50	95
50 but < 100	90
100 or more	80

carrying inventory is 20 percent of the value of inventory per year (.055 percent per day).

a. Simulate the following two inventory policies for 1 month (assume a 30-day month and a beginning inventory of 15 pairs, with no skis on order).

(1) Order 15 pairs when inventory reaches 10 pairs.

(2) Order 25 pairs when inventory on hand plus on order reaches 20 pairs.

b. Which of the two policies is better? Explain.

c. What other experiments should be run?

15.6 *Laundromat.* The owner of a large laundromat is considering the opening of a second store. The location she has in mind can accommodate 20 washers and 10 dryers. At peak times she has found arrivals to be Poisson-distributed at a mean rate of 6 customers per hour. The number of washers used by 1 customer is random and distributed according to the table. Dryers can accommodate 2 loads of washing. Both washers and dryers take 30 minutes. The owner has found that to make a profit, the washers must be operated at 40 percent capacity during peak hours. Simulate manually for 2 hours. Should the new laundromat be installed at the proposed location? Assume that there are 5 customers waiting when the doors are opened for business.

Number of washers	Relative frequency
1	.20
2	.35
3	.20
4	.15
5	.05
6	.03
7	.01
8	.01
	1.00

15.7 *Automobile parts department.* Consider a parts department in an auto dealership. At the present time, one clerk operates the parts department, but the owner-manager of the dealership has noticed rather long lines of mechanics waiting for parts. Mechanics arrive to the parts counter at a rate of 10 per hour in a Poisson manner. Service times are exponential, with a mean of 5 minutes. By simulating 25 arrivals, analyze the desirability of adding a second parts clerk.

15.8 *Manufacturing machine shop.* A machine shop has two machine centers. Jobs arrive at the shop according to the following distribution:

Number of jobs per 8-hour day	Relative frequency
0	.40
1	.20
2	.20
3	.10
4	.05
5	.05
	1.00

Time required for jobs at each machine center behave according to the following probability distributions.

Machine center 1

Time (hr)	Relative frequency
1	.10
2	.10
3	.15
4	.20
5	.10
6	.10
7	.08
8	.07
9	.07
10	.03
	1.00

Machine center 2

Time (hr)	Relative frequency
1	.10
2	.15
3	.20
4	.20
5	.15
6	.10
7	.03
8	.03
9	.02
10	.02
	1.00

A given job can take one of the following four possible paths through the machine shop, with the indicated relative percentages.

- machine center 1 only—25 percent
- machine center 2 only—10 percent
- machine center 1, then machine center 2—50 percent
- machine center 2, then machine center 1—15 percent

Simulate the machine shop for ten 8-hour days using the following machine loading rules.

1. First come, first served.
2. Priority based on the amount of processing time left for the job. For example, if 2 jobs are waiting for machine center 2 and one has 5

hours of processing left and the other has 7 hours left, the job with 5 hours left would have priority.

15.9 *Medical insurance.* The AAA Health Insurance Company is concerned with its cash outflows on a weekly basis. AAA is being considered for a large group policy. If AAA wins the contract and insures the group, the daily frequency of claims is estimated as follows:

Number of claims	Relative frequency
0	.05
1	.06
2	.08
3	.10
4	.33
5	.14
6	.11
7	.07
8	.04
9	.02
	1.00

The probability distribution of the cost of each claim has been estimated using historical data. The probability distribution is as follows:

Cost per claim	Probability
$800	.30
900	.24
1,000	.22
1,100	.18
1,200	.06
	1.00

a. Manually simulate 7 days to estimate weekly cash outflow.

b. Write a program that will output a frequency distribution of monthly cash outflows.

15.10 *Newsstand.* A newsstand proprietor is trying to decide how many copies of a weekly news magazine to stock. The magazines sell for $1 and he purchases them for $.60. If he has old magazines at the end of the week, they must be discarded and the proprietor loses his total purchase cost. The demand distribution for the papers is shown in the table.

Number of magazines	Probability
50	.10
55	.15
60	.20
65	.30
70	.15
75	.10
	1.00

Use simulation to determine the number of magazines to be purchased for sale at the newsstand.

15.11 *Agriculture.* Although other factors affect the yield per acre, the amount of rain is the most significant factor in the growing of corn on an Iowa farm. The per acre yield can be estimated by the following regression equation:

$$y = 35x + 50$$

where

$$y = \text{yield per acre}$$
$$x = \text{monthly rainfall (inches)}$$

The monthly rainfall for the growing season is distributed as reflected in the table. Estimate the mean yield per acre by simulating 10 growing seasons.

Average monthly rainfall	Probability
1.0	.08
1.5	.10
2.0	.15
2.5	.21
3.0	.20
3.5	.12
4.0	.08
4.5	.03
5.0	.02
6.0	.01
	1.00

15.12 *Project scheduling.* Consider the project information shown in the table.

Task	Immediate predecessor	Expected time (weeks)
A	—	5
B	A	4
C	A	3
D	B	4
E	C	5
F	D	2
G	E	3

a. Simulate the completion of this project 10 times to estimate the probability distribution of project completion times. Assume an exponential distribution for each task time.

b. Write a simple program to perform the simulation and simulate the project completion 1,000 times.

15.13 *Manufacturing.* The Chigger Lawn Mower Company manufactures a small tractor frame exclusively for a local hardware store chain. The frame is produced by a two-stage process. Stage 1 (molding) has a setup cost per order of $1,000 plus a variable cost per piece of $100. Stage 2 (finishing) has a setup cost of $500 and a variable cost per piece of $80.

The anticipated average reject rate in the first stage is 4 percent (of the frames entering the first stage), and in the second stage it is 20 percent (of the pieces entering stage 2). Rejects are not detected until the end of each stage.

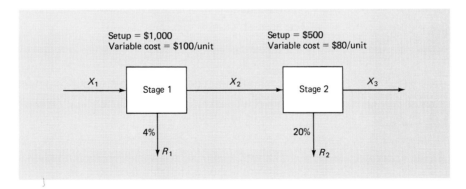

The diagram illustrates the situation, which can also be described using the following variables:

X_1 = the size of the batch ordered into production
R_1 = (stochastic) the number of frames rejected in stage 1
X_2 = the number of good pieces coming out of stage 1 and used as input to stage 2
R_2 = (stochastic) the number of X_2 pieces rejected in stage 2
X_3 = the number of good pieces of final product

How many pieces should be ordered into production (X_1) if the customer requires that exactly 10 good frames be shipped? If the process results in less than 10 good frames (X_2), the shortfall will be hand-crafted at a cost of $1,200 per frame.

For simplicity, assume that

□ All good pieces coming out of the first stage (X_2) will be processed in the second stage.
□ Even if the number of rejections in the first stage is high, a rerun of the first stage will not be made until after the good frames are processed in stage 2.
□ At the end of the second stage, all good frames in excess of the required 10 will be scrapped at zero value.

Write a computer program in the language of your choice to simulate the situation. The inputs to the program should be

□ Input batch size (X_1)
□ Required shipment size (S)
□ Number of batches to simulate (N)

The outputs should include the average cost per shipment and probability of a shortfall ($X_3 < S$).

Use this to determine

□ The minimum average cost batch size for $S = 10$ and 18.
□ The probability of a shortfall in each case.

Solve using trial and error, with $N = 500$ or larger.

BIBLIOGRAPHY

Fishman, George S., *Principles of Discrete Event Digital Simulation.* New York: John Wiley & Sons, Inc., 1978.

Gordon, Geoffrey, *System Simulation,* 2nd ed. Englewood Cliffs, N.J.: Prentice Hall, 1978.

Law, Averill M., and W. David Kelton, *Simulation Modeling and Analysis.* New York: McGraw-Hill Book Company, 1982.

Pritsker, Alan B., *Introduction to Simulation and SLAM,* 3rd ed. New York: John Wiley & Sons, Inc., 1986.

Schriber, Thomas J., *Simulation Using GPSS.* New York: John Wiley & Sons, Inc., 1974.

Shannon, Robert E., *Systems Simulation: The Art and Science.* Englewood Cliffs, N.J.: Prentice Hall, 1975.

Solomon, Susan L., *Simulation of Waiting Line Systems.* Englewood Cliffs, N.J.: Prentice Hall, 1983.

Watson, Hugh J., *Computer Simulation in Business.* New York: John Wiley & Sons, Inc., 1981.

16

Inventory Systems

AMERICAN AIRLINES, INC.

American Airlines has an investment of over $650 million in spare aircraft parts. Efficient management of this huge inventory is one of the key factors that helps insure that American retains its excellent on-time performance and maintenance record. In addition to sophisticated real-time systems that continuously monitor inventory levels for each and every part in inventory, American utilizes advanced decision support systems that perform key decision-making functions.

Spare parts in the airline business are classified as expendable parts and rotable parts. Expendable parts are generally not repaired, whereas rotable parts are parts that are removed from an airplane and sent to a repair facility. The decisions that must be made regarding expendable parts are basically when to order and how much to order. These two decisions are made on a part-by-part basis using models similar to these discussed in this chapter. Making these relatively simple decisions intelligently saves American millions of dollars each year.

The decison problem associated with rotable parts is more complex. In addition to deciding how many spares is the optimal number, American must decide how to distribute these typically high-value parts to the various stations. American Airlines Decision Technologies has built a PC-based model that optimizes the quantity of parts to own system-wide and then allocates those parts to the various stations in an optimal manner.

Once the allocation is made, a model imbedded in the real-time rotable parts tracking system monitors actual inventory levels versus planned and recommends station transfers in order to reduce temporary exposure to stockouts.

The goal of both the expendable parts inventory system and the rotable parts inventory system are the same—to provide a high level of service at the minimum cost. Without the models imbedded in both systems, achieving current service levels with the same investment in inventory would be impossible.

INTRODUCTION

An inventory is a stock of goods that is held for the purpose of future production or sales. Raw materials, work in process, and finished goods can all be classified as inventory items, and the decisions about them are similar. Obviously, such decisions often have a critical effect on the health of the firm.

Reasons for Carrying Inventory

Organizations carry inventories for a number of the following reasons.

Smooth production   Often, the demand for an item fluctuates widely due to a number of factors such as seasonality and production schedules. For example, 50 percent of all the toys manufactured in one year may be sold in the three weeks before Christmas. If toy manufacturers were to try to produce 50 percent of a year's output in three weeks, they would need a tremendous influx of labor as well as huge manufacturing facilities. Instead, firms find it more economical to produce goods over a longer, slower schedule and store them as inventory. Thus, they keep the labor force fairly stable, and expenditures for capital equipment are lower.

Product availability   Most retail goods and many industrial goods are carried in inventory to ensure prompt delivery to customers. Not only does a good inventory provide a competitive edge, it often means the difference between success and failure. If a firm gains a reputation for constantly being out of stock, it may lose a significant number of customers.

Advantages of producing or buying in large quantities   Most production runs involve machine setup time and production time. If setup time is significant, real savings can be achieved by producing in large lots. In addition, many firms offer quantity discounts for buying in large quantities.

lead time **Hedge against long or uncertain lead times**   The time between ordering and receiving goods is known as *lead time*. Firms do not want to stop manufacturing or selling goods during lead time; so it is necessary to carry inventory.

Importance of Effective Inventory Management

In many organizations the importance of effectively controlling inventories is difficult to overestimate. In a manufacturing environment poor inventory control can result in production stoppages thus wasting expensive labor and capital equipment resources. In a retail environment the availability of stock can make the difference between success and failure. Too much inventory could be an impossible financial burden and not enough inventory could result in losing the customer goodwill necessary to succeed. In a service industry such as the transportation industry, lack of critical spare parts can cause canceled service or delayed departures. The U.S. Air Force manages a spare parts inventory valued at billions of dollars. Obviously, even marginal improvements in inventory management can save hundreds of millions of dollars for the U.S. taxpayer.

Gene Woolsey, writing for *Interfaces,* emphasizes the importance of controlling inventories:

> The second stop on the required tour is the production line of machinists making part X. We proceed as follows. First look for a 5 by 5 by 3 foot bin of gears or parts that looks like it has been there awhile. Pick up a gear and ask, casually. "How much is this worth?" You then ask, "How many of these are in the bin?" followed by, "How long has this bin been here?" and, "What's your cost of money for this company?" I recall one case in a nameless South American country where the unit cost times the number of parts times the time it had been there times the interest rate resulted in a cost per day figure that would insure a comfortable retirement for the plant manager on the bank of the Rio de la Plata at one of the better resorts to be found there. The plant manager suddenly realized that what he was holding was not just a chunk of high-test steel, but was *real money*. He then pointed out that *he* now understood the value of the inventory but could I suggest a way to drive the point home to upper management? I suggested that he go to the accounting department and borrow enough money to be equal to the bin's value for as long as it had been sitting there, and pile it on the top of the bin. I further suggested that he do that for every bin on the production line. We rapidly figured out that by the time we had the money piled up on

the bin, you would not even be able to *see* the bin. My opinion was that if the upper managers were given a tour of the line with the money piled up, they would *never forget it.*

Inventory Decisions   Inventory and purchasing managers are charged with making the following basic decisions which will affect inventory service level and the cost of inventory:

- **When to order**   Questions such as whether to order periodically (e.g., monthly) or when stock of an inventory item has reached a specified point must be answered.
- **Where to order from**   Questions like make or buy and if we decide to buy, which vendor should be selected must be answered.
- **How much to order**   Questions such as what is the most cost effective order quantity and should we take advantage of a quantity discount must be answered.
- **What are the proper logistics**   How should the order be shipped and if there are multiple demand points within the inventory system how should the inventory items be allocated among the various demand centers.

To answer these questions and manage the inventory effectively, medium to large organizations needs sophisticated computer-based decision support systems.

Inventory Management Systems

physical inventory system Inventory systems can be classified as physical or continuous. A *physical inventory system* is a system in which management periodically reviews inventory levels of the various items to make inventory decisions. A common example of this type system might be in the small grocery store. Each day, various delivery people stop at the store to replenish inventory. For example, the milkman may come daily, take a physical inventory, and decide what he needs to leave in the dairy case. Each week it may be necessary to order canned goods and other relatively nonperishable items. In order to do this, the manager must look at each item and make a decision on whether to order the item and how much to order.

continuous inventory systems   *Continuous inventory systems* are typically more sophisticated than periodic ordering systems. They keep track of the inventory level of each item on a continuous basis. In other words, as items are added to or drawn from inventory, these events are recorded and the new inventory level is computed.

Continuous inventory accounting systems can range from the extremely simple manual system to very sophisticated computer-based systems. An example of a manual but continuous inventory system might be the local blood bank. For each type of blood, there might be a card on which is recorded the number of units in inventory. As units are demanded or added to inventory, a clerk merely makes the appropriate notation on the card. Hence, there is a permanent record of the inventory status of each blood type at all times.

batch processing inventory Computerized inventory systems can be classified as batch-processing systems or real-time systems. A *batch processing inventory system* is a system in which inventory transactions (additions to and withdrawals from inventory) are collected periodically, batched together, and processed to update the current inventory master file. Typically an inventory control clerk creates a transaction document each time an item is drawn from inventory and each time an order is received. Periodically, these documents are "batched" together and sent to data processing, where the information is transcribed into machine-readable form. These data are then processed against the current inventory master file to create an updated master file. Output from this processing would include a list of items that need to be ordered, a list of the status of all inventory items, purchase orders, a value-of-inventory report, suggested order quantities, and so on. Therefore, in a batch processing environment, the inventory master file is only as current as the date of the last update.

real-time systems *Real-time systems* keep the inventory master file continuously up to date. When a unit is drawn out of or added to inventory, that event is recorded immediately and the master file reflects the change immediately. Typically, real-time systems are significantly more costly than batch systems, but as the cost of computing continues to decrease, the number of real-time inventory systems will inevitably increase. Regardless of the mode of processing, a computer-based inventory system can vary according to the amount of inventory decision making that is delegated to the system.

Figure 16.1 is a functional schematic diagram of an inventory management system in which the basic decisions are being made or at least recommended by the decision-making modules of the system. The basic functions of a decision support system for inventory management are:

- **Inventory accounting** Keeping track of quantities on hand and on order for each inventory item is a major function of any inventory management system. This requires a data base and transaction processing software.

- **Demand forecasting** To make intelligent replenishment and allocation decisions the system must forecast demand for each item. Failure to predict demand accurately will seriously degrade the effectiveness of any inventory system. Some of the models discussed in Chapter 13 are often imbedded in progressive inventory management systems.

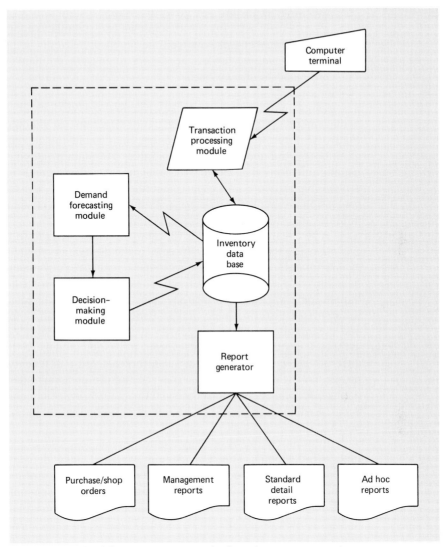

FIGURE 16.1   **Decision support system for inventory management**

☐ **Inventory decision making**   In systems where the demand for an item is in one place, this decision-making function is focused on how much to order and when. When there is more than one demand point, it is often necessary to make decisions concerning how to allocate a given number of units to the various demand points. The models discussed in this chapter address the replenishment decision.

◻ **Inventory reporting** A good inventory system will produce standard reports for use by inventory analysts and summary reports that will tell senior management how well the inventory asset is being managed. In addition, ad hoc reports necessary to analyze problem areas are often produced by the system.

The management scientist has a key role in the development of an inventory management system. Of the four major functions or modules depicted in Figure 16.1 the management scientist must build the demand forecasting module and the decision-making module. The data processing professional usually develops the data base management software and builds the input processing software and report generator. In addition, the data processing professional is typically charged with the responsibility of integrating all the modules together into a cohesive system.

As we learned in Chapter 13, there are many ways to forecast demand, and choosing the appropriate forecasting technique is crucial to the success of any inventory management system. For this reason management scientists typically evaluate the effectiveness of a variety of forecasting techniques for a variety of inventory items. The demand forecasting analysis usually uses historical data and statistics such as mean absolute deviation and mean squared error to identify the best forecasting model. Often, an inventory system will contain several forecasting models so that demand for different categories of inventory can forecast using different models. Some progressive inventory systems use adaptive forecasting where each time a demand forecast is required the system analyzes historical demand data and decides which forecasting technique is best for that inventory item at that point in time.

In addition to being responsible for the development of the demand forecasting module, the management scientist must decide what kind of replenishment model or models should provide the decision-making function for the system. As with forecasting models, a wealth of inventory replenishment decision models have been developed and deciding which model or models to use in the inventory management system is critical to the cost effectiveness of the system. The remainder of this chapter introduces you to the types of models that are commonly used.

ABC Analysis

Obviously, using a computer-based inventory information system and sophisticated operations research techniques to control the paper-clip inventory might be absurd. For this reason, many organizations choose to classify inventory items into three basic categories, usually according to annual dollar volume. The logic of this classification scheme (*ABC classification*) is to

TABLE 16.1   *Annual dollar-volume usage*

Item no.	Annual demand	Per-unit cost	Total annual value
22213	100	$10,000	$1,000,000
22157	2,000	500	1,000,000
22545	200	1,500	300,000
22432	400	500	200,000
22511	150	700	105,000
22457	240	100	24,000
22111	300	50	15,000
22331	10	100	1,000
22471	10	100	1,000
22512	25	25	625
25531	30	20	600
22122	50	10	500
			$2,647,725

spend money and time closely controlling only important inventory items, in the realization that the cost of closely controlling relatively unimportant inventory items cannot be justified. To give you a feeling for how this classification is effected, let us assume that a firm has only 12 individual inventory items. These items and their annual dollar volume are shown in Table 16.1.

The ABC classification typically seeks to put approximately 15 percent of the items in category A, 35 percent in category B, and 50 percent in category C. There is nothing sacred about these percentages, but these are often used. Since in our example we have 12 items, 2 would make up 16.6 percent and 4 would be 33.3 percent. Therefore, you might put items 22213 and 22157 in category A, and 22545, 22432, 22511, and 22457 in category B, with the remaining items in category C. Table 16.2 shows that if we closely controlled only 2 items, we would be controlling 75.5 percent of the annual inventory dollar volume.

TABLE 16.2   *ABC analysis*

Category	Total annual volume	Percent of total
A	$2,000,000	75.5
B	629,000	23.8
C	18,725	.7
	$2,647,725	100.0

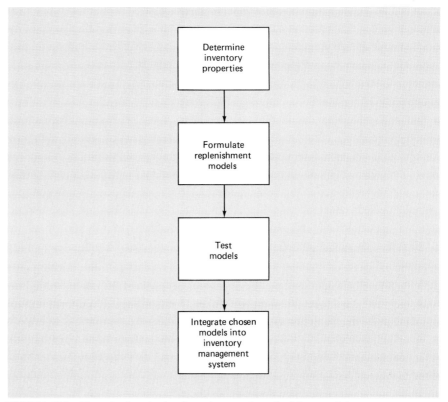

FIGURE 16.2 Steps in developing inventory system decision module

Models for Inventory Decision Making

In this section, we discuss the essential steps to developing the decision module of an inventory management system. These steps include categorizing inventory items into logical categories and for each category of inventory determine relevant properties, formulating candidate replenishment models, testing model performance using simulation, and finally integrating the models selected for each category of inventory item into the inventory management system. These steps are depicted in Figure 16.2.

Determining Inventory Properties

Inventory properties can be classified into four categories: demand properties, replenishment properties, cost properties, and constraints. To prevent the misapplication of an inventory model, it is extremely important for you to identify and consider each property of an inventory system properly.

size of demand **Demand properties**   These characteristics include the size of demand, the rate of demand, and the pattern of demand. The *size of demand* can be constant or variable depending on the nature of the good. A constant demand merely means that, for each time period, the quantity of goods demanded is constant. The size of demand for a good can be deterministic or stochastic. Given a production schedule, for example, it may be a simple calculation to determine demand for a particular period of time. However, the demand of many inventory items cannot be predicted with any degree of certainty; hence, the problem is a stochastic or probabilistic problem rather than a deterministic one.

rate of demand   The *rate of demand* is the size of demand over a particular unit of time. For example Worldwide Widgets has a total demand for the year of 600 widgets, and its records verify that the monthly demand rate is $\frac{600}{12}$, or 50 units per month. Clearly, demand rate can be variable or constant, deterministic or stochastic.

demand pattern   The *pattern* of demand refers to the manner in which units are drawn from inventory. Some items may be drawn from inventory at the beginning of the time period, others at the end, still others at a uniform rate during the period. Many variations of demand pattern are possible, and it is important to try and identify the demand pattern of the inventory item in question. Figure 16.3 shows some common demand patterns.

scheduling period **Replenishment properties**   When you analyze replenishment properties, it is necessary to define the *scheduling period*. The scheduling period is the length of time between decisions concerning replenishments. This time period can be prescribed or variable. For example, the local supermarket or-

FIGURE 16.3 **Demand patterns**

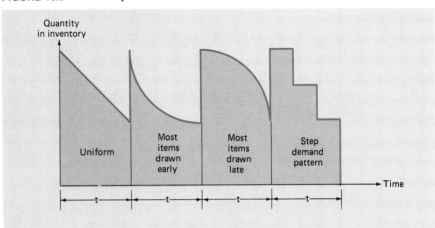

ders fresh lettuce twice a week (prescribed), whereas canned kidney beans are ordered when the inventory reaches a certain reorder point (variable). Variable scheduling periods require a continuous accounting for inventory.

lead time   *Lead time,* you will recall, is the time between ordering a replenishment of inventory and actually receiving the goods into inventory. Lead time can be either a constant, a variable, or a stochastic variable. If lead time is known with a high degree of certainty, its existence is easily treated in inventory modeling. On the other hand, if lead time is stochastic with a large variance, the difficulty in finding an appropriate inventory model is greatly increased.

replenishment,   Like demand, the *size of replenishment* can also be stochastic. In other
or lot, size words, the quantity ordered may not be the same as the quantity received. Replenishment size is often called *lot size.*

replenishment   The *replenishment period* is the time during which units of a particular
period order are added to inventory. In a purchasing situation, the replenishment period may be insignificant, but in a production environment, units are added to inventory over a period of time (that is, as they are produced). If a
replenishment significant replenishment period exists, then units are added to inventory
pattern according to some *replenishment pattern.* Replenishment patterns are similar to demand patterns except the flow of goods is going in the opposite direction.

order   Often, instead of specifying the lot size, an inventory policy specifies
level an *order level.* An order level is the total quantity that will be in inventory after replenishment.

Cost properties   Inventory models, such as the ones to be discussed in this chapter, seek to minimize the total cost of the inventory system. These costs fall into three basic categories: ordering costs, carrying costs, and shortage costs.

ordering   *Ordering costs* are the costs involved in ordering and receiving inven-
costs tory. These costs typically consist largely of salaries in the purchasing and accounting departments and wages in the receiving area; they also include purchase and transportation charges. If a firm produces its own inventory instead of purchasing from an outside source, production setup costs are analogous to ordering costs. Ordering costs are usually expressed by a dollar amount per order.

carrying,   Carrying costs, also referred to as *holding costs,* are the costs that
or holding, holding inventory entails. Components of carrying costs are both direct and
costs indirect, including

- ☐ Interest on the money invested in inventory
- ☐ Storage or warehousing costs, including rent, electricity, wages, insurance, security, data processing, and so on

□ Obsolescence (if the good is held too long in inventory, its value may decrease substantially)

Carrying costs are typically calculated as a percentage of inventory value or a dollar value per unit of inventory.

shortage, or   The third category of inventory costs is *shortage,* or *stockout costs.* If
stockout demand for an off-the-shelf good exists and a firm does not have the good in
costs inventory, there is an inevitable loss of customer goodwill as well as loss of the profit from the sale. The dollar value of this loss of goodwill is, at best, difficult to measure. If you had to assess it, relevant questions would include: Will the firm lose the sale? Will the firm lose the customer? What are the probabilities of these losses? What is the dollar value of that particular customer?

If the inventory is being carried for internal use (that is, production), a stockout can have very serious effects. A stockout can shut down an assembly line, and to shut down a typical automobile assembly line, for example, can cost thousands of dollars per minute. The shortage cost is typically expressed as dollar cost per unit of inventory per unit of time.

System constraints   In addition to determining system properties, before you can decide on solution methodology you must analyze system constraints. For example, if the inventory storage area holds only 100 units, an optimal order quantity of 1,000 units is irrelevant. Similarly, if working capital is severely limited and the optimal inventory policy calls for carrying a huge inventory, the optimal policy may not be feasible. Typical inventory system constraints are

□ **Space**   The amount of storage space may put limits on the order quantity.

□ **Scheduling period**   If the scheduling period is prescribed, many inventory models cannot be used.

□ **Shortage**   Management may make a decision that stockouts cannot be allowed. On the other hand, shortages may be allowed and may or may not result in lost sales.

□ **Continuous nature of inventory units**   Most analytical models used for optimizing inventory systems depend on the calculus for their derivation. Consequently, if inventory units are not, or cannot be considered, continuous in nature, a majority of the analytical optimization models cannot theoretically be applied. Usually however, when large quantities are involved, the assumption of continuity is not damaging.

Determining properties is crucial to analyzing inventory systems. If we expect to find or develop an appropriate model of the inventory system in question, we must carefully analyze the system properties and characteristics.

Formulating the Model

The second step in developing the inventory replenishment decision module is to discover or derive the appropriate model. Basically, there are two types of inventory models: deterministic models and stochastic models. The parameters of deterministic inventory models are assumed to be known with certainty. For example, demand is assumed to be perfectly predictable. Stochastic inventory models contain uncontrollable variables, such as demand or lead time, that are probabilistic in nature. Generally, stochastic inventory models are mathematically more difficult to derive and solve. As the number of stochastic variables increases, it becomes increasingly difficult to derive an analytical optimization model. In addition, if a stochastic variable is not distributed according to a known probability density function, the likelihood of finding or deriving an analytical inventory model is drastically reduced.

Often, an analytical model that strictly conforms to all properties of any category of inventory cannot be found or derived. In this case the management scientist must choose the model or models that he or she thinks ''fit'' the situation the best.

Testing the Models

Once the candidate replenishment models have been identified the next step is to evaluate those models and to fine tune their parameters. This testing can be done using deterministic simulation where the demand forecasting model, and the various replenishment models are implemented into the simulation so that the cost of effectiveness using the candidate replenishment models can be compared objectively. Once the best model has been identified using the simulation results, the parameters of this model can be fine-tuned using the simulation.

Integrating the Model

As we mentioned earlier in this chapter, integrating the model into the inventory control system is typically the job of the data processing professional, not the management scientist.

ANALYTICAL MODELS FOR REPLENISHMENT DECISIONS

In this chapter, we are going to consider several deterministic analytical models and one stochastic model. These models represent only a small sampling of the inventory models that have been developed and used since the first one was introduced in 1915.

Basic Economic Order Quantity Model (EOQ)

Before examining it, we must identify the assumptions of the basic EOQ model so that you will know under what conditions to apply it. If the following assumptions cannot be accepted, thereby indicating that the real-world inventory system may not be adequately represented by the basic EOQ model, the EOQ model will yield at best an approximate solution.

- **Deterministic demand**   It must be possible to predict demand with a high degree of confidence.
- **Constant rate of demand**   Not only is it necessary to know the total demand, but units must be drawn from inventory at a uniform rate. For example, if 365 units are used each year, these items must be drawn 1 per day during the year to strictly satisfy this assumption.
- **No shortages**   Inventory replenishments are made whenever the inventory level reaches zero. Shortages are not allowed to occur. This assumption implies that, of the three costs involved in an inventory system, stockout cost does not exist in the basic EOQ model.
- **Constant replenishment size**   The replenishment size, denoted by q, is the only decision variable in the basic EOQ model. The other decision variable—when to reorder—is fixed because demand is at a constant rate and replenishments occur when the inventory level reaches zero.
- **Zero lead time**   It is assumed that no appreciable time elapses between placing an order and receiving that order. This assumption can be easily dealt with as we explain later.
- **Infinite replenishment rate**   Replenishment rate is defined as the rate at which units are added to inventory. An infinite replenishment rate implies that inventory replenishment occurs at one time. In other words, it takes zero time to receive an order. This assumption is reasonable for most purchased goods but is often unreasonable for manufactured goods. Typically, manufactured goods are put into inventory at some finite rate.
- **Constant inventory costs**   Both costs in the basic EOQ model are constant. Ordering cost is expressed as dollars per order and holding cost is expressed as dollars per unit per time period.

These assumptions for the basic EOQ model determine the graph in Figure 16.4.

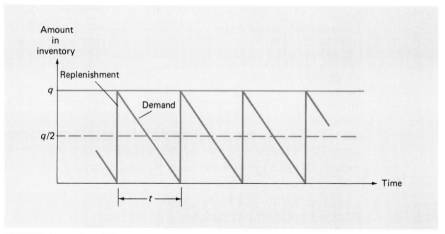

FIGURE 16.4 **Graphic representation of the basic EOQ model**

Inventory models in which the decision variable is the order quantity have the objective function in equation (16.1):

$$\text{Minimize} \quad C(q) = A(q) + B(q) + D(q) \tag{16.1}$$

where

$C(q)$ = total cost function
$A(q)$ = function of q that defines the holding cost
$B(q)$ = function of q that represents the shortage cost
$D(q)$ = function of q that defines the ordering cost

To determine the optimal value of q, it is necessary to develop the functions $A(q)$, $B(q)$, and $D(q)$ for the basic EOQ model,

$$A(q) = C_1(q/2)$$

where C_1 = holding cost per unit of inventory.

A look at Figure 16.4 will reveal to you that $q/2$ represents the average number of units in inventory. In other words, half the time there are more than $q/2$ units in inventory, and half the time the amount in inventory is less than $q/2$ units. Therefore, if we multiply a per unit holding cost by the average number of units in inventory, that product is the holding cost. Since no shortages are allowed in the basic EOQ model due to the zero lead time and zero reorder point assumptions, $B(q)$ is not present in the total cost function. Ordering cost can be thought of as the cost of placing an order multiplied by the number of orders placed in a particular time period. More specifically,

$$D(q) = C_3(r/q)$$

where

$$C_3 = \text{cost of processing one order}$$
$$r = \text{total demand for a given period of time}$$
$$r/q = \text{number of orders}$$

Given the preceding defined functions, the total cost function can be written as shown in equation (16.2).

$$C(q) = A(q) + D(q) \qquad (16.2)$$
$$C(q) = C_1(q/2) + C_3(r/q)$$

Remember, the goal is to determine the value of q that minimizes the objective function $C(q)$. Figure 16.5 graphs the three functions $A(q)$, $C(q)$, and $D(q)$. From Figure 16.5, it is apparent that the minimum of $C(q)$ occurs at the same level of q where functions $A(q)$ and $D(q)$ intersect. It is possible, therefore, to set $A(q)$ equal to $D(q)$ and solve for q to find q^*, the optimal value of q. It must be noted that this relationship is not universally true for other inventory models.

FIGURE 16.5 Inventory cost basic EOQ model

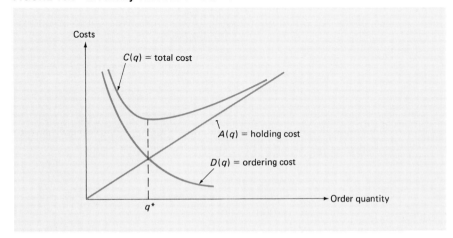

$$A(q) = D(q) \tag{16.3}$$
$$C_1(q/2) = C_3(r/q)$$
$$C_1(q^2/2) = C_3 r$$
$$q^2/2 = C_3 r/C_1$$
$$q^2 = 2C_3 r/C_1$$
$$q^* = \sqrt{2C_3 r/C_1}$$

The majority of inventory models are derived using the differential calculus. The basic methodology involves deriving a cost function, which is differentiated with respect to the decision variable. The derivative is set equal to zero and the function is solved for the optimal value of the decision variable. This methodology is illustrated in the appendix at the end of this chapter.

EXAMPLE   Now, let us look at an example of how to use the basic EOQ model. The XYZ Company uses 10,000 valves per year. Each valve costs $1. The Materials Department estimates that it costs $25 to order a shipment of valves and the Accounting Department estimates the holding cost is 12.5 percent of the value of inventory. All the assumptions of the basic EOQ model are valid.

$$C_1 = \$.125 \text{ per valve per year } [(.125)(\$1.00)]$$
$$C_3 = \$25 \text{ per order}$$
$$r = 10,000 \text{ valves}$$
$$q^* = \sqrt{2C_3 r/C_1}$$
$$= \sqrt{2(25)10,000/.125}$$
$$= \sqrt{4,000,000}$$
$$= 2,000 \text{ valves}$$

If the XYZ Company buys 2,000 valves every time inventory reaches zero, the total annual cost of this policy is

$$C(q^*) = .125(2,000/2) + 25(10,000/2,000)$$
$$= 125 + 125$$
$$= \$250$$

Once q^* is calculated, it is a simple matter to calculate the optimal number of orders per year and the time between each order.

$$N^* = \text{optimal number of orders}$$
$$= r/q^*$$
$$= 10,000/2,000$$
$$= 5$$

$t^* =$ optimal time between orders (optimal reorder schedule)

$\quad =$ planning period$/N^*$

$\quad = 365/5 = 73$ days

Sensitivity of the Basic EOQ Model

As indicated in Figure 16.5 the shape of the total cost curve, $C(q)$, is relatively flat. Consequently, $C(q)$ is not very sensitive to small changes in q. To illustrate this fact, let us assume that the XYZ Company orders 1,000 valves in each order instead of the optimal 2,000 valves.

$$C(1,000) = .125(1,000/2) + 25(10,000/1,000)$$
$$= 62.50 + 250$$
$$= \$312.50$$

Hence, a change of 50 percent in q resulted in only a 25 percent increase in the total inventory cost. (See Table 16.3 for a more complete sensitivity analysis.) This means that if total demand, r, is incorrectly estimated, thus causing a suboptimal q to be calculated, the consequences are not as critical as they would be if the shape of the total cost curve were more peaked.

Basic EOQ System with Finite Replenishment Rate

Often, it is unrealistic to assume an infinite replenishment rate. If a firm is purchasing off-the-shelf items for its inventory, typically when an order is delivered the entire replenishment quantity is delivered at one time; hence,

TABLE 16.3 *Sensitivity analysis of order quantity*

Order quantity	Order cost	Carrying cost	Total cost
100	$2,500.00	$6.25	$2,506.25
500	500.00	31.25	531.25
750	333.33	46.88	380.21
1,000	250.00	62.50	312.50
1,250	200.00	78.13	278.13
1,500	166.67	93.75	260.42
1,750	142.85	109.38	252.23
2,000	125.00	125.00	250.00
2,250	111.11	140.63	251.74
2,500	100.00	156.25	256.25
3,000	83.33	187.50	270.83
4,000	62.50	250.00	312.50
10,000	25.00	625.00	650.00

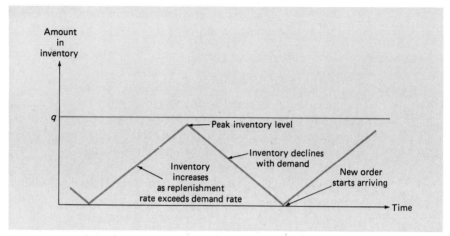

FIGURE 16.6   **Basic EOQ system with uniform replenishment rate**

an infinite replenishment rate. If, however, a company is producing for inventory, units are added to inventory over a finite period of time. Therefore, the inventory system has a finite replenishment rate. If it can be assumed that this replenishment rate is uniform and all other assumptions of the basic EOQ model hold, the appropriate model is the basic EOQ system with a finite replenishment rate. The graphic representation of the model is given in Figure 16.6.

The total cost function of the inventory system depicted in Figure 16.6 is

$$C(q) = \frac{C_1 q(1 - r/p)}{2} + \frac{C_3 r}{q} \qquad (16.4)$$

Following a procedure similar to the one set forth in the appendix at the end of the chapter, the expression for the optimal order quantity shown in equation (16.5) can be derived.

$$q^* = \frac{\sqrt{2rC_3/C_1}}{\sqrt{1 - (r/p)}} \qquad (16.5)$$

where

r = total demand for a given period of time
C_3 = setup cost per setup
C_1 = carrying cost per unit
p = uniform replenishment rate expressed in units per time period

The minimum total inventory cost is given by the following function:

$$C^* = \sqrt{2rC_1C_3} \sqrt{1 - (r/p)} \qquad (16.6)$$

where C^* = the minimum inventory cost.

EXAMPLE   Let us change our previous example just slightly so that the replenishment rate changes from infinite to a uniform 500 valves per day. To restate, the XYZ Company uses 10,000 valves per year. Each valve costs $1. The Production Engineering Department estimates setup costs at $25, and the Accounting Department estimates that the holding cost is 12.5 percent of the value of inventory.

$$r = 10,000 \text{ valves}$$
$$C_3 = \$25 \text{ per order}$$
$$C_1 = \$.125 \text{ per valve per year}$$
$$p = 125,000 \text{ valves per year}^2$$
$$q^* = \sqrt{\frac{2rC_3/C_1}{1 - (r/p)}}$$
$$= \sqrt{\frac{2(10,000)25/.125}{1 - (10,000/125,000)}}$$
$$= \sqrt{4,000,000/.92}$$
$$= \sqrt{4,347,826}$$
$$= 2,086$$

Therefore, the XYZ Company should order 2,086 valves every time inventory for the valves reaches zero. The total inventory cost of this ordering policy is calculated as follows:

$$C^* = \sqrt{2rC_1C_3} \sqrt{1 - (r/p)}$$
$$= \sqrt{2(10,000).125(25)} \sqrt{1 - (10,000/125,000)}$$
$$= \sqrt{62,500} \sqrt{.92}$$
$$\cong \$239.79$$

Therefore, if the XYZ Company orders 2,086 valves approximately five times a year, inventory cost related to this particular valve is minimized at about $240 per year.

---

[2] It was necessary to convert the per day production of valves to per year production of valves because the time units must be compatible; that is, r was expressed in units per year. Assumes a 5-day week and a 50-week year.

Basic-Order-Level System

The basic-order-level system is very similar to the basic EOQ system previously described. In fact, all properties are the same except that shortages are allowed and back-ordered and the scheduling period is prescribed. This type of system is very common in the real world when an organization places orders for certain inventory items on a regularly scheduled basis, such as once a month. An advantage of a prescribed scheduling period is that it does *not* necessitate continuous monitoring of inventory levels.

The basic-order-level system has the following properties:

- Demand is deterministic.
- The rate of demand is constant; that is, it is a linear demand function.
- The scheduling period is prescribed.
- The lead time is zero.
- The replenishment rate is infinite.
- Shortages are made up; that is, there are no lost sales.
- The decision variable is the order level, S; that is, the decision variable is the amount of inventory after replenishment.
- Holding cost is constant and is expressed as dollars per unit per time period.
- Shortage cost is constant and expressed as dollars per unit per time period.

The basic-order-level system is depicted in Figure 16.7.

FIGURE 16.7 Basic-order-level system

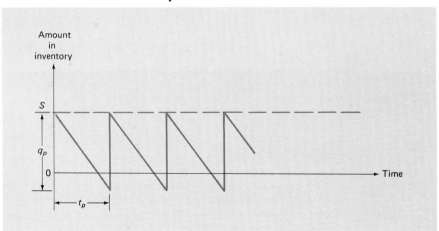

Since the scheduling period is prescribed, the only controllable inventory costs are the carrying and shortage costs. Since order level is the decision variable in this inventory model, the total cost function is a function of order level, S. It can be shown geometrically, using similar triangles, that the total cost function is

$$C(S) = C_1 S^2/2q_p + C_2(q_p - S)^2/2q_p \qquad (16.7)$$

where

$C_1 =$ carrying cost per unit
$S =$ order level
$q_p =$ prescribed lot size (rate of demand multiplied by the prescribed time period)
$C_2 =$ shortage cost per unit

Minimizing this total cost function, the optimal order level is

$$S^* = q_p C_2/(C_1 + C_2)$$

EXAMPLE   A local television store reviews its stock of 25-inch color television sets every month, then orders for the next month. Last year, it sold 120 25-inch color sets ($q_p = 10$ sets per month), and sales were spread evenly throughout the year. Predictions are that this year's sales will be approximately the same. Lead time is effectively zero, and shortages are made up. The holding cost is $80 per set per year, and shortage cost has been determined to be $10 per set per month. The optimal order level, therefore, is

$$S^* = 10(120)/(80 + 120)$$
$$= 6 \text{ sets}$$

To find the minimum cost of this solution, merely substitute S^* into the cost function:

$$C(6) = 80[6^2/(2 \cdot 10)] + 120(10 - 6)^2/(2 \cdot 10)$$
$$= \$240$$

In summary, the inventory policy of the local television store is to order 10 25-inch color TV sets whenever back-orders reach 4. This policy costs $240 per year in inventory cost; any other policy would cost the TV store more. The graph of this inventory policy is shown in Figure 16.8.

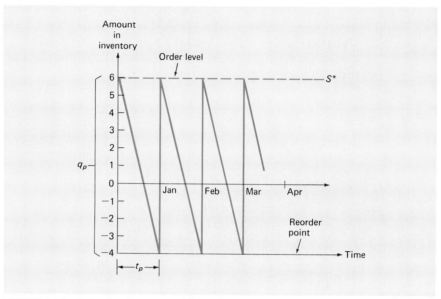

FIGURE 16.8 **Order-level system with stockouts**

Basic EOQ Model with Discrete Price Breaks

It is often advantageous to procure inventory items in large quantities to get quantity discounts. A supplier often sells a product at a price that fluctuates with the quantity purchased. Usually, the price-break scheme is discrete in nature. For example, the per unit cost of an item might be $25 for quantities of 50 or less, $22 for quantities of less than 100 but more than 50, and $20 per unit for more than 100 units. As reflected in Table 16.4, buying in large quantities has several advantages and disadvantages.

Buying large quantities has advantages other than merely lowering the per unit cost of the particular inventory item. Obviously, because fewer

TABLE 16.4 *Quantity buying advantages and disadvantages*

Advantages	Disadvantages
1. Lower unit cost	1. Higher holding cost
2. Lower ordering cost	2. Higher capital requirements
3. Fewer stock-outs	3. Increased risk of deterioration and
4. Preferential treatment by suppliers	obsolescence
5. Lower transportation cost	4. Older stock on hand
6. Increased uniformity in goods	
(coming from the same shipment)	
7. Security (against such factors as strikes	
and price increases)	

orders are placed, ordering costs are reduced when an organization takes advantage of quantity discounts and buys in larger quantities. Transportation costs, also, are usually lower for a few large shipments rather than many small shipments. If demand is stochastic and lead time is not zero, buying in larger quantities results in fewer stockouts.

As you have probably realized, buying in large quantities has some very important disadvantages, too. The most obvious is that, because the average amount in inventory is increased with large orders, the carrying cost of the inventory item is increased. In addition to increased carrying cost, more capital is required to buy larger quantities. For firms with limited capital, this can be a critical drawback, and sometimes it prevents taking advantage of quantity discounts. If the inventory item is perishable or has an otherwise limited life, buying in larger quantities may also be disadvantageous to a firm. High-fashion, ready-to-wear clothing is an example of such an inventory item. Even if a manufacturer is willing to give a quantity discount that would ordinarily minimize the retailer's total inventory cost, it may be wiser to buy the smaller quantity due to the potential obsolescence of the article.

The model we describe in this section is a simple, discrete price-break model. The assumptions concerning demand and replenishment properties are the same as the basic EOQ model except that in this model there exists the condition of discrete prices based on the quantity ordered. Since the cost of goods purchased is no longer constant but is a function of the price, the objective function is composed of ordering cost, carrying cost, and the cost of goods. More specifically,

$$C(q_i) = fb_iq_i/2 + (C_3r/q_i) + rb_i \qquad (16.8)$$

where

$$f = \text{carrying cost fraction}$$
$$q_i = \text{order quantity for price-break } i$$
$$b_i = \text{unit cost for price-break } i$$
$$C_3 = \text{ordering cost per order}$$
$$r = \text{total demand}$$

If you look carefully at the objective function in equation (16.8), you can see that it closely resembles the total cost function of the basic EOQ model. In fact, the first two terms are identical if you realize that the carrying cost (C_1) in dollars per unit per time period is simply the cost fraction (f) multiplied by the unit cost (b_i). The only difference is the existence of more than one price level and the addition of the cost of goods.

As depicted in Figure 16.9, the total cost function for the price-break model is not continuous. Therefore, it is not possible to use the calculus to

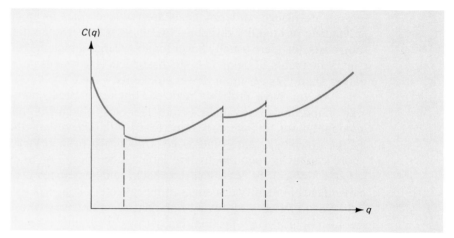

FIGURE 16.9 **Discontinuous cost function**

derive a simple formula to compute the optimal order quantity. Instead, we need an algorithm. The algorithm for the discrete price-break model is presented in flow-chart form in Figure 16.10. The first step in the algorithm is to compute the EOQ for each price level, starting at the price level that has the lowest cost per unit, until an EOQ fits in the relevant range of its price level. In other words, let q_o be the largest EOQ for which $q_i \le q_o < q_{i+1}$, where q_i = minimum order quantity for price level i. The next step is to compare the

FIGURE 16.10 **Discrete price-break algorithm**

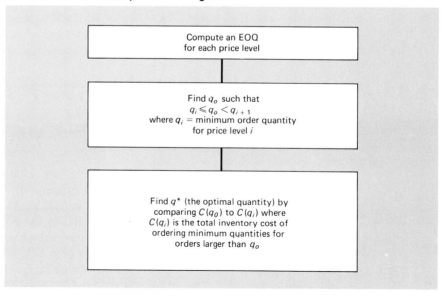

total cost of q_o with the total cost of all price break quantities for orders larger than q_o. In other words, compare $C(q_o)$ to $C(q_j)$ for $j > i$, where $q_j =$ the minimum order quantity for price-level j and $i =$ the price level for q_o.

EXAMPLE   A manufacturing company has planned its production schedule for the coming year based on forecast demand, back-orders, and plant capacity. Instead of making a particular hydraulic pump that goes into the final product, the company has decided to buy the pump. There are two such pumps in the end product, and the production schedule calls for producing 10,000 units of the end product. Therefore, 20,000 pumps will be needed next year. Ordering costs are estimated at $50 per order, and the carrying cost fraction for the firm is .20. A request for bids has yielded only one supplier, Victor Pumps, Inc., who is approved by the Engineering Department; hence, the Purchasing Department has only one basic decision. That decision concerns the quantity to be ordered. Victor Pumps, Inc., has submitted the price schedule shown in Table 16.5 together with its technical proposal.

$$EOQ_5 = \sqrt{\frac{2(20,000)50}{.2(11.50)}} \qquad b_5 = 11.50$$
$$\cong 933$$

$$EOQ_4 = \sqrt{\frac{2(20,000)50}{.2(12)}} \qquad b_4 = 12.00$$
$$\cong 913$$

$$EOQ_3 = \sqrt{\frac{2(20,000)50}{.2(12.50)}} \qquad b_3 = 12.50$$
$$\cong 894$$

$$EOQ_2 = \sqrt{\frac{2(20,000)50}{.2(13.50)}} \qquad b_2 = 13.50$$
$$\cong 861$$

$$EOQ_1 = \sqrt{\frac{2(20,000)50}{.2(15)}} \qquad b_1 = 15.00$$
$$\cong 817$$

TABLE 16.5 *Victor Pumps, Inc., price schedule*

Quantity ordered	Unit price
1–1,999	$15.00
2,000–4,999	13.50
5,000–7,999	12.50
8,000–19,999	12.00
20,000 and over	11.50

The largest EOQ that falls in the relevant range of order quantities is $q_0 = 817$, falling between 1 and 1,999. What remains to be done is to compare the total cost of $q_0 = 817$ to order quantities equal to the minimum levels of all price breaks greater than 817. This is done by substituting the various order quantities into equation (16.8).

$$C(817) = \frac{.2(817)15}{2} + 50\left(\frac{20,000}{817}\right) + 20,000(15)$$

$$= \$302,449.49$$

$$C(2,000) = \frac{.2(2,000)13.50}{2} + 50\left(\frac{20,000}{2,000}\right) + 20,000(13.50)$$

$$= \$273,200$$

$$C(5,000) = \frac{.2(5,000)12.50}{2} + 50\left(\frac{20,000}{5,000}\right) + 20,000(12.50)$$

$$= \$256,450$$

$$C(8,000) = \frac{.2(8,000)12}{2} + 50\left(\frac{20,000}{8,000}\right) + 20,000(12)$$

$$= \$249,725$$

$$C(20,000) = \frac{.2(20,000)11.50}{2} + 50\left(\frac{20,000}{20,000}\right) + 20,000(11.50)$$

$$= \$253,050$$

According to the foregoing analysis the manufacturing company should order 8,000 pumps to minimize total inventory cost for the pump. In addition to the assumptions described for this simple price-break model, it must be noted that buying in quantities of 8,000 is going to require significantly more capital investment in inventory and, consequently, may not be the wisest choice if money is tight for the firm.

Stochastic Demand Model

Until now, we have assumed that all demand parameters of an inventory system are known with certainty. In addition, we have assumed that lead time is zero. If we loosen only this latter assumption, very little has to change except that we must order prior to running out of inventory to prevent stockouts. (Figure 16.11 illustrates the basic EOQ system with nonzero lead time.) In this situation, let us say, for example, that demand is 10 units per day and lead time is known to be five days; then the reorder point, s, is equal to 50 units. Therefore, whenever inventory reaches 50 units, an order for q units should be processed.

If we loosen the assumption of known or certain demand, then the problem of when to order becomes more complicated. As you can see in Figure 16.12 there is now the danger of stockouts.

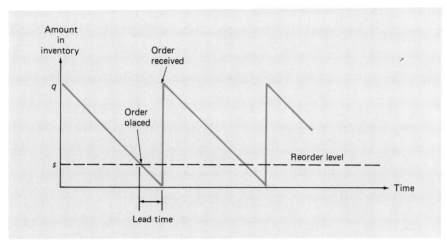

FIGURE 16.11 **Basic EOQ with nonzero lead time, deterministic demand**

If an inventory system has all the properties of the basic EOQ system except that lead time is not zero and demand is not deterministic and constant, we can proceed in the following manner. The problem is still how much, and when to order. If we assume that a reasonable estimate of the optimal order quantity can be calculated using the basic EOQ formula, then the problem reduces to merely determining the reorder point. In most real situations, using the EOQ formula when demand is not known with certainty has little effect on total inventory costs because of the relative insensitivity of total costs to moderate changes in the order quantity.

FIGURE 16.12 **Stochastic demand**

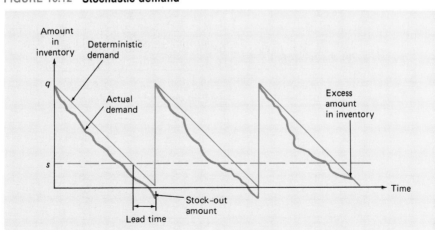

Since the order quantity is given, ordering costs should not be affected by changes in the reorder point. The inventory costs affected by changes in the reorder point are the carrying costs and the stockout costs. The problem, however, is that when stockout costs are lowered by increasing the safety stock, carrying costs are increased because the average value of inventory is increased.

To illustrate how to determine the reorder point, let us consider the following problem. A sporting goods store wants to determine the proper reorder point for a Prostaff Wilson tennis racket. Annual demand is for 1,000 rackets sold at a rate of approximately 4 per day. It takes 5 days between the day the order is placed and the receipt of the shipment from Wilson. The question is, at what point does the sporting goods store order Prostaff tennis rackets? In order to answer the question, it is necessary to have some idea of the probability distribution of the number of rackets demanded in any 5-day period. This information is summarized in Table 16.6. To determine a good reorder point, it is possible to look at six reorder points and calculate the expected cost of each, then simply choose the reorder level with the smallest total cost. In order to determine this total cost, it is necessary to ascertain a per unit stockout cost. Let us assume this stockout cost is $10 per racket, carrying cost is $5 per racket per year and ordering cost is $25 per order.

$$q = \sqrt{[2(1{,}000)(25)]/5}$$
$$= \sqrt{10{,}000}$$
$$= 100$$

If the sporting goods company reorders when inventory hits 10 rackets, there is a high probability (90 percent) of having a shortage before the shipment is received. The shortage cost associated with this policy can be calcu-

TABLE 16.6 *Frequency distribution of five-day demand for Prostaff tennis rackets*

Demand for five-day periods	Frequency of specified demand	Relative frequency	Cumulative relative frequency
10	5	.10	.10
15	15	.30	.40
20	20	.40	.80
25	5	.10	.90
30	4	.08	.98
35	1	.02	1.00
	50	1.00	

lated in the following way:

$$C_2 = \left[\sum_{i=1}^{n} x_i P(x_i) c_2 \right] \left(\frac{r}{q} \right) \qquad (16.9)$$

where

$$
\begin{aligned}
C_2 &= \text{shortage cost for year} \\
x_i &= \text{number short during lead time} \\
P(x_i) &= \text{probability of being short } x_i \text{ units} \\
c_2 &= \text{per unit shortage costs} \\
r &= \text{total annual demand} \\
q &= \text{order quantity} \\
n &= \text{number of reorder points to be examined}
\end{aligned}
$$

Given that the reorder point is 10

$$
\begin{aligned}
C_2 &= [0(.1)10 + 5(.3)10 + 10(.4)10 + 15(.1)10 + 20(.08)10 \\
&\quad + 25(.02)10](1{,}000/100) \\
&= \$910.00
\end{aligned}
$$

Stockout costs for other reorder points are shown in Table 16.7.

The incremental carrying costs for the various reorder points under consideration are represented by

$$\Delta C_1 = \sum_{i=1}^{n} y_i P(y_i) c_1 \qquad (16.10)$$

where

$$
\begin{aligned}
\Delta C_1 &= \text{incremental carrying cost} \\
y_i &= \text{number of units in inventory at the time of replenishment} \\
P(y_i) &= \text{probability of } y_i \text{ units in inventory at the time of replenishment} \\
c_1 &= \text{per unit carrying cost} \\
n &= \text{number of demand levels}
\end{aligned}
$$

TABLE 16.7 *Stockout costs*

Reorder point	Stockout costs
10	$910
15	460
20	160
25	60
30	10
35	0

TABLE 16.8 *Cost of reorder point policies*

Reorder point	Expected stock-out costs	Expected incremental carrying costs	Total cost, $C_2 + \Delta C_1$
10	$910.00	0	$910.00
15	460.00	$2.50	462.50
20	160.00	12.50	172.50
25	60.00	32.50	92.50
30	10.00	55.00	65.00
35	0	79.50	79.50

Given a reorder point of 10,

$$\Delta C_1 = 0(.1)5 + 0(.3)5 + 0(.4)5 + 0(.1)5 + 0(.08)5 + 0(.02)5$$
$$= 0$$

For a reorder point of 25,

$$\Delta C_1 = 15(.1)5 + 10(.3)5 + 5(.4)5 + 0(.1)5 + 0(.08)5 + 0(.02)5$$
$$= 32.50$$

Table 16.8 reflects total incremental costs per year based on reorder point. Since the total incremental cost of the various reorder point policies is minimized when the reorder point is 30, the optimal inventory policy for the sporting goods company is to order 100 tennis rackets 10 times a year whenever the inventory level reaches 30 rackets.

This approach works quite well when demand is stochastic and stockout cost can be accurately estimated. Unfortunately, stockout costs are almost always difficult to estimate accurately. Consequently, inventory managers often are more comfortable specifying a minimal acceptable service level such as 95 percent of the time the inventory unit should be in stock. There are two basic approaches to achieving specified service levels. First, the management scientist might formulate a model that relies on stockout cost to specify a reorder point or an order quantity and then use simulation to determine what stockout costs provide the desired service level. The second way of achieving a given service level is to use a replenishment model that does not explicitly consider stockout cost such as a basic EOQ model and dictate a reorder point. Selection of the reorder point can be determined using simulation and is often expressed in days of supply.

SIMULATION APPROACH

If a satisfactory model cannot be identified, it is possible to use a simulation approach to evaluate different reorder policies for important high-dollar-value inventory items. These reorder policies once they are identified can then be imbedded into an automated inventory management system.

EXAMPLE   You can gain specific insight into how simulation is used to answer inventory questions by working through a simple inventory simulation. A ski shop carries a particularly popular pair of skis that sells for $120 and wishes to know how much, and when, to order. Because demand is not known with certainty (see Table 16.9) and lead time is not known with certainty (see Table 16.10), simulation appears to be a proper approach to the problem. The cost of the skis, which depends on the quantity ordered, is reflected in Table 16.11. Ordering cost is estimated at $25 per order, and the carrying cost fraction is .2. Stockout cost is assumed to be $25 per unit.

TABLE 16.9   *Historical frequency of demand*

Demand per day	Number of observations	Relative frequency
0	19	.095
1	27	.135
2	42	.210
3	49	.245
4	34	.170
5	17	.085
6	9	.045
7	2	.010
8	1	.005
	200	1.000

TABLE 16.10   *Historical frequency of lead time*

Lead time (days)	Number of observations	Relative frequency
4	11	.22
5	7	.14
6	3	.06
7	21	.42
8	5	.10
9	2	.04
10	1	.02
	50	1.00

TABLE 16.11   *Price schedule*

Order	Price per pair of skis
Less than 25	$100
25 or more	95
50 or more	90
100 or more	80

TABLE 16.12   *Demand generating function*

Random-number range	Demand per day
0–.095	0
.095–.230	1
.230–.440	2
.440–.685	3
.685–.855	4
.855–.940	5
.940–.985	6
.985–.995	7
.995–1.00	8

TABLE 16.13   *Lead-time generating function*

Random-number range	Lead time (days)
0–.22	4
.22–.36	5
.36–.42	6
.42–.84	7
.84–.94	8
.94–.98	9
.98–1.0	10

To utilize simulation to solve this inventory problem, we must develop functions that can be used to generate the two stochastic variables in the problem, namely, demand and lead time. Let us assume that no known probability distribution can be fitted to the two sets of historical data and that we are forced to use these empirical distributions. Hence, the generating functions we need can be found merely by using the cumulative frequency distribution of the two stochastic variables. (See Tables 16.12 and 16.13 for these distributions.) You can refer back to Chapter 15 if necessary, for an explanation of how the two generating functions were derived.

Once we have the generating functions, the next step is to experiment with a particular inventory policy. For example, let us compare two inventory policies:

□ Order 25 pairs of skis when inventory reaches 10 pairs of skis.
□ Order 25 pairs of skis when inventory reaches 15 pairs of skis.

For illustrative purposes, we first simulate one month manually. Then, using a computer, we simulate a number of different policies to determine a good inventory policy. Tables 16.14 and 16.15 reflect the results of the manual

TABLE 16.14 *Simulation: reorder point = 10, order quantity = 25*

Day	Random number	Demand	Amount ordered (pairs)	Random number	Lead time (days)	Amount received (pairs)	Ending inventory	Carrying cost*	Stockout cost	Cost of goods	Order cost	Total cost
1	.134	1					14	$1.06				$ 1.06
2	.909	5	25	.344	5		9	.68		$2,375	$25	2,400.68
3	.204	1					8	.61				.61
4	.906	5					3	.23				.23
5	.387	2					1	.08				.08
6	.045	0					1	.08				.08
7	.894	5					0	.00	$100			100.00
8	.172	1				25	24	1.82				1.82
9	.380	2					22	1.67				1.67
10	.390	2					20	1.52				1.52
11	.513	3					17	1.29				1.29
12	.563	3					14	1.06				1.06
13	.670	3					11	.84				.84
14	.428	2	25	.633	7		9	.68				.68
15	.589	3					6	.46				.46
16	.040	0					6	.46				.46
17	.738	4					2	.15				.15
18	.460	3					0	.00	25			25.00
19	.007	0					0	.00				0.00
20	.775	4					0	.00	100			100.00
21	.421	2				25	23	1.75		2,375	25	2,401.75
22	.072	0					23	1.75				1.75
							Total	$16.19	$225	$4,750	$50	$5,041.19

* Note: Carrying cost assumes 250 days per year.

TABLE 16.15 *Simulation: reorder point = 15, order size = 25*

Day	Random number	Demand	Amount ordered (pairs)	Random number	Lead time (days)	Amount received (pairs)	Ending inventory	Carrying cost	Stock-out cost	Cost of goods	Order cost	Total cost
1	.134	1	25	.344	5		14	$1.06		$2,375	$25	$2,401.06
2	.909	5					9	.68				.68
3	.204	1					8	.61				.61
4	.906	5					3	.23				.23
5	.387	2					1	.08				.08
6	.045	0					1	.08				.08
7	.894	5				25	21	1.60				1.52
8	.172	1					20	1.52				1.44
9	.380	2					17	1.29				1.29
10	.390	2	25	.633	7		15	1.14		2,375	25	2,401.14
11	.513	3					12	.91				.91
12	.563	3					9	.68				.68
13	.670	3					6	.46				.46
14	.428	2					4	.30				.30
15	.589	3					1	.08				.08
16	.040	0					1	.08				.08
17	.738	4					0	.00	$75			75.00
18	.460	3				25	22	1.67				1.67
19	.007	0					22	1.67				1.67
20	.775	4					18	1.37				1.37
21	.421	2					16	1.22				1.22
22	.072	0					16	1.22				1.22
							Total	$17.79	$75	$4,750	$50	$4,892.79

simulation for both inventory policies we established. Look at the carrying cost and the stockout costs for the two policies simulated in Tables 16.14 and 16.15. (Ordering costs and the cost of goods are constant for the two policies.) You can see that, by increasing the reorder level five units, the stockout cost is decreased by $150 with only a $1.60 increase in the month's carrying cost.

FIGURE 16.13 **GPSS program**

```
            REALLOCATE BLO,50,XAC,50,FAC,1,STO,1,QUE,1
            REALLOCATE LOG,5,TAB,1,FUN,3,VAR,30,BVR,1,FSV,15
            REALLOCATE HSV,10,BVR,1,FMS,1,HMS,1,CHA,5,COM,5000
            SIMULATE
* X1 = CARRYING COST
* X2 = STOCKOUT COST
* X3 = COST OF GOODS
* X4 = ORDER COST
* X5 = TOTAL COST
* X6 = ENDING INVENTORY
* X7 = REORDER POINT
* X8 = ORDER QUANTITY
* X9 = COST PER UNIT
            INITIAL      X6,30
            INITIAL      X9,8000
            INITIAL      X7,10
            INITIAL      X8,100
    1       VARIABLE     X9*X6*2/2500  CARRYING COST
    2       VARIABLE     X6*(-2500)  STOCKOUT COST
    3       VARIABLE     X9*X8  COST OF GOODS
    4       VARIABLE     X1+X2+X3+X4  TOTAL COST
    1       FUNCTION     RN2,D9  DEMAND FUNCTION
.095,0/.23,1/.44,2/.685,3/.855,4/.94,5/.985,6/.995,7/1,8
    2       FUNCTION     RN3,D7  LEAD TIME FUNCTION
.22,4/.36,5/.42,6/.84,7/.94,8/.98,9/1,10
            GENERATE     1,0,,1000  GENERATE 1 DAY
            SAVEVALUE    6-,FN1  ADJUST ENDING INVENTORY
            TEST GE      X6,0,NEG  CHECK FOR STOCKOUT
            TEST GE      X6,X7,ORDER  CHECK FOR REORDER LEVEL
            SAVEVALUE    1+,V1  ACCUMULATE CARRYING COST
            TERMINATE    1
    NEG     SAVEVALUE    2+,V2  ACCUMULATE STOCKOUT COST
            SAVEVALUE    6,0  ZERO ENDING INVENTORY
    TEM     TERMINATE    1  END THE DAY
  ORDER GATE LR        1,TEM  HAS ORDER BEEN MADE??
            LOGIC S      1  SET THE ORDER SWITCH
            SAVEVALUE    4+,2500  ACCUMULATE ORDERING COST
            SAVEVALUE    3+,V3  ACCUMULATE COST OF GOODS
            SAVEVALUE    1+,V1  ACCUMULATE CARRYING COST
            PRIORITY     10  SET PRIORITY OF AN INCOMING ORDER
            ADVANCE      FN2  LEAD TIME
            SAVEVALUE    6+,X8  INCREMENT ENDING INVENTORY
            LOGIC R      1  RESET ORDER SWITCH
            TERMINATE    1
            GENERATE     1001  GENERATE TIMER TRANSACTION
            SAVEVALUE    5,V4  ACCUMULATE TOTAL COST
            TERMINATE    1
            START        1001
```

TABLE 16.16   *Simulation results: total adjusted inventory costs (including cost of goods)*

Order quantity	Reorder level				
	10	15	20	25	30
25	$283,258	$276,738	$271,863	$269,611	$269,055
50	$263,589	$259,330	$256,271	$255,367	$254,937
100	$232,559	$229,395	$228,529	($227,777)	$227,828

Obviously, other inventory policies need to be examined and the number of days simulated must be significantly increased before we can have much faith in the results of the simulation experiments. To give you some idea of what it costs to "solve" the ski inventory problem using computer simulation, we wrote and ran a simulation program to determine the effects of various inventory policies. The program, reflected in Figure 16.13, was written in GPSS, a special-purpose simulation language. It took approximately 2 hours to write and debug. One experiment simulating 4 years took less than 6 seconds on a small mainframe computer. In all, 15 experiments were run at a total computer cost of less than $5.00. As you can see in Table 16.16, the best inventory policy concerning skis is to order 100 pairs whenever inventory level reaches 25 pairs.

MATERIAL REQUIREMENTS PLANNING— A METHOD FOR DEPENDENT-DEMAND ITEMS

Thus far in this chapter, we have examined a sampling of classical analytical inventory methods. These methods are useful for managing distribution inventories or items subject to independent demand. Demand for a given inventory item is *independent* when it is unrelated to demand for other items. Thus, end products and items stocked to meet customer demand are subject to independent demand. Since independent demand is not known exactly, it must be forecasted, and statistical order-point or EOQ methods are appropriate.

independent demand

materials requirements planning (MRP)

Now let us examine the *materials requirements planning (MRP)* approach to dependent-demand items. An item has *dependent demand* whenever its demand depends on the demand for another item or product. For example, the demand for automobile engines or transmissions depends directly on the demand for the final product, automobiles. The MRP approach is particularly appropriate for manufacturing operations in which the demand for subassemblies, component parts, and raw materials is dependent

dependent demand

upon an end product. These dependent-demand items have a demand pattern that is not smooth over time, but lumpy. Demand that is lumpy occurs in discrete batches at different points in time. This type of pattern is very unlike the steady-demand-rate assumption of the basic EOQ models. Thus, MRP was developed to better cope with the lumpy demand patterns of dependent-demand items.

The Development of MRP

In the 1970s, MRP had the distinction of being hailed by many as the new way of life in production and inventory management. It is a methodology that has been developed "on the firing line" in industry rather than by academicians and theoreticians. It has been in use by some companies for many years, and is now finding its way into academic courses. MRP has been successful largely because it addresses some of the basic time-phasing problems that confront the inventory manager. It is concerned with an all-important problem: getting the right materials to the right place at the right time.

MRP has grown out of a certain disenchantment of practitioners with classical inventory methods for dependent-demand items. Some practitioners felt a need for better data processing and timing rather than better statistical or mathematical methods. MRP has experienced a very rapid growth and level of acceptance since 1970. This growth is partly attributed to the *APICS* "MRP crusade" carried out by the *APICS* (*American Production and Inventory Control Society*). APICS is a 12,000-member professional society for the advancement of the practice of production and inventory management. The APICS effort to promote the utility of MRP was spearheaded by such professionals as Joseph Orlicky of IBM, Oliver Wight, George Plossl, and Walter Goddard. The list of firms using MRP has grown rapidly from 700 in 1975 to well over 1,000 today, and all indications are that the list will continue to grow.

The Nature of MRP

MRP is a technique for determining when to order dependent-demand items and how to replan and reschedule orders to adjust for changes in demand estimates from the master production schedule. The MRP system consists of inventory records, bills of material, and usually computer programs that translate the master production schedule into time-phased net requirements and planned coverage of these requirements for each component item needed. Because of the large amounts of data that usually need to be manipulated, MRP systems are computerized; they are, in a sense, a data processing approach to dependent-demand inventory control. Successful MRP systems are taking the systems approach to inventory; they coordinate not only inventory, but purchasing, manufacturing, scheduling, and planning.

MRP avoids the "averaging process" of statistical inventory methods in managing inventory and calculates a specific quantity of what parts to order and when. Thus, an essential feature of MRP is the *calculation* of *bill of* exact inventory needs rather than a statistical estimation. The calculation is *materials* based on a planned production quantity of an end item and the *bill of materials* (*BOM*) for that item, which specifies a list of all subassemblies and parts required to produce the end item. The MRP systems interact with production scheduling to time the release orders correctly for all required items.

The purpose of an MRP system is more than to maintain inventory levels by ordering the right quantities of items at the right time. A properly functioning MRP system aids in priority and capacity planning. It helps to establish valid order priority by revising due dates that have been invalidated. An MRP system is an integral part of the priority planning system. It provides valuable information for both purchasing and production operations. However, it cannot cause due dates for purchasing or operations to be met. Thus, MRP must be supplemented by a priority control system in the factory. The control system provides the means to enforce adherence to plans.

Prerequisites and Assumptions of MRP

MRP is primarily intended for manufacturing operations and has been used in such general applications as assembly operations, general machine shops, and fabrication assembly operations. It can be applied to any operation provided that certain assumptions or prerequisites are satisfied. The following conditions are the primary prerequisites for using MRP:

- □ The existence of a realistic master production schedule that can be stated in bill-of-material terms.
- □ An accurate bill of material for each product that not only lists all components of the product, but also reflects how the product is actually made in steps.
- □ Having each inventory item identified with a unique code or part number.
- □ Data-file integrity pertaining to inventory status data and bill-of-material data. The system will not function properly without accurate input data.
- □ Known lead times on all inventory items.

Benefits and Costs of MRP

The benefits and costs of using an MRP system will vary with individual companies, and efficiency increases will depend on how well the company was doing with its previous inventory system. However, successful adopters of MRP have noted the following potential benefits:

- Lower inventories. The ability to plan ahead and the flexibility to reschedule rather than maintain large safety stocks allows significant reduction in inventory levels; reductions of up to 50 percent are not unusual.
- Improved customer service. The percentage of late orders and stockouts is reduced, sometimes up to 75 percent.
- Reduced overtime and idle time—the result of smoother and better planned production.
- Reduced sales price and improved response to market demands.
- Ability to modify the master schedule and respond to unanticipated changes in demand.
- Ability to aid in capacity and priority planning. MRP not only aids the expediting of "hot orders," but also helps in deexpediting orders that must be delayed.
- Reduced subcontracting and purchasing costs.

The largest cost or disadvantage of any MRP system is the computing cost to support the function. However, with increasing inventory and production costs, along with decreasing computation costs, an MRP system is getting easier to justify. An MRP system will also require personnel with MRP expertise and computer programmers to interact with the system, although the actual MRP system software is usually purchased from major computer manufacturers. Additional costs include system maintenance costs and the trials and tribulations of a system changeover.

But once functioning smoothly, the MRP system offers really significant advantages to weigh against the costs. The actual benefits depend upon how bad the performance of the current system really is. For example, one company that had some serious inventory problems installed an MRP system and achieved a 12 percent reduction in finished inventories, a work-in-process inventory reduction of 30 percent, and a 35 percent increase in the number of on-time deliveries.

Illustration of Lumpy Demand

Having briefly discussed the nature of MRP and its potential benefits, let us look at an example of dependent or lumpy demand (requirements) to demonstrate the superiority of MRP in handling this type of inventory problem. Let us assume we are to produce a final product A whose demand is uniform at the rate of 4 units per week. From Figure 16.14, which illustrates the product structure tree for product A, we can see that it takes 1 unit of component B and 2 units of component C to make 1 unit of A. Also, each B requires 3 Ds, and each C requires 1 D. Even though demand for product A is uniform, the

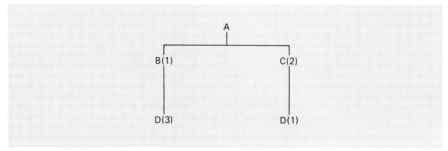

FIGURE 16.14   **Product structure for A**

	Week 1	Week 2	Week 3	Week 4	Week 5	Week 6
Demand for Product A	4	4	4	4	4	4
Production	20					20

FIGURE 16.15   **Master production schedule for product A**

production of A occurs in lot sizes of 20 units every 5 weeks. This is shown in Figure 16.15.

Given that 20 units of A take 1 week to produce and that parts B, C, and D have lead times (for internal production or external ordering) of 2, 4, and 1 week respectively, when should we release orders so that 20 units of A can be ready for distribution at the end of week 6? We are faced with the basic problem of time phasing and getting the right parts to the right place at the right time.

To have 20 units of product A ready at the end of week 6 (we are concentrating only on these 20 units in week 6), we can see from the product structure in Figure 16.14 that we will need 20 units of B and $2 \times 20 = 40$ units of C at the beginning of week 6. Given the lead times of B and C, we should place orders for 20 units of B at the beginning of week 4 and 40 units of C at the beginning of week 2. This in turn would require 60 units of D to be ordered (for the assembly of B) at the beginning of week 3 and 40 units of D to be ordered (for the assembly of C) at the beginning of week 1. These order release dates are summarized in Figure 16.16. Looking at the gross requirements for part D in that figure, we see that the requirements follow a "lumpy pattern" of 0 40 0 60 0 0. In spite of the fact that the demand for the end product A is uniform at 4 per week, the resulting dependent demand for part D is quite lumpy.

Figure 16.17 illustrates the large amount of error that can result in trying to forecast demand statistically when in fact you can calculate it after

ITEM B Leadtime 2 weeks	1	2	3	4	5	6
Gross requirements						20
Planned order releases				20		

ITEM C Leadtime 4 weeks	1	2	3	4	5	6
Gross requirements						40
Planned order releases		40				

ITEM D Leadtime 1 week	1	2	3	4	5	6
Gross requirements		40		60		
Planned order releases	40		60			

FIGURE 16.16 Lumpy demand

end-item production quantities have been established. The forecast in Figure 16.17 is based on exponential smoothing, where forecast = previous period forecast + α(previous demand − previous forecast), where α = the smoothing constant. For example, using an α of .2, and assuming a previous period

FIGURE 16.17 MRP-calculated demand versus statistically forecasted demand

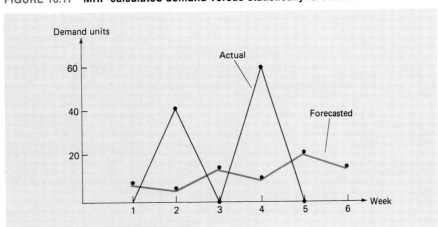

forecast of 10 units and demand of 0 units, we obtain

$$\text{forecast in period } 1 = 10 + .2(0 - 10) = 8$$
$$\text{forecast in period } 2 = 8 + .2(0 - 8) = 6.4$$
$$\text{forecast in period } 3 = 6.4 + .2(40 - 6.4) = 13.12$$
$$\text{forecast in period } 4 = 13.12 + .2(0 - 13.12) = 10.5$$
$$\text{forecast in period } 5 = 10.5 + .2(60 - 10.5) = 20.4$$
$$\text{forecast in period } 6 = 20.4 + .2(0 - 20.4) = 16.32$$

It is clear from the figure that dependent-demand quantities should be calculated once firmed production quantities have been determined from the master production schedule.

Principles of MRP

The example dealing with lumpy demand illustrates the basic process in MRP—working backward from the scheduled completion dates of end products to determine the dates when the various component parts and materials are to be ordered, and the quantities to be ordered. Of course, the example was a simple one, but the basic process is the same for large-scale real-world manufacturing operations.

The calculations of dependent-demand quantities and order dates are performed by the MRP computer program. The computer program is but one aspect of the overall MRP system, whose structure Figure 16.18 depicts. Chronologically, the MRP system begins with the aggregate production plans, which are refined into a master production schedule. Forecasts of independent-demand items such as end products serve as input to aggregate plans and the master schedule. The master schedule is broken down into firm and tentative plans. Firm production schedules are needed for short-range time frames covering up to a month or two; tentative production plans may range from a month up to a year. Tentative plans are sometimes revised according to market reactions, new forecasts, and capacity output reports of the MRP computer program.

The MRP computer program has three major sources of input—the master production schedule, the inventory records file, and the product structure or bill-of-materials file. Using these three inputs, the MRP computer program schedules order releases and production dates for the entire manufacturing operation. The MRP computer program must schedule not only orders for regular customer demand, but also random orders or orders external to the planned master schedule. These external orders can include service and repair parts, interplant orders, and items specially selected for experimentation or testing.

Given random demand, the MRP computer program schedules orders by combining information from the master schedule, the bill-of-materials

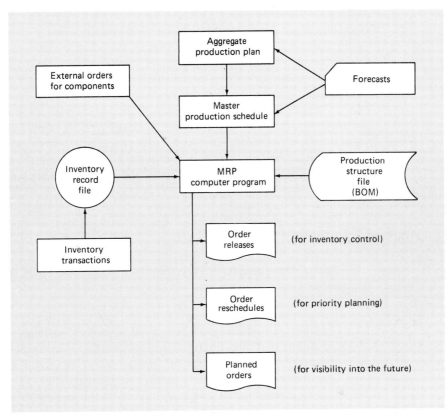

FIGURE 16.18 **Structure of MRP system**

file, and the inventory record file. The master schedule specifies production quantities and due dates, the inventory record file states the number of units on hand and on order for each item, and the bill-of-materials file lists all the items needed to produce a given end product. The logic processor within the MRP computer program then "explodes" the net requirements for the production of the end product and schedules order releases, taking into account any lead times of items.

As can be seen in Figure 16.18, there are three important output reports from the MRP computer program. Order release reports are the principal output, and they represent planned orders in the current period. They form the basis for new shop orders, new purchase requisitions, and due dates for production scheduling. The order reschedule reports call for changes in due dates for open orders. These reports are major input for priority planning and rescheduling, and they also provide expediting information. The planned order reports tentatively schedule orders for release in future periods. These provide information in forecasting inventory and future work center loads. This visibility into the future is very helpful in capacity planning and the development of realistic master schedules. Other, secondary reports not shown in Figure 16.18 can include performance reports for forecasted usages and costs, and exception reports, which signal errors such as late orders, nonexistent parts numbers, or a due date of an open order outside the planning horizon.

Our purpose here has not been to give you an in-depth understanding of MRP and how it works. Rather, we hope you have gained some insight into the nature of MRP, some of its advantages, and where it can be successfully applied. Joseph Orlicky's book and other MRP references listed at the end of the chapter are recommended to the student seeking more material on MRP.

COMPUTER IMPLICATIONS

The role of the computer in the effective management of inventories can be categorized into three areas:

- □ **Inventory record keeping** With the increased availability of microcomputers and the proliferation of inventory software, it is the rare company that does not or should not have their inventory record keeping automated. Even small businesses and professional offices are turning to the computer to help manage their inventories. The major retardant of computerized inventory record keeping is not computer cost or software availability but the attitude and education of many smallbusiness managers and professional people.

- □ **Inventory decision making** Models like those described in this chapter have been integrated into many large-scale computer-based inventory systems. However, the majority of today's automated inventory systems are still primarily record keeping systems with no replenishmentdecision-making or decision-aiding capabilities. To be effective, models similar to those described in this chapter should be integrated into a firm's computer-based inventory system.

- □ **MRP systems** As was mentioned earlier in this chapter, MRP systems are the computer professional's solution to dependent demand inventory problems. Without the computer and associated software an MRP approach to inventory management is simply not viable.

In short, the effective management of an organization's inventory requires the intelligent use of the computer. This means combining analytical models with today's computer hardware and software to transform mere recordkeeping inventory systems into intelligent systems that support cost-effective inventory decision making.

SUMMARY

For many firms, the effective management of their inventory can have a significant impact of the bottom line. Today's major challenge is not merely to push the state of the art in management science or computer science but to take existing hardware, software, and analytical tools that are available and successfully apply them. To apply existing technology successfully, a manager must beware of two potential pitfalls.

☐ The manager must avoid the misapplication of various inventory models by carefully examining the properties of an existing inventory system and making sure system properties adequately match model assumptions. Too many firms do not distinguish between dependent and independent demand items in their inventory. Consequently, models are being misapplied with very costly consequences.

☐ To implement a decision-making inventory system, many human factors must be dealt with carefully. People naturally resist change, especially when it threatens their security or self-image. Many times, it is more effective, for example, to have the management information system suggest an order quantity rather than automatically print the purchase or production order. A major reason why management science has not progressed faster in most organizations is a failure to take into consideration the human factors connected with organizational change. Unless the people in an organization are in favor of a change, that change, regardless of its individual merits, will not succeed.

DERIVATION OF THE
BASIC EOQ MODEL APPENDIX

From equation (16.2)

$$C(q) = C_1(q/2) + C_3(r/q)$$

To optimize, take the first derivative with respect to q, set it equal to zero, and solve for q. Thus

$$\frac{dC(q)}{dq} = \frac{C_1}{2} - \frac{C_3 r}{q^2}$$

$$\frac{C_1}{2} - \frac{C_3 r}{q^2} = 0$$

Solve for q:

$$\frac{C_1}{2} = \frac{C_3 r}{q^2}$$

$$q^2 = \frac{2C_3 r}{C_1}$$

$$q^0 = \sqrt{2C_3 r / C_1}$$

To determine whether q^0 is a maximum or a minimum, take the second derivative: If it is greater than zero, q^0 is a minimum; if $d^2C(q)/dq^2$ is less than zero, q^0 is a maximum. Thus,

$$\frac{d^2C(q)}{dq^2} = \frac{2qC_3 r}{q^4} = \frac{2C_3 r}{q^3}$$

Since C_3, r, and q are all greater than zero, the second derivative is greater than zero. Therefore, q^0 is a minimum.

SOLVED PROBLEMS

PROBLEM STATEMENT

A local TV distributor has found from experience that demand for a certain model TV is fairly constant at a rate of 50 sets per month. Lead time is effectively zero and no shortages are to be allowed. If the sets cost $300, the carrying-cost fraction is .20 per year, and ordering cost is estimated to be $50, how many sets should be ordered and how many orders must be processed per year?

SOLUTION

Using the basic EOQ model, the optimal order quantity is

$$q^* = \sqrt{\frac{2C_3 r}{C_1}}$$

where

$$C_3 = \$50 \text{ per order}$$
$$r = (12)(50) = 600 \text{ sets per year}$$
$$C_1 = (.2)(300) = \$60 \text{ per set per year}$$

$$q^* = \sqrt{\frac{(2)(50)(600)}{60}}$$

$$= 31.62 \text{ sets per order}$$

Owing to the relative insensitivity of q^*, we can round q^* up or down with little effect. Let $q^* = 32$ sets per order. This means that the number of orders processed per year is

$$N = 600/32 = 18.75 \text{ orders}$$

PROBLEM STATEMENT

A basket factory has decided to try to apply an inventory model to its most popular item. Demand is fairly deterministic at a rate of 5,000 baskets per month. Lead time is zero and no shortages are allowed by management. The factory can produce the baskets at a rate of 15,000 per month. Carrying costs are \$.20 per basket per year, and setup costs are \$100. What is the optimal lot size?

SOLUTION

Using the finite replenishment-rate model, we obtain

$$q^* = \frac{\sqrt{2rC_3/C_1}}{\sqrt{1 - (r/p)}}$$

where

r = annual demand = (5,000 baskets per month)(12) = 60,000 baskets
C_3 = setup cost = \$100
C_1 = per basket carrying cost per year = \$.20
p = replenishment rate—15,000 baskets/month = 180,000 baskets per year

$$q^* = \frac{\sqrt{(2)(60,000)(100)/.2}}{\sqrt{1 - (60,0001/180,000)}}$$

$$\cong 9,487 \text{ baskets}$$

The minimum cost of implementing an order quantity of 9,487 is

$$C^* = \sqrt{2rC_1C_3} \sqrt{1 - (r/p)}$$

$$= \$1,264.91$$

The QSB computer solution to this problem is

```
                    EOQ Results for BASKET

EOQ Input Data:
    Demand per year (D) =   60000
    Order or setup cost per order (Co) =   100
    Holding cost per unit per year (Ch) =   .2
    Shortage cost per unit per year (Cs) =   ∞
    Shortage cost per unit, independent of time (π) =   0
    Replenishment or production rate per year (P) =   180000
    Lead time for a new order in year (LT) =   0
    Unit cost (C) =   0

EOQ Output:
    EOQ                    =        9486.834
    Maximum inventory =             6324.556
    Maximum backorder =             0.000
    Order interval     =            0.158 year
    Reorder point      =            0.000
        Ordering cost =             632.455
        Holding cost  =             632.456
        Shortage cost =             0.000
    Subtotal of inventory cost per year      =        1264.911
    Material cost per year                   =        0.000
    Total cost per year                      =        1264.911
```

PROBLEM STATEMENT

A glass company has patented an extra-strength glass and currently sells it in 25-square-foot sheets. Because the product is patented, being out of stock does not result in a lost sale. A stockout, however, is bad for customer goodwill, and management has assigned a stockout cost of $50 per sheet per month. The sheets cost $1,000 to make, but because of the unusual process, orders can be filled in less than one day. Demand for the glass has averaged 150 sheets per month. Annual holding costs for the company are assumed to be 15 percent of the value of inventory. Lot sizes are 150 sheets (owing to production scheduling, the hi-test glass can be produced only once monthly). The pertinent question is, What is the optimal order level?

SOLUTION

$$S^* = \frac{q_p C_2}{C_1 + C_2}$$

where

$$q_p = 150 \text{ sheets}$$
$$C_2 = (50)(12) = \$600$$
$$C_1 = (1,000)(.15) = \$150$$

$$S* = \frac{(150)(600)}{150 + 600}$$
$$= 120$$

In other words, back orders would reach 30 sheets of glass before inventory was replenished.

The cost of the solution is

$$C* = \frac{C_1 S^2}{2q_p} + \frac{C_2(q_p - S)^2}{2q_p}$$
$$= \frac{(150)(120)^2}{2(150)} + \frac{600(150 - 120)^2}{2(150)}$$
$$= \$9,000$$

REVIEW QUESTIONS

1. List four reasons for carrying inventory.
2. Why is it critical to manage an organization's inventory effectively?
3. What are the two major functions that must be performed to control an organization's inventory effectively?
4. In your own words, explain the rationale behind ABC analysis.
5. Classify inventory accounting systems into two categories.
6. Distinguish between real-time inventory control systems and batch processing systems.
7. Why is it likely that the number of real-time inventory systems will increase in the future?
8. What is the object of inventory models?
9. What are the two major decision variables in inventory models?
10. Describe the three components of inventory cost.
11. Briefly explain the five basic steps in analyzing an inventory system.
12. Why is the determination of system properties so important?
13. What is meant by demand patterns?

14. Define "lead time."
15. Distinguish between stochastic demand and deterministic demand.
16. Define "replenishment period."
17. Distinguish between order level and reorder level.
18. Why is it sometimes necessary to simulate an inventory system?
19. Why is sensitivity analysis an important step in analyzing inventory systems?
20. List the assumptions of the basic EOQ model.
21. Distinguish between finite and infinite replenishment rate.
22. What is the major difference between the basic EOQ model and the basic order-level model?
23. Why is simulation often used for inventory problems?
24. What are two major disadvantages of using a simulation approach to inventory problems?
25. What distinguishes a management information system from an inventory accounting system?
26. Why haven't inventory models been more widely applied?
27. List four advantages and two disadvantages of buying in large quantities.
28. What is the difference between dependent and independent demand?
29. Explain how errors can arise in applying statistical order point procedures to lumpy demand.
30. Where did MRP originate?
31. What are the three main inputs to any MRP computer program?
32. What kind of information is held in the BOM file? The inventory records file?

PROBLEMS

16.1 Given the following information, perform an ABC analysis on the data. Discuss your results.

Item no.	Annual demand	Cost per unit
157	100	$25
222	50	30
315	1,000	50
719	250	15
244	300	20
367	400	25
219	2,000	20
234	345	20
577	500	25
619	750	10
621	1,000	35
322	900	5
357	432	10
192	150	15
334	225	30

16.2 *Blood bank.* You are asked by the manager of a blood bank to study its inventory problem and make recommendations for optimizing costs. The manager has been taking some night courses; she has been taught the following formula and wonders if it might be applied to the problem:

$$q^* = \sqrt{2C_3r/C_1}$$

Specifically, do the following:

a. Indicate to the manager what an inventory model is meant to do.

b. Discuss properties of this inventory problem.

c. Recommend use of the aforementioned formula or state specific reasons why it should not be used.

16.3 *Drill-rig manufacturer.* A drill-rig company has a contract with Saudi Arabia to produce 60 drill rigs during the next year. The plan is to produce these rigs at a rate of 5 per month. A valve used in the drill rig is purchased off the shelf from a nearby supplier; no lead time is required. Each drill rig requires 4 valves. The valves cost $100 each. Holding cost for the valves is $10 per year per valve. In addition, it costs $75 to order these valves and receive them from the vendor.

a. What is the optimal order quantity?

b. What is the optimal number of orders per year?

c. How frequent should the orders be?

d. What is the total inventory cost of ordering the optimal order quantity?

e. Perform a limited amount of sensitivity analysis on the order quantity.

16.4   *Auto Manufacturer.* An automobile manufacturer plans to produce 30,000 cars in the next month. All cars planned for production use the same headlamps; therefore, demand for the headlights for the next month is known to be 60,000. The purchasing agent wants to know how many headlamps to buy at one time. Historically, headlamps have been received on the same day they were ordered. It costs $35 to order headlamps, and the carrying-cost fraction used by the auto company is .15 per year. The lamps cost $.87 each.

a. What is the optimal order quantity?

b. What is the optimal number of orders per year?

c. What is the frequency of orders? Assume 22 working days.

d. What is the total inventory cost of ordering the optimal order quantity?

e. Show the inventory cost for q's of 10,000, 20,000, 25,000, 30,000, and 40,000 units.

16.5   *Drill-rig manufacturer.*

a. Referring to Problem 16.3, what should the drill-rig company do if lead time is 1 month rather than zero? In other words, what should the inventory policy be?

b. Does the existence of lead time change the total inventory cost of the valves? If so, what is the total cost of the new inventory policy?

16.6   *Drill-rig manufacturer.* Management has decided to make the valves in Problem 16.3 rather than buy them from an outside vendor. The demand is for 240 valves for the next year, or 20 valves per month. To make the valves costs the company $90 each, and setup time amounts to $100 per set up. Holding cost remains at $10 per valve. Since these valves are not being bought off the shelf, replenishment of inventory is not simultaneous. In fact, the production department says it can produce 200 valves per month given present human and capital resources.

a. What is the optimal order quantity?

b. What is the optimal number of setups per year?

c. What is the optimal time between orders? Assume 250 working days.

d. What is the total inventory cost of the optimal order policy?

16.7 *Auto manufacturer.* The automobile manufacturer in Problem 16.4 has decided to make the headlamps. It has been determined that 150,000 headlamps per month can be produced, but owing to various resource constraints, management has decided to buy half the necessary quantity of headlamps and make the other half. It costs the company $.75 to make each headlamp, and setup costs are $50 per setup. Refer to Problem 16.4 for the parameters of the purchasing decision.

a. What is the optimal order quantity to be purchased from the outside supplier?

b. What is the EOQ for in-house production?

c. What is the total inventory cost for the headlamps?

d. What is the optimal number of purchase orders per month?

e. What is the optimal number of production runs per month?

16.8 *Mail-order supply.* A mail-order stereo firm reviews its stock of amplifiers each month and orders for the next month. Its most popular amp last year was the SEA-700. Last year, 600 amps were sold; these sales were spread evenly throughout the year. Predictions are that this year's sales will be approximately the same. Lead time from the manufacturer is effectively zero, and no sales are lost owing to shortages; instead, the amps are merely delivered one month later. A recent market survey revealed that 60 percent of the customers surveyed would not buy amps again from this firm if they were made to wait an extra month. Profit on an SEA-700 amp is $50. Management, therefore, has estimated stockout cost to be .6 (profit on two future sales), or $60, or $720 per amp per year. Holding cost per amp is $75 per year.

a. What is the optimal order level?

b. What is the minimum inventory cost for the SEA-700 amp?

c. What is the order-level sensitivity?

16.9 *Bicycle manufacturer.* A deluxe-bicycle store sells a particular model men's bike for $200. The bike costs the store $150, including selling cost. The wholesale cost of the bike is $125. Demand for the bike is stochastic; past demand is reflected in the table. Total demand for 1 year is forecast to be 52 units. Stockout cost is assumed to be the profit lost, or $50. Lead time is 1 month. Ordering costs are $50 per order. Carrying cost is 20 percent per year of the inventory value.

a. What is the best inventory policy for the bicycle in this problem?

b. What are the expected stockout and incremental carrying costs of the selected inventory policy?

Monthly demand	Frequency
0	1
1	3
2	6
3	7
4	8
5	11
6	7
7	5
8	2
	50

16.10 Given the policy you recommended in Problem 16.9, simulate manually 1 year's activity. Interpret your simulation results. Assume a beginning inventory of 10 units.

16.11 *Charter airline.* A small charter airline company wants to know how much aviation fuel to buy. Demand for flight fuel has been somewhat constant at 50,000 gallons per month. Fuel costs are $.75 per gallon, and the company's annual carrying-cost fraction is .10. If it costs $100 to get a delivery with no lead time required:

a. What is the optimal order quantity?

b. What assumption did you make in answering part (a)?

c. If storage capacity for the fuel were limited to 10,000 gallons, how would you analyze the problem?

16.12 *Hospital.* Demand for pacemakers has been running at a rate of 10 per month. The cost of a pacemaker to the hospital is $1,000. It costs $50 to place an order, and the hospital's annual carrying cost is 12 percent of inventory value.

a. What information would you need to determine the optimal order quantity?

b. Assuming the basic EOQ model, what are q^* and the minimum inventory cost?

c. If lead time were 7 days, what is the proper reorder point, assuming a constant rate of demand?

16.13 *Hospital.* If lead time for the pacemakers in Problem 16.12 is 1 day and daily demand is distributed according to the following table, what is the reorder point if stockouts are not allowed?

Daily demand	Probability
0	.30
1	.40
2	.15
3	.10
4	.05
	1.00

16.14 *Sawmill.* A sawmill has been operating at peak capacity for several years. To keep the mill running takes 2,000 trees per day. The supplier of raw material (trees) can deliver 10,000 trees per day. Trees cost an average of $100. Ordering costs are extremely high at $5,000 per order. The annual carrying cost fraction is .12. Assume a 365-day operation of the mill.

a. What is the optimal order quantity?

b. What is the total inventory cost?

c. What assumption about system properties did you make in calculating the optimal order quantity?

16.15 *Aerospace.* An aerospace company has a contract with the U.S. Navy to produce 120 airplanes during the next year. The plan is to produce these airplanes at a rate of 10 per month. An actuating cylinder used to move the wing flap is purchased off the shelf from a nearby supplier; no lead time is required. Since there are two wings, two cylinders are needed per airplane. The actuating cylinders cost $200. Holding cost for the cylinders is $20 per year per cylinder. In addition, it costs $75 to order these cylinders and receive them from the vendor.

a. What is the optimal order quantity?

b. What is the optimal number of orders per year?

c. What is the optimal time between orders?

d. What is the total inventory cost of ordering the optimal order quantity?

e. Perform a limited amount of sensitivity analysis on the order quantity.

16.16 *Aerospace*. Referring to Problem 16.15.

a. What should the aerospace company do if lead time is 1 month rather than zero? In other words, what should the inventory policy be?

b. Does the existence of lead time change the total inventory cost of the actuating cylinders? If so, what is the total cost of the new inventory policy?

16.17 *Mail-order supply*. A mail-order, auto supply firm reviews its stock of tires each month and orders for the next month. Its most popular tire last year was the XR-100 radial. Last year, 1,600 sets were sold; these sales were spread evenly throughout the year. Predictions are that this year's sales will be approximately the same. Lead time from the manufacturer is effectively zero, and no sales are lost due to shortages. Instead, the tires are merely delivered 1 month later. A recent market survey revealed that 50 percent of the customers surveyed would not buy tires again from this firm if they were made to wait an extra month. Profit on a set of tires is $70. Management, therefore, has estimated stockout cost to be .5 (profit on two future sales), or $70, or $840 per set per year. Holding cost per set of tires is $75 per year.

a. What is the optimal order level?

b. What is the minimum inventory cost for the XR-100 radial tire?

c. What is the order-level sensitivity?

16.18 *Automobile Dealer*. An automobile dealer has the exclusive rights to market a foreign car. For this reason, no sales are lost if he is out of stock when a customer wants to buy. Demand for the car has been running at 20 units per month. The dealer orders one time per month and receives the order within a day or two. The dealer's subjective estimate of the cost of the loss of customer goodwill is $100 per month. The dealer cost on the cars is $4,000 and her carrying-cost fraction is approximately .15 per year.

a. What is the optimal order level?

b. What is the minimum inventory cost for the foreign car?

c. What is the sensitivity of the order level?

16.19 *Hospital*. A large hospital's nursery uses disposable diapers for its newborn babies at a rate of 60 cases per day. Ordering costs have been estimated at $50 per order. The hospital's Accounting Department has assigned an annual carrying cost fraction of .15 to the nursery supplies. All the assumptions of the basic EOQ model, such as zero lead time, are applicable. The purchasing agent for the hospital has an opportunity to take advantage of one of several quantity discounts. The pricing schedule is listed in the table.

Quantity ordered (cases)	Unit price
0–1,999	$2.50
2,000–4,999	2.45
5,000–9,999	2.40
10,000 and over	2.35

a. What is the optimal order quantity?

b. What is the minimum inventory cost?

16.20 *Restaurant.* A large restaurant sells 600 16-ounce strip steaks each week. It costs the restaurant $25 to order steaks from a local meat packer, and since the meat packer is close there is effectively no lead time involved. The restaurant's accountant has estimated the annual carrying cost fraction to be .2. The local meat packer has submitted the price schedule listed in the table. Assume that the restaurant has ample freezing capacity.

a. What is the optimal order quantity?

b. What is the minimum total cost?

c. How much initial investment capital would it require to implement the optimal inventory policy?

d. What policy would you recommend to the restaurant manager?

Quantity ordered	Price per pound
Less than 500	$2.00
500–999	1.90
1,000–1,999	1.85
2,000–3,999	1.80
4,000–6,999	1.75
7,000–9,999	1.73
10,000 and over	1.70

16.21 *Retail chain store.* A large retail chain store sells a vacuum cleaner, model LX-1002, for $150. The cost of the vacuum cleaner, including selling cost, is $120. Cost of goods is $100. Demand for this vacuum cleaner model is stochastic; past demand is reflected in the table. Total demand for 1 year is forecast to be 260 units. Stockout cost is assumed to be the profit lost, or $30. Lead time is 7 days. Ordering costs are $40 per order. Carrying cost is 23 percent of the inventory value.

Weekly demand	Frequency
0	2
1	7
2	10
3	7
4	12
5	20
6	14
7	10
8	9
9	7
10	2
	100

a. What is the best inventory policy for the model LX-1002 vacuum cleaner?

b. What do the expected stockout and incremental carrying costs of the selected inventory policy total?

16.22 *Retail chain store.* Given the policy you recommended in Problem 16.21, simulate manually 1 month's activity. Interpret your simulation results.

16.23 Compute the net requirements for items A, B, and C if we want to produce 40 units of X.

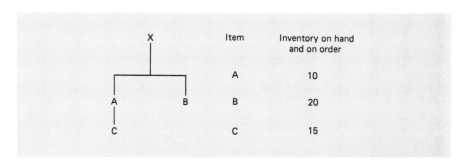

	Item	Inventory on hand and on order
	A	10
	B	20
	C	15

16.24 Calculate the gross and net requirements for the following BOM and quantities. Assume that you want to produce 50 end items.

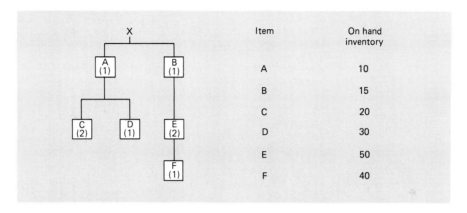

Item	On hand inventory
A	10
B	15
C	20
D	30
E	50
F	40

16.25 *Retail.* A local bicycle store has a very successful line of chromo alloy dirt bikes that are selling an average of approximately two per day. The demand for the past two months is summarized in the two tables:

Date	Demand	Date	Demand
10/1/88	1	11/1/88	2
2	2	2	1
3	0	3	1
4	4	4	1
5	1	5	2
6	3	6	3
7	1	7	4
8	2	8	0
9	7	9	1
10	2	10	2
11	1	11	1
12	0	12	3
13	3	13	5
14	2	14	2
15	5	15	4

Date	Demand	Date	Demand
10/16/88	5	11/16/88	5
10/17/88	1	11/17/88	4
10/18/88	1	11/18/88	2
10/19/88	2	11/19/88	1
10/20/88	1	11/20/88	0
10/21/88	2	11/21/88	1
10/22/88	3	11/22/88	2
10/23/88	1	11/23/88	2
10/24/88	2	11/24/88	2
10/25/88	3	11/25/88	1
10/26/88	4	11/26/88	0
10/27/88	0	11/27/88	4
10/28/88	1	11/28/88	2
10/29/88	2	11/29/88	2
10/30/88	2	11/30/88	1
10/31/88	4		

The bike wholesales for $150 and retails for $199. Because of competition, the owner of the store thinks it is very important to not run out of stock. Vendor lead time varies uniformly from 10 to 20 days. Ordering cost is minimal at about $20 per order and carrying cost averages 20 percent of inventory value. Given this information, analyze the problem and recommend an inventory policy to the owner of the bicycle store. Be sure to justify your recommendations.

16.26 *Retail.* The bike manufacturer in Problem 16.25 has just initiated a volume discount for its most popular bike (see the accompanying table). Given the situation described in Problem 16.25, what is the best reorder policy for the owner of the bike store?

Discount schedule

Quantity	Price
0–49	$150
50–99	140
100 and over	130

BIBLIOGRAPHY

Buffa, Elwood S., and Jeffrey G. Miller, *Production Inventory Systems,* 3rd ed. Homewood, Ill.: Richard D. Irwin, Inc., 1979.

Chase, Richard B., and Nicholas J. Aquilano, *Production and Operations*

Management: A Life Cycle Approach, 4th ed. Homewood, Ill.: Richard D. Irwin, Inc., 1985.

Naddor, Eliezer, *Inventory Systems.* New York: Krieger, 1982.

Orlicky, Joseph, *Materials Requirement Planning.* New York: McGraw-Hill Book Company, 1975.

Plossl, G. W., and O. W. Wright, "Materials Requirement Planning by Computer." Washington, D.C.: APICS, 1971.

——, *Production and Inventory Control,* 2nd ed. Englewood Cliffs, N.J.: Prentice Hall, 1985.

Wagner, Harvey M., *Principles of Operations Research,* 2nd ed. Englewood Cliffs, N.J.: Prentice Hall, 1975.

Wight, Oliver W., *Production and Inventory Management in the Computer Age.* Boston: Cahners Books, 1988.

Decision Support Systems

BETHLEHEM STEEL CORPORATION[1]

American steel companies have been hard pressed by foreign competition during the last decade. The Japanese, Koreans, and others have invested heavily in new plants and new technology that, combined with their relatively low labor costs, afford tremendous competitive advantages. The message is clear: American steel companies must implement productivity improvements and cut their costs dramatically if they are to survive.

As with many industries, the domestic steel industry is increasingly turning to the computer for assistance in reducing costs and making better decisions. Each year Bethlehem Steel ships millions of tons of raw material by ocean-going vessels from mines throughout the world to its steel plants. Bethlehem's Marine Operations has the responsibility for handling the bulk cargo requirements for the company. Bulk cargo is shipped using company-owned or -controlled vessels or noncontrolled vessels that are chartered for a trip or set of trips. In addition, Marine Operations can contract to transport non-Bethlehem bulk commodities. Consequently, management has a high degree of flexibility in making individual transportation decisions.

[1] Kenneth L. Stott, Jr., and Burnie W. Douglas, "A Model-Based Decision Support System for Planning and Scheduling Ocean-Borne Transportation," *Interfaces,* 11, no. 4 (August 1981), 1–10.

Because of the nature and importance of the decision-making process, Bethlehem's management decided several years ago to integrate basic systems concepts and some rather traditional operations research/management science (OR/MS) techniques to create a decision support system that would provide a tool to assist in long-range planning as well as day-to-day operations scheduling. The Marine Operations Planning and Scheduling System (MOPASS) is used by scheduling personnel on a daily basis to make scheduling decisions that tend to minimize transportation costs given shipping requirements and a specific ocean-going fleet. The same system is used by senior management for fleet planning and financial reporting purposes. In short, Bethlehem Steel Corporation has implemented a decision support system that has aided management in acquiring and scheduling ocean-going transportation resources in a near optimal manner.

INTRODUCTION

The term decision support system (DSS) was invented more than a decade ago and has taken on a wide range of meanings. One author has defined DSS as any system that provides support to decision making. Gerry Wagner has defined a DSS as "a tool, usually computer-based, for the purpose of executive mind support." Others consider that the key attributes of a decision support system are:

- ◻ Top-management decision support
- ◻ Flexible financial data bases
- ◻ High-level languages such as EXPRESS and IFPS

For purposes of this chapter, let us define a decision support system as simply a computer-based system that possesses some decision-making or decision-aiding capability. A DSS goes beyond aiding the decision-making process by merely providing the decision maker with timely and relevant information.

As illustrated in Figure 17.1, a DSS usually consists of a data base, information processing software, and appropriate decision models. These decision models are what differentiates a DSS from a more conventional information system. In addition to the standard reports and inquiries that typically are produced by conventional systems, decision support systems often provide daily operating decisions and the answers to complex "what if" questions.

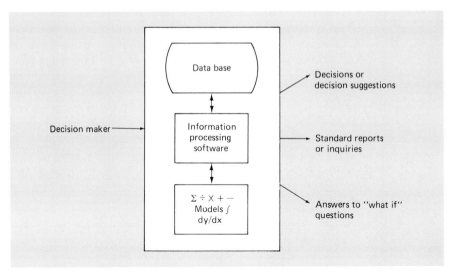

FIGURE 17.1   **Decision support system**

Let us illustrate these concepts with the following example. A small manufacturing company was in desperate need of a production scheduling and control system. The problem was a common one for small companies. This particular company had experienced a rapid rate of growth during the past five years and had simply outgrown its informal information system. Management was experiencing great difficulty in ascertaining the status—indeed the location—of each job or work order. The status and backlog at each workstation could only be determined by actually walking into the factory and visiting each workstation. The traditional data processing solution to this problem might have been to design and implement a work order tracking system that would effectively report on job status and work center status so that management would have the information necessary to make their day-to-day decisions. A decision support system solution to the problem would provide more than timely reporting of job and work center status. The enhanced DSS that was implemented actually schedules each work order on each machine center in such a way that attempts to maximize productivity and minimize the occurrence of missed shipping dates. In addition to the daily decision-making capability of the system, management can use the system to answer "what if" type questions such as

- What is the effect on the shop and the other work orders in the shop of accepting a large order with a specific promised date?
- What is the effect of increasing the priority of a specific job?
- What is the effect of working overtime on various machine centers?

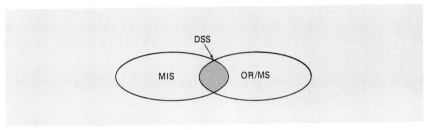

FIGURE 17.2   **The MIS OR/MS interface**

There has been much discussion in the OR/MS literature devoted to the controversy of whether DSS is really a unique concept or just a new acronym for MIS (management information system). Several highly respected scholars have suggested that DSS is merely another name for MIS or no more than a subset of OR/MS. It is our opinion that DSS can be thought of as where the MIS discipline and the OR/MS discipline meet. As pictured in Figure 17.2, DSS must have the attributes of an MIS as well as the decision-making or decision-aiding capability of OR/MS models.

As illustrated in Figure 17.3, decision support systems can be classified on a continuum according to their degree of decision-making capability. At the far left of the continuum is the pure information system that is devoid of any decision-making capability and on the far right is a pure DSS that was created for the sole purpose of aiding the decision-making process. The great majority of installed decision support systems fall somewhere in between these two extremes. The production scheduling system described earlier in this chapter is a good example of the type of DSS which falls between the two extremes.

In the remainder of this chapter, we will describe

- ☐ The evolution of information systems
- ☐ The key characteristics and structural framework of a DSS
- ☐ Implementation issues
- ☐ Computer implications of the DSS movement

FIGURE 17.3   **Decision support system continuum**

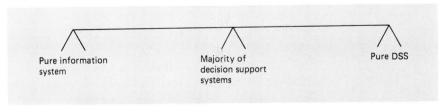

TWO CATEGORIES OF OR/MS APPLICATIONS

OR/MS applications can be divided into two distinct categories:

- Decision-oriented applications
- Decision-process applications

Decision-oriented applications are studies that assist management in making one-time, nonrecurring decisions. Corporate mergers or acquisitions are nonrecurring decisions where a modeling approach is often very useful. Other examples of these types of OR/MS applications include

- **Self-maintenance of delivery trucks** Management of a large geographically dispersed soft drink bottling and distribution company wanted to build and staff a central truck maintenance facility. A simulation approach to studying the economic feasibility of the proposed facility revealed that the cost of transporting the trucks to the facility was prohibitive. Rather than saving maintenance cost, self-maintenance would cost the company almost twice what the company was currently paying to contract out the maintenance of their fleet of over 300 trucks.

- **Airline fleet decisions** The swap of 8 American Airlines' Boeing 747 aircraft for 15 DC10 aircraft from Pan American was a one-time decision that was extremely complex. The decision was supported by a multitude of OR/MS and financial models which indicated where the new airplanes would be used and what the revenue and operating consequences of the swap would be.

Decision-process–oriented applications are those applications where OR/MS models make or suggest solutions to recurring problems. Progressive inventory systems are good examples of analytical systems that address a decision process. Examples of these types of applications include:

- **Pipeline scheduling** Scheduling a petroleum products pipeline is a classic OR/MS application that can potentially save pipeline companies millions of dollars a year. The model is used to make critical scheduling decisions that determine the energy requirement to run the pipeline.

- **Airline seat allocations** All airlines overbook their flights because a percentage of the passengers that hold confirmed reservations fail to show up for their flight. Without overbooking, those seats would be flown empty. If the airline overbooks too lightly it will lose revenue and if the overbooking is excessive the airline will lose money through the payment of denied boarding compensation. Many airlines have decision support systems that forecast demand, cancellations, and boarding rates and which attempt to optimize the overbooking procedure for each flight. In addition, these systems attempt to maximize revenue by deciding how many seats to authorize for sale in each of up to six discount classes. Major airlines have spent millions developing these decision support systems which have been given a large amount of the credit for defeating the low-cost entrant carriers during the years following airline deregulation. American Airlines estimates that their yield management decision support system generates in excess of $300 million in additional revenue.

Successful decision support systems can be applied to both types of applications. These systems often take the form depicted in Figure 17.4. The front-end module interacts with one or more data bases, extracting necessary data elements and performing appropriate manipulations on that data. The intelligence of this type of system is provided by statistical or management science models imbedded in the system. Often, the output from the decision-making module needs to be processed by a back-end module that presents the information in a "user-friendly" format.

FIGURE 17.4 **DSS schematic**

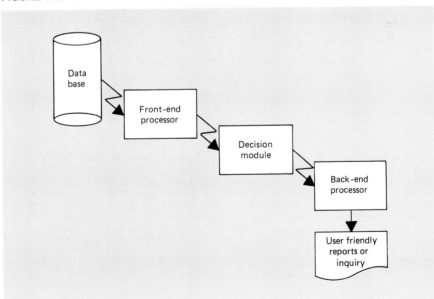

EVOLUTION OF INFORMATION SYSTEMS

During the past 25 years, information systems have evolved at an extremely rapid pace. Progress has been so rapid that many firms and organizations have lagged far behind the state of the art. Where an organization is with respect to the state of their information systems can have a decisive effect on their competitive position. In this section, we will describe the evolution of information systems in an organization by defining the stages of information system development reflected in Figure 17.5. It should be noted that most organizations have a wide variety of information systems and that these systems are not uniform with respect to their sophistication or progressiveness. In other words, some systems within an organization could be second-generation transaction processing systems whereas others could be progressive decision support systems.

Manual Transaction Processing Systems

A transaction is an event that affects an organization. Examples include sales, purchases, inventory withdrawals, and airline reservations. Before the computer revolution, transactions were recorded manually. Today, many small organizations still record their transactions manually. With the advent of the microcomputer, however, the organization with manual transaction processing systems is a vanishing breed.

EAM-Based Transaction Processing Systems

There was a brief period before computers became commonplace when large organizations used electronic accounting machines (EAM) to process their transactions. These types of systems became extinct during the 1960s with the development of first- and second-generation computers.

FIGURE 17.5 **Evolution of information systems**

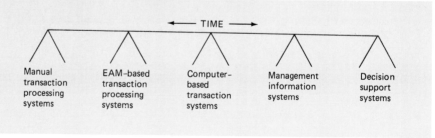

Computer-Based Transaction Processing Systems

A great majority of the computer-based processing systems are of the transaction processing variety. Many of the advances in computer processing systems have been at this level. Examples include

- Computerized payroll systems
- Dividend calculation systems
- Airline reservation systems
- Customer billing systems

Transaction processing systems are not decision oriented, but two types of reports can be generated that do provide some information. Control reports can provide information on errors that were detected during the transaction processing. Monitoring reports provide information that allows various activities to be observed or summarized. Examples include payroll summaries and basic accounting performance reports. These reports do not aid directly in the decision-making process; true management information systems are characterized by providing information for specific decision problems.

Management Information Systems

Unlike a transaction processing system, a true information system contains information and not just data. It contains the kind of information that is pertinent for a specific decision-making problem. An effective management information system will provide the required information in a meaningful form and at the right time.

An information system differs from a mundane data processing system by having its own data base, information retrieval capabilities, and report-generating software. The extent to which an information system is successful is measured by the degree that it supports the management and decision-making functions of the organization.

The typical information system performs two basic functions. These functions are information retrieval and preparation of reports. *Information* *information* *retrieval* refers to the accessing of specific data or information stored in the *retrieval* data base. This information may be used to answer a specific inquiry but is usually retrieved to prepare a specific report. A list of the typical types of reports is shown in Table 17.1.

The output of these types of reports support such decision situations as

- Inventory reordering and status reporting
- Quality control

TABLE 18.1   *MIS-generated reports*

Type of report	Purpose
Special retrieval requests	To answer a specific question or provide information for a specific problem.
Regular report	To support the operating and control functions on a regularly scheduled basis.
Exception report	To signal an out-of-control or unusual situation.
Special report	To support a specific one-time decision problem. Prepared only on request.

- Budget analyses
- Sales analyses
- Depreciation decisions
- Projected income statements

Decision Support Systems

The most recent stage of development for information systems is the advent of systems that employ decision models to support the decision process. As information systems become more sophisticated, they will increasingly rely upon appropriate decision models. No longer will the models be used in an ad hoc, nonintegrated basis. They will need to become part of an integrated system composed of decision models, decision maker, and data base.

decision support system   This relatively new breed of information system has been labeled a *decision support system* (*DSS*). It is an exciting concept which extends the range of decision problems that OR/MS and MIS can support. In particular, it promises to help decision makers deal with *unstructured problems* which are often encountered in real-world decision making. Just as early MIS helped to extend OR/MS applications by providing accurate timely data, DSS extends OR/MS by dealing with problems that do not have enough structure to be "solved completely" by any particular OR/MS model or MIS report.

Most problems encountered by real-world decision makers require some degree of human judgment or input; very few real decision problems can be completely solved by the straightforward application of a decision model. It is the incorporation of the human judgmental process that further distinguishes decision support systems from other information systems. There is definitely some overlap among MIS, OR/MS, and DSS, especially since DSS is an integration of MIS and OR/MS. However, these disciplines are differentiated in terms of their relative emphasis and relevance to managers. In their book, Keen and Morton further delineate the differences among the three approaches.[2] They explain the differences in emphasis and impact as follows:

1. Management information systems:
   a. The main impact has been on structured tasks where standard operating procedures, decision rules, and information flows can be reliably predefined.
   b. The main payoff has been in improving efficiency by reducing costs, turnaround time, and so on and by replacing clerical personnel.
   c. The relevance for managers' decision making has mainly been indirect; for example, by providing reports and access to data.
2. Operations research/management science:
   a. The impact has mostly been on structured problems (rather than tasks) where the objective, data, and constraints can be prespecified.
   b. The payoff has been in generating better solutions for given types of problems.
   c. The relevance for managers has been the provision of detailed recommendations and new methodologies for handling complex problems.
3. Decision support systems:
   a. The impact is on decisions in which there is sufficient structure for computer and analytic aids to be of value but where managers' judgment is essential.
   b. The payoff is in extending the range and capability of managers' decision processes to help them improve their effectiveness.
   c. The relevance for managers is the creation of a supportive tool, under their own control, which does not attempt to automate the decision process, predefine objectives, or impose solutions.

One of the key differences in decision support systems is that the decision maker's insights and judgments are used at all stages of problem solving—from problem formulation, to data selection, to model building and

[2] Peter G. W. Keen and Michael S. Scott Morton, *Decision Support Systems: An Organizational Perspective* (Reading, Mass.: Addison-Wesley Publishing Company, 1978).

selection, and to solution evaluation, It should be clear by now that categorizing a specific information system may be difficult for two reasons:

- There are no universally accepted definitions of MIS or DSS. Indeed, some respected scholars in the field make no distinction.
- Even if we can agree on the definition of these types of systems, there are very few real systems that fit neatly into one category or the other.

Decision Support Systems and Expert Systems

Some authors have stated that expert systems are the natural extension of decision support systems. As we shall discuss in Chapter 18, it is our opinion that an expert system has a role to play in a decision support system but is not merely an extension or the evolutionary offspring of DSS. If we define an expert system as a computer program that emulates the decision-making behavior of a human expert, then we can think of an expert system as being imbedded in a DSS in much the same way as an OR/MS model. It is quite conceivable that as expert systems continue to evolve, the designer of a decision support system will turn to the knowledge engineer rather than to the OR/MS professional to build key decision-making modules of the DSS. Indeed, the decision support system of the future may have a combination of OR/MS decision modules and expert systems decision modules that provide the system with the necessary intelligence. It is for this reason that the OR/MS professional must adapt so that he or she can take an expert system approach to those decision problems that cannot be modeled with more traditional OR/MS techniques. In the words of Nobel Prize laureate Herbert Simon, "We should aspire to increase the impact of MS/OR by incorporating the AI kit of tools that can be applied to ill-structured, knowledge-rich, nonquantitative decision domains that characterize the work of top management."[3]

IMPLEMENTATION ISSUES

Although the DSS movement is more than 15 years old, progress toward DSS implementation remains relatively slow in most organizations. A survey of 114 industrial firms completed several years ago indicated only 3 percent of installed systems could be classified as decision support systems. Several writers have discussed the gap between what the data processing community is providing today's decision maker and what that decision maker wants and needs to make better decisions. Robert Alloway states, "A

[3] H. A. Simon, "Two Heads Are Better than One: The Collaboration Between AI and OR," *Interfaces*, 17, no. 4 (July–August 1987), 8–15.

search for the cause of user dissatisfaction with DP need go no further than this mismatch between user managers' important needs and the installed base of applications.''

According to a recent survey, of the 120 transaction processing systems examined, management felt that 34 (28 percent) should have been designed as decision support systems. Survey respondents (user and data processing managers) indicated that when the known backlog and invisible backlog for decision support systems are implemented, the number of DSS's will grow by over 1,000 percent. This contrasted with 88 percent growth projected for monitoring-type transaction processing systems.

Impediments to DSS

Why are decision support systems so scarce? The major reason is that the installed base of computer applications is so large that the conversion of these relatively unintelligent systems will take years to accomplish. Other reasons for the slow growth of installed decision support systems relate to answering the question of why nonprogressive informations systems are still being designed and implemented. These reasons include

- **Lack of user demand** There is a lack of understanding on the part of user management concerning what they should be able to expect out of their informations systems. The typical user is often delighted if the DP professional staff merely automates the manual system successfully and on time.

- **Lack of system designer motivation** If users do not demand more progressive decision support systems, there is little motivation for the system designer to think creatively. In addition, DP management often lack a clear understanding of the quantitative aspects of a DSS and consequently fail to motivate their professional staff to integrate appropriate modeling techniques into their system designs.

- **Lack of system designer expertise** A lack of modeling or quantitative skills on the part of the system designer often eliminates the possibility of designing a progressive DSS. Integrating a linear programming model or a forecasting model into the design of an information system is often not considered primarily due to the lack of experience of the system designer or project leader.

- **Reluctance to change** Human beings have a natural reluctance to change. This built-in inertia has resisted the use of structured design and structured programming techniques. It is also resisting the change from traditional transaction processing systems to decision support systems.

- **Increased risk of failure** Designing and implementing a DSS typically has a greater risk of failure than do less complex information systems.

Consequently, system analysts have a strong tendency not to venture into the unchartered waters of DSS. This increase in risk is usually not as large as it is perceived and the added risk is usually outweighed by the increase in the system's utility.

Motivation

Why design and implement decision support systems? The major reason is that a DSS is often more cost effective because either the system can make better decisions than a manager or more commonly the manager can make better, more cost effective decisions with the aid of a DSS. In addition, the benefits of a DSS are often tangible. In most new information systems, the benefits of the new system cannot be quantitatively predicted before the implementation, and often even after installation, benefits cannot be quantified in dollars. This is not true of many decision support systems. Financial benefits of a DSS can often be predicted and measured.

Who should motivate the design and implementation of a DSS? The answer to this question is threefold.

□ **The user/decision-maker** The manager that is requesting information to support his or her decision making should not be satisfied with the traditional DP approach to his or her request for information. He or she should demand an analytical DSS when it is appropriate.

□ **The DP professional** The systems analyst that has been asked to design a system should ask questions such as:

What decisions does the information being requested support?

Of those decisions, which can be better made using some modeling or heuristic technique?

For which decisions can some form of heuristic or model be used to aid the decision-making process?

□ **The OR/MS professional** The management scientist was advised several years ago by Gene Woolsey to develop a close working relationship with a firm's cost accountant. With the advent of DSS our advice is for the OR analyst to develop good working relations with the firm's data processing applications development staff. A systems analyst is more apt to design a DSS if he knows and trusts someone that can assist in developing the decision-making or decision-aiding modules of the system.

COMPUTER IMPLICATIONS

Recent developments in computer hardware and software have opened the door for widespread proliferation of DSS. Fourth-generation data base access software such as DBII, FOCUS, and RAMIS, together with flexible financial and statistical modeling languages such as IFPS, EXPRESS, Lotus 1-2-3, and SAS, provide the software tools necessary to provide management with flexible and up-to-date decision support systems. This explosion of user-friendly software is expected to continue during the 1990s.

The advent of microcomputers encourages the wide distribution of DSS within large organizations and makes it possible for small businesses and nonprofit organizations to develop meaningful and effective decision support systems. In short, the hardware and software technology of today is sufficient to support a DSS explosion. The important challenge is to overcome the organizational impediments to DSS implementation and for decision makers, DP professionals, and OR/MS professionals, to work as a team to develop tomorrow's intelligent systems.

SUMMARY

In this chapter we have discussed the interface between OR/MS and MIS. Using a fairly broad definition, this interface can be described as decision support. We have defined a DSS as a system that goes beyond merely providing the decision maker with timely, useful information. Rather, the DSS, through the employment of heuristic, statistical, or operations research models, provides analytical support. Our definition of DSS is broader than those that consider a system a DSS only if it is for senior management, only if it uses fourth generation software and only if it deals with nonrecurring unstructured decisions.

Although the term DSS has been around for more than 15 years, we are still in the embryonic stage of development. Many of today's traditional information systems need to be transformed into more useful decision support systems, and many new analytical systems need to be developed. The challenge of the future for the DP and OR/MS professional is to work together to develop a new generation of systems that take full advantage of existing hardware and software technology to close the gap between what management needs for effective decision making and the existing information systems.

REVIEW QUESTIONS

1. What is a decision support system?
2. List three categories of output from a DSS.
3. Distinguish between a pure information system and a pure DSS.
4. Comment on the MIS and OR/MS interface.
5. Define the two major categories of OR/MS applications.

6. What is an MIS?
7. Distinguish between transaction processing systems and management information systems.
8. List three examples of transaction processing systems.
9. Describe the four types of MIS-generated reports.
10. What is the role of an expert system in DSS?
11. List five impediments to the development of decision support systems.
12. What are some of the potential benefits of DSS?
13. Who should motivate the development of DSS within an organization?
14. Briefly describe the interface between DSS and expert systems.

BIBLIOGRAPHY

Alter, Steven L., *Decision Support Systems: Current Practices and Continuing Challenges,* pp. 123–182. Reading, Mass.: Addison-Wesley Publishing Company, 1980.

Barr, A., and E. Feigenbaum, *The Handbook of Artificial Intelligence,* Vol. 2. Los Altos, Calif.: Kaufmann Publications, 1982, contains excellent survey of expert systems.

Davis, Gordon B., and M. H. Olsen, *Management Information Systems: Conceptual Foundations, Structure and Development,* 2nd ed. New York: McGraw-Hill Book Company, 1985.

———, and Gordon C. Everest, *Readings in Management Information Systems.* New York: McGraw-Hill Book Company, 1976.

Davis, Randall, and Douglas Lenat, eds., *Knowledge-Based Systems in Artificial Intelligence,* pp. 229–490. New York: McGraw-Hill Book Company, 1982.

Hayes-Roth, F., et al., *Building Expert Systems.* Reading, Mass.: Addison-Wesley Publishing Company, 1983.

Keen, Peter G. W., and Michael S. Scott Morton, *Decision Support Systems: An Organizational Perspective.* Reading, Mass.: Addison-Wesley Publishing Company, 1978.

Pearl, J., *Heuristics: Intelligent Search Strategies for Computer Problem Solving.* Reading, Mass.: Addison-Wesley Publishing Company, 1984.

Reitman, W., *"Applying Artificial Intelligence to Decision Support."* In *Decision Support Systems,* ed. M. J. Ginsberg et al. Amsterdam: North-Holland, 1982.

Senn, James A., *Information Systems in Management,* 3rd ed. Belmont, Calif.: Wadsworth Publishing Co., 1987.

Sprague, Ralph H., Jr., and Eric D. Carlson, *Building Effective Decision Support Systems*. Englewood Cliffs, N.J.: Prentice Hall, 1982.

———, and Hugh J. Watson, *Decision Support Systems: Putting Theory into Practice*. Englewood Cliffs, N.J.: Prentice Hall, 1986.

Vazsonyi, Andrew, and Herbert Spirer, *Quantitative Analysis for Business*. Englewood Cliffs, N.J.: Prentice Hall, 1984.

## 18

Heuristics, AI, and Expert Systems

DIGITAL EQUIPMENT CORPORATION[1]

As a major computer vendor of minicomputer systems, Digital Equipment Corporation must configure thousands of hardware systems for its customers. In the past, technical editors would review a customer's order to determine what computer components needed to be substituted in order to make the order consistent and complete.

In conjunction with AI researchers at Carnegie-Mellon University, Digital developed an expert system called XCON to configure all VAX™ family systems. XCON performs at a level similar to that of an experienced technical editor. For each order, XCON determines necessary modifications, produces diagrams showing the spatial and logical relationships between hundred of components, and defines exact cable lengths required between system components. Configurations which required 20–30 minutes of a technical editor's time can be accomplished by XCON in less than one minute.

XCON is a rule-based expert system with several thousand rules. It is implemented in OPS-5, a general-purpose rule-based language. XCON has evolved and improved over time. The system required four person-

[1] J. Bachant and J. McDermott, "R1 Revisited: Four Years in the Trenches," *AI Magazine,* 5, no. 3 (Fall 1984).
Note: The trademarks of Digital Equipment Corporation: VAX and the Digital logo.

years to build and approximately the same level of effort each year to enhance and maintain. By 1985 all VAX℠ family system orders in U.S. and European plant operations were configured by XCON.

Digital had set a performance goal of 90 to 95 percent perfect configurations. XCON has evolved to exceed that goal with accurate configurations 98 percent of the time. Regardless of its stage of development XCON will never have all the knowledge it needs to be 100 percent accurate.

The high level of performance of XCON has allowed Digital to increase its order throughput rate and smooth production. It has been able to redeploy skilled senior technicians to work on more technically difficult tasks. Cost savings to Digital are estimated to be $15 million per year.

INTRODUCTION

In this text, we have focused on traditional OR/MS modeling and optimization techniques. Those methods include the simplex method, goal programming, MODI method, network algorithms, dynamic programming, and branch and bound. Whereas these methods are often the foundation of OR/MS analysis, the concept of optimization is not always appropriate in decision making. In many decisions, uncertainty and the decision maker's attitude toward risk preclude problem solution through optimization.

In applying the scientific method to decision making, alternatives to optimization include heuristics, satisficing through goal programming, interactive decision support systems, simulation, and expert systems, or the application of artificial intelligence. We have looked at several heuristics throughout the text. For example, we used a greedy heuristic to solve the knapsack problem, and the ROW MINIMUM rule and VAM to approximate transportation problem solutions. MINSLK was used to solve resource constrained PERT problems, and LP with rounding was used to obtain feasible integer solutions. Heuristics play an important role in both OR/MS and the emerging field of artificial intelligence. In this chapter we take a look at the relationship among OR/MS, heuristics, and artificial intelligence.

HEURISTICS REVISITED

In Chapter 6, we defined a heuristic as a rule-of-thumb procedure for determining a solution to a problem. Not all heuristics yield good solutions to problems, however, and even effective heuristics vary in the quality of their solution to different problems. At best, a heuristic can guarantee its results only probabilistically or within certain margins of uncertainty. Empirical testing can yield estimates of the heuristic's mean percentage deviation from the optimal solution.

You may wonder why heuristics are used in OR/MS since they provide approximate or even suboptimal solutions to problems. There are two primary reasons why heuristics are used:

1. A problem might not be amenable to optimization. For instance, a mathematical model formulation is feasible, but its solution might require excessive amounts of computer memory or execution time. This situation is common in really large-scale applications or in problems that are nonlinear or combinatorially complex.

2. A problem might be amenable to optimization, but optimization is not cost effective. In this case management may not require an optimal solution and therefore the ease and simplicity of a heuristic approach is preferred. It is also possible that the effort, time, and expense required of an optimization approach is not justified given the expected level of benefits.

Heuristics can be a valuable addition to the management scientist's repertoire of tools for solving practical real-world problems. Heuristics are usually based on human insight into the nature of a problem. Good heuristics are usually intuitive and easy to explain. Other properties of effective heuristics include the following:

1. An effective heuristic should yield solutions that consistently approximate optimal solutions. There should be little or no dependency on data or problem structure to yield good solutions.

2. The heuristic should be relatively easy to use and cost effective in terms of human and computer resources.

Some problems require more than one heuristic for their solution. For example, an analyst might use the VAM heuristic to obtain an initial solution to a transportation-type network problem and then apply another heuristic to get closer to optimality. A collection of heuristics combined to solve a problem *heuristic* is called a *heuristic program*. Many of the more complex decision problems *program* are approached with highly refined heuristic programs.

We now present examples that represent each of the two main reasons for using heuristics. The first example is a combinatorial problem called the traveling salesman problem. The second example involves inventory problems having dynamic demand.

The Traveling Salesman Problem

The traveling salesman problem was briefly discussed in the supplement to Chapter 6. It is a classical combinatorial problem that is extremely difficult to solve optimally.

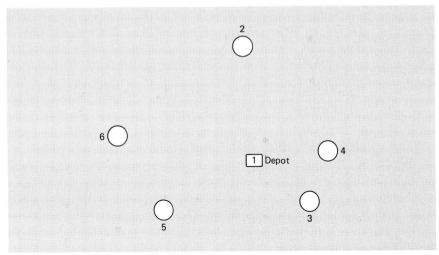

FIGURE 18.1   Graph of points in traveling salesman problem

The traveling salesman problem involves the creation of a tour that passes through n points. One of these points is designated as the home base. The problem is to leave the home base, visit each of the points once, and then return to the home base while minimizing the total distance traveled during the entire tour. The problem is a sequencing problem. Its computational complexity derives from the fact that there are $(n - 1)!$ possible sequences or tours for a problem with n points. As n gets large the number of possible solutions becomes astronomically large. In terms of computational complexity, the problem is "NP complete." The term NP complete means that the number of steps required to obtain an optimal solution is not bounded by a polynomial function of the problem size. Until recently, the largest traveling salesman problem that could be solved optimally had approximately 100 points. Researchers have recently been able to solve some

TABLE 18.1   *Distance matrix*

From \ To	Distance in miles					
	1	2	3	4	5	6
1	—	42	20	31	29	33
2	42	—	58	45	68	47
3	20	58	—	28	32	51
4	31	45	28	—	57	61
5	29	68	32	57	—	34
6	33	47	51	61	34	—

traveling salesman problems involving several hundred points. Nevertheless, heuristic solutions are common in practice and necessary for most large-scale problems.

As an illustrative example consider a delivery problem in which a vehicle must leave a depot or warehouse and deliver to each of five customers. The graph of the problem is shown in Figure 18.1, and the associated distance matrix is shown in Table 18.1.

Nearest Neighbor Heuristic

Many heuristic procedures have been developed for solving the traveling salesman problem. The nearest neighbor rule is easy to describe and quite intuitive since it attempts to link points that are close together. The steps of the nearest neighbor heuristic are as follows:

Step 1: Start with any node as the beginning of a path

Step 2: Find the node closest to the last node added to the path. Add this node to the path.

Step 3: Repeat step 2 until all nodes are contained in the path. Then, join the first and last nodes.

1. To illustrate the heuristic let's start with node 1, the depot in Figure 18.1.
2. Scanning the distance matrix, we see that point 3 is the closest to node 1. Therefore, send the vehicle from node 1 to node 3.
3. Excluding node 1, the closest point to node 3 is node 4. Therefore, send the vehicle to its next delivery at node 4.
4. Excluding nodes 1 and 3, the node closest to node 4 is node 2.
5. From node 2 the closest unvisited customer is node 6.
6. From node 6 the only remaining customer is node 5.
7. From node 5 the only choice is to return to the depot.

Figure 18.2 shows the final tour determined by the nearest neighbor heuristic.

The tour may or may not be optimal. In computational testing[2] on $n = 100$ node problems, the nearest neighbor rule was not a particularly good performer; its tours were typically 13 to 16 percent longer than the best known solutions. However, the heuristic is very efficient, requiring on the order of n^2 computations to obtain a solution.

[2] B. Golden, L. Bodin, T. Doyle, and W. Stewart, Jr., "Approximate Traveling Salesman Problems," *Operations Research,* 28 (May–June 1980), 694–711.

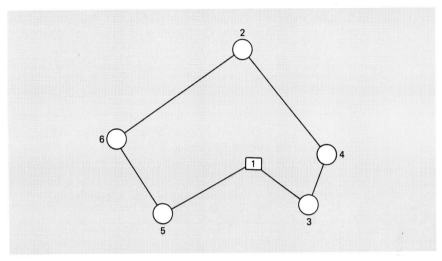

FIGURE 18.2   **Graph of final tour**

Inventory Planning with Dynamic Demand

In some cases optimization is possible, but a heuristic is used for simplicity and cost considerations. This is often the case in inventory planning with dynamic or time-varying demand. In Chapter 16 on inventory systems we described the EOQ model for determining optimal order quantities under the assumption of constant demand. In most real-world applications, demand is not constant and varies seasonally or randomly over time.

Time-varying or "lumpy demand" is most often the rule in requirements planning for manufacturing inventories. In this case, an important decision is to determine the appropriate lot size to order so that all requirements are met and costs are minimized. The standard EOQ model could be used by averaging the forecasted demand over several time periods. However, other heuristic rules have performed better in practice.

The Silver-Meal Heuristic

In this section we present the Silver-Meal heuristic (named after its developers E. A. Silver and R. Meal). It is superior to the EOQ heuristic, especially when demand is highly variable over time. Consider the following six-week demand forecast:

Week	1	2	3	4	5	6
Demand forecast	10	10	10	40	60	30
Cumulative demand	10	20	30	70	130	160

Suppose that the carrying cost is $2 per unit per year and that the order cost is $5. Extrapolating the demand to a 52-week-year yields

$$EOQ = \sqrt{\frac{2(1,386)5}{2}} = 83$$

A fixed EOQ ordering policy would order 83 units. Assuming a zero lead time, the EOQ policy would be to order 83 units at the beginning of period 1 and also at the beginning of period 5.

The Silver-Meal heuristic attempts to minimize the combined costs of ordering and carrying inventory by computing the order quantity that would minimize the total costs per unit of time. Specifically,

> The Silver-Meal heuristic specifies the order of *n* consecutive periods of demand where the resulting quantity ordered minimizes the combined cost of carrying and ordering per time period.

Table 18.2 illustrates the calculation of carrying cost for various periods ordered. The weekly carrying cost = $2/52 = $.038 per unit per week. Note that carrying costs are paid only on inventory that is carried over from one period to the next.

The calculation of the Silver-Meal order quantity requires the combining of carrying costs and ordering costs in order to compute the total cost per week. Table 18.3 shows the remaining calculations. The Silver-Meal solution is obtained when three periods worth of demand is ordered or 30 units.

The Silver-Meal heuristic results in the ordering of 30 units in week 1. Orders for subsequent weeks (from week 4 on) would be planned by reapplying the heuristic's logic. The Silver-Meal heuristic is effective and often results in lower cost ordering decisions than other lot size rules. However, it considers only consecutive periods of demand. For example, it does not consider a policy such as order in period 1 for periods 1 through 4, and

TABLE 18.2 *Calculating carrying costs for n periods of demand*

Periods ordered	Quantity	Inventory carrying costs
1	10	$.038 × 0 = 0
1 and 2	20	.038 × (10 + 0) = $.38
1, 2, and 3	30	.038 × (20 + 10 + 0) = $1.14
1, 2, 3, and 4	70	.038 × (60 + 50 + 40 + 0) = $5.70
1, 2, 3, 4, and 5	130	.038 × (120 + 110 + 100 + 60 + 0) = $14.82
1, 2, 3, 4, 5, and 6	160	.038 × (150 + 140 + 130 + 90 + 30 + 0) = $20.52

TABLE 18.3 *Calculations of the Silver-Meal heuristic*

Periods ordered	Inventory carrying costs	Order cost	Total cost	Number of weeks	Total cost per week
1	$ 0	$5.00	$ 5.00	1	$5.00
1 and 2	.38	5.00	5.38	2	2.69
1, 2, and 3	1.14	5.00	6.14	3*	2.05
1, 2, 3, and 4	5.70	5.00	10.70	4	2.68
1, 2, 3, 4, and 5	14.82	5.00	19.82	5	3.96
1, 2, 3, 4, 5, and 6	20.52	5.00	25.52	6	4.25

reorder in period 5 for periods 5 through 6. The determination of an optimal order policy that considers all possible sequences can be achieved by the application of dynamic programming.

The Wagner-Whitin algorithm is the name of a dynamic programming optimization approach to the dynamic inventory ordering problem. It is more expensive and more difficult to implement than heuristics. It is not used very often (though perhaps it should be used more often than it is). However, heuristics such as the Silver-Meal rule are often within 1 to 2 percent of optimality. Given less than perfect inventory cost estimates, and hundreds or possibly thousands of inventory items, it is easy to understand why many managers weigh simplicity and minimization of computer time over optimality.

AI AND OR/MS

The field of artificial intelligence has received a great deal of attention lately. The interest is reflected not only in levels of research activity but also the promise of commercial applications. The total market for AI products is projected to reach $1 billion by 1990. AI and OR have at least two things in common. They both are dedicated to problem solving/decision making, and they both make use of heuristics.

Traditionally, OR/MS has made use of models, heuristics, and other quantitative tools to solve decision problems. Historically, these problems have been relatively structured and amenable to analysis by algorithms. In the previous chapter, we looked at decision support systems and how they have united the subjective powers of the decision maker and the analytical powers of quantitative tools in one interactive system. Decision support systems have helped to expand the boundaries of the problem-solving domain by enabling decision makers to utilize computers in addressing less well-structured or semistructured problems. Still, some complex problems elude successful solution by approaches that employ only quantitative information. The promise of AI has always been great, but historically the payoff has been low. However, with millions of dollars being spent on AI research, it is worthwhile to take a closer look at AI, its relationship to OR/MS, and what the future might hold.

What Is AI?

There are many different definitions of AI. Perhaps the simplest one is

> AI is the science and technology concerned with creating behavior by a machine that, if performed by a human being, would be called intelligent.

Another more detailed explanation of AI is given by AI pioneer and Nobel laureate Herbert Simon.[3]

> Artificial intelligence is the application of methods of heuristic search to the solution of complex problems that
>
> a. defy the mathematics of optimization
> b. contain nonquantifiable components
> c. involve large knowledge bases (including knowledge expressed in natural language)
> d. incorporate the discovery and design of alternatives of choice
> e. admit ill-specified goals and constraints

The latter explanation emphasizes the aspiration of AI to deal with all the aspects of managerial decisions that stretch beyond the limits of classical OR/MS.

Historically, the AI field got its start at a conference conducted at Dartmouth College in 1956. The term "artificial intelligence" was coined there as well as some predictions that in 10 years computers would be as smart as people. Early successes in AI were confined to relatively small structured problems such as puzzles and games such as checkers or chess.

After failure in the AI field to achieve earlier predictions, the discipline began to pick up momentum in the mid-1970s with the success of several expert systems. Two developments were fundamental to advancements in AI. First, software tools such as LISP and PROLOG evolved to handle AI problems much more effectively than traditional data processing methods and languages. LISP (LIST Processing language) expresses complex objects such as rules, sentences, and names, not just numbers. Therefore, LISP

---

[3] Herbert A. Simon, "Two Heads Are Better than One: The Collaboration Between AI and OR," *Interfaces,* 17 (July–August 1987), 8–15.

facilitates the development of flexible systems that can accommodate complex relationships among data. PROLOG (PROgramming in LOGic) is another AI development tool. A PROLOG program essentially consists of a knowledge base of facts and rules (clauses). A PROLOG system provides a way to ask for logical deductions to be made using the data base. A key characteristic of PROLOG is that it enables programs to be written focusing on the description of the problem rather than on the algorithms for solving the problem.[4] Additionally, computer hardware with fast processing capabilities and large memories have become much less expensive and more readily available. Symbolic processors that have a logical architecture specifically to support LISP applications now facilitate AI program development and execution.

A second development responsible for the advancements in AI is the integration of several different sciences and technologies. Artificial intelligence is so broad a concept that no single discipline can hope single handedly to create intelligent behavior. The primary disciplines involved in AI include linguistics (computational linguistics and socialinguistics), psychology (cognition and psycholinguistics), philosophy (logic), mechanics, hydraulics, optics, computer science (hardware and software), electrial engineering (image processing, control theory, and robotics), statistics (pattern recognition), management and organization theory (decision making, implementation), operations research/management science (heuristic programming, fuzzy logic, and cost effectiveness), and MIS.[5] The various disciplines that overlap and interact in the field of AI are so diverse that it is not possible to classify the field according to any one discipline. It is perhaps more meaningful to look at AI in terms of the major areas of development and application.

Major Areas of Application

Although the following list is not all inclusive, it does cover the primary areas of commercial application:

1. Computer vision/sensory systems
2. Robotics
3. Speech recognition
4. Natural language processors
5. Expert systems

The last two areas of natural language processing and expert systems have the most impact on OR/MS and decision support systems.

[4] R. Bharath, "Logic Programming: A Tool for MS/OR?" *Interfaces,* 16 (September–October 1986), 80–91.

[5] Efraim Turban, *Decision Support and Expert Systems: Managerial Perspectives* (New York: Macmillan Publishing Company, 1988).

Natural language processing has a major impact on the perceived usability of computer-based systems. The lack of a natural dialogue between computer and user limits the number of potential users for many systems. Unfamiliar command phrases, intricate software instructions, and keyboards discourage system usage by some managers and decision makers.

Current natural language processors can recognize and interpret phrases and sentences relating to very restricted topics. Their capabilities, however, fall short of the goal of allowing users to communicate with a computer in their native language.

Probably the two most fruitful areas for the application of natural language processors are as interfaces to data bases and to decision support and expert systems. Natural language interfaces allow users to query data bases in a natural language context rather than having to use a formal and unfamiliar command language. Several natural languages interfaces for DBMS software currently exist. One example is CLOUT from Microrim, Inc., Bellevue, Washington. CLOUT is designed to be used with R : Base 5000, another Microrim product. Using CLOUT, the user can pose a query such as: "Give me the names of all students with a G.P.A. over 3.5." This phraseology is much more natural than is relational data base terminology using SELECT, JOIN, or PROJECT commands.

A natural language processor is a type of expert system. The processor contains knowledge pertaining to understanding a human language. Expert systems are the most active area of AI development and are most related to OR/MS and DSS and consequently we focus the remainder of this chapter on expert systems.

EXPERT SYSTEMS

The scientific approach and quantitative tools have enabled OR/MS to have great success in solving many different kinds of decision problems. However, there are many types of decision problems that are best handled by human expertise and knowledge. These kinds of problems tend be less structured, qualitative problems as opposed to more structured problems amenable to solutions by algorithms.

Expert systems have evolved as computer-based systems that can provide intelligent or mechanical but not human expertise in solving a specific problem. Rauch[6] describes knowledge-based expert systems as

> A class of computer programs intended to serve as consultants for decision making. These programs use a collection of facts,

[6] H. Rauch, "Probability Concepts for an Expert System Used for Data Fusion," *AI Magazine*, 5, no. 3 (1984), 55–60.

rules of thumb, and other knowledge about a limited field to help make inferences in the field. They differ substantially from conventional computer programs in that their goals may have no algorithmic solution, and they must make inferences based on incomplete or uncertain information. They are called expert systems because they address problems normally thought to require human specialists for solution, and knowledge-based because researchers have found that amassing a large amount of knowledge is largely responsible for the success of the approach.

Expert systems are valuable because they capture, store, and distribute expertise. They can also help solve problems whose complexity (or knowledge required) exceeds that of the intended user.

Knowledge Representation

knowledge engineering The process of capturing knowledge and building an expert system is often called *knowledge engineering*. It involves the interaction between a knowledge engineer and one or more experts who possess the knowledge in a specific domain or problem area. The knowledge engineer "extracts" procedures, strategies, and heuristics for problem solving and represents this knowledge in the expert system. Figure 18.3 illustrates the knowledge engineering process.

The extraction and assimilation of knowledge can be a labor-intensive and time-consuming process. Months or even years can be required to develop a sophisticated expert system. The extraction process is further complicated by the fact that some experts have difficulty specifying precisely how they make certain types of decisions.

Another issue in expert systems is the representation of knowledge. How can knowledge be represented so that intelligent inferences can be made about a specific problem? Some of the methods for storing expertise include frame-oriented structures and semantic nets. However, the most widely used form of knowledge representation is a rule set. A rule set contains a collection of rules, each of which captures some piece of knowledge about how to reason in the specific problem area addressed by the expert

FIGURE 18.3 **The knowledge engineering process**

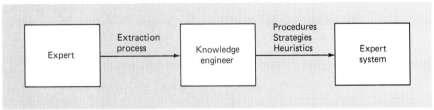

system. These rules (commonly called production rules) describe an inference that can be made about a specific situation.

The premise or IF part of each rule describes the conditions that must be met for the rule to apply. The action, or THEN part, of each rule describes the conclusions that can be made when the premise is valid. For example, a production rule for a chemical spill expert system might be:

RULE: R1
  IF: If the pH of the spill is less than 6
THEN: The spill material is an acid

Production rules have some advantages as representations of knowledge. They are easy for humans to relate to, they are modular and easy to change, and they allow for an explanation of system conclusions. It is clear, however, that much of human reasoning cannot be represented as a collection of IF-THEN rules.

Expert System Structure

Expert systems must contain more than a collection of rules. Some means of deciding which rules apply and controlling the "reasoning" process is required. Most rule-based or production-type expert systems are composed of the following five parts:

1. A knowledge base consisting of rules or heuristics about the problem
2. A data base containing facts about the problem
3. An inference engine or reasoning mechanism for interpreting and applying the knowledge
4. An explanation mechanism
5. A set of control strategies

Figure 18.4 illustrates the basic structure of a production expert system.

The inference engine is the "brain" of the expert system. In rule-based expert systems the inference engine is a control structure or rule interpreter. It is essentially a computer program that provides a methodology for reasoning about information in the knowledge base. It contains an interpreter that decides how to apply the rules to infer new knowledge and a scheduler that decides the order in which the rules should be applied.

The power of the inference engine is related to the kinds of rules it can process. A low-power engine can only deal with rudimentary rules. A higher-power engine can deal with more sophisticated rules. Reasoning in the inference engine can be based on forward chaining or backward chain-

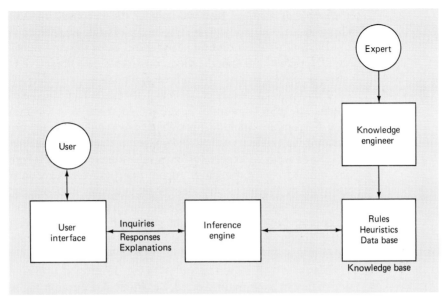

FIGURE 18.4 **Structure of a production expert system**

ing. Forward reasoning involves looking first at each rule premise. The rule's conclusion is ignored until the premise is determined to be true. Backward chaining is a "goal-directed" approach that starts with an expectation of what is to happen, then seeks evidence that supports it. An engine that can run in either direction is more powerful and offers more versatility for expert system development.

Another important property of an inference engine is its ability to deal with uncertainty. There are many kinds of uncertainties that may need to be factored into decision making. In some expert systems, a probability or reliability factor is offered with the various conclusions offered by the system.

Expert System Applications

Expert systems are still at a relatively early development stage. The present systems are applied primarily in three categories: diagnosis/categorization, design, and planning.[7]

Diagnosis/categorization is the dominant paradigm of expert systems. These types of systems answer questions. Such a system diagnoses or classifies the situation under investigation (an illness, a chemical compound, a drilling prospect, the financial profile of a customer) as one of several possi-

---

[7] M. Rychener, "Expert Systems for Engineering Design," *Expert Systems,* 2, no. 1, 85, 30–44.

ble categories that, in turn can trigger the recommendation of an action. Examples include medical, electronic, mechanical, and software diagnosis.

Design involves several of the same kinds of constraints as categorization. Given cost and specification constraints, the objective is to configure a system or object to meet overall design goals.

Planning is a design process whose result is a procedure or sequence of actions. The plan sometimes has to include provision for unexpected occurrences. Examples include project management, routing, communications, product development, military applications, and financial planning.

Other areas of expert system application include interpretation, prediction, monitoring, debugging, repair instruction, and control. Table 18.4 lists some of the most popular expert systems that have been developed. MYCIN, for example, is considered the granddaddy of expert systems. It now contains over 400 production rules and has evolved over two decades. Though successful, MYCIN is still not as effective as a competent medical staff in diagnosing infectious blood diseases.

Many of the expert systems being developed are not very sophisticated. They consist mainly of very-high-level programming techniques with only a few characteristics of true AI systems. The fact that they utilize a knowledge base or rule system is the primary characteristic which allows them to be classified as artificially intelligent.

The recent proliferation of these knowledge-based systems has occurred not only because of increasing recognition of the field, but also because of the increasing availability of expert system development tools.

TABLE 18.4 *Representative expert systems*

Expert system	Development organization	Problem area
MYCIN	Stanford University	Diagnoses and prescribes treatment for bacterial blood infections
PROSPECTOR	Stanford Research Institute	Determines major types of ore deposits present in a geological site
ACE	AT&T Bell Labs	Provides trouble shooting reports and analysis for telephone cable maintenance
XCON	Digital Equipment Corporation	Configures VAX family of computer systems
ISIS-II	Westinghouse Corporation	Does job scheduling, factory automation
YES/MVS	IBM	Helps computer operator monitor the MVS operating system
DELTA	General Electric Co.	Helps diagnose and repair diesel electric locomotives

These tools are expert system shells (or skeletal systems) and usually consist of two modules: a rule set manager and an inference engine. Given a shell, virtually anyone can produce a knowledge-based system by loading production rules relevant to a specific problem domain. However, consistency of knowledge and reasonableness of system conclusions are not guaranteed. Examples of expert system shells include Expert Ease, M.1, OPS 5+, Personal Consultant, and Insight 2. However, such developed systems usually are more closely related to decision trees than to true AI concepts.

Expert Systems and OR/MS

Expert systems are able to address qualitative and fuzzy-type decision problems that have previously been unapproachable through OR/MS methodologies as well as decision support systems. Though both ES and OR/MS approaches are intended to help the decision maker, one attempts to move problem domain knowledge from the human being to the computer while the other incorporates normative models and other sharp quantitative tools that provide the decision maker with solutions which are often superior to those he or she could determine.

At the present, ES methodologies are effective only for relatively simple applications in approximately a dozen generic categories. Most systems developed are capable of offering significant help to someone who is a novice to the problem domain. However, end users who have some expertise often find that the expert system lacks the depth of knowledge to provide significant help. A future goal of expert systems is to solve problems whose complexity exceeds human ability. The current state of the art is that there are a few expert systems that are able to solve problems where the required scope of knowledge exceeds that of any one individual.

The development of expert systems thus far has occurred almost entirely within the AI community of computer scientists and AI researchers. Many of these developers have been unfamiliar with classical OR/MS tools. Future developments in both ES and OR/MS can benefit from the integration of these two fields. In some problem domains such as pure categorization there is probably little need for integration of ES and OR/MS tools. However, there are some problem domains such as scheduling where the two fields have begun to overlap. For example, ISIS-II has been developed at Carnegie-Mellon University and used at Westinghouse to construct factory job shop schedules. Another example is the ES called Calisto, also in development at Carnegie-Mellon. Calisto is designed to help schedule complex engineering projects.

The more advanced expert systems can benefit from the incorporation of quantitative tools from OR/MS. Knowledge need not be limited to what can be extracted from a human being. OR/MS has long been involved with heuristics and other techniques such as branch and bound that can help to search for solutions to subproblems. The treatment of uncertainty in facts and production rules is another area where OR/MS and statistics can make contributions.

Combining OR/MS methods and artificial intelligence techniques can lead to the implementation of an intelligent DSS. An intelligent DSS could contain problem-solving modules from both OR/MS and expert systems. Such systems will be able to draw upon the capabilities offered by both approaches to problem solving. If intelligent DSS also incorporate AI capabilities for natural language processing and voice (pattern) recognition, they could offer new levels of "suggestion," "learning," and "understanding" in dealing with managerial decision problems.

In the face of emerging technologies, the OR/MS analyst must continue to adopt a problem-oriented point of view. That is, he or she must let the problem determine the method that best applies to it, instead of letting familiar techniques determine what problems he or she is willing and able to tackle. The OR/MS profession has been quick to adopt promising new approaches in the past. The assimilation of and collaboration with AI and expert systems should enlarge the repertoire of the OR/MS bag of decision tools. This is especially important in real-world management problems most marked in knowledge-rich domains whose qualititative as well as quantitative information has to be taken into account.

SUMMARY

Heuristics are valuable tools in both OR/MS and AI. They can be used to provide solutions when optimization techniques are either not practical or not cost effective. Heuristic programming is concerned with developing solution procedures which use a combination of heuristic algorithms. In AI, heuristics are often used to guide search procedures to find acceptable solutions.

AI is a rapidly evolving field that has potential for collaboration with OR/MS. Of particular interest to OR/MS are the subfields of natural language processing and expert systems. Natural language processing is important as it impacts the user interface in computer-based systems. Expert systems offer new ways to tackle qualitative and less well-structured problems.

Expert systems differ from traditional computer-based systems mainly in their ability to do simple reasoning and to offer explanations. Expert systems use knowledge bases extracted from human experts and inferential reasoning techniques to solve problems. Most expert systems to date solve only simple problems and are limited to a very narrow problem domain. However, some early applications have shown the potential for future applications.

The integration of OR/MS heuristics and normative models in expert systems will help to improve expert systems in areas where some quantitative analysis is required. The incorporation of AI technology and expert systems in decision support systems offers the potential for a "super DSS." These integrated systems could provide previously unattainable levels of decision-making support.

REVIEW QUESTIONS

1. Define a heuristic in your own words.
2. State the advantages and disadvantages of using a heuristic compared to an optimization technique.
3. What are the two main reasons heuristics are used in OR/MS?
4. What are the five main areas of AI?
5. Define artificial intelligence in your own words.
6. What is the primary benefit of natural language processing to OR/MS?
7. For what kinds of decision problems are expert systems likely to be more appropriate than traditional OR/MS techniques.
8. Discuss the state of the art in expert system capabilities.
9. Discuss the potential contributions of OR/MS to expert systems and vice versa.

BIBLIOGRAPHY

Harmon, Paul, Rex Maus, and William Morrissey, *Expert Systems: Tools & Applications*. New York: John Wiley & Sons, Inc., 1988.

Hayes-Roth, F., et al., *Building Expert Systems*. Reading, Mass.: Addison-Wesley Publishing Company, 1983.

Holsapple, Clyde W., and Andrew B. Whinston. *Business Expert Systems*. Homewood, Ill.: Richard D. Irwin, Inc., 1987.

McDermott, C., and E. Charniak, *Introduction to Artificial Intelligence*. Reading, Mass.: Addison-Wesley Publishing Company, 1985.

Pearl, Judea, *Heuristics: Intelligent Search Strategies for Computer Problems Solving*. Reading, Mass.: Addison-Wesley Publishing Company, 1984.

Rauch-Hindin, Wendy B., *A Guide to Artificial Intelligence: Fundamentals and Real-World Applications*. Englewood Cliffs, N.J.: Prentice Hall, 1988.

Simon, Herbert A., and A. Newell, ''Heuristic Problem Solving: The Next Advance in Operations Research,'' *Operations Research,* 6 (January–February, 1958), 1–10.

Tonge, F. M., ''The Use of Heuristic Programming in Management Science,'' *Management Science,* 7 (1961), 213–237.

Turban, Efraim, *Decision Support and Expert Systems: Managerial Perspectives.* New York: Macmillan Publishing Company, 1988.

Waterman, Donald A., *A Guide to Expert Systems.* Reading, Mass.: Addison-Wesley Publishing Company, 1986.

Appendix A
Cases

CASE 1
ALLYN FOOD COMPANY*

The Allyn Food Company is a midwestern processed frozen beef supply house. The market for their products includes the states of Missouri, Nebraska, Kansas, Iowa, and Colorado. To compete in these states which are known for quality beef products, the company has developed a product mix of five different beef products. These products differ on their percentage content of high-quality beef cuts (e.g., low fat content meat), low-quality beef cuts (e.g., high fat content meat), and filler (i.e., soy bean meal). The five products and their percentages of beef content are listed in Table 1 along with the wholesale prices the Allyn Food Company charges its customers.

During the first two years of operations, the management planned their production in pounds of beef on a monthly basis. As their company's sales and product line grew, they realized that some type of planning aid was needed to ensure a continued increase in sales. A consultant was hired to develop the monthly planning system that management desired.

The consultant began by researching the markets of the Allyn Food Company to determine the best approach to plan the utilization of the pro-

---

* Mark Schniederjans, *Case Studies in Decision Support Systems.* Copyright 1987 by Petrocelli Books. Reprinted with permission.

TABLE 1 *Percentage of beef content and prices*

Product name	Percentage of beef content per pound			Current wholesale price per pound
	High-quality cuts	Low-quality cuts	Filler	
Super prime	100	0	0	$1.50
Super deluxe	70	30	0	1.20
Super	50	50	0	1.00
Deluxe	10	70	20	.80
Regular	0	70	30	.65

duction resources and their use in meeting customer demand requirements. The company sells frozen one-pound packages of beef to government agencies and retail frozen beef stores. The government agencies contract their requirements a year ahead of time, whereas the retail stores place their orders on a weekly and sometimes daily basis. Fortunately, the former represented about 75 percent of the total business and so minimum product demand was predetermined for a full year. This fixed government demand minimized planning problems for Allyn's management and kept monthly production in pounds of meat at a fairly constant rate. As the retail store demand increased, Allyn management tried to adjust their production to match the fluctuation inherent in retail sales. As Allyn grew, so did the size of their customers and their orders. The consultant noted that Allyn had no problem in acquiring new retail customers. Based on current government agencies contracts, the minimum monthly demand for the company's five products is presented in Table 2. The consultant combined realistic short-run physical plant limitations with optimistic forecasts of Allyn's management to generate the maximum demand estimates also presented in Table 2. The Allyn Food Company viewed the government product demand as essential to their success in the beef business. The retail sales were viewed as supplemental and, while important, were to be achieved only if excess supplies were available.

TABLE 2 *Monthly demand in pounds*

Product name	Demand in pounds by product	
	Minimum	Maximum
Super prime	50,000	320,000
Super deluxe	55,000	330,000
Super	75,000	345,000
Deluxe	80,000	355,000
Regular	100,000	370,000

The production resources used to service the demand appeared to be more limiting to profit maximization than any possible market response. The materials used in the manufacture of their food products were contracted on a yearly basis with Allyn Food Company suppliers. In accordance with the current contract which had eight more months to run, Allyn would receive a monthly shipment of 450,000 pounds of high-quality meat cuts, 440,000 pounds of low-quality meat cuts, and 380,000 pounds of filler. Unused portions of these shipments were sold at cost each month to employees and local markets. In addition to the raw materials, labor and machine processing time are used in the manufacture of the company's products. Both skilled and unskilled labor are used in production processes. The consultant found that time study analysis and stopwatch techniques are currently used in the Allyn plant to control and monitor labor costs. The labor usage by product and by type of laborer is presented in Table 3. Under existing union contracts, the minimum number of hours for skilled workers required per month is 40,000 and the maximum number is 70,000. Unskilled workers have no maximum, but a minimum of 60,000 hours. To process the beef products, machines are used that mix the beef content proportions and grind the beef to differing degrees of texture. Indeed, one of the Allyn Food Company's major marketing features is their quality of texture due to the processing machines they use. Two types of machines are used—fine texture machines and coarse texture machines. The number of processing machine runs necessary for the beef products to meet customer texture requirements is also presented in Table 3. A total of 12 coarse texture machines and 15 fine texture machines represent the total available processing machines at the company. The consultant who estimated breakdowns and normal maintenance requirements forecasted the maximum number of lot runs per month for all coarse texture machines at 8,000 and all fine texture machines at 24,000 runs.

The consultant found that no other resources, such as finances or plant space, posed any significant constraint to Allyn's short-run monthly produc-

TABLE 3 *Labor and machine utilization*

Product name	Per pound hourly labor usage		Number of machine processing runs*	
	Skilled	Unskilled	Coarse	Fine
Super prime	0.085	0.164	1	5
Super deluxe	0.082	0.140	1	4
Super	0.078	0.130	2	3
Deluxe	0.070	0.110	2	2
Regular	0.068	0.105	2	3

* The processing machines process the meat in 100-pound lots.

tion planning problem. After a careful review of numerous planning aids that might be useful to management, the consultant decided to use a monthly linear programming model to help determine the sales-maximizing production levels for the company's five food products. Each month, the next month's per-pound production for the five products would be determined by modeling the estimated demand, material, labor, and machine constraints to determine optimal production levels to achieve maximum sales contributions. To illustrate the use of linear programming as a planning aid, the consultant decided to structure the model for the next month's production based on the data collected.

Case Questions

1. What assumptions is the consultant making concerning the applicability of linear programming as a decision aid for planning in this case situation?
2. What is the linear programming model formulation for next month's production? Clearly define the decision variables and label the constraints used in the model that represent production resources.
3. What is the sales-maximizing production level for each product?
4. What resources inhibited sales maximization the most?
5. To implement this type of planning system, what type of monthly information is necessary?

CASE 2
RED BRAND CANNERS*

On Monday, September 13, 1965, Mr. Mitchell Gordon, Vice-President of Operations, asked the Controller, the Sales Manager, and the Production Manager to meet with him to discuss the amount of tomato products to pack that season. The tomato crop, which had been purchased at planting, was beginning to arrive at the cannery, and packing operations would have to be started by the following Monday. Red Brand Canners was a medium-size company that canned and distributed a variety of fruit and vegetable products under private brands in the western states.

Mr. William Cooper, the Controller, and Mr. Charles Myers, the Sales Manager, were the first to arrive in Mr. Gordon's office. Dan Tucker, the Production Manager, came in a few minutes later and said that he had picked

* Reprinted from *Stanford Business Cases 1965* with the permission of the publishers, Stanford University Graduate School of Business. Copyright © 1965 by the Board of Trustees of the Leland Stanford Junior University.

TABLE 1 *Demand forecasts*

Product	Selling price per case ($)	Demand forecast (cases)
24–2½ whole tomatoes	4.00	800,000
24–2½ choice peach halves	5.40	10,000
24–2½ peach nectar	4.60	5,000
24–2½ tomato juice	4.50	50,000
24–2½ cooking apples	4.90	15,000
24–2½ tomato paste	3.80	80,000

up Produce Inspection's latest estimate of the quality of the incoming to-matoes. According to their report, about 20 percent of the crop was Grade "A" quality and the remaining portion of the 3,000,000-pound crop was Grade "B."

Gordon asked Myers about the demand for tomato products for the coming year. Myers replied that they could sell all of the whole canned tomatoes they could produce. The expected demand for tomato juice and tomato paste, on the other hand, was limited. The Sales Manager then passed around the latest demand forecast, which is shown in Table 1. He reminded the group that the selling prices had been set in light of the long-term marketing strategy of the company, and potential sales had been fore-casted at these prices.

Bill Cooper, after looking at Myers's estimates of demand, said that it looked like the company "should do quite well (on the tomato crop) this year." With the new accounting system that had been set up, he had been able to compute the contribution for each product, and according to his analysis the incremental profit on the whole tomatoes was greater than for any other tomato product. In May, after Red Brand had signed contracts agreeing to purchase the grower's production at an average delivered price of 6 cents per pound, Cooper had computed the tomato products' contribu-tions (see Table 2).

Dan Tucker brought to Cooper's attention that, although there was ample production capacity, it was impossible to produce all whole tomatoes as too small a portion of the tomato crop was "A" quality. Red Brand used a numerical scale to record the quality of both raw produce and prepared products. This scale ran from zero to ten, the higher number representing better quality. Rating tomatoes according to this scale, "A" tomatoes aver-aged nine points per pound and "B" tomatoes averaged five points per pound. Tucker noted that the minimum average input quality for canned whole tomatoes was eight, and for juice it was six points per pound. Paste could be made entirely from "B" grade tomatoes. This meant that whole tomato production was limited to 800,000 pounds.

TABLE 2 *Product item profitability*

Costs ($)	24–2½ Whole tomatoes	24–2½ Choice peach halves	24–2½ Peach nectar	24–2½ Tomato juice	24–2½ Cooking apples	24–2½ Tomato paste
Selling price	4.00	5.40	4.60	4.50	4.90	3.80
Variable costs						
Direct labor	1.18	1.40	1.27	1.32	.70	.54
Variable overhead	.24	.32	.23	.36	.22	.26
Variable selling	.40	.30	.40	.85	.28	.38
Packaging material	.70	.56	.60	.65	.70	.77
Fruit*	1.08	1.80	1.70	1.20	.90	1.50
Total variable costs	3.60	4.38	4.20	4.38	2.80	3.45
Contribution	.40	1.02	.40	.12	1.10	.35
Less allocated overhead	.28	.70	.52	.21	.75	.23
Net profit	.12	.32	(.12)	(.09)	.35	.12

* Product usage is as given below

Product	Pounds per case
Whole tomatoes	18
Peach halves	18
Peach nectar	17
Tomato juice	20
Cooking apples	27
Tomato paste	25

Gordon stated that this was not a real limitation. He had been recently solicited to purchase 80,000 pounds of Grade "A" tomatoes at 8½ cents per pound and at that time had turned down the offer. He felt, however, that the tomatoes were still available.

Myers, who had been doing some calculations, said that although he agreed that the Company "should do quite well this year," it would not be by canning whole tomatoes. It seemed to him that the tomato cost should be allocated on the basis of quality and quantity rather than by quantity only, as Cooper had done. Therefore, he had recomputed the marginal profit on this basis (see Table 3), and from his results, Red Brand should use 2 million pounds of the "B" tomatoes for paste, and the remaining 400,000 pounds of "B" tomatoes and all of the "A" tomatoes for juice. If the demand expectations were realized, a contribution of $48,000 would be made on this year's tomato crop.

TABLE 3 *Marginal analysis of tomato products*

	Product		
Costs ($)	*Canned whole tomatoes*	*Tomato juice*	*Tomato paste*
Selling price	$4.00	$4.50	$3.80
Variable cost (excluding tomato costs)	2.52	3.18	1.95
	1.48	1.32	1.85
Tomato cost	1.49	1.24	1.30
Marginal profit	($ .01)	$ .08	$ .55

Z = cost per pound of "A" tomatoes in cents
Y = cost per pound of "B" tomatoes in cents
(1) (600,000 lbs. $\times$ Z) + (2,400,000 lbs. $\times$ Y) = (3,000,000 lbs. $\times$ 6)

(2) $\dfrac{Z}{9} = \dfrac{Y}{5}$

Z = 9.32 cents per pound
Y = 5.18 cents per pound

Case Questions

1. Before any systematic analysis can be performed on the Red Brand Cannery problem, the issue of relevant data must be resolved. With which cost-and-profit data do you agree—Table 2 or Table 3? Does the fact that Red Brand has already purchased the 3-million-pound crop at planting affect your answer?

2. Do you think that the allocated overhead should be subtracted from the profit contribution per case as shown in Table 2?

3. Propose a systematic procedure for developing a good solution for the production of tomato products. Model the problem to obtain an optimal product mix. Solve the problem using an LP computer package. Be sure to include a sensitivity analysis of whether Red Brand should purchase the additional 80,000 pounds of grade A tomatoes.

4. Reformulate the model to explicitly consider the additional purchase of the 80,000 pounds of grade A tomatoes. How many pounds should be purchased? Does the answer agree with your answer in part 3?

5. If the marketing manager wanted to increase the demand for juice by 20,000 cases, how much should Red Brand be willing to pay for an advertising campaign?

6. Suppose that the price of juice increased 8 cents per case. Does your computer output tell you whether the optimal production plan will change?

CASE 3
SOUTHERN PETROCHEMICAL COMPANY*

Introduction

Southern Petrochemical Company produces many products. Along with plastic films and resins, an antifreeze—Summit—is produced. This antifreeze is composed essentially of one compound, ethylene glycol, which is a by-product of the natural gas industry. The antifreeze industry is maturing as the production of automobiles has leveled off and the average engine size appears to be decreasing. Due to this, and other factors, the director of

TABLE 1 *SPC plants*

#	City	Cost	Min (000)	Max (000)
P01	Oakton	2.4900	1,000	1,200
P02	Lowlands	2.7125	500	10,000
P03	River Lake	2.3925	1,000	5,000
P04	Rogers Ferry	2.5534	500	1,000
P05	Baytown	2.5231	200	1,000

TABLE 2 *SPC warehouses*

#	City	In/out cost	Maximum capacity (000)
W01	Los Alamos	.015	200
W02	Birmingham	.017	200
W03	Fox Heights	.013	1,000
W04	Akron	.012	500
W05	Columbus	.016	200
W06	Irving	.013	1,000
W07	Grand Junction	.013	200
W08	Lansing	.017	500
W09	Twoen	.010	900
W10	Jersey City	.018	—
W11	Nashville	.009	500
W12	Linden	.014	—
W13	Liverpool	.013	230
W14	Los Diablos	.008	—
W15	Omaha	.008	500
W16	Cape Giraudeau	.013	—

* Condensed from *Southern Petrochemical Company Transshipment Problem: An IFPS/Optimum Case Study Analysis* by Jodean Meisinger Gesell and Roger Hayen.

Product Transportation and Shipping at Southern Petrochemical is trying to cut costs wherever possible.

Statement of the Problem

The Vice-President of the Petrochemicals Division has issued a mandate to cut costs. As part of this new austerity program, the director of the Product Transportation and Shipping Department is looking for ways to control expenses. Three issues have come to his attention as potential cost-cutting measures: minimizing the cost of the product that is shipped to the distribu-

TABLE 3 *SPC distribution points*

#	City	Demand (000)
D01	Mobile	189.2
D02	Tempe	172.1
D03	Los Angeles	707.3
D04	Hartford	96.4
D05	Wilmington	11.0
D06	Alexandria	16.4
D07	Leesburg	229.4
D08	Pocatella	29.5
D09	Terre Haute	100.1
D10	Des Moines	70.0
D11	Hays	30.0
D12	Lexington	65.7
D13	New Orleans	202.5
D14	Gardiner	18.4
D15	Bethesda	318.8
D16	Tupelo	40.2
D17	St. Louis	245.0
D18	Omaha	71.2
D19	Las Vegas	12.5
D20	Dover	31.1
D21	Newark	184.2
D22	Albuquerque	32.4
D23	Toledo	197.2
D24	Norman	274.0
D25	Erie	438.9
D26	Lawrence	97.0
D27	Dallas	450.3
D28	Odessa	172.0
D29	Salt Lake City	134.0
D30	Wilmington	26.2
D31	Norfolk	283.3
D32	Spokane	114.6
D33	Kingwood	21.3

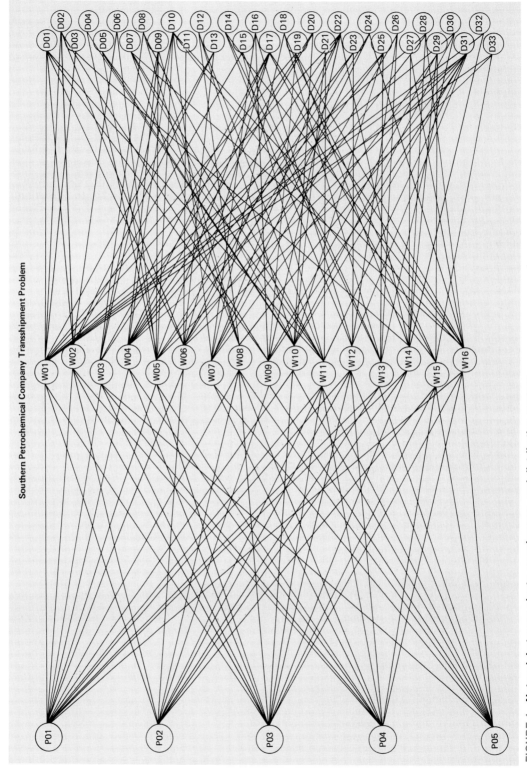

Southern Petrochemical Company Transshipment Problem

FIGURE 1   Network between plants, warehouses, and distribution centers

tion centers, closing warehouses that are underutilized, and the possible renegotiation of contracts with the plants involved.

The current method used for shipping Summit antifreeze from the plants where it is manufactured to the warehouses where it is stored and on to the distributors is simply by "best guess." This method is very time-consuming to perform manually, it does not guarantee optimal costs, and at times the distribution centers do not have adequate supplies to meet the demand due to miscalculations. The cost to transport the antifreeze has currently been averaging about $16 million using this manual, "best-guess" method. A transshipment problem could be set up and solved, which would generate an optimal solution that would minimize the cost and also satisfy the demand. In addition, a tremendous amount of time would be saved.

Southern Petrochemical company has five plants where antifreeze can be produced. Associated with each plant is a cost of producing the anti-freeze, a minimum amount of antifreeze that can be realistically produced, and a maximum amount of antifreeze that can be accommodated at the facility. This data is shown in Table 1.

TABLE 4   *SPC shipment costs (from plant to warehouses)*

#	City	Cost (in dollars)
	Warehouse	
W01	Los Alamos	From P01 = .343, P02 = .300, P03 = .381
W02	Birmingham	From P01 = .223, P02 = .239, P03 = .230, P04 = .194
W03	Fox Heights	From P01 = .275, P03 = .249, P04 = .198, P05 = .152
W04	Akron	From P01 = .187, P03 = .183, P04 = .115
W05	Columbus	From P01 = .153, P03 = .123, P04 = .140
W06	Irving	From P01 = .266, P02 = .137
W07	Grand Junction	From P04 = .232, P05 = .187
W08	Lansing	From P01 = .210, P02 = .169, P03 = .301, P04 = .198, P05 = .221
W09	Twoen	From P02 = .219, P04 = .177, P05 = .276
W10	Jersey City	From P01 = .243, P03 = .244, P05 = .360
W11	Nashville	From P01 = .154, P02 = .187, P03 = .201, P04 = .198, P05 = .232
W12	Linden	From P01 = .236, P02 = .149, P03 = .209, P04 = .218, P05 = .165
W13	Liverpool	From P01 = .213, P02 = .175, P05 = .227
W14	Los Diablos	From P01 = .311, P02 = .283, P03 = .332
W15	Omaha	From P02 = .569, P03 = .241, P04 = .209, P05 = .058
W16	Cape Giraudeau	From P01 = .349, P03 = .292, P04 = .308, P05 = .196

TABLE 5 *SPC shipment costs (from warehouses to distributors)*

#	Warehouse City	Cost (in dollars)
W01	Los Alamos	To D01 = .532, D02 = .219, D03 = .467, D13 = .477, D19 = .421, D22 = .131, D28 = .286, D32 = .522, D33 = .421
W02	Birmingham	To D01 = .113, D06 = .347, D13 = .421, D15 = .599, D30 = .672, D31 = .444
W03	Fox Heights	To D08 = .223, D09 = .294, D10 = .489, D17 = .251, D20 = .421
W04	Akron	To D09 = .187, D10 = .383, D17 = .215, D20 = .442, D21 = .434, D23 = .113, D25 = .198, D31 = .301
W05	Columbus	To D04 = .422, D05 = .476, D06 = .231, D09 = .153, D10 = .323, D17 = .240, D23 = .125, D25 = .228, D31 = .299
W06	Irving	To D01 = .466, D02 = .378, D11 = .247, D13 = .175, D17 = .289, D22 = .192, D24 = .142, D27 = .102, D28 = .156, D33 = .168
W07	Grand Junction	To D10 = .332, D16 = .131, D18 = .287, D22 = .254, D24 = .436, D26 = .324, D29 = .348
W08	Lansing	To D07 = .210, D08 = .189, D09 = .301, D12 = .298, D31 = .232
W09	Twoen	To D02 = .233, D03 = .137, D16 = .467, D19 = .336, D22 = .451, D29 = .339, D32 = .397
W10	Jersey City	To D04 = .267, D05 = .298, D06 = .167, D07 = .215, D12 = .367, D20 = .245, D21 = .102, D25 = .451, D30 = .321, D31 = .299
W11	Nashville	To D01 = .454, D04 = .431, D05 = .520, D06 = .387, D07 = .151, D08 = .198, D12 = .132, D15 = .328, D21 = .321, D31 = .270
W12	Linden	To D14 = .346, D16 = .169, D23 = .309, D26 = .208, D31 = .465
W13	Liverpool	To D14 = .309, D15 = .221, D18 = .233, D25 = .275, D26 = .137, D30 = .435
W14	Los Diablos	From D03 = .143, D19 = .219, D22 = .500, D27 = .221, D28 = .208, D29 = .448, D32 = .621
W15	Omaha	From D10 = .131, D11 = .111, D17 = .254, D18 = .010, D29 = .488, D33 = .521
W16	Cape Giraudeau	From D07 = .369, D10 = .214, D11 = .309, D14 = .485, D17 = .101, D18 = .332, D24 = .343, D27 = .497, D28 = .467

There are 16 warehouses in the Southern system. Each of these warehouses has an associated "in/out" cost for handling the antifreeze, and some have maximum limits that are set on their capacity. There is no need for inventories, or any accumulation of items at the warehouses. The warehouse information is shown in Table 2.

There are 33 distribution points for the antifreeze. Each one of these points has a required demand for the product. Table 3 highlights the demand for each distribution point.

There are shipment paths from various plants to warehouses and from warehouses to various distribution points. A cost is associated with the transportation of Summit across each of these paths. Because of logistics, a path does not exist from every plant to every warehouse, nor from every warehouse to every distribution point. The network between the plants, warehouses, and distribution centers is presented in Figure 1. The costs associated with transportation from plants to warehouses is shown in Table 4. Table 5 lists the costs incurred when transporting from warehouses to distribution centers.

Case Questions

1. Determine the optimal solution and cost for Southern Petrochemical's distribution problem.
2. Which warehouse would you recommend for capacity expansion?
3. Would you recommend closing any warehouse?
4. The director of Product Transportation and Shipping is considering renegotiating the contract with Plant P02 in Lowlands, which currently produces the most costly antifreeze. The Lowlands personnel are receptive to a lower price agreement, but they feel that in order to accommodate this request they must be guaranteed a market for a larger proportion of their antifreeze. They are willing to decrease the price from $2.7125 to $2.4840, if the minimum number of units shipped is increased from 500,000 to 1,500,000. What do you recommend?

CASE 4
JULIAN RESEARCH ASSOCIATES*

Julian Research Associates is a private, independent product research organization. Julian Associates tests new products against existing competitive products. Their research efforts are supported by the manufacturers of the new products they test. Julian provides new product manufacturers a means

---

* Mark Schniederjans, *Case Studies in Decision Support Systems.* Copyright 1987 by Petrocelli Books. Reprinted with permission.

by which their products can be independently tested without risk of public awareness. When research is concluded, the findings are reported only to the manufacturing company that employed their service. If the results of the research on a new product turns out not to favor that product, the manufacturer can shelve the research report or use the findings to improve the new product's marketability. On the other hand, if the report favors the product, the manufacturer can claim their new product was tested by an independent research organization and was proven superior to its competition.

Julian Associates has shown continued success since its inception 10 years ago. During the last four years, a national union became the agent for all labor (i.e., researchers) in the product-testing areas of their business. Through negotiation with the union over the years, Julian management found themselves with a significant number of work assignment rules limiting the types of work that can be performed. While the rules had been placed in operation for the protection of both labor and management, they posed considerable complications for managers who had to implement them. As a result, numerous complaints from both research laborers and managers had been filed in protest of alleged work rule violations. Labor relations continued to be strained for a year-and-a-half, and it appeared that Julian was destined for a strike. As a last resort, a consultant was called in by the management of Julian to see if a solution to their problem could be found.

The consultant began by researching the type of jobs the 10 researchers that make up the staff were expected to perform. The titles and job duties of researchers are listed in Table 1. The consultant found that the 10 research-

TABLE 1 *Researcher titles and job duties*

Researcher number	Title	Job duties
1	Supervisor	Supervise Department 1 research staff, monitor workflow, fill out reports, and evaluate research staff for promotions.
2, 3	Assistant Supervisor	Assist Department 1 supervisor and perform basic research activities.
4, 5	Researcher	Perform basic research activities in Department 1.
6	Supervisor	Supervise Department 2 research staff, monitor workflow, fill out reports, and evaluate research staff for promotions.
7, 8	Assistant Supervisor	Assist Department 2 supervisor and perform basic research activities
9, 10	Researcher	Perform basic research activities in Department 2.

TABLE 2 *Researcher hourly wages; maximum and minimum contracted weekly hours*

Researcher number	Hourly wage	Controlled weekly hours	
		Maximum	Minimum
1	$8.95	40	25
2	8.95	40	20
3	8.75	40	10
4	8.65	40	*
5	8.50	40	*
6	8.25	40	30
7	8.25	40	25
8	8.00	40	25
9	7.50	40	*
10	7.25	40	*

* Other minimum restrictions apply.

ers were divided into two departments. Department 1 performs physical product testing, such as finding out how many times a door handle on a refrigerator will work before it breaks. Department 2 performs consumer product testing, such as food store survey work to determine consumer reaction to a new food product. The consultant was surprised to see that most of the researchers had supervisory duties. Further research revealed those duties were just one of the many work rules defined in the labor contract at Julian Associates. The supervisory duties consisted more of providing job education and leadperson (i.e., junior foreman) type task direction than actual management responsibilities.

The management of Julian Associates asked the consultant to develop a staffing schedule of hours that would define the cost-minimizing number of hours each researcher would work each week. Hourly wages for each researcher are presented in Table 2. As can be seen, for example, Researcher 1 has an hourly wage of $8.95, can work a maximum of 40 hours per week, but must be allowed to work a minimum of 25 hours per week. Of particular importance to management was the desire that this schedule be structured to comply with all of the union-negotiated work rules. This schedule would not have to define when the researchers would have to work during a particular day, just the total number of hours each week. In response to the request for the staffing schedule, the consultant decided to structure the work rules into a decision model that could be used on a weekly basis. In developing the model from the rules, the following points of information were considered relevant for inclusion:

1. Each researcher is not permitted to work more than 40 hours per week because of possible hazardous conditions occasionally required in their

work environment. Management did not want to pay overtime, so this rule was well received by both labor and management.

2. Researchers who performed some supervisory duties were required to work a minimum of hours each week, depending on their seniority with the company. The specific minimum number of hours, per researcher, is presented in Table 2. This rule insured that one or more researchers would be supervising each department's weekly activities.

3. Management can define which days of the week a researcher may work and how long each day a researcher may work. While hours of work can be defined in fractions, whole-hour assignments are preferable. This permits a supervisory researcher to be scheduled throughout the week to ensure adequate supervisory coverage, as well as scheduling other researchers for the convenience of customer demand.

4. Every week, the total available hours for researcher labor can be changed. Over the planning horizon of the next few weeks, the total maximum available hours permitted per week will be 375. This allows management to adjust labor resources to meet customer demands of their services.

5. The number of hours per week for both department supervisors must be the same.

6. The number of hours per week for both second supervisors (researchers 2 and 7) must be the same.

7. The minimum total number of hours for all Department 1 researchers must be 100 or more.

8. The minimum total number of hours for all Department 2 researchers must be 175 or more.

9. The minimum total number of hours for the two lowest-paid researchers in Department 1 must be 50 hours or more.

10. The minimum total number of hours for the two lowest-paid researchers in Department 2 must be 50 hours or more.

Case Questions

1. Which quantitative method can be used to model this scheduling situation? Why would the Transportation Method not be appropriate for allocating the researcher hours?

2. What is the formulation of the model that could be used to generate the assignment schedule desired by Julian Associates management?

3. What is the cost-minimizing assignment schedule?

CASE 5
SMU PARALLEL PROCESSING CASE

In 1987, The Operations Research Department at Southern Methodist University began a project that attempted to solve a variety of mathematical programming problems using a special type of computer called a parallel processor. These computers have several central processing units, with both shared and private memory. The CPUs can perform their operations simultaneously, with the result that a complex computer algorithm can be greatly speeded up by dividing the work among the several processors.

One of the problems chosen for research was the binary integer programming problem. These problems are characterized by restricting the variables in the linear program to values of either 0 or 1. Integer problems of this sort cannot be solved by traditional linear programming methods because the optimal solution is not necessarily an extreme point. These problems are solved by iterative methods such as branch and bound (Chapter 9), which base effectiveness on the fact that if any of the integer requirements are relaxed, the solution to the resulting linear program produces an optimal value of the objective function which is a lower bound on the optimal integer solution.

The analyst at SMU studying this problem realized that his first step was to analyze the serial algorithm that was being used on a single CPU computer and see what effect additional CPUs produced. The algorithm is outlined in Table 1. The analyst wanted to know two things:

1. Given a test problem of N variables, what is the average time to solution using one processor.
2. What is the critical path and average solution time using two processors.

A test problem with six variables was run and the algorithm solved the problem with the steps outlined in Table 3. Answer the foregoing two questions for the test run. Calculate the speed-up (runtime for one processor − runtime for two processors).

A *critical step* is one which must be executed by only one processor at a time. If, say, processor 2 arrives at a critical step and processor 1 is executing the step, then processor 2 must wait until processor 1 has finished.

It is also important to note that if a processor arrives to select a problem from an empty candidate list, the processor must wait until other processors have completed their work before testing for termination.

Source: Case prepared by William K. Stripling.

TABLE 1

Step 0: Initialize the algorithm and relax the original problem by allowing all variables to range between 0 and 1. Add the relaxed problem to the candidate list.
Step 1: Select a candidate subproblem from the candidate list.
Step 2: Solve the linear programming relaxation of the candidate subproblem.
Step 3: Test the solution to the subproblem:
    1. If the solution is integer:
        a. If solution is less than the incumbent (best integer solution so far), then replace the old incumbent with the new solution.
        b. If solution is greater than or equal to the incumbent, discard the subproblem.
        c. Go to step 5.
    2. If the solution is greater than or equal to the present incumbent, the relaxation exceeds the lower bound and the subproblem is discarded.
        a. Go to step 5.
    3. If the solution is less than the present incumbent, the subproblem still might contain a better integer solution.
        a. Go to step 4.
Step 4: Branch on the subproblem:
    1. Create two new subproblems by selecting a free variable and setting it equal to 0 for one subproblem and to 1 for the other subproblem.
    2. Add the two new problems to the candidate list.
    3. Go to step 5.
Step 5: Test the candidate list:
    1. If candidate list is empty, present incumbent is optimal.
        a. Terminate algorithm.
    2. If candidate list is not empty, go to step 1.

TABLE 2

Activity	Critical step	Mean time	Best time	Worst time
Step 0:				
Initialize	Yes	$5N$	$5N$	$5N$
Step 1:				
Select a candidate subproblem	Yes	$4N$	$3N$	$6N$
Step 2:				
Solve original LP relaxation	Yes	$48N$	$39N$	$63N$
Solve subsequent subproblems	No	$17N$	$11N$	$28N$
Step 3:				
Test the solution	No	17	16	18
Step 4:				
Create new subproblems	No	18	16	19
Update candidate list	Yes	$6N$	$4N$	$10N$
Step 5:				
Test for optimality	No	13	10	16

TABLE 3

Activity	Step
Initialize problem: Allow all variables to range between 0 and 1, and set the value of the incumbent integer solution to infinity. Put the relaxed problem (SP1) in the candidate list.	0
Select SP1 from the candidate list.	1
Solve the relaxed LP.	2
Testing the solution indicates that the LP solution is lower than the incumbent integer solution, so go to step 4.	3.3
Create SP2 and SP3 by setting $X1 = 0$ and $X1 = 1$.	4.1
Add these problems to the candidate list.	4.2
Test for termination: Candidate list is not empty, so go to step 1.	5
Select SP3 from the candidate list.	1
Solve the relaxed LP.	2
Testing the solution indicates that the LP solution is lower than the incumbent integer solution, so go to step 4.	3.3
Create SP4 and SP5 by setting $X2 = 0$ and $X2 = 1$.	4.1
Add these problems to the candidate list.	4.2
Test for termination: Candidate list is not empty, so go to step 1.	5
Select SP2 from the candidate list.	1
Solve the relaxed LP.	2
Testing the solution indicates an integer solution. It is less than the incumbent, so make it the new incumbent and go to step 5.	3.1.a
Test for termination: Candidate list is not empty, so go to step 1.	5
Select SP4 from the candidate list.	1
Solve the relaxed LP.	2
Testing the solution indicates its value is higher than the present incumbent, so abandon this problem and go to step 5.	3.2.a
Test for termination: Candidate list is not empty, so go to step 1.	5
Select SP5 from the candidate list.	1
Solve the relaxed LP.	2
Testing the solution indicates its value is higher than the present incumbent, so abandon this problem and go to step 5.	3.2.a
Test for termination: Candidate list is empty, so the algorithm terminates with the incumbent SP5 as the optimal integer solution.	5

CASE 6
SOUTHERN HYDRAULIC SUPPLIES COMPANY*

The Southern Hydraulic Supplies Company was a distributor of hydraulic supplies in the Gulf states area. Southern handled standard hydraulic fittings, tubing, and similar items. Generally Southern carried an entire line for each manufacturer whose products it handled and provided local stock for rapid delivery to customers. The items that Southern stocked were mainly used in the maintenance, modification, and manufacture of trucks, off-highway construction equipment, and machine tools.

Southern had grown from a small two-person operation to a $75-million-per-year business in a span of 25 years. The growth of its dollar volume was based on an excellent reputation for good service coupled with the general expansion of industry in the Gulf states. From its inception Southern had been a profitable business in sound financial condition.

Despite the continued growth of profits in absolute terms, however, Southern found that profits as a percentage of sales had declined from 11.3 percent of sales to 6.4 percent of sales. When management became aware of the seriousness of the problem, it was decided to undertake a thorough review of policies and procedures in the areas that could have significant influence on costs and profits—namely, product line, sales methods, stock handling and storage methods, billing and record keeping, and inventory replenishment. The last area was included as a major area for study because the company had been experiencing increasing difficulty with out-of-stock situations and unbalanced inventories.

Inventory Replenishment Procedures

Up until the time that the review of the inventory replenishment policies and procedures was begun, there had been no formal study of this phase of the company's operations. Since maintaining inventories was one of the company's major functions, Southern had always used experienced personnel to control the placing of orders and had relied on their judgment to make correct decisions. One thing that became immediately apparent as this phase of Southern's operations came under scrutiny was that the inventory replenishment problem had become vastly more complicated in recent years as the variety of items carried had tripled from what it had been five years previously to more than 15,000 separate stock items. Because no formal study had been made previously of the inventory replenishment operations, it was decided as a first step to get some general information about order placement

---

* Johnson Meier and Schrieber Newell, *Cases in Production and Operations Management,* © 1982, pp. 232–235. Reprinted by permission of Prentice-Hall, Inc., Englewood Cliffs, N. J.

costs and inventory carrying costs and also to analyze in detail several typical items of inventory.

Several years earlier Southern had installed a small computer for maintaining inventory records, writing purchase orders, and other record-keeping functions. To use this equipment efficiently, the master inventory records were updated only once weekly. Purchase orders were also prepared on a schedule of once each week. Purchase requisitions were turned in by the supervisors responsible for various types of stock, and these were accumulated until Friday when they were used to initiate purchase orders. In effect this meant that review of the inventory levels occurred once every five days as the supervisors turned in most of their purchase requisitions only once each week immediately before the scheduled machine run. In total, the cost of preparing and processing a requisition, preparing a purchase order, and making necessary record changes was estimated to be $12.50 per order.

Analysis of company records indicated that the following were reasonable estimates of the variable cost per year of carrying inventories (as a percentage of dollar value of average inventory):

Cost category	% of total
Capital cost	18
Obsolescence	5
Insurance	3
Taxes	2
Storage and handling	11
Total	39

One of the typical items of inventory analyzed in detail was a small hydraulic fitting. The fitting was purchased for $14.00 and sold for $19.50. The manufacturer from whom Southern procured the fitting did not offer any quantity discount on the fitting, but it would not fill orders for less than 50 fittings without adding a flat charge of $25.00 to the order. For this particular item, there were other distributors in Southern's immediate vicinity that could supply a comparable fitting made by another manufacturer. Because of this, orders that Southern could not fill immediately were lost.

The fitting was ordered from the manufacturer located about 1,500 miles away and shipped to Southern by truck. An analysis of the time taken to receive the fittings from the day the purchase order was prepared until the fittings were received indicated that this varied between 5 and 14 working days. The historical record of the time between the preparation of the purchase order and receipt of the fittings is shown in Table 1. It was estimated

TABLE 1 *Analysis of procurement lead times**

Working days between order issue and delivery of fittings	
8	11
12	14
6	9
5	8
7	9
8	7
8	6
9	8
13	13
9	10
10	7
8	7
11	12
7	10
8	9
5	10
7	7
6	8
9	14
7	6

* Average lead time = 8.7 days.

that inspection of the shipments, preparations of receiving reports, and related activities cost Southern $12.25 per order.

Customer orders filled each day for one year (260 working days) were tabulated for this fitting and are shown in Table 2. No record was kept of customer orders that were cancelled because the fitting was out of stock. Further analysis of the records pertaining to this fitting revealed the fact that replenishment orders for the fitting were always for lots of 750 and that the amount of stock on hand averaged about 115 units on the days that purchase orders were issued for replenishment stock.

Case Questions

1. Analyze the cost of the system currently used for maintaining the inventory of this fitting.
2. What is the minimum cost of maintaining the inventory of the fitting if the once-a-week ordering system is used?
3. What would be the advantage, if any, of revising the computer procedures so that replenishment orders could be placed every day?

TABLE 2 *Analysis of orders for one year**

Orders filled per day					
35	9	17	16	20	0
0	8	4	0	0	19
0	0	28	11	13	29
17	17	25	16	7	18
36	0	27	0	0	11
6	28	20	13	14	29
0	0	0	24	0	14
5	29	7	11	10	0
11	9	0	0	41	19
18	0	8	27	8	31
0	0	0	26	0	10
4	0	18	0	9	16
16	23	28	6	22	0
25	0	20	0	0	27
0	17	22	26	0	18
19	8	0	13	44	14
14	13	0	0	24	0
32	31	16	21	0	0
15	8	31	17	7	38
0	0	24	22	40	3
17	25	16	0	9	17
18	11	0	10	0	0
10	0	0	42	0	21
30	43	14	0	0	15
15	9	36	18	21	0
0	0	11	0	16	9
12	12	0	12	0	14
21	22	3	27	23	0
23	15	30	4	19	6
15	0	12	19	25	23
12	7	0	17	0	12
0	15	10	0	2	22
19	10	0	34	15	0
37	33	20	17	12	34
0	26	14	21	0	5
13	0	21	0	32	
0	6	0	18	8	
18	20	17	13	0	
20	13	37	24	5	
14	7	19	33	15	
19	0	0	26	20	
18	0	0	0	30	
0	39	35	18	23	
10	19	16	0	0	
15	16	13	16	11	

* Average orders filled per day = 13.1

4. Based on the analyses in the preceding questions, what possibilities appear to be present for improving the management of inventories?

CASE 7
BUFFALO ALKALI AND PLASTICS

Buffalo Alkali and Plastics, a prominent producer of soda ash, began operations in the United States in 1880 using the Solvay Process.[1] Buffalo, New York, was selected as the site for the soda ash operation because of the close proximity of both brine wells (permitting solution mining of salt) and limestone deposits. The initial complex was later expanded for the production of chlorine, caustic soda, chlorinated solvents, industrial detergents, and polyvinyl chloride. Having experienced considerable success in this initial operation, Buffalo Alkali and Plastics built eight additional plants in the central and southern regions of the United States during the first half of the twentieth century.

Even with this diversification and expansion, Buffalo Alkali and Plastics' principal product continues to be soda ash. Until the 1960s, soda ash was almost exclusively produced by the Solvay Process. However, huge deposits of trona, or natural soda ash, have been discovered in Wyoming. (Trona ore is mined directly and is purified by dissolution, evaporation, and recrystallization. Production costs for natural soda ash are much lower than those for synthetic soda ash produced by the Solvay Process.) Thus, Buffalo Alkali and Plastics' plants remain competitive only because of their close proximity to markets. Freight charges incurred in shipping soda ash from Wyoming to markets served by the synthetic plants tend to offset the lower production costs of mining/purification operations. (Principally, soda ash is used in the manufacture of glass by combining certain ratios of sand and soda ash and fusing the mixture under high temperature.)

The Calciners

Even when freight charges are considered, synthetic soda ash producers remain competitive with trona producers only if their plants maintain high volume operations. Synthetic plants have large investments in fixed costs and must sustain high production rates to remain above the break-even point. Area markets support these high rates. Glass manufacturers and other

Source: By Professors Jerry Kinard and Joe Iverstine, Southeastern Louisiana State University. Used by permission.

[1] The Solvay Process for producing soda ash involves exposing sodium bicarbonate (soda) to intense heat. Soda is initially formed through the carbonation of ammoniated brine. (Ammonia gas is absorbed in brine; then the ammonia-brine solution is saturated with carbon dioxide gas from the burning of limestone in kilns.)

users of soda ash consume the entire output of local synthetic plants and supplement this source of supply by purchasing higher priced trona ash.

Production rates for the synthetic plants are usually dependent on the number of calciners (pronounced cal-cī-ners) available for operation.[2] The Buffalo, New York, complex has 32 calciners, each with a daily capacity of 100 tons of soda ash. The plant capacity is 3,000 tons per day; hence, 30 of the 32 calciners must be available for service to maintain maximum output.

The Problem

Because of the intense heat in the fire zone, the one-inch thick steel shell eventually is oxidized and cracks. When this occurs, the shell is pulled from the brick housing and the burned-cracked section (approximately 15 feet) is cut out and a new section is welded into place. The repaired shell is reinstalled in the brick housing; drive mechanisms are attached; and the calciner is returned to service. (Heat resistant alloys are judged to be impractical for this operation because of the enormous cost and prolonged delivery dates for such alloy shells.)

The central problem for this operation is the determination of appropriate maintenance forces to effect calciner repairs. A large number of recent shell failures has reduced the number of calciners available for service to 25. A check of maintenance logs for the past ten years revealed 180 shell failures. Upon further examination of these logs, monthly failure probabilities were developed. These are included in Table 1. Repair procedures involve laying 100 feet of railroad track at the end of a failed calciner on which a crane rides to remove the cracked shell. The repair procedure averages three weeks (15 working days) with a standard deviation of three days. A schedule of repair time vs. cumulative probability is in Table 2. (The dispersion is usually a result of working overtime.) The crane track cannot be permanently installed at each calciner because of obstruction of other equipment repairs.

Repairs can be expedited, however, by renting a large mobile crane. The rental cost of this crane is $1,500 per day with a minimum charge of $12,000 per rental. With the rented crane, two calciners may be repaired simultaneously. Moreover, the average time for repairs using the rented crane is reduced from three weeks to two weeks (ten working days) with a standard deviation of two days. A schedule of repair times vs. cumulative

---

[2] A calciner is comprised of a steel pipe, 60 feet in length and six feet in diameter. This pipe, or shell, is fitted with a drive sprocket at one end and is supported by tines (steel rollers) at both ends. Through a gear drive mechanism, the shell is rotated about 30 rpm on fixed rollers. The shell lies horizontal in a fire brick housing. Approximately 30 feet of the shell are included in a fire-box or gas-fired furnace. Sodium bicarbonate (soda) is fed into one end of the shell and is conveyed to the other end by internal flights. When the soda passes through the fire zone, it is converted into sodium carbonate or soda ash. This process is called calcination.

TABLE 1   *Monthly shell failure probabilities*

Failures	Probability
0	0.22
1 or less	0.55
2 or less	0.80
3 or less	0.92
4 or less	0.96
5 or less	0.97
6 or less	0.98

TABLE 2   *Repair time probabilities utilizing normal repair procedures (crane track)*

Time	Probability
6 days or less	0.001
9 days or less	0.02
12 days or less	0.16
15 days or less	0.50
18 days or less	0.84
21 days or less	0.98
24 days or less	0.999

TABLE 3   *Repair time probabilities utilizing accelerated procedures (rental crane)*

Time	Probability
4 days or less	0.001
6 days or less	0.02
8 days or less	0.16
10 days or less	0.50
12 days or less	0.84
14 days or less	0.98
16 days or less	0.999

probability is included in Table 3. Other maintenance material and labor costs for these two repair approaches (rented crane and installed crane) are estimated to be equal. Profit and overhead contribution from a ton of soda ash is estimated to be $12.00.

Case Question

As a maintenance manager, develop a plan of action for the restoration of the failed calciners and present a policy that will be implemented in the future.

CASE 8
DRAKE RADIO

Drake Radio got its start during World War I by manufacturing radio communications equipment for the military. By the start of World War II, Drake was one of the largest suppliers of military communications equipment. After World War II, Drake diversified into the following three market areas:

1. Military Communications Equipment
2. Amateur Radio Equipment
3. CB Radios and Equipment

Using its technology and experience gained from manufacturing military communications equipment, Drake became known as one of the best producers of amateur radio equipment. Drake especially excelled with its single sideband radios and its two-meter radios for amateur use. Although these radios were expensive, they were of the finest quality and always in demand.

In developing CB radios, however, Drake decided to mass produce cheap units that would have a wide appeal and a low price. To help protect its good name in military communications equipment and amateur (ham) radios, these inexpensive CB radios were marketed under the brand name of Hustler.

In 1975, George Populas, the president of Drake Electronics, decided to investigate the possibilities of entering into the market of home stereo systems. These stereo systems would be high quality, highly priced, and marketed with the Drake name.

The most remarkable stereo system that Drake manufactured was the DR-2000, which was a sophisticated stereo receiver. The demand for the DR-2000 was fairly constant from month to month. (See Figure 1.)

The DR-2000 had all the features of a stereo receiver that carried a price tag of $765. Some of these features included the ability to connect four different speaker systems, loudness control, flatness control, blend control, and completely digital read out. Of course, it could be connected to one or

Source: By Professor Ralph M. Stair, Jr., Florida State University.

January	February	March	April
801	807	795	797

FIGURE 1 **Demand for DR-2000's in units**

more receivers, tape units, turntables, etc. Instead of having a base control to regulate the low frequencies and a treble control to regulate the high frequencies, the DR-2000 had five separate controls that regulated five frequency ranges. One control regulated frequencies from 0 to 500 Hz; another control regulated frequencies from 500 to 5,000 Hz; a third regulated the frequencies between 5,000 to 10,000 Hz; a fourth regulated frequencies between 10,000 to 15,000 Hz; and a fifth, the frequencies between 15,000 and 50,000 Hz.

One of the biggest selling features of the DR-2000 was its ability to use the DR-2000 RC, the remote control device for the stereo receiver. Because all of the switching and components were solid state, the engineers of Drake Electronics were able to develop a complete remote control station that was no bigger than a cigarette pack. The basic idea for the remote control device was borrowed from that of television, and Drake engineers were able to control *all* functions by the DR-2000 RC. Each remote control box cost $75, and many people purchased more than one unit. The ability to control the stereo system from literally anywhere in a house was one of the system's biggest selling features, but it also caused some problems in homes with children. As a result, Drake developed a master control unit that parents could keep and that would override all other remote control units and the controls on the stereo receiver.

Another outstanding feature of the DR-2000 was its completely modular design, shown in Figure 2. Each module was contained in a completely separate, color-coded box. By unlatching four hidden slides, the top of the cabinet could be removed, giving access to all of the modules.

The control module contained a microprocessor chip that monitored the operations of all of the other modules. If one of the modules stopped functioning correctly, the control module would activate a warning light on the front panel that indicated which module was not working properly. The owner could pull out the appropriate module and replace it with a new module from a nearby Drake dealership. If a Drake dealership was not close, Drake promised two-day, COD delivery. The malfunctioning module could even be sent to Drake or given to a Drake dealership to be repaired or for a refund.

All of the modules, except the FM tuner, were manufactured by Drake and stored until they were needed. Annual carrying cost was estimated to be

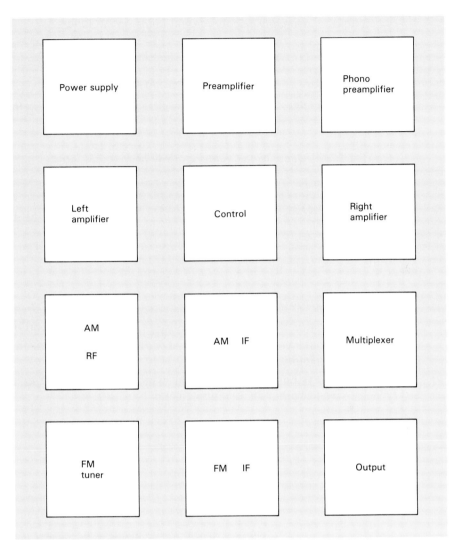

FIGURE 2 **Modules for the DR-2000**

25 percent for all modules. The FM tuner modules were supplied by Collins Electronics, which also adjusted and sealed them. The cost to place an order was estimated at $50 per order, and the time to receive an order from Collins was approximately two weeks. Collins also offered quantity discounts on its FM tuners. (See Table 1.)

Nitobitso Electronics also manufactured FM tuners compatible with the DR-2000. Because of its location in Japan, the time to receive an order was about two months, and the ordering cost was $100 because of the additional required paperwork. (See Table 2.)

TABLE 1   *Quantity discount from Collins on FM tuners*

Quantity	Price
0–100	$25
101–500	24
501 and over	22

TABLE 2   *Quantity discount from Nitobitso on FM tuners*

Quantity	Price
0–200	$25
201–800	23
801–2,000	22
2,001 or more	21

Case Questions

1. What is the optimal reorder point for Collins and Nitobitso?
2. Would you recommend that Drake get FM tuners from Nitobitso? Explain your answer.
3. Everything else being equal, which supplier of FM tuners would you want with a fluctuating demand?

Appendix B
Solving Simultaneous
Linear Equations with
Gaussian Elimination

Solving simultaneous linear equations is often important in the world of business. The following example illustrates the utility of being able to simultaneously solve a system of n linear equations with n unknowns.

EXAMPLE   Let us assume that the amount of corn that buyers are willing to buy is defined by the function

$$d = 50,000 - 7,500p \qquad 1.00 < p < 5.00$$

where d = demand (bushels)
p = price (dollars per bushel)

Furthermore, the amounts farmers are willing to supply is s:

$$s = -15,000 + 11,000p \qquad 1.00 < p < 5.00$$

where s = supply (bushels)
p = price (dollars per bushel)

Often, it is desirable to know the point at which supply is equal to demand. Economists call this point the equilibrium point. Figure 1 graphs the supply and demand functions.

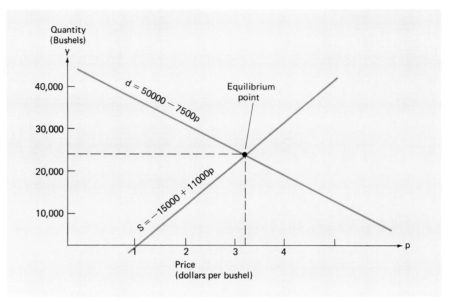

FIGURE 1 **Equilibrium point**

If we wish to find the equilibrium point (where $d = s$), we can equate d and s to another variable y and we have two simultaneous equations with two unknowns, $y = 50,000 - 7,500p$ and $y = -15,000 + 11,000p$. To find the value of the two unknowns (y and p) that simultaneously satisfy the foregoing equations, we could read the values for p and y off the graph or we could solve the two simultaneous equations. Obviously, when we have more than two equations and two unknowns, graphical procedures become impractical or impossible and an algebraic procedure is required. One of the most useful business applications of matrices is solving simultaneous linear equations.

You might be familiar with the methods of substitution or elimination from previous courses in algebra. (If you are willing to date yourself, you might even admit to being exposed to a method using determinants and co-factors!) These methods are useful for solving small 2×2 or 3×3 systems of linear equations. In this appendix we want to develop a systematic procedure that will solve linear systems of equations. The procedure is called Gaussian elimination and is a generalization of the simple elimination method for solving a 2×2 system. Gaussian elimination will determine whether there is a unique solution, no solution, or an infinite number of solutions to a system of equations. It is easily programmed for implementation on a computer.

Consider the following 2×2 system of equations:

$$2x_1 + 3x_2 = 19$$
$$6x_1 + 8x_2 = 54$$

The solution to the system of equations is not obvious, but can be transformed into an equivalent system in which the answer is obvious. Suppose we convert the 2×2 system into the system shown below:

$$2x_1 + 3x_2 = 19 \quad \longrightarrow \quad 1x_1 + 0x_2 = 5$$
$$6x_1 + 8x_2 = 54 \qquad\qquad 0x_1 + 1x_2 = 3$$

The solution to the second system of equations is obvious (we hope!) and can be specified as $x_1 = 5$ from the first equation and $x_2 = 3$ from the second equation. The second system of equations is mathematically equivalent to the first system in that all properties of the system and the solution are the same. How do we convert one system of equations into another one that has an obvious solution? The answer is by using elementary row operations and Gaussian elimination.

elementary *row opera-* *tions*   There are 3 *elementary row operations* that can be used to transform a system of equations into a different but mathematically equivalent system of equations. These row or equation operations are:

1. Multiply any equation by a nonzero constant
2. Interchange the position of any two equations
3. Multiply any equation by a constant and add it to any other equation in the system.

In using these elementary row operations, our objective will be to convert all equation coefficients to a 0 or 1. In a square $n \times n$ system we will want the coefficient of variable x_j to be a 1 in row j and 0 in every other row.

Let us solve the previous 2×2 system in order to illustrate the procedure. We start with

$$2x_1 + 3x_2 = 19$$
$$6x_1 + 8x_2 = 54$$

Remember, we want a coefficient of 1 for x_1 in row 1 and a coefficient of 1 for x_2 in row 2; all other coefficients need to be zero. Our first step will be to achieve a coefficient of 1 for x_1 in row 1. We multiply equation 1 by $\frac{1}{2}$.

$$\frac{1}{2}(2x_1 + 3x_2 = 19) \quad \longrightarrow \quad 1x_1 + \frac{3}{2}x_2 = \frac{19}{2}$$
$$6x_1 + 8x_2 = 54 \qquad\qquad 6x_1 + 8x_2 = 54$$

We next eliminate x_1 from the second equation by using elementary row operation number 3. Multiply the first equation by -6 and add the resulting equations to the second equation.

$$
\begin{array}{ll}
6x_1 + 8x_2 = 54 & \text{old second equation} \\
\underline{(-6)(1x_1 + \frac{3}{2}x_2 = \frac{19}{2})} & \\
0x_1 - 1x_2 = -3 & \text{new second equation}
\end{array}
$$

The system now is written as:

$$1x_1 + \tfrac{3}{2}x_2 = \tfrac{19}{2}$$
$$0x_1 - 1x_2 = -3$$

The next step is to achieve a coefficient of $+1$ for x_2 in row 2. We can accomplish this by multiplying row 2 by -1.

$$1x_1 + \tfrac{3}{2}x_2 = \tfrac{19}{2} \qquad \longrightarrow \qquad 1x_1 + \tfrac{3}{2}x_2 = \tfrac{19}{2}$$
$$(-1)(0x_1 - 1x_2 = -3) \qquad\qquad 0x_1 + 1x_2 = 3$$

The final step will be to eliminate x_2 from the first row. To do this we multiply row 2 by $-\tfrac{3}{2}$ and add it to row 1.

$$1x_1 + \tfrac{3}{2}x_2 = \tfrac{19}{2} \qquad \text{old first row}$$
$$\underline{(-\tfrac{3}{2})(0x_1 + 1x_2 = 3)}$$
$$1x_1 + 0x_2 = \tfrac{10}{2} \qquad \text{new first row}$$

The system of equations is finally in the form:

$$1x_1 + 0x_2 = 5$$
$$0x_1 + 1x_2 = 3$$

and is solved with $x_1 = 5$ and $x_2 = 3$.

Let us now turn to a more formal development of the Gaussian elimination procedure. The process can be streamlined by using a matrix notation to represent the system of equations. If we detach the coefficients of the system:

$$2x_1 + 4x_2 + 2x_3 = 2$$
$$3x_1 + x_2 - x_3 = 5$$
$$x_1 - 3x_2 + 2x_3 = 4$$

we obtain the following matrix of coefficients

$$\begin{bmatrix} 2 & 4 & 2 \\ 3 & 1 & -1 \\ 1 & -3 & 2 \end{bmatrix}$$

Now, if we augment the coefficient matrix by adding the right hand side columns, we have

$$\begin{bmatrix} 2 & 4 & 2 & \vdots & 2 \\ 3 & 1 & -1 & \vdots & 5 \\ 1 & -3 & 2 & \vdots & 4 \end{bmatrix}$$

augmented Notice how the *augmented matrix* represents the system of equations with
matrix each row representing an equation in the original system.
We want to transform the augmented matrix to the form

$$\begin{bmatrix} 1 & 0 & 0 & \vdots & a \\ 0 & 1 & 0 & \vdots & b \\ 0 & 0 & 1 & \vdots & c \end{bmatrix}$$

where the solution is $x_1 = a$, $x_2 = b$, and $x_3 = c$.

In order to achieve this transformation we will proceed a column at a
time using elementary row operations. That is, we will first convert column
one to $\begin{pmatrix} 1 \\ 0 \\ 0 \end{pmatrix}$, then column two to $\begin{pmatrix} 0 \\ 1 \\ 0 \end{pmatrix}$ and finally column three to $\begin{pmatrix} 0 \\ 0 \\ 1 \end{pmatrix}$.

We summarize the steps in the Gaussian elimination procedure as follows:

1. Begin with the first row and multiply the row by the multiplicative
   inverse of the coefficient of variable x_1.
2. Use the new row 1 to eliminate variable x_1 from all other rows using

   elementary row operations. This will achieve a unit vector $\begin{pmatrix} 1 \\ 0 \\ 0 \\ \vdots \\ 0 \end{pmatrix}$ for

   column one.
3. Go to the second row and multiply the row by the multiplicative inverse of the x_2 coefficient.
4. Use the new row 2 to eliminate variable x_2 from all other rows using

   elementary row operations. This will achieve a unit vector $\begin{pmatrix} 0 \\ 1 \\ 0 \\ \vdots \\ 0 \end{pmatrix}$ for

   column two.
5. Go to the next row and repeat the process for the next variable.
6. Continue the process until each variable x_j has a coefficient of 1 in row j
   and a 0 coefficient in every other row.
7. The final solution can be read from the far right column of the augmented matrix.

To illustrate the procedure let us solve the 3×3 system:

$$\begin{bmatrix} 2 & 4 & 2 & \vdots & 2 \\ 3 & 1 & -1 & \vdots & 5 \\ 1 & -3 & 2 & \vdots & 4 \end{bmatrix}$$

We will highlight the key element or pivot element in each row by circling it. The pivot element must first be converted to a 1 and then used to create zeros for the remaining coefficients in the column.

Step 1.   Convert pivot element to 1 (Multiply row 1 by $\frac{1}{2}$)

$$(\tfrac{1}{2}) \begin{bmatrix} ② & 4 & 2 & \vdots & 2 \\ 3 & 1 & -1 & \vdots & 5 \\ 1 & -3 & 2 & \vdots & 4 \end{bmatrix} \rightarrow \begin{bmatrix} 1 & 2 & 1 & \vdots & 1 \\ 3 & 1 & -1 & \vdots & 5 \\ 1 & -3 & 2 & \vdots & 4 \end{bmatrix}$$

Step 2.   Multiply row 1 by -3 and add to row 2

$$\begin{bmatrix} 1 & 2 & 1 & \vdots & 1 \\ 3 & 1 & -1 & \vdots & 5 \\ 1 & -3 & 2 & \vdots & 4 \end{bmatrix} \rightarrow \begin{bmatrix} 1 & 2 & 1 & \vdots & 1 \\ 0 & -5 & -4 & \vdots & 2 \\ 1 & -3 & 2 & \vdots & 4 \end{bmatrix}$$

Step 3.   Multiply row 1 by -1 and add to row 3

$$\begin{bmatrix} 1 & 2 & 1 & \vdots & 1 \\ 0 & -5 & -4 & \vdots & 2 \\ 1 & -3 & 2 & \vdots & 4 \end{bmatrix} \rightarrow \begin{bmatrix} 1 & 2 & 1 & \vdots & 1 \\ 0 & -5 & -4 & \vdots & 2 \\ 0 & -5 & 1 & \vdots & 3 \end{bmatrix}$$

We have now converted column 1 to a unit vector. The following operations must convert other columns to unit vectors and at the same time leave column one unchanged.

Step 4.   Establish coefficient of 1 for pivot element in row 2 (Multiply row 2 by $-\frac{1}{5}$)

$$(-1/5) \begin{bmatrix} 1 & 2 & 1 & \vdots & 1 \\ 0 & ⊖5 & -4 & \vdots & 2 \\ 0 & -5 & 1 & \vdots & 3 \end{bmatrix} \rightarrow \begin{bmatrix} 1 & 2 & 1 & \vdots & 1 \\ 0 & 1 & \frac{4}{5} & \vdots & -\frac{2}{5} \\ 0 & -5 & 1 & \vdots & 3 \end{bmatrix}$$

Step 5. Eliminate x_2 from row 1 (Multiply row 2 by -2 and add to row 1)

$$\begin{bmatrix} 1 & 2 & 1 & \cdot & 1 \\ 0 & 1 & \frac{4}{5} & \cdot & -\frac{2}{5} \\ 0 & -5 & 1 & \cdot & 3 \end{bmatrix} \rightarrow \begin{bmatrix} 1 & 0 & -\frac{3}{5} & \cdot & \frac{9}{5} \\ 0 & 1 & \frac{4}{5} & \cdot & -\frac{2}{5} \\ 0 & -5 & 1 & \cdot & 3 \end{bmatrix}$$

Step 6. Eliminate x_2 from row 3 (Multiply row 2 by 5 and add to row 3)

$$\begin{bmatrix} 1 & 0 & -\frac{3}{4} & \cdot & \frac{9}{5} \\ 0 & 1 & \frac{4}{5} & \cdot & -\frac{2}{5} \\ 0 & -5 & 1 & \cdot & 3 \end{bmatrix} \rightarrow \begin{bmatrix} 1 & 0 & -\frac{3}{5} & \cdot & \frac{9}{5} \\ 0 & 1 & \frac{4}{5} & \cdot & -\frac{2}{5} \\ 0 & 0 & 5 & \cdot & 1 \end{bmatrix}$$

Step 7. Establish coefficient of 1 for pivot element in row 3 (Multiply row 3 by $\frac{1}{5}$)

$$\begin{matrix} \\ \\ (\frac{1}{5}) \end{matrix} \begin{bmatrix} 1 & 0 & -\frac{3}{5} & \cdot & \frac{9}{5} \\ 0 & 1 & \frac{4}{5} & \cdot & -\frac{2}{5} \\ 0 & 0 & ⑤ & \cdot & 1 \end{bmatrix} \rightarrow \begin{bmatrix} 1 & 0 & -\frac{3}{5} & \cdot & \frac{9}{5} \\ 0 & 1 & \frac{4}{5} & \cdot & -\frac{2}{5} \\ 0 & 0 & 1 & \cdot & \frac{1}{5} \end{bmatrix}$$

Step 8. Eliminate x_3 from row 1. (Multiply row 3 by $\frac{3}{5}$ and add to row 1)

$$\begin{bmatrix} 1 & 0 & -\frac{3}{5} & \cdot & \frac{9}{5} \\ 0 & 1 & \frac{4}{5} & \cdot & -\frac{2}{5} \\ 0 & 0 & 1 & \cdot & \frac{1}{5} \end{bmatrix} \rightarrow \begin{bmatrix} 1 & 0 & 0 & \cdot & \frac{48}{25} \\ 0 & 1 & \frac{4}{5} & \cdot & -\frac{2}{5} \\ 0 & 0 & 1 & \cdot & \frac{1}{5} \end{bmatrix}$$

Step 9. Eliminate x_3 from row 2. (Multiply row 3 by $-\frac{4}{5}$ and add to row 2)

$$\begin{bmatrix} 1 & 0 & 0 & \cdot & \frac{48}{25} \\ 0 & 1 & \frac{4}{5} & \cdot & -\frac{2}{5} \\ 0 & 0 & 1 & \cdot & \frac{1}{5} \end{bmatrix} \rightarrow \begin{bmatrix} 1 & 0 & 0 & \cdot & \frac{48}{25} \\ 0 & 1 & 0 & \cdot & \frac{14}{25} \\ 0 & 0 & 1 & \cdot & \frac{1}{5} \end{bmatrix}$$

The desired form of the augmented matrix has been achieved and the final solution can be read directly as

$$x_1 = \frac{48}{25}$$
$$x_2 = \frac{14}{25}$$
$$x_3 = \frac{1}{5}$$

In this appendix we have applied Gaussian elimination to 2×2 and 3×3 examples. Understanding these procedures will enable you to solve for steady state probabilities in Markov Chains and to better understand the simplex method calculations for linear programming. Gaussian elimination can also be applied to non-square $m \times n$ systems. The interested student should refer to a book on linear algebra for a more advanced theoretical treatment of the solution of simultaneous linear equations.

Appendix C
Areas of a Standard Normal Distribution

An entry in the table is the proportion under the entire curve that is between $z = -\infty$ and a positive value of z.

z	.00	.01	.02	.03	.04	.05	.06	.07	.08	.09
0.0	.5000	.5040	.5080	.5120	.5160	.5199	.5239	.5279	.5319	.5359
0.1	.5398	.5438	.5478	.5517	.5557	.5596	.5636	.5675	.5714	.5753
0.2	.5793	.5832	.5871	.5910	.5948	.5987	.6026	.6064	.6103	.6141
0.3	.6179	.6217	.6255	.6293	.6331	.6368	.6406	.6443	.6480	.6517
0.4	.6554	.6591	.6628	.6664	.6700	.6736	.6772	.6808	.6844	.6879
0.5	.6915	.6950	.6985	.7019	.7054	.7088	.7123	.7157	.7190	.7224
0.6	.7257	.7291	.7324	.7357	.7389	.7422	.7454	.7486	.7517	.7549
0.7	.7580	.7611	.7642	.7673	.7703	.7734	.7764	.7794	.7823	.7852
0.8	.7881	.7910	.7939	.7967	.7995	.8023	.8051	.8078	.8106	.8133
1.9	.8159	.8186	.8212	.8238	.8264	.8289	.8315	.8340	.8365	.8389
1.0	.8413	.8438	.8461	.8485	.8508	.8531	.8554	.8577	.8599	.8621
1.1	.8643	.8665	.8686	.8708	.8729	.8749	.8770	.8790	.8810	.8830
1.2	.8849	.8869	.8888	.8907	.8925	.8944	.8962	.8980	.8997	.9015
1.3	.9032	.9049	.9066	.9082	.9099	.9115	.9131	.9147	.9162	.9177
1.4	.9192	.9207	.9222	.9236	.9251	.9265	.9279	.9292	.9306	.9319
1.5	.9332	.9345	.9357	.9370	.9382	.9394	.9406	.9418	.9429	.9441
1.6	.9452	.9463	.9474	.9484	.9495	.9505	.9515	.9525	.9535	.9545
1.7	.9554	.9564	.9573	.9582	.9591	.9599	.9608	.9516	.9625	.9633
1.8	.9461	.9649	.9656	.9664	.9671	.9678	.9686	.9693	.9699	.9706
1.9	.9713	.9719	.9726	.9732	.9738	.9744	.9750	.9756	.9761	.9767
2.0	.9772	.9778	.9783	.9788	.9793	.9798	.9803	.9808	.9812	.9817
2.1	.9821	.9826	.9830	.9834	.9838	.9842	.9846	.9850	.9854	.9857
2.2	.9861	.9864	.9868	.9871	.9875	.9878	.9881	.9884	.9887	.9890
2.3	.9893	.9896	.9898	.9901	.9904	.9906	.9909	.9911	.9913	.9916
2.4	.9918	.9920	.9922	.9925	.9927	.9929	.9931	.9932	.9934	.9936
2.5	.9938	.9940	.9941	.9943	.9945	.9946	.9948	.9949	.9951	.9952
2.6	.9953	.9955	.9956	.9957	.9959	.9960	.9961	.9962	.9963	.9964
2.7	.9965	.9966	.9967	.9968	.9969	.9970	.9971	.9972	.9973	.9974
2.8	.9974	.9975	.9976	.9977	.9977	.9978	.9979	.9979	.9980	.9981
2.9	.9981	.9982	.9982	.9983	.9984	.9984	.9985	.9985	.9986	.9986
3.0	.9987	.9987	.9987	.9988	.9988	.9989	.9989	.9989	.9990	.9990
2.1	.9990	.9991	.9991	.9991	.9992	.9992	.9992	.9992	.9993	.9993
3.2	.9993	.9993	.9994	.9994	.9994	.9994	.9994	.9995	.9995	.9995
3.3	.9995	.9995	.9995	.9996	.9996	.9996	.9996	.9996	.9996	.9997

Appendix D
Selected Values of the Binomial Cumulative Distribution Function

$$F(c) = P(X \le c) = \sum_{r=0}^{c} \binom{n}{r}(1 - p)^{n-r}p^r$$

EXAMPLE If $p = .20$, $n = 7$, $c = 2$, then $F(2) = P(X \le 2) = .8520$.

n	c	0.05	0.10	0.15	0.20	p 0.25	0.30	0.35	0.40	0.45	0.50
2	0	0.9025	0.8100	0.7225	0.6400	0.5625	0.4900	0.4225	0.3600	0.3025	0.2500
	1	0.9975	0.9900	0.9775	0.9600	0.9375	0.9100	0.8775	0.8400	0.7975	0.7500
3	0	0.8574	0.7290	0.6141	0.5120	0.4219	0.3430	0.2746	0.2160	0.1664	0.1250
	1	0.9928	0.9720	0.9392	0.8960	0.8438	0.7840	0.7182	0.6480	0.5748	0.5000
	2	0.9999	0.9990	0.9966	0.9920	0.9844	0.9730	0.9571	0.9360	0.9089	0.8750
4	0	0.8145	0.6561	0.5220	0.4096	0.3164	0.2401	0.1785	0.1296	0.0915	0.0625
	1	0.9860	0.9477	0.8905	0.8192	0.7383	0.6517	0.5630	0.4752	0.3910	0.3125
	2	0.9995	0.9963	0.9880	0.9728	0.9492	0.9163	0.8735	0.8208	0.7585	0.6875
	3	1.0000	0.9999	0.9995	0.9984	0.9961	0.9919	0.9850	0.9744	0.9590	0.9375
5	0	0.7738	0.5905	0.4437	0.3277	0.2373	0.1681	0.1160	0.0778	0.0503	0.0312
	1	0.9774	0.9185	0.8352	0.7373	0.6328	0.5282	0.4284	0.3370	0.2562	0.1875
	2	0.9988	0.9914	0.9734	0.9421	0.8965	0.8369	0.7648	0.6826	0.5931	0.5000
	3	1.0000	0.9995	0.9978	0.9933	0.9844	0.9692	0.9460	0.9130	0.8688	0.8125
	4	1.0000	1.0000	0.9999	0.9997	0.9990	0.9976	0.9947	0.9898	0.9815	0.9688

Source: From Irwin Miller and John E. Freund. *Probability and Statistics for Engineers*, © 1965 by Prentice-Hall, Inc.

Selected values of the binomial cumulative distribution function

n	c	0.05	0.10	0.15	0.20	p 0.25	0.30	0.35	0.40	0.45	0.50
6	0	0.7351	0.5314	0.3771	0.2621	0.1780	0.1176	0.0754	0.0467	0.0277	0.0156
	1	0.9672	0.8857	0.7765	0.6554	0.5339	0.4202	0.3191	0.2333	0.1636	0.1094
	2	0.9978	0.9842	0.9527	0.9011	0.8306	0.7443	0.6471	0.5443	0.4415	0.3438
	3	0.9999	0.9987	0.9941	0.9830	0.9624	0.9295	0.8826	0.8208	0.7447	0.6562
	4	1.0000	0.9999	0.9996	0.9984	0.9954	0.9891	0.9777	0.9590	0.9308	0.8906
	5	1.0000	1.0000	1.0000	0.9999	0.9998	0.9993	0.9982	0.9959	0.9917	0.9844
7	0	0.6983	0.4783	0.3206	0.2097	0.1335	0.0824	0.0490	0.0280	0.0152	0.0078
	1	0.9556	0.8503	0.7166	0.5767	0.4449	0.3294	0.2338	0.1586	0.1024	0.0625
	2	0.9962	0.9743	0.9262	0.8520	0.7564	0.6471	0.5323	0.4199	0.3164	0.2266
	3	0.9998	0.9973	0.9879	0.9667	0.9294	0.8740	0.8002	0.7102	0.6083	0.5000
	4	1.0000	0.9998	0.9988	0.9953	0.9871	0.9712	0.9444	0.9037	0.8471	0.7734
	5	1.0000	1.0000	0.9999	0.9996	0.9987	0.9962	0.9910	0.0812	0.9643	0.9375
	6	1.0000	1.0000	1.0000	1.0000	0.9999	0.9998	0.9994	0.9984	0.9963	0.9922
8	0	0.6634	0.4305	0.2725	0.1678	0.1001	0.0576	0.0319	0.0168	0.0084	0.0039
	1	0.9428	0.8131	0.6572	0.5033	0.3671	0.2553	0.1691	0.1064	0.0632	0.0352
	2	0.9942	0.9619	0.8948	0.7969	0.6785	0.5518	0.4278	0.3154	0.2201	0.1445
	3	0.9996	0.9950	0.9786	0.9437	0.8862	0.8059	0.7064	0.5941	0.4770	0.3633
	4	1.0000	0.9996	0.9971	0.9896	0.9727	0.9420	0.8939	0.8263	0.7396	0.6367
	5	1.0000	1.0000	0.9998	0.9988	0.9958	0.9887	0.9747	0.9502	0.9115	0.8555
	6	1.0000	1.0000	1.0000	0.9999	0.9996	0.9987	0.9964	0.9915	0.9819	0.9648
	7	1.0000	1.0000	1.0000	1.0000	1.0000	0.9999	0.9998	0.9993	0.9983	0.9961
9	0	0.6302	0.3874	0.2316	0.1342	0.0751	0.0404	0.0207	0.0101	0.0046	0.0020
	1	0.9288	0.7748	0.5995	0.4362	0.3003	0.1960	0.1211	0.0705	0.0385	0.0195
	2	0.9916	0.9470	0.8591	0.7382	0.6007	0.4628	0.3373	0.2318	0.1495	0.0898
	3	0.9994	0.9917	0.9661	0.9144	0.8343	0.7297	0.6089	0.4826	0.3614	0.2539
	4	1.0000	0.9991	0.9944	0.9804	0.9511	0.9012	0.8283	0.7334	0.6214	0.5000
	5	1.0000	0.9999	0.9994	0.9969	0.9900	0.9747	0.9464	0.9006	0.8342	0.7461
	6	1.0000	1.0000	1.0000	0.9997	0.9987	0.9957	0.9888	0.9750	0.9502	0.9102
	7	1.0000	1.0000	1.0000	1.0000	0.9999	0.9996	0.9986	0.9962	0.9909	0.9805
	8	1.0000	1.0000	1.0000	1.0000	1.0000	1.0000	0.9999	0.9997	0.9992	0.9980
10	0	0.5987	0.3487	0.1969	0.1074	0.0563	0.0282	0.0135	0.0060	0.0025	0.0010
	1	0.9139	0.7361	0.5443	0.3768	0.2440	0.1493	0.0860	0.0464	0.0232	0.0107
	2	0.9885	0.9298	0.8202	0.6778	0.5256	0.3828	0.2616	0.1673	0.0996	0.0547
	3	0.9990	0.9872	0.9500	0.8791	0.7759	0.6496	0.5138	0.3823	0.2660	0.1719
	4	0.9999	0.9984	0.9901	0.9672	0.9219	0.8497	0.7515	0.6331	0.5044	0.3770
	5	1.0000	0.9999	0.9986	0.9936	0.9803	0.9527	0.9051	0.8338	0.7384	0.6230
	6	1.0000	1.0000	0.9999	0.9991	0.9965	0.9894	0.9740	0.9452	0.8980	0.8281
	7	1.0000	1.0000	1.0000	0.9999	0.9996	0.9984	0.9952	0.9877	0.9726	0.9453
	8	1.0000	1.0000	1.0000	1.0000	1.0000	0.9999	0.9995	0.9983	0.9955	0.9893
	9	1.0000	1.0000	1.0000	1.0000	1.0000	1.0000	1.0000	0.9999	0.9997	0.9990

Selected values of the binomial cumulative distribution function (continued)

n	c	0.05	0.10	0.15	0.20	p 0.25	0.30	0.35	0.40	0.45	0.50
11	0	0.5688	0.3138	0.1673	0.0859	0.0422	0.0198	0.0088	0.0036	0.0014	0.0005
	1	0.8981	0.6974	0.4922	0.3221	0.1971	0.1130	0.0606	0.0302	0.0139	0.0059
	2	0.9848	0.9104	0.7788	0.6174	0.4552	0.3127	0.2001	0.1189	0.0652	0.0327
	3	0.9984	0.9815	0.9306	0.8389	0.7133	0.5696	0.4256	0.2963	0.1911	0.1133
	4	0.9999	0.9972	0.9841	0.9496	0.8854	0.7897	0.6683	0.5328	0.3971	0.2744
	5	1.0000	0.9997	0.9973	0.9883	0.9657	0.9218	0.8513	0.7535	0.6331	0.5000
	6	1.0000	1.0000	0.9997	0.9980	0.9924	0.9784	0.9499	0.9006	0.8262	0.7256
	7	1.0000	1.0000	1.0000	0.9998	0.9988	0.9957	0.9878	0.9707	0.9390	0.8867
	8	1.0000	1.0000	1.0000	1.0000	0.9999	0.9994	0.9980	0.9941	0.9852	0.9673
	9	1.0000	1.0000	1.0000	1.0000	1.0000	1.0000	0.9998	0.9993	0.9978	0.9941
	10	1.0000	1.0000	1.0000	1.0000	1.0000	1.0000	1.0000	1.0000	0.9998	0.9995
12	0	0.5404	0.2824	0.1422	0.0687	0.0317	0.0138	0.0057	0.0022	0.0008	0.0002
	1	0.8816	0.6590	0.4435	0.2749	0.1584	0.0850	0.0424	0.0196	0.0083	0.0032
	2	0.9804	0.8891	0.7358	0.5583	0.3907	0.2528	0.1513	0.0834	0.0421	0.0193
	3	0.9978	0.9744	0.9078	0.7946	0.6488	0.4925	0.3467	0.2253	0.1345	0.0730
	4	0.9998	0.9957	0.9761	0.9274	0.8424	0.7237	0.5833	0.4382	0.3044	0.1938
	5	1.0000	0.9995	0.9954	0.9806	0.9456	0.8822	0.7873	0.6652	0.5269	0.3872
	6	1.0000	0.9999	0.9993	0.9961	0.9857	0.9614	0.9154	0.8418	0.7393	0.6128
	7	1.0000	1.0000	0.9999	0.9994	0.9972	0.9905	0.9745	0.9427	0.8883	0.8062
	8	1.0000	1.0000	1.0000	0.9999	0.9996	0.9983	0.9944	0.9847	0.9644	0.9270
	9	1.0000	1.0000	1.0000	1.0000	1.0000	0.9998	0.9992	0.9972	0.9921	0.9807
	10	1.0000	1.0000	1.0000	1.0000	1.0000	1.0000	0.9999	0.9997	0.9989	0.9968
	11	1.0000	1.0000	1.0000	1.0000	1.0000	1.0000	1.0000	1.0000	0.9999	0.9998
13	0	0.5133	0.2542	0.1209	0.0550	0.0238	0.0097	0.0037	0.0013	0.0004	0.0001
	1	0.8646	0.6213	0.3983	0.2336	0.1267	0.0637	0.0296	0.0126	0.0049	0.0017
	2	0.9755	0.8661	0.6920	0.5017	0.3326	0.2025	0.1132	0.0579	0.0269	0.0112
	3	0.9969	0.9658	0.6820	0.7473	0.5843	0.4206	0.2783	0.1686	0.0929	0.0461
	4	0.9997	0.9935	0.9658	0.9009	0.7940	0.6543	0.5005	0.3530	0.2279	0.1334
	5	1.0000	0.9991	0.9925	0.9700	0.9198	0.8346	0.7159	0.5744	0.4268	0.2905
	6	1.0000	0.9999	0.9987	0.9930	0.9757	0.9376	0.8705	0.7712	0.6437	0.5000
	7	1.0000	1.0000	0.9998	0.9988	0.9944	0.9818	0.9538	0.9023	0.8212	0.7095
	8	1.0000	1.0000	1.0000	0.9998	0.9990	0.9960	0.9874	0.9679	0.9302	0.8666
	9	1.0000	1.0000	1.0000	1.0000	0.9999	0.9993	0.9975	0.9922	0.9797	0.9539
	10	1.0000	1.0000	1.0000	1.0000	1.0000	0.9999	0.9997	0.9987	0.9959	0.9888
	11	1.0000	1.0000	1.0000	1.0000	1.0000	1.0000	1.0000	0.9999	0.9995	0.9963
	12	1.0000	1.0000	1.0000	1.0000	1.0000	1.0000	1.0000	1.0000	1.0000	0.9999
14	0	0.4877	0.2288	0.1028	0.0440	0.0178	0.0068	0.0024	0.0008	0.0002	0.0001
	1	0.8470	0.5846	0.3567	0.1979	0.1010	0.0475	0.0205	0.0081	0.0029	0.0009
	2	0.9699	0.8416	0.6479	0.4481	0.2811	0.1608	0.0839	0.0398	0.0170	0.0065

Selected values of the binomial cumulative distribution function (continued)

n	c	0.05	0.10	0.15	0.20	0.25	0.30	0.35	0.40	0.45	0.50
14	3	0.9958	0.9559	0.8535	0.6982	0.5213	0.3552	0.2205	0.1243	0.0632	0.0287
	4	0.9996	0.9908	0.9533	0.8702	0.7415	0.5842	0.4227	0.2793	0.1672	0.0898
	5	1.0000	0.9985	0.9885	0.9561	0.8883	0.7805	0.6405	0.4859	0.3373	0.2120
	6	1.0000	0.9998	0.9978	0.9884	0.9617	0.9067	0.8164	0.6925	0.5461	0.3953
	7	1.0000	1.0000	0.9997	0.9976	0.9897	0.9685	0.9247	0.8499	0.7414	0.6047
	8	1.0000	1.0000	1.0000	0.9996	0.9978	0.9917	0.9757	0.9417	0.8811	0.7880
	9	1.0000	1.0000	1.0000	1.0000	0.9997	0.9983	0.9940	0.9825	0.9574	0.9102
	10	1.0000	1.0000	1.0000	1.0000	1.0000	0.9998	0.9989	0.9961	0.9886	0.9713
	11	1.0000	1.0000	1.0000	1.0000	1.0000	1.0000	0.9999	0.9994	0.9978	0.9935
	12	1.0000	1.0000	1.0000	1.0000	1.0000	1.0000	1.0000	0.9999	0.9997	0.9991
	13	1.0000	1.0000	1.0000	1.0000	1.0000	1.0000	1.0000	1.0000	1.0000	0.9999
15	0	0.4633	0.2059	0.0874	0.0352	0.0134	0.0047	0.0016	0.0005	0.0001	0.0000
	1	0.8290	0.5490	0.3186	0.1671	0.0802	0.0353	0.0142	0.0052	0.0017	0.0005
	2	0.9638	0.8159	0.6042	0.3980	0.2361	0.1268	0.0617	0.0271	0.0107	0.0037
	3	0.9945	0.9444	0.8227	0.6482	0.4613	0.2969	0.1727	0.0905	0.0424	0.0176
	4	0.9994	0.9873	0.9383	0.8358	0.6865	0.5155	0.3519	0.2173	0.1204	0.0592
	5	0.9999	0.9978	0.9832	0.9389	0.8516	0.7216	9.5643	0.4032	0.2608	0.1509
	6	1.0000	0.9997	0.9964	0.9819	0.9434	0.8689	0.7548	0.6098	0.4522	0.3036
	7	1.0000	1.0000	0.9996	0.9958	0.9827	0.9500	0.8868	0.7869	0.6535	0.5000
	8	1.0000	1.0000	0.9999	0.9992	0.9958	0.9848	0.9578	0.9050	0.8182	0.6964
	9	1.0000	1.0000	1.0000	0.9999	0.9992	0.9963	0.9876	0.9662	0.9231	0.8491
	10	1.0000	1.0000	1.0000	1.0000	0.9999	0.9993	0.9972	0.9907	0.9745	0.9408
	11	1.0000	1.0000	1.0000	1.0000	1.0000	0.9999	0.9995	0.9981	0.9937	0.9821
	12	1.0000	1.0000	1.0000	1.0000	1.0000	1.0000	0.9999	0.9997	0.9989	0.9963
	13	1.0000	1.0000	1.0000	1.0000	1.0000	1.0000	1.0000	1.0000	0.9999	0.9995
	14	1.0000	1.0000	1.0000	1.0000	1.0000	1.0000	1.0000	1.0000	1.0000	1.0000
16	0	0.4401	0.1853	0.0743	0.0281	0.0100	0.0033	0.0010	0.0003	0.0001	0.0000
	1	0.8108	0.5147	0.2839	0.1407	0.0635	0.0261	0.0098	0.0033	0.0010	0.0003
	2	0.9571	0.7892	0.5614	0.3518	0.1971	0.0994	0.0451	0.0183	0.0066	0.0021
	3	0.9930	0.9316	0.7899	0.5981	0.4050	0.2459	0.1339	0.0651	0.0281	0.0106
	4	0.9991	0.9830	0.9209	0.7982	0.6302	0.4499	0.2892	0.1666	0.0853	0.0384
	5	0.9999	0.9967	0.9765	0.9183	0.8103	0.6598	0.4900	0.3288	0.1976	0.1051
	6	1.0000	0.9995	0.9944	0.9733	0.9204	0.8247	0.6881	0.5272	0.3660	0.2272
	7	1.0000	0.9999	0.9989	0.9930	0.9729	0.9256	0.8406	0.7161	0.5629	0.4018
	8	1.0000	1.0000	0.9998	0.9985	0.9925	0.9743	0.9329	0.8577	0.7441	0.5982
	9	1.0000	1.0000	1.0000	0.9998	0.9984	0.9929	0.9771	0.9417	0.8759	0.7723
	10	1.0000	1.0000	1.0000	1.0000	0.9997	0.9984	0.9938	0.9809	0.9514	0.8949
	11	1.0000	1.0000	1.0000	1.0000	1.0000	0.9997	0.9987	0.9951	0.9851	0.9616
	12	1.0000	1.0000	1.0000	1.0000	1.0000	1.0000	0.9998	0.9991	0.9965	0.9894
	13	1.0000	1.0000	1.0000	1.0000	1.0000	1.0000	1.0000	0.9999	0.9994	0.9979

Selected values of the binomial cumulative distribution function (continued)

n	c	0.05	0.10	0.15	0.20	p 0.25	0.30	0.35	0.40	0.45	0.50
14		1.0000	1.0000	1.0000	1.0000	1.0000	1.0000	1.0000	1.0000	1.0000	0.9997
15		1.0000	1.0000	1.0000	1.0000	1.0000	1.0000	1.0000	1.0000	1.0000	1.0000
17	0	0.4181	0.1668	0.0631	0.0225	0.0075	0.0023	0.0007	0.0002	0.0000	0.0000
	1	0.7922	0.4818	0.2525	0.1182	0.0501	0.0193	0.0067	0.0021	0.0006	0.0001
	2	0.9497	0.7618	0.5198	0.3096	0.1637	0.0774	0.0327	0.0123	0.0041	0.0012
	3	0.9912	0.9174	0.7556	0.5489	0.3530	0.2019	0.1028	0.0464	0.0184	0.0064
	4	0.9988	0.9779	0.9013	0.7582	0.5739	0.3887	0.2348	0.1260	0.0596	0.0245
	5	0.9999	0.9853	0.9681	0.8943	0.7653	0.5968	0.4197	0.2639	0.1471	0.0717
	6	1.0000	0.9992	0.9917	0.9623	0.8929	0.7752	0.6188	0.4478	0.2902	0.1662
	7	1.0000	0.9999	0.9983	0.9891	0.9598	0.8954	0.7872	0.6405	0.4743	0.3145
	8	1.0000	1.0000	0.9997	0.9974	0.9876	0.9597	0.9006	0.8011	0.6626	0.5000
	9	1.0000	1.0000	1.0000	0.9995	0.9969	0.9873	0.9617	0.9081	0.8166	0.6855
	10	1.0000	1.0000	1.0000	0.9999	0.9994	0.9968	0.9880	0.9652	0.9174	0.8338
	11	1.0000	1.0000	1.0000	1.0000	0.9999	0.9993	0.9970	0.9894	0.9699	0.9283
	12	1.0000	1.0000	1.0000	1.0000	1.0000	0.9999	0.9994	0.9975	0.9914	0.9755
	13	1.0000	1.0000	1.0000	1.0000	1.0000	1.0000	0.9999	0.9995	0.9981	0.9936
	14	1.0000	1.0000	1.0000	1.0000	1.0000	1.0000	1.0000	0.9999	0.9997	0.9988
	15	1.0000	1.0000	1.0000	1.0000	1.0000	1.0000	1.0000	1.0000	1.0000	0.9999
	16	1.0000	1.0000	1.0000	1.0000	1.0000	1.0000	1.0000	1.0000	1.0000	1.0000
18	0	0.3972	0.1501	0.0536	0.0180	0.0056	0.0016	0.0004	0.0001	0.0000	0.0000
	1	0.7735	0.4503	0.2241	0.0991	0.0395	0.0142	0.0046	0.0013	0.0003	0.0001
	2	0.9419	0.7338	0.4797	0.2713	0.1353	0.0600	0.0236	0.0082	0.0025	0.0007
	3	0.9891	0.9018	0.7202	0.5010	0.3057	0.1646	0.0783	0.0328	0.0120	0.0038
	4	0.9985	0.9718	0.8794	0.7164	0.5187	0.3327	0.1886	0.0942	0.0411	0.0154
	5	0.9998	0.9936	0.9581	0.8671	0.7175	0.5344	0.3550	0.2088	0.1077	0.0481
	6	1.0000	0.9988	0.9882	0.9487	0.8610	0.7217	0.5491	0.3743	0.2258	0.1189
	7	1.0000	0.9998	0.9973	0.9837	0.9431	0.8593	0.7283	0.5634	0.3915	0.2403
	8	1.0000	1.0000	0.9995	0.9957	0.9807	0.9404	0.8609	0.7368	0.5778	0.4073
	9	1.0000	1.0000	0.9999	0.9991	0.9946	0.9790	0.9403	0.8653	0.7473	0.5927
	10	1.0000	1.0000	1.0000	0.9998	0.9988	0.9939	0.9788	0.9424	0.8720	0.7597
	11	1.0000	1.0000	1.0000	1.0000	0.9998	0.9986	0.9938	0.9797	0.9463	0.8811
	12	1.0000	1.0000	1.0000	1.0000	1.0000	0.9997	0.9986	0.9942	0.9817	0.9519
	13	1.0000	1.0000	1.0000	1.0000	1.0000	1.0000	0.9997	0.9987	0.9951	0.9846
	14	1.0000	1.0000	1.0000	1.0000	1.0000	1.0000	1.0000	0.9998	0.9990	0.9962
	15	1.0000	1.0000	1.0000	1.0000	1.0000	1.0000	1.0000	1.0000	0.9999	0.9993
	16	1.0000	1.0000	1.0000	1.0000	1.0000	1.0000	1.0000	1.0000	1.0000	0.9999

Selected values of the binomial cumulative distribution function (continued)

n	c	0.05	0.10	0.15	0.20	p 0.25	0.30	0.35	0.40	0.45	0.50
19	0	0.3774	0.1351	0.0456	0.0144	0.0042	0.0011	0.0003	0.0001	0.0000	0.0000
	1	0.7547	0.4203	0.1985	0.0829	0.0310	0.0104	0.0031	0.0008	0.0002	0.0000
	2	0.9335	0.7054	0.4413	0.2369	0.1113	0.0462	0.0170	0.0055	0.0015	0.0004
	3	0.9868	0.8850	0.6841	0.4551	0.2630	0.1332	0.0591	0.0230	0.0077	0.0022
	4	0.9980	0.9648	0.8556	0.6733	0.4654	0.2822	0.1500	0.0696	0.0280	0.0096
	5	0.9998	0.9914	0.9463	0.8369	0.6678	0.4739	0.2968	0.1629	0.0777	0.0318
	6	1.0000	0.9983	0.9837	0.9324	0.8251	0.6655	0.4812	0.3081	0.1727	0.0835
	7	1.0000	0.9997	0.9959	0.9767	0.9225	0.8180	0.6656	0.4878	0.3169	0.1796
	8	1.0000	1.0000	0.9992	0.9933	0.9713	0.9161	0.8145	0.6675	0.4940	0.3238
	9	1.0000	1.0000	0.9999	0.9984	0.9911	0.9674	0.9125	0.8139	0.6710	0.5000
	10	1.0000	1.0000	1.0000	0.9997	0.9977	0.9895	0.9653	0.9115	0.8159	0.6762
	11	1.0000	1.0000	1.0000	1.0000	0.9995	0.9972	0.9886	0.9648	0.9129	0.8204
	12	1.0000	1.0000	1.0000	1.0000	0.9999	0.9994	0.9969	0.9884	0.9658	0.9165
	13	1.0000	1.0000	1.0000	1.0000	1.0000	0.9999	0.9993	0.9969	0.9891	0.9682
	14	1.0000	1.0000	1.0000	1.0000	1.0000	1.0000	0.9999	0.9994	0.9972	0.9904
	15	1.0000	1.0000	1.0000	1.0000	1.0000	1.0000	1.0000	0.9999	0.9995	0.9978
	16	1.0000	1.0000	1.0000	1.0000	1.0000	1.0000	1.0000	1.0000	0.9999	0.9996
	17	1.0000	1.0000	1.0000	1.0000	1.0000	1.0000	1.0000	1.0000	1.0000	1.0000
20	0	0.3585	0.1216	0.0388	0.0115	0.0032	0.0008	0.0002	0.0000	0.0000	0.0000
	1	0.7358	0.3917	0.1756	0.0692	0.0243	0.0076	0.0021	0.0005	0.0001	0.0000
	2	0.9245	0.6769	0.4049	0.2061	0.0913	0.0355	0.0121	0.0036	0.0009	0.0002
	3	0.9841	0.8670	0.6477	0.4114	0.2252	0.1071	0.0444	0.0160	0.0049	0.0013
	4	0.9974	0.9568	0.8298	0.6296	0.4148	0.2375	0.1182	0.0510	0.0189	0.0059
	5	0.9997	0.9887	0.9327	0.8042	0.6172	0.4164	0.2454	0.1256	0.0553	0.0207
	6	1.0000	0.9976	0.9781	0.9133	0.7858	0.6080	0.4166	0.2500	0.1299	0.0577
	7	1.0000	0.9996	0.9941	0.9679	0.8982	0.7723	0.6010	0.4159	0.2520	0.1316
	8	1.0000	0.9999	0.9987	0.9900	0.9591	0.8867	0.7624	0.5956	0.4143	0.2517
	9	1.0000	1.0000	0.9998	0.9974	0.9861	0.9520	0.8782	0.7553	0.5914	0.4119
	10	1.0000	1.0000	1.0000	0.9994	0.9961	0.9829	0.9468	0.8725	0.9507	0.5881
	11	1.0000	1.0000	1.0000	0.9999	0.9991	0.9949	0.9804	0.9435	0.8692	0.7483
	12	1.0000	1.0000	1.0000	1.0000	0.9998	0.9987	0.9940	0.9790	0.9420	0.8684
	13	1.0000	1.0000	1.0000	1.0000	1.0000	0.9997	0.9985	0.9935	0.9786	0.9423
	14	1.0000	1.0000	1.0000	1.0000	1.0000	1.0000	0.9997	0.9984	0.9936	0.9793
	15	1.0000	1.0000	1.0000	1.0000	1.0000	1.0000	1.0000	0.9997	0.9985	0.9941
	16	1.0000	1.0000	1.0000	1.0000	1.0000	1.0000	1.0000	1.0000	0.9997	0.9987
	17	1.0000	1.0000	1.0000	1.0000	1.0000	1.0000	1.0000	1.0000	1.0000	0.9998
	18	1.0000	1.0000	1.0000	1.0000	1.0000	1.0000	1.0000	1.0000	1.0000	1.0000

Appendix E
The Cumulative Poisson Distribution

$$P(r \le r_0 | \mu)$$

μ \ r_0	0	1	2	3	4	5	6	7	8	9	10
0.02	980	1000									
0.04	961	999	1000								
0.06	942	998	1000								
0.08	923	997	1000								
0.10	905	995	1000								
0.15	861	990	999	1000							
0.20	819	982	999	1000							
0.25	779	974	998	1000							
0.30	741	963	996	1000							
0.35	705	951	994	1000							
0.40	670	938	992	999	1000						
0.45	638	925	989	999	1000						
0.50	607	910	986	998	1000						
0.55	577	894	982	998	1000						
0.60	549	878	977	997	1000						
0.65	522	861	972	996	999	1000					
0.70	497	844	966	994	999	1000					
0.75	472	827	959	993	999	1000					
0.80	449	809	953	991	999	1000					
0.85	427	791	945	989	998	1000					
0.90	407	772	937	987	998	1000					
0.95	387	754	929	984	997	1000					
1.00	368	736	920	981	996	999	1000				
1.1	333	699	900	974	995	999	1000				
1.2	301	663	879	966	992	998	1000				
1.3	273	627	857	957	989	998	1000				
1.4	247	592	833	946	986	997	999	1000			
1.5	223	558	809	934	981	996	999	1000			
1.6	202	525	783	921	976	994	999	1000			
1.7	183	493	757	907	970	992	998	1000			
1.8	165	463	731	891	964	990	997	999	1000		
1.9	150	434	704	875	956	987	997	999	1000		
2.0	135	406	677	857	947	983	995	999	1000		
2.2	111	355	623	819	928	975	993	998	1000		
2.4	091	308	570	779	904	964	988	997	999	1000	
2.6	074	267	518	736	877	951	983	995	999	1000	
2.8	061	231	469	692	848	935	976	992	998	999	1000
3.0	050	199	423	647	815	916	966	988	996	999	1000

The cumulative Poisson distribution (continued)

r_0 / μ	0	1	2	3	4	5	6	7	8	9	10	11	12	13
3.2	041	171	380	603	781	895	955	983	994	998	1000			
3.4	033	147	340	558	744	871	942	977	992	997	999	1000		
3.6	027	126	303	515	706	844	927	969	988	996	999	1000		
3.8	022	107	269	473	668	816	909	960	984	994	998	999	1000	
4.0	018	092	238	433	629	785	889	949	979	992	997	999	1000	
4.2	015	078	210	395	590	753	867	936	972	989	996	999	1000	
4.4	012	066	185	359	551	720	844	921	964	985	994	998	999	1000
4.6	010	056	163	326	513	686	818	905	955	980	992	997	999	1000
4.8	008	048	143	294	476	651	791	887	944	975	990	996	999	1000
5.0	007	040	125	265	440	616	762	867	932	968	986	995	998	999
5.2	006	034	109	238	406	581	732	845	918	960	982	993	997	999
5.4	005	029	095	213	373	546	702	822	903	951	977	990	996	999
5.6	004	024	082	191	342	512	670	797	886	941	972	988	995	998
5.8	003	021	072	170	313	478	638	771	867	929	965	984	993	997
6.0	002	017	062	151	285	446	606	744	847	916	957	980	991	996
6.2	002	015	054	134	259	414	574	716	826	902	949	975	989	995
6.4	002	012	046	119	235	384	542	687	803	836	939	969	986	994
6.6	001	010	040	105	213	355	511	658	780	869	927	963	982	992
6.8	001	009	034	093	192	327	480	628	755	850	915	955	978	990
7.0	001	007	030	082	173	301	450	599	729	830	901	947	973	987
7.2	001	006	025	072	156	276	420	569	703	810	887	937	967	984
7.4	001	005	022	063	140	253	392	539	676	788	871	926	961	980
7.6	001	004	019	055	125	231	365	510	648	765	854	915	954	976
7.8	000	004	016	048	112	210	338	481	620	741	835	902	945	971
8.0	000	003	014	042	100	191	313	453	593	717	816	888	936	966
8.5	000	002	009	030	074	150	256	386	523	653	763	849	909	949
9.0	000	001	006	021	.055	116	207	324	456	587	706	803	876	926
9.5	000	001	004	015	040	089	165	269	392	522	645	752	836	898
10.0	000	000	003	010	029	067	130	220	333	458	583	697	792	864
10.5	000	000	002	007	021	050	102	179	279	397	521	639	742	825
11.0	000	000	001	005	015	038	079	143	232	341	460	579	689	781
11.5	000	000	001	003	011	028	060	114	191	289	402	520	633	733
12.0	000	000	001	002	008	020	046	090	155	242	347	462	576	682
12.5	000	000	000	002	005	015	035	070	125	201	297	406	519	628
13.0	000	000	000	001	004	011	026	054	100	166	252	353	463	573
13.5	000	000	000	001	003	008	019	041	079	135	211	304	409	518
14.0	000	000	000	000	002	006	014	032	062	109	176	260	358	464
14.5	000	000	000	000	001	004	010	024	048	088	145	220	311	413
15.0	000	000	000	000	001	003	008	018	037	070	118	185	268	363

The cumulative Poisson distribution (continued)

14	15	16	17	18	19	20	21	22	23	24	25	26	27	28	29
1000															
1000															
1000															
999															
999	1000														
999	1000	1000													
998	999	1000													
997	999	1000													
997	999	999	1000												
996	998	999	1000												
994	998	999	1000												
993	997	999	999	1000											
991	996	998	999	1000											
989	995	998	999	1000											
986	993	997	999	1000											
983	992	996	998	999	1000										
973	986	993	997	999	999	1000									
959	978	989	995	998	999	1000									
940	967	982	991	996	998	999	1000								
917	951	973	986	993	997	998	999	1000							
888	932	960	978	988	994	997	999	999	1000						
854	907	944	968	982	991	995	998	999	1000						
815	878	924	954	974	986	992	996	998	999	1000					
772	844	899	937	963	979	988	994	997	999	999	1000				
725	806	869	916	948	969	983	991	995	998	999	999	1000			
675	764	835	890	930	957	975	986	992	996	998	999	1000			
623	718	798	861	908	942	965	980	989	994	997	998	999	1000		
570	669	756	827	883	923	952	971	983	991	995	997	999	999	1000	
518	619	711	790	853	901	936	960	976	986	992	996	998	999	999	1000
466	568	664	749	819	875	917	947	967	981	989	994	997	998	999	1000

Appendix F
The Chi-Square Distribution

Degrees of freedom	Level of significance								Degrees of freedom
	$\chi^2_{.995}$	$\chi^2_{.99}$	$\chi^2_{.975}$	$\chi^2_{.95}$	$\chi^2_{.05}$	$\chi^2_{.025}$	$\chi^2_{.01}$	$\chi^2_{.005}$	
1	.0000393	.000157	.000982	.00393	3.841	5.024	6.635	7.879	1
2	.0100	.0201	.0506	.103	5.991	7.378	9.210	10.597	2
3	.0717	.115	.216	.352	7.815	9.348	11.345	12.838	3
4	.207	.297	.484	.711	9.488	11.143	13.277	14.860	4
5	.412	.554	.831	1.145	11.070	12.832	15.086	16.750	5
6	.676	.872	1.237	1.635	12.592	14.449	16.812	18.548	6
7	.989	1.239	1.690	2.167	14.067	16.013	18.475	20.278	7
8	1.344	1.646	2.180	2.733	15.507	17.535	20.090	21.955	8
9	1.735	2.088	2.700	3.325	16.919	19.023	21.666	23.589	9
10	2.156	2.558	3.247	3.940	18.307	20.483	23.209	25.188	10
11	2.603	3.053	3.816	4.575	19.675	21.920	24.725	26.757	11
12	3.074	3.571	4.404	5.226	21.026	23.337	26.217	28.300	12
13	3.565	4.107	5.009	5.892	22.362	24.736	27.688	29.819	13
14	4.075	4.660	5.629	6.571	23.685	26.119	29.141	31.319	14
15	4.601	5.229	6.262	7.261	24.996	27.488	30.578	32.801	15
16	5.142	5.812	6.908	7.962	26.296	28.845	32.000	34.267	16
17	5.697	6.408	7.564	8.672	27.587	30.191	33.409	35.718	17
18	6.265	7.015	8.231	9.390	28.869	31.526	34.805	37.156	18
19	6.844	7.633	8.907	10.117	30.144	32.852	36.191	38.582	19
20	7.434	8.260	9.591	10.851	31.410	34.170	37.566	39.997	20
21	8.034	8.897	10.283	11.591	32.671	35.479	38.932	41.401	21
22	8.643	9.542	10.982	12.338	33.924	36.781	40.289	42.796	22
23	9.260	10.196	11.689	13.091	35.172	38.076	41.638	44.181	23
24	9.886	10.856	12.401	13.848	36.415	39.364	42.980	45.558	24
25	10.520	11.524	13.120	14.611	37.652	40.646	44.314	46.928	25
26	11.160	12.198	13.844	15.379	38.885	41.923	45.642	48.290	26
27	11.808	12.879	14.573	16.151	40.113	43.194	46.963	49.645	27
28	12.461	13.565	15.308	16.928	41.337	44.461	48.278	50.993	28
29	13.121	14.256	16.047	17.708	42.557	45.722	49.588	52.336	29
30	13.787	14.953	16.791	18.493	43.773	46.979	50.892	53.672	30

Appendix G
One-Tailed Table of Critical Values for the Kolmogorov-Smirnov Test

Values of $d_\alpha(N)$ such that $Pr[\max|S_N(x) - F_0(x)| > d_\alpha(N)] = \alpha$, where $F_0(x)$ is the theoretical cumulative distribution and $S_N(x)$ is an observed cumulative distribution for a sample of N.

Sample size (N)	Level of significance (α)				
	0.20	0.15	0.10	0.05	0.01
1	0.900	0.925	0.950	0.975	0.995
2	0.684	0.726	0.776	0.842	0.929
3	0.565	0.597	0.642	0.708	0.828
4	0.494	0.525	0.564	0.624	0.733
5	0.446	0.474	0.510	0.565	0.669
6	0.410	0.436	0.470	0.521	0.618
7	0.381	0.405	0.438	0.486	0.577
8	0.358	0.381	0.411	0.457	0.543
9	0.339	0.360	0.388	0.432	0.514
10	0.322	0.342	0.368	0.410	0.490
11	0.307	0.326	0.352	0.391	0.468
12	0.295	0.313	0.338	0.375	0.450
13	0.284	0.302	0.325	0.361	0.433
14	0.274	0.292	0.314	0.349	0.418
15	0.266	0.283	0.304	0.338	0.404
16	0.258	0.274	0.295	0.328	0.392
17	0.250	0.266	0.286	0.318	0.381
18	0.244	0.259	0.278	0.309	0.371
19	0.237	0.252	0.272	0.301	0.363
20	0.231	0.246	0.264	0.294	0.356
25	0.21	0.22	0.24	0.27	0.32
30	0.19	0.20	0.22	0.24	0.29
35	0.18	0.19	0.21	0.23	0.27
over 35	$\dfrac{1.07}{\sqrt{N}}$	$\dfrac{1.14}{\sqrt{N}}$	$\dfrac{1.22}{\sqrt{N}}$	$\dfrac{1.35}{\sqrt{N}}$	$\dfrac{1.63}{\sqrt{N}}$

Appendix H
Multiserver Poisson-Exponential Queuing System: Probability That the System Is Idle, p_0

$\dfrac{\lambda}{s\mu}$	Number of channels, s								
	2	3	4	5	6	7	8	10	15
.02	.9608	.9418	.9231	.9048	.8869	.8694	.85214	.81873	.74082
.04	.9231	.8869	.8521	.8187	.7866	.7558	.72615	.67032	.54881
.06	.8868	.8353	.7866	.7408	.6977	.6570	.61878	.54881	.40657
.08	.8519	.7866	.7261	.6703	.6188	.5712	.52729	.44933	.30119
.10	.8182	.7407	.6703	.6065	.5488	.4966	.44933	.36788	.22313
.12	.7857	.6975	.6188	.5488	.4868	.4317	.38289	.30119	.16530
.14	.7544	.6568	.5712	.4966	.4317	.3753	.32628	.24660	.12246
.16	.7241	.6184	.5272	.4493	.3829	.3263	.27804	.20190	.09072
.18	.6949	.5821	.4866	.4065	.3396	.2837	.23693	.16530	.06721
.20	.6667	.5479	.4491	.3678	.3012	.2466	.20189	.13534	.04979

Multiserver Poisson-exponential queuing system (continued)

$\dfrac{\lambda}{s\mu}$	Number of channels, s									
	2	3	4	5	6	7	8	10	15
.22	.6393	.5157	.4145	.3328	.2671	.2144	.17204	.11080	.03688
.24	.6129	.4852	.3824	.3011	.2369	.1864	.14660	.09072	.02732
.26	.5873	.4564	.3528	.2723	.2101	.1620	.12492	.07427	.02024
.28	.5625	.4292	.3255	.2463	.1863	.1408	.10645	.06081	.01500
.30	.5385	.4035	.3002	.2228	.1652	.1224	.09070	.04978	.01111
.32	.5152	.3791	.2768	.2014	.1464	.1064	.07728	.04076	.00823
.34	.4925	.3561	.2551	.1821	.1298	.0925	.06584	.03337	.00610
.36	.4706	.3343	.2351	.1646	.1151	.0804	.05609	.02732	.00452
.38	.4493	.3137	.2165	.1487	.1020	.0698	.04778	.02236	.00335
.40	.4286	.2941	.1993	.1343	.0903	.0606	.04069	.01830	.00248
.42	.4085	.2756	.1834	.1213	.0800	.0527	.03465	.01498	.00184
.44	.3889	.2580	.1686	.1094	.0708	.0457	.02950	.01226	.00136
.46	.3699	.2414	.1549	.0987	.0626	.0397	.02511	.01003	.00101
.48	.3514	.2255	.1422	.0889	.0554	.0344	.02136	.00820	.00075
.50	.3333	.2105	.1304	.0801	.049	.0298	.01816	.00671	.00055
.52	.3158	.1963	.1195	.0721	.0432	.0259	.01544	.00548	.00041
.54	.2987	.1827	.1094	.0648	.0831	.0224	.01311	.00448	.00030
.56	.2821	.1699	.0999	.0581	.0336	.0194	.01113	.00366	.00022
.58	.2658	.1576	.0912	.0521	.0296	.0167	.00943	.00298	.00017
.60	.2500	.1460	.0831	.0466	.0260	.0144	.00799	.00243	.00012
.62	.2346	.1349	.0755	.0417	.0228	.0124	.00675	.00198	.00009
.64	.2195	.1244	.0685	.0372	.0200	.0107	.00570	.00161	.00007
.66	.2048	.1143	.0619	.0330	.0175	.0092	.00480	.00131	.00005
.68	.1905	.1048	.0559	.0293	.0152	.0079	.00404	.00106	.00004
.70	.1765	.0957	.0502	.0259	.0132	.0067	.00338	.00085	.00003
.72	.1628	.0870	.0450	.0228	.0114	.0057	.00283	.00069	.00002
.74	.1494	.0788	.0401	.0200	.0099	.0048	.00235	.00055	.00001
.76	.1364	.0709	.0355	.0174	.0085	.0041	.00195	.00044	
.78	.1236	.0634	.0313	.0151	.0072	.0034	.00160	.00035	
.80	.1111	.0562	.0273	.013	.0061	.0028	.00131	.00028	
.82	.0989	.0493	.0236	.0111	.0051	.0023	.00106	.00022	
.84	.0870	.0428	.0202	.0093	.0042	.0019	.00085	.00017	
.86	.0753	.0366	.0170	.0077	.0035	.0015	.00067	.00013	
.88	.0638	.0306	.0140	.0063	.0028	.0012	.00052	.00010	
.90	.0526	.0249	.0113	.0050	.0021	.0009	.00039	.00007	
.92	.0417	.0195	.0087	.0038	.0016	.0007	.00028	.00005	
.94	.0309	.0143	.0063	.0027	.0011	.0005	.00019	.00003	
.96	.0204	.0093	.0040	.0017	.0007	.0003	.00012	.00002	
.98	.0101	.0045	.0019	.0008	.0003	.0001	.00005	.00001	

Appendix I
Random Numbers

04433	80674	24520	18222	10610	05794	37515
60298	47829	72648	37414	75755	04717	29899
67884	59651	67533	68123	17730	95862	08034
89512	32155	51906	61662	64130	16688	37275
32653	01895	12506	88535	36553	23757	34209
95913	15405	13772	76638	48423	25018	99041
55864	21694	13122	44115	01601	50541	00147
35334	49810	91601	40617	72876	33967	73830
57729	32196	76487	11622	96297	24160	09903
86648	13697	63677	70119	94739	25875	38829
30574	47609	07967	32422	76791	39725	53711
81307	43694	83580	79974	45929	85113	72268
02410	54905	79007	54939	21410	86980	91772
18969	75274	52233	62319	08598	09066	95288
87863	82384	66860	62297	80198	19347	73234
68397	71708	15438	62311	72844	60203	46412
28529	54447	58729	10854	99058	18260	38765
44285	06372	15867	70418	57012	72122	36634
86299	83430	33571	23309	57040	29285	67870
84842	68668	90894	61658	15001	94055	36308
56970	83609	52098	04184	54967	72938	56834
83125	71257	60490	44369	66130	72936	69848
55503	52423	02464	26141	68779	66388	75242
47019	76273	33203	29608	54553	25971	69573
84828	32592	79526	29554	84580	37859	28504

Random numbers (continued)

68921	08141	79227	05748	51276	57143	31926
36458	96045	30424	98420	72925	40729	22337
95752	59445	36847	87729	81679	59126	59437
26768	47323	58454	56958	20575	76746	49878
42613	37056	43636	58085	06766	60227	96414
95457	30566	65482	25596	02678	54592	63607
95276	17894	63564	95958	39750	64379	46059
66954	52324	64776	92345	95110	59448	77249
17457	18481	14113	62462	02798	54977	48349
03704	36872	83214	59337	01695	60666	97410
21538	86497	33210	60337	27976	70661	08250
57178	67619	98310	70348	11317	71623	55510
31048	97558	94953	55866	96283	46620	52087
69799	55380	16498	80733	96422	58078	99643
90595	61867	59231	17772	67831	33317	00520
33570	04981	98939	78784	09977	29398	93896
15340	93460	57477	13898	48431	72936	78160
64079	42483	36512	56186	99098	48850	72527
63491	05546	67118	62063	74958	20946	28147
92003	63868	41034	28260	79708	00770	88643
52360	46658	66511	04172	73085	11795	52594
74622	12142	68355	65635	21828	39539	18988
04157	50079	61343	64315	70836	82857	35335
86003	60070	66241	32836	27573	11479	94114
41268	80187	20351	09636	84668	42486	71303
48612	62866	83963	14045	79451	04934	45576
78812	03509	78673	73181	29973	18664	04555
19472	63971	37271	31445	49019	49405	46925
51266	11569	08697	91120	64156	40365	74297
55806	96275	26130	47949	14877	69594	83041
77527	81360	18180	97421	55541	90275	18213
77680	58788	33016	61173	93049	04694	43534
15404	96554	88265	34537	38526	67924	40474
14045	22917	60718	66487	46346	30949	03173
68376	43918	77653	04127	69930	43283	35766
93385	13421	67957	20384	58731	53396	59723
09858	52104	32014	53115	03727	98624	84616
93307	34116	49516	42148	57740	31198	70336
04794	01534	92058	03157	91758	80611	45357
86265	49096	97021	92582	61422	75890	86442

Random numbers (continued)

65943	79232	45702	67055	39024	57383	44424
90038	94209	04055	27393	61517	23002	96560
97283	95943	78363	36498	40662	94188	18202
21913	72958	75637	99936	58715	07943	23748
41161	37341	81838	19389	80336	46346	91895
23777	98392	31417	98547	92058	02277	50315
59973	08144	61070	73094	27059	69181	55623
82690	74099	77885	23813	10054	11900	44653
83854	24715	48866	65745	31131	47636	45137
61980	34997	41825	11623	07320	15003	56774
99915	45821	97702	87125	44488	77613	56823
48293	86847	43186	42951	37804	85129	28993
33225	31280	41232	34750	91097	60752	69783
06846	32828	24425	30249	78801	26977	92074
32671	45587	79620	84831	38156	74211	82752
82096	21913	75544	55228	89796	05694	91552
51666	10433	10945	55306	78562	89630	41230
54044	67942	24145	42294	27427	84875	37022
66738	60184	75679	38120	17640	36242	99357
55064	17427	89180	74018	44865	53197	74810
69599	60264	84549	78007	88450	06488	72274
64756	87759	92354	78694	63638	80939	98644
80817	74533	68407	55862	32476	19326	95558
39847	96884	84657	33697	39578	90197	80532
90401	41700	95510	61166	33757	23279	85523
78227	90110	81378	96659	37008	04050	04228
87240	52716	87697	79433	16336	52862	69149
08486	10951	26832	39763	02485	71688	90936
39338	32169	03713	93510	61244	73774	01245
21188	01850	69689	49426	49128	14660	14143
13287	82531	04388	64693	11934	35051	68576
53609	04001	19648	14053	49623	10840	31915
87900	36194	31567	53506	34304	39910	79630
81641	00496	36058	75899	46620	70024	88753
19512	50277	71508	20116	79520	06269	74173

Appendix J
Answers to Selected Problems

Chapter 1

1. $y = 8.14 + .66(40,000) - .17(250) = 26,365.64$

3. Maximize $\quad 60x_1 + 40x_2 + 10x_3 + 20x_4 + 10x_5 + 3x_6$

   s.t. $\qquad 50x_1 + 4x_2 + .01x_3 + 4x_4 + 3x_5 + .5x_6 \leq 10$

   $$x_i = 0 \text{ or } 1 \text{ for } i = 1, 2, \ldots, 6$$

   The optimal solution is to take tent, food, matches, and snake bite kit for a value of 113.

5. One systemic procedure to use is to calculate the expected profit for stock decision.

   $E(50) = 1.0(50)(.08) = \$4.$

   $E(75) = .90(75)(.08) + .10[50(.08) - 25(.12)] = \$5.50$

   $E(100) = .40(100)(.08) + .40[75(.08) - 25(.12)]$
   $\qquad\qquad + .10[50(.08) - 50(.12)] = \$4.20$

   $E(125) = .15(125)(.08) + .35[100(.08) - 25(.12)]$
   $\qquad\qquad + .40[75(.08) - 50(.12)] + .10[50(.08) - 75(.12)] = \$2.75$

   Using expected value as the decision criterion, we should stock 75 newspapers.

10. Let x = the location of the bin in feet from 0

$$\text{Min} \quad (x - 5)^2 + (13 - x)^2 + (22 - x)^2$$

Using calculus,

$$2(x - 5) - 2(13 - x) - 2(22 - x) = 0$$
$$6x = 80 \quad \text{or} \quad x = 13.33$$

Chapter 2

2. x_1 = lbs. mix 1

x_2 = lbs. mix 2

Obj.: Max $\$1.065x_1 + \$1.265x_2$

s.t.

$$.5x_1 + .6x_2 \leq 30,000$$
$$.5x_1 + .25x_2 \leq 12,000$$
$$.15x_2 \leq 9,000$$
$$x_1, x_2 \geq 0$$

4. x_1 = amount invested in bonds

x_2 = amount invested in stock

x_3 = amount invested in gold

x_4 = amount invested in real estate

Obj.: Max $.085x_1 + .09x_2 + .10x_3 + .13x_4$

s.t.

$$x_1 + x_2 + x_3 + x_4 = 5,000,000$$
$$x_1 + x_2 \geq 2,000,000$$
$$x_4 \leq 1,000,000$$
$$x_1 \leq 3,000,000$$
$$x_2 \leq 3,000,000$$
$$x_3 \leq 2,000,000$$
$$x_4 \leq 1,000,000$$
$$x_i \geq 0 \text{ all } i$$

9. x_1 = units of T.V. adv.

x_2 = units of Mag. 1 adv.

x_3 = units of Mag. 2 adv.

Obj.: Max $(1.8(1,000,000) + (1,000,000)x_1 + (1.8(750,000)$
$+ 250,000)x_2' + (1.8(400,000) + 200,000)x_3$

s.t. $35,000x_1 + 25,000x_2 + 15,000x_3 \leq 250,000$ Budget

$$x_1, x_2, x_3 \geq 0$$

16. x_1 = no. of small stores leased

x_2 = no. of medium stores leased

x_3 = no. of large stores leased

Obj.: Max $\quad 20{,}000x_1 + 170{,}000x_2 + 265{,}000x_3$

s.t. $\qquad\qquad 2500x_1 + 100{,}000x_2 + 250{,}000x_3 \leq 1{,}000{,}000$

$$x_3 \geq 1$$

$$x_2 - \qquad 3x_3 = 0$$

$$2500x_1 - 150{,}000x_2 - 375{,}000x_3 = 0$$

$$x_i \geq 0 \text{ all } i$$

Chapter 3

4.

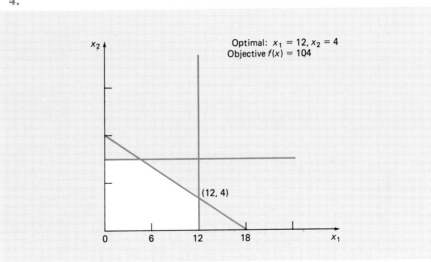

Optimal: $x_1 = 12$, $x_2 = 4$

Objective $f(x) = 104$

(12, 4)

6.

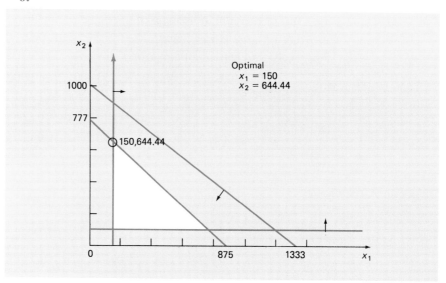

10. $x_1 = 0$, $x_2 = 250$, profit $= \$1750$

14. a.

Point	x_1	x_2
A	1	−2
B	0	2
C	2	2
D	3	2
E	1	0
F	4	0

    b. Feasible points include C, D, E, and F
    c. $C - 14$, $D - 17$, $F - 12$
    d. D is the optimal point with $x_1 = 3$, $x_2 = 2$

18. No feasible solution

23. a. $x_1 = 162$, $x_2 = 0$ profit $= \$56,700$
    b. $x_1 = 105$, $x_2 = 28.5$ profit $= \$35,200$
    c. $x_1 = 130$, $x_2 = 16$ profit $= \$34,000$

25. $x_1 = 10$, $x_2 = 0$, Cost $= 80$

29. a. The second and third constraints are binding.
    b. The slack in the first constraint is 36.67; zero slack in last two constraints
    c. No, the solution stays the same, however, the associated profit is lowered to $\$48,666$

32. a. $y_1 = 0$, $y_2 = 25$, obj fun $= 900$
  b. They are the same
  c. Resource 2

Chapter 4

1.

c_j		6	8	0	0	0	
c_B	Basic	x_1	x_2	S_1	S_2	S_3	Sol.
0	S_1	①	0	1	0	0	12
0	S_2	0	1	0	1	0	10
0	S_3	2	3	0	0	1	36
	z_j	0	0	0	0	0	0
	$c_j - z_j$	6	8	0	0	0	

c_j		6	8	0	0	0	
c_B	Basic	x_1	x_2	S_1	S_2	S_3	Sol.
6	x_1	1	0	1	0	0	12
0	S_2	0	1	0	1	0	10
0	S_3	0	③	−2	0	1	12
	z_j	6	0	6	0	0	72
	$c_j - z_j$	0	8	−6	0	0	

c_j		6	8	0	0	0	
c_B	Basic	x_1	x_2	S_1	S_2	S_3	Sol.
6	x_1	1	0	1	0	0	12
0	S_2	0	0	2/3	1	−1/3	6
8	x_2	0	1	−2/3	0	1/3	4
	z_j	6	8	2/3	0	8/3	104
	$c_j - z_j$	0	0	−2/3	0	−8/3	

4. $x_1 = 4$, $x_2 = 6$, $s_3 = 2$, obj fun $= 42$

7.

	c_j	1.065	1.265	0	0	0	
c_B	Basic	x_1	x_2	S_1	S_2	S_3	Sol.
0	S_1	.5	.6	1	0	0	30000
0	S_2	.5	.25	0	1	0	12000
0	S_3	0	.15	0	0	1	9000
	z_j	0	0	0	0	0	0
	$c_j - z_j$	1.065	1.265	0	0	0	

	c_j	1.065	1.265	0	0	0	
c_B	Basic	x_1	x_2	S_1	S_2	S_3	Sol.
0	S_1	−.7	0	1	−2.4	0	1200
1.265	x_2	2	1	0	4	0	48000
0	S_3	−.3	0	0	−.6	1	1800
	z_j	2.53	1.265	0	5.06	0	60270
	$c_j - z_j$	−1.465	0	0	−5.06	0	

10. $y_1 = 0$, $y_2 = 62.5$, $y_3 = 250$, obj fun = 35,250

15. a. one

b. $x_1 = 7/4$, obj. fun. = 35/4

22. The computer solution is $x_2 = 30$, $x_3 = 12.5$, $x_4 = 25$, $x_7 = 15$ with a waste measurement of 990 units.

27. $x_1 = 2330$, $x_2 = 300$, $x_3 = 0$, obj fun = 30,100

Chapter 5

1. Min: $52y_1 + 40y_2$

s.t. $3y_1 + 14y_2 \geq 16$

  $-4y_1 + 7y_2 \geq 10$

  $8y_1 + 4y_2 \geq 9$

  $y_1, y_2 \geq 0$

3. The dual, it has fewer constraints

6. $x_1 = 0$, $x_2 = 2$, Max value = 16; $y_1 = 2$, Min value = 16

9. a. $(-\infty, \frac{3}{2}]$ for S_1, $(-\infty, 2]$ for S_3

b. [0.4] for x_1, $[-\frac{1}{5}, \frac{1}{2}]$ for S_2, $[6, \infty)$ for x_2

c. greater than $7

11. a. resources 1 and 2

b. Either resource 1 or 2; both shadow prices are $1

    c. Resource 1 could be increased by 12, Resource 2 could be increased by 2, no limit on Resource 3

15. **a.** .74 gals. milk, .639 lbs. spinach per day, $1.39, no.
    b. vitamins C and D exactly, A and iron are overdoses
    c. $[29.36, \infty]$ **d.** $c_1[.156, \infty), c_2[0, \infty), c_3[0, \infty), c_4[0, 2.9]$

18. Constraints 2 and 3 are tight. Shadow price 1 is zero.

20. **a.** RHS 1 $[0,9]$ RHS 2 $[12, \infty)$ **b.** $y_1 = 1, y_2 = 1$
    c. Cost range for $S_1(-\infty, 3]$ Cost range for $x_1[0,6]$
    Cost range for $x_2[3\frac{1}{2}, \infty)$

Chapter 6

2. Two solutions are possible: Min cost is 304. One solution is $x_{11} = 11$, $x_{13} = 7, x_{14} = 2, x_{23} = 10, x_{32} = 13, x_{34} = 12$

4.

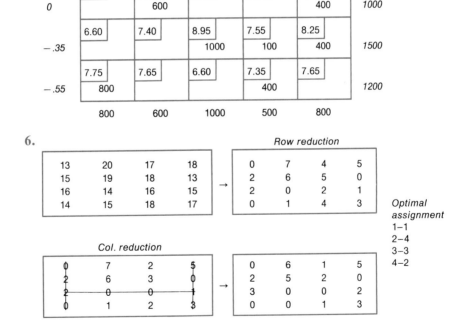

12. Total cost with two factories is $32,000 (transportation cost is $12,000); total cost with three factories is $35,750 (Transportation cost is $14,750).

14. Let **W** represent the warehouse and **D** the dummy node. The constraints are:

$$X_{11} + X_{12} + X_{1W} + W_{13} + X_{14} = 100$$
$$X_{21} + X_{22} + X_{2W} + X_{23} + X_{24} = 150$$
$$X_{31} + X_{32} + X_{3W} + X_{33} + X_{34} = 120$$
$$-X_{1W} - X_{2W} - X_{3W} + X_{WD} = 0$$
$$-X_{WD} + X_{D1} + X_{D2} + X_{D3} + X_{D4} = 0$$
$$-X_{11} - X_{21} - X_{31} - X_{D1} = -80$$
$$-X_{12} - X_{22} - X_{32} - X_{D2} = -100$$
$$-X_{13} - X_{23} - X_{33} - X_{D3} = -90$$
$$-X_{14} - X_{24} - X_{34} - X_{D4} = -100$$
$$0 \le X_{WD} \le 90$$
$$0 \le X_{ij} \le 80 \quad \text{all other i and j}$$

S6.1 VAM solution in 6.2 is optimal

S6.5 $x_{15} = 5$, $x_{27} = 7$, $x_{36} = 4$, $x_{47} = 2$

S6.6 1, 5, 2, 3, 4, 1

S6.7 1–x, 2–y, 3–Z

S6.9 1–5, 2–2, 3–1, 4–3, 5–4, Min cost = $155,000. If more than one contract can be awarded to a bidder then 2–1, 2–2, 1–3, 5–4, 1–5, Min cost = $141,000

Chapter 7

1.

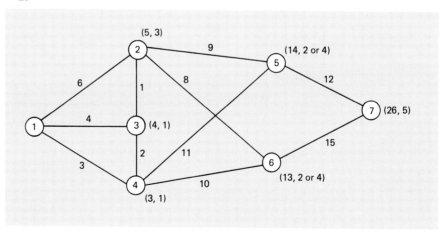

2. Arcs in tree are 1,4, 4,3, 3,2, 2,5, 2,6, 5,7 Length = 35

3.

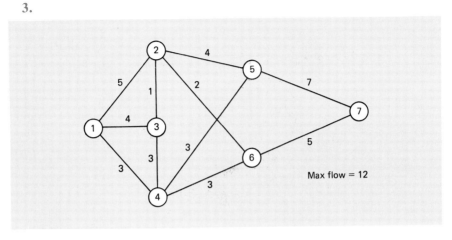

Max flow = 12

6. Max flow = 7,000 vehicles per hour

$$1\ 3\ 4\ 5\ 7 \quad \text{flow} = 3$$
$$1\ 2\ 4\ 6\ 7 \quad \text{flow} = 2$$
$$1\ 3\ 6\ 7 \quad \quad \text{flow} = 2$$

9. Yes, shortest route is now 1–5–7

13. Max shipment is 31,000 barrels.

Chapter 8

3. b.

Task	ES	EF	LS	LF	Slack
A	0	5	1	6	1
B	0	4	0	4	0
C	5	8	6	9	1
D	4	11	4	11	0
E	8	10	9	11	1
F	11	12	11	12	0

Critical path is B–D–F

c. 12 days

d. No, the critical path would remain B–D–F. The length of the project would increase by 4 days.

e.

Time	Activities eligible to start	Slack	Start	Finish
0	A	1	—	—
	B	0	0	4
4	A	0	4	9
	D	3	—	—
9	C	2	9	12
	D	0	9	16
12	E	2	12	14
16	F	0	16	17

5. b.

Activity	$\bar{t}$	σ^2	ES	EF	LS	LF	Slack
A	4.833	.25	0	4.833	0	4.833	0
B	4.333	.444	4.833	9.167	5.167	9.500	.333
C	3.000	.444	4.833	7.833	4.833	7.833	0
D	4.167	.694	9.167	13.333	9.500	13.667	.333
E	5.000	1.000	7.833	12.833	7.833	12.833	0
F	2.167	.250	13.333	15.5	13.667	15.833	.333
G	3.000	.111	12.833	15.833	12.833	15.833	0

c. A–C–E–G   **d.** 15.833   **e.** .267   **f.** 0.93   **g.** 19 weeks

9. a. 15 weeks   **b.** $1275   **3.** $600

Chapter 9

3.

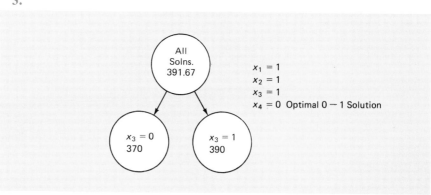

4. a. 0–1 integer   **b.** mixed integer   **c.** linear   **d.** pure integer

7. $x_1 = 4,\ x_2 = 2$

8. 63

9. a.

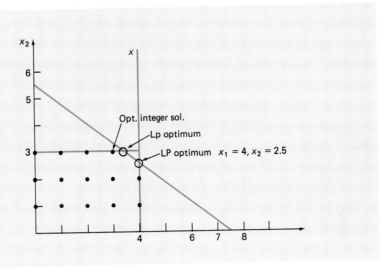

b. LP optimum is $x_1 = 4$, $x_2 = 2.5$ Alternative optimum is $x_1 = 3.33$, $x_2 = 3$.

c. Upper bound is given by LP solution value or 22, lower bound is provided by any feasible integer solution such as $x_1 = 4$, $x_2 = 2$, or 20.

d. By inspection, the optimal integer solution is $x_1 = 3$, $x_2 = 3$, value = 21

12. Let x_1 = no. of mag. ads
   x_2 = no. of T.V. ads

Min $P_1 d_1^+ + P_2 d_2^- + P_3 d_3^- + P_4 d_4^-$

s.t. $12,000 x_1 + 20,000 x_2 + d_1^- - d_1^+ = 500,000$

$350,000 x_1 + 1400000 x_2 + d_2^- - d_2^+ = 35,000,000$

or some large number

$x_2 + d_3^- - d_3^+ = 10$

$+ d_4^- - d_4^+ = 8$

$x_i, d_i^-, d_i^+ \geq 0$

Chapter 10

3. There are 4 stages; each project is a stage
   Let x_i = no. of foremen assigned to project i
      s = no. of foremen still available for allocation
   $f_i(S, x_i) = t(x_i) + f_{i-1}(S - x_i)$ where $t(x_i)$ = time for project i given x_i foremen.

Stage 1: Min $f_1(S,x_1) = t(x_1)$ for project A

S	$f_1^*(S,x_1)$	x_1^*
1	5	1
2	3	2
3	2	3

Stage 2: Min $f_2(S,x_2) = t(x_2) + f_1(S - x_2)$

S	$x_2 = 1$	$f_2(S,x_2)$ $x_2 = 2$	$x_2 = 3$	$f_2^*(S,x_2)$	x_2^*
2	12	—	—	12	1
3	10	10	—	10	1 or 2
4	9	8	8	8	2 or 3

Stage 3: Min $f_3(S,x_3) = t(x_3) + f_2(S - x_3)$

S	$x_3 = 1$	$x_3 = 2$	$x_3 = 3$	$f_3^*(S,x_3)$	x_3^*
3	21	—	—	21	1
4	19	20	—	19	1
5	17	18	19	17	1

Stage 4: Min $f_4(S,x_4) = t(x_4) + f_3(S - x_4)$

S	$x_4 = 1$	$x_4 = 2$	$x_4 = 3$	$f_4^*(S,x_4)$	x_4^*
6	28	27	29	27	2

Optimal allocation 1–A, 2–B, 1–C, 2–D, or 2–A, 1–B, 1–C, 2–D.

6. The optimal purchase and storage strategy is to buy all 10 kits.

8. a. There are 6 stages, x_i = no. of items of type i loaded
There are 2 state variables,
$$S_1 = \text{volume capacity remaining}$$
$$S_2 = \text{weight capacity remaining}$$
recursive relationship
$$\text{Max } f_i(S_1, S_2, x_i) = \max P_i x_i + f_{i-1}(S_1 - w_i x_i, \, S_2 - V_i x_i)$$
where $P_i x_i$ represents the profit of x_i units of type i.

b. There are many standard IP computer codes that could easily be used to solve the cargo loading problem. There is no such thing as a standard dynamic programming software package. Also, there are two state variables that would make the combinations of possible states rather large. Integer programming appears to be the more desirable approach.

10. Optimal decision is to purchase at end of year 0 and keep until end of year 4 or to purchase at end of year 0 and year 1 and keep until end of year 4.

13. The optimal strategy is to allocate $300,000 for direct mailing, and $100,000 to T.V. and magazine ads. Nothing is to be spent on radio advertising.

Chapter 11

1. a. $(\frac{1}{2})(\frac{1}{2})(\frac{1}{2})(\frac{1}{2}) = \frac{1}{16}$ b. $(\frac{1}{2})^4 = \frac{1}{16}$ c. $\frac{1}{2}$

3. $\frac{1}{2}$

6. a. $\frac{210}{390} = .5385$ b. $\frac{60}{390} = .1538$

    c. $.60$ d. $\frac{50}{210} = .2381$

9. a. $(.8)(.1) = .08$ b. $(.2)(.1) = .02$

13. a. $.1204$ b. $.8541$ c. less than $.0001$

19. $.90(.50) + .10(.80) = .53$

22. Binomial $p = .1$ $n = 10$
    a. $P(2) = .1937$
    b. $p = .1$ $n = 15$ $P(2) = .2669$
    c. $p = .1$ $n = 10$ $P(x > 3) = 1 - P(x \leq 3)$
    $$= 1 - (.3487 + .3874 + .1937 + .0574)$$
    $$= .0128$$

    d. $p = .1$ $n = 12$

x	$P(x)$
0	.2824
1	.3766
2	.2301
3	.0851
4	.0213
5	.0038
6	.0005
7	0
8	0
9	0

36. a. $.007$ b. $.176$ c. $.068$

Chapter 12

1. a. d_2 b. d_4 c. d_3

3. c. $16,666.50

6. c. Buy 3 dozen balls early EMV = $301.70

10. c. Go without research

14. c. Take test and do not drop

Chapter 13

1. $F_{1989} = \dfrac{457{,}000 + 481{,}000 + 492{,}000 + 505{,}000}{4} = \$483{,}750$

3. $F_{1989} = 505{,}000 + .25(505{,}000 - 500{,}00) = 501{,}250$

5. $\alpha = .15; \beta = .20$ $F_{1988} = 500{,}000$
$F_{1989} = 500{,}000 + .15(5000) = \$500{,}750$
$t_{1989} = 500{,}750 - 500{,}000 = 750$
$T_{1989} = 0 + .2(750) = 150$

$F'_{1989} = \$500{,}750 + \dfrac{(1 - .2)}{.2}(150) = \$501{,}350$

8. $\displaystyle\sum_{i=1}^{19} x_i = 190$ $\displaystyle\sum_{i=1}^{19} y_i = 7{,}564{,}000$

$\displaystyle\sum_{i=1}^{19} x_i y_i = 82{,}650{,}000$ $\displaystyle\sum_{i=1}^{19} x_i^2 = 2470$

$$\begin{array}{rl}
7{,}564{,}000 = & 19b + 190m \\
82{,}650{,}000 = & 190b + 2470m \\
\underline{-75{,}640{,}000 =} & \underline{-190b - 1900m} \\
7{,}010{,}000 = & 570m
\end{array}$$

$m = 12298$

$b = 275125$

$\therefore y = 12298x + 275125$

$y_{1990} = (12298)(21) + 275125 = 533383$

22. a. Not applicable

b.

x_i	y_i	$x_i y_i$	x_i^2
1	55.125	55.125	1
2	57.250	114.500	4
3	57.500	172.500	9
4	59.375	237.400	16
5	65.000	325.000	25
6	63.250	379.500	36
7	68.750	481.250	49
8	69.125	553.000	64
9	72.125	649.125	81
10	73.375	733.750	100
11	72.125	793.375	121
12	75.250	903.000	144
$\overline{78}$	788.250	5397.520	650

$$788.25 = 12b + 78m$$
$$5397.52 = 78b + 650m$$
$$\underline{-5123.62 = -78b - 507m}$$
$$273.90 = 143m$$
$$m = 1.915$$
$$b = 53.24$$

Therefore, $y = 1.915x + 53.24$
$$y_{13} = 1.915(13) + 53.24$$
$$= \$78.135 \text{ per share}$$

Chapter 14

4. $\lambda = 10$ cars per minute; $\mu = 4$ cars per minute. Let $s = 3$.

$$P(0) = \cfrac{1}{\cfrac{\left(\frac{5}{2}\right)^0}{0!} + \cfrac{\left(\frac{5}{2}\right)^1}{1!} + \cfrac{\left(\frac{5}{2}\right)^2}{2!} + \cfrac{\left(\frac{5}{2}\right)^3}{3!}\left[\cfrac{1}{1 - \frac{5}{6}}\right]}$$

$$= \frac{1}{1 + 5/2 + 25/8 + 15.625}$$

$$= \frac{1}{31.625} = .0449$$

$$L_q = \cfrac{(.0449)\left(\frac{10}{4}\right)^3\left(\frac{10}{12}\right)}{3!\left(1 - \frac{10}{12}\right)^2} = 3.508 \text{ cars}$$

∴ Since 1 or 2 toll booths would lead to an infinite queue the smallest number of booths acceptable is 3.

8. λ = 45 customers per hour; μ = 60 customers per hour

 a. ρ = 45/60 = .75 The manager spends 75% of his time cashing checks.

 b. $W_q = \dfrac{45}{60(60 - 45)}$ hours = expected time spent waiting in line

$$= .05 \text{ hours} = 3 \text{ minutes}$$

$W_s = \dfrac{45}{60 - 45}$ hours = expected total time spent waiting

$$= .0667 \text{ hours} = 4 \text{ minutes}$$

 c. $L_q = \dfrac{45^2}{60(60 - 45)}$ = expected number of customers in line

$$= 2.25 \text{ customers}$$

$L_s = \dfrac{45}{15}$ = expected number of customers waiting including the

customer being waited on = 3 customers

 d. $P(0) = 1 - 45/60 = .25$

 e. The effect of the addition of the assistant manager to the check cashing function could be predicted by utilizing the basic multi-server model to produce queuing statistics similar to those statistics reflected above.

10. $N = 5$; $\lambda = 3$ failures per week; $\mu = 16$ machine repairs per week; $s = 1$

$$P(0) = \cfrac{1}{\dfrac{5!}{5!0!}\left(\dfrac{3}{16}\right)^0 + \dfrac{5!}{4!1!1^0}\left(\dfrac{3}{16}\right)^1 + \dfrac{5!}{3!1!1^1}\left(\dfrac{3}{16}\right)^2 + \dfrac{5!}{2!1!1^2}\left(\dfrac{3}{16}\right)^3 + \dfrac{5!}{1!1!1^3}\left(\dfrac{3}{16}\right)^4 + \dfrac{5!}{0!1!1^4}\left(\dfrac{3}{16}\right)^5}$$

$$= \dfrac{1}{3.212} = .311$$

$$P(1) = (.311)\dfrac{5!}{4!1!}\left(\dfrac{3}{16}\right)^1 = .292 \qquad P(2) = (.311)\left(\dfrac{5!}{3!1!1^1}\right)\left(\dfrac{3}{16}\right)^2 = .219$$

$$P(3) = (.311)\dfrac{5!}{2!1!1^2}\left(\dfrac{3}{16}\right)^3 = .123 \qquad P(4) = (.311)\dfrac{5!}{1!1!1^3}\left(\dfrac{3}{16}\right)^4 = .046$$

$$P(5) = (.311)\dfrac{5!}{0!1!1^4}\left(\dfrac{3}{16}\right)^5 = .009$$

13. $\lambda = 5$ per day $\sigma^2 = 0.333$ (days)^2 $\dfrac{1}{\mu} = .125$ days $\mu = 8$ per day

$$L_q = \dfrac{(5^2)(.0333) + \left(\dfrac{5}{8}\right)^2}{2(1 - 5/8)} = 1.6308 \text{ ships}$$

$$\rho = \frac{5}{8} = .625$$

$$L_s = .625 + 1.6308 = 2.2558 \text{ ships}$$
$$W_q = 1.6308/5 = .3262 \text{ days} = 156.5 \text{ minutes}$$
$$W_s = 156.5 + 60 = 216.5 \text{ minutes}$$
$$P(0) = 1 - \frac{5}{8} = \frac{3}{8} = .375$$

Chapter 15

11. The function necessary to generate rainfall is as follows:

RN	Average monthly rainfall
0 – .08	1.0
.08– .18	1.5
.18– .33	2.0
.33– .54	2.5
.54– .74	3.0
.74– .86	3.5
.86– .94	4.0
.94– .97	4.5
.97– .99	5.0
.99–1.00	6.0

Growing season	RN	Rainfall	Yield per acre
1	.319	2.0	120.00
2	.223	2.0	120.00
3	.594	3.0	155.00
4	.494	2.5	137.50
5	.904	4.5	207.50
6	.636	3.0	155.00
7	.460	2.5	137.56
8	.772	3.5	172.50
9	.485	2.5	137.50
10	.934	4.0	190.00
			1532.5

Therefore the mean yield per acre is 153.25 bushels.

Chapter 16

3. a. $q^* = \sqrt{\dfrac{(2)(75)(240)}{10}} = \text{EOQ} = \sqrt{3600} = 60$

b. $N^* = \dfrac{240}{60} = $ optimal number of orders $= 4$

c. $t^* = 12/4 = $ optimal time between orders $= 3$ months

d. $C^*_{(q)} = (10)\left(\dfrac{60}{2}\right) + (75)\left(\dfrac{240}{60}\right) = 300 + 300 = \$600$

e.

q	Carrying cost	Ordering cost	Total cost
30	150	600.00	750.00
40	200	450.00	650.00
50	250	360.00	610.00
60*	300	300.00	600.00
70	350	257.10	607.10
80	400	225.00	625.00
90	450	199.95	649.95

8. a. $S^* = \left(\dfrac{600}{12}\right)\dfrac{(60)(12)}{(75) + (60)(12)} = (50) \cdot \dfrac{720}{795} = 45.28 \cong 45$

b. $C^*(S)^* = (75)\dfrac{45^2}{(2)(50)} + (720)(50 - 45)^2/(2)(50) = 1518.75 + 180.00$
$\qquad = \$1698.75$

c.

S	Holding cost	Stockout cost	Total cost
35	918.75	1620.00	2538.75
40	1200.00	720.00	1920.00
45*	1518.75	180.00	1698.75
50	1875.00	0	1875.00

14. $r = 730{,}000$ trees per year
$p = 3{,}650{,}000$ trees per year
$C_1 = \$12$ per tree
$C_3 = \$5{,}000$ per order

$q^* = \sqrt{\dfrac{(2)(730{,}000)(5000)/12}{1 - 730/3650}}$

$\qquad = 27{,}575.65$ trees

a. $= 27{,}576$ trees

b. $C^* = \sqrt{(2)(730{,}000)(12)(5000)} \ \sqrt{1 - 730/3650}$
$\qquad = \$264{,}600$ per year

c. Assumptions made include: all the assumptions of the basic EOQ model with the exception that a constant and finite replenishment rate is assumed instead of an infinite replenishment rate. In addition, it is assumed that adequate storage capacity and inventory capital exists to pursue the inventory policy of ordering 27,576 trees at a time.

18. a. $S^* = (20)\dfrac{1200}{(.15)(4000) + 1200} = 13.33 \cong 13$

b. $C^*(S) = \dfrac{(.15)(4000)(13)^2}{40}\ \dfrac{(1200)(7)^2}{40} = 2535 + 1470 = \$4005$

c.

S	Holding cost	Stockout cost	Total cost
10	$1500.00	3000.00	$4500.00
13*	2535.00	1470.00	4005.00
14	2940.00	1080.00	4020.00
17	4335.00	270.00	4605.00
20	6000.00	0	6000.00

20. $EOQ_7 = \sqrt{\dfrac{(2)(600)(52)(25)}{(.2)(1.70)}} \cong 2142$

$EOQ_6 = \sqrt{\dfrac{(2)(600)(52)(25)}{(.2)(1.73)}} \cong 2123$

$EOQ_5 = \sqrt{\dfrac{(2)(600)(52)(25)}{(.2)(1.75)}} \cong 2111$

$EOQ_4 = \sqrt{\dfrac{(2)(600)(52)(25)}{(.2)(1.80)}} \cong 2082$ in relevant range

$C(2082) = \frac{1}{2}((.2)(2082)(1.80)) + \dfrac{(25)(600)(52)}{2082} + (600)(52)(1.80)$

$\qquad = \$56,909.40$

$C(4000) = \frac{1}{2}((.2)(4000)(1.75)) + \dfrac{(25)(600)(52)}{4000} + (600)(52)(1.75)$

$\qquad = \$55,495.00$

$C(7000) = \frac{1}{2}((.2)(7000)(1.73)) + \dfrac{(25)(600)(52)}{7000} + (600)(52)(1.75)$

$\qquad = \$55,298.43$

$C(10,000) = \frac{1}{2}[(12)(10,000)(1.70)] + \dfrac{(25)(600)(52)}{10,000} + (600)(52)(1.70)$

$\qquad = \$54,818.00$

a. Order 10,000 lbs. each order
b. $54,818.00
c. $17,000.00

Chapters 17 and 18 Not Applicable

Glossary

additive law Axiom pertaining to the union of two events.

algorithm A systematic procedure used to derive a solution to a problem.

all integer programming model A linear mathematical model in which all the decisions variables are restricted to be integer values.

alternative optima Occurs whenever an LP problem has more than one optimal solution. The condition can be observed whenever a nonbasic variable has a zero $c_j - z_j$ value in the optimal simplex tableau.

analog model A physical model that substitutes one property for another; thus, it does not look like the object or phenomenon that it represents.

arc capacity The maximum allowable flow on an arc in a network.

artificial intelligence The science and technology concerned with creating behavior by a machine that, if performed by a human, would be called intelligent.

artificial variable Dummy variable added to an = or $\geq$ constraint in order to get a starting feasible solution. At optimality all artificial variables must have a zero value or the LP problem has no solution.

basic feasible solution A basic solution that also satisfies all constraints of an LP problem; geometrically, it corresponds to an extreme point of the feasible region.

basic solution A solution to a linear programming problem with n variables and m constraints in which $n - m$ of the variables are set equal to zero and the m equations are solved in terms of the remaining m variables.

basis In an LP problem with m constraints and n variables, the basis consists of those m variables which are not set automatically to zero and are used to determine the solution to the problem.

batch-processing system A data-processing system in which transactions are accumulated and master files are updated periodically.

Bayes theorem A mathematical theorem used to revise the probability of an event given new information.

Bayesian strategy The optimal decision strategy with respect to expected value.

Bernoulli trial A random phenomenon involving two mutually exclusive and exhaustive events.

beta distribution A continuous probability distribution often used in stochastic PERT analysis.

bill of materials (BOM) A list that specifies all component items that a product comprises.

binding constraint A constraint whose left-hand side equals its right-hand side.

binomial distribution A discrete probability distribution.

branch and bound A partial enumeration procedure

for integer or other combinatorial problems in which the set of feasible solutions is partitioned into smaller and smaller subsets until the optimal solution is found.

calling population (also called input source) Consists of all customers or calling units that can arrive to a queuing system. When the calling population is finite, it is referred to as a finite calling population or limited-source calling population. An infinite calling population refers to a calling population containing an infinite number of calling units.

carrying cost (also called holding cost) One of three components of inventory costs. Carrying costs are those costs incurred for holding inventory.

cell Cell (i,j) in a transportation tableau is associated with the route from origin i to destination j.

certainty Conditions under which all parameters of a decision problem are known exactly.

chi-square test A nonparametric goodness-of-fit test used to test the hypothesis that a random variable is distributed in a specified manner.

$c_j - z_j$ **row** A row in the simplex tableau that gives the opportunity cost of bringing each variable into the basis. This row is used to check for optimality.

collectively exhaustive events A group of events that together include all the sample points in the sample space.

column vector A matrix consisting of only one column.

complementary event Consists of all points in the sample space not included in the event.

compound event Consists of more than one simple event.

computer hardware The physical equipment comprising a computer system such as CPU, disks, memory, and so on.

computer simulation A numerical technique that involves modeling a stochastic system on a digital computer with the intention of predicting the system's behavior.

computer software The computer programs and procedures used to process data and enable the computer to function.

conditional probability Probabilities that depend on the outcome of another event.

constraints Mathematical expressions that state resource limitations or other physical restrictions in a particular decision model.

continuous inventory system A system of accounting for inventory that updates inventory levels whenever there is an inventory replenishment or decrement.

crashing The process of reducing the time necessary to complete a project by adding resources.

critical activities Activities in a PERT network that are on the critical path and consequently have zero slack time.

critical path The longest path through a PERT net-

work. The critical path is composed of activities with zero slack time.

critical-path method A project scheduling and control method similar to PERT.

cumulative probability distribution A function of some random variable that defines the probability of the random variable being less than or equal to a specific value.

data base An integrated and organized collection of stored files and data useful in the operation of an organization.

decision support system (DSS) A type of computer-based system which involves the decision maker himself, a data base, and some decision models to aid in the decision process.

decision tree A network representation of a decision problem containing decision nodes and chance nodes.

decision variables Variables whose values (when determined) will solve a given problem.

degeneracy A condition in which one or more basic variables assume a zero value in the simplex solution to an LP problem.

delphi method A qualitative forecasting technique that utilizes a panel of experts and a series of questionnaires to develop a forecast.

dependent demand Demand whose magnitude depends on the demand for another item or product.

destination A customer or demand location in a transportation problem.

deterministic PERT A project-scheduling technique in which the activity times are assumed to be known with certainty.

deterministic problem Problem in which all the data and relevant parameters are known with certainty.

deterministic simulation Simulation with no stochastic events.

deviation variable A variable used in goal programming to measure the extent to which an associated goal is violated.

dual price Another term for shadow price.

dual problem A counterpart LP problem associated with the primal formulation. Unique relationships exist between the primal and dual, such as the fact that the solution to one yields the solution to the other.

dual variable A variable in the dual of a linear programming model. Its optimal value determines the shadow price for the associated primal constraint.

dummy destination A destination added to make demand equal to supply in a transportation problem. The fictitious demand is equal to the excess of supply over demand.

dummy source An origin added to a transportation problem whenever demand exceeds supply. It is assigned a fictitious supply so that supply and demand are equal.

dynamic programming A serial optimization method that decomposes a problem into smaller interrelated problems in order to find the overall optimum solution.

elementary row operations Operations that can be performed on a system of linear equations without changing the solution to the system of equations.

equilibrium condition Occurs when additional transitions do not affect the probabilities of finding a Markov process in the various states.

event In PERT analysis, the completion of an activity or task.

expected critical path The path in a stochastic PERT network that would be the critical path if the length of each activity were the expected time.

expected value of perfect information (EVPI) Measures the economic value of perfect information.

expected value of sample information (EVSI) Measures the economic value of new information.

expert system A class of computer based systems that provides human expertise and serves as a consultant for decision making.

extreme point A vertex of the convex region defined by the constraints of a mathematical model.

feasible In mathematical programming, feasible means within the region defined by the constraints or physical limitations.

feasible region The set of all feasible solutions.

feasible solution A solution that satisfies all the constraints.

Gantt chart A simple bar chart depicting the starting time and completion time for various project tasks.

Gaussian elimination An algebraic procedure for solving a set of simultaneous linear equations.

goal programming A mathematical programming technique that solves optimization problems having multiple and sometimes incompatible goals.

grass-roots forecasting A qualitative forecasting technique in which individual forecasts are generated at the end of the distribution channel and are aggregated to generate the total forecast.

greedy algorithm An algorithm that proceeds at each step by making the maximum improvement possible.

gross requirements The quantity of an item that will have to be disbursed to support the production of a parent item.

heuristic A method or rule of thumb that determines good but not necessarily optimal solutions to a problem.

historical analogy A qualitative forecasting technique that forecasts demand based upon past experience with a similar product or service.

holding costs (See carrying costs.)

homogeneous Markov chain A specific type of stochastic process.

Hungarian method An algorithm used to determine an optimal solution to an assignment problem.

iconic model Physical replica or representation of the object it represents.

independent demand Demand that is not dependent on the demand for an end item.

independent events Events whose probability of occurrence is not affected by the occurrence of another event.

infeasibility A condition which exists when an LP problem has no feasible solution; that is, there are no points which satisfy all constraints.

input source (See calling population.)

integer programming A type of mathematical programming in which the decision variables are restricted to whole number values.

inventory A stock of goods that is held for the purpose of future production or sales.

iterative technique Is a solution process that repeats certain phases of the solution process until a solution is found.

joint probability The probability of two or more events occurring.

knowledge engineering The process of capturing knowledge and building the knowledge base of an expert system.

Kolmogorov-Smirnov test A nonparametric goodness-of-fit test.

lead time The time between the release of an order and the time the goods start being added to inventory.

least-squares method A method for deriving a function that best fits a set of data.

linear programming A mathematical technique that can be used to maximize or minimize a linear objective function subject to certain linear constraints.

lower bound A value which is less than or equal to the value of an optimal solution to a problem.

LP relaxation An LP problem that is derived from the integer programming problem by ignoring the integrality constraints.

management information system (MIS) An integrated human/machine system for providing information to support operations, management, and decision-making in an organization.

management science The discipline devoted to studying and developing scientific procedures to help in the process of managerial decision making (see operations research).

marginal probability Probabilities that do not depend on other events.

market research A family of qualitative forecasting techniques that is helpful in revealing predictions about the size, structure, and configuration of markets for various goods and services.

Markov process A stochastic process where the probability of moving from one state to another depends only on the present state of the system.

materials requirements planning (MRP) A system of

logically related records, procedures, and decision rules that translate the master schedule into time-phased net requirements and planned coverage of these requirements for all component items needed.

mathematical model Mathematical symbols and equations used to represent a given situation.

mathematical programming The art of developing mathematical models to solve various types of decision problems.

matrix A rectangular arrangement of numbers.

matrix addition The algebraic operation of adding two matrices of the same dimensions.

matrix multiplication The algebraic operation of multiplying two matrices.

maximal flow The maximum amount of flow that can enter into or out of a network system per unit of time.

maximax criterion The decision criterion that maximizes the maximum payoffs of various decisions.

maximin criterion The decision criterion that maximizes the minimum payoffs of various decisions.

mean absolute deviation (MAD) Measurement of forecast accuracy which is computed as the average absolute deviation from the forecasts.

minimax regret criterion A decision criterion that minimizes the maximum opportunity losses of various decisions.

minimum spanning tree A tree of minimal total arc length that spans or connects all nodes in a network.

MINSLK heuristic A priority decision rule that is used to schedule a PERT project with resource constraints. Priority is given to those activities having minimum slack.

mixed integer programming model A linear mathematical model in which some but not all variables are required to have integer values.

model Representation or an abstraction of an object or phenomenon.

model relaxation The dropping of certain restrictions in a model. For example, a linear relaxation of an integer model is implemented when the integer restrictions are dropped.

modified distribution method (MODI) A streamlined simplex algorithm used to find the optimal solution to a transportation problem.

Monte Carlo simulation A simulation using a sampling technique that consists of the generation of random variates from a specified probability distribution.

most likely time A PERT activity time estimate management believes to be the most likely.

multiple choice constraint A constraint requiring the sum of 0–1 variables to equal 1; any solution thus selects one alternative out of several.

multiple objective linear programming (MOLP) An LP model with more than one objective function.

multiplicative law Axiom pertaining to the intersection of two events.

mutually exclusive events Events that cannot occur at the same time.

net requirements The quantity of additional component items to procure in order to support the production of a parent item. Net requirements = Gross requirements − Scheduled receipts − Inventory on hand.

netform concept The concept of exploiting the network substructure of a problem whenever possible to gain computational efficiency.

network A graphical representation of a problem or situation consisting of a collection of nodes connected by links.

nonnegativity conditions Conditions that require all variables in a model to be nonnegative.

0–1 integer programming model A linear mathematical model in which the decision variable values are restricted to 0 or 1.

objective function An equation or mathematical expression that is used to measure the effectiveness of proposed solutions to a problem.

objective function ranging The process of determining how much each objective function coefficient c_j can be increased and decreased before the basis would change.

objective probability A probability measure for which there is definitive historical information or rigorous analysis.

on-line Being under direct control of the computer at that point in time. Thus, users who interact directly with the computer via a remote terminal are on-line as opposed to submitting a job for batch processing.

operations research The discipline devoted to studying and developing scientific procedures to help in the process of making decisions (see Management science).

optimistic time A PERT activity time estimate based on the assumption the activity will progress ideally.

order costs The costs incurred when processing an order for inventory.

order level The inventory level after replenishment.

origin A source or supply location in a transportation or transshipment problem.

panel consensus A qualitative forecasting technique that involves assembling a panel of experts for the purpose of jointly developing a forecast.

parameters The input data that together with a model's structure define a model.

pareto optimality The principle that states that a state of the world A is preferable to a state of the world B if at least one person is better off in A and nobody is worse off.

path A sequential series of activities in a PERT network.

payoff table A matrix of payoffs for a decision problem.

PERT (See Program Evaluation and Review Technique.)

PERT chart A network diagram of a project.

PERT/Cost A methodology for planning, scheduling, and controlling the cost of a project.

pessimistic time A PERT activity time estimate based on the assumption that the most unfavorable conditions will occur.

physical inventory system An inventory accounting system in which management periodically reviews levels of the various items in inventory in order to make inventory decisions.

pivot element In the simplex method, the element of the simplex tableau that is in both the pivot row and pivot column.

pivoting The process of updating the simplex tableau in the simplex method.

Poisson probability density function A discrete probability function that yields the probability of n events occurring in a given time interval.

Poisson process Usually refers to a random arrival process where the number of arrivals in a time period is distributed according to a Poisson probability distribution.

posteriori probabilities The revised conditional probabilities of the various states of nature after applying Bayes theorem.

postoptimality analysis Analysis performed after an optimal solution to a mathematical model has been obtained. Also called sensitivity analysis.

primal problem The original formulation of a linear programming problem.

principle of optimality In dynamic programming, an optimal policy has the property that whatever the initial state and initial decision are, the remaining decisions must constitute an optimal policy with regard to the state resulting from the first decision.

probability density function The function that describes a continuous probability distribution.

probability distribution A function that relates a probability to the values a random variable can take on.

probability mass function A function describing a discrete probability distribution.

process generator A function that transforms a uniformly distributed random number into a nonuniform random variate.

Program Evaluation and Review Technique (PERT) A technique for scheduling and controlling large projects.

project scheduling The scheduling of major tasks that require a significant amount of time to accomplish.

queue discipline (also called service discipline) The decision rule that determines which calling unit in the queuing system receives service.

queuing system Any system that has a waiting line as an element of the system.

queuing theory A branch of operations research that

through mathematical models describes the behavior of queuing systems.

random variable A function whose numerical value depends on the outcome of some random event.

real-time system A computer-based system that is on-line to the computer. This enables instantaneous response to inquiries and often instantaneous update of a data base.

recursive relationship An equation in which a function at one stage is used to evaluate the same type of function at the next stage.

redundant constraint A constraint that does not affect the feasible region. It can be deleted from the model without affecting the optimal solution.

regression analysis A forecasting technique yielding a forecasting equation that predicts the dependent variable as a function of one or more independent variables.

reorder level The inventory level at the time of placing the order.

replenishment period The time it takes to replenish inventory once replenishment has begun.

return function The value or measure of effectiveness of a specific decision at stage n given state S_n in a dynamic programming problem.

right-hand side ranging The process of determining how much each r.h.s. in the primal LP model can be increased and decreased before the current basis becomes infeasible.

row-minimum method A heuristic used to find an initial feasible solution to a transportation problem.

row vector A matrix consisting of only one row.

sample point (See simple event.)

sample space Collection of all possible sample points.

satisficing The process of getting as close as possible to the achievement of a goal, possibly without reaching the goal completely.

scalar A constant.

scalar multiplication The multiplication of each matrix element by a scalar.

sensitivity analysis The analysis of how an optimal solution and the value of its objective function are affected by changes in the various inputs or parameters of the decision model.

service discipline (See queue discipline.)

service facility A server in a queuing system.

shadow price The marginal value of a resource associated with a linear programming constraint at optimality.

shortage costs (also called stockout costs) Inventory costs associated with being out of stock.

shortest route Shortest path between two nodes in a network.

simple event Consists of a single possible outcome of a random phenomenon.

simplex method An algebraic procedure for iteratively solving LP models. It begins with a feasible extreme point and moves from one adjacent extreme point to another making successive improvements until the optimal solution is determined (if it exists).

simplex tableau A tabular form used to perform hand calculations to carry out the simplex method. It contains all equation coefficients plus other information needed to check solution quality.

sink A destination node in a network that has a demand.

slack time In PERT analysis, the amount of time an activity can be delayed without delaying the entire project.

source An origin node in a network that has a positive supply.

stage A subproblem in a dynamic programming formulation that corresponds to a situation where a decision must be made.

stage variable A variable whose value describes the status of the system at any stage in a dynamic programming problem.

standard form of an LP model The form in which all constraints have been converted to equations.

steady state A queuing system is in a steady-state condition when its behavior is not a function of time.

stochastic PERT A project-scheduling technique in which the activity times are of a probabilistic nature.

stochastic problem Problem in which the data and parameters are not known with certainty, but a probability distribution is known.

subjective probability A probability which is based on someone's experience.

systems approach A modern integrated approach to decision making in which all relevant factors (including intra-organizational and environmental or external factors) are considered in the decision process. The objective is to achieve the goals of the organization as a whole.

time phasing The process of timing inventory needs to arrive at the point in time when they are needed.

tracking signal A measure used to identify those forecasts which are failing to keep pace with trend.

transaction processing system A computer based system that primarily handles simple data processing and clerical activities such as sales, purchases, and inventory changes.

transition matrix A matrix describing single-period conditional probabilities.

transition probability The transition probability p_{ij} is the probability of moving from state i to state j in one transition period.

transportation tableau A table used to facilitate the solution to a transportation problem. Its rows correspond to origins, its columns to destinations, and its cells to costs.

transshipment node A node in a network that has entering and exiting arcs; it is neither a source nor a sink.

unbounded solution A solution to an LP problem in which the value of some variable can be made arbitrarily large without violating any of the constraints.

uncertain problem Problem in which the data or parameters are uncertain or unknown.

uniform distribution A continuous probability distribution.

upper bound A value which is greater than or equal to the value of an optimal solution to a problem.

Vogel's approximation method (VAM) A heuristic used to find an initial feasible solution to a transportation problem.

work package The smallest element in the work-breakdown structure.

Index